C0-ARW-677

GANDHI

VOICE OF A NEW AGE REVOLUTION

Genealogical Tree of Mohandas Karamchand Gandhi

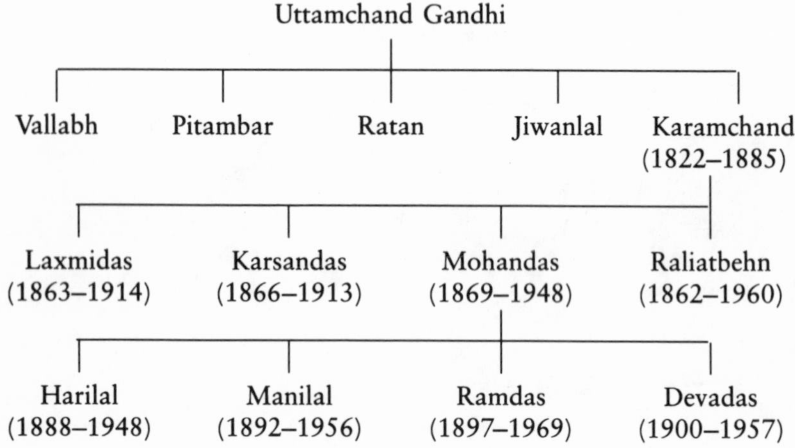

GANDHI

VOICE OF A NEW AGE REVOLUTION

MARTIN GREEN

CONTINUUM · NEW YORK

To U. R. Ananthamurthy,
my first Indian friend

1993
The Continuum Publishing Company
370 Lexington Avenue, New York, NY 10017

Printed in the United States of America

Library of Congress Cataloging-in-Publication Data

Green, Martin Burgess, 1927–
Gandhi : voice of a new age revolution / Martin Green.
p. cm.
Includes bibliographical references and index.
ISBN 0-8264-0620-3 (acid free)
1. Gandhi, Mahatma, 1869–1948. 2. Statesmen—India—Biography.
3. Nationalists—India—Biography. 4. New Age movement. I. Title.
DS481.G3G7314 1993
954.03'5'092—dc20
[B] 92-46986
CIP

CONTENTS

Acknowledgments

I have been helped in various ways by a number of people. In particular I should like to cite: Deborah Baker, Chitrita Banerji, Diane Carmody, Ganesh Davy, Jitendra Desai, Mahendra Desai, Stephen Hay, Jim Hunt, Lin Haire-Sargent, Digish Mehta, Uma Mesthrie, Ramanibhai Modi, Constance Putnam, Lloyd and Susanne Rudolph, Hassim Seedat, Mr. Shiromany, Suresh Shukla, N. Vasudevan.

Author's Note

This biography gives most space to its subject's personal relationships and private life—but the latter was a life of ideas, so this is an intellectual biography, by ordinary standards. It also makes preferential use of certain new raw materials which have become available in the last ten or twenty years. Those biases acknowledged, the author claims to have given, or tried to give, a broad and steady view of Gandhi's extremely shifting and far-ranging life.

INTRODUCTION

THE NEW AGE SCENE AND SCENARIO

A Problematic Hero

I describe Gandhi as problematic here to acknowledge not only that many people dispute his claims to be a hero, but that today the standing of heroism, even or especially pious heroism, is shaky. "Mahatma Gandhi" is today one of the most frequently and emptily invoked of all names; in many ways resembling "Jesus Christ" and "Mother Teresa." All three of those names, but perhaps "Gandhi" most of all, lay claim to sanctity, haloed virtue, an impossible loftiness; and arouse corresponding feelings of disgust and resistance. This is partly because Gandhi's authority is invoked so glibly and ignorantly, but also because of the nature of that authority, however knowledgeably defined. This reaction is not to be found in everyone, of course, but it is to be expected in a group of people who particularly concern a writer—a group I would like to call "professional readers."

I use that phrase to mean people in the professions (historians, political scientists, lawyers, psychoanalysts, and so on) who have to read a lot, and who acquire the habit of reading documents critically, analytically, testingly; expecting either to accept or reject an argument more completely than the ordinary reader; so that their reading itself becomes professional, even in areas outside their own specialty. We often use the term *intellectuals* for this group, but that term has too much tendentiousness to be useful to me here.

I am a writer for professional readers in that sense, and also a professional reader. I myself feel that instinctive resistance to Gandhi, as I read him, as well as to the empty invocation of his name. I don't want heroes, or saints or martyrs, with their totalitarian claims on my attention. On the other hand, at certain moments (moments in his life, moments in my life) I feel translated into Gandhi's presence, and then I deeply regret the habits of thought that keep me at such a distance from him in my ordinary life, and deny me another sort of experience—the *extra*ordinary sort. Using as cool a tone as possible about the matter, I would say that the Gandhi experience teaches professional readers how much they lose in exchange for their advantages.

As I write about him, I am addressing both those professional readers and that larger group who read looking for enthusiasm, inspiration, pious consolation—looking for direct moral authority. These are the people who keep Gandhi's autobiography (and the New Testament, and pamphlets about Mother Teresa) permanently in print. One of the attractions of this subject for me is that it puts the two audiences into tacit confrontation. Here for once a professional writer/reader can address also that larger audience, or at least a topic dear to that audience.

Everyone in both audiences knows Gandhi's image, the skinny figure in the loincloth, the toothless grin, the spinning wheel; and most people have heard of his *satyagraha* (nonviolent activism), his fasting, his marches, and his successful resistance to the British empire, in South Africa and India. He stood and stands for causes popular with many professional readers today—anticolonialism, appropriate technology, multiculturalism. What then makes those readers feel so hostile? The ultimate answer I think is that Gandhi believed in adults "being good," as children are told to be good—and he defined goodness in terms of ascetic self-denial and self-punishment—and he talked of "being bad" as evil and sin. All these concepts are deeply repugnant to us today, as being too simple, too didactic, too moralistic.

Moreover, Gandhi looked like a victim, and an intentional victim, who tried to exert power over the rest of the world through his sufferings. The most obvious example of that is his fasting, but also his meeting blows and bullets with no resistance. The same is also implicit in his costume, his gauntness, his toothlessness, and so on. One could point out that his conversation was eminently sane, cheerful, lively—but still it was part of his intention, his philosophy, to suffer in this masochist way. *Victim* and *martyr* are at best ambivalent terms for the readers I am speaking of. Gandhi was a man of sorrows, a suffering savior, and the death's-head at the feast; he refused to join us in our hedonism—including intellectual hedonism. It is our resentful experience of that refusal that gives the deeper resonance to our denial of whatever he was saying.

These are respectable reasons for us to turn away from him, since they are rooted in our serious convictions. But I hope to persuade you that they are insufficient.

Why a New Biography?

There is a great deal already in print about Gandhi. There will ultimately be ninety-five volumes of his own *Collected Works,* most of them as long as five hundred pages each. They include books, political documents, journalism, but also a high proportion of informal, spontaneous notes to friends—things that other people would only speak, Gandhi on his days of silence wrote down, and so recorded. This constitutes an enormous data bank on his behavior—of both the considered and the unconsidered kinds; and then there are all the books about him, the works of scholarly commentary and interpretation; and then the biographies, themselves amounting, when I began to work on Gandhi (more than twenty-five years ago) to some four hundred.

So why add another one? I will offer three reasons, out of the many possible. First because we have recently learned much that is new about him. For instance, the Gandhi-Kallenbach correspondence, and the Gandhi-Polak correspondence, Gandhi's side of which is shortly to appear in a supplementary volume to the *Collected Works*, show us a Gandhi we had not seen before; a young man discovering his powers, and dealing boldly in the personal emotions (making European friends, arranging their marriages, delighting in their and his own reciprocal fondness).

Second because, as one becomes familiar with what Gandhi did, and what he and others said about it, one can recognize things he is not putting into words, and which therefore have passed unnoticed. These are of various kinds. Some have to do with the vow of *brahmacharya,* which he took in 1906, and which we usually translate as celibacy or chastity, but was not so simple. For over forty years, Gandhi renounced sexual excitement; but believed in a trans-sexual loving intimacy that involved acts of touch and embrace that would normally be called sexual. For about half of that period it seems that he believed in that freedom without practicing it; but in the second half the practice grew increasingly dramatic, till he slept naked with a naked woman. This was not kept secret in any ordinary sense (at least, not by him) but neither was it publicly avowed. It is now time to break that silence.

Some other silences amount to a sort of moralist's self-denial. For instance, soon after his return to India in 1914, his friend C. F. Andrews asked him how he, as a reformer, could swallow in silence the slaughter of animals in the Kali temple in Calcutta as a sacrifice to the goddess. Gandhi replied by telling how deeply he felt that horror, and how he had recently asked his son, Harilal, not to settle in that city for just that reason; how he "writhed in agony" to think of such sacrifices—but: "I cannot speak or write about it."[1]

In January 1921, Andrews wrote him a similar reproach about the Untouchables problem, and Gandhi replied again that that was too sensitive an issue for him to take up; he could talk about a British crime like the massacre at Amritsar, but not an Indian one of even greater magnitude. "I began to think about you and the question at 2 a.m. Not being able to sleep I began to write to you at 4 a.m. I have not written all I want to say on the question. . . . I sometimes writhe with agony when I think of it. But I do not speak or write about it" (19:289).[2] Such silences are a part of Gandhi's presence, which needs to be brought out.

A third reason for writing about him again is because I now see even the familiar sides of Gandhi in a new light. I see his early experience of fear and anger as lying at the source of his political leadership, but also at the source of his spiritual strength, his scrupulous innocence and his power of love. In political matters, for instance, he "shook with rage" to see his proud culture humiliated by the British. (Remember also how he "writhed with agony.") Those emotions, which burned from sources stoked very early in his life, were his authority to lead a national campaign, primarily among caste Hindus. But he also identified (self-reproachfully) with the Untouchables humiliated by the caste Hindus. While in his own personal relations he strove to avoid all pride—to "reduce the I to O."

I Shook with Rage

Gandhi shook with rage, by his own account, more than once; and both in South Africa and in India; as he read the drafts of government legislation that he then called on his countrymen to resist. But a stream of anger ran underground through his experience, all his life.

It began with the humiliating experience of his own cowardice. This he admitted again and again, in formulas like this of 1924: "As a coward, which I was for years, I harboured violence."[3] Thus he presented nonviolence as a way to achieve courage, and vice versa. Without denying the moral truth of Gandhi's equation, I shall look at this complex of feelings from a different angle.

In Porbandar, in 1893, the young Gandhi asked a favor, on his brother's behalf, of the English political agent, who refused to listen to him. "He called his peon, and ordered him to show me the door. I was still hesitating when the peon came in, placed his hands on my shoulders and put me out of the room." Gandhi went home and immediately wrote and sent over a note: "You have insulted me. You have assaulted me through your peon. If you make no amends, I shall have to proceed against you" (A:98).

The reply he got was dismissive, and Gandhi's brothers and friends could think of nothing for him to do. Beside himself, he appealed for help and advice to Sir Pherozeshah Mehta, the great Bombay lawyer; who said Gandhi should swallow the insult: he would gain nothing by proceeding, and would very likely ruin himself. "The advice was as bitter as poison to me, but I had to swallow it. I pocketed the insult, but also profited by it. 'Never again shall I place myself in such a false position, never again shall I try to exploit friendship in this way,' said I to myself. . . . This shock changed the course of my life" (A:99).

This was a semipolitical occasion; but the anger in Gandhi was not exclusively political. One of the newly acquired, not yet published, letters to Kallenbach, written in April 1914, gives us a fuller account of a marital quarrel between Gandhi and his wife than we have elsewhere, and reveals the force of personal bitterness in him.

An incident of the day before, Gandhi writes to his friend, has proved that Kasturba has "both the devil and the divine in her in most concentrated form." She made a "venomous" remark, asking who had opened a certain drawer, implying that an Indian girl who lived with them had tampered with it. "She spits fire on Jeki [the daughter of his friend, Dr. Mehta]: I gently remarked that I had opened it. 'Why?' was the growling answer. I said, 'In order to see whether I could find a sheet for you.' [Kasturba had been very ill, and Gandhi had been nursing her.] 'That does not contain sheets,' was the retort, so much as to convey to me that I was telling a fib to shield Jeki. This was too much and I gently but rebukingly remarked that she was sinful in her thoughts and that her disease was largely due to her sins. Immediately she began to howl. I had made her leave all the good food in order to kill her; I was tired of her, I wished her to die, I was a hooded snake." And so on.

He continues: "She is the most venomous woman I have ever met. She never forgets, never forgives. She is quite normal today. [Here without transition his tone changes.] But yesterday was one of the richest lessons of my life. All the charges she brought against me she undoubtedly means. She has contrary emotions. I have nursed her as a son . . . but my love has not been sufficiently intense and selfless to make her change her nature. What wonder if Anglia [one of his political rivals] and others cannot respond to my skin-deep love? . . . She has been my best teacher [of patience and forgiveness]." She is not, he says, a particularly bad wife or woman; on the contrary. But you cannot attach yourself to a particular woman, and yet work for humanity. The two don't harmonize. "That is the real cause of the devil waking in her now again."

In such scenes Gandhi reminds us of his great precursor, Tolstoy, and *his* quarrels with his wife—in scenes that were played out at almost the same moment, in Russia. The spokesman for peace and love is provoked by his life partner into an exchange of hate and malice; the effect of which is to damage him much more than her in the eyes of onlookers. In Sonia Tolstoy's case, I think one can say that that effect was intended. In Kasturba's case, we don't know enough to say. In any case, both men admitted the truth of the implicit accusation. Each was part of a system of reciprocal anger and malice. Some years later, in India, Gandhi wrote to a friend, "I remember that [Kasturba] often charged me with having poison in my heart. How can I deny that charge? . . . [since] she felt the poison" (53:117).

Part of the unpleasantness for the reader is that, at least in personal matters, Gandhi tried to suppress and overcome and deny such feelings—he did not enjoy his rage—and so his reports of his feelings sound hypocritical. It was not often that Gandhi directly expressed accusation or even grief or self-dissatisfaction, within a concrete and personal situation. He was not a very expressive personality, even in the sense that Nehru was; he had too strong a sense of decorum, for one thing. But he led a stormy emotional life deep within. There is another newly discovered letter of April 1914, written after the discovery of misdoing at Phoenix (sexual misconduct by some of the boys) and during the fourteen-day fast he then imposed on himself.

"Never perhaps have I spent such days of agony as I am doing now. I can do no writing whatever. The heart seems to have gone dry. The agony I am going through is unspeakable. . . . I have often wanted to take out the knife from my pocket and put it through my stomach. . . . I have a strain of cruelty in me, as others say, such that people force themselves to do things, even to attempt impossible things, in order to please me. . . . Even Gokhale used to tell me that I was so harsh people are terrified of me."

The reader takes a violent shock from the contact with Gandhi at such moments as this. But we sense that same volcanic emotion, in controlled and refined form, behind his reflections on nonviolence, which strike us as going as far as the human mind can go in the direction of peace and truth.

On June 7, 1918, he wrote to his English friend, Florence Winterbottom, about his recruiting campaign: "I am going through perhaps the severest trials of my life. I had hoped whilst I was here to be able in India to retire from the War. Now I find I am in the thick of it. To be true to myself, I feel I dare not avoid it. I want to raise men to fight, [he was recruiting Indian soldiers for the British army, to fight in the war] to deal death to men who, for all they know, are as innocent as they. And I fancy that through this sea of blood I shall find my haven. The nearest analogy is 'If I want a man to have a clear, lustless eye, I must give him sight first. I cannot preach the virtue of a pure sight to a blind man. I cannot descant upon the efficacy of silence before a dumb man.' I find men are incapable through cowardice of killing. How shall I preach to them the virtue of non-killing? And so I want them to learn the art of killing! This is all awful. But such is the situation in front of me. Sometimes my heart sinks within me and I feel like throwing the whole thing overboard and seek solace in silence and retirement. But I soon rise from the despondency and stick to action."[5]

This is Gandhi the thinker at his very best, and to know him means to understand the connection between such reflections and his righteously angry nationalism, for that connection is the key to everything else. That psychological truth sheds much new light on Gandhi.

The New Age Mentality

Another light emanates from a historical movement—the New Age that flourished at the end of the nineteenth century, and to which Gandhi belonged. This was a period in the history of consciousness that has been scanted of serious attention; a period when many people made a naive act of faith in self-renewal, both for the individual and for society—naive in the sense that they felt no need for the massive support usually taken by ideas from armed power or instituted theory. Once we see Gandhi in this setting, we better understand not only him but the forces behind him, and some of the great patterns of world history.

Gandhi has struck most commentators as being very unlike themselves. *Enigmatic, elusive, paradoxical, mystical, medieval, oriental,*—these are words often used about him. In 1939 several contributors to a volume of essays about him expressed that feeling: one Englishman, for instance, wrote, "Mr Gandhi's attitude to sex is more completely opposed to modern psychology and medicine than one could have imagined it possible for any man to be."[6] In fact, however, Gandhi belonged to a human type that is in some sense familiar to us, throughout history. More than that, he belonged to a recurrent historical movement, the New Age.

It will help us to understand him if I define that type and that movement here in this introduction, before beginning his biography proper. This is because, to demonstrate my idea, I need to break with the chronological order of Gandhi's biography, and to range freely over history and geography for examples. In later chapters I shall describe the leading features of the New Age in the order in which Gandhi encountered them. But it will let us proceed more smoothly at those points if I say something general here about the concept, and the mentality it embodies.

Terms like *New Age* have mostly been used about the West, which means—when we are thinking of Gandhi—about England. Some phenomena of related kinds were to be seen in India, but in less-concentrated form, and confused by an appearance of revivalism. One of the features of New Ages is Orientalism—substituting features of Eastern culture for Western equivalents in one's life—and so in India New Age activities looked like a revived traditionalism.

In England *New Age* was widely used about the period of Gandhi's young manhood, 1880–1910. He was in London 1888–91; and again in 1906, 1909, and 1914; and from 1893–1914 he lived in South Africa, in a British colonial environment, where many of his close friends were New Agers. He himself wrote in 1947, "For twenty years I was in closest touch with the West in South Africa"; and he went on to cite his familiarity with New Age writers on sex like Havelock Ellis and Bertrand Russell (87:90).

The period was given that name both by the people who took part in New Age activities, and by those who observed such activities from outside, so it had both favorable and unfavorable connotations. The same is true today; for we have a New Age going on around us now, at the end of the twentieth century. And at the end of the eighteenth century, the period of Blake, Paine, Godwin, Wollstonecraft, was also a New Age (though they did not use that phrase). At the end of centuries, as we see again today, such phenomena often become more assertive, and attract more attention. We shall see that Blake and Shelley were the English poets Gandhi most often quoted—because they were the main New Age poets—that is, the most popular reading amongst the New Agers at the end of the nineteenth century, though themselves of the earlier period. Gandhi sometimes addressed the crisis in India in the language of, for instance, Blake's "Jerusalem."

Thus, in 1923 Gandhi writes: "This land of ours, we are told, was once the abode of the gods. But it is not possible to conceive of gods inhabiting a land made hideous by the smoke and din of mill chimneys and factories, and whose roadways are traversed by rushing engines. . . . Factories are risen on the corpses of men, women and children to create what we call civilization" (23:197).

In another book I have suggested that New Ages are periods of cultural history when the naive mind or mentality finds powerful expression: naive not meaning any lack of knowledge or of analytic power, but a readiness to act on one's beliefs and hopes—as if one person, or a small group, could alter life, without using power or force against others, and without developing elaborate analytic theory, simply by beginning to live differently, between one day and the next. They are life-experimenters.

The title Gandhi gave to his autobiography was "My Experiments with Truth." He liked to feel he was starting from scratch, almost every day and on every side of life. (This is not to say that he did not value tradition, but he valued it as raw material for his experiments.) And at the end of his life all he achieved was almost destroyed in a great scandal over what he called his experiments in brahmacharya, which we in the West would be likely to call experiments in sex.

But if Gandhi experimented in the forbidden, he and most New Agers believed just as strikingly in values that other people think of as sentimental or idealistic or religious. For instance, his English disciple, Madeline Slade, was a lover of vegetable as well as animal life. "Many and many a time have I gained comfort and guidance from our forest brethren. Often have I put my arms around the trunk of an old mighty tree and listened to his hushed words of wisdom and peace" (42:239). That idea was a part of Gandhism, and also a part of our own New Age's thinking.

By commonsense standards, this is at best romanticism, as are other aspects of Gandhism. Politically speaking, Madeline Slade, and other of Gandhi's English disciples, such as C. F. Andrews and Reginald Reynolds, came to him in order to "atone" to India for the harm which England had done it. Philosophically speaking, Gandhi refused to believe in the "hard facts" of his time, such as the greatest good of the greatest number, or the survival of the fittest (50:157).

For obvious reasons, the naive tend to believe in human perfectibility, something that was often called "Creative Evolution" in the period being discussed—creative meaning non-Darwinian—the ascent of man, as opposed to the descent. In the process of his evolution, Gandhi said, man will come to resemble his ideal. We can see that beginning in the history of the Quakers and the Dukhobors (a nonviolent sect in Russia, assisted by Tolstoy). Those who disagree with him, Gandhi continued, are people who cannot believe that Christ's teaching was meant for the world at large. They think it was esoteric, and meant only for his twelve disciples. (They have, we might say, "given up on the world.")

To make the point clearer, I will contrast two other sorts of mind, each operating primarily in a certain part of society or primarily conspicuous in a certain period. These are the systematic mind (which does deal in elaborate, would-be scientific theory) and the authoritarian (which does deal in force and violence, individual or societal). During a New Age, these two find themselves ignored or insulted. After a New Age they take their revenge, making naïveté seem ridiculous. In times of war, especially when a nation's existence seems at stake, the authoritarian mind is conspicuous; in places of study, think tanks and research laboratories, the systematic mind is dominant.

The systematic mind is that proper to the professional reader, and so, as I said, is one of the meanings of the term *the intellectual.* Gandhi once remarked that intellect had had "very little share" in shaping his life. "I believe that I have a rather poor intellect" (51:1). In Spring 1932, he wrote that he could not write out his ideas in a *smitri* (a treatise). "What I write or say has not been thought out in conformity with a system. I have only enough strength to enable me to meet every situation as it arises" (49:256). He was suspicious even of sustained reading, when that was separate from action. "Many of us read and read until they almost lose the power of thinking." He reproached his secretaries, Desai and Pyarelal, with this failing.

In *Gandhi and Marx,* his friend Kishorelal Mashruwala says that Gandhi refused to write a treatise because that would call forth other treatises. "Armament by one country encourages armament by another, and so with the war of words about scholarly systems."[7] He relied on intuition or instinct.

Gandhi more than once claimed to know the mind of "the people" better than others did, quasi-mystically. "I have one qualification which many of you do not possess. I can almost instinctively feel what is stirring in the heart of the masses."[8] How shall we understand this "instinct" he speaks of? By noting the negative proposition, the criticism of his counsellors, linked to the positive one. I think we can translate his claim into "I instinctively feel the limits—the habits—of your systematic thinking, and recoil away from it towards other kinds of intelligence."

Gandhi himself used the term *simple-hearted* where I use naive, though—like other people—he sometimes used it to suggest "simpleminded." (The two ideas are quite distinct, but they are after all connected.) Gandhi deliberately made himself simple-hearted—a satyagrahi, who practices satyagraha, must be—but he was also congenitally subtle and even suspicious. His secretary Krishnadas wrote a book about his time with Gandhi, called *Seven Months with Mahatma Gandhi* (published in 1929). It is written in a naive style, full of worshipful enthusiasm. Gandhi commented skeptically, "How far Krishnadas himself believes in what he has written in these volumes is the question that agitates me" (UC).

I hope it will, nevertheless, seem plausible to say that Gandhi was a naive mind; that one of his great opponents in imperial politics, Winston Churchill, was an authoritarian; while one of his great opponents in the struggle for the mind of India, Karl Marx, was a systematic mind. Neither of the latter pair belonged to New Ages. Gandhi's achievement, one might say, was to make naïveté more intensive and extensive, to the point where it could infect other people, and at least temporarily checkmate both the power of force and the power of theory.

Culture as a whole, and each individual mind, is composed of elements of all three types. Most people use naive language to describe the ultimate utopian perspective, what the perfect life would look like; and for genial complaints about the authoritarian or the oversystematized. But these are little more than rhetorical elements, of sentiment, or irony, in the general language. And everyone has traits that belong to all three mentalities, even though we (rightly) assign individual cases to one or other of the three. For instance, though Gandhi was naive, he spoke of India often in the authoritarian-patriotic voice—he spoke *as* India, just as Churchill spoke *as* England; while in Gandhi's political/legal documents he was pedagogical and rational to the point of pedantry—he spoke as a systematic mind. He was, after all, by training a lawyer.

Most people think of Gandhi as a political figure, and he certainly deployed political skills on a very large scale. But he—and others, including his enemies—often said he was *not* a politician, and it helps us in understanding the man, to regard him as in some ways split, between that identity and the one I call naive—the New Ager. The split goes deep. For instance, as a politician he appealed often to the manhood of his followers, and spoke of India's weakness as an emasculation. As a New Ager, he said he felt more at ease with women than with men, and even felt himself to be a woman. Both were strong drives in him, toward the masculine and toward the feminine.

In the world of religious ideas the authoritarian mind was often associated with Jehovah, the Father God of the Bible. Common to many kinds of New Ager was a hostility to Jehovah. Madame Blavatsky, the Theosophist, disavowed all interest in him or any other "celestial aristocrat." Stanton Coit, the leader of the Ethical Culture movement, spoke of "the vengeful tribal deity of ancient Israel." Gandhi himself spoke of how Jehovah was invoked to justify bloodshed as soon as war broke out in 1914: "The old formula of Jehovah thirsting for the blood even of children was revived" (29:278).

As for his own theology, he said: "We need no king-like gods"; and to think that we do is to put a limit to the infinite powers of the *atman,* which can come to its fullness in the humblest of us (22:93). And in another place he says we know Mother and God intimately: it is only Father we fear and address formally (11:355). These dispositions of his mind would work against "Jehovah" worship.

The second alternative realism I associate primarily with intellectuals, such as the followers of Marx, Freud, and Weber, the founders of the nineteenth- and twentieth-century social sciences. We do not associate them with patriotic war, with exploits of glory or cherishings of tradition. Their sense of reality is marked by its unmasking of ideology, and by its systematic and rational character: the mutual consistency of its defined terms. Its legendary ancestor is the hard sciences, the triumphant achievement of modern civilization. In society its practical manifestation is the law.

Gandhi confronted the systematic mind in various forms, including traditional Hindu philosophy, but most importantly in socialism. He read Marx himself during his last jail sentence, trying to understand Marx's power to fascinate young Indians. His political heir, Jawaharlal Nehru, was an enthusiastic admirer of Marxist socialism. Gandhi's response of bafflement is expressed in a letter to Nehru, of 1936, in which he says, "Why can't I, with all the will in the world, understand what is so obvious to you? I am not, so far as I know, suffering from intellectual decay" (63:249). Nehru too could not understand many things that were clear and important to Gandhi; things Nehru often labeled as religious. The two mentalities differed.

One might say that the systematic mind, in a pure form, does not believe in nature (or the unconscious, or God, or whatever). It understands everything so much in the terms of social codes that it *cannot* believe in such reservoirs of pure being, out of the reach of human manipulation. The authoritarian mind, understood in the same way, *cannot* believe in innocence; and the naive mind *cannot* believe in realpolitik. Gandhi was a very various mind, composed of elements of all three types. But he was naive with such a passion of intention that he must be understood primarily in terms of God and innocence and the denial of realpolitik.

A Final Contrast

Gandhi and A. K. Coomaraswamy, the art historian, were allies, concerned with the same values, in the decade before 1914, but Coomaraswamy gradually turned away from activism and developed those values into an intellectual system, which he called "the tradition." The contrast with Gandhi becomes clear a propos of a stanza of Blake, the great New Age poet.

> I give you the end of a golden string
> Only wind it into a ball,
> It will lead you in at Heaven's gate
> Built in Jerusalem's wall.

In 1946 the English feminist Emmaline Pethick-Lawrence sent a copy of these lines to Gandhi on his birthday, and added, "You also have put this thread in our hands." Gandhi replied, "Have you ever noticed that my ball is an unending ball of cotton thread instead of Blake's 'golden string'? Blake's was the imagination of a poet, mine can become now and here the gateway if the billions of the earth will but spin the beautiful white ball of the slender and unbreakable thread."[9]

Coomaraswamy, writing of the same stanza, in an article on Literary Symbolism, traced the symbolism of the golden string back through Dante's "Paradiso," St. John's Gospel, Philo, Plato, and Homer. He preserved the tradition, in mummified form.[10] Gandhi used it, as he said, "here and now." That is the difference between the systematic and the naive mind.

Tolstoy the Precursor

I have in other books already aligned Gandhi with Tolstoy, who was in fact his great teacher in the last few years of Tolstoy's life, as two naive minds. This was not the great author of *War and Peace,* but the late Tolstoy, of the years after 1880, a leader of the New Age, who turned away from his work as a novelist, and devoted himself to religious moralism. He and Gandhi belonged to the same branch of the New Age—the ascetic. The moral style of the ascetic New Age (as opposed to the erotic branch) involves a turn back toward childhood teachings.

Thus these two complex minds both said they had been closest to the truth, and at the height of their powers, when they were children; that education, even in the broadest sense of that word, had obscured the truth for them. Tolstoy saw in one of his own children who died very young spiritual powers that he himself could not achieve. Gandhi said that Jesus must have been at the height of his powers as a child, when he talked with the teachers in the temple.

They must be said, therefore, to have tried to be naive. They saw religion (at its supreme moments) in very simple terms. When Gandhi read the Sermon on the Mount in the New Testament in London, he recognized it as the faith he had seen practiced around him as a child—a religion of compassion and renunciation. He and Tolstoy tried later in life to retrieve their childish faith by an eager assent to the moral teachings of Christianity on the one hand, Hinduism on the other; taking those teachings in what seems to most of us the brightly coloured picture-book form of, say, the Gospels and the Parables.

The vegetarianism they shared, for example, was under one aspect simply a literal application of "Thou shalt not kill." Most of us learn as adolescents not to apply that commandment to the food on our plates. Indeed, Tolstoy and Gandhi learned that "adult" lesson too; but then rebelled against it.

Thus the word *naive* shows its appropriateness to the New Age temperament in the latter's childish attachment to goodness; its stubborn insistence on the primary-school or catechetical virtues. Tolstoy in his old age thought he had been taught the crucial values as a child, and then had them obscured (ridiculed and replaced) in adolescence. Gandhi was taught to recite the name of Rama by his nurse, gave it up as a young man, and rediscovered its virtues when he was sent to jail.

At the age of twelve, he tells us, he was taught not to hate his enemies, and for the rest of his life he went on trying to apply that lesson. He told, admiringly, the story of Queen Victoria promising to be good, when she was told she was queen. Victoria was sometimes known as "Victoria the Good," and Gandhi chose as his political guru the man he called "Gokhale the Good." Most people find that word inappropriate for adults. (A popular appeal to goodness, in a tag that in Gandhi's time came to be used ironically, was "Be good, sweet maid, and let who will be clever.")

Naiveté also means Tolstoy's saying that we have only to want no more war, and we shall have no more war. We find the same faith in Gandhi—the moment Indians really want *swaraj,* self-rule, they will have it. The two men's heroic personalism was also voluntarism: man must live by will, not habit.

"Gandhi was an incarnation of voluntarism," is the way J. P. Narayan began his essay of 1970, "Gandhi and Social Revolution."[11] But their sense that everything depends on the individual act of will also contained a component of lightness, which facilitated that heroism: a sense that the world only exists as it does because we allow it to—because we assent to its claims. Much of what we call, or allow to be called, the world's substance—"human nature" and "our situation" and "what history teaches"—is quite insubstantial. Reality could perfectly well be absolutely different tomorrow, and we do not need to take it seriously. Gandhi once refused to "judge mankind on the scanty evidence of history." He was a realistic politician, as Tolstoy was a realistic moralist, but it was a paradoxical, New Age realism in both cases.

It is also a contradiction of common sense. A New Age must be radically different from the traditional and the accustomed. Nonviolence is obviously a contradiction of violence, which at least in its institutional form is something taken for granted. Nonviolence may sound utopian or sentimental, but to believe it demands a powerful skepticism about accepted truths, and a ruthlessness of feeling and action. Tolstoy and Gandhi lived, for instance, on intimate terms with the idea of death.

Paradox is one of Gandhi's characteristic traits, in literary style (calling the prisons he was locked up in His Majesty's hotels, for instance) in self-presentation (he labeled himself a crank and a quack and a faddist) and in political philosophy. He more than once quoted a South African friend who said he would always support Gandhi as long as the latter was in the minority (24:180). And Gandhi himself professed to feel uneasy whenever he found himself surrounded by a large following. This of course is profoundly self-contradictory for a political leader.

Minds in Conflict

The mutual antagonism between these three mentalities takes many forms. One of the most striking is the resentment felt by the systematic for the naive, and vice versa. Academia, guardian of systematic realism, regards Gandhi as grade-school pablum, to be rejected by the brighter high-school student, and on no account to be allowed into college, except to be reductively analyzed. To reject Gandhi, along with many other New Age enthusiasms, is an intellectual rite of passage.

Gandhi encountered the same hostility in his own time and place. In 1921 he remarked that the educated classes in India had not taken up his nonviolent noncooperation because they were skeptical—being soaked in modern or Western civilization—and lacked the religious fire of the people (19:266). In 1925 he reported a student telling him that he and his friends could not take the interest in spinning that Gandhi wanted, because: "There is no excitement about the wheel. Our education has unfitted us for any such work" (27:196).

K. M. Munshi, a Bombay lawyer and politician, reports that Gandhi said to him, "I do not understand educated men, and they do not understand me; but the masses know me and I know them."[12] Munshi adds, "He was right; educated men have come to believe in him because what he says comes true, not because they are convinced."

Another of those skeptical intellectuals was M. R. Jayakar; he first encountered Gandhi around 1920, and was then very impressed by him, saying how different he was from our idea of a politician, with his: "deep-seated modesty, restraint, asceticism, simplicity, refinement and culture. . . . Political life is to Gandhi only an extension of domestic life, governed by the same ideals of truth, justice, . . . love, generosity, and refinement."[13]

Later, however, reacting against his early enthusiasm, Jayakar said that in politics Gandhi lived in a world of his own, and could not bring his critical faculties to play upon his own "theories." Tolstoy, Christ, and Buddha, said Jayakar, held a "singular sway" over Gandhi (354). Jayakar decided that the other man's doctrine of ennoblement by suffering, and of persuading the opponent by one's suffering, "has no scope in public affairs" (356). In other words, Gandhi dissolved politics away, by reducing public values to domestic ones.

That division between public and private was paralleled by another between political and religious. Gandhi himself said in 1919 that to get certain political reforms passed was less important to him than to defeat the punitive Rowlatt Acts: because the latter were *moral poison* (16:36). He was a man of religion rather than of politics, and so the reforms affected him more superficially. This self-description as a "man of religion," and not a politician, is a recurrent motif of Gandhi's self-presentation, and means something like "naive mind."

Many Indian politicians shared Jayakar's opinion. Srinivasa Sastri, a leading liberal, wrote Gandhi in 1935, "To my unaided mind you appear to be opening the first campaign of an endless and quixotic war against modern civilization.

Long ago you proclaimed yourself its sleepless enemy, and now you would, if you could, turn it back on the course it has pursued for some millennia. I reel at the mere thought" (60:54). And in 1938 Gandhi himself reported that Nehru "is convinced that I have put back the clock of progress by a century or thereabout by my Rajkot misdeeds. [One of Gandhi's civil disobedience campaigns was held in Rajkot.] . . . He thinks I am impossible for an organization. He is right there" (69:369).

But this opposition was more than a matter of politics and progressivism. Even in matters of music, for instance, Jayakar remarked that Gandhi knew nothing of Indian music, and would probably not have been attracted to it, because of its complexity.[14] It is true that Western classical music was too complex for him.

The difference was a matter, then, of mentality, not just of politics in the narrow sense. In January 1942, Gandhi gave a speech at Benares Hindu University, and said, "A feeling of nervousness overpowers me when I am in the midst of learned men. . . . In your midst I feel tongue-tied." He said that half-musingly, as he looked for a topic; and then, "The inspiration has come, but I do not know how you will welcome my plain-speaking" (75:241). The topic he found was a complaint against the students speaking English instead of an Indian language. He wanted them to resist the modern world with all of their minds. He wanted them to join the New Age. He spoke of making the world stop spinning, to start again in the opposite direction.

New Age Themes and Concerns

In April 1910, Gandhi's South African paper, *Indian Opinion,* reproduced a satirical cartoon entitled "The March of Civilization," which had originally appeared in the London magazine, *New Age*. The title *New Age* was an easily read signal of that magazine's contents; it was considered England's leading journal not so much of left-wing politics as of cultural radicalism; and the link between it and *Indian Opinion* is appropriately symbolized by a satire on "Civilization."

Equally appropriate was the fact that these were both journals and not books. In any New Age, journalism or pamphlets are likely to be more important than in periods dominated by the authoritarian or systematic minds. This is because, to the naive mind, ultimate truth may be embodied in living persons and may take the form of contemporary events, the news of the day; and because it can be told in language simple enough for everyone to understand. (In other periods theological or theoretical documents, written in sacred or technical language, defer the ultimate truths.) That is presumably why some journalists have such high prestige in New Age places and times. Both the systematic and the authoritarian mind tend to scorn journalism.

In the eighteenth-century New Age we had Tom Paine; in our own New Age we have Norman Mailer; and in Gandhi's New Age we had Gandhi. And before he began to write, there were also famous names like George Bernard Shaw, G. K. Chesterton, Annie Besant, and Robert Blatchford, to name only those we find referred to by Gandhi. There were also H. G. Wells and Hilaire Belloc and others; the line separating journalism from literature was fuzzier than at other times. When such an age ends, that line is redrawn more firmly, and the controversy between, for instance, Wells and Henry James is reread, to James's advantage.

But we will here concentrate on substance rather than process, and analyze the nineteenth-century New Age in terms of its concerns. The New Age was, amongst other things, a reaction against the imperialism that became rampant in Europe at the end of the nineteenth century. The British Empire was the greatest single case of that imperialism, and India was the jewel in the crown of Empire. For an Indian, therefore, it was natural (easier than for a white-skinned man) to make himself central to the New Age. In 1909 Gandhi read Edward Carpenter's diagnosis of modern civilization with enthusiasm, but added that Carpenter half-knew what he was talking about; only an Indian could really know.

Historians speak of a New Imperialism that developed in England at the end of the nineteenth century, differentiated from earlier imperialism by its jingoism among other things.[15] It called into being its antithesis, a new radicalism, which deeply affected Gandhi. A leading radical of that generation was J. A. Hobson, the economist and author of *Imperialism* and *The Psychology of Jingoism.* Hobson's inspiration and principal teacher, even in economic theory, was Ruskin, the most important single English name in the New Age.

Hobson's friends, who included the future prime minister, Ramsay MacDonald, belonged to the Union of Ethical Societies, which took up the cause of the Indians in South Africa, and in 1909 Gandhi became a member of the union, and made friends amongst the members.

That union, founded in 1896, had aims much broader than party politics, which covered much of the New Age spectrum. It aimed to give religion a scientific basis, to impose the rule of morality on politics, and to give philosophy an anthropocentric synthesis: all of them ideas congenial to Gandhi. The journal the *National Reformer* discussed New Age topics like free love, vegetarianism, vivisection, and so on. Edward Carpenter was a regular contributor, as well as Hobson. The journal was edited by Hypatia Bradlaugh Bonner, the daughter of Charles Bradlaugh, the famous member of parliament who was known as "the Member for India."

These radicals were not in every sense anti-imperialist. On issues like the Anglo-Boer War, for instance, they found it difficult to be on the Boer side; because the British Empire had a more liberal philosophy than the Boers or other white colonists. But they were very critically interested in imperial issues. They made use of new kinds of knowledge, which had been unavailable to Victorian liberals, Porter says; including the field reports of anthropologists. They sat in judgment on Western culture.

It will be noted how often the word *new* is used by Porter: new knowledge, new radicals, new imperialism. This is a sign that he is discussing the New Age. Another sign is the heterogeneous subject matter. There is no system to New Age theory, but a number of ideas, and a number of names, like Hobson and Ruskin, which knit themselves together into a movement of thought.

The concerns of the New Age (a dozen of which are discussed more fully in *Prophets of a New Age*) ranged from Orientalism and what we now call Environmentalism to Nature Cure and Nonviolence. The last-named, which is associated especially with Gandhi, was one of the major concerns of his period, but also of that later period at the end of the twentieth century. That does not mean that everyone who can be called New Age was or is nonviolent; the greatest spokesman for Gandhi's New Age, Ruskin, saw the arts as all founded on war. But peace was a widespread and passionate wish, and there was a marked relation of leadership, or at least of affinity, between that particular aspiration and the others.

The promise of peace has of course been traditionally one of the consolations of religion, devised by the victims of empire. Christianity, for instance, was seen in Gandhi's time (and other times) as a movement of protest within the Roman Empire; as having been originally *founded* as a New Age reaction against imperialism. For instance, George Santayana, in an essay of 1900, described its early impact in terms of newness and naïveté: "Therein was a new poetry, a new ideal, a new God. . . . It carried the imagination into a new sphere; it sanctified the poverty and sorrow at which Paganism had shuddered; it awakened tenderer emotions. . . . It was a whole world of poetry descended among men. . . . The consciousness of new loves, new duties, fresh consolations, and luminous unutterable hopes."[16] Santayana was speaking *of* the atmosphere of the first century A.D., but he wrote *in* a comparable atmosphere at the end of the nineteenth century. Though not himself susceptible of Gandhian kinds of enthusiastic action, he was very alert to them.

Gandhi even saw crucifixion as part of his fate, or his ambition. He began his movement in South Africa with the vow to resist the government's regulation to the death; and only a day or two before he was in fact assassinated, forty years later, he told his friends that he would not have deserved the title Mahatma if he died of an illness—only if he were killed by a bullet and died with God's name on his lips. From early on, his most understanding friends—Henry Polak, Emily Hobhouse, Florence Winterbottom—told him he would die on the scaffold; and others like Isabella Mayo and Mira Behn, Charlie Andrews and Verrier Elwin, drew the world's attention to many other parallels between his story and Jesus Christ's.

In a less-emotive style, William James wrote an essay on nonviolence, "The Moral Equivalent of War," which appeared in the same year as Gandhi's main statement, *Hind Swaraj*. The American philosopher said that so far war had been the only force that could discipline a whole community, and preserve its "manliness of type"; but he believed that a different social movement could be developed to be just as effective for that purpose. In effect, Gandhi offered satyagraha, firmness in truth, as that movement.

"The Moral Equivalent of War" was a New Age document using rational and liberal language. Gandhi's idea was linked, for good and ill, to the more emotional and mythic language of a crucified savior. He was a victim, a figure of renunciation, an embodied call for compassion, in the most exalted style.

His teaching was often compared with the Buddha's; and Buddhism too was in this period the object of very general interest.

This tremendous pathos became a part of Gandhism, and to some degree of the whole New Age. Romain Rolland said in the 1920s that Gandhi's life was the strongest stimulant that European Christianity could get (31:571). And Americans were even more fascinated by the parallel. John Haynes Holmes gave a famous sermon in New York, after Gandhi's Salt March, entitled "Gandhi before Pilate"; and introduced a collection of Gandhi's letters to Madeline Slade, *Letters to a Disciple,* by comparing the woman they were addressed to with the women who stayed loyal to Christ when his men disciples fled.

But nonviolence was only one of the New Age concerns. The New Agers rebelled in a sense against everything—against "reality," the old sense of reality that was embodied in all sorts of institutions, from parliament to the local police station, from individual factories to the stock exchange or the Royal Navy.

Two such features of the age were especially often discussed as rapidly growing powers; one was imperialism abroad, and the other was bureaucratization and industrialization at home. Because the latter was a case of and for grim realism, while the former declared itself romantic, the two often seemed to be in conflict. But in the work of the great proconsuls, like Milner in South Africa, and the viceregal government in India, they came together. And in Kipling's stories and poems about the imperial caste, both the romantic and the realistic were celebrated.

Gandhi was an enemy of the British Empire in the second half of his life. In the first half he was its friend. Even more strikingly, there was something in his moral style that derived from that of British Imperialism. His most massive biography, written by his devoted secretary, Pyarelal, begins with a quotation of Kipling's poem, "If," which celebrates the Kipling virtues; and Pyarelal says, "If the poet had had for his pattern the man whom it was my privilege to serve and follow to the end of his days, the picture could not have been truer to life. Calm in the midst of storm, awake when others were lulled into false security . . . by the alchemy of his detachment he transmuted his anguish into a relentless drive for self-denial, self-purification, and self-surrender."[17] This kind of moral melodrama (as a critic might see it) that soon rang false in England itself after 1900, flourished amongst the Anglo-Indians. It was in the empire that—as Paul Scott amongst others has remarked—the greatest drama of "the English" was played out, and the Indian resisters, including Gandhi himself, responded to it in something like the empire's style.

Looking at one of the other colonies, however, Gandhi also saw the empire as the home of bureaucracy—in South Africa. When the Transvaal was taken over by British officials (many of whom had worked in India) after the Anglo-Boer War, its bureaucracy grew more rigid. "A good officer has not under the British Government as much scope for the exercise of his goodness as he had under the Boer regime." The British officers had to work like machines. "Their liberty of action is restricted by a system of progressive checks." This was the idea of system made concrete—the Iron Cage—and Gandhi like other New Agers resisted it.

This second idea was at first associated with Max Weber and his perception of Central Europe. Watching the unification and organization of Germany after 1870, Europeans were made disturbingly aware that the modern state brought with it a great number of restrictions, regulations, and frustrations, for the individual citizen. These resistances, to imperialism and to bureaucracy/industrialism, were two of the leading characteristics of the New Age.

New Age politics needed its own images. Some of these I have suggested were traditionally religious; others were supplied by the Tolstoy Farms and simple life "colonies," which sprang up everywhere in this period. One of these, at Ascona in Switzerland, has been called the capital city of Europe's counterculture: it is not clear how much Gandhi knew about Ascona, but it was the subject of excited curiosity in the vegetarian circle he belonged to.

As far as the world scene went, the political imagery was supplied notably by Gandhi himself, in India, and in South Africa in the first decade of the twentieth century; the imagery of his loincloth and sandals, his arrests by the police and sentences to jail, and the whole satyagraha movement. In 1908, for instance, he was marched through Johannesburg from the railway station to the fort, in convict clothes and carrying a prison kit. He had been a highly successful lawyer in that city, earning as much as five thousand pounds a year, and people on the street stared at his humiliation; but for some of them he was now charged with a greater value. They saw suffering and sacrifice entering into politics.

Another example of such idealism was to be found in the Zionist aspiration to reclaim the Holy Land of Palestine, which Gandhi saw a lot of in South Africa. The Jews Gandhi himself knew saw being Jewish as a special calling to a universal moral obligation. Henry Polak said he had taken part in Gandhi's satyagraha campaigns because the Indian problem seemed to him the Jewish problem all over again, and he attacked his coreligionists for their indifference or hostility to the Indian movement. Polak was not only Gandhi's lieutenant in South Africa; at Gandhi's suggestion he (an Anglo-Jew) also toured India as the spokesman to Indians at home for the Indians in exile. That international and peripatetic agitation (like Tom Paine's) was a very New Age political gesture.

A number of interests, in diet, reformed clothing, nature cure, sunbathing, and so on—in opposition to city life and scientific medicine and factory production—came together to form a cult of nature and of simplicity. One symbol within this powerful system was the knitted wool clothing with which Dr. Gustav Jaeger promised to save his customers from physical degeneracy. (George Bernard Shaw wore Jaeger suits.) The homespun *khadi* that Gandhi's followers wore was very similar, and was recommended in very similar terms.

There were also the sandals that Edward Carpenter got from India, and which the Gandhians in South Africa made for themselves. It was of course possible to go completely barefoot, as some Simple Lifers did, but even sandals stood in powerful contrast to leather boots or shoes, and became a sign of the New Age. A book of 1901 by Ernest Crosby, an American Tolstoyan, says that sandals "free the human foot from the stiff, impermeable leather boxes in which it is at present deformed and befouled."

A quite different kind of the Simple Life was to be found among Nonconformist working-class Christians. Wilfred Wellock was one of those who became an English Gandhian. He wrote an autobiography called *Off the Beaten Track* (published by a Gandhian press in India in 1963) that gives us interesting details of this kind of Simple Living. He was born in 1879 in Nelson, a cotton-mill town in Lancashire. There was no smoking or drinking in the family home, and Wilfred's recreation was a Saturday afternoon walk of ten or fifteen miles, and some carpentry or painting in the evenings.

For the decade 1892–1902 his Nonconformist church was the hub of Wellock's life. At the age of twenty he was preaching every Sunday. And besides the Bible, he was teaching the lessons of the New Age—of Ruskin, Tolstoy, Kropotkin, Emerson. He came to see Jesus as a man, not a god, and translated Christian feeling into the terms of socialism.

Everyone he knew before 1914, he says, was an optimistic idealist; they saw their enemies as only remnants of feudalism, and were inspired by a fine galaxy of poets; notably Blake and Shelley. But then, "As I reached middle life I began to notice that the idealists were declining in number . . . some years later came the biggest shock of all when I discovered that I had been swerved into a backwater. . . . People like me were relegated to the back stage."[18] He was a member of parliament from 1927 to 1931, but the New Age was over, and he was living in a social wilderness.

But if we look at how Wellock's story got published, we get a less-gloomy picture. He kept in touch with Gandhi, and after the latter's death was asked to write his story by the editor of the Gandhian Sarvodaya Press, and a foreword is contributed by J. P. Narayan, who became the greatest Gandhian political leader of the 1960s and 1970s. Narayan says he had begun to read Wellock's *Orchard Lea Papers* in 1954, and went to his cottage home in 1958, where he found the old man still living the simple life. He followed a vegetarian diet, kept his income below income-tax level, and so on. Narayan concludes that he hopes Wellock's book will find its way into the hands of every college student in India. Thus we see—as we saw in Gandhi's own case, fifty years earlier—how New Age ideas, in some sense starved to death in England after 1918, found their way to a more fertile soil in India.

Edward Thompson, the son of a Methodist missionary and a friend to Indian nationalism, gave a similar account of the side of England he belonged to, writing to Nehru in 1937. "I belong to that joyous (once-joyous, that is) confident Liberal movement which before the War did manage to get something done for our working classes (at any rate, practically all that ever has been done for them), which believed that *by peaceful methods* we could do away with every kind of injustice everywhere. Most of us are in our graves, and the rest of us disillusioned and prematurely broken in spirit."[19] He is talking about the New Age.

The Garden Cities conceived and even brought to birth in England in this period—a radical attempt to redeem the nineteenth-century urban scene from its dreary ugliness—appealed to the Nonconformist sects like the ones to which Wellock and Thompson belonged, and provided a congenial environment for lovers of the Simple Life. A typical citizen of the first of them, Letchworth, for instance, was vegetarian and Theosophist, had a photograph of Madame Blavatsky on the mantelpiece, and books by her, William Morris, Tolstoy, and H.G. Wells on the shelves. (So we are told in "From a Letchworth Diary" in *Town and Country Planning,* in 1953.) Many of the later citizens would have Gandhi pictures and pamphlets. These are the Socialists Stanley Pierson calls "Ethical Socialists," as opposed to scientific or Marxist Socialists. New Age summer schools were held there, and after the war, Ebenezer Howard organized another such city at Welwyn. The Theosophists ran a coeducational, vegetarian boarding school at Letchworth, to which Henry Polak sent his sons.

Howard was a long-term adherent of the South Place Ethical Society, and sometimes led its Sunday excursions into Epping Forest, which took the place of church services. He was a friend of Shaw and of Sidney Webb, the Fabian, and influenced by Thomas Davidson of the Fellowship of the New Life. The same names turn up in the membership of most of these activities, and—more broadly—each group knew about the others. The New Age was a subculture of its own. The Garden Cities are an example of the New Age mind at its mildest, its most moderate, and compatible with ordinary respectable life.

Gandhi spread news of the Garden City movement while in South Africa, and read and wrote to one of its leaders, Patrick Geddes, about civic festivals and ideal cities in India. He said in 1924 that he had intended when he settled there, to work to make Ahmedabad an ideal city, opening up parks, providing pure milk to all the population, and ensuring the planned growth of the city by building new suburbs. It was the demands of the nationalist movement that "blew away such schemes" (25:40–41).

Passing from life-style to religion and philosophy, we come to the Orientalism and Theosophy so popular in Garden Cities. As in our own New Age, the people of that earlier one took a strong interest in the religions of the East, especially in Buddhism, Hinduism, and Taoism. Edward Carpenter visited India, and in the careers of Annie Besant and Gandhi, we see that interest taking on a political dimension, as major New Age enterprises. The first leading congressmen were many of them Theosophists, as Gandhi remarked (85:514).

Among the Theosophical sects, the one with which Gandhi had most to do was the Hermetic Society, later called the Esoteric Christian Union, founded by Edward Maitland and Anna Kingsford. One of their concerns was humanitarianism and vegetarianism—the horror of carnivorousness. One sentence of Anna Kingsford's about meat-eaters stuck in Gandhi's mind, and he quoted it more than once: "As I walk about the streets of Paris, I seem to see before me divers lions and tigers personified" (28:21, 1925). Kingsford, who took a degree in medicine in Paris, believed she had cured herself of tuberculosis by following a vegetarian diet. Maitland was another Shelley-enthusiast, and a figure in several aspects of the New Age. He was, for instance, one of the founding members of Salt's Humanitarian League.

Maitland was a declared reincarnation of John the Baptist, as Kingsford was of Mary Magdalene. But she had been a man previously, and Christ had been a woman—such alternations of gender were a regular feature of the Theosophists' sense of self. Each person has several layers of identity, of both genders. In 1890 the pair published *The Perfect Way; or, The Finding of Christ,* which had considerable vogue, and also *The Perfect Way in Diet.* Both of these were praised by Gandhi, and one can see what would appeal to him in their teaching. For instance, Kingsford and Maitland said that Christ had probably been an adept of the religious science of Egypt and India.

More radically, they said that God is twain in gender; He is the Life, and She is the Substance. Man, too, is a dual being, both man and woman—but woman is superior. Man is Understanding, woman is Intuition. All truths, such as the multiple rebirths of the ego, are discovered by intuition. Such ideas obviously have much in common with the erotic and unconscious-life ideas of apparently remote contemporaries like D.H. Lawrence. These conjunctions are signs of the New Age's kind of connection or convergence.

Gender is always a focus of anxiety and speculation in New Ages. Edward Carpenter took up the cause of homosexuality. But the period from 1880–1910 was the time above all of the New Woman, symbol of a movement for the liberation of women, imaginatively as well as politically. She was depicted by women artists and writers like Olive Schreiner (a friend of Gandhi's) but also by men like Shaw, Wells, Ibsen, and Hardy.

This was by a natural correspondence the period of the women's suffrage movement, and Gandhi attended some of its meetings in England. One part of the movement was led by Mrs. Pankhurst and her daughters. Gandhi criticized their violence, and the Pankhursts resented his criticism. But other English feminists were in sympathy with him; for instance, the Quaker Emmaline Pethick-Lawrence, already mentioned, and the suffragist leader Gandhi knew and liked best, Charlotte Despard, also a Theosophist.

Thus there was a variety of ways in which women struggled for freedom, and Gandhi was a hero to many of the activists. In South Africa, Millie Polak wrote: "Most women love men for such attributes as are usually considered masculine. Yet Mohandas Gandhi has been given the love of many women for his womanliness." They found in him a fellow traveller.[20]

In India, he often sounded like a feminist. He wanted to remove from the Hindu wedding vows taken by a bride the promise to regard the groom as a guru and a god (43:9). In 1929 he had an article in his weekly, *Navajivan,* entitled "An Unfortunate Daughter." He described a case history and generalized: many girls suffer this one's fate. "Selfish and bigoted parents push her into the sea of matrimony as soon as she begins to take an interest in studies and games" (41:160). Many of the friends and coworkers closest to him were women eager to prove themselves in action.

A variety of attitudes toward the erotic can be linked to the New Age; there is a range all the way from enthusiasm to rejection; but to qualify as New Age, the attitude must express some intensity of feeling. Both the other kinds of realism can often take life's sexual element for granted, at least more often than the New Age can. Because of the latter's assertively naive and spontaneous values, anything that has as much as sex has the character of "unconscious" or "animal" truth is bound to seem to be of the utmost importance, whether as a manifestation of the inner life, or as an interruption of that life.

On the whole, Tolstoy and Gandhi were sharply separated from most other members of the New Age over this, because of their asceticism. But Gandhi read Havelock Ellis and Bertrand Russell on sex, in the first part of his life, and experimented with sex in the last part. Ascetics, after all, are very interested in sex: we shall describe a Purity Campaign that took place in this period.

Marriage was an institution under severe attack, usually in the name of erotic fulfillment. It was depicted as a black hole of lovelessness in novels and the lives of novelists: see, for instance, the semipublic misery of Tolstoy's marriage in this period—and the Gandhis' not entirely private misery. In the teachings of Tolstoy and Gandhi marriage suffered an opposite rejection, the preferred state for them being celibacy or renunciation. Whether that or sexual freedom was recommended, however, sexuality became quite generally the object of great interest, moral and intellectual.

In New Ages there are always bold experiments in the salvation of the individual, which correspond to the group movements in politics and economics. The "unconscious life" is, as was just said, very important to New Agers. Gandhi's ashram always contained a number of disturbed people, whom he was looking after.

In the West, the most famous names in the history of psychotherapy came to be Sigmund Freud and Carl Jung, but the most extreme New Age psychoanalyst was Otto Gross of Ascona, who carried the ideal of individual liberation as far as it could go. As a result, Gross moved quickly away from the orthodox position of the ordinary medical man as servant of society, and toward the position of accuser of society (which often meant the sick one's family) in the name of the patient. This was a New Age idea of medicine, comparable with Nature Cure. Gandhi encouraged some of those who came to him to escape from the bondage of conventional family and sex roles.

Early on in his life, Gandhi wanted to become a doctor, because of his love of healing. But he could not accept Western medicine's experiments with animals. His was a nonviolent medicine, and one friendly to the other species. But he acted as a therapist to many of the inmates of his ashrams and to others who came to him to find relief from torment. He was even ready, on occasion, to diagnose repressed sexuality as the source of their problems. With certain friends, his correspondence is full of therapeutic recommendation and consolation; this was a sizable part of his total activity.

The New Age is therefore a cloud of tendency, not embodied completely in any one person, though partly in everyone. But if there were to be a search made throughout history for representatives of the idea in all its ramifications—

and quite apart from the fact that he magnified the concept with his extraordinary abilities—Gandhi would surely be one of those chosen. He is therefore in no sense unique and peculiar, twisted or crazy; much less born out of his due time and place. On the map of culture, he took up a familiar position, and used an easily recognized voice, indeed one of the most important of all voices, to be heard lifted up in all times and places in our recurrent debates over "What then must we do?"

ONE

PORBANDAR AND THE PAST

· 1869–1876 ·

Mohandas Karamchand Gandhi was born on October 2, 1869, in a three-story house in Porbandar; which is a town on the Arabian Sea coast of India, north of Bombay, in the province of Gujarat. In earlier centuries, it had traded with Persia, Arabia, Java, Africa. A hundred yards from the water a road runs around three sides of the town, and a quarter of a mile inside the circle still stands the Gandhi home. The house is a fortresslike structure of limestone, whose walls bear the marks of cannon fire. About thirty years before Gandhi's birth, his grandfather, the chief administrator of the little state of Porbandar, had quarreled with the ruling monarch, Rupali Ba, who had thereupon besieged his house and fired cannon at it, till the British agent in Rajkot intervened.

It is a house of many rooms, most small and dark. A suite of two rooms on the ground floor were occupied by Gandhi's father and his immediate family; plus a small kitchen and veranda. Gandhi's mother had a room twenty-by-thirteen feet; but the inner room occupied by her mother-in-law was twelve-by-twelve feet. The house stood on three sides of an underground tank of rainwater that measured fifteen-by-twenty-by-ten feet. This was a valuable resource in time of siege. Drinking water was scarce in Porbandar, and the lime in the soil purified the rainwater and made it potable. Mohandas Gandhi was married on the front veranda of that house.

The Arabian Sea therefore almost surrounded the town of Porbandar. Before the nineteenth century, there had been a lot of piracy on that ocean, and the city walls were built up to be twenty feet thick, to resist attack. They were constructed, as was the Gandhi house, of the local limestone, which gradually turned white and hard like marble, when it was exposed to the open air. Ships approaching Porbandar saw a flash of white in the sky before they saw the harbor.

In his autobiography, Gandhi does not describe the town, but implicitly presents it as a suitable background to his parents' traditional and respectable family life. In other places, however, he gives us saltier images of Porbandar. In one speech he said he had grown up in a village of fishermen, and so he knew what fishermen were like; "I suppose it is from their habits that we have got the phrase 'he drinks like a fish'" (57:209). When addressing an audience in Cocanada, moreover, he referred to the many prostitutes of his native town (19:503).

So we gather that it had some of the social characteristics of a British or American port. His family's Porbandar, on the other hand, probably was remote from that of the sailors and prostitutes. His father was a man of high social and moral standing. Mohan's elder brother, Karshandas, however, was a somewhat disreputable character, and *his* life may not have been so far removed from theirs.

In any case, Gandhi was in some ways highly critical of the family he was born into. It was a family of politicians, he said, always involved in secret alliances and mutual promotions (24:170). Even early in the morning, his father was surrounded every day on the veranda by squatting groups who stayed till he went to his office.

Gandhi must have been proud at first of his family heritage, but he reacted against it in later years. In South Africa he wrote his nephew, Chhaganlal, that the Gandhis had been a famous, or perhaps notorious family: "that is, we are known to belong to a band of robbers" (12:381). He meant, of course, that they had lived on, or off, the people.

More moderately and analytically, he wrote: "I knew then, and know better now, that much of my father's time was taken up in mere intrigue. Discussions started early in the morning and went on till it was time to leave for the office. Everyone talked in whispers" (24:170).

The talk was of how to get an official appointment, how to promote the Gandhi family interests, or how to advance the Modh Bania caste they belonged to, as against other people. The experience sickened Mohandas of politicians. "I am atoning for their sin of clever talking by . . . the philosophy of action . . . my dislike of this [scheming] was even one of the reasons for my leaving the country." Gandhi hated that atmosphere, and in South Africa tried to take on a different identity, as farmer—and later as weaver and sweeper.

At times he extends this "politician" image from his family to the whole region of Kathiawar. "I know how turbid Kathiawari politics is. This unfortunate sub-province is notorious for its intrigues" (69:13). "You will not see anywhere else the fierce hatreds you see in Kathiawar" (50:422). The very word *Kathiawari,* he claimed, suggested crookedness. In the last year of his life he quoted a saying that Kathiawaris have as many twists in their hearts as they have in their *puggrees*—their turbans (35:215).

The house had been bought in 1777 by Mohandas's great grandfather, and about twenty to twenty-five people lived there in his childhood. They acquired their family name at the time when Uttamchand (our Gandhi's grandfather) gave offense to Rupali Ba. He then had to flee to the neighboring state of Junagadh with his five children, and his work there was as a grocer—which is what the word *Gandhi* means. But that was a short episode of commerce in a family history of administration.

In 1841 Rupali Ba died, and her successor invited Uttamchand to return as *diwan* (chief minister) again, but he recommended his son Karamchand instead. The latter was the fifth son in his generation, and yet—like *his* son, our Gandhi—he was preferred over his older brothers. Other men in the family had lesser administrative jobs; four out of five of our Gandhi's paternal uncles were so employed. Karamchand was diwan of Porbandar for about thirty years, until the ruler imposed a punishment (on someone else) that Karamchand thought unjust. He resigned, acting as a man of principle, and pride, on this as on other occasions; when, for instance, the Rajah of Wankaner tried to settle the accounts between them by offering him less than he should have, Karamchand refused to take anything.

So the Gandhis were not untouched by the risks and responsibilities of power, and the rivalries of patronage. Explaining his family to Englishmen, Gandhi usually said that his father was the prime minister of the state, but Karamchand had nothing to do with elections and parliamentary debates or Liberal vs. Conservative parties. He gave advice to the royal family of Porbandar, considered applicants for jobs and contracts, and supervised appointments.

In the first biography of Gandhi, which derived directly from his own account, we are told that the Porbandar princes traced their line back to Hanuman, the monkey god, and were strange, fantastic, choleric characters. They represented traditional or legendary power and force, and in the "modern" times of the pax britannica were often out of touch with reality—so could be called "fantastic." The Gandhis could be said to represent moral and rational realism in Porbandar, in contrast to that fantasy.

This background is something to keep in mind as we follow Gandhi's life-story. J. C. Heesterman, in *The Inner Conflict of Tradition* (University of Chicago, 1985) says that according to Indian tradition, the king must seek to ally himself to the brahmin, but the latter must reject the alliance (7). "The pivot of Indian tradition [is] the irreconcilability of 'brahmin' and 'king'" (15). Interdependence would be fatal to the brahmin, as it would have been to the Jewish prophets. We shall see Mahatma Gandhi acting as brahmin advisor, opponent, denouncer, to the British "kings" first of all, and later to the Indians in power.

In class terms, it has been suggested, the Gandhis could have found in the English novel—had they read such things—the voice of a social identity in some ways like their own. (In fact, Gandhi did read *Pride and Prejudice* at school.) The novels of Jane Austen, and those of her nineteenth-century successors, come out of an experience of cultural responsibility like that of the Gandhis. C. D. S. Devanesan describes the family as "impoverished gentry," and says, "respected but poor, friendly with the rich and powerful but alienated from them, they would naturally develop a contempt for the nouveau riche and lean towards radicalism in politics."[1] It is of course the Mahatma Devanesen is primarily thinking of.

Mohandas was the third son and last child of Putliba, the fourth and last wife of Karamchand Gandhi. (The familiar form of his name was Kaba.) The latter's third wife had proved infertile, and he married again at the age of thirty-seven or so, while she was still alive; and could not, for that reason, aspire to an equal match, socially. Putliba, who was only thirteen at the time of the marriage, was a village girl of a somewhat lower caste.

The offspring of Karamchand's earlier marriages, and other branches of the family and servants, were stowed away in that house's warren or honeycomb of dark, hot rooms. The coasts of Kathiawar are both warm and humid. Reminiscing later, Gandhi remembered how much pleasanter the top story was, being built of wood, and exposed to the winds of the sea.

The sociologist Fatima Meer paints a vivid picture of what the birth itself must have been like.[2] The still-young mother would lie isolated from the family in the long dark lying-in room, attended only by a midwife of the washerwoman caste, an Untouchable. Her mother-in-law, Tulsima, when she heard the news, must have climbed down from the swing on the roof, where she lay every morning, making the day's supply of *pan* (a traditional Indian snack). The father/husband was away from home.

For ten days the new mother lay there alone, polluted by the carnal act of giving birth, the room lit and heated by an oil lamp. When Tulsima was given the newborn baby to hold, it would be on a towel fetched from elsewhere. Everything in the lying-in room was considered contaminated. (The idea of pollution, and the opposite cleansing, material and moral, was installed in many rituals of Hindu culture.) The baby was given an auspicious horoscope by the family astrologer, and his name was compounded from letters supplied by the same priest.

In such families a child was often breast-fed until much later than was common in the West, according to some Indian autobiographies. A youngest child might conceivably still be given the breast when as old as five. In cases like Gandhi's, one has the right to speculate about the effects of such a history, because the relations between Putliba and her youngest child were unusually close, her hopes for him unusually high. According to Ranjit Shahani, in *Mr. Gandhi,* Putliba used to pray that God would make Mohan a hero among heroes—a man the like of whom had not appeared on earth. It seems clear that she—and Kaba—saw something remarkable in their youngest child. He felt himself recognized by them, as he did not by his peers.

Gandhi was apparently somewhat afraid of his father, although full of respect. He told his first biographer that Karamchand could be cruel and stubborn, though he was firm and chaste. Ranjit Shahani says (perhaps a bit imaginatively) that Karamchand liked a square meal, and expressed satisfaction with a series of loud belches. When there was only a silence at the end of his meal, the wife and children would scatter in alarm.[3]

The father must also have been a somewhat remote figure, since he went to live and work in another state when Mohandas was five years old (by some reports, only four) and the family was reunited only when the latter began to attend school in Rajkot. As a child, he was the responsibility of his mother, his seven years older sister, a servant girl, and generally of all the extended family. He had three boy cousins who were older than he, a half-cousin also older, and two younger cousins. In such joint families, there were many people, young and old, who might pick up and cherish a child. And Hindu families in general differed from Western families, according to some sociologists, because there were many caste regulations to be observed (which united parent and child in equality) and few personal obligations to set them in mutual opposition. The superego formed was powerful, but familial rather than individual.

Mohan shared with his mother especially a naive religious and moral piety; a devotion to being good, which involved maintaining tradition in social and religious matters. Putliba had been brought up in the Pranami sect of Hinduism, a sect that incorporated certain features of Islam. Its temple in Porbandar contained a copy of the Koran, as well as of the Puranas, and no idols. But Putliba in fact most often visited the Vaishnavite temple next door to the Gandhi house, as was traditional in the Gandhi family. She made offerings twice a day there, and on holy days would visit also other temples, including the Pranamis', which was two hundred yards away.

There were many sects and about a hundred temples in Porbandar, which held about 14,500 people in 1872, when the whole state held about 72,000. Vaishnavism, the cult of Vishnu or Krishna, is one of the great devotional religions of Hinduism. (Vishnu is one of the three great divinities of Hinduism, along with Brahma and Shiva; Krishna is one of the main avatars of Vishnu.) Family prayers at the Gandhis might last, on and off, from six to eight a.m., prayers alternating with the consultations described; and a Brahmin came at the end to conduct a prayer; and every day twenty or thirty people came for alms or something to eat. Karamchand [or Kaba] sat in the temple and peeled vegetables as he listened to his clients or petitioners. His relative Prabhudas Gandhi says that "a kind of *ashram*" came into being during "Kaba Kaka"'s lifetime, even in the family home. (*Kaba Kaka* means something like Uncle Kaba.)[4]

The emotional and moral tone of the piety itself would probably sound familiar enough to those in the West who have any memory of religious tradition. "He is the true Vaishnava who knows and feels another's woes as his own. Always ready to serve, he never boasts. He bows to everyone and despises no-one, keeping his thought, word, and deed pure. Blessed is the mother of such a one. He looks upon all with an equal eye," wrote Narasimha Mehta, a Kathiawar poet of the fifteenth century.

The Gandhis' particular Vaishnavite sect (called the Vallabhacharya sampradaya) worshipped Vishnu under the name of Krishna, the bringer of bliss. Theirs was a kind of devotion full of light and color, and sometimes criticized for an implicit hedonism. Dishes were prepared for the god every day, and flowers presented. Its temples were unlike most temples in being the property of the princes, and were opened to the people only at certain hours, for congregational worship. Besides the temple, each family had a shrine-room, where they gathered to sing hymns, and Krishna was worshipped as, amongst other things, the Holy Child, Bala-Krishna.

Gandhi tells us he was repelled by the masses of flowers left to rot in the temple, and by the rumors of immorality attaching to the place. As he grew up, he preferred another version of Vishnu, as a warrior figure, sometimes called Rama. This current of Vaishnavite piety was more ascetic and popular, and used quotations from the *Ramayana* of Tulsidas.

It is important for our understanding of Gandhi that Putliba was a pious woman, and that the character of her piety—like her son's—was moralistic and ascetic. But this does not mean that she and he were not keenly interested in worldly affairs and values. Putliba and Mohandas joined Karamchand in taking pride in his exercise of administrative and advisory power. (As a child Mohandas was petted and flattered by strangers in the street, because he was the son of the diwan.) Putliba also was a notable figure in Porbandar, consulted as a sage by other women.

Gandhi once told his secretary, Mahadev Desai, that his mother was more worldly than his father, and that she was fascinated by money and by fame. From the same source we hear a story about a state celebration in Rajkot, when Karamchand's two sons were assigned to the inferior of two places, and Putliba was indignant at this affront to the family honor. She sent the boys to the Thakore to ask for a change in the arrangements, but Karamchand insisted they should accept the inferior option (26:151). So also she got angry with Mohan because he would not put himself forward, and claim his rights (UC).

However, Gandhi's more "official" account of his mother was quite different. In his autobiography he says "the outstanding impression my mother has left in my memory is that of saintliness . . . [whereas Father] to a certain extent might have been given to carnal pleasures" (A:4, 3). This impression derived from her asceticism. Putliba ate only from other people's leavings, and often fasted. She was, like her son, very fastidious about cleanliness, and purity in general. She is reported to have envied the bee, which turns all its food into fragrant honey and leaves no smelly waste behind; and she pitied the fate of the food we eat, degraded in our stomachs from being attractive to being repulsive. Like her son also, she suffered from constipation, a problem we must see as at least analogous with that fastidiousness and refinement of temperament.

Erik Erikson tells us that as a little boy Mohandas used to take down the image of the Rana from its stool, and install himself in its place. He did so when his father was not there, and the significance of the game, Erikson says, was that the little boy was installing himself in the position of authority over his father; reversing the actual relationship. (It is the psychoanalyst's thesis that Gandhi was always in rebellion against father figures, but enacted his rebellion in the form of taking care of them—for instance, nursing his actual father.)[5]

A story Gandhi himself tells also indicates a privileged and playful child. "I roamed about the villages in a bullock cart. As I was the son of a diwan, people fed me on the way with *juwar roti* and curds and gave me eight anna pieces."[6] And he could be playful and energetic, by himself. There is a story of his being found up in the branches of a mango tree, and explaining that he was bandaging the mangos. Erikson tells this story, and he sees in it a typical combination of the adventurous with the responsible and nursing interests of the child (and the man).[7]

In 1876, Mohan started going to the Dhooli Shala, or Dust School, where he traced the letters of the Gujarat alphabet in the dust with his finger, and recited verses and tables by heart. According to J. M. Uphadyaya, this was probably Virji Kamdar's. Gandhi remembered till late in life the rude rhymes the boys recited about their teacher. The school was near the Vaishnava Haveli, and he went to the temple every day, though it was for him a place to play—even, on occasion, dragging down the idols from their places. Probably (again according to Upadhyaya) he was tutored by Anandji Tulsi Acharya, tutor to the Porbandar princes. After a year, he and the rest of the family moved to Rajkot, where Karamchand and Lakshmidas already were.

The Gandhis were of the *Bania* or commercial caste, which was widespread and powerful in Gujarat, in its various subcastes. (The Gandhis belonged to the Modh Banias, so called in reference to the town of Modh.) In the distant past they had been moneylenders. But in the historical record they were like Brahmins, who have traditionally been the advisers to rulers. The latter are considered to belong to the Kshattriya caste; in Gujarat often, and for instance in Porbandar, they were Rajputs, whose family origins lay in Rajputana rather than in Gujarat.

The Gandhis emerge into the light of historical records in the eighteenth century, as minor officials attached to the princely family of the Jethva Rajputs. They probably arrived in Porbandar with that family in the 1750s, since they bought their house there twenty years after that. Gandhi told his first biographer, Joseph Doke, that one of his earliest memories was of the learning and repetition, as a child, of the family pedigree, with all its ramifications and offshoots.[8]

Uttamchand Gandhi was made Diwan by the Rana Khimatji (*rana* means prince). He persuaded the neighboring state of Junagadh to sign over its customs rights to Porbandar; and also irrigated the area by building a dam, thus increasing its revenue considerably. As a result of his efforts, Porbandar (about six hundred square miles) was given a Class One classification by the British when they took over Kathiawar.

Uttamchand also found an escape clause in a mortgage that had bound the Rana to the trading firm of the Sundarjis, to whom the Rana had long been in debt. Thus Uttamchand rescued the state of Porbandar from serious financial difficulties and set it on a firm foundation of prosperity. The legend of his achievements was an important part of our Gandhi's family heritage.

Karamchand too was a deeply respected figure in the state, as we have seen. He was not a man of education, and his political horizons seem to have been limited to Porbandar and the adjacent little states (there were about two hundred "independent" states in Kathiawar then) but he was a serious man. In matters of religion, he liked to hear the priests of all the Indian religions recite their texts and expound their creeds.

There were earthquakes, famines, and plagues (of both rats and locusts) in the Kathiawar Mohan grew up in. Lions and panthers still roamed the forests; there were *dacoits* (robbers) and ghosts. Dacoits hid from justice in the Gir Forest and the Bard Hills, and the British government in Bombay stationed troops in Porbandar, to suppress them. Gandhi actually met one of these robbers, Mowar, and remembered hearing tales of Mudu Manik, one of the most famous (24:23). There were also the Angria sea-pirates, the widow of one of whom was still alive in Gandhi's day.

All these categories, animal, social, and supernatural, included items that frightened Mohan as a child. He lists ghosts, robbers, and snakes among the things he was afraid of. This timidity was an important psychological fact about him, which will be explored later, but here it must be understood as a cultural phenomenon; in being timid, Gandhi was being Gujarati. At least, he felt that, and so did others. Geographical theories of cultural psychology are an important part of Indian culture. In *The Discovery of India,* Jawaharlal Nehru surveys the various social groups, saying: "the Gujaratis are soft in body, gentler, richer, and perfectly at home in trade and commerce."[9] And later he says, "The Gujaratis were essentially a community of peaceful traders and merchants, influenced by the Jain doctrine of *ahimsa* (nonviolence). . . Other parts of India had been influenced much less by this" (460).

Gujaratis felt themselves to be soft, gentle, and nonviolent in comparison with other cultural types, though Mohandas Gandhi, as we shall see, felt himself be those things in comparison with other Gujaratis. However, according to some family traditions, the young Mohandas (called Mohan or Moniya) was a very lively infant. Certainly his sister, who looked after him as a little boy, described him as energetic and restless. He was hard for those in charge of him to keep track of. He was also playful and high-spirited—always ready to play with dogs, and teasing them by twisting their ears.

On the other hand, some traditions of his childhood describe him as timid and self-occupying, with a passion for washing his clothes, and for growing plants. There are many anecdotes about his shyness and withdrawnness, mostly referring to a little later in his life. Presumably he, like others, had both these rather strikingly different sides to his character. But perhaps also a change came about when he moved from infancy into boyhood—a change we might associate with the move to Rajkot—for it seems that it was then that he had to deal with the rougher aggressions of boyhood. When lads try out the various styles of manly forcefulness, some are likely to be coarse and ugly and violent; and a sensitive child like Mohan is likely to recoil from them—as we shall see was in fact the case. To some degree he withdrew from boyhood, and reached manhood by a moralistic short cut, acting the adult while still a boy.

In *Gandhi's Truth,* Erikson says that from early on Gandhi felt isolated in a group, and sought one-to-one relationships, or relationships in which he had the moral advantage. Thus he often did not play with his schoolmates, but made peace between them when they quarreled. The peace-making role, and the truth-telling role (both well-defined in Hindu culture) were those he preferred. Naturally, this did not make him popular in the school-yard. Prabhudas Gandhi tells us of an occasion when Mohan thus told the truth at all costs: "The incident convinced Mohan's companions that he could not be treated as one of them because of his simplicity and outspokenness." When he did not like "the other boys' rough handling of one another even in play, he would stand aloof and say: 'Carry on, but I cannot join you.'"[10]

He told Edward Thompson that he was at his profoundest at seven or eight, before education and society clipped his wings; a date that seems to set a crucial break between infancy and boyhood, and that coincides exactly with the move to Rajkot. He wished he could have heard the boy Jesus arguing with the priests in the temple: "Then and then alone uninhibited truth must have come out."

Erikson says that Gandhi could play, could be genial, only when he felt morally dominant, because he was doing good to the others concerned. As a child he preferred to serve his mother rather than play with his brothers. (Serving one's elders also is a clearly defined activity in Hindu culture.) And although Erikson's analysis may not be quite satisfactory, what he says is echoed in Gandhi's own declarations, that he ran home from school so no one should speak to him. He disliked both cricket and football, and stood in the corner at sports time; he went for long walks by himself. He accepted adult standards, was proud of his moral character, upset when aspersions were cast on it, obedient and pious.

According to Amrit Kaur, a woman disciple who acted as his secretary in the 1930s and 1940s, he said he had been a dull child, shy, and hating to be part of a crowd of other boys. In consequence, his teachers knew him as a good boy, a conscientious pupil, but not a brilliant one. On other occasions he used the word *silent:* he had been a silent boy and a silent student. He later found reason to be glad about that—he valued silence—but it was a humiliation to him when young.

He seems to have been somewhat separate even from his siblings. The oldest brother, Lakshmidas, went with the father to Rajkot in 1874, and was anyway considerably older, being born in 1863. He seems to have been a mild personality, later described as genial and feckless, with many friends. According to Stephen Hay, he probably protected Mohan from the aggressions of the other brother. With Karshandas, this second brother, Mohan had a strong bond of affection, in their early years, and the elder was upset when the younger would not follow his lead; but that happened often, because the two were very different, in gifts and temperament. Mohandas was the more quick-witted and intelligent, and much more susceptible to moral enthusiasm. Vigorous and willful, Karshandas led his three years younger brother into mischief. Later in life, he was often in the kind of trouble that must have been a disgrace to the family in general, and a grief to Mohan in particular.

So we may see in Gandhi from the beginning a moral enthusiast and a lively intelligence; who was, however, hampered or crippled, in the world of boyhood, by fears and inhibitions that his peers—and no doubt he himself—regarded as disabling. His parents, and particularly his mother, probably protected him from the pressure of his peers; but then she too used to scold him for being so timid and silent, quoting an old song: "You must shout to sell your wares."

In congenial company, however, he could be humorous and playful. He joined his friends in mild forms of rebellion, including secret smoking, and indulged in at least one session with bhang, the drug most widespread among Indians. (The experience left him feeling a loss of power, not a gain; while he was under the drug's influence, he said, anyone could have played fast or loose with him.) He resented some of the rules his elders laid down, and even agreed with some friends, who felt similarly oppressed, to commit suicide by swallowing *datura* leaves. Neither Gandhi nor his biographers take this episode seriously, but it surely testifies to a significant tension. Thus the main drama of these early years, as the reports come down to us, was a conflict between the desire to be good, and the attractions of boldness and adventure, held out by his brother Karshandas, and later by Karshandas's friend, Sheikh Mehtab.

The Social and Political Scene

Many communities, of caste and sect, were represented in Porbandar, and even as a boy Gandhi was interested in those unlike himself. The Muslims were, in Porbandar, the ones who took to the seas and had the adventures. They carried the silks and cottons woven by the Hindus of Porbandar in their homes, to Aden, Zanzibar, and Cape Town, and sold them there. Hindus were forbidden by their religion to cross the "great black waters," though of course some did so. The Muslims also figured in tales of combat. Gandhi's great grandfather had a Muslim in his personal bodyguard, Ghulam Mohammed Makrani, who gave his life for his lord. There was a memorial to him in the temple. Thus in Gandhi's experience (which was corroborated by tradition) Muslims were bolder and more adventurous than Hindus or Jains or Buddhists, and we shall find that idea reflected in his own thinking again and again. Muslims are good fighters, he said, and have a long history of aggression, inside and outside India. He would often describe them as "stalwart," and as men of strong likes and dislikes. This was a factor in his very important relations with his first Muslim friend, Sheikh Mehtab.

Porbandar was a small place, left behind by world and even national history. The Rana had an eleven-gun salute, and the power of life and death over his subjects, but the British residents and political agents in Kathiawar represented the iron of modern reality, which when it showed made the manifold small states seem all crumbling stucco. Iron railways were built there in the 1880s, and iron bridges, iron ships, and iron machinery, were introduced all over India.

The actual British presence in Porbandar was concentrated in the Christian missionaries, who had been in Kathiawar ever since 1815, in the form of the London Missionary Society, and in Ahmedabad in the form of the Society for the Promotion of Christ's Kingdom. The former handed over its mission to the Irish Presbyterians, who settled in Bombay in 1846, and brought out a translation of the New Testament into Gujarati in 1857, and the Old Testament in 1861. It has been suggested that Gandhi may have attended the school they maintained in Porbandar, though he does not say so.

Writing about those years, he remembers Christian missionaries standing at a street corner and "pouring abuse" on Hindus and their gods (A:33). He could not endure to listen to them. And he heard talk of a Hindu convert to Christianity who was made to eat beef and drink liquor, and wear European clothes, including a hat, which seemed a humiliation (A:34).

Gandhi's attitude to the Christian missions, through most of his life, remained uncharacteristically hostile—even though he had many admirers and some followers among the missionaries, and he read the New Testament with enthusiasm. But he was always a cultural patriot, and he belonged to a generation that was devoted to restoring cultural pride—the pride that India should take in all its institutions; and which saw no religious need for conversions, since the best part of any religion was almost identical with the best of all others. The missions seem often to have been a center of hostility to Indian culture, while the British political agents, confining themselves to official dealings, trod on fewer toes.

They were also much admired for their enforcement of various reforms and of a "pax britannica" between the native states. For instance, Colonel R. H. Keatinge, who was political agent in Kathiawar from 1863–67, began a period of reforms there that lasted until 1882. He intervened energetically in state affairs, limited the powers of the chiefs, organized police forces, and so on, but at the same time, revived Rajput traditions. He assigned the rajas their gun salutes and built a college to educate their sons. Thus he both limited and reinforced the powers of the native rulers. He reinvigorated their rule in the service of the English. One of the new institutions was the Rajasthanik Court, where Karamchand Gandhi acted as assessor, and where, it has been suggested, Mohandas may have first found his ideal of law being practiced as reconciliation.

Perspectives

The hero of this story was a world-historical figure. His antagonists included an empire, which he confronted on three continents, and a historical process that was political, economic, and technological. So let us now situate Gandhi within the larger world he was born into, by gradually pulling back from the house in Porbandar to a provincial, a national, a continental perspective.

Kathiawar (also called Saurashtra) was, we have seen, a historical backwater, with all its modes of power and men of power, whether rulers or hereditary advisers, left over from the past. The present-time or modern power was that of the English, embodied in their political agent, who was not even resident in Porbandar, but kept an eye on things from afar, and intervened if any of the player kings went too far. In Gandhi's birth year, for instance, the state was degraded to the third class, in punishment for bad behavior by the Rana.

This situation was a profoundly humiliating one for the Indians, and especially for one with a political and moral sensitiveness like Gandhi's. When he was asked in 1929 why he addressed his satyagraha campaigns always to the rulers of British India, and not to "the native states," he replied that it was because he could not exert influence there; the princes did not acknowledge the moral principles he appealed to. They could not be shamed into good behavior. (Indeed, his major attempt at such a satyagraha, in Rajkot, was a failure.) Usually, of course, he avoided that topic—it was one of the things he was silent about—but it was a bitter truth to chew even in silence.

Nevertheless, even in *Hind Swaraj,* his most radical political statement, Gandhi declared himself content to let the British remain in India as administrators, provided they would leave the culture of the country under Indian control. He often saw Kathiawar in legendary, rather than social-science terms, as a land of temples and pilgrimages, Jain, Vaishnavite, Shaivite; but also as the land of Rajput rulers, whose hereditary bards, the Chavans and Bhats, recited their heroic deeds in ballads. Devanesan says that Gandhi wanted India to be like what he thought Kathiawar had been in the past, an "idealized Rajput state," where "the martial Rajput aristocracy and the peaceful Bania oligarchy lived in a kind of dialectical tension with each other."[12]

Prosperity came to Gujarat during the American Civil War, just before Gandhi's birth, when the supply of cotton from the American South to England and the rest of the world dried up. India, and especially Gujarat, supplied the markets that had been America's. In 1860 to 1861 the cotton Bombay exported was worth 7,000,000 pounds; in 1865 to 1866 it was worth 355,000,000 pounds. But it was of course British India, and the British in India, who benefited primarily from this prosperity.

Moreover, not all the cotton went to the Lancashire mills as raw material. More and more was spun and woven in Gujarat factories. And the development of the cotton mills doubled the rate of decline of the traditional textile industries. Gandhi remembered seeing, as a child, handwoven, brilliantly colored cloths in Rajkot—he hoped, once, that his father would buy him a turban made from them. In those days, Gandhi said, the homemade satins of Kathiawar had competed with the mill-cloths of Ahmedabad. He had seen the local weavers bring their tie-and-dye work to the temples, to make good use of their time there.

In Ahmedabad (the largest city in Gujarat, the sixth largest in India) as in Calcutta or Bombay, one could see the factories and bridges and railways of the modern world, and modern institutions, political and religious. It was a major junction of the Western Railway, and from it roads ran to Bombay and central India, to Kathiawar, and to Rajasthan. At the same time, the city had an ancient guild system, and was built in a series of "pols," rectangular enclosures of houses, each with a temple in the center. The presence of the modern world was seen and felt directly in the city center; but only here and there in the pols and the smaller towns. There were, for instance, no banks and no insurance agents in Kathiawar in the 1880s.

Erik Erikson compares Ahmedabad with Pittsburgh in America, because both cities are highly industrialized and unionized; financed by local investment, and managed by a few powerful families. In Ahmedabad, many of these are Jains, and included some who supported Gandhi in his early work in India. In the twentieth century, Erikson says, it has the most modern welfare institutions in India.

Gandhi was a son of Gujarat, by his criticism of as well as his loyalty to that province. Though he also belonged to India, he had to be seen by the other provinces as different from their sons. Even he himself had to see the loincloth and the spinning wheel, his gaunt frail body and low flat voice, as defined against those backgrounds—those grand landscapes of Gangetic delta or Rajasthan desert, those rich textiles of Bengal or Madras.

If we take that wide historical and geographical perspective, we can contrast Gujarat as a province in the West with Bengal, the Punjab, and Maharashtra. Bengal, in the East, was traditionally the land of intellectuals, poets, and revolutionaries, the intellectually sophisticated. Calcutta was an enormous city, the capital of British India, and the birthplace of the Brahmo Samaj, a reform movement within Hinduism. The Brahmo Samaj was comparable with and in touch with the Unitarian congregations in Boston, London, and Bristol. For them, Gandhi remained always very provincial.

Bengal and Gujarat were very different. In 1924 Gandhi said that Gujarat had been and still was a most backward province, intellectually. The Gujaratis are comparatively unlettered, he said; they only know how to trade (24:488). He spoke, for instance, of valuable religious manuscripts locked away in the possession of rich merchants, who took no interest in them. "In Gujarat a priceless collection of books lies in the custody of the merchant class. Beautiful collections of Jain literature are wrapped up in their silk cloths. My heart is sore. . . . The Jain religion is also withering in their hands because they have reduced *dharma* to a formal business" (56:17).

The Punjab, in the North, was Kipling-country, the showplace of British India, because of the great engineering work done there, roads and railways and canals; and because of the tradition of Punjabi Hindus and Sikhs serving in the British army. It was also the birthplace of the Arya Samaj, another reform movement within Hinduism, but more communalist and reactionary—differing from the Brahmo Samaj in roughly the way that Lutheran reformers differed from Unitarians, within the varieties of Christianity. It was nationalist; Arya Samajists held classes in Hindi in order to spread a national language, and set out to convert non-or ex-Hindus. They were uneasy with the religious eclecticism of Gandhi and Gujarat.

Though the Arya Samajists were opposed to idol worship, they were fundamentalist in their reverence for the Vedas, which they thought contained all wisdom, including that which the Western culture claimed as its own possession. They also taught physical exercises, with military overtones, and were generally masculinist.[13] The leaders made much of Hindu causes, like cow-protection, for instance, which set the Hindus at odds with non-Hindu Indians. At about this time, cow protection became implicitly an anti-Muslim issue (not anti-British, as it might logically have been). Gandhi was in conflict with the Arya Samaj in a number of ways, but his sons were to be attracted to Arya ideas just for that reason.

Maharashtra, in the center, between Calcutta and Bombay, had been the home of a great historical movement that in the eighteenth century had organized Hindus to resist the Muslim invaders. That movement was led by the Chitpavan Brahmins, and the city of Pune (Poona) was their center. In Gandhi's youth, the chief leader of the reform movement in Congress, Gokhale, and the chief leader of the extremists, Tilak, both came from Pune. In his middle age, a bomb was thrown at Gandhi in Pune; and later the men who assassinated him were Chitpavan Brahmins, who came from Pune. These were men of fierce self-dedication and self-sacrifice in activist politics.

All three of the provinces just discussed had a more distinct tradition of resistance to the British than Gujarat did, and were more expected to produce a great national leader. And to look further afield, there was South India, all that part of the subcontinent below the Vindhya mountain range, which traditionally left national politics to the provinces just mentioned. In the south there were few Muslims, and the Brahmins were powerful. And then there were the northern reaches, where the Muslims and the Sikhs were large minorities; including the Northwest Frontier Province, the center of tribal war and international intrigue between England, Afghanistan, and Russia. That area was the home of the Pathans, the social group regarded by the Gujaratis (including Gandhi) as most opposite to themselves, out of all the Indian groups. Some Gujarati *banias* (traders) hired Pathans as watchmen, he warns his readers in 1928; such men are dangerous; they always carry knives, and some of them have beaten a buffalo to death (36:436).

Seen in this subcontinental perspective, Gujarat was a land of banias and a land of religions—perhaps characterized by the Jains, the most nonviolent of sects. Devanesen says that Gujaratis had the reputation of being meek and bashful, hardworking and unspending. There were peasants and farmers in Gujarat, but both Gandhi and most people who took a national perspective, saw the province in terms of traders—and devotees of religion. Gandhi often complained of his compatriots' lack of the soldierly virtues.

Looking at India as a whole, from a Western point of view, two reciprocal rhythms seem to constitute key images. The first is that of pollution and purification, which is so central to Hinduism, and which makes the social procedures of, for instance, eating, so elaborate. The sprinkling of water, the morning ablutions, the holiness of the Ganges and other rivers, the burning of corpses, the sacrificial fire, which is the heart of Brahmin religion; all this is purification. And it is the fear of pollution that expresses itself in the distance people preserve from other people, the strong feeling against meat and blood and feces, the ritual separation of castes, and, most dreadfully, the excommunication of pariahs. Hindus are forever becoming polluted, by their own and other bodies, and are forever having to purify themselves.

The second reciprocal rhythm is that of making and unmaking cloth. *Making* here does not mean only the spinning and weaving but the wrapping and unwrapping of sari and dhoti about the body (cloth and clothes are the same thing in traditional India). And *unmaking* does not mean unraveling, but the beating clean of clothes on river rocks. Always in India one is aware of cloth coming into shape and coming flat again, being beaten, being worn out. This of course gives another dimension to the meaning of Gandhi's spinning, and reminds us of another primary process that the West has locked behind factory walls and lost touch with. Both reciprocal rhythms can be seen at once in the women washing clothes on the banks of the Ganges.

A third feature is the mosaic of costumes and customs—each proclaiming a caste, sect, or race identity—visible on the city streets of India. This has suggested to many people the mutability of social roles, and the intoxication of disappearance and of disguise. This is reflected in English stories about India (most famously *Kim*) but it has also been felt by Indians. Gandhi himself may be said to have worn costume nearly all his life, and in the first half changed it frequently. He tells us an anecdote of another Gujarati politician, Vithalbhai Patel, which illustrates the general point.

When Gandhi first met Vithalbhai, on returning from South Africa, the latter wore a beard and a Turkish fez and jacket, and Gandhi had no idea that he was a Hindu. (Presumably he thought Vithalbhai was a Muslim.) Then, after they had got to know each other, in 1917, Gandhi came across Vithalbhai dressed like a fakir, in short dhoti, cap, and *paharaj* (shirt). And he laughed gleefully to see Gandhi fail to recognize him. Gandhi's own changes of costume, in South Africa and India, albeit serious, had something of the same challenging character. It is difficult to think of a Western equivalent for this.

India as a whole was of course a part of the British Empire, the most enormous political entity on the world scene, which was extending its tentacles further year by year. Gandhi was born in the year the Suez Canal was opened, built by France but soon largely owned by England. The years 1868 to 1885 were the period of rivalry between the two British parliamentary statesmen, Gladstone the Liberal and Disraeli the Conservative, when one of the two was always prime minister; and all England, and in a sense all the world, watched their parliamentary battles. For Gandhi, these were familiar names before he left India.

In 1877 Disraeli made Victoria empress of India, symbolizing the taking over of India from the East India Company by the British government. Imperialism became proudly self-conscious for the first time. In 1886 Joseph Chamberlain and his following of radicals split from the Liberals in a disagreement over whether Ireland should be allowed to rule itself, independently of the empire.

At the time of her Diamond Jubilee as queen, in 1897, Victoria ruled over 372 million subjects and over 11 million square miles; whereas Rome at the height of its power ruled 120 million subjects and 2½ million square miles. Because it possessed India, Britain was both the world's greatest Hindu power, and its greatest Muslim power. In the Jubilee procession of that year fifty thousand troops marched through London, including cavalrymen from New South Wales, Hussars from Canada, Carabiniers from Natal, camel troops from Bikaner, and Dyak headhunters from Borneo.

But that was pageantry, and the substance and the growth of the empire was economic and commercial. There were a thousand miles of railway in India when Gandhi was born; by the time he sailed for London there were fifteen thousand miles. In 1897, at any given moment, British ships were carrying two hundred thousand passengers, and two hundred thousand merchant seamen. Half the world's shipping flew the Red Ensign. A thousand new British ships were launched in the Jubilee year, and seven thousand tons, out of every ten thousand that passed through the Suez Canal, belonged to Britain. Another rapidly growing form of communication (which was to be much employed by Gandhi) was the overland and submarine cables. The cable from London to Calcutta was finished in 1865. In 1870 the Colonial Office spent eight hundred pounds a year on such cables; in 1897, eight thousand pounds.

England's triumph was India's humiliation, in a number of ways. In 1869, the year of Gandhi's birth, Bholanauth Chunder published *Travels of a Hindu*, in two volumes, in London. This was one of the first books by a modern Hindu to be read by Englishmen. It concluded that India had never had any political life, any political science, or any political reform. It had known nothing but crude despotism. Political life as Chunder understood it was exclusively European, and the British constitution was the greatest phenomenon in world history. This can stand for all the varieties of English pride and Indian humiliation that Gandhi was to feel and resist.

India was, nevertheless, adopting modern means of communication in the early years of Gandhi's life. In 1885 there were 160 English language newspapers, with a total circulation of 90,000; by 1905 there were 309 such papers, with a circulation of 276,000. The vernacular papers (employing one or another of the Indian languages) increased from 509 to 1,107, and the circulations from 299,000 to 817,000.

Education in English also was expanding. In 1886 4,286 students matriculated, and 708 got BA degrees. In 1905, the corresponding numbers were 8,211 and 1,570. At the top of all the educational ladders was a position in the Indian Civil Service. A few of these positions were made available to Indians, and the official expectation was that the number would increase. Some of these men were made knights, baronets, or peers—aristocrats of empire.

As a result of these changes, in 1911 30 percent of adult city-dwelling males in British India were literate in English, although only 1 percent of the total population were. The spread of English meant the establishment of a national language; but one that was imported, and that chained the Indian mind to the chariot wheels of England, or so Gandhi believed. Congress, the first national or All-India political organization, founded in 1885, was an English-speaking institution. It was also completely dominated by high-caste Hindus from the coasts. (There was a countermobilization, of Muslims in the Muslim League, founded 1906, and of an anti-Brahmin movement in the south.)

All this was of course done in the hope of, or in the name of, bridging the gap between the Indians and their conquerors. But there were forces working in the opposite direction, forces of racism in both groups. The racism of the English can be shown by this quotation from Sir Francis Younghusband, who once interviewed Gandhi in South Africa, for the *Times*.

> No European can mix with non-European races without feeling his superiority over them. He feels, from the first contact with them, that whatever

> may be their relative positions from an intellectual point of view, he is stronger morally than they are. And facts show that this feeling is a true one. It is not because we are any cleverer than the native of India, because we have more brains or bigger heads than they have, that we rule India, but because we are stronger morally than they are. Our superiority over them is not due to mere sharpness of intellect, but to the higher moral nature to which we have attained in the development of the human race.[14]

We can also find examples of British racism relating to the position of the Indians in South Africa, while Gandhi was there. Lionel Curtis wrote in a letter to the *Times* on May 4, 1907: "Englishmen who believe in the excellence of their civilization cannot really desire to see their Empire used as a means for propagating the society and institutions of the East in new countries, to the exclusion of their own."[15] The Convention of Associations of East Africa declared, "Whereas these people follow in all things a civilization which is eastern and in many ways repugnant to ours . . . [we must] avoid a betrayal to the Asiatic of a section of the African peoples whose destinies have fallen into our hands." The report of the Economic Commission called the Indian, "not a wholesome influence because of his incurable repugnance to sanitation and hygiene. The moral depravity of the Indian is equally damaging. . . . [He brings with him] the worst vices of the East" (16:358).

Finally, while considering South Africa, it should be noted that although the British Empire had abolished slavery—and taken a world-lead in doing so—the British had subsequently instituted, as far as Indians went, a kind of serfdom. In fact, Hugh Tinker's book on the export of Indian labor overseas between 1880 and 1920 is titled, *A New System of Slavery.* This serfdom in South Africa was to be one of Gandhi's first political concerns.

In his Introduction, Tinker says that as he studied the issue:

> Only gradually did the accumulation of evidence produce the conclusion that indenture and other forms of servitude did, indeed, replicate the actual conditions of slavery. It became apparent that for a period of seventy or eighty years British statesmen and administrators were being confronted with evidence that the planting interest was exploiting Indian workers in ways which could not be tolerated by a decent, humane society; and yet they continued to assure themselves that these wrongs were mere abuses and irregularities which could be amenable to reform.[16]

Between one and two million Indians emigrated to tropical countries between 1830 and 1870, according to Tinker. Many went to the island of Mauritius, from where they moved on to Natal later. In the mid-1850s a heavy annual migration to the Caribbean began, and the passage death-rate shot up. About 525,000 indentured men went to the French and British sugar colonies between 1842 and 1870. (Another 1,500,000 went to Ceylon, where about 250,000 settled down.) Indentured Indians were often put straight into the Nigger Yards and Camps des Noirs just vacated by the slaves. "The plantation meant the barracks, the huts where the workers spent their scanty hours of rest; and above all the canefields, where the fronded cane waved, as end-product of backaching toil under the burning sun; and the factory, where the juice was distilled into sugar and rum" (178). Essentially the same things happened in Natal, where Gandhi encountered them, only a little later.

Of course, England knew a more reputable kind of imperialism, in which Gandhi in fact believed. For that reason, he taught the schoolchildren of Rajkot to sing the British National Anthem in 1897. He quoted Ruskin saying that the ideal of empire was to produce "as many as possible, full-breathed, bright-eyed, and happy-hearted human creatures." Ruskin's inaugural lecture at Oxford, in 1879, called on his undergraduate listeners to found colonies as fast and as far as they were able.

To take the very widest political view, in that first decade of Gandhi's life, the British citizen saw that empire confronted by a number of other empires that were either decaying (like the Turkish, the Chinese, the Austro-Hungarian) or almost openly tyrannical (like the Russian). These empires, and France before 1870 and Germany after 1870, were ruled by men who wore uniforms and carried swords. The British Empire (ruled by a woman, a mother, and grandmother) was the only one that could plausibly claim to be different—the one on which liberals, like the young Gandhi, could focus their hopes.

In the very first years of his life the Franco-Prussian War had ended with the defeat of France, Britain's traditional enemy, and the emergence of a new nation state, Germany. The official liberal scenario of politics was that the subject nations of the old empires should break free, and become national states. Germany and Italy had thus been marked out for that development; and England, the liberal empire, had promised to give dominion status to—first of all—Canada. India hoped to follow in those footsteps. Because of the English view of nonwhite cultures, however, it was understood that would take longer to prepare.

In this attempt at a world perspective, we have now step-by-step removed ourselves from the baby and the boy Gandhi, scampering along the streets of Porbandar in the 1870s until we look down upon the whole globe, blotched with British red. It is a dizzying angle of vision, but one we have to employ. Gandhi's antagonist was in time to be that enormous entity, the British Empire; more than that, he was—to use his own image—to try to reverse the spin of that globe; to stop or alter the global progress of Westernization. But it is time to reverse our process of withdrawal, and to work our way back down toward him again; this time looking more at the leading ideas at different levels of generalization, rather than at the material facts.

Looking at the world historical process, probably the leading political idea of the second half of the nineteenth century was socialism in its various developments, and the leading event was the triumph, at the theoretical level, of the Marxist version. This kind of socialism had more of theoretical rigor than other kinds, more of social science. It also embodied more of anger and realpolitik. Gandhi was to meet this idea and make his own, almost opposite idea, prevail against it in India.

At the level of generalization next below, we have the idea of the iron cage, associated above all with Max Weber. He was especially concerned with what was happening in Europe as the different parts of Germany came under a common government and bureaucracy, and systems of industrialization, banking, and insurance developed their power. But something comparable was soon to be seen outside Europe, as we have said.

As for India, England's consciousness, and indeed all Europe's, of what the empire was doing, was shaped to a remarkable degree by the work of a single writer, Rudyard Kipling. He interpreted and harmonized the various voices of British India, including those of the land itself insofar as the British heard them. (Strictly speaking, Kipling began to write in the decade after the one we are concerned with.) He blended images of the iron cage of bureaucracy with images of the romantic splendor of empire. Gandhi knew and admired Kipling's work. He was of course offended by Kipling's racism, but he did not deny the truth of his picture of India. We shall see that Gandhi quite often shaped his own image in such a way as to both evoke and refute Kipling's legends.

Within India's indigenous culture, however, we can take the two great epic poems, or poem-systems, the *Mahabharata* and the *Ramayana*, to represent the life of ideas. The reform movements like the Brahmo and the Arya Samajes, reinterpreted those epics and renewed their influence. And although Gandhi did not study them until later, stories from these sources were recited by priests and *sanyasis* at the Gandhi home in Porbandar. Although there are elements of epic action in both, those elements were when interpreted subdued to allegorical moral meanings, of a naively ascetic kind. The great actions were said to happen inside the individual soul, and to be triumphs of self-sacrifice. More exactly, there are many interpretations; and some are revolutionary and violent; but moral-allegorical reading is a well-established tradition in India, and that is certainly how Gandhi understood the epics.

In the *Ramayana* Prince Rama is deprived of his heritage and goes to live in the forest with his wife Sita and his faithful brother Lakshmana; Sita is abducted by Ravana, a demon king, and the brothers pursue him and destroy his kingdom and rescue Sita. Rama, Sita, and Lakshmana are incarnations of dharma, duty; they are not, therefore, to Western eyes, either lifelike or heroic; their persuasive force lies in the elegance with which they represent a moral ideal; their religious and aesthetic submission to their fate, their obedient impersonality.

The version of the *Ramayana* Gandhi preferred was the North Indian one composed by Tulsidas, the most popular scripture in North India for three hundred years, and one of the legends about Tulsidas may help us to understand Gandhi. Being so passionately fond of his wife, Tulsidas followed her when she went, without his permission, to visit her parents. (The situation will remind Gandhi's readers of his own marital problems.) So she reproached him, "My body is nothing but skin and bone; and if such love as you have for it had been devoted to the Lord Rama, you would have no reason to dread re-birth." Hearing this, Tulsidas at once abandoned all his ties to his home, became an ascetic votary and pilgrim, and later composed this and other poems about Rama.[17]

Tulsidas's Hindi version is more devotional than, say, Valmiki's Sanskrit is.

The latter's Rama is royally strong—his arms are like bars of iron; Tulsidas's hero is divine rather than human, and his character is softened. This Rama does not send Sita into exile, and when she seems to be captured by Ravana she in fact enters into the fire of sanctity, and it is a mere image of her who is dishonored.

Rama creates the world as Maya; Sita is his *shakti*, his power—"she by the play of whose eyebrows the world comes into being." Tulsidas glorified the name of Rama above the person; the form of the Absolute is unknown until revealed in the name, and even mechanical utterance thereof can bring liberation. Morally, Tulsidas is severe and enthusiastic. "The acts of a saint are good, like the acts of a cotton plant, whose produce is dry and white and thread-like." (There is a pun hidden in the word *guna*, "act," which can mean both human quality and strand of thread.) The good man's triumph is inevitable but virtual: the ax cuts down the tree, but the sandal sheds its natural fragrance on the ax. This idealism is a clue to some of the things in Gandhi that puzzle Westerners.[18]

Women Tulsidas presents as inherently impure; "a night, impenetrably dark, to bring delight to all the owls of sin; a hook to catch all the fish of sense and strength and goodness and truth."[19] One can find similar passages in the *Mahabharata*, the other great Hindu epic. "There is nothing more evil than women; a wanton woman is a blazing fire; she is the illusion born of Maya; she is the sharp edge of the razor; she is poison, a serpent, and death all in one."[20] But Gandhi deplored such ideas. He was ready to see sensuality, including the sexual kind, as a threat to the life of the spirit, which should be strenuously guarded against; but he also saw women as exemplars of that life, and superior to men.

Two stories Gandhi mentions reading or hearing in his early childhood are that of Shravana and that of Harishchandra, the Hindu Job, who kept his faith despite terrible trials. The first was a very pious boy who gave his life to looking after his parents when they grew old and blind. He carried them both to the river to bathe, when they could no longer make their own way, and lost his own life. Gandhi saw a theatrical version of this legend, and learned the tune that went with the song, and sang the words to his own accompaniment on the concertina. He said he acted *Harishchandra* to himself, times without number (A:7).

Another story he heard and loved was that of Prahlad, a boy so dedicated to truth that he resisted all the commands and punishments of his father when they went against truth, and died in consequence. Gandhi says, "My common sense tells me today that Harishchandra could not have been a historical character. Still both Harishchandra and Shravana are living realities for me, and I am sure I should be moved as before if I were to read those plays again today." (There, incidentally, we see the adult Gandhi avowing his naiveté: he will recognize a living reality that goes against common sense, and will be, as an adult, as moved by the story as he had been when a child.)

Gandhi's life covered a period when writing for children was highly developed in England, from Lewis Carroll and Edward Lear to E. Nesbit and Enid

Blyton—not to mention A. A. Milne and Kenneth Grahame. These writers' stories have no connection to moral grandeur or tragic self-sacrifice. And then there were the boys' adventure tales, by Stevenson, Kipling, and Haggard, which have no connection to piety or asceticism.

Gandhi recognized the difference between such stories and those that he was given to read. As a father, in South Africa, he said he wanted his children to hear and read the story of Prahlad, because, "the ideas so common among us, which it faithfully reflects, are rarely to be found among English books reputedly great" (11:153).

But this contrast between English and Indian children's stories was to some degree a result of Gandhi's choice among the latter. Devanesan has told us how many legends of heroic warfare were recited amongst the Gandhis and similar families during the boy's childhood—stories of cannon fire, for instance, and bodyguards who died for their master. There are plenty of Western parallels to *those* tales, in the adventure stories mentioned. But the stories Gandhi retails to us are not of that active and romantic kind, but didactic legends of passive suffering.

Why he chose to make such selections will be something to understand as we follow his development. He was not himself simply inclined only to suffering or to passivity. It was he, amongst all his family, who desired and determined to go to England, to renew the family's fortunes, and when asked why he went he replied, "In a word, ambition." But just as strong as this ambition in him was a vein of ethical idealism, and that was dominant in his self-description.

Ramakrishna and Vivekananda

The preceding paragraph brought us back to Mohan in Porbandar and his experiences in those early years. That survey should have shown both how various India was and how similar the different parts were in their experience of humiliation at the hands of a great world power—which yet seemed like the mildest and most liberal representative of the West, and so the Indians' best available protector.

That complex feeling was at least what Gandhi felt, and so did all but the most fanatical of Indian extremists. In his first decade, in Porbandar, he was not, of course, sophisticated in the way he discussed these ideas, but it seems clear that he felt them: the resentment of the British missionaries, the admiration for the pax brittanica, the humiliation of national powerlessness, the glamour of railways and ocean liners, parliament and Jubilee—all were there.

Every serious conversation he held, from this point on, would lead Gandhi to ask how the other person—how he himself—was going to address that issue. That is how he would define himself and others, how he would understand politics and religion. And if we ask what was happening elsewhere in India, during Gandhi's boyhood years, which foreshadowed his own later activity, the best answer may be the religiopolitics of the Ramakrishna Mission (now called Vedantism).

That movement had a spiritual and cultural perspective more like Gandhism than that of either the Brahmo Samaj or the Arya Samaj, or the secular nationalism of Congress. The Ramakrishna Mission put into action the sense of a reciprocity between East and West that answers to Gandhi's New Age Orientalism. Although Gandhi read some of Vivekananda's writing, there is no evidence to prove that he studied him as fervently as he did, say, Tolstoy. But the two men worked on a number of large and parallel ideas.

Ramakrishna Paramahansa (1836–86) was a Brahmin priest of a village shrine near Calcutta in the mid-nineteenth century, who had ecstatic mystical experiences that recalled ancient legends of the saints, and who acquired a large following. He met Keshub Chandra Sen, a leader of the Brahmo Samaj, in 1875. And though Ramakrishna was neither an intellectual nor a Westernizer, the Brahmo Samaj adopted him; his doctrine included a receptivity to all religions, something that they agreed with. But he wanted intellectual disciples of his own, who would not, for instance, disapprove of religious idols, as the Brahmos did. He found what he wanted in Vivekananda, who was born in Calcutta in 1863, his original name Narendra Nath Datta, the son of a wealthy Kshattriya, and a natural leader.

Ramakrishna himself was, or seemed, untouched by modernity; an incarnation of traditional popular Hinduism in a form that scandalized but also dazzled skeptics and intellectuals. Vivekananda was a Westernized intellectual who had been—thanks to Ramakrishna—rerooted in Hinduism, and so was able to bring East and West together. He was of an ebullient temperament, at college an athlete and an organizer of, for instance, a theater troupe. At college he studied history and logic, and lost his faith; his intellectual heroes were English intellectuals like John Stuart Mill and Herbert Spencer, with whom he corresponded.

At their first meeting Ramakrishna claimed him as a disciple, embracing Vivekananda with tears; and at the second meeting, he put his foot upon him, which induced a mild ecstatic delirium. But all this was against Vivekananda's mind and will. There was much in it that was embarrassing for a forceful young man, trained in Western styles of intellect; for instance, Ramakrishna claimed to embody both genders. Thus Vivekananda fought off the other man's claim for six years—indeed, it was not until after the latter's death that Vivekananda accepted his claim to godhead. (There is a certain likeness between their relationship and that of Gandhi and Nehru; and Gandhi thought that Nehru would accept his ideas after his death.)

But before that, Vivekananda was gradually brought to accept certain truths that Ramakrishna imposed on him; such as the religious significance and value of physical contact, and the truth and holiness of the cult of Kali, the great Mother of Death, who was worshiped in Calcutta with animal sacrifices. As a student, Vivekananda had chosen the West; and he continued to take a great interest in the other world religions; but Ramakrishna won him back to belong to the East, also.

The dates of these men's lives, and of the key events in which they were linked, are very close to Gandhi's. When Ramakrishna began to suffer from cancer in 1885, he constituted an order of monks, to continue his work, and died just before Gandhi went to England. Vivekananda was the natural leader of this order, but for some years did not know what its work should be. Till 1893 (the year Gandhi went to South Africa) he wandered about India in the manner of the sadhus, and then saw it as his calling to bring together India, which was fundamentally religious, with the West, which was fundamentally scientific; each had what the other lacked, and his calling was to be to bring them to that exchange. He set off immediately for the Parliament of Religions, which was meeting in Chicago that year, and where he made a great impression, and acquired some wealthy American supporters.

Vivekananda's main work, however, was not to take the East to America, but to bring India to accept the science and practicality of the West. This involved teaching his compatriots to make a cult of strength, in which he came close to Gandhi. He taught that men in general, and Indians in particular, were lions who thought themselves sheep. (Gandhi was to use a very similar formula, in South Africa.) "Above all, be strong!" Vivekananda said in 1891. "Be manly! I have a respect even for one who is wicked, so long as he is manly and strong."

Gandhi went nearly that far, sometimes; he wanted Hindus to learn courage, and regretted that they were more upset by death than either Muslims or Christians (51:49–50). But he would never have said, like Vivekananda, "You will be nearer to Heaven through football than through the study of the *Gita*." When Vivekananda visited England in 1896 he described it as "a nation of heroes . . . the true Kshattriyas. . . . They have solved the problem of obedience without slavish cringing—great freedom with law-abidingness." And he declared that "the British Empire with all its drawbacks is the greatest machine that ever existed for the dissemination of ideas."[21]

The other great theme that united this man with Gandhi was Vivekananda's strong sense of social misery and the need to remedy it by changing society, though not using narrowly political means. His Order did a lot of social work. He invented the term *daridranarayana* (God-as-the-poor), which Gandhi took over from him. "Let these people be your God," he said, "Him I call a Mahatma whose heart bleeds for the poor. . . . So long as the millions live in hunger and ignorance, I hold every man a traitor who having been educated at their expense, pays not the least heed to them." He taught that India's Great Mother Goddess would never awake until the pariahs had been raised from their misery. "He alone serves God who serves all other beings. . . . There is no other god to seek."

All this was very close to Gandhi, and a disciple of Vivekananda's, Saraladevi Chaudhurani, became a close ally of Gandhi's after 1918. Indeed, Gandhi himself sought Vivekananda out on one of his trips home to India, during his years in South Africa. But he did not find him then, and Vivekananda died before Gandhi's Indian career began. However, Gandhi's name was known in India in those years, and it is worth noting that Vivekananda issued no statement commending him. This points us to the differences of principle between them; Vivekananda was nonpolitical, and nonascetic—he ate meat and deplored vegetarianism as a Buddhist fad.

Conclusion

Before we pass to Gandhi's years in Rajkot, we should note the fondness of some of his memories of Porbandar. Although, as we have seen, Gandhi rebelled against much in his family and city heritage, he did also cherish cultural memories, and used them to inspire his politics.

There were political traditions of resistance, specific to Kathiawar, which Gandhi was able to adapt to his own purposes. Kathiawaris used fasting and passive resistance and guerrilla warfare as political leverage by and against the government—for instance, in Surat in 1878 there was a five-day *hartal* or strike against a new license law. These were traditions known to India as a whole but kept alive longer than usual in Kathiawar.[22]

Moreover, everything in that Porbandar past was *substantial*; and he was trying to retrieve that past. He contrasted khadi, his homespun cloth, with mill cloth; saying the former was like the coarse *rotlas*, made of *bajra*, which Kathiawaris used to eat—so much better for them than modern tea and biscuits (22:93).

And in the last year of his life he gave some Socialist congressmen an idyllic description of that past: "In the old days in Kathiawar we didn't have even water-taps. The women used to fetch water from the river, with shining pots resting on supports studded with bright beads; it would be early morning and the women thus had a sun-bath daily and that kept them healthy. They used to grind the corn in the early dawn, singing *bhajans* the while, including prayers to God. These simple innocent songs. . . . Afterwards the whole family would go to work in the fields" (88:16). This Socialist idyll, described in a style comparable with William Morris's *News from Nowhere*, is one of Gandhi's debts to his Porbandar origins.

TWO

RAJKOT AND THE PRESENT

· 1876–1888 ·

During his years in Rajkot, Gandhi formed two relationships of major importance: with Kasturba, his wife, and with Sheikh Mehtab, his closest friend during the first part of his life. He lost his father and—so it would seem—his intimacy with his brother Karsandas. And he developed political, or protopolitical, feelings: against the British and for all those forces in India that enabled Indians to resist their conquerors.

Karamchand Gandhi left Porbandar at the end of 1874 (his brother stepping into the place he left vacant) and became an administrator for the nearby states of Rajkot and Wankaner alternately, till he finally settled in the former place in 1876, eventually building a house and transferring his family there. It was a large house, constructed in 1880, with high walls around its courtyard, and an imposing gateway. Karamchand was not very provident. This house and the one in Porbandar were almost all he owned when he died a few years later.

Rajkot is depicted by Robert Payne as being then a small, ugly, dusty town, in the arms of two small rivers. The general landscape around the town Gandhi himself once described as a treeless desert. Rajkot was certainly less picturesque and attractive than Porbandar, and indeed more provincial, less cosmopolitan, not being a port. (Gandhi said that during his childhood there was less drunkenness there than in Porbandar.) But Rajkot was more important politically, and its windows were more open on the forces of history in the nineteenth century, because the British political agent in Kathiawar had his headquarters there.

Rajkot was in effect two cities, one traditionally Indian and the other British. In the Indian city the houses were crowded together in crooked streets (built that way to facilitate street fighting in time of war) while in the British "Civil Lines" there were few houses, much space between them, and streets ran at right angles to each other; all was order and cleanliness. The Civil Station was eight hundred acres large and contained six thousand people; the Indian city was only 137 acres, into which were crammed fifteen thousand people.

Much of Karamchand's duty was to work as an assessor with the Rajasthanik Court, a legal court of appeal, set up by the British, in which boundary and revenue disputes between the landlords and rulers of the Kathiawar states were settled. This court, which seems to have functioned well until the end of the century, was perhaps an example of British administration at its best or most typical, since it ran on common sense and conciliatory principles, but tended to preserve old power relations and delay radical reforms in Indian society.

In Rajkot, at least in his dealings with its ruler, the Thakore, Karamchand was less happy than before in his work; an unhappiness that affected his health and his whole life, and "left a deep and lasting impression on his youngest son."[1] Mohandas for instance hated to see his father put on "whole boots" to attend state functions; and Karamchand himself expressed disgust at doing so. "Our household was turned upside down when my father had to attend the Durbar during a Governor's visit. He never [except on these occasions] wore stockings or boots or what were then called 'whole boots.' His general footwear was soft leather slippers. If I was a painter, I would paint my father's disgust and torture on his face as he was putting his legs into his stockings and feet into ill-fitting and uncomfortable boots" (71:132). As our Gandhi describes it, the disgust has a political or cultural bearing. English impositions were intruding into the very clothes on Kaba's back. "He had to do this!" his son exclaims. (Comparably, Putliba hated to see her sons wearing English trousers, which seemed indecent to her; Indians draped the hips and crotch with loose folds of cloth.)

There is one anecdote that can suggest the flavor of Kaba Gandhi's work there. This is the story of a nighttime abduction (complete with ladder and lookouts) planned by the Thakore, to procure himself an attractive woman recently married to one of his subjects. Kaba's cousin, who was superintendent of police in the city, got wind of the plan, and on Kaba's advice frustrated it (removed the ladder). Kaba then told the Thakore how and why he had interfered—among other things he pointed out that the woman's house was very close to the Civil Lines, so that the British were sure to have found out—and the Thakore apparently pardoned his interference.[2] That perhaps suggests the complex of moral and political constraints within which a diwan like Kaba operated.

Two of Mohandas's family anecdotes seem to show that Kaba dealt delicately with his youngest son—delicately meaning that he employed moral persuasion rather than physical punishment—despite the short temper and explosiveness for which he was known. (We don't know much about how he dealt with his other sons, but there is some indication that he may have been rougher with them.) One of these stories refers to a time of Kaba's sickness, when Mohandas asked, and was granted, permission to go to see a play. As he waited for the performance to begin, he began to be uneasy about his father, feeling that the latter had not really wanted to be left alone, so he went home again; and found that his feeling had been right. Telling his secretary this story, he added that he never went to see another play, during his father's lifetime.

The second story—again referring to the time of Kaba's sickness—is told in the autobiography. Karsandas had run up a debt of twenty-five rupees (according to one account, this was to pay for meat meals that a Muslim friend had lured him into eating). To pay the debt he wanted to clip a piece of gold off one of his bracelets, and Mohandas was commissioned to do it.

But then he felt guilty, and made up his mind to confess, but did not dare to do so in speech. He wrote his confession out and handed it to Kaba. The father "read it through, and pearl-drops trickled down his cheeks, wetting the paper. For a moment he closed his eyes in thought and then tore up the note. . . . Those pearl-drops of love cleansed my heart, and washed my sin away. . . . This sort of sublime forgiveness was not natural to my father. I had thought that he would be angry, say hard things, and strike his forehead" (A: 27–28).

We note that the worst Mohan had feared was that his father would have punished himself, and that Kaba, in dealing with Mohan, transcended even that. It is also typical that Gandhi communicated in writing; the pattern of dumbness in speech and fluency in writing was a prominent aspect of his behavior in his early years. He insists that he was not a great reader, but he seems to have been a son of the literacy-and-print culture nevertheless. It appears that he even picked up from published sources some of his ideas about sex and marriage.

To take another instance, he wrote in 1925 about what he called the peremptory rule of his personal religion. He said he was early convinced that it was wrong ever to hate anyone or anything, and had stayed true to that teaching. "I learned this simple but grand doctrine when I was twelve years old, through a school book, and the conviction has persisted up to now. It is daily growing on me" (28:29). So this too originally came to him from a book.

He began school in Rajkot in January 1879, and two years later transferred to the Kathiawar High School, called the Alfred High School. He attended the first, the City Taluka School, only 110 days out of the 238 days of the first year, and missed 48 days in the second year, presumably for reasons of sickness. He seems to have suffered from fever in that first year, and was prone to headaches and nosebleeds in general. His brother Karsandas, having failed to pass out of Standard 4, began it again when Mohan entered the school in Standard 3. There were 234 pupils there, altogether. They had thirty-three hours of teaching a week. A school report described Mohan as being good at English, fair at Arithmetic, weak at Geography; "conduct very good, handwriting bad." (The most detailed account of Gandhi's schooldays is given by Upadhyaya in the work cited.)

In this first school Mohan did not make friends. He felt "forlorn, unlike all the other schoolboys" (53:100). At the age of eleven he took the entrance examinations for the high school, in four subjects, and passed ninth out of the 70 who sat. Of the 38 who passed the entrance examination, only one other reached matriculation in 1877. Thus Mohan performed well, if not brilliantly, in school; but he always believed his success was due to conscientious obedience, not original talent.

This high school had been opened in 1866, supported by donations from the princes, and was quite highly esteemed. In 1875 a new building was erected, with twelve rooms, for 300 pupils; in each room the pupils sat on benches or desks, the teacher on a dais. Several of his teachers were Parsis; members of a small religious group, powerful in Bombay and Gujarat, because of their wealth, their high standards in education, and their control of journalism. There were twenty-nine hours of class a week, ten of them conducted in English. Mohan was younger than the class average by a year, but at the end of the first year he ranked fifth. He also won some small scholarships.

Being taught in English, what he learned separated him from his parents and his siblings, who did not know more than a few phrases of that language. In 1937 Gandhi wrote in his weekly, *Harijan,* "The English medium created an impassable barrier between me and the members of my family, who had not gone through English schools. My father knew nothing of what I was doing. I could not, even if I had wished it, interest my father in what I was doing. . . . I was fast becoming a stranger in my own home. I certainly became a superior person. Even my dress began to undergo imperceptible changes."[3] Throughout his adult life, Gandhi insisted on the harm that was done to Indians by their spending so much time learning English.

As for what information he acquired, he complained about the rote learning of, for instance, the names of the counties of England, and the rote teaching of chemistry, a subject in which he failed to pass the examination (28:363 and 26:301). All this brought him only headaches. But he did learn certain political principles and historical legends. "British history, which I was taught as a lad," he wrote in 1944, "had it that Wat Tyler and John Hampden, who had rebelled, were heroes" (77:92).

In May 1881 he was married to Kasturba Makanji, whose father was a friend of Karamchand. He was of the same Modh Bania caste as the Gandhis, but a merchant in cloth, grain, and cotton. The Makanji family had links to both Porbandar and Rajkot. They do not figure largely in Gandhi's story, but Kasturba had a brother whom Gandhi had to support later in life; and who had become a nuisance by the time of Kasturba's death.

The Makanji house was grander than the Gandhis', with inlaid ceilings, carved teak walls, and broad verandas opening on to gardens. Kasturba brought with her a dowry of jewels worth two or three thousand rupees. In such a house, the women were restricted to their own quarters, but little girls could run everywhere, and tradition has it that Kasturba was an energetic and wilful tomboy.

Before she was accepted as Mohan's betrothed, she must have been inspected by the women of her groom's family, for crucial attributes like clear skin, sweet breath, perfect limbs, luxuriant hair. But Kasturba was a pretty and healthy girl, though small, who became quite a beautiful woman. To give birth to a daughter rather than a son was theoretically considered a punishment for some past sin, but that did not mean that all girls lacked self-confidence. There is reason to suppose that in this marriage it was the boy who was self-doubtful and unsure of himself.

On the other hand, as husband he had some kinds of superiority over his wife. Gandhi reflected about his own case that he "naturally" took certain freedoms with regard to Kasturba that she did not with regard to him. He could—and did—send her back to her parents when she seriously displeased him (72:127). Much is also suggested by the fact that she, as his wife, would eat the leavings on his plate, but he would not eat hers.

As a fiancée, Kasturba had five great rules to learn; to tell the truth, to be chaste, to pray, not to steal, and not to grow attached to her possessions. Of those, the last ran counter to much in the family life-style. A wife's main work in life, she was taught, was to please her husband and direct the household, but once those aims were accomplished, jewelry, cosmetics, and clothes were the main centers of her interests. In the afternoons, we are told, the women of such families might take out of the chests the saris that lay folded there, to air them and admire them. Jewelry, to ward off evil, was to be worn at every orifice of the body. Oil was to be rubbed into the throat and knees, perfume in the hair, and the soles of the feet were to be stained red. Moreover, the conduct of the household was heavily ritualized by caste and other quasi-religious prescriptions. Cooking was elaborate and time-consuming, and cleanliness was religious in its implications. Being a wife and mother was a full-time job.

Gandhi was engaged for some time to Kasturba, and before that had been engaged to two other little girls, who died. The mutual affection of the two principals had little to do with such marriages. They were events in the social and economic history of the two families. Once it was decided that Mohandas's wedding should be celebrated, the ceremony was designed to include Karsandas, and a cousin of theirs, so that the quite crippling expense need be undergone only once.

The brides and grooms sat on a special platform, and then took the ritual seven steps together, symbolizing their mutual obligations, and offered each other *kansar,* a sweetened wheat cake.

Kasturba was a very strong-willed as well as pretty girl. She had received no school education, and was to resist all her husband's attempts to teach her. To the end she knew only how to read a little, simple Gujarati. She was however physically strong and brave, and delighted in her superiority over Mohandas in that regard. He was nervous, as we know, and afraid of the dark; after a dispute she would blow out the lamp and run away, leaving him to his fears. There were many humiliations for Mohandas in those years.

The Young Couple

Gandhi tells us in his autobiography that he was passionately fond of Kasturba, and the context seems to show that he is speaking of both the affections and sexual desire. In other places he is quite unequivocal. "As far as one's wife is concerned, you are not likely to find anyone as lustful as I was" (35:379). He was also possessive and dominating, and wanted to reshape all those he came close to. But Kasturba seems to have had a passion for independence equal to his for dominance. She did not want to shape *him,* but she was determined to remain herself, which meant to maintain the traditions in which she was brought up. She was determined—for instance—to reign supreme in the traditional wifely realms, in the household and the kitchen. Since he was a reformer, a changer of tradition, this brought them into conflict again and again. It was she who cherished the traditional image of the Indian wife, including all a wife's deference to her husband.

Of what the early experience of marriage meant to them, we know only that Gandhi, when he spoke of early marriages later in life, bitterly disapproved of them. In his articles on Hindu customs that he wrote for the *Vegetarian* in London in 1890, it was on early marriage that he blamed the physical weakness of the Indians when compared with the English.

Physically, by most people's accounts, Gandhi was no more attractive than self-confident. Short and tense and sickly, he was solitary in his habits, and nervous in many relationships. Fatima Meer tells us that Kasturba condescended to Mohan, and told him not to bother her when he approached her during the day.[4] She refused to pledge him fidelity, and resisted his authority, while his brothers' wives did not resist them.[5]

Meer also tells us that older women consulted the girl, valuing her advice, though it is not clear on what evidence she asserts this. Of Kasturba's mind and nature we know very little, except that she was a forceful but in some sense undeveloped person—understanding *developed* to refer to thoughts and analytical feelings, on either personal or general topics. She came from a less reflective, more hedonist family than the Gandhis.

In the long run, however, she was not untouched by her husband's mission. She was his faithful companion, even in jail, and took part in the Gandhi movement, at certain moments. He did not discuss ideas with her; she did not want to discuss; but because he was a naive mind, that was not as much of an inequality or barrier between them as we might think. He shared with Kasturba, as with his mother, a desire to be good, and to be faithful to the teachings they had both learned as children. He did not claim all the intellectual's or the man's freedoms. This side of Gandhi, which conversely made him alien to many political allies, kept him in sympathy with his wife, and on the same level with her.

In what terms (except clichés) she understood him and his mission, how she named to herself the difference between him and her, between him and other men, it is impossible to say, because she had no gift of speech about such matters. But we are bound to assume that her understanding of "issues" was intellectually primitive. Gandhi says, for instance, that she had no idea at all of what either Muslims or Christians believed. Scarcely literate, she yet passed her life in a whirlwind of letters, minutes, petitions, publications, arguments, speeches, constitutions, a snowstorm of rhetoric under which she sat silent for sixty or seventy years.

She refused to learn to read or write from him, often as he strove to teach her—at one time he hired a tutor to take on the work. And it seems that this was typical of a general resistance on her part. One can only assume, from his own attitude to sexuality, and from what he said about her, that she never responded to him sexually or dropped her initial reticence toward him. "There was never any want of restraint on the part of my wife. Very often she would show restraint, but she rarely resisted me although she showed disinclination very often."[6]

Gandhi explained her failure to learn, his failure to teach, as the result of his sexual passion for her. He told Margaret Sanger in December 1935: "I was not the ideal teacher because I was a brute. The animal passion in me was too strong and I could not become the ideal teacher" (699). He was also fairly explicit, on that occasion, about her sexual passivity.

In this matter of sexuality, Erikson thinks that Gandhi held his father guilty, first of involving Mohan in sexual activity so early, by arranging his marriage; and second of marrying several times himself; identifying himself, in his son's eyes, with sex. Sex thus became linked to masculinity and domination. Erikson points out that Gandhi himself never admitted to finding any joyful intimacy in sex; that he seemed to associate sex with excretion, as something dirty; and that he needed to establish his own gaiety, intimacy, and playfulness in an area as far as possible removed from sex. (There was ample precedent for this in Hindu moral literature.)

Some more light may be thrown on Gandhi's idea of marriage by the comments of two American missionaries about Indian marital psychology in a village near Agra, from 1925 to 1950. In *Behind Mud Walls,* W. W. and C. V. Wiser say how struck they were by the way babies, especially boys, are deified in Hindu families, how reluctantly the mothers lose them to the world of men; and how eagerly they recapture them in adolescence, when they marry. Thus the women of the household, including the boy's mother, encourage sexual excitement and erotic dreaming. The Wisers saw a mother delighted to get her son sent home from school, claiming to be vaguely unwell (because his wife had gone on a visit to her parents) and his uncle trying to persuade the boy to take the rest of the year off from school. School, meaning work, was set in opposition to sex, meaning play, and the mother favored the second.

If we transpose this to Rajkot in the 1880s, we shall find it easy to understand an extra reason why Gandhi disapproved marriage. He was taken out of school several months before the wedding, and missed almost a whole year of education because of it. The institution of Hindu marriage, instead of being a separating-off from their families of two individuals, to explore each other and create a new world between them (the ideal for the modern world) was a return from the exploration of the outer world, to a nursery of physical pleasures set in an inner chamber of the original family. Thus Karsandas Gandhi, for instance, never really returned to school after his wedding.

Gandhi's Self-Description

When Gandhi wrote his autobiography he presented his timidity and physical awkwardness as advantages: his silence and shyness, for instance, kept him from filling his head with all kinds of foolishness. Serving his elders instead of playing with his peers saved him from bad habits. The autobiography is, in certain respects, the self-portrait of a prig, by Western standards—and indeed by some Eastern standards. D. B. Kalelkar, quite a close disciple, once suggested to Gandhi that it was a pity his autobiography omitted to describe the turmoil of his youth, the self-analysis and mental struggle he had overcome in order to become gentle and chaste, to subdue his rebellious nature. Kalelkar's implication was that the book gave a dull or an unattractive picture of Gandhi.[7]

In reply, Gandhi professed to have known no such Sturm und Drang. He had suffered certain temptations but no enthusiasms, no inspirations, or other self-swellings. This idea was part of Gandhi's Hindu pietism, and his repudiation of Western styles; perhaps it was also a revenge on those criteria of vitality that he had suffered from. Whatever the reason, looking back, he claimed to see no poetic vistas of personal beauty, power, personality. He had envisaged no greatness of force, or size of self, except the spiritualized and self-denying kinds.

As we shall see, Gandhi's psyche did bear traces of an encounter with "storms and passions," but we should not read his denial as deceit or as a personal self-disguise. His self-image in the autobiography is like Judge Ranade's image of himself, as recorded in the remarkable biography by Ranade's widow. These are in some sense Brahmin self-images. Gandhi and Ranade are content to present themselves as quiet, obedient, children, anxious to win their elders' approval and merely repelled by the alternative standards represented by their peers. They wanted to be good; or at least, looking back on themselves as children, the men they became search out the signs of goodness, not those of vitality. They are not on the side of rebellion, or nature, or vitality or dialectic; they are not on the side of the child against adults. When Gandhi mentioned his experience with bhang, he spoke of it as a loss of self (33:424).

Moreover there was, it seems, little in that boy for the man to be proud of, looking back. There is plenty of evidence that Gandhi saw himself as frail and feeble all through his childhood, youth, and even later. At seventeen and eighteen, he told a friend in 1933, he was still scared of everything (56:421). He also seems to have despised his body in childhood. Perhaps this was because it betrayed him in the ways described—his headaches and fevers. In any case he tells us that he could not, at school, believe that gymnastics had anything to do with education. He took no interest in cricket or football, and (he said) had even watched a game only at his teachers' insistence. Later in life he made a cult of health and of the healthy body, though a New Age rather than a school sports kind of cult.

Another such sign is that he was ready to say "we are weak" about many groups he belonged to—about banias, about Kathiawaris, about Hindus as a whole; and when he confronts individuals or groups whom he sees as powerful—*Kshatriyas* or the martial races, the Muslims, the English—his tone is playfully challenging. As groups the Zulus and the Pathans (both on the Northwest Frontier and in South Africa) attracted Gandhi's attention for their physical power and fierceness; while the Muslims and the Englishmen were adventurers and conquerors and meat-eaters, and Gandhi himself was timid even vis-à-vis his brothers and his bride.

School and Sheikh Mehtab

The two younger Gandhi brothers began school together in Rajkot, but Karsandas was not a quick learner, and was often in trouble. Moreover he made friends with a Muslim boy, Sheikh Mehtab, who combined somewhat greater gifts with an equal or greater naughtiness. (He was the instigator of the meat meals for some of which Karsandas had to pay.) The school records show that they passed the entrance examination in November 1879, with scores of 59 percent and 62 percent—Karsandas getting the lower score. Both failed the terminal examination, in the following April. In the following September Mehtab was "struck off," for being absent without leave for four days, and was not readmitted until the following February.

In 1882, the year of their weddings, the Gandhi boys were absent 67 and 74 days, out of 222: Karsandas formally left school in February 1883: Mohandas and Sheikh Mehtab repeated a year, but the latter was struck off the roll again in February 1884, while Mohandas did well that year. It seems, though we have no full account of these matters, that Sheikh Mehtab gradually transferred his friendship from the older to the younger brother; which must have been a source of joy to Mohandas, but only in the short run.

Because Sheikh Mehtab became a close friend of Mohandas as well as Karsandas, we need to know as much as we can about him. It seems likely that he was a Meman Muslim. The Muslims of Gujarat were mostly either Voras, who were village laborers, or Memans, who were originally Kshatriya Hindus, driven out of Sind when they converted to Islam.[8] Most of those who went out to Natal as merchants were Memans.

Sheikh Mehtab was about a year older than Karsandas, and three years older than Mohandas. He lived in a house a few paces away from the Gandhis. But his father, Mahmedshah Umarmian, was employed by the Kathiawar political agency as a jailer in Gondal, a nearby town. He earned twenty rupees a month, very much less than Kaba Gandhi; who earned three hundred as diwan. Mahmedshah's son is recorded as coming to the high school from the Rajkot Civilian Station School, Karsandas as coming from the Rajkot Taluka—a Hindu school. And the Gandhi family was not connected with the British police, but with the state's police. (It is however worth noting that the Gandhis had several such connections with the police—that was another aspect of their family tradition—and Karsandas eventually became a policeman in charge of the jail in Porbandar.)

Thus there were ways in which Sheikh Mehtab was associated with the social group that ruled over the Hindus—as of course the Muslims themselves had done before the English, in North India. Gandhi said later that he consciously cultivated the friendship of Muslims, Parsis, and Jains at school (76:386) and that Muslims and Hindus went in and out of each other's houses in Rajkot. Presumably that refers to Mehtab, for there is no record of any other Muslim in Gandhi's social circle; nor of any other friend, of whatever religion, being half so intimate.

Gandhi says he *had* another friend at school in Rajkot, who was by one account a Parsi. In any case, Mohan lost this friend through Mehtab—because the Parsi disapproved of the Muslim or because the latter absorbed all of Gandhi's attention. As we shall see, the Gandhi family disapproved of Mehtab's influence upon Mohandas, and one is tempted to interpret a story of an early boyhood satyagraha as relating to the Muslim boy. The Gandhi family apparently invited people to a feast at the beginning of the mango season, but did not invite a particular friend of Mohandas; and in retaliation he forswore mangoes, of which he was very fond, for the whole season.[9]

The best chronicler of Gandhi's early years, J. M. Uphadyaya, tells us that Sheikh Mehtab was well-built and spectacular at sports, especially the long jump. He took the brothers swimming and displayed his skills, and cast a spell over them. He was a fighter and had a crowd of obedient followers among his peers. Pyarelal says Sheikh Mehtab "feared neither God nor Devil." Robert Payne says that Mehtab provoked and intimidated Mohandas in many ways.

Gandhi used strong language about his relationship to his friend, and though most writers who take an interest in Gandhi's emotional development have deprecated Gandhi's way of presenting it, their own language is quite dramatic. Erikson, for instance, says that Mohandas was "addicted to" Sheikh Mehtab.[10] In *Intimate Relationships,* the Indian psychiatrist, Sudhir Kakar, describes Mehtab as "physically strong, fearless, and rakishly handsome," and goes on to say that—despite Gandhi's description in the *Autobiography*—he does not seem to have been especially evil.[11] Kakar tries to interpret Gandhi's account of himself as sympathetically as possible, but resists him in this matter. "He [Sheikh Mehtab] is neither more nor less than an average representative of the world of male adolescence, with its phallic displays and the ethic of a devil-may-care bravery." The implication seems to be that therefore he was not to be taken seriously.

Since Gandhi was a self-confessed mama's boy, Kakar says, Sheikh Mehtab "must have been a godsend. He provided Mohandas with the adolescent haven where young men can be both dismissive and fearful of women and heterosexual love, where in the vague homoeroticism of masculine banter," and so on. This is probably a fair representation of the way most of us react to the two figures in the story Gandhi tells. His own point of view was different.

The chapter of Gandhi's autobiography in which he discussed Sheikh Mehtab is entitled "A Tragedy," and he writes that he regarded the friendship as "a tragedy in my life." In the Gujarati version of the *Autobiography,* Gandhi says that Mehtab polluted him by making him a meat-eater, and he himself calculated wrongly in staying friends with him. "One should not venture into deep waters even for the sake of reforming another" (39:476).

"Amongst my few friends at the high school I had, at different times, two who might be called intimate. One of these friendships did not last long, though I never forsook my friend. He forsook me, because I made friends with the other" (A:19). This latter was of course Sheikh Mehtab. The influence he exerted on Mohan was largely in the direction of rule breaking or disobedience, and various members of the Gandhi family warned Mohandas against him. Gandhi does not mention his father as so doing, which probably means that the friendship only grew strong after Karamchand died, but he does mention his mother, his eldest brother, and his wife, as issuing these warnings.

His own reply to their disapproval he represents thus: "I am sure that if he reforms his ways, he will be a splendid man." It seems clear that, as they saw each other, Mehtab had the advantages of splendor, and that Gandhi lacked them. He says he himself looked feeble-bodied by the side of Karsandas and the other. "They were both hardier, physically stronger, and more daring. . . . [Mehtab] would often display his exploits to me and, as one is always dazzled when he sees in others the qualities that he lacks himself, I was dazzled by this friend's exploits" (A:20). Mehtab was not afraid of the dark or of robbers, he could hold live serpents in his hand, and so on. He was a champion fighter as well as athlete, and sometimes generously defended younger boys against bullying.

He played tricks on his friends, and notably on Mohandas. On one occasion he persuaded a group of boys to eat pan together, but put something into the mixture that left black stains on their teeth and lips. Mohandas was held responsible, and scolded by his elders. In one place, Gandhi says Sheikh Mehtab often "threatened" him (72:127).

Robert Payne (who seems to have got his information from Pyarelal) calls Sheikh Mehtab the star athlete of the school, and says he had "followers" there. He represented "strength, guile, and domination" to the young Gandhi.[12] He would also, as we shall see, lead Mohandas in directions that even today we would probably regard as—for such a boy—dangerous. Besides inducing him to eat meat, against the wishes of his parents and the practice of his religion, he took him to a brothel, as part of a program of asserting his independence of, and dominance over, Kasturba. This was when he was fifteen (53:467). Fatima Meer says that the woman had faded henna on the soles of her feet, and was perfumed with pan and attar. (The episode apparently took place during one of Kasturba's lengthy returns to her parents' house; Mohan's experiment with smoking also took place while she was away; Mohan and his cousin resented their wives' absence, and protested by means of such acts of disobedience.)

It is clear that Mohan would almost certainly be badly upset by his visit to a brothel, even though no sexual acts took place. (He was, he says, "deprived of animal instinct" and so felt shamed in his manhood.) And his friend's over-persuading him to go there—apparently Mehtab paid the woman her fee—may well have had some strain of malice in it. Even so, most Western readers probably find the use of the word *tragedy* excessive, and we recognize here one of the places where we have to reach across a gap toward Gandhi. Indeed, this gap is not there only for Westerners, as Kakar's and Kalelkar's remarks show.

It is clear that Mohandas's feelings about this friend were mixed up with his feelings about his older brother, and his feelings about himself. Gandhi saw himself as physically feeble and often socially humiliated, and saw others among his friends as stronger than he in nearly every way. He set out to equal or surpass them, and failed.

Later, of course, he succeeded, but not by becoming like them—he learned to become stronger *in his weakness*. (This paradoxical transposition of strength and weakness, bold as it is, is commonplace in religious writings, in both East and West—for instance in Christian hymns.) That was the result of a reverse philosophy.

The pattern of Gandhi's feelings in boyhood—about himself and his friend—was not restricted to purely personal relations. The same was true of his sense of the Hindu's relations to the Muslim and the Englishman.

For instance, many of Gandhi's remarks about Indian Muslim psychology in general have an obvious bearing on his friend. "The Mussalman, being generally in a minority, has as a class developed into a bully . . . he exhibits the virility of a comparatively new system of life [compared with the Hindu system, that is] . . . thirteen hundred years of imperialistic expansion has made the Mussalmans fighters as a body. They are therefore aggressive. Bullying is the natural excrescence of an aggressive spirit" (24:270).

"Many [Muslims] regard themselves, quite wrongly, I think, as belonging to a race of conquerors" (26:442). Gandhi says he thinks that idea is wrong because he saw the Muslims as being mostly converted Hindus, and so of the same race. But he certainly saw the Muslims as fighters and conquerors. ("The general impression is that the Muslims can fight and fight well" 25:136.) And he saw them as braver than Hindus: "The Hindu is proverbially, almost contemptibly mild" (21:483).

Gandhi linked the Muslims in his mind with the other "martial races" of India, such as the Rajputs and the Sikhs and the Pathans; while the Hindus he linked to the Jains and the Parsis. He also believed that the martial races indulged in wine and meat, and allowed themselves sexual license, which the Hindus denied themselves (33:430). When he addressed Muslims, or spoke officially, he usually described them in other terms, but in informal talk he joined in this cultural typology that is a kind of Indian common sense. It forms a middle ground between Gandhi's personal relationships and his politics, and is an important bridge linking them.

Moreover, although we hear more about Mehtab's physical exploits and mischievousness, we should not forget that his propaganda for meat eating was political in its reference. Perhaps the insistence on gender dominance was, too. All over India, and indeed in Europe too, nationalist movements were also physical culture movements; there was a chain of strong connections of muscularity to aggression to manliness to patriotism.

In fact, Sheikh Mehtab's interests in later life included patriotic music and poetry—both as performer and composer—and history. He was a man of ideas (even though not, presumably, very clever) and the recklessness and fecklessness of his behavior are traits that go along with a love of ideas, in a popular stereotype (which, like other stereotypes, is true enough). We should not think of Sheikh Mehtab as merely a physique, or merely a rascal. All his varied interests were, like Gandhi's, connected to Indian patriotism. In South Africa he composed songs and gave lectures about national heroes. He was not primarily interested, any more than Gandhi was, in making money or having a career or a family. There were thus several dimensions to the attraction he had for Mohandas, and the power he held over him.

Not that Gandhi's feelings about Karsandas and Mehtab were simply admiring or imitative. We should note that he thought of himself as reforming Mehtab, which implies that *he* had the role of dominance. Of course, one wonders what Mehtab—a professedly tricky character—felt about that; but Gandhi went on, in the course of a long life, to charm many very difficult characters into "reform."

He may have been, in part he probably was, deceiving himself about the other boy's response, but it is quite likely that the other boy may have intermittently seen things in Mohan's way, too. He would have to have been very blackhearted, not to have wanted in some measure to be "reformed" by this warmly affectionate and insightful little friend. Later events seem to show Mehtab cynically exploiting that friend's affection, but it may be better to regard that as part of the to and fro of a struggle in which each side was partly closed to but partly open to the other's appeal, and appreciative of the other's strengths.

The way in which Gandhi first saw Mehtab is one familiar to readers of nineteenth-century novels about boys. In *Tom Brown's Schooldays,* for instance—an immensely popular book published in 1857—Tom is a big blundering impulsive boy who forms a friendship with physically frail, morally serious Arthur; and the latter reforms the former. It is worth noting that Tom is the story's central character; Arthur is right but Tom is "splendid." The hero embodies nature—good nature—and needs only to be made thoughtful by a more sensitive friend.

This dialectic, between goodness and nature, is to be found throughout the main line of English fiction: in Fielding's *Tom Jones,* for instance, and in most of Dickens. Any character, at least any male character, who speaks explicitly for virtue, is to be regarded with suspicion, and any "bad boy" is likely to win our hearts. (In American literature, *Tom Sawyer* is a famous example of this dialectic.) How much of such writing Gandhi may have read we do not know, but in jail in the early twenties, he read, and was impressed by, *Tom Brown's Schooldays,* just while he himself was writing his autobiography (23:146). His high-school reading was in English literature, and his schoolteachers favored cricket and the English public-school moral atmosphere. The headmaster was a Parsi—the most anglicized group among Indians—and in his last three years at school, Gandhi was taught by three Parsis, and exclusively in English.

Moreover, this way of understanding boys and boyhood, and this preference for nature over goodness, seems to be traceable in many cultures. Gandhi almost certainly shared that preference while he was a boy in Rajkot—however little it was to his own advantage—and he sometimes analyzed masculine types in the same way later. But he found that that *value* system (as opposed to the analytical system) let him in for a lot of misery and shame, and he had renounced it by the time he came to write his autobiography.

Even in boyhood, he was ethically very serious in this friendship. The idea of reform was a very important one to all young Indians interested in politics, and a complex idea. It could mean—as it did in the West—narrowly moral self-improvement; but it could mean something almost opposite, the indulgence of the appetites in the pursuit of a forcefulness that contemporary India had lost. This latter was of course what Sheikh Mehtab stood for.

Gandhi quotes to us a stanza popular among his schoolmates, which recommended eating meat:

> Behold the mighty Englishman
> He rules the Indian small
> Because, being a meat-eater,
> He is five cubits tall. (A:21)

In the Gujarati version of the autobiography, the verse continues, "And can defeat five hundred Indians."

This was a message Sheikh Mehtab endorsed. Being a Muslim—and so belonging to a race of conquerors—he was a meat-eater himself, and boasted of the manifold virtues of that diet, physical, sexual, political. He claimed, for instance, that meat-eaters would not suffer from boils—an argument that probably carried weight with Mohan, who always tested even moral prescriptions by their effect upon health and strength.

In any case, their friend persuaded the Gandhi brothers secretly to rebel against their parents' rules, and to eat goat meat at a restaurant. "To this day," Gandhi wrote in 1929, "I have no knowledge where he found the money to pay for meat banquets" (39:7). After eating, Mohandas had strong, even physical, reactions against the meat, but persevered in the experiment for a time, until the guilt he felt at deceiving his parents grew too strong. Then he told his friend that he would remain a vegetarian as long as his parents were alive, even though he was rationally convinced of the advantages of a meat diet.

Mehtab also persuaded Gandhi that he needed to establish himself as the master in his marital relationship, by making Kasturba take a pledge of obedience, promising to tell him wherever she went, and so on. Gandhi's suspicions of his wife were so strong that he once sent her back to her parents for a whole year. Writing in 1940, he does not say what he suspected her of, but it was something "worse than stealing." And why? "Sheikh Mehtab was behind this. He kept me under his thumb for more than ten years. . . . I broke her bangles, refused to have anything to do with her and sent her away to her parents" (72:127).

In 1928 he wrote that he had shown, in his autobiography, that he could be "a positive beast even though at the same time I claimed to be a loving husband. It was not without good cause that a friend once described me as a combination of sacred cow and ferocious tiger" (36:101). The masterful relation did not "come naturally" to Gandhi in relation to Kasturba, or to others at this time, for instance, to servants. It did come to him naturally in certain other relationships (with fellow idealists and disciples) but those relationships came into existence only after he had renounced the false wisdom—false as far as Gandhi was concerned—which Mehtab preached.

As was said, Sheikh Mehtab persuaded his friend to go to a brothel, in 1883, as part of his program of masterful masculinity. Gandhi said he went "out of false regard for the friend." Gandhi was too embarrassed to perform—and even more embarrassed by that failure, though he realized later that his "stupidity" had shielded him (27:108).

It was a cruel but fitting punishment that, as Gandhi understood things, his treatment of Kasturba, and his other misbehavior with Sheikh Mehtab at that time, should have shaped the soul of the child that Kasturba bore—Gandhi's eldest son, Harilal: who alternately denied and betrayed his father's moral teaching. For thirty or forty years Harilal increasingly played the rogue, quarreling bitterly with his father, semideliberately destroying himself by an addiction to drink and drugs and other vices, and once renounced Hinduism for Islam. (Erik Erikson points out that Harilal was a kind of rebirth of Sheikh Mehtab in Gandhi's life.) Thus Gandhi went on paying the price of his early mistakes throughout his life.

Gandhi remained suspicious of exclusive relationships ever after, even in friendship. In 1926 he wrote to a friend who had been reading the autobiography, speaking of "intimacy between two or more persons where . . . mutual help is the consequence of, not a motive for, friendship. The motive is some indefinable attraction. It is this exclusive relationship which I have considered to be undesirable and antagonistic to communion with God" (29:454). Also—in the same year—he says that friendship is contrary to dharma. "We are all bullocks together, and there can be no friend but God" (34:285).

Meanwhile, Karsandas Gandhi left school on February 4, 1883, and seems to have "gone downhill." Mohan told his secretary, "My brother was a drunkard, a thief, and addicted to smoking." Mohan used to warn Karsandas repeatedly of the direction he was moving in.[13] When Karsandas died, Mohan—in South Africa—said they had been of very different temperaments, and the elder had been hurt because the younger brother would not join in his projects. Our Gandhi had hoped, when they met, to apologize and to "remove the mental distance between us."[14]

Patriotic Heroism

To understand Mehtab's challenges to Mohandas fully, we should take into account the insurgent growth of nationalist feeling in India at that time. Different as are these two things, a friendship between two boys, and a set of widespread political ideas, both set up a strong polar opposition between masculinity and effeminacy; spurning the latter and promising the former, as a reward for political action. The boys aimed to become "Indian men," possessed of a virility that seemed to have been stolen from the motherland by her conquerors.

Outside Rajkot, they were of course two anonymous atoms of Indian humanity. But because they were more alert than most to the sufferings of their country and the philistinism of their conquerors, they were linked potentially to some famous names. If we think of the subcontinent as a triangular papier-mâché model, with the names of cities and provinces painted on, then we can imagine also a hidden electrical network that represents the excitement of nationalist pride, with heroes' names that light up at moments of crisis. How much Mehtab and Gandhi knew in 1888 about those names we can't be sure, but they felt that excitement.

Indian nationalist politics had a great variety of beginnings, in secret societies, open rebellions, newspaper polemics, and officially sponsored organizations like congress. But the theme of masculinity can be heard in all of them. We can look, for instance, at the lives of three leading figures—Balvantra Tilak, Lala Lajpat Rai, and Bipin Chandra Pal—who were shaping the tradition of political radicalism that Gandhi was to inherit. This famous trio, sometimes linked together as Bal, Lal, and Pal, were however of different types, and came from different parts of the country; and their politics were in some ways unlike. They represented the three politically active provinces mentioned before—Maharashtra, Punjab, and Bengal.

As we have noted, Gandhi was not politically precocious, in the sense of reading about current events or party programs. Before he left India, in 1888, he tells us, he did not read any newspaper regularly; and he seems to have taken no political action before he got to Natal in 1893. But he was from boyhood on deeply concerned with (Indian) humiliation and (English) arrogance. And these three radical leaders were certainly present to his imagination in later years. They all served terms in British jails before he did. As soon as he had established himself as a leader in South Africa, he went back to India and made himself known to them.

Tilak (1856–1920) was a Pune Brahmin, who began his career in education. His ideology was emphatically Hindu-nationalist. One of his most famous books described a scheme for dating the Vedas by means of the position of the stars mentioned in them; the point of which was to prove that the *Rigveda* was written around 4000 BC, and thus claim immense antiquity and superiority for the Aryan cultural tradition.

Apart from the Vedic Aryans, Tilak's other great enthusiasm in Indian history was the Marathis, and he built himself a house on Singagahr (a mountain whose name means "the fortress of the lion") where their great military hero, Shiva Maharaj, ensconced himself. Shiva Maharaj, 1627–80, was the leader of the Hindu Marathis against the Muslims.

Tilak made himself a latter-day bard of Shivaji, and of the eighteenth-century heroes of the same area, the Peshwa Brahmins. The last of the latter surrendered to the British only in 1818, and the government remained suspicious of Pune, their capital, their secret societies, and the violence of Maharashtran politics. (That violence was in time to be directed against Gandhi.)

In 1881 Tilak started up a Marathi magazine, called *Kesar,* the Lion, and leonine imagery was central to his politics. He wanted Indians to be lions. As this indicates, he had shifted his field of action from education to vernacular journalism, and to a revival of Hindu festivals, especially those connected with Shivaji.

The masculinism of Tilak's style emerged in the contrast he made with his rival and coeval, Gopal Krishna Gokhale, the leader of the moderates. The latter was an invalid and intellectual, who wore Western dress and glasses, plus a scarf and longer hair. Tilak was shorter, darker, tougher, louder-voiced. With a shaven head and a big mustache (the emblem of virility for Indians) he wore always traditional dress. He was known as a vigorous and inspiring teacher, harsh and turbulent, and determined to lead. Gokhale was soft-spoken, mild, sensitive, remote from crowds, diffident. The difference between the two was generally felt in gender terms. Gandhi acknowledged a primary affiliation to Gokhale, but bowed to Tilak also.

Tilak was not a reformer, in the sense of a Westernizer. The leader of the reforming party was Justice Ranade, whose heir was Gokhale, whose heir, in turn, was Gandhi. This lineage was sharply opposed to Tilak's, in various ways. Gandhi described Gokhale as a maternal presence, like the Ganges. Tilak wanted to revive Indian pride in Indian institutions, trusting that that pride would be enough to remove their imperfections. He cared primarily for male/caste/national pride and tradition, and often inspired aggressive protest to support his causes. "Individuals as well as institutions are of two kinds; those that take the circumstances as they are and compromise with them, and those that [create] favorable circumstances by robustly and steadily fighting their way up. . . . I cannot accept compromise."[15]

Lala Lajpat Rai (1865–1928) was a Punjabi, whose mother was a Sikh. Trained in the law, he was at first enthusiastic about the Brahmo Samaj ideas, but then—as would be likely to happen in the Punjab—the idea of "the ancient Aryan culture" became his guiding star, and he joined the Arya Samaj. The latter, Swami Dayanand's organization, was fiercer and more proselytizing than its rival. (Gandhi said it borrowed its idea of conversion, which he disliked, from the Muslims.)

Introducing his book, *The Story of My Deportation* (he had been deported in punishment for his part in the Bengal Partition protests) Rai said, "As a Hindu, it is my devout prayer that I may be born again and again in this land of the Vedas to contribute my Karma to the corporate Karma of the nation." That is the style of the Arya Samaj.

When Rai moved to Lahore, he found the local branch of the Arya Samaj split in two, and joined the more worldly and aggressive of the splinter groups. He became known as the Lion of the Punjab. Romain Rolland, when he met Rai in the 1920s, said he was the most un-Gandhian of men; finding him rougher and more aggressive than any of the other Indians he knew. In Indian history, Rai admired above all the military Rajputs, and the first book he bought after passing his law examination was James Tod's *Annals of Rajasthan.* Rai wrote that his love for the valorous deeds described therein "developed into an irresistible passion." Amongst nineteenth-century Europeans, he admired the Italian nationalists. Rai translated Mazzini's *Duties of Man;* but Garibaldi, the man of action, was even more his hero. He wrote biographies of both men. It is not surprising that Rai died as a result of being beaten up by the police in the course of a demonstration.

Finally, Bipin Chandra Pal (1858–1932) was a vivid example of the Indian revolutionary nationalist—Pal was known for a time as the Danton of Bengal—who first achieved and then lost his ideological virility, under the pressure of repression. Pal began as a reforming liberal, especially in matters of religion. He was librarian of Calcutta's city library. A member of the Brahmo Samaj, he loved Emerson and translated Theodore Parker, and in 1898 he was given a Unitarian scholarship to go to Oxford. (Tilak refused to consider the Brahmo Samaj faith as genuine Hinduism.) From there Pal went on to America, delivering speeches against the dangers of drink. He was one of the great Indian orators of that generation; Nehru wrote home from Cambridge to his father that Pal had thundered at his student group as if they had been ten thousand, instead of a dozen.

Pal thus began by praising Hinduism as a family of religions, and Hindu society as a social federation; concepts that imply a pacifist politics. But after 1895, and especially after 1905, when Lord Curzon, the viceroy, announced that Bengal would be partitioned, everybody in Bengal public life became politically aggressive, including Pal. Resistance to the partition became the cause of all those educated and well-to-do classes who had taken part in the Bengal Renaissance, including the Tagores. Pal became an activist, preaching passive resistance and *swadeshi.* (Swadeshi, the boycotting of all but native produce, had been a cry in Pune in the 1840s, and was revived in Gandhi's campaigns later.) In 1907 he even went to jail for refusing to testify against his fellow Bengali, Arabindo Ghose, who was involved in illegal activism.

From jail, however, Pal issued a statement that he was primarily a sociologist, a student of the science of society, and not an extremist. This was the first sign of a change in him, which paralleled a general sense among the well-to-do radicals in Bengal that they were in deeper water, politically, than they had intended. (They were afraid that their opposition to partition was arousing the mostly Muslim peasants against them.)

In 1908 Pal went to England again. Ironically, his passage was paid by a radical nationalist, Pandit Krishnavarma—a patron of revolutionary extremism. But while in England, Pal repeatedly repudiated terrorism, and said that India's future lay in belonging to the empire, as that evolved into a federation: India should appeal to England's civilized conscience. Pal was consequently denounced as a traitor by Krishnavarma, in October 1908, and scorned by all the young men who wanted to become heroes of nationalism.

In all three of these lives we see an attempt at a masculine activism within politics. At some moments that heroism is achieved, at others lost, but always the judgment of an audience—all India—is implicitly asked on the question: is this a man, or less than a man? Feelings of the same kind were running through the heads of the two boys of Rajkot, and were involved in their friendship and quarreling, their competition and comradeship.

Leaving Home

Karamchand Gandhi suffered an accident on his way to Porbandar for his sons' wedding. His Thakore Saheb had kept him busy in Rajkot till the last minute, and then ordered for him a stagecoach that could do the journey in three days, instead of the five it took by bullock cart. But the speed was dangerous. On the last of the three days (the roads being worse the further west one went) the coach overturned, and Karamchand fell and was injured. He appeared at the ceremony bandaged. This was an evil omen for the marriage, and in fact Karamchand never fully recovered from the injuries of that accident, developing a fistula that finally killed him.

In 1882, not long after his sons' wedding, Kaba sided against his prince in a dispute between the latter and a relative, and resigned. He was already sick much of the time. For the next three years, until his death at the end of 1885, when Mohandas was sixteen, the family's income dropped from three hundred to fifty rupees a month. It was because of the declining fortunes of the family (Devanesen refers to them as "impoverished gentry") that the plan of sending Mohandas to England to become a barrister was again mooted. Let us note again that it was the youngest son in whom the family's hopes were invested.

Kaba's resignation from his post with the ruler of Rajkot came on January 19, 1882, and he died on November 16, 1885. He spent the last three years of his life in bed. He refused to have the ulcerated boils on his neck lanced. In his last year he was preoccupied with religion, and priests sat by his bed from morning to night, Jain, Muslim, Parsi, Vaishnava, reading or expounding their various scriptures. Mohandas was much affected by hearing the Tulsidas *Ramayana* recited to his father by Lodha Maharaj of Bileshwar; who was rumored to have cured himself of leprosy by such recitations.

Mohandas took pleasure in nursing his father, and regarded that as a privilege. But on the evening his father died, the son was with his pregnant wife, and was making love to her when the servant came to fetch him—too late. This was a cause of intense grief and even of self-disgust to Gandhi; since, as we have seen, Kasturba never responded to his sexual advances, sexuality in his experience of it was merely an animal egotism, and offensive to a fastidious ethical idealist. Moreover, when Kasturba gave birth, shortly after Karamchand's death, the child lived only a few days (some say three). Thus injury and death, sexuality and animalism, failure toward his father and exploitation of his wife, were all entwined together for Mohandas while he was still only a teenager.

Kaba's death left the Gandhi family in something of a crisis, conscious of a diminished economic and social position. Prabhudas Gandhi tells us that on his deathbed, Kaba said, "Manu here will keep up my reputation. He will increase the fame of our lineage." It seems to have been agreed that some bold moves were required to restore the family's fortunes. Even some years before Kaba died, the plan of Mohan going to train in law in England had been discussed. (This possibility was referred to as early as 1879.)[17] This implies both a public and a private fact of great importance: we see that the family recognized the historical trend that made it necessary for a young man to get professional preparation in England, in order to do work that his father and grandfather did without it; and we see that the youngest son was expected to lead the family. Nobody expected so much of Karsandas or Lakshmidas.

As noted, Mohandas himself was full of self-doubts and inhibitions. He found it very hard to stand up in public and speak. When he made a little farewell speech to his schoolfellows, his head spun and he could only stammer out a few words. "I hope that some of you will follow in my footsteps and after your return from England you will work whole-heartedly for big reforms in India" (1:2). It was quite clear to everyone that going to England meant making a promise to return able to change things in India—to make Indian culture more vigorous—more like English culture. But this tiny speech was too much for Gandhi. Looking back, in London, he wrote: "When I spoke half of what I had to speak, I began to shake. I hope I will not do it again when I return to India" (1:10).

Before that decision was taken, however, he matriculated from high school, and began to study for his BA at Samaldas College in Bhavnagar, ninety miles southeast of Rajkot, in January 1888. In March 1885 he was third in the inspector's examination, out of the forty who took it; and in the matriculation he was placed 404th out of 3,000. His attention was being drawn more and more to England. In his prematriculation course he had to study two hundred pages of Addison's essays, and 750 lines of poetry—from Milton and others.

Samaldas was founded in 1884, and had only sixty students. Gandhi did not do well there, either in his studies or his health, and returned home after five months. Robert Payne suggests that he may have suffered a nervous breakdown, of a kind not uncommon among Indian students. Being suddenly so far removed from the support system of his family and home town, it was easy for such a student to panic.

The family consulted with Mavji Joshe, a Brahmin who seemed to know more about the world, and who recommended that Mohandas be sent to London. "If you wish to make headway in your country, and become, like your father, a man of importance, you had better relinquish the idea of graduating here. You must go to London and become a barrister."[18] He said that the total cost would be five thousand rupees (in fact, it turned out to cost the family thirteen thousand rupees). The money was found from various uncles and cousins in the extended family, but not without a good deal of intrigue and difficulty. X would lend a certain sum *if* Y approved the scheme—but was not this condition a subtle cheat?—was not Y already committed to disapproving?—and must not Z be consulted before even talking to X? Such were the moves and countermoves in this example of the "family intrigues" that Gandhi so disliked.

When asked in 1891 for his motive for going to England, Gandhi said, "In a word, ambition." But while he was in London, Gandhi kept a diary (it mounted to 120 pages) which gives a somewhat different motive for his move. "Before the intention of coming to London was actually formed, I had a secret design in my mind of coming here to satisfy my curiosity of knowing what London was" (1:3). He thought of it as the home of philosophers and poets, the very center of civilization. Mavji Joshe had merely "fanned the fire that was burning in me." Obviously the two motives were not mutually exclusive;

this one was secret and personal; but let us note that it is the timid Mohandas, rather than, say, Sheikh Mehtab, who formed this project.

The family had tried to keep their scheme a secret, but of course it could not be long before all the friends and relations knew about it. Besides the borrowings and bargainings mentioned before, Kasturba's jewelry was sold, and a scholarship was requested from the British agent. Mohandas had to engage in some fulsome flattery of the Thakore Saheb, which made him angry. And he had to deal with the religiocultural opposition of his caste, which is where Hindu conservatism, with its disapproval of overseas travel, concentrated its strength.

Putliba was on her son's side, but she was not easy about the moral dangers he would run in England. She consulted Becharji Swami, a Brahmin turned Jain monk, and spiritual adviser to the family. He said Mohandas should take three vows, not to eat meat, not to drink wine, and not to touch a woman, while he was in England; and if so he might go.

Erikson points out that these vows, taken to his mother, again identified temptation and self-indulgence with the male sex, strength of will and self-denial with the female. (The psychiatrist sees the exaggerations of Mohan's diet-puritanism as a concealed rebellion against his mother's sanctity. He certainly engaged later in competitions in self-denial.)

Sheikh Mehtab was much involved in all this, in characteristic ways. "Very full of tricks," as Gandhi puts it in the diary, Mehtab forged a letter as coming from Gandhi—while the latter was in Porbandar—and showed it to a cousin called Meghijibhai, who thereupon promised a contribution, but later found out he had been fooled (1:8). Gandhi also tells us that his quarrels with Mehtab were constant and preoccupied him. In consequence, on the eve of the journey to Porbandar, in quest of funds, "quite engrossed in thinking about the quarrel," Mohan fell and banged his head against a carriage; "I was always quarrelling with my friend Sheikh Mehtab" (1:6); and then, a little later, fell and injured himself again, so that he lay unconscious for five minutes. His companions thought he was dead, as he lay there. (These details are rather puzzling, but Gandhi calls it a serious accident and—partly just because he wrote the story down some time later—it seems to testify to the strength of the emotional involvement.)

Mehtab's seems to have been a consciously and admittedly mischievous and comical personality. This further defines the relationship between the two, for Gandhi loved to laugh. Although Mohan was very eager to go abroad, and suffered badly from all these obstacles, he himself seems to have treated them as the stuff of comedy. He boasts that he made his mother laugh heartily about these intrigues, when she should have been shedding tears because of them (1:10).

Nevertheless, he described the five months before his departure as full of terrible anxiety and torture. "These were indeed hard days," Gandhi writes, "I could not sleep well at night, was always attacked by dreams" (1:9). Everyone offered him advice, and often changed what they had given; his oldest brother especially wavered. Mohan got no financial support from official sources, and there were reports in the press of the plan, which aroused disapproval as well as inquisitiveness. Lakshmidas told Mohan to give up the whole plan on August 4. But the latter refused, and finally, on August 10, a group of five (including Mohan himself and Sheikh Mehtab) set off for Bombay. He said good-bye to his mother and wife and baby son in Porbandar.

He had intended to sail on August 21, but he encountered more opposition from his caste in Bombay. "My caste fellows tried their best to prevent me from proceeding further" (1:11). They objected both to his crossing the ocean and to his eating in the company of Englishmen, a kind of pollution. The boy—so slight and nervous—was pointed at and hooted in the streets, and a caste meeting was held, near the Bombay Town Hall, at which he was interrogated and reproached. This was a compulsory meeting, of all the Modh Banias, and those who did not attend had to pay a five-anna fine. Mohandas replied to his accusers that they were "as elders" to him, and deserved his obedience, but his mind was made up, and he was helpless to alter it. (This negative determination was very characteristic of him—his mind had been made up for him, and he *could not* change it.) In his diary he says he found the courage to tell them that malice was at the root of all their objections (1:60).

Though deeply distressed, his will was not shaken. But his brother returned to Porbandar, leaving the money in Kasturba's brother's keeping, and the ship sailed without Mohandas. Finally, he got a place on another ship, sailing in early September. Then the keeper of his money would not release it, fearing the caste's retribution, and perhaps Lakshmidas's displeasure. Mohandas found another friend of the family who advanced some money, counting on getting it back from Lakshmidas finally. (In effect, Mohandas forced his brother's hand.)

Mehtab then took letters from Gandhi back to the family; which sounds as though Mehtab had stayed on in Bombay after his friend's brothers left. "Before finishing this," the diary says, "I must write that had it been some other man in the same position which I was in, I dare say he would not have been able to see England" (1:12–13). It was indeed a triumph of determination, and we see that the young Gandhi was aware of and proud of this trait.

THREE

METROPOLIS

· 1888–1893 ·

Eighteen eighty-eight to eighteen-ninety-one were Gandhi's three years as a student in England, which were followed by a frustrating interlude in Rajkot again and Bombay, before he went to South Africa. Out of his multitudinous impressions in London, he picked up a number of ideas that formed a pattern for him, and a filter for later experience. He even began to act on those ideas, writing, speaking, organizing, on a small scale. But in 1893 he was still a timid and largely silent young man.

From Bombay to London

Mohandas sailed away from Bombay on September 4, on the SS *Clyde,* across the Arabian Sea, the Red Sea, the Suez Canal, the Mediterranean, and toward Malta and Italy, Gibraltar and Spain, and then into the cold Atlantic, and London.

He enjoyed the voyage, not suffering from seasickness at all, and striking up an immediate friendship with his cabin mate, Tryambakrai Mazmudar. On the first day this man talked to Gandhi "as if they were old friends," and borrowed his black coat to go to dinner. Gandhi himself stayed in his cabin, too shy to eat in public. He was surprised, but pleased, at the liberties Mazmudar took, and from that night on, "looked upon him as an elder brother" (1:12). Gandhi for some days did not speak a word to anyone but Mazmudar.

In London, later, he wrote that on the decks of such a ship, "You can mix with and talk with the fellow passengers, "if you are bold and have got that stuff" (1:13). Mazmudar, we can take it, had. He was, Gandhi tells us, "a very bold man" (1:19). Their relationship—not a significant one, for Gandhi was soon disillusioned about the other man—lasted only a few years. But the encounter illustrates the pattern of his early friendships—timidity attracted to boldness.

The journey took 3½ weeks. In the diary of these days which Gandhi wrote up in London, he described the ship, the sailors, the games on board (chess, cards, draughts) and the piano—on which Gandhi now and then played (1:12). He described admiring and envying the Arab boys at Aden, who dived for coins thrown by the passengers. (1:14). He was even more impressed by the canal. "The construction of the Suez Canal I am not able to understand. It is indeed marvellous. I cannot think of the genius of a man who invented it. I don't know how he would have done it" (1:15). Port Said showed him the sleazy side of empire (1:16). But he described the sights he saw in Malta and Gibraltar enthusiastically, particularly praising the engineering of the latter. He was appreciative of everything, and ready to be amazed by London.

But before we try to imagine the spectacle that the imperial capital offered to young Asians like Gandhi, we should place him among his rivals and allies to be. He was joining a sequence of young Indians, training in the imperial capital for the professions but also for nation building, which meant, as we know, introducing "reforms."

There were two hundred "Indian gentlemen" in London in 1890.[1] Immediately before Gandhi had come two Kathiawaris, Dalpatram Shukla and Pranjivan Mehta, whom he was to meet as soon as he got there; a few years after him came Mohammad Ali Jinah; and after *him,* Vinayak Rao Savarkar—two of Gandhi's inveterate enemies; and then his lieutenants, Jawarhalal Nehru, and Vallabbhai Patel; and others.

Moreover, we can fill out our sense of what he was leaving behind; by making acquaintance with two other gifted Gujaratis, of roughly the same age, on whom Gandhi was to lean, one making a career in politics, the other in religion, and whose life stories form complementary contrasts with his. These two represent each a different side of the manifold backdrop against which we must see Gandhi. In religion, for instance, we do not find the sequence of young men going to the West to be trained that we find in politics. Men like Ramana Maharishi and the Sage of Kanci—important in India's reigious life in Gandhi's time—remained rooted in Indian tradition. But Gandhi needs to be seen against that background too.

Raychandbhai

The first of the two contrasts was a man almost exactly the same age as Gandhi, called Raychandbhai. He and Ghandi were already following rather opposite-tending courses in 1888. Raychandbhai stayed at home in Kathiawar, did not learn English, devoted himself to his ancestral religion, and so on. But Gandhi sat at his feet when he returned to India, and came to rank the other man on a level with Tolstoy and Ruskin among his teachers, in fact promoting Raychandbhai above the other two in matters of religion. It will therefore be useful to follow the part of Raychandbhai's life story that ran parallel with Gandhi's. He and Gandhi were, for instance, both middle-school pupils in Rajkot at about the same time, though they first met and talked in 1891.

Raychandbhai or Shrimad Rajachandra (his family name, Mehta, is never used) was born in 1867, and his father was a Vaishnavite and his mother a Jain. The two religions intermingled in Gujarat, and such cross-faith marriages were not exceptional; many people with the name of Gandhi, for instance, were Jains. But Raychandbhai felt he had to choose between the two faiths.

His paternal grandfather, who came to live in the Kathiawar port of Vavania in the 1830s, was full of Vaishnavite enthusiasm, loving the songs about Krishna and his avatars, wearing a *kanthi,* a necklace of *tulsi* beads, and cherishing the many associated symbols. This picturesqueness attracted Raychandbhai in his childhood, but he eventually turned to the austerer Jainism.

He was allegedly a much more gifted child than Gandhi, and completed a seven-year school course in two years: at eight, composed five thousand lines of verse; and so on. (We should note that our sources about Raychandbhai are hagiographical, because he was early revered by a religious sect, and thus many of the "facts" about him are legendary.) However, although he began to learn English at the age of thirteen, he evidently did not persist. At twenty-two he said he didn't regret not knowing it, as it would have added to his doubts and perplexities. We see in his piety a more simply conservative or anti-Western drive than in Gandhi's. But for both, religion meant moral enthusiasm, and reform from within.

In those days the Jains were generally thought of as a rich sect in decay.[2] Their numbers were dwindling, they were self-divided, and their truths were crusted over with superstitions and vested interests. The one leader worthy of mention, according to Farquhar, was Raychandbhai (327–28).

The moral character of Jainism, in its pure form, was very attractive to Gandhi, and his own teaching was often said to be based on it. In 1901 Annie Besant, in her little book called *Jainism,* introduced the religion by saying how different it was from Islam and Sikhism. "We shall not now have round us the atmosphere of romance, of chivalry"; but instead a calm, philosophic, quiet atmosphere.[3] The Jain is taught to try to reach Nirvana (peace) by injuring no living creature; and "questions of conduct" must take up most of his energy. Fasting is frequent, and solemn vows are taken, on even trivial matters, to keep man morally self-aware.

Ideally, the Jain monk lived by begging, and died by starving, voluntarily. In practice, the discipline was much softened and accommodated to worldly considerations: according to Gandhi, Raychandbhai said that Jains were all banias at heart, and so had neither the courage of Kshatriyas nor the wisdom of brahmins.

Vavania is situated on the same ocean shore as Porbandar, and the two boys' backgrounds, as they grew up, were very similar. Like Karamchand Gandhi, Raychandbhai's father liked to sit with friends at leisure and hear wandering sadhus or fakirs, who sang devotional songs on a one-stringed *tanpura,* or recitations of folk-poems, about wars and warriors. The two boys both heard such songs and stories as part of their home life.

Vavania, in the little state of Morvi, practiced ship-building and trade, while Porbandar was mainly a fishing port. Before the days of steam, says Digish

Mehta, Raychandbhai's biographer, Vavania was very prosperous, but with few connections to the big events of "history." When wars occurred between kings, they did not much affect the rest of the population. (Gandhi thought this was always true in history.) The rulers brought in mercenaries to fight other mercenaries; and the stouter build and bonier features of those soldiers' descendants were still recognizable in the area, long after.

The atmosphere of Vavania is still sleepy, Digish Mehta tells us, the soil dark and gritty, with low shrubs and a few yellow cotton flowers, and the white of salt outcroppings.[4] A Jain monastery, an *upashraya,* stood almost next door to Raychandbhai's home. But nearby, among some *neem* trees, also stood the Hindu shrine of Rambai Ma, a female Vaishnavite saint. When Raychandbhai's mother was pregnant with him, hoping for a male child, she consulted Rambai Ma, who gave her visions of his future life. Mehta tells us that sacred cows still rest in the shade near the shrine, twirling their tails against flies, and sounding the bells on girdles round their necks. This is the richly sensual, heavily scented world of the Vaishnavites, Mehta tells us, and one-half of Raychandbhai's heritage. Jainism is the other half.

According to Annie Besant, there were less than two million of that faith in India, and most of them were to be found in Gujarat and especially in Kathiawar. They were important, despite being few, because of their commercial wealth. The key Jain virtues, very like those Gandhi prescribed, are *brahmacharya* (purity), *ahimsa* (nonviolence), *asteya* (no stealing), *aparigraha* (no possessions). A picturesque symbol of their ahimsa was the little mask, the *muhapatti,* which pious Jains should wear over their mouths, to prevent them from breathing in, and so killing, insects. They should also brush away insects from the path before them, with a feather broom, as they walk.

Much of this was reflected in Gandhism, in less purely picturesque fashion. So was the Jain prohibition on drink and drugs, and the practice of fasting. But the most striking case of congeniality is the Jain stress on taking vows—something that most of Gandhi's Eastern and Western friends could not understand in him, but to which he remained faithful to the end.

One or two anecdotes will give us the flavor of Raychandbhai's piety, which is much more traditional than Gandhi's. At the age of seven, he first encountered death, when a friend died from a snakebite. He was told that his friend's body would be burned, and climbed a tree to spy on the ceremony. He was then granted a vision of his own former births—a remembering of those earlier lives that most people forget. A surpassing peace descended upon him. He had other such visions, in which he saw his earlier selves involved in the vortex of relationships, now as a son, now as a wife, now as an insect. He allegedly claimed to know of nine hundred such births. Like other Jains (and Hindus) he saw it as his religious calling so to live as to end that sequence and cycle for himself; each good life is rewarded with reincarnation into a higher life-form, until finally the soul merges with Brahma.

When he left Vavania it was first for Morvi, where he made friends who were taking part in the late nineteenth-century cultural renaissance. The leading journal in Gujarat, *Buddhiprakash,* gave news of many new groups and new ideas. Some of Raychandbhai's poems were published there as early as 1885; which was three years before Gandhi left India. He was also already famous for his mental powers.

In 1881 Raychandbhai saw some exponents of what was called *shatavadana,* the art of attending to a number of things simultaneously. He first saw a performance by Shastri Shankarlal, who demonstrating the art of attending to eight such *kriyas,* or activities. But Raychandbhai showed almost immediately that he could do the same for twelve, then sixteen kriyas; and his displays began to be reported in the newspapers. He would turn from cards to chess, to multiplications, linguistic quizzes, poetical exercises, estimating the number of beads in a bag or of bells chiming together, distinguishing tastes and flavors, and so on, before an admiring audience. Finally, in Bombay, he mastered fifty-two and then a hundred kriyas, in 1886. The *Times of India* reported one such occasion on January 24, 1887. (Such feats of memory and awareness, very Indian in character, are briefly represented in *Kim*—at the jeweler's shop in Simla—as being an opposite to Western forms of intelligence and mastery.) It is said that Raychandbhai was invited to tour Europe giving displays as a Memory Man.[5]

Gandhi was not a *shatadavani,* in the literal sense. He was thoroughly Western in such matters. But he could be called a striking example of "Western shatadavana"; since he sometimes wrote fifty or more letters in a day, and dealt with a stream of seekers for spiritual counsel, and curiosity visitors; while also being consulted by local and national politicians, nature cure doctors, educationists, and so on.

Raychandbhai soon felt the moral vanity and the mechanicalness of shatavadana, and gave it up. (This too was a traditional turn in a career like his.) He had established his reputation for intellect—he was given honorary titles to that effect—but cared much more for spiritual things. He sought to escape from all attachment to this world. In a piece of autobiography he declared that he had been "exposed to the teeming variety of nature, to the waves of the world, to that which is the very root of endless suffering. . . . As a child he had had strange imaginings he did not understand. [Raychandbhai sometimes wrote about himself in the third person].[6] . . . I was one to place an immense deal of trust in others. I was deeply attached to the nature of the created world . . . [and felt]—sympathy for all in a spirit of deep humility" (30).

He makes no mention there of nonviolence, and his understanding of religion is more traditional and unpolitical than Gandhi's. Nevertheless they shared much in the way of ascetic moral teaching. In 1888 (the year Gandhi went to England) Raychandbhai wrote an essay on women that is full of the same ascetic distrust of sex as Gandhi shows. The defect does not lie with women in themselves (the essay is of course written from the masculine point of view) but the physical site of sex is "a place which is not fit even for vomiting on. Whatever things are revolting in their nature, why, these are all present in her." You should treat all women as your sister, and so exempt from your desires.

"Having come from that prison of infinite darkness, [the womanly body] weary of it, what prompts you to make friends with it yet again?" (38–39). The general law is to wean yourself of all attachment, even to your children.

Both Raychandbhai and Gandhi wanted to disentangle the soul from the body, in order to hold it steady. The steady state of the soul is *samadhi,* and unsteadiness is evil (this is a very Gandhian emphasis). "The means of deliverance is conscious thought. Deliverance lies in the knowledge of the soul." We must unlearn the habits of association "by which the soul believes that things are as they appear to be." And "Resignation alone is the true sister of all felicity, and it is also the mother of all true spirituality" (62).

Despite Gandhi's activism, such ideas often emerge in his writings, where at least the sexual attitudes often seem, to Western readers, to be personal eccentricities or flaws of temperament, that need to be explained by early misadventures. (We find this attitude for instance in Erikson's book, insightful as that is.) When we read Raychandbhai, we realize that Gandhi was following religious tradition in making those declarations.

Patel

The other young Gujarati whose mind-set compares interestingly with Gandhi's was called Vallabhbhai Patel, and was six years younger, being born in 1875. He was later to be one of Gandhi's two chief political lieutenants. He belonged to the Patidar caste, who constituted only a quarter of the population of their area, which lay between Ahmedabad and Baroda, but who employed other castes, like the more numerous Baraiyas and Patanvadiyas, to work for them.[7]

David Hardiman says the Patidars are characterized by "bluntness of speech, an unconcern about dress and appearance, a sense of equality within the fold that turned the village into 'a collectivity of Patidar brothers,' and a sense of superiority towards non-Patidars, a self-image of tough independent men . . . naturally given to ruling over others."[8]

It is worth noting here the flexibility or looseness of the Indian system of cultural geography. The Patidars of Gujarat have just been defined in terms very different from those in which the Gujaratis were presented before. The two sets of terms are equally traditional, and both are often employed by the same people, with no sense of self-contradiction. Since Gandhi, and his friends, used these terms, it is easiest for us to follow their example.

While Vallabhbhai was a child, his father joined the Swaminarayan sect, and became a religious recluse; and this choice could be seen as a spiritual intensification of the Patidar temperament. The Swaminarayans deserve a word to themselves, as an important presence on the religious scene in Gujarat at the time of Gandhi's childhood. Gandhi wrote in 1933 that the Gandhi family had had very close relations with Swaminarayans for many years.

They were a nineteenth-century reformist and puritanical foundation, which originated in Gujarat and was strong there. The movement's original enemy—the object of its reforms—was a tantric Shakti cult, associated with goddess-worship, and seen as a corruption of true Hinduism; one of those religious phenomena that everywhere oppose the ascetic tradition (which is sometimes called the Great Tradition, or the Sanskrit or Brahmin tradition within Hinduism). Founded after a time of famine and social chaos, the Swaminarayans offered a return to order by means of a rather severe discipline and sacrifice. Though they believed it wrong to take life, their leaders had an armed bodyguard.

The founder, Sahajanand Swami, who died in 1830, required five vows from his followers, renouncing meat and liquor, theft and adultery, and the taking of food from a lower-caste person. They were organized for social welfare, including relief and manual work. In a number of ways, therefore, they had something in common with what became Gandhism. This puritanism, then, was to be found in Vallabhbhai Patel's background along with the Patidar heritage.

Vallabhbhai followed his older brother Vithalbhai by becoming a lawyer—going to London, just like Gandhi—and the story of just how both brothers got themselves there illustrates the sternly fraternal/paternal discipline in Patidar families. Vallabhbhai first secretly conceived such a project; and when he had saved up enough money, and had bought the ticket, his brother found out by accident, and persuaded or ordered him to hand over both. Vithalbhai then sailed, without telling his wife and children; who came to live with Vallabhbhai. The latter moreover regularly sent money to England to sustain his brother there. Since the two wives did not get on together, Vallabhbhai sent his own wife back to her mother. Only after his brother returned did Vallabhbhai himself set off for London—this too, secretly. By this time his wife had died, but he lodged his two very young children with an English schoolteacher in Bombay.

As a lawyer, Vallabhbhai was stern and reserved with his clients and aggressive with his judges. Socially, he took up certain British habits, such as smoking and playing bridge, and speaking English, but he resented Britain's cultural dominance. (He seems to have shown no interest in English high culture, even in London.) Presumably he saw no chance of a successful revolt against the British, and resented those politically exciting figures who promised to lead one; until he met Gandhi, with his paradoxical and yet prosaic combination of the meek and the bold.

Patel was always a figure of power and contest. An observer described him thus in 1928: "a slight redness in the eye, a little hardness in the mustache and the face as a whole, an impatience that would not be encountered on a search in ten villages, a natural consciousness of power."[9] He told Mahadev Desai, "I know how to fight. . . . But I don't enjoy discussions about awards. At times they suffocate me" (125).

The viceroy, Lord Wavell, spoke of Patel's "Roman face, powerful, clever, uncompromising," and the English generally admired him, including those who scorned Gandhi. Patel's biographer sums it up thus, "Indians elegant in mind and manners were not hard for the Raj to lure, but of their backbone the empire-builders could seldom be certain, whereas with Vallabhbhai it was always his masculinity that struck the Raj's custodians. . . . The Raj would have given much for a Sir Vallabhbhai" (36). But as we shall see, Patel instead became one of the most devoted enemies of the Raj, and the most self-sacrificing of Gandhi's followers. It is one of the most brilliant paradoxes of Gandhi's career that he—so shy and vulnerable—should command this figure of power.

Patel and Raychandbhai belonged in the same cultural landscape, and features of the two personalities that puzzle or distress Westerners they could at least take for granted in each other. But they were almost totally exclusive of each other, and it is one way to describe Gandhi, to say that he reached out on the one hand to the former and on the other to the latter. He had something in common with each; they had nothing in common with each other, except a drive to reform and reanimate the world they were born into.

If we add these two men to Gandhi himself, we have a sampling of the culture he was leaving behind as he sailed from Bombay to London in 1888. Digish Mehta describes Raychandbhai leaving home at just the same moment (for Bombay): leaving Kathiawar, "with its slow pace of life, quaint and leisurely speech, and the irony and cynicism bred by a long history of feudal rule."[10] Raychandbhai and Vallabhbhai Patel and Mohandas Gandhi represent different modes of dealing with the wounds and the weaknesses of Gujarat (and all India) under the heel of empire at the end of the nineteenth century.

London

Gandhi arrived in London in September, 1888, having demonstrated on the journey—much to his own satisfaction and against the predictions of fellow passengers—that he could survive without meat and alcohol even aboard ship, and even in Europe in autumn. It was a part of modern European legend that a cold northern climate challenged man's physiology as much as free enterprise and parliamentary politics challenged his moral energy; so that a northerner needed more to support life, just as, of course, he made more of life. Gandhi himself said, in his "Guide to London," written in India in 1893: "In England, it does not do to be idle. You like to work for the sake of it. You cannot help working" (Revised 1:71, rev. ed.).

He arrived at Tilbury, about twenty miles from the center of London, on September 29, and went to the luxurious Victoria Hotel on Northumberland Street, near to Trafalgar Square. The floors were of marble, and the servants wore livery and the waiters frock coats. In his "Guide to London," we read: "When I first saw my room in the Victoria Hotel, I thought I could pass a lifetime in that room" (1:83, rev. ed.).

Gandhi was particularly impressed by the rows of electric lights and the elevator, which he at first thought was another room. About all these marvels of modern engineering, as about the engineering of the Suez Canal, the layout of Gibraltar, and so on, Gandhi was enthusiastic. He said to his secretary, in 1918, that he might have become an engineer, because of his interest in how things work and how they are built. "Whatever object I chance to look at, my eye immediately perceives it inside out, and I can detect the flaws and merits of the mechanism." People often remarked on his fondness for and ingenuity with gadgets.[12]

In this way, too, he was at that time a Westerner. George Orwell says that Westerners are so constituted that they cannot perform any job of work without their minds being haunted by visions of the machines or tools that would do the job for them—visions that derive not from physical laziness but from mental energy.

By a natural extension, Gandhi had appreciated the social organization of the ship, the efficiency with which passengers were served, and the profusion of comforts. On a later voyage, he commented on the falling off in standards when they were transferred to the *Assam,* at Aden, and the English crew were replaced by Portuguese. In these ways one might say he was a Northerner.

But Gandhi's time in England was to promote the growth in him of opposite feelings. He heard many voices criticizing England, and he listened eagerly to them, though it seems likely that at that time he could rebel only on nonpolitical issues. For instance, he arrived in England "a convinced meat-eater," abstaining from meat in fact, but only because of his vow to his mother. But the arguments of English vegetarian pamphlets (principally those written by Henry Salt) gradually gave his abstention moral and ideological substance. England also forced on him other changes of practice, which he then adopted as matters of principle. In diet, for instance, he could not get the Indian sweets and condiments, chutneys and chilis and pickles, which he was used to. Having stopped taking them, he felt himself the better for it. He had been in the habit of indulging himself: good food, he said, had been his main interest in life: "I was a good eater and had a capacious stomach" (A:46).

Being a vegetarian and an abstainer from drink gradually became a large part of Gandhi's identity. It set him apart from most of the Indians he met in England, who followed Western ways even if that meant breaking vows like those Gandhi had taken. It also gave him a moral role he enjoyed. He showed himself, while apparently meeker and less rebellious than they, to be really stronger and more defiant.

He went to live first in the suburb of Richmond, to be near Dalpatram Shukla, but after a month moved to an Anglo-Indian family at 20 Baron's Court Road, where he paid thirty shillings a week for room and board, but suffered from the meals. The household did not understand vegetarian cooking. He moved from there to a suite of rooms, and then to a single room on Tavistock Street, where he cooked for himself, and his expenses were only fourteen shillings a week. For his last months in London, when he was much taken up with vegetarian-society work, he lived with Josiah Oldfield in St. Stephen's Gardens in Bayswater.

According to Gandhi in 1928, he regularly wrote home letters to his elders (his mother and Lakshmidas) which gave a detailed description of everything he did and read (35:217). These were twenty to twenty-five pages long, according to another reference (50:404). He did not, it seems, write to Kasturba; perhaps because she was not literate enough. She heard a reading aloud of his letters to his elders, and other letters, written to Sheikh Mehtab and meant for her. Though extraordinary to our eyes, this secondhand character of the letters she received would not seem exceptional to a family in the Gandhis' situation.

Dr. P. J. Mehta, who knew of the family, and Dalpatram Shukla, a lawyer, came that first evening to Mohandas's hotel to meet him. (These were also

Kathiawaris, in fact from Morvi, like Raychandbhai.) Mehta, who was to be a lifelong friend, was square-faced, heavy-browed, and authoritative. Shukla was younger and looked rather like Mohandas, Payne tells us.[13] They tried to take charge of him. "What is the value," Shukla asked Gandhi, "of a vow made before an illiterate mother, and in ignorance of conditions here? It is no vow at all. You admit to having eaten and relished meat. You took it where it was absolutely unnecessary, and will not take it where it is quite essential.' . . . But I was adamant" (A:46).

Shukla, or one of the others, also brought more bookish philosophic arguments to bear, but Gandhi found their language too difficult to understand. "I said: 'Pray excuse me. These abstruse things are beyond me. I admit it is necessary to eat meat. But I cannot break my vow.' . . . The friend looked at me in surprise. He closed the book and said: 'All right. I will not argue any more'" (A:46–47).

But Shukla went on worrying; fearing that Gandhi would develop a weak constitution, and that "I should remain a duffer, because I should never feel at home in English society." (This question of Englishness was part of what was at issue; Gandhi was holding on to his Indian identity.) So he invited Gandhi to the Holborn restaurant (quite a luxurious place) and ordered a dinner. Gandhi asked the waiter—not daring to ask his friend—whether the soup on the menu was made from meat. Gandhi reports his friend's reaction: "'You are too clumsy for decent society,' he passionately exclaimed. 'If you cannot behave yourself, you had better go. Feed in some other restaurant, and await me outside'" (A:49). Gandhi, though he did not find any other restaurant, was glad to stand outside the Holborn, and then they went on to the theater together.

We should notice not only Gandhi's general meekness, but the negative character of his faith. He did not try to persuade others to renounce meat; he did not even argue that he was right to do so; he simply said no. "I had an eternal negative to face him with." This involuntary decisiveness was an important trait; we saw him tell his caste-elders that he *could not* change his mind about going to England.

More generally, negation is something we must take for granted among New Agers, especially those of the ascetic variety. Despite their naiveté of mind, and the bright-faced openness that often accompanies it, they are saying no to the world around them. That is a far-reaching action, and we must pay attention to their act of will—which, in Gandhi, was so deeply felt that it was experienced as beyond his control—as well as to their reasons.

But Gandhi was certainly not conscious of saying no to the whole modern world then. Up to this point, he had of course known only life in a small town in a small Indian state, and he was deeply impressed by what he saw of official imperial England. He had very little sense of India as an ancient imperial civilization, much less as a political entity that could rival the West. Morally, as became obvious, he could be stern, and would say no forever to what offended him, but imaginatively he was labile, ready to believe, and believe in, most of official England's tales of her material and moral greatness. He was, after all, there to learn English law, in one of the great English institutions, the Inns of

Court, which seemed to have endured forever. Medieval in origin, the Hall of the Inner Temple, to which he belonged, had been rebuilt in 1870. (His friends Mehta and Shukla belonged to the slightly less expensive Middle Temple.)

He first saw London as a city grouped around the Inns of Court, Buckingham Palace, the Tower of London, the Houses of Parliament, and Whitehall. India House must have been of special interest to him. It had been designed by George Gilbert Scott, who also designed the Foreign, the Home, and the Colonial Offices, all in a cinquecento style—polished granite columns and majolica friezes—a style that had replaced the Gothic, for imperial buildings.

We should not underestimate the power of England to strike the imagination of Indian students. In some articles in the September, January, and March issues of the *Indian Magazine and Review* in London, 1889 and 1890, Ram Gopal wrote of the immense stimulus of the spectacle of London. "Busy pedestrians walk fast, as if racing with time itself. Time is very valuable here," and "The amount of work these people do is wonderful."[14] (Ram Gopal was a law student, who later became chief justice of Hyderabad.) The same things impressed Gandhi: hard work, punctuality, the scrupulous use of time and hygiene, were virtues he always said he had learned in England.

It was no doubt the liberal reformers he learned most from, amongst the official heroes. From Gladstone, for instance, still then a famous name, Gandhi seems to have picked up a distinction he often employed in later life, between sinners and their sins—one should hate the sin but not the sinner (20:134). Gladstone's attempt to give home rule to Ireland was still a current political topic, and especially so with Indian nationalists. Gandhi read the *Pall Mall Gazette,* edited between 1883 and 1890 by W. T. Stead, a reforming journalist, and before that edited by John Morley, Gladstone's biographer, and later secretary of state for India.

Gandhi had absorbed at school, as we saw, the official version of English history, as a series of rebellions by which "the people" had, step-by-step, taken power away from their rulers. "English history teems with instances of bloody revolts whose praises Englishmen have sung unstintingly and taught us to do likewise" (44:82). It was a natural consequence of this idea that Indians should do the same: they must *take* their liberty in order to show that they deserved it. They must make the English their enemies in order to make them their friends.

On the other side, it could have seemed that Englishmen in England were spontaneously overcoming their racial prejudice. In the last mentioned *Indian Magazine* a Madras student wrote that the more different he was seen to be in England, the more he was respected. "Hence I wished my color turned from brown to black." (This was in April 1888, a little before Gandhi's arrival.) From 1877 on, Queen Victoria had two Indian servants, one of whom became her confidential secretary in 1889. It was known that she had studied Hindi, and Gandhi certainly thought of her for a time as a phenomenon of benevolent power. She had her Proclamation after the Mutiny redrafted, he tells us, to bring out the fact that she was a female sovereign, addressing her people after a tragedy (3:359).

Official England was then impressive in many ways. But the further we move away from the establishment and toward New Age radicalism, the more of English culture we shall find that Gandhi absorbed and used himself. This was the time of the Nonconformist Conscience. That phrase—a reproach, turned into a boast—became popular in 1890, at the time of Charles Stewart Parnell's disgrace. (This leader of Irish nationalism was ruined politically by being named in a divorce case.) The three features of "conscientious" politics, according to David W. Bebbington, were: the intervention of the state, on the side of morality; the stress on social purity, as in the Parnell case; and the elimination of boundaries separating religion from politics.[15]

Silvester Horne was a nonconformist minister and member of parliament who said he would henceforth follow Christ into society (i.e., into political action) not John the Baptist into the wilderness. The abolition of the slave trade and of slavery was the great historical cause these people looked back to. The politicians they worked with were liberal or radical, not conservative. At the Congregationalist Union, Joseph Parker, whom Gandhi went to hear preach, declared, "Toryism is wickedness," in 1886 (8). And the three features came together powerfully after 1890.

In 1902 the Baptist minister John Clifford (another social activist Gandhi admired) became president of the Liberal Society, with David Lloyd George as vice president. The latter was first elected to parliament in 1890, and seemed to promise to introduce the nonconformist conscience into national politics. (Gandhi later used that phrase to reproach him with falling away.) Another Free Church leader, Hugh Price Hughes, was called "the Day of Judgment in breeches" (37).

"Back to the Land" was one of the slogans of the radical branch of the Free Churches. A little book with that title was published in 1893 by J. B. Paton, of the Congregationalist Training Institute. When W. T. Stead helped General Booth of the Salvation Army write *In Darkest England—and the Way Out* (1890), he incorporated Paton's ideas about agricultural colonies and farms. As mentioned before, the garden city was another, more genteel idea generated in the same nonconformist circles, and subsidized by nonconformist business firms like Cadbury and Lever. In 1892 Ebenezer Howard brought out *Tomorrow,* the blueprint for the city of Letchworth, which opened in 1903.

The purity campaign of that period—which included crusades against prostitution, horseracing, drink, and so on—was a model Gandhi acknowledged for his own campaigns in India (20:46). In the national flag he designed for India, the white stripe stood for purity. He studied the campaign at the time, well enough to remember it long after. In 1931, arguing with his friend Andrews about quite a different matter, he recalled the controversy he had followed in the newspapers in 1889–90, between temperance reformers and total prohibitionists. He could cite Sir Wilfred Lawson, who led the latter group.

Speaking on prohibition in 1925, Gandhi recalled how he used to stand in front of "those great palaces called public houses in London, where people went in sober and came out . . . dead drunk" (26:389). In South Africa, later, he had known sea captains who sailed when they were drunk, and had had friends who struggled in vain against that temptation.

More radical in some ways (more evangelical, more alien to high culture) was the Salvation Army, which aroused suspicion in both the Socialists and the cultured classes; and was admired by right-wingers like Kipling and Haggard as well as New Agers. To judge by later references, Gandhi's mind was struck by the idea of the army's "Lassies" entering fearlessly "the dens of thieves and drunkards and murderers," to fall on their necks or at their feet (35:289). He must have liked the army's strategy of arriving at slum dwellings with soap, buckets, and scrubbing brushes. He also remembered the army going into public houses, to sing hymns and exhort the drinkers to repent; and like the army he used a reborn-military imagery in his own campaigns.

New Age intellectuals like George Bernard Shaw took a keen interest in the army. (Shaw discussed its music, for instance.) And the attention of Indians in particular was attracted by the fact that the army had branches in India, where its soldiers took Indian names and wore Indian costume. Gandhi remarked how the army won over other races by adopting their dress, their customs, and so on (8:155).

Political radicalism, of the Marxist kind, does not seem to have engaged him. We should, however, take note of a London event a few months before Gandhi arrived, "Bloody Sunday," a defiance of that official England, which brought together a number of the people to whom he would finally be closer in sympathy. "Bloody Sunday" took place on November 13, 1887, and was a clash between protesters and the authorities, of a kind we are familiar with in our own times. The former wanted to hold a rally in Trafalgar Square, but the latter had forbidden it, and fifteen hundred police and two hundred mounted Life Guards were called out to prevent it.

The protesters assembled at various points around the city. William Morris, George Bernard Shaw, and Annie Besant made speeches at Clerkenwell Green, before their section began its march. Shaw and Besant marched together. Edward Carpenter and Henry Salt were also among the protesters. Heroes of the day were the labor leader John Burns and the author Cunninghame Graham, who chained themselves to the railings outside a hotel. They and the Marxist, Maurice Hyndman, were sent to jail for their actions. Some of these were amongst the English people Gandhi came to admire most.

Gandhi's Life in London

Slender, broad-cheeked, glowing-eyed, Gandhi was full of maladroit enthusiasm and naive curiosity. He was nervous about the handling of a knife and fork. He had arrived in London dressed in white flannels, in late September, having been misdirected as to English dress codes, and then was mortified to be unable to change to something less conspicuous because his luggage was delayed. When Dr. Mehta came to his hotel to meet him, Gandhi played with this new friend's headgear, the symbolic top hat. "I casually picked up his top-hat, and trying to see how smooth it was, passed my hand over it the wrong way and disturbed the fur" (A:44). Dr. Mehta looked angrily at what Gandhi was doing and stopped him. He was lectured on being overfamiliar.

A recent book about Gandhi remarks on his tactile sensibility, even at the end of his life, when his habit of touching women gave rise to sexual scandal. "Like most Indians he was a highly tactile person and found physical touch irresistible. It is hard to find an informal photograph of him in which his hand does not rest on someone's shoulder or he is not patting someone on the back."[16] Smoothing that top hat, Gandhi was, I think we can guess, absorbing the magic of Victorian London from that strange black cylinder, through his fingertips; but he obediently put the hat down, and absorbed his friend's advice instead.

This confiding naiveté, both toward his friend and toward England, was situational in part; most young Indian students arriving in London must have displayed something like it; but in part it was Gandhi's special way of believing in himself (and so in other people) and was to remain a valuable tool or weapon of his to the end. He believed all they said, and expected to see their promises kept. Other students in much the same position, like his rival-to-be, Mohammed Ali Jinnah, mastered the forms of English life, and were mastered by them, much more brilliantly.

Gandhi, however, at first took lessons in Western dancing and violin playing and elocution. (He paid three guineas for dance lessons.) At some point in these years he learned to play bridge. He went to the theater every month, and remembered in 1931 that he had adored the incomparable Ellen Terry—"I worshipped her" (48:2) He sent home for a double gold chain for his watch. He formed the habit of combing his hair, and shining his shoes, and read his three papers a day. He followed the cross-examination in the Parnell divorce case, and the investigation of the Maybrick poison case. He even read that harbinger of modern cheap journalism, Alfred Harmsworth's *Answers to Correspondents,* which was, as Gandhi said, smutty but witty and very readable. He spent ten minutes before the mirror every morning, parting and brushing his hair. (At home in Rajkot, he saw a mirror only when the barber shaved him.) He was ready, out of a kind of love, to make himself into an Englishman of the official kind. His enormous change in this regard—to quite an opposite readiness—was halting and gradual.

For a time Gandhi wore elegant English clothes, including a top hat, patent-leather boots and spats, leather gloves, and a silver-mounted cane. He cultivated certain elegances of literary style. His London diary began, "The scene opens in April." His later "Guide to London" began: "Who should go to London? . . . all who can afford it should go to England. . . . The movements alike of students and laymen in London are shrouded in mystery. . . . The writer of the following pages proposes to uncover the mystery." Describing the situation of an Indian student there, he wrote: "While he is in England, he is alone, no wife to tease and flatter him, no parents to indulge, no children to look after, no company to disturb. He is the master of his time" (1:71). (There was in fact a growing audience for such a book; the total of 207 Indian gentlemen in London in 1890 was 47 more than there had been in 1887.)[17]

But Gandhi did not persist long in these attempts at elegance. He soon discontinued his private lessons in elocution, dancing, and playing the violin. About dancing he tells us, "I could not follow the piano [or] achieve anything like rhythmic motion" (A:51). We have already seen that he was clumsy in handling a knife and fork. This bodily clumsiness testifies to the shamefacedness we have noted before, which the elegances could not remedy.

What was to cure him was something almost opposite—his religious asceticism. He put himself on guard against his appetites, physical and social, he aimed at diminishing rather than expanding his size, and his bodily consciousness became as closed, contained, and undevouring as he could contrive. As far as social style went, he renounced those powers—of authority and anger, of infectious gaiety, voice and personality—which men associate with the body. More exactly, he employed them only in the service of duty.

His "Guide to London" employs its literary graces to recommend self-help and the simple life. "Cooking, as perhaps would be feared, is not at all a difficult or troublesome process. No smoke, no wood, no cowdung cakes and no blowing or fanning are associated with the idea of cooking as here advocated. A portable oil stove serves the purpose of the Indian *chulas*. On that stove one may cook almost anything that may be cooked on the Indian *chulas* for five or six persons" (1:20).

However much of a simple lifer he became, Gandhi remained sensually, intellectually, and socially very alert. *Refined* is one of the adjectives most often used about him. Had he persisted in the pursuit of dandyism, he could have made himself a good arbiter elegantiarum. He did not because he was more committed to the opposite.

He attended Christian church services, though mostly in nonconformist chapels; one of the famous preachers of the day he heard was Dr. Spurgeon, in the Tabernacle; another was Joseph Parker, at the City Temple Congregationalist Church, on Holborn Viaduct. Parker's Thursday-noon services brought merchant and clerk alike trooping in, we are told—the clerks took turns and drew lots to see who should be given the time off, to go. He was famous for his "appeal to the thoughts of young men," especially men of business. According to Joseph Doke, Parker converted Gandhi to theism.

It was still possible then in England to link Protestant piety and business efficiency, in the way that Defoe had linked them, as twin tendencies. And the idea would not be strange to Gandhi, because in India there were comparable phenomena. The Jains and the Parsis of Gujarat, and the Marwaris of Maharashtra, who gave valuable support to Gandhi later, were groups who combined commercial enterprise with notable piety, as if those were natural partners.

It is pleasant to think that Gandhi might have brushed shoulders with the future British prime minister, Lloyd George (who also attended Parker's services) at one of these occasions. Such commerce-minded evangelism was not in general to be counted as a New Age enthusiasm, but this was a time of group self-assertion for the dissenting sects, and a little later, as we shall see, their example was to stimulate Gandhi to social and political action of their kind.

According to Doke again, who was one of Clifford's protégés, Gandhi was influenced by the latter—though whether during this first visit to London or during the Anglo-Boer War, we do not know. (Clifford wrote against the war; he was a close friend of W. T. Stead, and a fierce critic of the British Concentration Camps.) Gandhi certainly read the New Testament during the first visit, and later credited that reading with reawakening his religious feelings. "That religion consists in renunciation appealed to me greatly" (39:481). The Sermon on the Mount echoed ideas Gandhi had learned in childhood, which had seemed to be practiced in the daily life around him.

However, Gandhi was also interested in secularism and atheism—an ideology far from "officially English"—and in them too his interest was then admiring. The two most prominent speakers and thinkers about atheism were Annie Besant and Charles Bradlaugh, and we know that Gandhi was much impressed with both. Bradlaugh was a working-class leader who signed his articles "the Iconoclast." He became president of the National Secular Society in the 1860s, and resigned only in 1890, the year before he died. He was a tall and charismatic presence, with a powerful voice. Shaw called him a great orator, and "the heavyweight champion of the platform"; Shaw spoke of Bradlaugh's terrific personal magnetism.[18]

Bradlaugh also took a keen interest in Indian affairs; which shows the way the various radical enthusiasms went together. He spoke at the Indian Congress in 1889, and there was a Bradlaugh Hall in Lahore. He and Mrs. Besant also took up the cause of birth control—though at least *her* conviction was not so much that artificial aids should be employed, as that information about birth control should be freely circulated. She and Bradlaugh conducted their various legal defences, and were brilliantly successful. Gandhi seems to have heard Annie Besant speak in 1889 on "Why I Became a Theosophist" at the Hall of Science (a typical New Age venue).[19]

Vegetarianism and the New Age

Thus Gandhi's attention and allegiance were engaged by many and very different aspects of English culture. Bewildered at first by so many challenges and solicitations, he began to orient himself and find his feet when he discovered a vegetarian restaurant in London. As he opened its door, he entered the New Age. There were about ten such restaurants in London then. Looking for the Porridge Pot, on High Holborn, he found the Central, just off Farrington Street, and within sight of St. Paul's Cathedral. It was next door to the Vegetarian Society, which had launched the *Vegetarian* weekly magazine earlier that year.

Besides literal food, these offered Gandhi reading matter, and discussion groups and social life. Above all, by refusing to eat the roast beef of old England, the vegetarians refused to join in the hearty rituals of English power. Beyond them, moreover, stretched perspectives of other groups with compatible interests, and other people ready to welcome a young Hindu. For instance, Gandhi met Edwin Arnold through vegetarianism. Arnold and Edward Carpenter both visited the Orient in this period. Arnold returned in February 1890, Carpenter in February 1891; after which the latter attended weekly vegetarian teas arranged by Henry Salt, for the Humanitarian Society, probably attended by Gandhi. Vegetarianism and Orientalism went together.

Vegetarianism was then not just a diet option; it was at the center of a web of idealistic thinking and action. A. F. Hills, 1857 to 1927, a successful businessman, was president of the Vegetarian Federal Union, formed in 1889. He described its aim as "to formulate the essential conditions necessary for the attainment of the ideal, first in the physical and then in the mental, moral, and spiritual life . . . man made one with God by obedience to His will."[20]

This was linked to Indian culture in various ways. In his little book on Gandhi of 1912, P. J. Mehta said that in the previous twenty-five years great progress had been made in London along the lines taught by Indian sages thousands of years before: including public baths, vegetarian and teetotal restaurants, and eating yogurt and whole wheat bread.[21]

The *New Age* was the title of an important radical journal, as we have seen. More generally the phrase was used, together with its alternate, the New Life, as the label for a powerful though diffuse movement of ideas, an idealistic faith. There was also a New Order publishing house and journal, a *New Era* magazine, and other such variants on the idea New.

Finally, there was a Fellowship of the New Life, the stimulus for which came from an itinerant Scottish teacher, Thomas Davidson. The meetings he convened in his rooms in Chelsea between 1881 and 1883 and said to be the *fons et origo* of ethical socialism in England. (Ethical socialism was the New Age alternative to scientific or Marxist socialism, and the Fabian Society in fact began as a branch of the fellowship.) Havelock Ellis and Hubert Bland are two members whose names have not entirely faded from the record.

A major name for all these people was John Ruskin, from whom Gandhi learned a great deal over the years. It is not clear that he read Ruskin's books at this time, but he certainly read *about* him in the *Vegetarian,* and probably in other places. The legend of Ruskin's life was widespread amongst New Agers. In the 1870s he had established St. George's Guild, a landowning community whose members were to take vows and contribute 10 percent of their individual incomes to the common project. (He had long played with the idea of a Protestant convent, a religious community of craftsmen.) The vows imposed on the members what Tolstoy called bread labor, what Gandhi was to call nonviolence, and the renunciation of machinery.

The *Vegetarian* began publication as a weekly in the January of the year in which Gandhi arrived in London. Under its masthead, its slogan was, "Vegetus—Vital, Healthful, Vigorous." Christ's example is invoked, as a prototypical vegetarian. The magazine will be a "radical, yet rational reformer, cutting at the roots of our national vices and sorrows . . . our pressing social questions . . . the congestion of our great cities, with its attendant curses of immorality, debauchery, and disease; the housing and feeding of our starving poor; and the land question." It was to teach agriculture, horticulture, and fruit-culture. Its collaborators will include Henry Salt, Dr. Anna Kingsford (the Theosophist), Howard Williams (whose book on diet had an introduction by Tolstoy), and T. R. Allinson.

This last was a physician Gandhi later consulted. He was also the inventor of a wholemeal bread, and a breakfast cereal. And he was a propagandist for birth control, publishing a book called *A Book for Married Women.* Hills objected to Allinson associating vegetarianism with this other cause, and got him expelled from the society, after a meeting in February 1891. Gandhi also disapproved birth control, but felt Allinson should not be expelled. He attended the meeting, and had a speech written out in advance, but was too nervous to deliver it.

Much that Hills says about the purpose of the Vegetarian Society could have been said by Gandhi later about *his* enterprises. And high-cultural and charitable features of the paper flesh out its idea: quotations from George Eliot and from *Paradise Lost;* plus friendly references to the Salvation Army and Dr. Barnardo's Homes for Orphans.

In the first month of publication there was a long quotation from Shelley's *Queen Mab,* and a biography of the poet, as one in a series of Vegetarian Biographies. In April of the same year, Salt's book on Shelley was reviewed with enthusiasm. Then Salt himself reviewed Carpenter's *Civilization: Its Cause and Cure,* a book that later had a profound effect on Gandhi.

A connected idea, as we know, was the Simple Life. Gandhi was always in love with simplicity, and hostile to the elaborate, gaudy, or luxurious. He scorned the palaces of the Indian princes; and when he was jailed during World War II in the Aga Khan's palace, suffered from the profusion of objects. "The heavy furniture, chairs, tables, sofas, bedsteads, innumerable looking glasses, all get on my nerves." It also felt unhygienic to him. He describes how six men beat one of the carpets all one afternoon, and "extracted ten pounds of dust from it" (77:36). That image of disgust expresses the heart of the Simple-Life enthusiasm.

The various German nature cures, promoted by Adolf Just, Louis Kuhne, Sebastian Kneipp, and some of the nature-cure colonies—for instance, the one in Ascona called Monte Verita—get described in the *Vegetarian.* And by a natural connection, there are many references to theosophy and to India. For instance, there was an article on "Buddhism and Vegetarianism" in August 1889. And in 1891 Gandhi began his career as a writer with articles on life in India.

He drew a contrast between the Kshatriyas, who ate meat, drank alcohol, smoked opium, and so grew weak from debauchery, and the Shudras (whom he calls shepherds, seeing nineteenth-century society in archaic terms). "I know a shepherdess who was more than a hundred years old in 1888. . . . Besides, the shepherd's figure is symmetrical. . . . It is rare to see any deformity in him. Without being fierce like a tiger, he is yet strong and brave, and as docile as a lamb" (1:32, first ed.). It is as a lamb that Gandhi himself writes, "It must at the outset be admitted that the Hindus as a rule are notoriously weak." But physical and mental strength cannot go together. "The law of compensation will require that what is gained in mental power must be lost in physical power. A Samson cannot be a Gladstone."

In 1889 Gandhi visited the Paris Exhibition, and saw the Eiffel Tower, and other sights; and agreed with Tolstoy that the tower was a monument to man's folly. Both men said that such a conception as the tower could never have occurred except to a people intoxicated with nicotine. Tobacco clouds man's intellect, and makes him build such castles in the air.

The movement was international, as the names of Tolstoy and Gandhi are enough to remind us; but it was especially English. The Russian noble and the Hindu bania came to know each other in the medium of English culture. In a list of the magazines he read, drawn up on March 15, 1890, Tolstoy put down a Swedenborgian journal called *New Christianity,* the American *World's Advance Thought,* the *Religio-Philosophical Journal,* the Orientalist *Open Court,* the Theosophical *Lucifer,* and *Theosophical Siftings,* and the Brotherhood Church's *Dawn Sower.* That is a very representative list of English language New Age periodicals; a similar list, but of books, can be found under "Recommended Reading" in many issues of Gandhi's *Indian Opinion,* 1894 to 1914.

Gandhi first heard Tolstoy's name in the vegetarian circles he moved in during his years in London, 1888–91; and first read him *(The Kingdom of God Is within You)* in South Africa in 1894; wrote to him (in English) in 1908, when Tolstoy was eighty; exchanged letters and documents with him, from London, in 1909 and 1910; and founded Tolstoy Farm in the Transvaal in 1910, the year the old man died. They read each other's writings in English, sent each other books and pamphlets printed in England, and wrote letters to each other in English and—sometimes literally—via London.

On December 21, 1889, the *Vegetarian* printed a picture of Tolstoy, and began a two-part biography, and on January 25 of the following year published a review of his recent writings. On December 20, 1890, there was an article on Ruskin. This selection of topics alone is enough to establish the *Vegetarian* as a major organ of the New Age during Gandhi's three years in London.

Mr. Hills financed the *Vegetarian* almost single-handed and was an enthusiastic and puritan idealist. His company built ironclad battleships, and he is said to have inspired Shaw's figure of the armaments manufacturer in his Salvation Army play, *Major Barbara.* He used quite a Shelleyan rhetoric about the great battle between good and evil in the world. Josiah Oldfield, editor of the *Vegetarian,* and a man with whom Gandhi shared rooms in St. Stephen's Gardens, also employed a Shelleyan or Blakean rhetoric. "When the inspiration of a diviner love has burned in the national life—when once the laws of men are made harmonious with the laws of God, then the new Jerusalem, perfect in its political purity, lovely in its moral strength, will descend as a bride adorned for her husband." This is something Oldfield wrote for the *Vegetarian* in November 1889, during Gandhi's time in London.

Oldfield invited Gandhi to attend the International Vegetarian Congress in September 1890, which seems to mark the beginning of Gandhi's intenser activity in the cause. In 1935, Gandhi described Oldfield as a fellow crank, who had been of the greatest help to him as a lad (60:357). This help included persuading Gandhi to speak to an audience, and generally to engage in public life. We are told that Mr. Hills was like a father to Gandhi, and persuaded him to write for the paper; but it was Oldfield with whom he was on the more equal and friendly terms. He cited Oldfield as an example of the Simple Life in his guide, mentioning his diet of bread and water and figs.

Oldfield was born in 1863, and took degrees at Oxford in both theology and civil law, being called to the bar in 1892; and in 1897 he qualified in medicine, and established a fruitarian hospital. He was much interested in how England acted toward its empire, and he visited India—and later the West Indies—to investigate the Christian missions there.

He was made editor of the *Vegetarian* in August 1890, and he and Gandhi shared rooms in Bayswater. Oldfield said that they went out in the evenings, lecturing in clubs; and arranged sample vegetarian suppers of lentil soup, boiled rice, and raisins. Both said such New Age work was Gandhi's first training in organization and agitation—in arranging lectures, passing out handbills, writing to newspapers, holding meetings to discuss issues. It was also a training in ceaseless activity. Gandhi said he had often seen Oldfield work sixteen hours a day; and when Gandhi went back to India, at his farewell banquet, he spoke of how much he owed his friend.[22]

Oldfield's later career is also of interest. In 1898 he had charge of a twenty-bed hospital on the edge of Epping Forest, where he experimented with meatless diets. Later he had a hospital in London, and finally for a long time, beginning in 1905, ran the Lady Margaret cottage hospital in Sittingbourne, Kent. This treated all patients along dietetic lines, using no violence and no "extracts from dead bodies," and specializing in the cure of digestive and nervous troubles. Gandhi sent Indian friends there, and made recurrent efforts (as late as the 1940s) to run such an establishment himself.

Oldfield published a little book called *The Cost of Living* in 1892, soon after Gandhi left London, and some of his later titles will show how many of Gandhi's interests he shared: *Tuberculosis; or, Flesh Eating a Cause of Consumption,* of 1897, and in the same year *The Voice of Nature; or, What Man Should Eat; The Claims of Common Life* of 1898, subtitled "The scientific relations of humans and non-humans"; *Fasting for Health and Life* of 1924 (chapter 2, "The Religious Fast," includes Native American and Zulu examples); and *The Ethics of Butchery* of 1895—our cruelty to animals an extension of slavery—a call to turn from Darwin to Kropotkin. This last was a publication of the Humanitarian League, and quoted Tolstoy.

Toward the end of Gandhi's stay in London he joined, or was a candidate to join, the Theosophical Society. There was a considerable crossover in membership and ideas between this and the Vegetarian Society. Gandhi was wary of the theosophists' occultism (for instance, the attempts at thought transference). He stayed interested in the society for many years, however, admiring its brilliant leaders, Helena Petrovna Blavatsky and Annie Besant, and its revival of Hindu religion.

Perhaps he was attracted also by the fact that those leaders were women. It was notable how prominent women were in many New Age enterprises; and also how often the men—like Henry Salt and Edward Maitland—deferred to female partners. This was quite different from the Indian nationalist movement and especially its terrorist wing, which Gandhi had to confront.

Theosophy was perhaps the major institutional form of a widespread orientalizing mood. It was a new religion, or philosophy of religion, officially founded in New York in 1875, by Blavatsky and Colonel Olcott. It derived from combining all the old religions and extracting the essence of each, but also from appealing to certain ancient, esoteric doctrines and powers handed down secretly through the ages from master to disciple and particularly associated with India and Tibet. Thus, if its one face was close to Unitarianism and Transcendentalism, the other was close to magic, alchemy, and witchcraft. (Only the first face was attractive to Gandhi.) Theosophy was a central New Age phenomenon: Blavatsky and Olcott set off to actually visit India in 1879—the birth year of that New Age. What they had heard about the Arya Samaj sounded to them exactly like what they were doing.

In its earliest origins, Theosophy was a dissenting branch of Spiritualism, but it developed into a form of religious knowledge, under the inspiration of Hinduism. So its reliance on supernatural phenomena was less crude. But the supernatural continued to fascinate many members, including the leaders, and prominently enough to lose Theosophy many of its soberer followers, including Gandhi. Mrs. Besant joined the society because it seemed able to explain phenomena like dreams, hypnosis, clairvoyance, and so on.

Blavatsky claimed to have studied under the Great White Brotherhood of Tibetan Masters. Her "scientific" and esoteric doctrines included the seven planes of the universe, the seven sheaths of man, the law of karma, the five successive races of men, and so on. She wrote critically of both Christianity and modern Western science. Some of her ideas found a permanent lodging in Gandhi. As late as 1946, he remarks, "As Madame Blavatsky puts it, man, in praying, worships the Great Power residing within him" (85:136).

By 1874 she knew that it was her mission to restore the ideal (combating the materialist influence of Darwin) and to defeat Spiritualism, by reintegrating its half-glimpsed truths into Theosophy. Spiritualism followed a different path of development, illustrated by Christian Science. Gandhi shared Blavatsky's dislike for "spiritual" therapy for physical diseases. "Ramanama [a prayer he recommended] is not meant for a boil, which can be cured with a poultice. Ramanama is meant for building a bridge across the sea, for making paper boats sail, for turning stone into water and water into stone" (UC).

Blavatsky's gnostic way of defending idealism and teaching creative evolution is like that of Tolstoy—whom she much admired. "The coming of Christ means the presence of Christos in a regenerated world, and not at all the actual coming in the body of 'Christ' Jesus."[23] Evolution meant man taking on a fresh type, more delicately organized as to the nervous system. She combined that with a quasi-Hindu idea that each person became perfect by means of a series of reincarnations—and some, who have attracted the attention of the spiritual guardians of mankind, move faster than the mass.

Her followers, Colonel Olcott and even more Annie Besant, were gifted organizers. The former became a culture hero to the Buddhists of Ceylon because of the schools and colleges he set up there. Besant worked on an even larger scale with Hindus in India and played a large part in public affairs in

India; founding a Home Rule League, for instance. Besant's life ran in some ways parallel to Gandhi's, and the two side by side illustrate the idea of the New Age, as we shall see.

The three official objects of the Theosophical Society were: to form a nucleus of the universal brotherhood of humanity, without distinction of race, etc.; to encourage the study of comparative religion, philosophy, and science; and to investigate the unexplained laws of nature and the powers latent in man. All three were congenial to Gandhi. He was alert to the dangers of the third, but we shall see that, in his way, he himself pursued powers beyond the ordinary.

An essay by Madame Blavatsky entitled "Civilization the Death of Art and Beauty" shows us the aspect of her thinking that most appealed to Gandhi. It warned Asian societies not to imitate Western models. "Like a hideous leprosy, our Western civilization has eaten its way through all quarters of the globe and hardened the human heart. . . . It is canting and deceitful, from its diplomats down to its custodians of religion, from its politics down to its social laws, selfish, greedy and brutal beyond expression in its grabbing characteristics." This appeared in her journal, *Lucifer,* in May 1891, the year of her death, and the year of Gandhi's return to India.[24]

This attack on Western civilization, in the name of Eastern spirituality, was immensely gratifying to Indians like Gandhi. (Bipin Chandra Pal spoke eloquently about the salve that Theosophy applied to Indian pride.) Blavatsky's essay is quite like his pamphlet of 1910, *Hind Swaraj,* in content. We know that he read her *Key to Theosophy,* of 1890, which was written as a dialogue, quite like his pamphlet in form; and which he said had been a powerful influence in sending him back to Hinduism. There too we find much to remind us of Gandhi in her attack on modern civilization; on materialism, on the misery and wretchedness of great cities, and on modern education; which breeds envy and jealousy, and trains people only to pass examinations.

As already noted, Gandhi's career ran parallel to Annie Besant's in several ways. Perhaps the main interest of that parallel to note here is the fascination that India held for both. Each had many interests and many opportunities, in religion and politics and other things; but in a way that is typical for other New Ages besides their own, Asia in general, and India in particular, drew them irresistibly. India was, perhaps is, *the* New Age country, for Westerners. Besant, like Madame Blavatsky, thought of India as her motherland even before she visited it; revered its past greatness and was indignant at its present ruin.

There were Theosophists at Ascona, the vegetarian and nature-cure colony in Switzerland that was a European capital of the counterculture or New Age. (There was an article about Ascona in the *Vegetarian* at a time when Gandhi was in London.) In 1889, Alfred Pioda, a liberal local politician with New Age ideas, proposed to found a colony of Theosophists there. He formed a joint stock company for the purpose, and one of his allies in the scheme was Countess Wachtmeister, a close friend of Madame Blavatsky. Another ally was Franz Hartmann, also a friend of Blavatsky, who translated, among other things, the *Bhagavad Gita* into German, in 1898. Hermann Hesse, who was reading the Theosophists at the time when he first came to Ascona, around 1907, was an enthusiastic admirer of Hartmann's *Gita,* as were many other Asconans. One of the founders of the nature-cure sanatorium, Ferdinand Brune, was a Theosophist (he went on from Ascona to India) and so was Gustav Nagel, a *Wanderprediger* (wandering preacher) who walked from one to another such settlement.

A heretical sect of the Theosophical Society was the Esoteric Christian Union, led by Edward Maitland and Anna Kingsford. Gandhi valued his 1894–97 correspondence with Maitland—it is the only lost correspondence he seems to have regretted losing—and so it is worth considering the man and his ideas. It was Maitland who sent Gandhi in South Africa a copy of *The Kingdom of God Is within You,* reading that had such a powerful effect on him.

Maitland was born in 1824, the son of a clergyman, and was brought up a Calvinist, but rebelled against the doctrine of original sin. He knew, he said, that, however weak and unwise he might be, he was not evil. This shift of moral target from sin to weakness was typical of the times, and corresponds, within religion, to the concentration on power and expansion in philosophy.

Maitland was oppressed by his father and older brother and later was estranged from his son. On the other hand, he won "the friendship of several noble women." On the whole we get a picture of a man in rebellion against male chauvinism and even maleness; who found in the womanly elements within him the best part of himself. As far as this goes, there was a likeness between him and Gandhi. But Maitland was spiritually, and even politically, expansionist. He believed that the means of man's perfection must inhere in his own system. And in his youth he went out to California and then to Australia, looking for adventure. He believed in the calling of the Anglo-Teutonic race to moral supremacy. He confidently foresaw China voluntarily becoming a British colony. We see in him the same mixture of incongruous elements as in Arnold.

His science-fiction novel, *By and By,* of 1873, was inspired by a Shelleyan enthusiasm for flight, amongst other things. Like other New Agers, Maitland often quoted from Shelley. But perhaps what is most striking about Esoteric Christianity is its stress on women. Woman, we are told, is the crowning manifestation of humanity. Simon Peter, the rock on which the church is founded, represents understanding, but woman is intuition. God is twain, both male and female. He is the Life, but She is the Substance. On the physical plane, Maitland said, Man is only Boy till he recognizes Her; on the spiritual plane he is only a materialist till he chooses Her, the soul, as his better half.

After her death, Maitland wrote a two-volume *Life of Anna Kingsford,* which appeared in 1895 (while Gandhi was in South Africa) in which he presented her as a "contemporary Revelator and Saviour." Born in 1846, she married a cousin but when her husband took orders in the Church of England, she converted to the Church of Rome, taking the baptismal name of Mary Magdalene. The harlot saint had appeared to her in a number of visions.

In 1873 she took up the study of medicine, and in 1875, under Maitland's protection (they met when she wrote him enthusiastically about his novel) she went to Paris as a medical student. She took up protesting against vivisection, converting Annie Besant to that cause, and studied the effect of diet on diseases like tuberculosis. She was one of the sponsors of the *Vegetarian* and the Vegetarian Association.

Theosophy and vegetarianism were thus two of the intellectual institutions of the New Age London of the 1880s. The ideas that finally had most influence on Gandhi were those embodied in two men: some in Tolstoy and others in Edward Carpenter; though his acquaintance with both was only superficial in this period. They belonged to opposite wings of the New Age, the ascetic and the erotic, but recognized each other as fellow campaigners, and were both recognized by Gandhi as masters.

Tolstoy and Carpenter

Tolstoy's *The Kingdom of God Is within You,* written in 1893, had the subtitle, *Christianity Not as a Mystical Teaching but as a New Concept of Life*—the last phrase making Christianity itself a New Age phenomenon. This book was first published in England, at the Free Age Press. Tolstoy's principal disciple, Vladimir Chertkov, was living in England, an exile from Russia, publishing the books Tolstoy could not bring out in his own country. The Tolstoyans, who were to be found in several countries, constituted one section of the international New Age public.

The person we call "the late Tolstoy" was in fact born in 1880 and died in 1910, so his life span was exactly the period of the New Age. In 1881 the famous author of *War and Peace* and *Anna Karenina* moved his large family from the country to Moscow, so that his children could have advantages and pleasures of life in the metropolis. But he himself had to meet the harsh and strenuous moral challenges of living in a large industrialized city, with a mixed population that included the very powerful and the very powerless. This was also the time of the assassination of the Czar Alexander II, by idealistic young radicals, and the execution of his assassins. The effect of these events was to bring the ugly facts of power close to Tolstoy—to upset for good the delicate balance of generous and self-preserving policies by which he had hitherto lived; a complex of interests and values (domestic and aesthetic) fairly typical of liberal intellectuals then. For the next thirty years, Tolstoy tried to discover both the theory and the practice of a different—and radically religious—attitude to life. *The Kingdom of God Is within You* records an important step forward in that progress.

Historically, the newness referred to in the subtitle means the way early Christianity differed from the Roman imperial culture in the midst of which it first developed; but ultimately it points to the incompatibility between Christian concepts and the Russian Empire of the nineteenth century (and modern Western civilization in general). It denounces that civilization, and prophesies its doom on the authority of true Christianity.

In the 1890s, the modern world seemed to many people to be trembling, in London as in Moscow, and a new idea to be burgeoning, which might in fact be that old idea of "true Christianity." Aylmer Maude, a member of the English New Age, named the period 1897–1907 as the Tolstoy period of history, when it seemed as if Tolstoy groups and colonies were springing up everywhere. A brief summary of the book will help us to understand what happened.

Tolstoy began by referring to the seventeenth-century Quakers as his spiritual ancestors—they could be called an example of the seventeenth-century New Age; and then to some of the nineteenth-century American abolitionists, quoting from William Lloyd Garrison's "Declaration of Sentiments" of 1838. Tolstoy described the Quakers' repudiation of patriotism, politics, and the courts, and contrasted with them the radicals of violence he called Jacobins or terrorists: "The spirit of Jacobinism is the spirit of retaliation, violence, and murder."[25]

Gandhi said later that reading Tolstoy had saved him from atheism and from violence. For the Tolstoy Centenary celebrations in 1928, he wrote, "When I went to England I was a votary of violence. I had faith in it and none in nonviolence" (37:261).

Carpenter, on the other hand, wanted a New Age that would be free from religious asceticism. He wrote in his autobiography that we should learn to understand Christianity as a version of a universal solar religion, and that the world was coming round again to a concrete appreciation of the value and beauty of actual life, and to a neopagan point of view. His *oeuvre* includes such titles as *Love's Coming of Age* and *The Art of Creation.*

The former is an argument for sexual liberation, including (discreetly) homosexuality. The latter begins:

> We seem to be arriving at a time when, with the circling of our knowledge of the globe, a great synthesis of all human thought on the ancient and ever engrossing problem of Creation is quite naturally and inevitably taking shape. The world-old wisdom of the Upanishads, with their profound and impregnable doctrine of the Universal Self, the teachings of Buddha or of Lao-Tzu, the poetic insight of Plato, the inspired sayings of Jesus and Paul, the speculations of Plotinus, or of the Gostics, etc. . . . all this, coming with . . . modern physical and biological Science and Psychology, are preparing a great birth, as it were.[26]

This sort of expansive speculation was New Age thinking, too; and was congenial to Gandhi, as far as its religious ecumenism went. The moral implications, on the other hand, are clearly quite different from Tolstoy's, and Gandhi was much closer to the latter, morally.

No single text by Carpenter was as important to Gandhi as the one by Tolstoy, but *Civilization, Its Cause and Cure,* of 1888, made a profound impact. Together with Tolstoy's, this was the most important of all books in forming Gandhi's philosophy. It is primarily an attack on modern medicine and health care. Health is wholeness and a positive presence, says Carpenter, and yet we treat it as the mere absence of disease. Medical science makes a fetish of disease, and dances round it. The wild races—the ancient Greeks, the Red Indians, the Africans—are at one with nature in their keenness of sense, and much more. We should eat primarily fruit and nuts, says Carpenter, and avoid even those vegetables which have to be uprooted, like cabbages. (Gandhi advanced many of these ideas, later.) In *Towards Democracy*, a long poem in Whitman-like blank verse, Carpenter presented himself, as Whitman had done, as a figure of perfect health.

Like Tolstoy, Carpenter began his New-Age career in the spring of 1881. It was then that he found his poetic voice and his philosophic message, in *Towards Democracy*. He explained later that he had been liberated by the sudden discovery of a new region of his self, which existed equally in others and which became the subject of his poetry. (Influenced by Hinduism, he understood the self rather as Hinduism understands the Atman.) He knocked together a sort of sentinel box in his garden, in which he sat to write—the free open air being as necessary as the free-verse form to his inspiration. He became the guru of the Simple Life.

In the twentieth-century New Age Tolstoy's ascetic moralism, seen especially in matters of sexuality, has come to seem at best eccentric, and it is Carpenter who probably seems to be the more authoritative voice of the New Age. But Gandhi made the opposite choice, and in order to understand that fact it is worth paying attention to something else that was going on in this same period.

The Purity Campaign

As noted, during Gandhi's time in London there was a Purity Campaign in England. E. J. Bristow, the historian of Purity Campaigns, in his book, *Vice and Vigilance*, describes the period 1880–1910 as the time of that campaign. (It is of interest that he also discusses two previous Purity Campaigns, of the 1690s and of 1780 to 1810; which is exactly the same historical pattern of recurrence as we find in the history of New Ages.)

The nineteenth-century Purity Campaign may be said to begin in the 1870s with Josephine Butler's work to repeal the Contagious Diseases Act, which condoned prostitution by establishing sanitary controls on the prostitutes. Her work, and that of Ellice Hopkins and her White Flag movement, was supported by the Quakers and the nonconformist sects. However, it was in the 1880s that the movement acquired a broad base. The White Flag League was founded in 1883, as was the Church of England Purity Society. (One of the leaders of the latter was Bishop Westcott of Durham, who was a strong influence on Gandhi's friend, Andrews.) It is worth noting how many purity campaigns attacked zones of privilege for men, like pubs and brothels; this was an antimasculinist trend very sympathetic to Gandhi.

Cardinal Manning and Hugh Price Hughes, the nonconformist leader, combined social reform with temperance and social purity work. The Salvation Army got involved in purity work in 1883, and it is said that General Booth's son, Branwell, interested W. P. Stead in it. The latter caused a great scandal in 1885, publishing articles in his *Pall Mall Gazette* on "The Maiden Tribute of Modern Babylon"—the purchase of young girls for sexual purposes. Stead went to jail for his actions.

One of Stead's most ardent supporters was Dr. Clifford, who was also the leader of the Baptists in their passive resistance to paying taxes to support Church of England schools. Clifford was a patron of Gandhi's friend, Joseph

Doke, and Gandhi asked him to read the competition essays about passive resistance in South Africa. Stead disapproved of England's part in the Anglo-Boer War, and Gandhi several times cited Stead's public protests against the war as a model of conscientious politics. We thus find involved in the Purity Campaign several people whom Gandhi admired and followed.

It would not be right to consider the Purity Campaign as a central part of the New Age: the campaign had a predominantly conservative character. But it was the expression of a naive mentality, seeking goodness. And Tolstoy and Gandhi *were* conservative in some ways, reminding contemporary readers of early fathers of the Christian church, like Tertullian, in matters of sex.

Narayan Hemchandra

We should not entirely neglect the nonintellectual, comic or crankish side of the New Age, for which also Gandhi had a strong appreciation. Chapter 22 of his autobiography is entitled "Narayan Hemchandra," and is about a traveling Hindu eccentric of that name.

"His dress was queer—a clumsy pair of trousers, a wrinkled, dirty, brown coat after the Parsee fashion, no necktie or collar, and a tasselled woolen cap. He grew a long beard. He was lightly built and short of stature. His round face was scarred with smallpox, and had a nose which was neither pointed nor blunt. With his hand he was constantly turning over his beard. Such a queer-looking and queerly dressed person was bound to be singled out in fashionable society" (A:72).

It is unusual for Gandhi to give so much detail in describing a person. Clearly he is moved, in remembering the man, as he was in meeting him, by a fond though humorous appreciation, which is admiring as well as protective. Gandhi offered to teach the other man English, and they became, in Gandhi's words, close friends. Hemchandra was a self-styled translator and literary scholar. He was in fact "innocent of grammar," but "was not to be baffled by his ignorance." He scorned Gandhi's instructions, saying that he himself had never felt the need of grammar. "Well, do you know Bengali? I know it. I have travelled in Bengal. It is I who have given Maharishi Devendranath Tagore's works to the Gujarati-speaking world. . . . And you know I am never literal in my translations. I always content myself with bringing out the spirit" (73).

He was going on to France (he had heard rumors that there was a literature in French) and then Germany and then America, for the same purpose. Gandhi is quite clear that the man's performance as a writer and intellectual was a joke, and says nothing of any spiritual or religious teaching, yet finds his naive originality, his courage in following his own line, impressive.

Gandhi asked where Hemchandra would find the money to do so much traveling. "What do I need money for? I am not a fashionable fellow like you. The minimum amount of food and the minimum amount of clothing suffice for me. . . . I always travel third class. While going to America also I shall travel on deck" (74). By the time he was writing his autobiography, Gandhi was of course a Hemchandra himself, in his simplicity of dress, food, traveling, and so on. Even at the time of their meeting, Gandhi says, there was "a considerable similarity between our thoughts and actions."

But at that time, he had much to learn from Hemchandra. He tells us that they met at Miss Elizabeth Manning's National Indian Association. Her teas, at Pembridge Crescent, Notting Hill, were a regular social occasion for Indians in London, where Gandhi used to sit tongue-tied, never speaking except when spoken to. "Miss Manning knew that I could not make myself sociable" (72). Hemchandra showed him how to shrug off such timidity, not by becoming polished, but by a New Age indifference to social etiquette.

Hemchandra came to Gandhi's lodgings one day in shirt and dhoti—which meant, no trousers. This alarmed the landlady, who announced him to her tenant as "some kind of crazy man." Gandhi asked his friend if the children in the street had not shouted at him. "'Well, they ran after me, but I did not mind them and they were quiet'" (75). Later, in America, Hemchandra was even prosecuted for being indecently dressed.

If he stayed a few years in Europe, he may have reached Ascona, where too there were often trouserless wanderers to be seen—who also were sometimes prosecuted by the Swiss authorities. (Gustav Nagel is an example.) Refusing trousers was like refusing meat, a gesture that made the Western world very uneasy, however serenely the gesture was performed.

Narayan Hemchandra exemplifies the comic side of the New Age, which gets lost when we study it just as intellectual history; and shows us Gandhi's attitude to that side, which is seriously as well as humorously appreciative. (Gandhi described himself as a crank, and encouraged people to laugh at him—it was one of his ways of making friends.) And he reminds us in how many ways Indians were part of the New Age.

New Age Leaders

Four of the New Age leaders in England who had especially interesting connections with Gandhi deserve some brief further introduction. They are Henry Salt, Olive Schreiner, Edwin Arnold, and Annie Besant. Gandhi knew all of them personally, though it was probably via their writings that they made their biggest impact on him.

It was Henry Salt's pamphlet, "A Plea for Vegetarianism," that persuaded Gandhi of the wrongness of eating meat. (He found the book for sale in his first vegetarian restaurant.) That change we have seen to be a very important one, which initiated many others in his life. For instance, the pamphlet began with a quotation from Thoreau, and later Salt's little book about Thoreau introduced the American to Gandhi as the theorist of civil disobedience also.

Salt was a long-term and close friend to George Bernard Shaw, though a much less brilliant figure. Shaw explained their friendship by saying that they had been Shelleyans and Humanitarians together. The love of Shelley was important to most New Agers; he was the poet of idealism. Thus the Asconan poet Harold Monro was interested in horses rather than books until, "like most of us," wrote his friend, F. S. Flint, "he met Shelley, and his entire life was changed. He became a gloomily serious young man."[27]

Salt's turn toward Shelley announced his literary radicalism. In fact his first book, of 1887, was a Shelley primer. As for humanitarianism, this was perhaps Salt's main cause. He founded the Humanitarian League, and edited the *Humanitarian Review*. The horror at vivisection and the distrust of modern medicine this implied, as well as the reverence for animal life in general, was as important an item as vegetarian diet in the humanitarian creed. Tolstoy sent Salt a vegetarian tract, and wrote an introduction to another one by Howard Williams, whom Gandhi knew.

The *Review* regularly attacked blood sports, corporal punishment, the death penalty, and the despoiling of the countryside. Shaw offered a sort of penitent tribute to Salt, and reproach to himself, saying that his pastime had been writing sermons in plays, sermons preaching what Salt practiced.

Salt's politics were what we would now call ecological, or New Age. Shaw called him a born revolutionist, but Salt himself said his profession was "looking for, and at, wild flowers." He loved Thoreau; to him, it has been said, *Walden* was as important as Whitman's *Leaves of Grass* was to Carpenter. Carpenter was also an admirer of *Walden,* and was sometimes called the English Thoreau. Salt edited a version of Carpenter's *Civilization: Its Cause and Cure,* as he edited other New Age classics, like Godwin's *Political Justice*. Thus he served the New Age on several fronts. We don't know what impression Gandhi made on Salt in their meetings—perhaps only an impression of shy nervousness—but Gandhi remembered his old teacher gratefully, corresponded with him, and saw him on his last trip to England, in 1931.

Olive Schreiner, on the other hand, did admire and support Gandhi in his New Age politics in her homeland, South Africa; and Gandhi referred to her as a close friend. He admired her simple life-style, and household work. She was a central figure in the New Age, from certain points of view. In 1881, the very beginning of the period, she arrived in London to make her literary debut. In 1883 she published her novel, *The Story of an African Farm,* famous in its day for its realism about marriage, and in our day for opening fiction up to the experience of women in colonial society. The central character, Lyndall, has been called the first wholly feminist heroine in English literature.

In 1884 Schreiner made friends with Havelock Ellis, and the two investigated sexual behavior together, and discussed all the current experiments in love and marriage. Their understanding of sex has been described as pre-Freudian, and was forgotten when Freud's more systematic ideas triumphed. Their understanding was unlike his because tied to progressive and evolutionary sympathies—to New Age ideas—and less "scientific." But in its day it was found just as subversive of sexual morals as his. Ellis and Schreiner belonged to the Men and Women Club, founded 1885, where sexual problems were discussed. This club, of about twenty members, met from 1885 to 1889. Gandhi's tone about sexual matters was usually quite different from theirs, but at the end of his life he engaged in what one can only call sexual experiments, and he cited Ellis as one of his precursors.

Schreiner's book *Woman and Labor* came out in 1911, at the very end of this period. She was almost alone in seeing the race conflict in South Africa as part of the worldwide struggle between capital and labor; but she was still a New Ager rather than a Marxist. Although she was a close friend of Eleanor Marx, she never read Karl Marx's *Capital,* and was averse from organizational or party politics. In 1914 she took a pacifist position on the war, and scolded Gandhi for raising an Indian ambulance corps to support the British. Thereafter there was little connection between them.

The third of these personalities was Edwin Arnold, with whom Gandhi worked together to found a new London branch of the Vegetarian Society. Arnold went out to India in 1857, when he was made principal of a government college in Pune, and became an Orientalist. He brought in Westernizing reforms there—he reduced the amount of Sanskrit taught, introduced science and the English classics, and admitted non-Brahmin students. However, he himself learned Sanskrit and Marathi, and studied the great religious poems of Hinduism.

In 1860, back in England, he became an editor of the Liberal *Daily Telegraph,* where he remained until 1889. This newspaper financed imperial expeditions, like Henry Stanley's three-year African journey west from Zanzibar to the mouth of the Congo. Arnold was much involved in promoting this journey, and Stanley named an African river after him. The imperialism of the *Telegraph* led to its going over to the Conservative party in 1878. Arnold wrote passages of Queen Victoria's Speech from the Throne in 1877, and was made a Companion of the Star of India.

However, most people then, including Indians, did not see this as imperialist in the bad sense. Victoria's proclamation to her Indian subjects, welcoming them as equal to Englishmen, was taken to be a new Magna Carta—as we know, Gandhi so took it. Indeed, the Orientalist was a whole other side to Arnold, which explains Gandhi's liking for him and their alliance.

In 1879 Arnold published *The Light of Asia,* a verse biography of the Buddha, which became very popular. It had appeared in thirty editions by 1885. In 1885 he produced *The Song Celestial,* largely a translation of the Bhagavad Gita, in which version Gandhi first met that classic of Hinduism. In the 1890s Arnold did some translations from the Qur'an published as *Pearls of the Faith* and *The Gulistan.* By then he was receiving rather scornful reviews both from scholars in religion and from literary critics; his account of Oriental religion was seen as popularization, and his poetry as simply derivative from Keats and Tennyson. He was however considered for the poet laureate's position when Tennyson died, and Gandhi reported in *Indian Opinion* the rumor that he had been passed over because of his sympathy for Oriental culture.

These affiliations made Arnold attractive to Gandhi, who cared little for fashions in poets or for scholarly exactitude, and he long felt indebted to Arnold, recommending his Orientalist work to Indian as well as English friends and disciples. And the two men came together over vegetarianism, as we saw. (Arnold was much influenced by Buddhism, giving up hunting as well as meat eating.) The first book of religion Gandhi was given in England, he says, was *The Light of Asia.* "I was an indifferent reader of literature, but I could not resist [it]" (27:62). The subtitle Arnold gave the poem was "The Great Renunciation," which is a clue to Gandhi's enthusiasm for the poem. He always declared *The Song Celestial* the best translation of the Gita. And in 1924 he said that all he knew about Buddhism he learned from Arnold (24:85).

Finally, Annie Besant was born of Irish stock in 1847, married a curate in the Church of England in 1867, but left him in 1873, joining the National Secular Society the following year. The variety and sequence of her interests (she also studied science and lectured on it) and something in the manner of her mind (the clear, quiet, simple prose of her pamphlets) makes her another parallel figure to Gandhi. She edited the Secular Society's publication, and made a close alliance with its leader, Charles Bradlaugh. They took up the cause of birth control, and Gandhi was for a time swayed by their arguments. (Gandhi much admired Bradlaugh, as one who stood alone against the world, and was himself a religious skeptic at this point.) She published *The Gospel of Atheism* in 1877, and was in consequence deprived of the custody of her daughter in 1878.

In 1885 she joined the Fabian Society, and helped organize the strike of London's women matchmakers in 1888. But then she left the Fabians and joined the Theosophical Society in 1890, carried away by one of Madame Blavatsky's books (which W. T. Stead gave her to review). Gandhi, as we saw, was much impressed by Annie Besant's account of her conversion. For him, too, Truth was the supreme value.

Besant entered nationalist politics in India, by her own account, in order to save India's youth from being corrupted by the anarchist revolutionaries of Bengal. This sounds very like what Gandhi said in *Hind Swaraj*. Also like him in South Africa, she taught Indian journalists how to make strong attacks on the government without being so violent as to provoke retribution by the law.

Thus Gandhi and Besant both were New Age heroes, though in their later political careers, in India, they were rivals, and seem to have been temperamentally incompatible. But he praised her in for instance 1928 in terms that would apply well to himself: referring to her simplicity of life and power of introspection; her bridging of the gulf between religion and politics; and her awakening of India from its deep slumber (37:321).

In 1893, the year Gandhi again left India, Besant arrived there, and made her home there. As she entered further into theosophy, she discovered her own earlier incarnations, which included two famous martyrs to truth, the woman intellectual Hypatia, and the Renaissance philosopher Giordano Bruno. (Bradlaugh named his daughter Hypatia, and Bruno, who was burned for heresy, was a hero to many New Agers then.) In 1895 Besant became absolute head of the society. Gandhi followed her career and recommended her writings, in his South Africa years.

Life-style

To return to the beginning of Gandhi's time in London, even in his period of dandyism he kept careful accounts of all he spent; bus fares, stamps, newspapers, all would be entered and the balance struck every evening. Moreover, he soon began to reduce his expenses. He moved out of the house where he paid for his meals, taking first two rooms, and then one, where he could prepare his own food. He chose a neighborhood from which he could walk to his place of work, and so walked eight to ten miles a day. He read some books on the Simple Life, and by following their advice reduced his expenditure by a half and more.

(Something he does not tell us is that he was sending home to Sheikh Mehtab in India money for his support, saved from what Lakshmidas sent *him*. Nor does he tell us that he was writing regularly to his old friend, and had him read aloud to Kasturba the accounts of his experience that she could not read herself. We should not confidently measure these facts by the criteria we would employ if Gandhi had been of our time and place; but both of them are surely very suggestive, especially when we recall the distrust of that intermediary felt by both Kasturba and Lakshmidas. Was Mehtab keeping watch on Kasturba for Gandhi? And if so, in what spirit was he doing so?)

Gandhi's work toward the bar examination did not take up much of his time or effort, so he took courses toward matriculating at London University, studying Latin and French, physics, and chemistry. (He failed some of the examinations in January 1890, but passed them in June.) He also read the newspapers regularly, and attended some of the occasions of English public life: hearing Annie Besant speak, and attending Charles Bradlaugh's funeral; where he would be one of the quietest of the audience.

Even in the world of vegetarianism, out of shyness he still could not speak at meetings of the society's executive committee. When an issue arose about which he had to make his feelings known, he wrote out what he had to say in advance; and then often could not bring himself to read it out, so had someone else do so. The same thing happened when he was invited to speak at a vegetarian meeting at Ventnor, and at his farewell banquet. Gandhi later felt that his shyness had been an advantage, as a kind of silence, but he was at the time determined to overcome it in the service of his ideas.

He made friends with women easily, but his relations with them were marked, and marred, by the same problem. Like most Indian students in England, he presented himself to English people as unmarried. (When he left he said that his friends would no doubt be surprised to hear that he was a husband.) As a result, he found an English friend promoting his marriage to a girl they both knew, and Gandhi had to explain and excuse himself—of course in writing. Outside the realm of public affairs, dharma did not help him to overcome his shyness.

He tells another anecdote about his stay at Ventnor, where his landlady's daughter took him out for a walk up a hill. (Gandhi went several times for holidays to the south coast resorts of Ventnor and Brighton.) "I responded to her chatter sometimes with a whispered 'yes' or 'no,' or at the most, 'yes, how beautiful!' She was flying like a bird whilst I was wondering when I should get back home." Moreover, "My cowardice was on a par with my reserve": when they had to get down the hill again, "This sprightly young lady of twenty five darted down the hill like an arrow. I was shamefacedly struggling to get down.

She stood at the foot smiling and cheering me and offering to come and drag me" (A:64).

These chapters of his autobiography are a record of constant humiliation, despite the lightness of their tone. The same is true of passages about sex in other writings, and about experiences in India and South Africa as well as England. Talking of his first visit to a brothel, with Sheikh Mehtab, he says the woman threw him out in contempt, because he was trembling and could not look her in the face: "What could that smart woman do to such a fool but turn him out?" And when, on one of his trips to South Africa, the captain and an English friend took him to a whorehouse, Gandhi was too embarrassed even to speak to the woman. Afterwards, "I certainly felt a little humiliated. They had seen that I was a fool in these matters. They even joked among themselves on this point. They pitied me, of course. From that day, I was enrolled among the fools of the world, as far as the captain was concerned" (27:111).

Finally, Gandhi tells us of a potentially sexual encounter while he was attending a Vegetarian Conference at Portsmouth, when playing bridge; his friend and their landlady (who was "as good as a prostitute"—[27:108]) began to make indecent jokes, in which Gandhi joined, and he was about to go "beyond the limit," when his friend Mazmudar warned him. It seems to be implied that the friend was ready to go "beyond the limit" himself, but felt that that would be wrong for Gandhi. Similarly, one of his friends, we are told, warned Gandhi against smoking and drinking, although he indulged in both himself. Thus we gather that Gandhi seemed to others to be morally more sensitive—more delicate or vulnerable—than they themselves.

Gandhi began his literary career in the *Vegetarian,* writing nine articles, starting in 1890. His political career also began in the Vegetarian Society. He became a member of the executive committee on September 19, 1890, and as we know, the following nine months were the period of his greatest activity in London. He read a paper on Indian food twice, spoke to a group of children in the Band of Mercy, and (nervously) hosted a farewell dinner. On June 10, 1891, he was called to the bar, on the eleventh he enrolled at the High Court, and on the twelfth sailed for India.

In an article for the *Vegetarian,* he said he regretted leaving dear London, which was a fit setting for someone like him, who was a traveler, a trader, and a faddist—"as a vegetarian would be called by his opponents" (1:64, first ed.). He clearly did feel some reluctance to exchange that setting for Porbandar, and those friends for Kasturba and Sheikh Mehtab.

In some ways Gandhi was indeed a natural Londoner, a natural citizen of a modern metropolis. He was full of curiosity and the itch to understand, an eager spectator of the play of conflicting forces, striking personalities, the varieties of men. (Those are the aspects of him that the Mahatma halo conceals.) But to call himself a trader (a Bania) is perhaps the most interesting, just because it was not literally true, and only made sense within the Hindu caste system. He was naming himself simultaneously in English and in Indian terms. He had acquired enough knowledge of English law to be able to rise high in India, and elsewhere in the empire; and enough knowledge of British politics and social issues—the sort of knowledge dispensed in serious newspapers—to prepare him for a life of public service. But he had also acquired interests and enthusiasms of another kind—New Age interests—which would sooner or later get in the way of his practice of the law and of any ordinary political career.

From London to Bombay 1891

He sailed from Tilbury on the *Oceana* on June 12, 1891, changing at Aden to the *Assam*. On the voyage back he wrote more articles for the *Vegetarian*, and he tore up and threw away various "certificates," testifying to what he had done and not done while away, which he had procured from friends, to show to his family in India. Acquiring such certificates was part of the routine or discipline of Indian students abroad, but Gandhi was now seeing such practices from outside. It is interesting also that he included adventurers in his list of the types among the passengers: some who, being disappointed at home, were going to pursue their adventure, God knows where. These were of course English men, or families. Gandhi saw the English, and not the Indians, as an adventurous race (1:70, first ed.). In 1925 he said that the sea was an epitome of adventures, and they, the Indians, needed the spirit of adventure in their national life (26:257). When India had swaraj her sons would certainly come forwards to climb the top of the Himalayas or discover the North Pole.

As one of a group who tried to organize social activities on the ship, he volunteered to give a talk on vegetarianism. When he confessed to feeling nervous, he was advised to make the talk humorous. He replied, he tells us, that "nervous I might be, but humorous I certainly could not be" (1:67). As that phrasing shows us, he was in fact a humorous man, but he could not, at that point in his career, stand up with a promise to entertain a random audience.

He still saw himself as a reformer, a Westernizer. On the way home, "as I was a reformer, I was taxing myself as to how best to begin certain reforms" (A:87). He was thinking generally about India; a country he had never looked at with the vision he was now bringing to it. He knew the Bhagavad Gita in Arnold's translation; he knew the faces of nationalist leaders from their photographs in English journals. For instance, he tells us he first saw a photograph of Pandit Malaviya in the magazine *India* in 1890. This magazine began to appear that year, put out by the British Committee of the Indian National Congress.

Congress was one institution he must have been thinking about. Its British Committee was founded in July 1889, at 25 Craven Street, the Strand. He had got to know one national leader in London, the Moderate Dadabhai Naoroji, three times president of congress, who in the following year was to be elected to parliament. A group of Liberals had got together in 1890 to promote his candidacy.

Gandhi admired Naoroji, and was to seek advice from him in South Africa. It does not seem that he saw much of him during these three London years; he was too shy to present a letter of introduction till he was about to leave; but he described Naoroji's office afterwards. Only eight feet by six, it had scarcely room for another chair. Naoroji wrote his letters in copying ink, and press-copied them himself. He was too mild a politician to please the younger revolutionary patriots, but to Gandhi he was a hero of efficiency, modesty, and moderation.

Congress had been formed in 1885, on the initiative of an Englishman, Allen Octavian Hume (a Theosophist, as were many of the first congressmen) and with the approval of a viceroy, Lord Dufferin. Before then, India had had a British Indian Association, founded in Calcutta in 1851, essentially an association of landlords; plus the Indian press, which especially for fifteen years after 1860 functioned as an opposition party.

Congress was a very parliamentary institution, and in its early years clearly imitative of things English. Its appeal was limited to the English-speaking middle class, and it met only once a year, with practically no full-time staff to work between sessions. After the turn of the century, Gokhale gave its discussions greater intellectual substance, with his addresses full of economic statistics, and Tilak gave it more political bite, with his demands for self-government. It became a wrestling ground for liberals or Moderates (following the former) against radicals or Extremists (following the latter). Once Gandhi had returned from South Africa, an experienced politician, he found congress an ineffective focus of the nation's political life, and reformed it radically.

India 1891–1893

Gandhi's ship reached Bombay in early July, having been delayed by storms, and he was met with the news of his mother's death, some weeks earlier. (She was only about forty years old, it would appear.) The family had kept the news from him, for fear he would be upset. Her death caused him great grief, but he tried, and apparently with success, to suppress all expression of it. Nor did he feel ashamed of that suppression; in certain areas, of grief and affection, Indian decorum as he had learned it was as emotionally chaste as that of the English.

In Bombay he was met by friends of Dr. Mehta, and by them introduced to Raychandbhai; who was now related by marriage to the doctor, and working as a jeweler in Bombay. Raychandbhai got married in 1891, much later in his life than Gandhi, and since he had much the same distrust of sex and marriage as Gandhi, this was inconsistent. Gandhi nevertheless found him calm, dignified, soft-voiced, and "full of inner joy."

Gandhi tested Raychandbhai's powers as a shatavadani, by reciting a number of words in European languages, which the other man was able to repeat without ever having heard them before. Gandhi confesses that he was vain of his linguistic skills, under the powerful spell of England. "Having been to England made a man feel that he was heaven-born." He wrote down a number of words in Latin and French, and read them out, and Raychandbhai recited them. "This was an excellent experience to break a little the binding spell of England on me. . . . I was all admiration. The power of memory is not sold in schools." Gandhi was the one who had gone to schools (32:5).

The two men must have quickly become more than acquaintances, for Gandhi was one of those who spoke at a public celebration of Raychandbhai's birthday in a public hall in Ahmedabad. His remarks were not recorded, but we know what he said at a similar occasion in 1921, after Raychandbhai's death; when he described Raychandbhai as the living embodiment of the religion of compassion. (He claimed that his own political activity was inspired by the same interest.) He also said that Raychandbhai's faith was founded on the bedrock of ahimsa, nonviolence (43:99).

Speaking of his friend as the Poet (one of Raychandbhai's honorary titles was *Kavi,* "the Poet") Gandhi said in 1921 that he had learned more from his friend's life than from any other source of the way of compassion. But as Gandhi (and presumably Raychandbhai) defined that quality, compassion involved severe discipline as well as self-discipline. "Let us suppose my son is a drink-addict, smoker and dissolute." Compassion would dictate that one prevent such a son from procuring drink or tobacco. (Such an example was bound, in 1921, to make his friends think of Gandhi's actual son, Harilal.) But Raychandbhai also taught that one should do what others of one's station in life do, unless it goes against conscience. Gandhi agreed with this, even though he broke so many rules; of course, for him, so much went against conscience.

Raychandbhai was what might be called anticlerical, or antisacerdotal. He used to say that of all his sufferings he could least bear being stabbed by the lies and hypocrisies masquerading as religion; and that if Jainism had not fallen into the hands of the Jains it would have filled the world with the marvels of its truths. This anticlericalism was a point of view congenial to Gandhi; who more than one said that Raychandbhai nevertheless was surrounded by "hypocrites." On another occasion he quoted Raychandbhai as warning others against religious revivalist fervor. Both of them were reformers and renewers of religion, who yet stood outside religious organizations. They agreed in their distrust of evangelism of the fundamentalist, Arya Samaj, kind (9:118).

Gandhi more than once said that the three people who had most influenced him were Ruskin, Tolstoy, and Raychandbhai; and that the last was the one who seemed to him most authoritative on the subject of religion (13:143). He used the title Mahatma about Raychandbhai. Perhaps the most revealing anecdote he tells about his conversations with him refers to their discussion of the use of leather. They agreed that in conscience it should be avoided. But then Gandhi said, "I have always been a man who would not miss a chance for a jest," so he asked his friend to take off the cap he was wearing; and there Raychandbhai found a strip of leather. His response was simply to tear it off, without either discussion or protest. That teasing challenge and irony is something very typical of Gandhi. It did not prevent his saying that he believed Raychandbhai had died because he could not bear the spectacle of the world's suffering (21:427–33).

In Kathiawar, Gandhi found that new European tastes like tea, coffee, and shoes, had been introduced into the family home. He himself added cocoa and oatmeal, and other European items of clothing. He was still a reformer. At least when he was present, his family now sat on chairs and ate from china plates, instead of squatting on the ground and eating off brass. According to Sudhir Kakar, Kasturba was also induced to wear European clothes for a time.

Lakshmidas had had the house whitewashed, put in new ceilings, and bought new crockery. The family looked forward to a rebirth of its former greatness, now that Mohandas had returned a barrister. Partly to please his brother, Gandhi went through the caste-prescribed forms of penance—expiating his sin in going to England—and so was reconciled with his castemen. He bathed in the holy river Godivari, at Nasik. But this did not satisfy all the Modh Banias. He was accepted among them in Rajkot but not in Bombay or Porbandar, so he remained excommunicated as far as his sister went. This contributed to his difficulties in finding clients for his legal practice.

He took the children of the extended family for walks, and it was apparently then that he began the practice of putting his hands affectionately on the shoulders of companions. This was clearly not the same gesture as his later leaning closely on young women, but it was in answering reproaches about the latter practice that Gandhi said it all began in 1891. He says this was when he returned from England, and it is probably significant that recreational walking was a New Age practice, and cross-gender contact a New Age freedom, alien to Indian decorum.

The autobiography tells us little of the terms on which he met with Kasturba or with Sheikh Mehtab. But the indications are that such things were surprisingly little changed, despite all that had happened in Gandhi's mind during the years away. There were again quarrels between husband and wife. "Once I went the length of sending her away to her father's house, and consented to receive her back only after I had made her thoroughly miserable" (A:91). The motive he describes as his "squeamishness and suspiciousness in respect of every little thing," which was deliberately exacerbated by Sheikh Mehtab, and which he later saw to be "pure folly on my part." On that occasion Gandhi broke her bangles, which was symbolically to repudiate her.

In November Gandhi applied for admission as advocate of Bombay High Court, but he was uneasy with his profession, both morally and psychologically. It involved him in serious collusion with the master race and the master class, and a betrayal of his Indian identity—a betrayal symbolized in the wig and gown he had to wear in court. He wanted, but did not want, to be an Englishman. He broke down when he had to cross-examine, returned his client's fees, and despite, or because of, his nervousness, fell asleep in the courtroom. When, once, he tried to speak, and stood tongue-tied, everyone laughed, and he "hastened from the room in shame." Another lawyer, who charged twice as much as he, took the case over and won it. In another reminiscence, which seems to refer to this occasion, Gandhi described how the oppression on his spirits was lifted, as he hastened away, by reciting to himself verses from the Gita. Reminding himself how necessary it was always to separate intention from result, duty from success, he soon felt ready to dance in the street.

Like other young England-returned barristers, he set up his office, and then had to wait for business to come to him. For various reasons, he did not do well as compared with his rivals—who included Mohammed Ali Jinnah, whose life history had been remarkably parallel up to this point. Jinnah was completely happy being a lawyer, and being a politician.

Gandhi's Jain friend, Virchand Gandhi, also a practicing lawyer, seems to have frightened him with tales of how clever and ruthless one had to be to succeed in the law in Bombay. (Virchand Gandhi—who must have been interested in Raychandbhai—spoke for Jainism at the Parliament of Religions in Chicago in 1893, where several Indian religions made themselves known to the West through gifted representatives.)

Not succeeding, Gandhi wound up his legal establishment in Bombay after six months, returned to Rajkot, and worked with his brother as a *vakil,* a solicitor, drawing up memorials and petitions, and earning up to three hundred rupees a month. Again, the written word was much easier for him than the spoken, and he did such work efficiently. But this was not what he had gone to London for, much less what he wanted to do with his life. And he was still required to take bribes, and to advance his own and his relatives' careers in the usual ways; for instance by acquiring powerful patrons.

In Bombay he had met Sir Pherozeshah Mehta, a Parsi lawyer who was known as the uncrowned king of the Bombay presidency, the Lion of Bombay, or Sir Ferocious, because of his dominant presence and domineering manner. Mehta was a good example of the kind of Indian Gandhi knew who was *not* weak, who admitted no connections with weakness, who embodied power, cunning, boldness, luxury, and largeness of style and appetite. He was an embodiment of the masculine principle, understood in cultural terms. In his autobiography, Gandhi remembers Mehta as always surrounded by a circle of admirers, and Gandhi "trembling with fear" while he addressed him. When Mehta encouraged him to speak louder, at a public meeting, Gandhi's voice "sank lower and lower."

There were many figures of power among the successful lawyers of India (like Motilal Nehru), men who had mastered the rules of the game of power, great orators with booming voices, Homeric laughter, cutting techniques of cross-examination, clever tricks, and dramatic changes of tone. Although Gandhi wanted to escape from weakness, he did not want to embody power. When Mehta organized a group of young lawyers who tested each other in imaginary legal situations, developing their skills in defending or accusing, without much scruple, Gandhi would not join.

In Porbandar, against his own wishes, Gandhi tried to intervene on his brother's behalf with Charles Ollivant, the British political adviser. Lakshmidas was secretary and adviser to Prince Bhavsingh, the heir to the throne, but the agent had formed a low opinion of him, and was ready to extend it to Gandhi himself. "Your brother is an intriguer," the Englishman said. "If he has anything to say, let him apply through the proper channel." He had Gandhi put out of his office (A:98). This is the event alluded to in this book's Introduction.

Gandhi was deeply humiliated; the sahib's peon had literally laid hands on him. "I had heard what a British officer was like, but up to now had never been face to face with one" (A:97). He sent for advice and help to Pherozeshah, but the latter sent the message that Gandhi must pocket the insult. Indeed Indian behavior pleased Gandhi no better than English. In Kathiawar, he said later, a brother would cut a brother's throat for a halfpenny; and "the atmosphere of intrigue was choking to me."

He was thinking about England. While he was in Rajkot he began to write his "Guide to London," employing quite a gay sophisticated tone. It must have aroused nostalgic feelings in him, considering his feelings about being home. On September 5, 1892—a year and a quarter after arriving in Bombay—he wrote to a friend regretting that he could not go abroad to practice because his brother was against it. Lakshmidas apparently said that Mohandas *could* get work without taking part in the *khutput* or intrigue; implying presumably that he was making too much moral fuss; but he himself was skeptical and unhappy (1:71).

The Gandhi family had always advanced itself by such intrigues, but he could not tolerate it. "This atmosphere appeared to me to be poisonous, and how to remain unscathed was a perpetual problem for me . . . without intrigue a ministership or judgeship was out of the question" (A:100). A call to go abroad was very welcome.

In April 1893 he sailed for Durban into Natal, readily grasping at the opportunity to do legal work there for a merchant called Dada Abdullah. The opportunity was offered him by a Kathiawari merchant. Dada Abdullah himself was born in Porbandar, and was one of those mostly Muslim merchants from West India who had gone to Mauritius or Zanzibar, and now on to Natal, following the indentured laborers in the sugar plantations, who would buy familiar Indian goods.

It was not a very advantageous move, as part of a legal career in India. Gandhi said in 1937 that he went to South Africa as a clerk. "I did not go anywhere, like Pherozeshah Mehta, charging Rs. 1000 [one thousand rupees] as a day's fee. I was to get £150 annually" (65:101). (In another place he says it was a hundred guineas.)

The opposition of his caste to such journeys was as great as ever, he said; "one man will do his best never to let me back in" (1:72). His commission was quite vague, moreover, and when he arrived in Durban, Gandhi's new employers wondered what to do with him. But it was an opportunity to escape from a bad situation—and to see more of the world—and Gandhi seized it eagerly. "I was fond of novel experiences. I loved to see fresh fields and pastures new" (S:37).

FOUR

DURBAN AND POLITICS

· 1893–1902 ·

During this period of his life Gandhi changes remarkably, and becomes a leader and a man of power. He escapes from the constraints and humiliations of his past, of his family's position, of his failed boyhood and adolescence, of being an Indian student in England, and of being an England-returned lawyer in India. He begins to design and implement the personality we know.

Gandhi left Bombay on April 19, 1893, aboard the steamer *Safari*, which took him as far as the former slave-trade center, Zanzibar, a major port of call for German as well as British ships trading with East Africa. This was the time of the Scramble for Africa, and the European countries were competing for commerce with the dark continent. In Zanzibar Gandhi had to wait about a week, and then embarked on the *Admiral* for the trip to Durban. The whole journey took him thirty-four days, but his subsequent trips to and from India were much speedier.

In Zanzibar the captain of the *Safari* took the unsuspecting Gandhi to patronize a native brothel; a visit that turned into another of the series of humiliations already discussed. When they saw how naive and innocent he was, Gandhi, in the eyes of the captain and his friend, was "enrolled among the fools of this world."

But the new theme in his life was something quite different. As he sailed from Bombay to Durban, he must have been preparing himself to see a new part of the empire—another British colony. No doubt he took some interest in Africa and the Africans, but that continent must have been to him, as it was to other people, primarily the site of British colonies, and the colonies of other European powers; and, before that, the destination of Indian traders setting out from Porbandar. Some Gandhis related to him had migrated to Natal, first to the town of Tongaat, and then Stanger, to trade, before he arrived.

However, Natal and the adjoining territories had their own African history. The Bantu-speaking peoples, spreading south, had slain or dispossessed the pygmy hunters they found there at the beginning of the seventeenth century. They arrived at Fish River in 1775, less than a hundred years before the English and Boers. One of their chiefs, Chaka, the Black Napoléon as Europeans called him, established a great empire, by bloodshed and torture, in the first half of the nineteenth century. He destroyed three hundred tribes, and extended his rule five hundred miles to the north and west. His story was told by H. Rider Haggard in more than one novel, very popular with English readers.

All this happened not long before, and during, the Indians' arrival in Natal. Chaka's successor, Dingaan, his brother and murderer, had been succeeded by Cetishwayo in 1856. The British led a Zulu War against him in 1879, and the king died in 1884. Zululand was annexed only in 1897, four years after Gandhi arrived. For the English, these events were part of the romance—or scandal—of empire.

Gandhi, and the Indians in general, seem to have paid little attention to that story, although many of them did regard the native Africans with alarm, as violent and uncivilized. (Kasturba was afraid of an attack by the Zulus who lived near the Gandhi colony of Phoenix.) But when one considers the image of Africa being propagated in the West, by Haggard and by quite different writers like Joseph Conrad in *The Heart of Darkness*, it is striking how little reflection of that horror is to be found in Gandhi's writings about Natal. Africa was never "the heart of darkness" to him.

Once a profitable crop was developed in the colony, the countryside was quickly transformed. By 1910 the coastal belt, which had been wooded, was planted with sugar cane, while inland what had been grassland became dark with trees; mostly the fast-growing wattle, cultivated after the 1880s for the tannin it yielded, and eucalyptus, cultivated to make railway sleepers and mine props. Natal had begun to flourish economically in the 1860s, when it was discovered how to grow sugar there.

The West Indies sugar industry had been severely injured in the middle of the nineteenth century by the ending of slave labor (proscribed by law in 1834) and sites for new plantations had to be sought. Sugar was first planted thirty-five miles north of Durban in 1850. But the English found that though the Zulus made good servants, they were unreliable as field workers, and so labor had to be brought in from outside. India supplied this labor to the sugar industries of the whole empire. Hundreds of thousands left that country for the West Indies, Mauritius, Fiji, as well as Africa.

Natal sent recruiting agents to India (where they had their greatest success in the south) and a steady stream of laborers began to arrive. The first shipload arrived from Madras in 1860, and by 1866 there were five thousand of these laborers in Natal. In a few years they were followed by merchants, who scented a new field for commerce, with the Indian laborers but also with the other races in South Africa.

With the merchants came racial conflict. The Indians turned out to be acceptable to the white colonists as plantation workers, but too competitive as traders. They were too parsimonious—they lived on "the smell of an oil-rag"; and too hardworking—the men were said to take their wives and go out weeding their patch even by moonlight. The Natal and Tanganyika English quickly grew to resent their success.

There was also something of a scandal among people of conscience about the conditions under which the Indian laborers lived, the primitive huts they had to build for themselves, and the high rate of suicide among them. In 1869, the year of Gandhi's birth, the Indian government renewed the contract to supply laborers, but stipulated that after the end of their indentures, the latter should have equality of status in that country. But in 1893, the year of Gandhi's arrival, Natal was granted responsible self-government; which meant, amongst other things, that the whites of the colony had the right to keep down the blacks and the browns.

It was a crucial test for the empire, to supervise such a mass movement from one continent to another, and to help the white settlers and plantation owners, but also to protect the laborers from exploitation by employers who were supposedly their fellow citizens. There was an immigration officer in Durban, and emigration officers in India, but the former in particular was little more than an agent for the planters.

The laborers were offered a five-year indenture, to begin the day they arrived in the colony; and, if they stayed a second period of five years as free laborers, a free passage home was available to them; or in place of the passage—up to 1890—a plot of land. Fifty-two percent of the laborers stayed on, and they or their children, called "colonial-born," often drifted north, to work in the Transvaal, the Boer colony, where there were—above all in Johannesburg—higher wages but worse conditions, especially as far as civil rights went. The Indians counted as foreigners there, and there was no one to protect their interests, amid the lawlessness of a mining-camp town.

Gold had been discovered on the Witwatersrand in the Transvaal in 1886, and Gandhi wrote in one of his pieces for the *Vegetarian*, "People here think of very little else than gold. The gold fever . . . has smitten the highest and the lowest, the spiritual teachers included" (1:287, first ed.). That gold was the source of the rapid prosperity of some of the Indians; up to 1891 the importation of gold into India was not officially controlled; and when it was, smuggling became rife. Diamonds moreover had been found at Kimberley in the Orange Free State in 1870.

Both the Great Powers and some economic adventurers based in the Cape province wanted to exploit this mineral wealth as fast as possible. The conflict between them and the largely conservative Boers would finally lead to war. Because of the Boers' fear of gold fever, the first finder had been sworn to secrecy, and the rush only began in 1884. By 1890 the easily workable veins had been exhausted, but just in time the MacArthur-Forrest cyanide process was invented, which had an extraction value of 90 percent as against 60 percent. This made lower-grade ore economically workable, and the process was declared "not dangerous to natives." With this, mining became more scientific and mechanical and efficient.

But in Natal, the major economic problems derived from sugar. The Indian merchants, nearly all Muslim and from Gujarat, like Dada Abdullah, began to arrive in Natal in numbers about 1875. They were called "passengers," meaning that they had paid for their passage, to distinguish them from the laborers. In that year there were ten thousand Indians in Natal, and ten Indian stores in Durban; by 1885 there were thirty thousand Indians and sixty stores—very few of which were *not* Indian. Dada Abdullah's company had fifteen branches in the 1890s, and also owned two steamships and traded directly with Germany and England. The suit for which Gandhi was engaged, against Abdullah's cousin, was for forty thousand pounds; an enormous sum, which had been accumulated in only twenty years. Such wealth brought certain kinds of power, but also resentments.

Natal

Gandhi arrived at the end of May. He wore a frock coat, striped trousers, and a black turban, the very picture of an Anglicized babu, a son of the empire. He sported a watch and chain, and attached to the latter was a locket that contained photographs of his father and his eldest brother (44:192).

Durban had a humid, semitropical climate, which must have reminded Gandhi of Porbandar. What he saw as his ship approached port we can imagine from what H. Rider Haggard says about Durban in *King Solomon's Mines*.

> It is a lovely coast all the way along from East London, with its red sandhills and wide sweeps of vivid green, dotted here and there with Kaffir kraals, and bordered by a ribbon of white surf which spouts up in pillars of foam where it hits the rocks. But just before you get to Durban there is a peculiar richness about it. There are the deep kloofs cut in the hills by the rushing rains of centuries, down which the rivers sparkle; there is the deepest green of the bush, growing as God planted it, and the other greens of the mealie-gardens and the sugar patches, while here and there a white house, smiling out at the placid sea, puts a finish and adds an air of homeliness to the scene.[1]

Haggard's description was published in 1886, only a few years before Gandhi arrived. (*King Solomon's Mines* was popular reading in the colony, and Gandhi's friend, Joseph Doke, wrote a novel that Gandhi enjoyed, strikingly like it.) The infusion of Boer and Bantu words in that description reminds us of the many layers of imperialist invasion, but even more significant is the invocation of nature—the bush growing "as God planted it." Men merely rest on the surface of Africa, in this picture. In England (and India) the land belonged to men, not to God—the land had been colonized, the soil had lost its otherness. Haggard said this explicitly, about England, and Gandhi had a similar feeling about India, in contrast with Africa and the Zulus.

Haggard's hero, Allan Quatermain, lives in Durban in a three-room shanty, built of green brick with a galvanized iron roof, while he accommodates visitors in a tent in a grove of orange trees. Thus the novelist stresses the primitiveness of the housing and the emptiness of the landscape; but Durban was estimated to have a population of twenty-seven thousand at that time; thirteen thousand whites, seven thousand Indians, and seven thousand Africans. By the end of Gandhi's time in South Africa, Durban was a resort town, with hotels and lodgings looking out on the sea, for Boer- and Englishwomen avoiding the cold months in Johannesburg; and with a large Indian population with a number of rich merchants, like the one who had hired Gandhi. Even in 1893 there was a charge of political electricity around the Indians.

The arrival of an Indian barrister was announced in the *Natal Mercury* on June 20, which reported also the rumor that he had already drafted an indictment of the colony's treatment of Indians, which had been presented by Dadabhai Naoroji to the secretary for the colonies in London.

Gandhi's new employer, Dada Abdullah, came to the quay and aboard the *Admiral* to meet him. The grand patriarchal figure of the "rich Muslim merchant" (it was already a social cliché) becomes pictorial to us in photographs of Dada Abdullah and Adam Jhaveri; calm and massive countenances, wearing white turbans and with white beards and whiskers so trimmed as to seem to flow out of the nostrils and frame the mouth.

Dada Abdullah greeted Gandhi with some reserve, or at least some doubt, wondering why he had been sent, and what use he could be put to. Gandhi noticed this, and also noticed that the Indians coming aboard to meet their friends, including his new and rich employer, "were not treated with much respect" by the whites (A:105). These were both parameters of his new situation. Perhaps in reaction to them, Gandhi began to act politically from the moment of arrival. Attending court within a week of landing, he was told by the judge to remove his turban; and left the building rather than comply; and wrote a letter of protest to a newspaper, which attracted considerable attention.

These were more clear-cut acts of protest than he had executed in his three years in London, or his many more years in Gujarat. Then, a few days after his arrival, Abdullah sent him in his own place to Pretoria where the case was being heard, the capital city of the Boer republic of the Transvaal. Gandhi started the journey by train, but this was a new and incomplete railway line, which had then been in operation only six months, and which ran only as far as Charlestown.

At Pietermaritzburg, moreover, a station up on the plateau that begins a few miles inland from the coast—and therefore a much colder place than Durban—Gandhi was ordered to leave the first-class compartment of the railway coach, because he was not white. He refused, and was put off the train, to pass the night on the platform. This was a replay, in somewhat more dramatic terms, of his being put out of the political agent's office in Porbandar.

He was indignant, and on behalf of his fellow Indians as well as himself. But he was also scared. Retelling the story in 1939, Gandhi wrote, "I was afraid for my very life. I entered the dark waiting room. There was a white man in the room. I was afraid of him" (48:171). He found the courage to act, as we shall see; but we must understand the fear as well as the courage.

He sent off a wire of complaint to the head office of the railway, and another wire to the Indians who were expecting him at Charleston. (As we know, he had a facile command of written language.) But he had also to decide something larger; for this society was more crudely racist than the others he had known. He had plenty of time that night to reflect on the path that lay ahead of him, if he remained and became politically active.

The next day he continued his journey by train to Charlestown, and then had to take a stagecoach (the service was run by George Heys and Co.) for a hundred and fifty miles from Charlestown to Johannesburg. On the first leg of the journey (before an overnight stop at Standerton) he refused to get down from his seat at the guard's command, and was beaten and threatened. He clung to his seat, while the driver struck him and pulled him down and threw him off. (The policy of simply holding on, ready to let one's wrists be broken rather than let go, was one he recommended later, for the passive resisters of the salt campaign, in 1930. It was a physical equivalent of his "eternal negative.") After he arrived in Pretoria, he convened a meeting of the Indians there and discussed their situation—no longer inhibited by the shyness that had made him largely voiceless up to now.

Why this change? In his autobiographical writings, and in letters, Gandhi himself indicates that it was because there was nobody else for him to leave the task to, and so he had to take it on. In a letter of July 5, 1894, he wrote to Dadabhai Naoroji, "I am the only available person who can handle the question . . . [even though] I am yet inexperienced and young and . . . quite liable to make mistakes. The responsibility undertaken is quite out of my ability . . . . You will, therefore, oblige me very greatly if you will kindly direct and guide me and make necessary suggestions" (1:106).

The historian, Maureen Swan, however, has produced evidence that—to the contrary—some Indians in Natal, and more in the Cape Province, were already politically active. Both Gandhi and she could be right. Those Swan speaks of were political beginners, and in need of leadership. From Gandhi's point of view, he saw in Africa none of those figures, so much better qualified than he—like the Bombay lawyers—who had intimidated him before.[2]

Following Gandhi's lead, most biographers have taken the night on the Maritzburg railway platform to be an absolutely pivotal event; but it is worth noting that his decision was simply to persist—it was another of his negative decisions, not to return to India. It was not followed by more political activity than before, rather by less. He wrote letters to the newspapers, and gave a talk about cleanliness and honesty in business, but initiated no political action. These months in Pretoria were a time of reading for him—notably of Tolstoy's *The Kingdom of God Is within You*—and for Gandhi reading was always a sign of political disengagement. He says he read some eighty books, and many of them about religion.

With some Theosophists he read Vivekananda's *Raja Yoga* and Patanjali's *Yoga Sutra*, and for a time learned two or three verses of the Bhavagad Gita every day. He also conducted an unsuccessful New Age experiment in eating nothing but "vital foods"—uncooked grains, vegetables, and fruits. These things occupied his time, rather than politics.

Of course, *The Kingdom of God Is within You* was radical reading. Gandhi says about Tolstoy's book: "I was at that time a believer in violence. Reading it cured me of my skepticism and made me a firm believer in Ahimsa" (37:261) [written in 1928, on the centenary of Tolstoy's birth]). But that skepticism and then belief was religious rather than political. Joseph Doke says that Gandhi also read Tolstoy's famous story, "Ivan Ilych," in 1893—it would be easily related to the book, in moral tone—and that suggests the level of imagination at which Gandhi was responding to his reading. This is not a matter of interpretation. He himself says, "But I did nothing beyond occasionally talking to the Indians of Pretoria on the subject" (S:39). And, "During the first year, therefore, I was merely the witness and the victim of these wrongs. I *then* awoke to a sense of my duty" [My emphasis] (S:38).

He ran up against racial prejudice and injustice in Pretoria, but did not translate the incidents into political campaigns. There were regulations forbidding Indians to use certain footpaths in the town, and Gandhi was kicked off such a path near President Kruger's house; but he refused to sue his assailant, saying he would never go to law for a merely personal grievance.

Many of his interests had to do with Nonconformist and evangelical Christianity, which attracted him in some ways. The attorney Gandhi had to work with in Pretoria, Mr. Baker, was a Methodist, who helped train missionaries for the South African General Mission. A friendly Quaker called Albert Coates invited Gandhi to prayer meetings with some ladies, Miss Bragg and Miss Harris. They hoped to convert him. Gandhi gave Coates his religious diary every week, and the ladies used to narrate their "sweet experiences" and talk about the peace they had found (A:122).

When he moved back to Durban, one of Gandhi's acquaintances was a man called Downes, a Seventh Day Adventist who was also an enthusiast for the Simple Life. He stayed with Gandhi in 1894, and announced a lecture on that topic at a chapel in Mercury Lane, with Gandhi presiding. As the latter had warned him, Downes drew a small audience—only one listener when he began, and not ten by the end—but the incident is interesting, because it shows the alliance of Nonconformist Christianity with the Simple Life, and Gandhi's interest in both (85:165).

Gandhi was also interested in other forms of religion. In April 1895 he paid a visit to a Trappist monastery at Mariann Hill, and was very impressed both by the education the monks were giving the native Africans, in several kinds of industrial work, and by the ascetic life of the monks and nuns. They were famous for maintaining silence, even with each other, and that was a rule Gandhi was to apply himself later, in modified form. They made their own furniture, used the cheapest cutlery, and renounced meat. He had heard about the Trappists' vegetarianism in *The Perfect Way in Diet*, and wrote about them for the *Vegetarian* in London. It was from them that Gandhi and his friends learned how to make sandals, when they experimented with the simple life.

He was in touch with Theosophists in Pretoria, and corresponded with Edward Maitland until the latter's death in 1897. Many colonists were Orientalist in some measure. Mr. Laughton, a Durban lawyer whom Gandhi consulted quite often about matters of Roman or Dutch law, on more than one of those occasions brought out his treasured copy of *The Song Celestial*, which his father had annotated with parallel passages from the New Testament (79:279).

There was thus a spirit of experiment among some of the Natal colonists, even in intellectual and spiritual matters. Perhaps the most striking proof of that is the case of the Anglican Bishop Colenso, famous for his book on the Pentateuch, which was condemned as heretical, and for his liberal interpretation of the sacramental and supernatural elements in Christianity.

John William Colenso, born in 1814, was appointed bishop of Natal in 1854. He saw his prime mission as being to the Zulus rather than the colonists. He started a school for chiefs' sons in 1856, and produced a Zulu dictionary, grammar, and readers. He was ready to adapt Christianity to Africans to some degree; he accepted even polygamous candidates for baptism in the church. He also became great friends with Theophilus Shepstone, the diplomatic agent to the native tribes, who set up the location policy of ruling through tribes and chiefs. Both Englishmen were deeply interested in Zulu culture.

Colenso's policies were innovative; they tended toward setting up autonomous missionary churches; and a long-term result of the controversy surrounding him was the future Anglican Communion of independent national churches, which was in its turn a forerunner of the idea of a British Commonwealth of nations. But in the immediate future, Colenso was tried for heresy in 1863, and in 1866 excommunicated. However, his admirers in Natal continued to consider him their bishop, and rebelled against the dean who was officially in charge at Pietermaritzburg Cathedral. Colenso died in 1883, just ten years before Gandhi arrived.

Indians too felt freer in Africa than at home. Gandhi quoted an Indian woman friend who wrote in every letter that in India she felt in prison, because of the rules of caste and sect. And of another returnee he wrote, "She will not be able to live there with that spiritual and physical freedom which she enjoys here" (10:312). When it came time for the Phoenix settlers to sail home, he gave instructions for the children to be taught, on the ship, to make obeisance to their elders, to eat with the right hand only, to sit cross-legged on the floor, and so on. For both the English and the Indians, the colony was a place of freedom and experiment. The greatest example of that was Gandhi himself, as we shall see in his New Age activities.

In November 1894 Gandhi wrote two letters to the *Natal Mercury*. One was about the Esoteric Christian Union, of which he was the official representative. He announced the availability of some of their books, and said he would like to chat with those interested. "The system of thought expounded by the books advertised is not by any means a new system but a rediscovery of the old, presented in a form acceptable to the modern mind" (1:139–40). This system taught universal values, and was not based on mere facts, and so was for those people dissatisfied by materialism.

The second letter said that the phenomenal success of the Theosophical Society was a sign of a general reaction against materialism. It referred to modern civilization's invention of the most terrible weapons of destruction, the awful growth of anarchism, the frightful disputes between capital and labor, the wanton and diabolical cruelty inflicted on innocent, dumb, living animals. This was the rhetoric of Theosophy, indeed of the New Age. Clearly Gandhi had even then only a short distance to move, conceptually, to the cultural radicalism for which he is famous.

An author Gandhi seems to have read with enthusiasm at about this time was Henry Drummond, born in Scotland, and a lecturer in science at a Free Church College. His *Natural Law in the Spiritual World* of 1883, translated into many other languages, argued that the laws of the spiritual world are also the (undiscovered) laws of nature. His chapters have epigrams from Ruskin and the Bible. This was a message easily combined with that of Theosophy.

Drummond's *Ascent of Man*, a popular reversal of Darwin and affirmation of creative evolution, must have appealed to all New Agers. The struggle for life is only the villain in the drama of evolution, says Drummond; the struggle for the life of others, *altruism,* is also part of the story. We must save sociology, by giving it spiritual values. Moreover, he says—like Maitland and Kingsford—that hitherto the world has belonged to the father. Henceforth it will belong to the mother. This New Age and feminist version of evolution is a subduing of social Darwinism's grim materialist logic to progressive and optimistic faith.

Meanwhile, Gandhi drew some attention in Natal by his letters to the newspapers. As early as September 1893, he had written to the *Natal Advertiser,* complaining about a leading article in that paper that had spoken of "the wily wretched Asian traders," and "the real canker that is eating into the very vitals of the community," and "these parasites who live a semi-barbarous life" (1:74). The passage that follows is Gandhi at his most literary—his least New Age.

> But they spend nothing, says the leading article under discussion. Don't they? I suppose they live on air or sentiments. We know that Becky lived on nothing a year in *Vanity Fair.* And here a whole class seems to have been found doing the same. It is to be presumed they have to pay nothing for shop rents, taxes, butcher's bills, grocer's bills, clerks' salaries, etc., etc. One would indeed like to belong to such a blessed class of traders, especially in the present critical condition of the trade all the world over. . . . It seems, on the whole, that their simplicity, their total abstinence from intoxicants, their peaceful and above all their businesslike and frugal habits, which should serve as a recommendation, are really at the bottom of all this contempt and hatred of the poor Indian traders. And they are British subjects . . . . Is this Christian-like? . . . Is this civilization? I pause for a reply (1:76).

Several months later, having succeeded at the legal task given him, and having brought the two parties to agree out of court, Gandhi was ready to return from Durban to Porbandar, when he read in a newspaper of a proposed act to disfranchise the Indians of Natal. He read this at the very last minute, by his account, both of the legislative process and of his stay in the country. (Some scholars feel that he compressed and dramatized the sequence of events.) The article said, in explanation of the action proposed: "The Asiatic comes of a race impregnated with an effete civilization with not an atom of knowledge of the principles or traditions of representative government. As regards his instinct and training he is a political infant of the most backward type, from whom it is an injustice to expect that he should . . . have any sympathy with our political aspirations."[3]

That no Indians had opposed the bill was urged as proof of their political unfitness, and indeed, when Abdullah's attention was drawn to the article, he only said, according to Gandhi, "We are after all lame men, being unlettered. We generally take in newspapers simply to ascertain the daily market rates, etc. What can we know of legislation? Our eyes and ears are the European attorneys here" (A:139). But Gandhi told him and his other merchant sponsors that they must fight this insult to Indian culture. They said that if so, he must lead them in the struggle, and he agreed. *This* was the crucial decision; to stay in Natal, to devote his energies to politics. He refused to be paid for such public work, but asked the merchants to guarantee him enough legal work to earn three hundred pounds a year.

He was immediately immersed in action. On June 27, he sent the government telegrams asking that the Franchise Law Amendment Act not be considered by the legislative assembly until the Indian petition was presented, and was granted two days grace. On the twenty-eighth he submitted a petition, signed by five hundred people, asking for a commission of inquiry. On the twenty-ninth he led a deputation to the premier, asking for a further week's delay, in order to present their case more exhaustively. On July 1 he addressed a meeting of Indians. On the third he led another deputation, to the governor. From this point on, the pace of Gandhi's life was to be of this frantic order.

It is worth noting that in that first petition, Gandhi cited Sir Henry Maine, Sir George Birdwood, Professor Mueller, and Sir Thomas Munro, the standard Western authorities on the dignity of Indian culture, the people he was still citing at the end of his time in South Africa. He was already an Orientalist.

The issue of the vote, as Gandhi conceived it, was broader than electoral politics. It might have been called a cultural or historical issue; were the Indians first-class citizens of the empire, or were they in Africa merely to supplement the English—to do the dirty work *they* would not? In the pamphlet, "Indian Franchise: An Appeal to Every Briton in South Africa," of December 16, 1895, Gandhi cited the Indian Immigrants Commission Report, which had said that white men would not settle in South Africa merely to become hewers of wood and drawers of water.

Every Englishman now identified himself, outside the British Isles, as upper caste—even as aristo-military—not as a trader. Lord Selborne, who succeeded Sir Alfred Milner as high commissioner in 1905, was to say, "What is wanted more than anything else in these two colonies are British subjects, who, if need be, can fight, which is the same thing as saying white British subjects. For in these colonies a white man must always be a fighter, whereas this is the one thing the Asiatic can never be, both owing to the peculiar circumstances of the country and to the fact that the Asiatics who come here are not of any martial race . . . but as trader the white British subject is hopelessly beaten out of the field by the Asiatic."[4] This was a definition of the cultural psychology of both the British and the Indians. The Indians were Banias, the English were Kshatriyas.

But the history Gandhi had been taught made the English out to be traders, heroes of free trade and the work ethic, a mutually competitive "people" who defended themselves against both their native aristocracy and militarist autocracies like France and Spain. A good deal of Gandhi's account of the Indians in South Africa amounts to an argument that by 1900 *they* had more of the work ethic—of the spirit of *Robinson Crusoe*—than the South African English did, and so better deserved to represent the modern world.

The trading Indians who were not merchants (that term was kept for wholesalers) were either hawkers, carrying the merchants' goods for sale on their backs, or *dukawallahs,* keepers of a shop or *duka*. The native Africans bought and sold almost exclusively with the Indians. We have one description of an Indian duka in Africa.

> Inside, the store was dark. Heavy striped blankets, the personal necessity of the Zulus, hung over wires stretched from wall to wall, next to colorful silks and cottons, the material for Indian saris and dhouries. Bags of *dal,* beans and masala powder, spices of the East, held up in confused array by bags of green and crushed mealies, *m'dombies* and samp. Bunches of Natal tobacco hung from the ceiling; green mealie cobs heaped on the floor with heavy stalks of bananas. The counter was heavy with cheap Indian jewelery.

The writer goes on to describe the rich and mingled smells of such a place.[5] It was in such a store, in Tongaat, that Gandhi's nephew, Maganlal, began his life in Natal.

Most of the shopkeepers and hawkers were not politically active. And in the immediate future Gandhi was asking for quite limited benefits for the Indians politically. He explicitly and repeatedly renounced all political ambition on their behalf, saying that the property qualification would prevent their theoretical franchise from counting politically, and that no Indian would object to the imposition of even a larger qualification of that kind, or an educational qualification. He three times kept his own name off the voters' lists. What he objected to in the franchise bill was the cultural insult; it was the honor of India he was concerned to preserve, not any democratic right (2:305).

The political community that Gandhi began by serving has been estimated by Maureen Swan to amount to two thousand in Natal (which meant only 3.5 percent of the Indian males there) and to one thousand in the Transvaal (which meant 15 percent of the same group there). The wage workers and the hawkers and so on, were not represented in this politics or its institutions, such as the Indian Committee, the Natal Indian Congress, and the Transvaal British Indian Association.

The merchants had petitioned the British government as early as 1885, and began systematic political activity in 1891, as Swan tells us. It was in 1891 that they were expelled from the other Boer Republic, the Orange Free State, and began to feel threatened even in the Transvaal. They appealed to the British empire, of which they were citizens, against the treatment they received in those foreign lands, where they had money invested. This was a source of great anxiety: one of them had property worth as much as fifty thousand pounds in the Transvaal in 1890. They collected a list of their grievances, which they sent to the merchants of Bombay, and in 1892 they prepared a pamphlet and wrote to the colonial secretary. They objected to being identified with the indentured laborers, though they included in their protests some account of how the latter were treated.

Such was the political situation into which Gandhi stepped when he agreed to stay in Natal. He acted energetically on behalf of his masters, the group led by Dada Abdullah. It was for them he preserved the franchise, and created political institutions to resist the oppression of the English and the Boers. But—after a time—he also took up the cause of the colonial-born and the indentured.

As we have seen, however, he was not professionally or at least by primary vocation, a politician. He wanted to change the world more profoundly than political means could encompass. He had spent a lot of his time in Pretoria reading about religion, and the book that had the greatest effect on him was *The Kingdom of God Is within You.*

It is now time for society as a whole to change its life, Tolstoy wrote, because material conditions now make that possible, and because the contradiction between Christian ideals and social facts, above all those of war, is now so great. There is a contrast between our (New Age) consciousness and our life, and the latter needs to catch up with the former. But this does not mean that people of culture should be our leaders, for Tolstoy found culture in that sense a kind of caste privilege, which lost people their naïveté, their capacity to act. "The indefiniteness, if not the insincerity, of the relation of the cultured men of our times to this phenomenon [war and conscription] is striking."

A man need only make the new life concept his own, Tolstoy said, for all his chains to fall off. But this means that he must not let the state make moral decisions for him. Indeed, a man must never take an oath of obedience to an army or to the state, however Socialist the latter may be, because the individual belongs to God. A Christian need not, must not, pass judgment on a government, but he must for himself refuse to support it. "Christianity in its true meaning destroys the state." That is why Christ was crucified.

These were ideas that had little to do with the kind of political work Gandhi was about to embark on; and in 1894 he could find little scope of expression for them, or even his own version of them (which was somewhat different from Tolstoy's). But they were at work within him from this time on, and dearer to him than those he did first act on.

The first thing he did, as we saw, was to organize very large petitions first to the government of the colony (which had newly been granted responsible government) to delay the disfranchizing legislation; and then to the secretary for the colonies in London. Then he set up the Natal Indian Congress, superficially on the model of the Indian National Congress, but described by Devanesen as being more like the National Union of Uitlanders in the Transvaal or the Irish Association in Natal. Like them, the NIC was an immigrant organization struggling to defend the rights of a minority.

What Gandhi had to do for the merchants of Durban and—increasingly as time passed—for his other fellow countrymen in Natal, was to make them engage in democratic politics of a reformist and protest kind. Most of them had everything to learn about how formally to debate an issue, how to draw up a petition or a constitution, simply how to stay interested—for instance, to keep paying or collecting from others the institution's dues. This was a radically new activity for them, though it was merely a belated entry into nineteenth-century parliamentary politics.

He had to teach the members of the Natal Indian Congress how to debate, how to listen and speak in an orderly fashion, how to raise points of order, how to amend motions and abide by votes, and even how to keep the records and balance the accounts of a political institution.

Private Life

When he decided to stay in Natal, Gandhi thought it important to live in some style. It was the source of much anti-Indian feeling amongst the whites that even the rich Indians did not, for instance, keep a horse and carriage, that they "lived on the smell of an oil-rag," as noted above, and that their streets and the outside of their houses were dirty. This was one of the ways in which the Indians were thought to resemble the Jews, and British anti-Semitism extended itself to cover them.

Gandhi took a house on the beach, called Beach Grove Villa; a semidetached, two-storeyed house, with an iron gate and a side entry with a passage. He was next door to the attorney general, who became later the prime minister. He wore a lounge suit and a turban to go to his office; and a wing collar, a striped tie, and brightly shined shoes. This was the most highly Westernized period of his life. He set up what he later referred to as a gymnasium in his house; we know of swings and parallel bars in the backyard. Some of Gandhi's clerks and other Indians lived with him. One we shall hear of again was Vincent Lawrence, a South Indian Roman Catholic, and Franciscan tertiary.

His house had a lounge, a drawing room, a dining room with eight chairs, and five bedrooms. In the bookcase were the works of Tolstoy, Madame Blavatsky, Edward Maitland, the Koran, the Bible, and the biographies of leaders in Indian public life. In his bedroom were photographs of his father and elder brother. In the evenings other Indians came to talk, and a few Europeans, notably missionaries. There was discussion of political and religious issues, joined in by Gandhi's friends and employees; and by Sheikh Mehtab.

When Gandhi left India for Natal, he did not take Kasturba and his sons, and in 1894 when he decided to stay in Durban, he did not send for them. But he did, in that year, send for Sheikh Mehtab, whom he asked to help him in the running of the house; there was a good deal of hospitality, and a variety of guests, as has been noted. Mehtab received board and lodging, and a little pocket money.

How he had been earning a living in Rajkot, and what kind of a career he had had or attempted, since Gandhi's return from London, is not known. We can only assume that he had drifted; and perhaps the reputation of South Africa as the site of a gold rush attracted him; though, if so, he seems not to have acted on the attraction, since he stayed in Durban. We see again his lesser energy and decisiveness compared with Gandhi, even in worldly matters, and this suggests to us another strand in the complex connection between the two men. It also indicates the change in their respective strengths that came with time. By this point, Gandhi was more the figure of masculine force, at least in political and economic terms.

In his autobiography, Gandhi offers no explanation for his sending for his trouble-making friend—whom indeed he does not name—except that he introduces the topic by saying: "A good servant is essential in every household. But I have never known how to keep anyone as a servant" (A:162). The implication seems to be that Gandhi found it difficult to exercise ordinary authority, and that Mehtab could manage servants, not having any such problem. "I had a friend as companion and help, and a cook who had been a member of the family. . . . The companion was very clever and, I thought, faithful to me." This cleverness was of course not "intellectual ability" but a sinister kind of deviousness.

In the same mischief-making way as before, Mehtab made trouble and betrayed Gandhi in a number of ways. One of the most striking was a repetition of what had happened in Rajkot; he cost Gandhi the trust and affection of another close friend, a loss Gandhi later tried but failed to retrieve. This time it was another of the Indians living in the house, against whom Mehtab sowed seeds of suspicion in Gandhi's mind, so that a quarrel ensued, and the other man left. A pattern of suspicion, jealousy, conspiracy, accusation—alleging a treachery the accuser himself was to be guilty of—such was the life of the emotions, of the "exclusive relationship," as Gandhi knew it. It is no wonder he felt he had to renounce that life.

Soon after the third man left the house, "heartbroken," the cook came to Gandhi's law office in the middle of the day, and insisted that his employer come home; where he found that Mehtab had a prostitute in his room—and not for the first time. Gandhi told Mehtab to leave the house, and a bitter quarrel took place, Mehtab at least shouting, and laying hands on Gandhi. One of the other men, Vincent Lawrence, had to intervene to protect Gandhi. Mehtab threatened to "expose" him; this is an enigmatic word, but it seems most likely that he meant only "ridicule."

Mehtab—though Gandhi does not tell us this—took refuge with Camroodin, one of the richest merchants in Durban, in some employment vaguely defined as "master of ceremonies"; some of such merchants regularly served dinner to fifty or more guests. M. C. Camroodin was the principal Indian firm in South Africa, 1880–1910, owning eighteen to twenty thousand pounds of property, and extending twenty-five thousand pounds in credit.[6]

According to Gandhi, that was the end of the relationship between him and Sheikh Mehtab. But we shall see that each of the two men continued for some years after to have his eye on the other's activities, and to act upon him. Payne says that Gandhi sometimes made inquiries about Mehtab; and circumstances brought them together, willy-nilly.[7]

The episode just described must have taken place in 1895 or 1896, for in the latter year Gandhi asked leave of his merchant friends to go back to Gujarat for six months, in order to bring his wife and children to settle in Natal.

Durban to Calcutta 1896

As he sailed toward India, on the *Pongola*, Gandhi must surely have been reviewing his emotional history, and pondering its lessons. He was now going to install Kasturba in the Beach Grove Villa—in some sense in Sheikh Mehtab's place. It was not to be, in the short run, any happier a relationship. The successful episodes in Gandhi's emotional life—and there were to be some very successful episodes—were with people who got to know him after he had grown up.

His relationship to Mehtab was already fifteen or sixteen years old. His comments on the most recent episode, in his autobiography, written twenty years later, are worth commenting on. "The companion was very clever and, I thought, faithful to me." Mehtab had flattered Gandhi by the implication that however "bad" he was to the rest of the world, he would be faithful to Gandhi. This must have given Gandhi a sense of power; the idea was implicit in his earlier defense of the other in Rajkot. He was going to cure this richly endowed friend of his moral weaknesses, and so—though this was only implicit—Gandhi would share in or appropriate those strengths that he envied him. *Moha* (enthusiasm, self-intoxication) was a failing Gandhi often accused himself of—he was carried away, past all prudence or reason, by the excitement of what he was doing. In another place he says, "But I would ride all the horses, and that is why God ordained my fall" (12:210).

To continue: "He [Mehtab] became jealous of an office clerk who was staying with me." Jealousy implies again that Mehtab felt he was competing against others for Gandhi's affection or at least attention—that even in their acting upon each other, the initiative or the power was in some ways with Gandhi.

"This evil genius"; it would be wrong to stress the word *genius,* but Gandhi does say the friend was very clever; and the phrase is anyway a highly dramatic one, which will remind us of "tragedy." Again "I believed in his faithfulness to me. . . . Infatuation had completely blinded me." Infatuation here means not necessarily personal fondness for Sheikh Mehtab, but "the power to keep me in the dark and to mislead me." Power, darkness (implying blindness) misleading—we note again the quasi-religious rhetoric (A:164).

From the same source we take the idea that, but for this break, Gandhi would never have been able to dedicate himself to service—"the companion would have obstructed my progress." He also said, "The incident purged my life of much impurity." It is not possible to know what he means by "impurity" there (39:487). But it sounds as though Mehtab's mockery and hedonism had drawn Gandhi in his wake, and prevented his committing himself to his "experiments with truth."

Moreover, although Gandhi describes these events, or at least their importance, so frankly and fully in some ways, he does not say that this companion was Sheikh Mehtab. He must have had his reasons—perhaps several, and perhaps just points of decorum—for suppressing the name; he avoids people's names in other parts of the autobiography. But one effect of the suppression on us must be to enhance the emotional resonance and suggestiveness of the episode. Perhaps because we know so little about Mehtab, and perhaps because what we do know is "merely" personal or anecdotal, he has been overlooked by most biographers. But he is surely one of the three or four keys to Gandhi's emotional development.

This 1896 passage to India is also a suitable place to mention Gandhi's correspondence with Raychandbhai about fundamental questions of religion; a correspondence that Gandhi initiated while in South Africa, and that he said convinced him that Hinduism was a religion in no way inferior to Christianity. The attentions of the missionaries in Pretoria induced a "mental churning" in Gandhi and he drew up a list of twenty-seven fundamental questions about religions, which he sent to his friend. Raychandbhai replied, on October 20, 1894; and in a later letter of February 15, 1895, boiled down Jainism into six tenets—tenets that he himself then used as the subject of a religious poem. So we see that the two men stimulated each other in their work. Unfortunately, Gandhi lost some of Raychandbhai's letters, and a manuscript, on a bus in London, so we don't know as much as we would like of what he said.

In the letter of September 20, 1894, Raychandbhai wrote in answer to the question, What is the soul? that there is an entity called the Atman, whose essence is knowledge; and that *Ishvar* (God) is another name for the Atman—Ishvar is *not* a different being of greater power. Not all knowledge derives from the Vedas (as the Arya Samaj claimed) and the Jain thinkers have revealed truths as deep as or deeper than the Hindu teachers. As for Christianity's claims to ultimate truth, "No country has gone so deep as India and discovered a religious path which can rival the one discovered by the great seers of India." Christianity does not give a true account of karma or the *anadi* (without a beginning) state of the soul (32:593–98). This promotion of East over West was something Gandhi wanted to hear; it is surely one of the things that made him prefer Raychandbhai over Tolstoy and Ruskin in matters of religion.

A third letter, of October 9, 1896, discussed the question of whether Gandhi should move back to India or stay in South Africa. On the one hand, Raychandbhai says, Gandhi is free in South Africa from "routine preoccupations," and can stay aloof from "personal considerations." (This presumably refers to the caste and family intrigues.) On the other hand, he may not get the right companionship, conducive to his moral growth. (This—judging by the date—may have some reference to Sheikh Mehtab.)[8]

South Africa was certainly an environment opposite to the one Raychandbhai had chosen for himself. Mystical tradition contrasted with Western-style experiment. Raychandbhai's disciples felt unutterable things in his presence, and greeted him with the traditional taking of his dust or prostration before him. Gandhi did not allow that from his followers, at least in South Africa, where he was Europeanized.

Raychandbhai and Gandhi met in Gujarat, during this six-month stay. We don't know what passed between them, but it seems likely that they and the friend who first brought them together, Pranjivan Mehta, were all in fairly regular contact. Soon thereafter, in 1899, Raychandbhai's religious career came to a climax in a legendary period of wandering and mystical experiences in the rocky countryside of Idar, one of the Jain holy lands of Kathiawar, full of temples and sadhus' caves, and sacred palm-leaf manuscripts, where he preached to devoted *munis* or disciples. (There were seven munis, to whom he addressed discourses, and he appeared and disappeared from before them semimiraculously.)

Dr. Mehta was an officer of Idar State at that time—chief medical officer—and it was he who invited Raychandbhai there. The latter accepted on condition that his sojourn in Idar be kept secret, especially from the orthodox Jains; he was always at odds with the ecclesiastical hierarchy, like other religious innovators. He died of dysentery—in Rajkot—in April 1901.

Raychandbhai's influence or at least presence in Gandhi's life persisted. On a later visit to London, Gandhi was carrying some of the other man's letters, and a translation of one of his poems. A son of Raychandbhai's corresponded with Gandhi later, and one of his disciples, Punchabbhai, who lived in Ahmedabad, constituted himself a financial adviser to Gandhi's ashram there: he found the land on which the ashram was to be built, guaranteed its credit, and got things at a good price (51:282). And at least one of the ashram hymns was of Raychandbhai's composition: one with a liberal moral message, despite his own asceticism. "Innocent joy may be derived from anywhere," including boys and girls playing together. "There cannot be one rule for this. Life is full of risks and will continue to be so" (82:425).

India

While in India in 1896, Gandhi lived for two months of Chaturmas, the penitential rainy season, with his oldest brother in Rajkot. The daily religious ritual in Lakshmidas's house, from four to six PM, was conducted by Nathuram Sharma, who had made a Gujarati translation of the Gita. Everyone assembled on the lower veranda to listen, and Mohandas also took part in the joint family religious life. He read the *Ramayana* to himself in the afternoons, and to the household in the evenings.[9]

His activity was more than merely political. He took the children for walks, and taught them to sing the English National Anthem, in preparation for the queen-empress's Diamond Jubilee in the following year. He also helped the state of Rajkot prepare to fight the infection of a plague; one had broken out in Bombay, and it was feared it might spread. Public health was a cause he held dear.

He was often at cross-purposes with his brother, who was eager to amass wealth, but at the same time improvident (404). Lakshmidas wanted Mohandas to rebuild the family treasury, restoring the jewels that had been gradually disposed of (partly to send Mohandas to England) since their father's death. He also disapproved of his younger brother engaging in the plague work. He feared Mohandas might become infected and die, leaving Lakshmidas with extra responsibilities. The younger brother bought an insurance policy of ten thousand rupees, to allay his elder's anxieties. It was an American agent who sold him the policy, which can remind us of the many ways the modern world was entering traditional India, under the sponsorship of the Anglo-Saxon nations.

He talked with Haridas Vora (whose daughter was to marry Harilal Gandhi) about nature cure, and took over the nursing of his own brother-in-law in his last illness—a task to which Gandhi's sister was not equal. He talked to Pherozeshah Mehta, who told him that he would not succeed as a lawyer in Bombay. Mehta had established a "moot" where lawyers might try out sharp practices and tricky cases; an idea that Gandhi disliked, because it made the law into the temple of untruth.

He made some speeches and wrote some public letters, about the condition of the Indians in Natal. He wanted to organize protests in India that could persuade the viceroy to intervene with the colonial secretary in London. Seeking political sponsors for this cause, he spent October 12 in Pune, and met the famous nationalist leaders, Tilak, Gokhale, and Bhandarkar. In Calcutta also he briefly, and humbly, met the leaders of Bengal.

Above all he wrote a pamphlet, usually referred to because of its color as the Green Pamphlet, entitled "The Grievances of British Indians in South Africa." It began: "This is an appeal to the Indian public on behalf of the hundred thousand Indians in South Africa. I have been commissioned by the leading members representing that community in South Africa to lay before the public in India the grievances" (2:2). Again the main burden of his argument was that South African law treated the Indians as barbarians; for instance by requiring registration. "There is a very good reason for requiring registration of a native, in that he is yet being taught the dignity and necessity of labor. The Indian knows it and he is imported because he knows it." This pamphlet aroused a lot of attention, by the specific description it gave of Indian sufferings, and ten thousand copies were printed. (Gandhi enlisted the help of children in Rajkot in mailing it out, and paid them with used stamps, of which he had apparently made a collection.) The "Pioneer," in Allahabad, printed a summary of the pamphlet, and the international news agency, Reuters, sent newspapers across the world a three-line sensationalist account of what Gandhi had said, which was printed in Natal.

On November 12 Gandhi got a wire from Durban, asking him to return immediately, because the parliament was to open in January, and the Transvaal *Volksraad* was recommending that Indians be confined to "locations." There was a lot of fierce anti-Indian feeling, much of it aroused by the news of the Green Pamphlet.

It is worth noting that while Gandhi was in India, at the beginning of this surge of anti-Indian anger, in September 1896, Sheikh Mehtab wrote a letter to the *Natal Advertiser*. Its tone was jocular, but it was a serious intervention on Gandhi's side. The newspaper had asked, on September 16, "Was this [a passage from the Green Pamphlet] written by Mr Gandhi?" Mehtab, writing from Sheth Abdul Cadir Camroodin's address in fashionable Stanford Hill, replied, "Why do you ask? Have you not read the 'Open Letter' and 'An Appeal,' which were published by Mr Gandhi in Natal?"[10] In politics, then, the two men remained allies.

Bombay to Durban

The family sailed from Bombay on November 30, on the *Courland*, a steamship recently purchased by Dada Abdullah—another mark of how the Indians' wealth was putting them on the same level as the English. It was a 760-ton ship, and carried 255 passengers. By Gandhi's wish, as part of his plan to improve the Indian image in South Africa, they wore Parsi coats and saris, and shoes and stockings, the most respectable Indian costume in the eyes of the colonists.

The *Courland* arrived in Durban Harbor at the same time as the *Naderi*, which also carried Indian immigrants. It was said in Durban that there were eight hundred immigrants on the two together. (Harry Sparks was the leader in spreading this alarmist rumor.) In fact there were five hundred, and, by Gandhi's count only sixty-two were men looking for jobs.

On Christmas Day there were the usual celebrations, and Gandhi was invited to give a speech at the dinner. "I spoke on Western civilization. I knew that this was not an occasion for a serious speech. But mine could not be otherwise. I took part in the merriment, but my heart was in the combat that was going on in Durban. For I was the real target" (A:189).

We must therefore imagine the Indian-owned steamer anchored in the Durban Harbor, and Gandhi rising from the Christmas dinner table to "deplore the civilization of which the Natal whites were the fruit, and which they represented and championed." To taste the full flavor of the event, we should note that the ship had been held in quarantine for a week already; and that paramilitary groups of townsmen were marching up and down the quays shouting slogans of hostility to the Indians.

Gandhi described Western civilization as being, "unlike the Eastern, predominantly based on force." In reply, the captain asked how Gandhi could exert nonviolent force against the violent, and "smiled, possibly distrustfully," at his answer (A:189). According to Erikson, the captain actually asked what Gandhi would do if faced by a lynch mob when he got ashore. Gandhi of course said he hoped he would forgive them.[11]

Natal

The ship was kept in quarantine, because of the plague in Bombay, for five days initially, which were gradually prolonged to twenty-three days, with the excuse of waiting to see if there were plague germs aboard the ship that might become active; and during that time agitation developed ashore. Rumors had spread that the Indian artisans would drive the British equivalents out of work, because they would take lower wages (2:201). It was said that the *Courland* was carrying a printing press, thirty compositors, and fifty smiths. As early as November there had been a meeting to set up a Colonial Patriotic Union, at which Gandhi's name had been hissed.

The leaders of the five thousand "men of Durban" included Harry Sparks of the Mounted Rifles, and Dr. Mackenzie. The latter declared that the *men* of Durban were united against the Indians, even though there were a few old women knocking about the place (2:208).

There was also another racial element to the situation. A band of five hundred African blacks had been recruited to support the whites, though the former were "kept quiet" by being given a dwarf mascot leader, to march up and down in front of them, while they danced and whooped.

The authorities were not ready overtly to back up the rioters, and the delay had some pacifying effect. By the time the Indians did disembark, there was no violence directed at anyone but Gandhi. He went ashore alone, after the others. But he was recognized, followed by a mob, pelted with fish and stones, his turban torn off, his ear and eye struck, and was in some danger of being killed. He was rescued—his life perhaps saved—by the intervention of an English lady, who sheltered him with her parasol. She stood and walked beside him, so that the mob would have had to stone her in order to reach him. He hid in a private house, and was smuggled out of it, disguised as a constable, to a police station.

His near lynching was followed by a reaction in Gandhi's favor. He refused to prosecute his attackers, and the newspaper editorials commented on his dignity, and on the lawlessness of the mob. Among the Indians, too, his position as leader was enhanced. But the incident marked the raising of the political stakes, and the political temperature, in Natal.

In 1897 the colonial premiers gathered in London for the Diamond Jubilee of Queen Victoria's reign, and stayed on for a conference on imperial affairs on July 24. It was a favorable opportunity for the Natal Indians to make their grievances and anxieties known. Gandhi sent Mansukhlal H. Nazar as a deputation of one, who made contact with people who could be useful to the cause later as well as then; including Dadabhai Naoroji, Sir Munchajee Bhownagree, formerly a Conservative MP, and Sir William Hunter, India editor of the *Times* newspaper. A list of "Friends of India in England," for Nazar to contact, has been found and analyzed by James Hunt.[12]

Hunt points out that the list contained no radicals—no Irish nationalists and no Socialists, much less any vegetarians or theosophists. The list was heavily biased toward the conservative East India Association, which was made up of retired Indian civil service officials. They were the voice of India, as far as England was concerned—and many were indeed devoted to the Indian people, as they understood them (45). This was the force Gandhi maneuvered into supporting him during Nazar's deputation, and the two later deputations he himself was to lead. Sir Lepel Griffin, the president of the EIA, was to lead the deputation to the colonial secretary in 1906.

Family Life

The year 1898 was one of crisis in Gandhi's relations with his wife. The house Kasturba had to live in, though luxurious by Western standards, was ill-adapted to Hindu ideas of refinement. There was, for instance, no internal enclosed place where the women were secure from men; and there were no gutters in the bedroom to allow water and urine to run outdoors. The rituals of Indian household life all had some religious resonance, and Kasturba found it difficult to accept European habits or experiments, such as were dear to Gandhi, and to have non-Hindus in the house.

Gandhi still had a number of his colleagues and employees staying with him from time to time, and one of them was an Indian Christian clerk who was there more than four years altogether. This was perhaps the man, Vincent Lawrence, who had defended Gandhi against Sheikh Mehtab when the two men came to blows. Most Indian Christians had been born into a very low caste, and all had lost their caste by renouncing Hinduism. Kasturba refused to clean out the chamber pot used by this man in his bedroom. (We must remember how important pollution and cleansing are in Hinduism, and that human excreta are considered the extreme of filth.) The two quarreled, and Gandhi was putting her out of the house until she recalled him to a sense of what he was doing.

Another and long-lived cause for Kasturba's discontent was the disappointment felt by her sons, especially Harilal, that they were not being educated in a way that would prepare them to enter one of the professions. Gandhi was adamant, and we see here the hard side of the naive temperament. Because Gandhi acted on his beliefs, whatever the common sense of an issue was, he was indifferent to even those arguments that everyone assured his sons were invincible. Kasturba and her sons felt doubly aggrieved, to enter into his domain of moral principle, only to find him still unpersuadable.

Gandhi had ceased to believe in the professions, and in college education generally—this disbelief was part of the New Age faith, though it was very rarely acted on. Moreover, at this time he could find no Gujarati tutors for his sons, and they had no teaching at all, except what he could give them as they trotted along beside him as he went to his office. They felt (again this was most true of Harilal) that they were not taken seriously. Harilal and Gokuldas—Gandhi's sister's son, who had accompanied the family to Natal aboard the *Courland*—were sent back to India to school, but it was not many months before Gandhi wrote for them to come to South Africa again.

In 1898, meanwhile, P. J. Mehta came to South Africa, and stayed with Gandhi in the house on the beach in Durban. He saw for himself both the way in which the Indians were treated, and the way his former protégé was becoming their leader, in an increasingly tense situation. He gave Gandhi valuable support, moral and financial.

Largely because of an implicit alliance between the British government and various speculators in the Transvaal who resented the interference of the authorities in their development of the country's mineral wealth, the Anglo-Boer War broke out in 1899. Gandhi persuaded his countrymen to form an ambulance corps—in which he served, with the rank of sergeant major—to support the British army nonviolently. (As for Indian soldiers, Delhi sent ten thousand of them to fight for the empire in South Africa; this was an imperial war.) Gandhi always seized opportunities to serve others in a medical or nursing way; and he felt that the Indians must take every opportunity to show themselves responsible citizens of the empire, and people of courage. On October 19 a hundred Indians volunteered at Gandhi's suggestion, and Gandhi felt that they gradually overcame the prejudice of the English soldiers in the army.

He spoke in the name of the manly virtues, including those of the soldier. "We do not know how to handle arms. It is not our fault; it is perhaps our misfortune" (October 19, 1899). In his speech at the Calcutta Congress December 27, 1901, he said that the colonists had thought that in time of danger the Indians would scuttle off like so many rabbits (3:215).

This mobilizing of the corps was largely a symbolic act. The men served for only about two months. There was certainly some gracious official acknowledgment of what Gandhi had done, and a poem was published in *Punch*, with the refrain, "We are sons of the Empire, after all." It was, of course, an important fact that the Indians were in Africa as sons of the empire, and they based their case for better treatment on that fact. Indeed, one of the official reasons the English offered for making war on the Boers, was the ill-treatment the latter gave to the Indians in the Transvaal.

Gandhi's feelings about the Anglo-Boer War were however complex. He saw in the Boers of the Transvaal and the Orange Free State an epitome of white-racist empire building, and none of his friends, personal or political, were Boers. But his attitude was complicated by two kinds of sympathy and admiration he felt for them. He liked their resistance to modern civilization, their desire to preserve a patriarchy, in the sense of a consciously traditional and archaic society: he wanted India to resist England in the same way. And he also admired their manliness, which included their militariness. The Indians, by contrast, could not bear arms—could not march in step—could not maintain discipline.

Every Boer is a good fighter, Gandhi wrote in *Satyagraha in South Africa.* They do not need elaborate drilling to turn them into soldiers. When the war broke out, "amongst the Boers, the entire male population joined the war. Lawyers gave up their practice, farmers their farms, traders their trade, and servants left their service" (S:65). They knew by heart the Old Testament descriptions of battles, he said, though they did not know the New Testament.

The Boers' self-reliance when war broke out therefore made a striking contrast with the Indians'. So also, if to a less degree, did the British colonists' (35:65). In the Boer War, every important lawyer in Natal went to the front, Gandhi wrote in 1927. "I could almost read the magistrate's anger in his eyes as he saw me linger on. And I tell you, I found it impossible to continue my practice for sheer shame." Like Ruskin, Gandhi measured himself by military standards, amongst others.

The British, according to Gandhi, called the Indians moneygrubbers because they stayed at home to make money. "Like worms which settle inside wood and eat it up hollow, the Indians were in South Africa only to fatten themselves upon them [the British]." Gandhi apparently felt the shame that his British colleagues wanted him to feel.

When the war dragged to its end, Gandhi decided to return to India, where he always felt that his real work must be done. He assumed, as did everyone, that the position of the Indians in South Africa would now be significantly improved, above all in the two Boer-inhabited states that were newly under British rule. In October 1901 he sailed away from Durban. However, he promised his friends that he would return to Africa, if they needed him.

The community made him and Kasturba traditional gifts of jewelry; of the sort that would normally be kept for the brides of the family's sons when they married. (There was a gold necklace, a diamond pin and ring for Kasturba; and a gold watch, chain, and a purse containing coins.) But instead of that Gandhi insisted on depositing these jewels as a reserve source of funds for the community cause. This occasioned another bitter quarrel with Kasturba, and no doubt angered Lakshmidas too.

Durban to Bombay 1901

As they sailed from Durban toward Bombay, Gandhi must have been reflecting on the paradoxes of empire. J. A. Hobson had been reporting the war for the *Manchester Guardian*; he was a New Age Englishman, whose books on the empire, *The Psychology of Jingoism* and *Imperialism*, were very acute analyses of the evil done in its name. W. T. Stead was publicly known to have prayed for England's defeat. So had John Clifford. These men were New Agers, whom Gandhi claimed as comrades.

Emily Hobhouse was a New Age Englishwoman who had come out to South Africa during the war to help the Boers and to protest against the British concentration camps. (During the First World War, she went secretly to Germany in the cause of peace, and was denounced as a traitor at home.) Gandhi admired her enthusiastically. Olive Schreiner was another such. Both of them had health problems, and were living proof of the triumph of the spirit over the body.

Such men and women as these were Gandhi's teachers and/or friends, and opponents of the new imperialism. The opposite philosophy seems to have been expounded to Gandhi by General Smuts.

Gandhi had several conversations with Smuts, and some of them philosophical and speculative, as well as the negotiations in which they opposed each other. Smuts had studied law in London at much the same time as Gandhi, and was a citizen of the empire in the same, rather special sense. For instance, they were both non-English citizens of that empire, and both more "philosophical" than the majority of their colleagues.

As Gandhi remembered it, Smuts declared that it was not color or race prejudice that held the whites apart from the Indians, but the fundamental difference beween the two cultures. The Indian civilization was different from the Boers', and must not be allowed to overwhelm it. There was a fundamental difference between East and West.

Gandhi's notes on a conversation with Smuts in 1911 translate East and West into traditional and modern. Smuts said: "You are a simple-living and frugal race, in many respects more intelligent than we are. You belong to a civilization that is thousands of years old. Ours, as you may say, is but an experiment. Who knows but that the whole damn thing will perish before long. But you see why we do not want Asia here."[13]

In *Satyagraha in South Africa*, Gandhi sums up what Smuts said to him thus:

> South Africa is a representative of Western civilization while India is the centre of Oriental culture. Thinkers of the present generation hold that these two civilizations cannot go together. If nations representing these rival cultures meet even in small groups, the result will only be an explosion. The West is opposed to simplicity while Orientals consider that virtue to be of primary importance . . . the Indian question cannot be resolved into one of trade jealousy or race hatred. The problem is simply of preserving one's own civilization . . . political thinkers believe and say that the very qualities of Indians count for defects in South Africa. The Indians are disliked in South Africa for their simplicity, patience, perseverance, frugality and otherworldliness. (S:83–84)

Smuts's remarks are flavored with moral paradox, a taste for which was another trait the two men shared. Of course they were essentially on opposite sides, but there was a good deal in Smuts's way of seeing the confrontation that Gandhi shared—which accorded with his Orientalism: for instance, the stress on the age of Indian civilization, and its love of simplicity.

India 1901–1902

Returning to his family home in Rajkot, Gandhi noted a change, a gradual impoverishment of the region during his lifetime. Britain's spoliation of India was a theme of all nationalists, and perhaps associated even more with the moderates, like Naoroji and Gokhale, because they dealt more than the extremists in economic statistics.

Soon after his arrival in India, he attended, for the first time, a meeting of congress—that year it was held in Calcutta and was presided over by Dinshaw Wacha, right hand man to Sir Pherozeshah Mehta. Gandhi traveled from Bombay on the same train as Sir Pherozeshah, who had as he usually did engaged a special saloon. Gandhi wanted the great man's support in presenting the plight of the South African Indians to the assembly. He had, he says, his orders, to report to this saloon for an interview, to be granted between two specified stations. But Mehta said he could not help advance his cause at the congress.

Gandhi found the organization of the meeting deplorable, with much waste of time, and physical disorder; he particularly objected to the dirtiness of the latrines. That had been a major object of his concern in Rajkot in 1896, when he was fighting the plague. Cleaning out latrines, Gandhi implicitly criticized all of Hindu culture.

He volunteered to do latrine work, and also to do clerical work in the congress office; and the second offer was taken up by one of the secretaries, called Ghosal, whom he describes as "talkative" and "naive", meaning something worse (A:226). Gandhi answered Ghosal's mail, listened to his chatter, and buttoned up his shirt, since the latter claimed to be so busy he had no time to do it for himself. Gandhi's tone in reporting all this is lightly ironic about the other man's self-importance, and about the amateur character of the congress proceedings in those days. It is the tone a friendly Englishman (say E. M.

Forster) might have taken about congress. Later, of course, he took those failings much more seriously, when he reformed congress.

Gandhi himself, however, for instance at meetings chaired by Pherozeshah Mehta in Bombay, or at the congress meeting, was not much more effective. He found himself overcome with the same shyness as had paralyzed him as a public speaker before, in India. "[My voice] was but a feeble pipe amongst those veteran drums"; and he read out his resolution trembling (A:227). He felt out of his own milieu, and so unable to lift up his voice to be heard. He could speak in Africa; and he could speak amongst New Agers; but if he was to speak in India he had to create a new context—to change congress, for instance.

The themes of his speech included the need for the Indians to demonstrate their manliness, as was indicated; and the need for educated Indians to establish Indian culture there. As it was, he said, it was European doctors, lawyers, architects, and missionaries whom the Indians had to consult or appeal to. Culturally, as well as economically, the Indians were serfs (3:216).

Gandhi's implication that he met a lack of sympathy in Mehta and Wacha is amply confirmed in a 1920 letter by the latter, saying that both men had soon seen Gandhi to be full of overweening conceit and personal ambition. "Time will be the avenger of the wrongs this madman is now inflicting on this poor country in his mad and arrogant career."[14] They, and Jinnah, and many others, thought that Gandhi was destroying the infant political system in India, by his New Age idealism—which certainly did include a skepticism about traditional politics.

His efforts did, however, catch the sympathetic attention of Gokhale, the only man there he really respected and felt at home with; and this developed into a valuable friendship. Gandhi stayed on in Calcutta for a month after the congress, in order to meet the chamber of commerce, and various other people, in connection with the South African situation. Gokhale was there too, and invited Gandhi to stay with him. He exhorted him to overcome his shyness; but praised Gandhi's perseverance and regularity, and his personal asceticism.

Gandhi had his reservations about, for instance, Gokhale's invalidism, but he was very grateful to be recognized and appreciated; and admired much about Gokhale, above all his gentleness. Gokhale's power was of Gandhi's kind, if somewhat less moral and more intellectual. Gandhi also cites the fact that (like him) Gokhale was a dedicated man; he never wasted a minute, and his private relations and friendships were all engaged in for the public good. The two men were significantly different: Gokhale was a systematic mind—a man of intellect, in that sense that did not apply to Gandhi; and had a narrower temperament—was not a hero in that strange sense that did apply to Gandhi. But they were alike, as Gandhi said, in their love of peace and truth.

While in Calcutta, Gandhi visited the Kali temple, and was horrified by the spectacle of bloodshed in the name of religion. He tried to meet Vivekananda, but the latter was ill. He also met some of the leaders of the Brahmo Samaj. Having heard Pratap Chandra Mozumbar preach, and met Pandit Shivrath

Shastri, he felt that the Brahmo Samaj was meant for a small group of the educated classes. But he attended a celebration at the Tagore house, where fine Bengali music was played. The Tagores were deeply identified with the Brahmo Samaj, although their religious fervor was turning toward aestheticism. Gandhi admired what he called their stupendous contribution to the intellectual and spiritual life of Bengal and India (37:192).

Among those he met at the congress was Saraladevi, the daughter of the congress secretary, Ghosal, and with her he was to have close relations later. She was at that time editor of the journal, *Bharati*, which published articles of a nationalist kind, and saw Gandhi only as a possible contributor. Through her mother, Saraladevi was a Tagore, and she was manifoldly gifted like so many of them, and especially her uncle, Rabindranath. Moreover, she employed her artistic talents in the service of the nationalist cause. The congress session opened with a song she had composed, sung by fifty-eight singers chosen from different regions, and from different religions, all over India. She herself conducted the orchestra, and the melody was taken up by a chorus of four hundred, all singing "Hail to Hindustan."[15] She no doubt cut a more brilliant figure at the meeting than Gandhi.

When he left Calcutta, he decided to make a tour, traveling third class on the railway, a class that was used only by the poorest travelers. Gokhale first tried to dissuade him, but then yielded, in admiration. He came to the station to bid Gandhi farewell, having made him a present of the metal tiffin box he needed for his travels. The first place Gandhi went to was Benares, the holy city of Hinduism, where he was as upset by the dirt, superstition, and venality, as he had been at the Calcutta temple. He also had a brief visit with Mrs. Besant at her Hindu Central College.

Gokhale had recommended him to set up office again as a barrister in Bombay, but Gandhi was afraid to take that risk. "The unpleasant memories of past failure were yet with me, and I still hated as poison the use of flattery for getting briefs" (A:243). So he returned first to Rajkot, and then, when he had some professional success there, was persuaded to move to Bombay. In that city, however, Manilal had a severe attack of typhoid, dealing with which took up most of Gandhi's energy. The doctor wanted him to give Manilal eggs and chicken broth, but Gandhi had of course a conscientious objection to meat. (Many Hindus had the same objection, but overrode it in medical emergencies.)

He persuaded the doctor to let him try his own nature-cure methods, while the doctor used his diagnostic skills to check the progress of the cure. Gandhi treated Manilal with Kuhne hip baths, and when the boy's temperature rose dangerously high, wrapped him in a wet sheet pack. He suffered great anxiety, knowing that he was risking his son's life, but the fever finally broke.

He did not get any work in the High Court, and though he attended meetings of Sir Pherozeshah's moot, he "never ventured to take part in it" (A:249). And then came a cable from Durban, asking him to return, to help his friends put their case to the colonial secretary, Joseph Chamberlain, who was about to pay a visit to South Africa. Gandhi left his wife and children behind temporarily, but took four or five young relatives, including Maganlal Gandhi, with him. "My father used to accommodate a number of [young relatives] in some state service. I wanted them to be free from this spell. I neither could nor would secure other service for them; I wanted them to be self-reliant" (A:250). We see there how the colonies represented the chance of freedom even to Gandhi.

FIVE

JOHANNESBURG AND SATYAGRAHA

· 1902–1914 ·

In this twelve-year period Gandhi developed all his major ideas, and achieved some of his large political successes. He became internationally famous. Besides that, moreover, he developed his personality, so that nearly everyone who met him after 1914 received an impression of power; and for many that was not only a power of asceticism or inspiration, but also of charm, gaiety, and affection.

The period being richer in hitherto unpublished documents than early ones, the chapter is long, and so it seems best to divide it into three, of which the first part covers the years 1902 to 1906. During these years Gandhi moved from Natal to the Transvaal, a more exciting part of the world, began to publish a weekly newspaper, *Indian Opinion,* and took a stand on a number of issues. And as a result of his leadership of the Indians, he attracted to him a number of enthusiastic European followers.

From Bombay to Durban

In 1902, Gandhi must have known that he was returning from India to a difficult political problem, complicated by racial conflicts. With the Anglo-Boer War won, it was clear that English statesmen would like to unite the four colonies of South Africa into a single dominion, which would then become a major unit of the British Empire. For Gandhi the primary question or anxiety of course was, what would be the position of the Indians there? As long as there were four small colonies, each treating separately with Whitehall, a certain balance of power would be in favor of the imperial statesmen. The latter could to some degree intervene to defend the right of the Indian minorities—for whom at least the viceroy and the India Office felt some responsibility. Once the South African colonies became one large political entity, power over the Indians would fall more into the hands of its white majority—Boer and English.

That calls to mind other difficulties caused by such a major historical development. The Boers formed a conservative community that was also reactionary. They were the remnant of an early phase of imperialist adventure, fossils or flotsam left behind by a receding wave of history. Holland ceased to be an expanding power at the end of the seventeenth century, and the South African colonists, losing touch with their homeland, turned inwards defensively, away from modern ideas. They became traditionalists, in religion and economics and politics. They relied on African slave labor. One of their disputes with their English rivals at the beginning of the nineteenth century, which led to their making the Great Trek away from the Cape Province into the interior, had to do with the English desire to put an end to slavery.

At the end of the century, one of their most liberal leaders was Jan Smuts, who acquired the title of general in the war; but as we have seen, his liberal ideas lifted him only above communalism and not above racism. He made his first important speech at Kimberley on October 29, 1895, before the Anglo-Boer War. He said there that the task of the white men in South Africa was to consolidate into a nation, in order to face the colored population united. Democracy was not an idea practicable by the latter; nor was intellectual education. He concluded, "Let us defy negrophilists, optimists, and well-meaning mischief-makers. . . . As Asia was the home of religious despotism, and Europe that of feudal monarchy, so the mission of the Newer World—if I may use the word—is a grand racial aristocracy."[1] Such was the ideology of the man with whom Gandhi was to confer so often, on related matters, from 1902 up to 1914.

Smuts was however not a typical Boer. He was intellectually sophisticated, interested in the phenomenon of the new imperialism, and ready, in private, to name things as they were. He had seen a good deal of J. A. Hobson, who had written *The Philosophy of Jingoism,* and he seems to have been ready to see the new imperialism in Hobson's terms. Jingoism, undeniably part of the new imperialism, implied the worship of power and force, and the glorification of war.[2] When imperialism was discussed, authors like Macchiavelli, Nietzsche, and Kipling were quoted, and slogans like "Might is right," and "Beyond good and evil," and "Blessed are the strong, for they shall prey upon the weak." These slogans were often used by the radicals to explain their enemies' policies. Indeed, they were tacitly or indirectly admitted by the imperialists (for instance, Kipling) despite the amoral bravura of such language.

In other cases, the hearty joviality of the new imperialism was intellectually naive enough to betray a brutality beneath. A new-imperialist epigram more than once cited came from *Aids to Scouting;* where the founder of the scouts movement, Robert Baden-Powell, said, "Football is a good game, but better than it, better than any other game, is that of man-hunting" (88).

Jingoism was a mood widespread in the colonies, and ominous for the Indians of South Africa.

As well as a political prize, South Africa was also economically valuable. It was the source of great mineral wealth, and it was often cited as a good example of the profitability of colonies. In an African colony railways were said to give investors a profit of between 10 and 20 percent, while in Western Europe the profit was only 2 to 3 percent. Similar profits were connected to the process of "civilizing the natives." In a speech to the Manchester Chamber of Commerce, Henry Stanley said that if the natives of the Congo learned to dress decently even only on Sundays, that would mean a sale of 320 million yards of Manchester cloth; while if they dressed properly on weekdays the profit would be twenty-six million pounds a year. "There are forty million of people beyond the gateway of the Congo, and the cotton spinners of Manchester are waiting to clothe them. Birmingham foundries are glowing with the red metal that will presently be made into iron work for them and the trinkets that shall adorn those dusky bosoms, and the ministers of Christ are zealous to bring them, the poor benighted heathens, in the Christian fold."[3]

We should note the religious coloring of this language (ripe for mockery by 1902) and its conjunction with the "320 million yards of Manchester cloth." That was the mill cloth Gandhi was to fight with his spinning wheel; he would give a different religious coloring to homespun.

The article on South Africa in the 1911 edition of the *Encyclopaedia Britannica* presents the country as essentially a source of raw materials for European industry. The drama of the Indians there is diminished to invisibility, as is the greater drama of the black population. "The history of South Africa is, almost entirely, that of its colonization by European powers, of their conflicts with, and influence over, its native inhabitants, and of the struggle for supremacy between the British and Dutch settlers."

The racial situation was complex as well as uneasy. The principal aim of the British being to reconcile the Boers to their new political situation, and to heal the wounds of war, the other races, black and brown, sometimes became little more than bargaining chips between them. There were also problems connected with the European Jewish immigrants. Unlike the Indians, the Jews *were*—some of them—intimately involved in the mining speculation; they took a share of its profits, and gradually won for themselves the status of "white." They did so partly by distinguishing themselves from the Indians.

Gandhi Establishes Himself in the Transvaal

Arriving in Durban on December 28, Gandhi led a deputation of Natal Indians to see Joseph Chamberlain, the visiting colonial secretary, and later prepared a written memorial for Transvaal Indians to present to Chamberlain in January. (Chamberlain refused to meet Gandhi personally a second time, as leader of the second group: Natal Indians were one thing, Transvaal Indians were another—it was a standard imperial tactic, to divide in order to rule.)

It was soon clear that the new colonies were going to maintain the Boer laws or impose others just as hard on the Indians. Law Three of the Transvaal denied its eleven thousand Indians both the vote and the right to own real estate; demanded they register and reside on locations. On May 9, 1903, there was a public meeting of Indians and a resolution was passed protesting the anti-Indian laws. But still, in a petition to the Transvaal government, of June 8, Gandhi declared that British Indians "ask for no political power. They admit the British race should be the dominant race in South Africa." All they asked for was freedom from restrictions on trade, movement, property, and an end to legislation directed against brown skins (3:330).

Gandhi had also to deal with immigrants from India, of more than one sort, but all of them hard for him to handle. He found the officials in charge of the new Asiatic Department in Pretoria (to whom the Indians now had to apply in all sorts of official matters) to be "adventurers who had accompanied the army from India to South Africa during the war and had settled there in order to try their luck" (S:77). About fifty Pathans had also arrived there in the same way. (Both groups belonged to Kipling's India, and his story, "A Sahibs' War," describes their migration.) These were groups Gandhi was going to have to confront, politically, and for both a Gujarati babu was just what they despised.

The Asiatic Department set out to displace Gandhi. It told the Indians of the Transvaal that they no longer need apply to him for advice or help. These officers brought with them the caste haughtiness of the Indian administration. The Pathans Gandhi explained thus: "To kill and get killed is an ordinary thing in their eyes, and if they are angry with anyone, they will thrash him and sometimes even kill him. . . . A Pathan's anger becomes particularly uncontrollable when he has to deal with anyone whom he takes to be a traitor. When he seeks justice he seeks it only through personal violence" (S:151).

This is very much the way Kipling characterized Pathans in his story, and the Indians and the whites shared many such stereotypes. The Pathans were widely seen as loyal allies to the British and hereditary enemies to babus like Gandhi. In Gujarat Pathans were employed by the government to repress revolts; just as the Cossacks were employed in Russia. It was one of Gandhi's tasks to overcome such aspects of those stereotypes.

Gandhi now established himself in Johannesburg, instead of in Durban. It was in the Transvaal that Indians most needed defending. And since Johannesburg was a very fast-growing city, Gandhi was moving into a crisis center or maelstrom of modern history. He became an attorney of the supreme court in that city, where he had a large practice. He tells us that he hired a Scottish woman, Miss Dick, to supplement the four Indian clerks he employed, because none of the latter could type. He established warm relations with her, as he usually did with his employees, and gave the bride away when she married (A:283). One of this firm's letter-books, covering a three month period, included a thousand letters. He is estimated to have earned five thousand pounds a year—his share of the gold-and-diamonds boom.

But he was still an untouchable. Though he lived in Johannesburg, Gandhi never thought of going to visit the mines, he said, "partly because I was afraid lest as an 'untouchable' I should be refused admission and insulted" (33:25). During Gokhale's visit to South Africa in 1912, however, the authorities there invited him and a party of Indians, including Gandhi, who saw unforgettable scenes. "Mountains upon mountains of excavated earth and stones and no diamonds!" Only after millions of pounds had been sunk in machinery was there any return. The mines, and the town built round them, were a striking image of capitalized industry in all its monstrous greeds and powers.

Gandhi called the Transvaal the El Dorado of the Western world, and Johannesburg "the golden city of South Africa. Only fifty years ago, the site on which it now stands was desolate and covered with dry grass" (S:3). In the streets, everybody ran, nobody walked, so great was the fever, he said.

The first biography of Gandhi (published in 1910) evokes the city as a backdrop to the man. The writer, Joseph Doke, is sitting in a Johannesburg park, thinking about Gandhi.

> But even now the roar of the batteries along the reef, like the roar of surf breaking on a distant shore, attracts the ear. At night it comes nearer. On some cold night, when the wind blows from the mines, the sound is like the roll of thunder, as though the rocks and sands and surf were battling with each other for victory down there on "the Wanderers." That roar never ceases. On calm, hot, sunny days it almost dies; it sinks away into a lazy hum like the drone of bees in the clover. But it is always there. The batteries of the reef are never still. Night and day, and every night and every day, without rest, the crushing of the great machinery goes on, and the rocks and stones and sand yield their golden treasure in response.[4]

It is a landscape of power.

A 1940 *History of South Africa* gives a similar picture:

> Upon those parts of the town that are within earshot of the roar of the crushing mills, the sudden winds of August drop their charge of fine white dust, carried from the dumps. The dumps are the physical sign of the Witwatersrand's great dependence upon the gold which makes men live constantly in the present, with their eyes constantly on monthly statements of gold production, their fingers on the pulse of the stock exchanges, and their ears cocked for news of international happenings.[5]

This gold fever brought other social consequences. The Australian journalist, Ambrose Pratt, wrote about South Africa in 1910, saying that "ancient Nineveh and Babylon have been revived. Johannesburg is their twentieth century prototype." Charles van Onselen has taken up Pratt's phrases in his *Studies in the Social and Economic History of the Witwatersrand* (London: Longmans, 1982); his two volumes are entitled "The New Babylon" and "The New Nineveh" respectively.

In 1890, he says, Johannesburg had little domestic life or social respectability. The miners lived in boardinghouses, and worked in compounds, which were male-dominated. Those who could not stand the conditions of work in the mines were employed as barmen, billiards men, skittle alley men, thieves. By 1896 drunkenness had reached enormous proportions. Distillery was one of the industries that went with gold mining; another was prostitution. Van Onselen quotes R. I. Evans, "large-scale, conspicuous prostitution was a by-product of the first explosive stage in the growth of the industrial city."[6] Many of the women came from Germany and Austria on the steamship lines in the 1890s. They also came from London, and ultimately New York, where there was a purity campaign that drove them out. Hundreds of "undesirables," many of them Jews, left the Lower East Side for London and the Rand.

Another consequence was a growth in organized crime. In his second volume, van Onselen describes the "Regiment of the Hills—Umkozi Wezintaba." The prisons and the mine compounds, sociologically similar environments, helped form a lumpen proletarian army of criminals. "Redundant miners, unemployed clerks, failed businessmen, ex–colonial troopers and British deserters," gradually turned into a population of pimps, illicit liquor-sellers, and so on.

The most lurid cases, in the eyes of respectable citizens, were the black gangs. Mzoozepi Mathebala, born 1876, called himself Jan Note when he got employed as a Johannesburg houseboy, and made contact with a world of crime. He joined a community of two hundred blacks who preyed on other blacks. Having read the Bible in jail and heard about Nineveh—the great state that rebelled against the Lord—he applied the word to his own group.

The gangs made recruits in the prisons, and were largely homosexual. Note, whose years of ascendancy were 1906–12, was in Volksrust jail in 1907–8, as Gandhi was. And in 1913 Note became native warder in Durban Jail until 1917. The prisons must have brought the Indian satyagrahis together with these other breakers of the laws. It is likely that Gandhi knew of Note, and possible that Note knew of Gandhi.

Gandhi spoke in 1922 of having been in the same prison with one of the greatest murderers in South Africa: "I know the prison life. Only a pitch-black wall separated one of the greatest murderers in South Africa and me. We were both in isolation cells by design, for we were both considered dangerous to society. I had to suffer [much] in that cell for nearly two months." (22:245). He is also quoted by P. J. Mehta as saying that he got "very nervous and terror-stricken" in jail.[7] Prabhudas Gandhi remembered the bad reputation of Durban Jail, and the murderers locked up there.[8]

Johannesburg therefore in various ways embodied an opposite to the social ideals promoted by the purity campaigns and the New Agers. Olive Schreiner described the city to Edward Carpenter as "a great, fiendish, hell of a city which, for glitter and gold and wickedness, carriages and palaces and brothels and gambling hells, beats creation."[9] However, the New Age had its representatives in the Transvaal, for instance the Theosophists.[10] The three sponsors of the Johannesburg Lodge were Herbert Kitchin and Louis Ritch, Gandhi's close friends, and Louis Playford, who conducted the marriage ceremony for Polak and his bride.

The Theosophists met at Miss Bissicks's vegetarian cafe, decorated with her own paintings. There were close connections with the headquarters of the society in London. Mr. Cordes, a German who lived with Gandhi at Phoenix, was a friend of Colonel Olcott. Madame Blavatsky's friend, Countess Wachtmeister, was the correspondent for the new lodge. Ritch said that he had come to Theosophy via socialism, in the way that his friend, Herbert Burrows, and Mrs. Besant herself, had.

One of the lodge's major activities was public lecturing. Ritch lectured on Judaism, Gandhi on Hinduism; but the more popular topics involved spiritual or extrasensory phenomena. Major Peacocke's lectures on such topics attracted audiences of three to four hundred at the Masonic Hall. In 1903 the membership grew from 16 to 123. On the other hand, in 1904 many members resigned because of the rumors of "dubious occult arts" (16).

Two more of Gandhi's acquaintances, W. P. Wybergh and Gabriel Isaacs, were members who signed the invitation to Mrs. Besant to become president of the whole society in 1907. In 1909 the South African Theosophical Society was formed, with a national secretary and seven lodges.

A 1910 report to the Theosophical headquarters at Adyar mentions that Mr. Gandhi remained always interested in the society's work. But his interest was critical. In 1905 he gave the society a lecture on "The Real Life"; summarized by Henry Polak. Gandhi said the Theosophists stressed mental studies and occult powers too much, neglecting their two spiritual ideas, the brotherhood of man and his moral growth. Students should study the control of their passions before they studied esoteric doctrines; for all people harbor in themselves the robber and the murderer, and should not see evil only in others. Theosophists should not seek to extend their scope but to intensify it. The Real Life is not to be lived in libraries. (35)

The *South African Theosophist* began to publish in April 1903, and seems to have had some connection with the Phoenix settlement. Cordes said that the Indian Opinion Press helped to print it. Miss E. Knudsen, a pioneer of Swedish massage, advertised in it, and in 1928 went to India and saw Gandhi there. (If she introduced him to Swedish massage, in South Africa, that was an important step in his career of accepting physical contact with women.)

Johannesburg harbored other aspects of the New Age, as well as theosophy. One of the results of the new wealth, as we have seen, was an immense immigration, of a kind quite different from the indentured Indians who were brought in to work the sugar plantations—and from the English settlers encouraged by the imperial government. The city was often called "Jo'burg" and sometimes "Jewburg," for the obvious reason. Forty thousand people of Jewish origin entered South Africa during the years that Gandhi was there; from England, from Germany, and from the Russian Empire.

Anti-Semitism developed in conjunction with other aspects of white racism. In London in 1906 one of Gandhi's sponsors was Sir Lepel Griffin, a retired Indian civil service official, who blamed the plight of the Indians in the Transvaal on the Jews there—"the offscouring of the international sewers of Europe." He was referring to those attracted by the gold and diamond mines.

A small subset of these people, however, were intellectuals, though in a sense rather different from the one we employ today. That is, they were not people with doctorates or academic jobs, but autodidacts, with an interest in life-experiment. Many of them were New Agers, and ready to exchange ideas with

Gandhi. They had been uprooted from the landscape in which they had been born, and had been even in that landscape wanderers, being Jews. Among the social experiments they were interested in was Zionism, the setting up of a Jewish community in Palestine. A great number of meanings were attached to the idea of Zion, all the way from Martin Buber's idealism to the militarist meaning. The former was quite close to Gandhism.

In this decade, Gandhi's social and intellectual world was composed largely of such people, more than of Indians or Englishmen. Zionism, the agelong sufferings of the Jews, Judaism's prayers and rituals, the relation of Judaism to Christianity, the pogroms in Russia, the reconciliation of tradition with experiment—such themes were discussed amongst his friends; and so were New Age ideas already described, especially the nonviolence of Tolstoy, and nature cure and vegetarianism.

Gandhi's closest friends were not Zionists, at least not during these years, but they were liberal in their Judaism, and saw the history of the Jews as constituting a call to them to recognize and alleviate the sufferings of similar groups—such as the Indians in the British Empire. Henry Polak, for instance, saw the Jews as the most Western of Eastern peoples, whose calling was to interpret East to West and vice versa, and whose sufferings had been to that end. "If a Jew does not stand up eminently for ethical principle, what raison d'être has he in the scheme of things . . . for what purpose is his the chosen race?"[11]

This very broad historical and religious perspective, and the keen dialectic and bold experimentation of these people, were very congenial to Gandhi, and gave him an apprenticeship to idealistic politics quite different from the training of other Indian politicians of his generation.

The three principal figures were Henry Polak, Hermann Kallenbach, and Sonja Schlesin. Kallenbach had been born on the border between East Prussia and Russian Poland; he was trained as an architect in Germany, and came to South Africa because some cousins had settled and made money there.

Polak was of a rabbinical family; he was born in England, but, as his name indicates, his paternal ancestors were Polish. His mother was of a Spanish Jewish family. He too came to Africa because of a family connection and a hope of more opportunity. Before joining Gandhi, he worked on a paper set up by a Jewish board of deputies, the *Transvaal Critic*.

Schlesin, about whose family origins we know nothing, was only seventeen in 1902, when she replaced Miss Dick as Gandhi's secretary. She worked for Gandhi, but also with him, taking on major responsibilities within the Indian movement. A short stocky figure, she wore severely cut costumes, with a dark-colored shirt and tie. (In some photographs she resembles the young Emma Goldman.) She was a feminist and in one message she sent to a meeting of Indians, read out by Gandhi, she compared the *satyagrahis* with "my sisters in England," the suffragists. She talked and acted toward Gandhi and the other men—though she was so much younger—with an aggressive freedom of manner.

Besides these close friends, there were Jewish allies and sympathizers: Theosophists like Gabriel Isaacs, a vegetarian jeweler who lived with Gandhi at his Phoenix settlement, and Louis Ritch, who did a lot of legal work for the Indians' cause; Morris Philipson and Morris Alexander, Jewish members of the South African Parliament, who represented their interests there; Mr. and Mrs. Vogl, and others. Few of these people were religiously orthodox, but from them Gandhi got glimpses of Jewish tradition and an infusion of the modern-intellectual temperament.

Polak said that the Indian problem in South Africa seemed to him the Jewish problem in Christendom all over again, and he reproached his countrymen with failing to recognize the obligations that brought. In 1911 he wrote in the *Jewish Chronicle* that as soon as they set foot in South Africa, Jews did not hesitate to join the hue and cry raised against the disinherited residents of the subcontinent (82). Polak is characterized by Payne as having a great capacity for indignation, and by Gandhi as having a will to change the world.[12]

Henry Polak was born in 1882 in Dover. His father, a clever and strong-willed man, was a justice of the peace and a member of the Port of London Immigration Board. Henry was educated partly in Switzerland, where he read Tolstoy and the *Ramayana* in English translation. He was already a New Ager, an admirer of Ruskin, and a member of the South Place Ethical Society, where he had met the woman he was to marry. Like many New Agers, he took an interest in India; besides some translation of the *Ramayana,* he had read the *Light of Asia.* He first saw Gandhi in the vegetarian restaurant in Johannesburg (where Gandhi also made the acquaintance of another faithful English disciple, Albert West.)

It was part of Polak's duty at the *Critic* to read the rival exchange journals, and so he had read and admired Gandhi's articles in *Indian Opinion.* He finally met him at the vegetarian Miss Bissicks's At Home. (Gandhi contributed to keeping her restaurant open.) Polak asked Miss Bissicks to introduce him to Gandhi.

When they discussed vegetarianism, at this first meeting, Polak said it was Tolstoy who had convinced him not to eat meat. Gandhi replied that he had a shelf full of Tolstoy's books in his office, and Polak must come to look at them. Thus theirs was a New Age union, cemented in the presence of the New Age icons in Gandhi's office. In return, over the years, Polak gave Gandhi two New Age books that were important to him. One was Thoreau's "Civil Disobedience," which preached a New Age political activism like Gandhi's own; and the other was Ruskin's *Unto This Last,* which inspired Gandhi to found his first ashram-commune, at Phoenix.

Unto This Last was a book of political economy so radical in its tendency that Ruskin's father had feared it would ruin his son's reputation. The book was in fact confidently dismissed by earlier reviewers. In the first decade after it appeared, 1862–72, only nine hundred copies were sold. But by 1910—after thirty years of the New Age—a hundred thousand had been bought, and there had been pirated editions. Hobson, a brilliant professional economist, expounded many of the same ideas.

Polak was also interested in the nature cure and diet experiments that were particularly advanced in Germany and Switzerland then. (He may have visited the several colonies of that kind in Switzerland.) He and Gandhi read books by Just and Kuhne, and followed their recipes for bread (grinding their own grain) their vegetarian diets and their mud and water therapies. At their very first meeting Gandhi and Polak discovered that both had read Adolf Just's *Return to Nature,* and neither had till then met a fellow enthusiast. This rebellion against scientific medicine was profoundly important for its symbolic rejection of elements of Western culture of which most people were most proud.

Hermann Kallenbach was born in 1871, studied architecture in Strelitz and Munich, and practiced it in Johannesburg. When he arrived in 1896 he brought with him New Age ideas in architecture—for instance, van de Velde's ideas, which were used in Ascona for the sunroof sanatorium building. For himself and his brother Kallenbach designed a home composed of several of the round huts found in Bantu villages—what was called the Rondavaals style—and had them built by native builders.

He built the white Sacke Building on Joubert Street in 1903 and 1904; for his uncles, the Sacke brothers. This was a building in a rather fanciful German-Swiss style, with a mansard roof and Jugendstil ornament, a tower and gables. Over the rest of his life, he belonged to one of South Africa's busiest architectural firms. Herbert Baker, the arts and crafts movement architect, active in Garden City design, inspired Kallenbach's design for a Christian Science Church in 1909–10. (Kallenbach's firm later designed Orlando, the first of the black townships around Johannesburg.)

Kallenbach joined the other two in many of their diet experiments, and when Gandhi fell ill wanted him to go—at Kallenbach's expense—to take a cure at Jungborn, Dr. Just's establishment in Germany. (Gandhi tried to get Gokhale to go there in 1912.) Kallenbach was also in touch with the Zionist movement. An uncle of Kallenbach's was a friend of Leo Pinsker in Odessa, the author of *Auto-emancipation.* He bought land in Palestine, and his daughter married Michael Halperin, who aroused the Jews there to the need for self-defense.

All Zionists had strong elements of idealism, and for many that idealism was of a pacific, simple-life, New Age kind. Someone Gandhi quite often referred to, as a spokesman for the Jews of England, was the novelist Israel Zangwill (1864–1916). Zangwill did not think Judaism any longer a viable religion (he said a Jew is "like a mother clasping a dead child to her bosom") but he cherished a nostalgic love for both the religion and the ghetto where it had been so humbly practiced. Zangwill wanted Zion to be a superghetto, an enclave within world society, which would preserve the best of Jewish pacifism and passivity. This was like Gandhi's vision of the international role of a free India.

Thus both men embraced what seemed weakness in the world's eyes, and admired New Testament Christianity. "The history of the ghetto," Zangwill said, "is from more than one aspect the story of the longest and bravest experiment that has ever been made in practical Christianity."[13] He also wanted to see a melting of Judaism into a religion of the future, fusing together Christianity,

Hellenism, and Hebraism. In all this, Gandhi must have found much to admire, although his own politics was much more activist.

At *their* first meeting, Gandhi and Kallenbach discussed Buddha and his teaching of renunciation. (We don't know if Kallenbach had then read Arnold's poem, but it is very likely.) They became very fond of each other and influential upon each other; and lived together for a time in a cottage seven miles from Johannesburg. Kallenbach had been used to spend seventy-five pounds a month on his person, Gandhi says; but under the latter's influence he reduced that sum to eight pounds a month (79:301). (In his autobiography, Gandhi said that when they met, Kallenbach was spending twelve hundred rupees a month, apart from rent) (A:329).

About Sonja Schlesin we know less, because she left no memoir, and apparently did not preserve the letters between her and Gandhi. He describes her as of difficult temperament, but with remarkable gifts of an executive kind. She contradicted and criticized him freely, and he liked her freedom. Gandhi wanted her to be articled to him, and so to become a lawyer, as other of these friends did (Polak, for instance). His application to the Law Society on her behalf was rejected on the grounds that she was a woman.

Letters and Literature

The letters that have been preserved between Gandhi and these friends begin—except for one or two earlier ones—in 1909. Gandhi was then separated from Polak and Kallenbach, having been sent to London to represent the South African Indians there.

Most of these letters therefore belong chronologically in the third part of this chapter. But they grow out of relationships that started much earlier; so let us sample some of those early ones that derive their interest from Gandhi's personal relationships or life-experiments. His letters from London to Kallenbach in Johannesburg start with two that make reference to novels. This is very interesting, for the novelistic note is just what is missing from most of Gandhi's autobiographical writing (you might think he'd never read a Western novel).

But in the first letter preserved between him and Kallenbach, he tells the latter that his daughter-in-law, Chaneki, is fretting over the imminent departure of her husband, Harilal. "She is very romantic and passionately fond of him. You meet with such characters in novels. Evidently she is living the heroine of her best novel" (UC). And in the second letter he reports reading *David Copperfield* "with avidity." Kallenbach had recommended the book to him with some comments on Uriah Heep, the archetype of hypocrisy. Gandhi, however, wants Kallenbach to reflect rather on Steerforth, David's boyhood hero and Little Em'ly's seducer—Steerforth who exploits the rich man's privilege and ruins the village beauty.

That Victorian gestalt of temptation, seduction, and ruin, with its implicit erotic psychology, had ceased to convince or to interest sophisticated novel-readers by 1909. They stood on the verge of *Sons and Lovers* and *A Portrait of the Artist as a Young Man,* erotic worlds with no place for those ideas. But Gandhi and Tolstoy remained nineteenth-century readers.

This was a matter of the larger imagination, not just of literary taste. Why did Gandhi choose Steerforth for Kallenbach to consider, out of all that variety of figures and themes? Because they both saw the latter as a past or future Steerforth. In 1913, Gandhi exhorted his friend not to revert to the rake's life (letter of Jan. 8, UC). When Kallenbach went to Europe in 1911, he drew up a contract with Gandhi, in which he vowed neither to marry, nor even to look lustfully upon a woman, while he was away.

Even so, he had to report, by mail, severe temptations. Gandhi replied, "Your experience about your cousin is disconcerting. . . . You are there in the midst of the subtlest temptation. The people you want to serve may unconsciously be your death-traps. Your very abstemiousness—the leaving off of salt, etc., may surround your life with romance and a halo and may then be itself a temptation. Yes, the path of those who want to live and think right is narrow like the edge of a sword. They may not swerve an inch from the path, they may not even lift their fixed gaze from the goal." He went on to speak of ropedancers in India, carrying bamboo poles to balance them, twenty feet above the ground. "You are one of these spiritual rope-dancers."

This sort of spiritual-ascetic thought about sexual experience has become alien to us, and perhaps we are inclined to think it could not be employed by anyone capable of appreciating the values of erotic love. But one person who was still thinking in those terms in 1909 was that great erotic novelist, Tolstoy. One can find that conceptual and imagistic language in such a story as his "Father Sergius," and in the third of his long novels, *Resurrection.*

Perhaps the character of Steerforth fascinated Gandhi also because of a prior seduction—at school—Steerforth's seduction of David rather than of Em'ly. This was of course a moral seduction, though not without its erotic elements. David's blindness to Steerforth's faults—so clear to the reader—must surely have recalled Mohan's blindness to Mehtab's faults; and what had dazzled the younger boy was the same in both cases—a strong, handsome, sophisticated masculinity. When Gandhi met Mehtab, he was, like David, a forlorn schoolboy, weak and lonely, needing a protector. But in the Kallenbach/Gandhi version of the story—as opposed to the Mehtab/Gandhi and the Steerforth/David versions—the moral enthusiast was able to reform his sophisticated friend. And if he and Kallenbach each saw his own identity in terms of *David Copperfield,* that made them both (belated) sons of nineteenth-century idealism.

We know that Kallenbach saw himself as like the unregenerate Tolstoy. When Gandhi corresponded with Tolstoy he passed on Kallenbach's message that he had recognized himself in Tolstoy's *A Confession.* (Tolstoy replied, via Chertkov, that "all you say about Kallenbach has greatly interested Tolstoy" [10:511].) And one can see a similarity between the two men. Kallenbach had apparently a big strong physique, and developed his muscles, following the methods of the famous strong man, August Sandow. (Tolstoy when young frequented gymnasia and hoped to become the strongest man in the world.) He was an extravagant man, both financially and emotionally, given to both succumbing to temptation and repenting the deed. He was an imaginative life-experimenter, a seeker after truths, and disciplines, and masters. And he was erotically very susceptible. The figures Tolstoy depicted in his fiction as autobiographical were all those things. We are not surprised that when Kallenbach bought land near Johannesburg, and put it at Gandhi's disposal in 1910, they called it Tolstoy Farm.

The first letter in the Gandhi-Polak Papers is addressed to Millie Graham in England in 1905. She was about to come out to South Africa to marry Henry Polak (Gandhi had promoted the match, countering the arguments of Polak's father, who thought Millie not strong enough). Gandhi wrote to welcome her to their "busy hive" of activity, and to tell her whom to get to know in England, to prepare herself for their work. She should call on Dadabhai Naoroji; she should go to meet Josiah Oldfield and see his fruitarian hospital; and Miss Nicholson of the Vegetarian Society in Farringdon Street; and the Tolstoy Farm somewhere near London (this is presumably either Whiteway or Maude's place at Purleigh).

Millie Graham arrived at Johannesburg on December 30, 1905, and was married that day. Kasturba and the younger boys had arrived earlier in the year. Millie Polak was to act as their governess for a time. She later described Gandhi's Turkish bath for nature cures, the attempt at a sanatorium, and the grinding of wholemeal flour, with which they then made unleavened bread according to Kuhne's recipe.

The names Gandhi sent Millie in 1905 give some sense of the network of the New Age; and in 1911 Henry Polak wrote to Gandhi from London about the groups he was addressing on the plight of the Indians. There was the Ethical Society at Holloway, where Miss Winterbottom was present—she was the corresponding secretary of the Union of Ethical Societies. There was the Harringay Ethical Society, the West Islington Women's Liberal Association, the New Reform Club, and the Hampstead Peace and Arbitration Society.

As that list suggests, Polak was concentrating his personal efforts on the political issue. But he remained generally a son of the New Age, and his politics, especially in his early years, fitted in with his other interests. He was not only Gandhi's lieutenant in the satyagraha movement; he made three trips to India, as spokesman for the Indians of South Africa. That was New Age or Gandhian politics; to have an Englishman speak on behalf of Indians, or (as Gandhi himself later attempted) to have a Hindu speak for Muslims.

New Enterprises

In June of 1903, Vyaharik Madanjit began to publish the weekly, *Indian Opinion,* which Gandhi took over and later transferred to an agricultural settlement called Phoenix. The object of the paper, he wrote in the issue of December 24, 1904, was to bring the European and the Indian subjects of King Edward closer together. Phoenix, on the other hand, was an attempt to combine the ideas of Ruskin and Tolstoy with "strict business principle." Again we see Gandhi espousing both politics and New Age experiment, which are separate but combined.

At first the paper came out in four languages, English, Gujarati, Hindi, and

Tamil, but it proved too difficult to keep the latter two editions going. Of the two that persisted, the Gujarati edition tended to be more factual, detailed, and down-to-earth than the English; also to be more gossipy and more forthright in its political statements. Gandhi wrote a commendation of Polak in the Gujarati pages that he thought it prudent to keep out of the English pages (UC, June or July 1911). The bulk of the editorial material—at least on sensitive issues—was written by Gandhi. Its principal function was to give information about the fortunes of the Indian cause and to shape Indian response.

Along with this material, Gandhi introduced quite a few Indian fables, poems, proverbs, cultural news, and so on. But there were also articles of a wider and less-direct interest, articles on other Eastern countries, like Japan, then rising to prominence through her successful self-modernization, and on leaders of other oppressed races, like Booker T. Washington; and on April 23 and 30, there were, for instance, extracts from Tolstoy's essays on science.

Perhaps just as interesting is what was not in *Indian Opinion*. Gandhi said writing for it must be an exercise in self-discipline, and he was on guard against rumor, paranoia, exaggeration, and falsification. He also eschewed, on principle, all bitter and biting rhetoric. He told Polak to imitate the *London Times* in his articles. *Indian Opinion* was an exercise in clarity, sobriety, and plain speaking.

He finally took over complete financial responsibility for the paper (debts that amounted to 3,500 pounds) in October 1904, and in January 1905 wrote Gokhale that his legal office was being run in the paper's interest. Albert West, whom Gandhi asked to report on it, found the paper's financial condition to be so bad that Gandhi set off from Johannesburg to Durban, to investigate. Reading Ruskin's *Until This Last* on the journey, he became enthusiastic about the idea of founding an agricultural settlement (he had already seen and envied his nephew Maganlal's orchard in Tongaat) and the next day set about buying a hundred acres at Phoenix, fourteen miles from Durban. There the paper could be produced (when somewhat reduced in size) while agriculture was also practiced, and the simple life followed. Twelve compositors worked on the press, which Gandhi called a village industry. The Phoenix settlement came into existence that November and December, and it marked an important stage in Gandhi's progressive self-disentanglement from city life and from the ordinary circumstances of secular modern life.

Polak resigned from the *Critic,* and became editor of *Indian Opinion,* at first under Herbert Kitchin. (Kitchin was an eccentric and hot-tempered engineer, who had lived with the Gandhis in Durban, after the war drove him out of the Transvaal. He had a drink problem from which Gandhi saved him for a time.) Three months later Gandhi persuaded Polak to become articled clerk to him—though he continued to work at the journal, and at all kinds of other things, in a more desultory way.

Gandhi himself became a skilful journalist, although much of the time he was concerned with exhortation and persuasion, rather than with informing and amusing. A description of a strike in the gold mines in 1913 is an excellent example of effective newspaper writing (12:132–35). It is worth noting that his account is implicitly on the side of law and order; and he was generally not ready to join in the hostility of the workers to employers and government.

In February 1904 he visited the Indian location of Johannesburg, which was in an unsanitary area, and on the fifteenth warned the medical officer of health about it, repeating the warning on the twentieth—again in vain. There had been heavy rains, and the drainage was bad. On March 1 he wrote to say that plague had in fact broken out there, and during the following month, with minimal help from the city, he organized a hospital and a quarantine. It was his work against the plague that won him the friendship of Albert West, a working-class Englishman who became a resident at Phoenix and a worker on *Indian Opinion*.

Meanwhile the political situation was getting worse for the Indians. Gandhi commented on the Immigration Restriction Act: "The colonies have become very powerful, and are becoming more and more so day by day. The Indian subjects of the King-Emperor therefore, have to patiently and quietly submit." But in other articles his language grew more prophetic, denunciatory, and inflammatory. In *Indian Opinion* for October 8, 1903, under the heading "Mockery of God in the Orange River Colony," he said that the state's Day of Humiliation had been proclaimed without the proclamation giving any hint of sacrifice or repentance, and he called the colony's color prejudice "a national sin before God."

Even then, however, his aggression was tempered by other tones, proper to the naive mind; he called the Orange proclamation "in itself a sign of a godly heart." We are a long way from Marx's or Lenin's tone about their opponents. All Gandhi will say about "the central sin spot of civilization" (Johannesburg was sometimes so called) is, "No one has the leisure to look at any one else, and every-one is apparently engrossed in thinking how to amass the maximum wealth in the minimum of time" (S:4).

Gandhi tried to create a unified Indian culture in South Africa, which combined Hindus and Muslims, and reconciled the various castes. For instance, he began to serialize an English-language biography of the Prophet in *Indian Opinion*. He had to cancel the scheme, however, because the Muslim readers objected to having Hindus and Englishmen speaking about their religious leader.

The enemies of the Indians were organizing themselves into white leagues and vigilantes' committees. The Johannesburg White League was formed in 1902, because the city was being "flooded with undesirables." Gandhi could of course prove that the proportion of Indians was very small, and could suggest that many of the European immigrants were not very desirable. But he knew that such arguments had little effect, and by 1905 (on June 28) he was speaking of a life-and-death struggle that lay ahead for British Indians in South Africa.

During the Bambata Rebellion, later called the Zulu War, Gandhi again raised an Indian Ambulance Corps, and served in it. In fact he raised a group who were ready to serve the authorities in any capacity; it was the government who decided it should be ambulance work. The rebellion broke out when a

Zulu chief killed a tax collector with an assegai, and it was quelled by means of machine guns as well as of floggings and hangings. Even General Smuts was appalled at the lengths to which the Natal government went in its panic.

Gandhi's support of the British was much resented by Indian radicals and enemies of the empire. In New York the *Gaelic American* called Gandhi's cooperation with the English army "contemptible beyond expression," and in London the *Indian Sociologist* called it "disgusting." Polak said Gandhi "must have had searching of conscience as to the propriety of his allying himself, even in that merciful capacity, with those capable of such acts of revolting and inexcusable brutality."[14] One of the British commanders, Colonel Sparks, was the Harry Sparks who had organized the men of Durban against Gandhi in 1897. Polak and Doke both say that Gandhi would never talk about the experience of serving in that campaign, and Erik Erikson suggests that the spectacle of the bodies of blacks killed and wounded by whites—and killed by machine guns against which they stood no chance—may have reinforced his revulsion against this white, male, cruel civilization, and his self-identification with opposite forces, with women and passivity and suffering.[15]

Certainly, during the marches of the Ambulance Corps in the Zulu War, Gandhi came to the conclusion that a public worker like himself should be a *vanaprastha;* that is, one who has renounced the cares and responsibilities of marriage and a family. And so that year he took the vow of *brahmacharya,* or abstinence in deed and thought from sexual pleasures. "Procreation and the consequent care of children are inconsistent with public service." He had been attempting this abstinence since 1900.

The vow of brahmacharya meant many things to Gandhi, and his renunciation of sexual love was in the service of greater spiritual love—a way to promote the triumph of *caritas* over *eros*. In his book on health, he said, "It is my full conviction that, if only I had lived a life of *Brahmacharya* all through, my energy and enthusiasm would have been a thousand fold greater" (H:152). Within the range of ordinary human experience, it was the love of a mother for her children that came closest to what Gandhi aimed at. He and his friends took brahmacharya to be a part of Indian culture. In his book on Gandhi, P. J. Mehta said that *brahmacharis* could be found everywhere in India, and he agreed with Gandhi that the practice was necessary to one who would serve the motherland.[16]

The full meaning of brahmacharya only gradually became apparent. In the last decade of his life, he talked of it in semimystical terms. "There is something very striking about a full-fledged brahmachari. His speech, his thought, and his actions, all bespeak possession of vital force . . . a man whose sexual desire has been burned up, ceases to make a difference between men and women. . . . Even his sexual organs will begin to look different . . . he never gets erections" (77:20–22). As such a man gets older, Gandhi says, his intellect gets clearer. (In the Gujarati, he added: "The lustre on his face should also increase. One in whom this lustre is not seen is to that extent lacking in brahmacharya.")

In natural parallel, Gandhi's sense of his own vocation grew more religious. On May 27, 1907, he replied to an angry letter from his elder brother Lakshmidas, who was by then treasurer of the state of Porbandar. Gandhi declared that he had not given up all family responsibilities and that he would look after his brothers' children and wives if that became necessary. But he could not be primarily a family man, and he could not devote himself to making money.

Gandhi moved from Johannesburg to Natal in summer 1906, though he kept his office in Johannesburg. *Indian Opinion* catered to the general interest in the Zulu War; carrying Notes from "Our Special Correspondent at the Front"—Gandhi. This is another of those moments when we are bound to think of Kipling. Politically, Gandhi was concerned with the Transvaal Draft Asiatic Ordinance, which if passed would require that all Indians register themselves and give ten fingerprints to do so. This struck Gandhi as the ultimate insult, the infliction of the status of criminal upon his countrymen, and he urged all Indians to resist it. He himself promised to die rather than comply. This was the birth of satyagraha. Having read and expounded Thoreau's civil disobedience theory, Gandhi offered a prize for an Indian word to express the same idea, and took the best offered, and adapted it himself to this one, which is usually translated as "firmness in truth."

His leadership had won a response. The draft was published on August 12, 1906, Gandhi led a deputation to the colonial secretary on September 3, and on September 11, 1906, there was a mass meeting of three thousand in the Empire Theatre in Johannesburg. This was organized by the Hamidiya or Ahmadiya Islamic Society (a missionary Islamic organization from the Punjab) according to one account. At the meeting Sheth Haji Habib made a motion that Indians must go to jail rather than submit. He and the seconder, Haji Ojer Ally, invoked God's name, and Gandhi seized the chance to call for an oath. The other leaders, Gandhi continues: "all dwelt upon their own responsibility and the responsibility of the audience . . . at last all present, standing with upraised hands, took an oath with God as witness not to submit. . . . I can never forget the scene, which is present before my mind's eye as I write. The community's enthusiasm knew no bounds" (S:100).

These two men, Ally and Habib were, one at a time, to accompany Gandhi to London on his deputations, the former in 1906, the latter in 1909. Both had strong reservations about passive resistance, and suspected Gandhi of primarily Hindu loyalties. (The Muslims as a whole tended to regard passive resistance as a Hindu strategy.) Ally was born in Mauritius in 1853, and had been politically active in Capetown before Gandhi arrived in South Africa. Habib was born in Porbandar and was one of the founders of the Natal Indian Congress. Both worked *against* Gandhi at crucial moments, right up to 1914.

This was a scene out of the international nation-building legend—to be found in Green's *Short History of the English People,* for instance. (Gandhi refers to that work occasionally.) The representatives of the people rise to their feet under the influence of moral inspiration and begin a new life of political liberty. The *Daily Mail* compared the Indians' subsequent burning of registration cards with the Boston Tea Party, and that must have seemed to Gandhi exactly right.

On September 11, 1906, therefore, Gandhi discovered the power and the beauty of public political vows; for to *vow* resistance to the law, even at the cost of imprisonment, was a solemn and religious act for Gandhi. He warned his listeners: "Personally, I hold that a man who deliberately and intelligently takes a vow and then breaks it forfeits his manhood" (S:97). But of course, by the same token to keep a vow was to achieve manhood, and manhood of an intensity that would save India from her long history and destiny of humiliation. His friend, Rajendra Prasad, said that once Gandhi had taken a decision, he held to it, whatever the opposition; it took on a life of its own inside him. This was the chaste man's version of virility.

1906–1909

In 1906 Gandhi was sent by his countrymen to London to make their case against the colonists to the imperial government. This shows the striking development in him; he now cut a very different figure from the timid young law student who sailed from India to London in 1888. He was acknowledged as the leader of the Hindus of the Transvaal and Natal, and—less securely—of the Indian non-Hindus there.

Of course, no leader commands a 100 percent support. Even as representing the Hindus, Gandhi was liable to challenge. Before he sailed, William Godfrey, an Indian Christian who had hoped to be one of the deputation, conspired with C. M. Pillay to arouse Tamil and colonial-born resentment against Gandhi, and sent to London news of partly fraudulent mass petitions, declaring that he did not represent them.

From Durban to London 1906

Gandhi was eager to see New Age London again; to renew his friendship with Josiah Oldfield, and to visit Whiteway. But he was to be in England only six weeks, and what time he could spare from his official business was largely absorbed by encounters with, not friends but the spokesmen for violent revolution. He seems to have planned it that way, and to have prepared himself for those encounters.

There was a long history of revolutionary action in India, but a new generation and somewhat new ideas had come to the fore during Gandhi's years outside the country. Important figures in that movement were now living in London. And Gandhi's trip took place at a time when events inside and outside India had a big impact on the self-image of Indians.

One of these was the partition of Bengal decreed by Lord Curzon in 1905—or more exactly the large-scale and prolonged agitation, mostly in Bengal, against that partition. This was the first large political action against the British since the Mutiny/War of Independence, and it made famous names that were to be important throughout Gandhi's lifetime, like Arabindo Ghose and Rabindranath Tagore, as well as older men like Surendranath Banerjee and Bipin Chandra Pal. It also employed methods of agitation that Gandhi was to use, notably the recommendation of *swadeshi* (things made in India) and the boycott and burning of foreign cloth. One of the participants, Saraladevi Chaudhurani, was to help Gandhi in his swadeshi campaign.

Perhaps even more important, though geographically remote, was the Russo-

Japanese War of 1904–5, in which, for the first time, a nation of the East defeated a nation of the West. There was also a dramatic difference between the two countries in geographical area, in size of population, and in length of participation in the modern system. Japan seemed a boyish David up against the Goliath, the colossus, of Russia. But it was above all the spectacle of yellow-skinned men handling the weapons of modern war and turning them against whites successfully that excited the patriots of other Asian nations, including India. Saraladevi Chaudhurani tried to organize an Indian Red Cross corps to serve alongside the Japanese.

So as we follow Gandhi's campaigns, we should compare the contemporary ones in India, and among Indians in exile, for national liberation by violent means. In October 1906, while Gandhi was in London, Bipin Chandra Pal was sentenced to six months jail in Bengal for refusing to give evidence in the sedition case against Arabindo Ghose; in December there was a terrorist attempt on a train carrying a lieutenant governor; in the following April there was an assassination in Muzaffarpur; and in May a bomb factory was discovered in the offices of the newspaper *Navashakti,* and Arabindo and fifty others were again arrested. Saraladevi Chaudhurani, who trained bands of young men in activist methods, was shadowed by the police. It was against this background of "the Russian method" in Bengal that Gandhi began to devise his own policy and political style.

The most striking of such personalities in India were Bengali, but the terrorist/anarchist/revolutionary option was represented in London in 1906 by a predominantly Maharashtran group around Pandit Shyamji Krishnavarma. This man had been successful in two spheres of action before he became a revolutionary. He had taught at Oxford, and married the daughter of a Bombay shipping magnate. He was in a position to promote the causes he believed in, and in 1904 he gave one thousand pounds to found a Herbert Spencer Lectureship at Oxford. Spencer was a hero of the young radicals, so this endowment combined bold with safe implications. But Krishnavarma soon moved toward the more dangerous options.

He had been sent by the government of India to represent India at the Leyden Oriental Congress of 1883, and qualified at the bar in 1884. He had served as diwan of Udaipur, but had left India for good in 1897, because of the government's prosecution of Tilak. He settled in London and founded a journal that was entitled *The Indian Sociologist* and whose ideology was frankly Socialist and nationalist. He had been a member of the Arya Samaj, and some members of that sect, like Bhai Parmanand, lived with him. Others of his associates were more specifically linked to Tilak, such as Vinayak Rao Savarkar, who had arrived that July.

Gandhi wanted to meet these people, but knew that he and they could not cooperate together—unless one of them converted the other—because their principles were mutually opposed. His own protest movement owed more to British New Age activists like the suffragists and the nonconformists.

The women's movement was the object of great interest to Gandhi. James Hunt points out that he was citing to his followers the example of the "suffragettes" a full year before he cited Thoreau's "Civil Disobedience."[17] He reported their activities in *Indian Opinion,* and attended at least one meeting of theirs in London in 1906.

The Nonconformists too were at that time engaging in New Age political action in England. Objecting to the imposition in 1902 of local taxes that benefited Church of England schools, and so promoted Anglican doctrine, they were practicing civil disobedience, by refusing to pay those taxes, and were being arraigned or going to jail as a result. This was an inspiration to Gandhi, who got in touch with their leader, Dr. Clifford, who had been taken to court several times for his actions. Gandhi asked him to judge an essay competition on the topic of passive resistance in South Africa.

Clifford was well-known to the National Council of Free Churches, and Robertson Nicoll, another powerful figure there, suggested that the National Council should endorse the antitax campaign. This did not occur, but many individual Nonconformists joined it, and a national newspaper called the *Crusader* did regularly carry its news.[18] Dr. Clifford went to court forty-one times between 1903 and 1914. He was an inspiring speaker, and it was said that his personality was stamped on a phase of English history (145).

Clifford was the Nonconformist conscience incarnate; he appealed to the example of Cromwell to legitimize his introduction of politics into religion. But he explained the Bible nondogmatically, in literary and spiritual terms, and the chief foe he acknowledged was "priestcraft." He often said that the same battle was being fought all over the world, against clericalism.

These were the two main kinds of radical activism, Indian and British, facing Gandhi as he sailed toward England in October 1906.

London 1906

Gandhi and his Muslim colleague, Haji Ojer Ally, arrived at Southampton on October 20, on the *Armadale Castle.* In London they both stayed at the Hotel Cecil, only ten years old, next door to the Savoy, and claiming to be the most magnificent in Europe. But Ally was sick even before they arrived, and Gandhi, after treating him himself, sent him to Josiah Oldfield.

Gandhi himself spent his first day in London with Henry Polak's family, who had arranged a press interview for him, and who were to be his close allies and sympathizers (Henry's two sisters especially) throughout his stay in England. But he also immediately met Krishnavarma and visited his India House, at 65 Cromwell Avenue, Highgate, where Savarkar was then living. Gandhi stayed two nights at India House, as soon as he arrived, and returned for three discussions on Sunday evenings. Also present were Bhai Parmanand, who had been to South Africa on an Arya Samaj mission the previous year, and several South African students.

Krishnavarma and his friends were more militant in their hatred of England than Gandhi was. They had objected bitterly to the ambulance corps he raised in the Zulu War. Now they criticized Gandhi's choice of the conservative Sir Lepel Griffin as spokesman for his delegation; and—because they wanted Tilak to be given the presidency of congress in the next election—charged Gandhi with persuading Naoroji to withdraw from the contest.

What they made of him, and what else he and they said to each other we have largely to guess, on the basis of what Gandhi wrote in 1909, after his second visit to London. To a man like Savarkar, already familiar with conspiracy, and training others in assassination, Gandhi must surely have looked a political innocent or simpleton, in the world of direct action. (Our own slang offers the word *wimp*—Gandhi's equivalent then was *duffer.*) Could Savarkar have sensed the political power that Gandhi was to generate—a power that was to frustrate the other man's ambitions? It is impossible to guess.

Gandhi and they differed profoundly from each other. But they were all extremists, to use the terms of Indian politics. Passive resistance, for instance, had been a plank in the extremists' platform of the most recent congress, of 1905. In that context it did not imply nonviolence, and was associated with Arabindo, Tilak, and Pal, not with Naoroji and Gokhale, who believed in traditional parliamentary politics. Gandhi's position was distinct from both, though his declared master was Gokhale.

Indian Opinion had some time before introduced Krishnavarma to the readers of *Indian Opinion* politely, as "An Indian Philanthropist," and said that his *Indian Sociologist* was "fearlessly edited." It also reported the opening of India House in its August 5 issue of 1905. Krishnavarma had then awarded his first five scholarships, of two thousand rupees each, to students who vowed not to take service under the government subsequently. He had space for twenty-five students, and hoped to increase that number to fifty. India House was to be like a college, but with a severe discipline; no drinking was to be allowed. The leading Marxist Socialist H. M. Hyndman (the hero of Bloody Sunday) attended the opening, and the India House library was named after him. The editors of *Justice* (a Communist journal) and the *Positivist* attended the opening; so too did Lala Lajpat Rai and Madame Cama, among the Indian radicals. Dadabhai Naoroji was present, but remained silent among the speeches. Krishnavarma however thanked him for coming, saying: "though tied down as he was by certain political views . . . [he] had the catholicity and generosity of mind to give encouragement by his presence" (5:506–7).

In fact Naoroji and Gokhale were bitterly criticized by the people of India House. The two groups represented opposite policies. Gokhale had founded his Servants of India Society the same year as Krishnavarma founded India House. This society's members were also dedicated reformers, working to improve society from within, but by constitutional means, and scrupulously moral. There were sixteen members, who had renounced so much they were in effect secular monks. To India House this seemed morally inert and politically conservative.

Gandhi's attitude to the Servants of India was almost as hostile as Krishnavarma's. He said in 1909 that the society was simply an indifferent imitation of the West. And why did the members have servants? Why did they make a university degree necessary? His experimental settlement at Phoenix was much better than the pomp and show of Pune. (10:138–39).

Mr. Ally was sick much of the time they were in London, and Gandhi himself needed medical attention. He proposed that Oldfield should operate on his nose. But he never had time for anything but a tooth-extraction, which Oldfield performed in the middle of a committee meeting, without anesthetic. Gandhi carried the burden of the deputation's work. This included writing five thousand letters in forty days, addressing a meeting of a hundred Liberal MPs; meeting the prime minister and the colonial secretary; meeting John Morley, the Secretary for India, and Curzon-Wyllie, the latter's political secretary.

We have only partial records of all this activity. James Hunt says that out of twenty-one letters written on a randomly chosen day, only six have survived.[19] Gandhi's main task, as Hunt explains it, was to form a deputation of authoritative British citizens to approach the colonial secretary on behalf of the South African Indians. Gandhi's strategy was an extension of the one he had devised for Nazar in 1897—to avoid alliance with extremists and to build a coalition of highly respected names across a spectrum of opinion. He had wanted Sir George Birdwood to be the leader. Birdwood was an authority on Indian folk art, and politically neutral. But in fact the lead was taken by Sir Lepel Griffin, president of the East India Association, a very conservative but respectable body.

Gandhi did not manage to get a commission of inquiry appointed, but he did set up a permanent South African British Indian Committee in London, to look after their interests. Louis Ritch was put in charge, with a room at Queen Anne's Chambers in Westminster.

On November 27, at the end of his stay, Gandhi met Winston Churchill, who was under secretary for the colonies, and more effectively in charge there than his official superior, Lord Crewe. The meeting was not a significant one, except in the light of subsequent events: Churchill's hostility was to confront Gandhi as persistently as Savarkar's. The two of them were both men of authoritarian power, of the oratorical and the practical kinds; in fact Savarkar was sometimes—in later years—called the Churchill of Maharashtra. And both, though different in other ways, represented a revived but unregenerate nationalism, one in England, the other in India, which Gandhi called on everyone to transcend.

Gandhi's political activities in London were radical in the sense that he was pressuring the empire to live up to its promises to grant brown-skinned citizens the same rights as whites; but they were in style and principle entirely orthodox. They were not revolutionary—which was just the complaint of Savarkar's friends, of course. He was much commended in the London papers for his parliamentary correctness and assiduity in presenting his case. But he also pursued New Age ideas, which were reaching a much wider public than before in England.

We see this in the world of journalism; besides those mentioned, there were the magazines the *New Age* and *Commonweal,* and the newspaper the *Daily Chronicle*. The famous journalists H. W. Massingham and W. T. Stead were Tolstoyans for a time. The *New Age* began in 1898, and *New Order* in 1899; the latter gave accounts of experimental communities; and the same function was performed by Joseph Edwards' *Labor Annual,* a publication Tolstoy read. It was in that direction that Gandhi was going to have to look in the future.

The general election of 1906 had returned a large Liberal majority to parliament, which included a proportion of Nonconformists much larger than before. The Liberals took 377 of the 670 seats, with another 53 going to various Labor candidates and 83 to the Irish Nationalists. The secretary for India was John Morley, who had fought for Irish Home Rule, like his master, Gladstone. He soon disappointed the Indians' hopes, by declaring that the partition of Bengal could not be reconsidered. Indeed, in the January 6 issue of *Indian Opinion* Lala Lajpat Rai had recommended Indians to set their hopes in the Labor members rather than the Liberals.

There was a striking number, over three hundred, of members of parliament who had never before been elected, and of them a goodly proportion were readers of *Unto This Last,* the radical tract that had inspired Gandhi to found his settlement at Phoenix. One of them was Ramsay MacDonald, a New Ager and also a Socialist, and later to be prime minister when Gandhi came to London in 1931 to take part in the Round Table Conference.

As for the nonparliamentary side of Gandhi's interests, he met Florence Winterbottom and Charles F. Cooper, of the International Committee of the Union of Ethical Societies, on November 12. Miss Winterbottom became a good friend; he asked her to arrange meetings he could address; and they saw each other again in 1909. She gave him a letter of introduction to Ramsay MacDonald.

Mrs. Pankhurst, moreover, had persuaded the Women's Social and Political Union, founded in 1903, to take up militant suffrage action. That happened in 1905, and in the same year H. G. Wells led a revolt of the radicals inside the Fabian Society. These were all signs of New Age activity.

Gandhi's mission was superficially successful. He left London on December 1, on the *Briton*, and on the third Churchill announced in the House of Commons that the government would not approve the Transvaal Ordinance. Gandhi's deputation got the news at Mauritius, and were overjoyed.

From London to Capetown 1906

On the voyage home, Gandhi must have been trying to estimate the strength of those New Age elements in England from whom he might expect some support, both in his South African activities and more generally. Two of those deserve some description.

Gandhi was not actively a Tolstoyan at the time of this visit, but he was soon after; and Tolstoy and Tolstoyans were major sponsors of the New Age movement in England. John C. Kenworthy, who has been mentioned before, was writing about Tolstoy. His book *A Pilgrimage to Tolstoy,* was published in 1896 by the Brotherhood Publishing Company, and written in the form of letters home from Russia.

Kenworthy was pastor of the Croydon Brotherhood Church, and editor of the publishing company. "Brotherhood" stood for "Brotherhood of Man," and such churches were sometimes called Labor Churches. This one, founded 1894, ran a store, a laundry, a dressmaking establishment, as well as a farm.

Kenworthy had founded that publishing house together with Vladimir Chertkov. Gandhi corresponded with Chertkov and with the British Tolstoyan, Mrs.

Mayo—who took up the Indians' cause—and read the publications of the Brotherhood Press and its successor, the Free Age Press.

In 1893 Kenworthy joined the committee of the Fellowship of the New Life, and published his *Anatomy of Misery*, which Tolstoy admired. (All these groups were deeply concerned with the social misery of the cities.) He was also a member of the Land Colonization Society, which encouraged and helped people to escape from the city to the country. The Croydon Church sent members out to farm Whiteway, on the Cotswold Hills. This was an enterprise that Gandhi visited later. He referred to it as Tolstoy Farm, which was also the name he gave to his own enterprise outside Johannesburg. He described his aim there as being "to implant the spirit of Tolstoy, and then of country life, and of the way to make the best use of it."[20]

The other aspect of the New Age that came to Gandhi's attention on this trip was the Ethical Culture movement, whose main center was the South Place Chapel. Polak and his wife both belonged to that society, and it may have been noted that an earlier quotation from Polak included the phrase "ethical principle." The word had a number of meanings for members of the movement. The first aim of the Ethical Society was to develop the "science of ethics."[21]

Ethical Culture was a movement with both a practical commitment, to working with the poor, and a philosophical position, based on the conviction that moral tenets need not be grounded in religious dogma. The first can be associated with the settlement house movement; the second with neo-Hegelianism. It was founded in New York by Felix Adler in 1876, and another American, Stanton Coit, brought it to South Place, where it took a prominent place in the congeries of New Age activities.

Felix Adler was the son of a Reform rabbi, and many members of the society were Jewish in origin. The success of the society in Hampstead was attributed to the number of Jews in that suburb of London. Gandhi found the Ethical Culture Union congenial and friendly; several of the constituent societies supported the cause of the Indians in South Africa; and in 1912 he translated and abridged a sixpenny reprint of one of the movement's key texts in his weekly, *Indian Opinion*.

That book was W. M. Salter's *Ethical Religion*. Salter was another American, living in Chicago, and active in applying his religion there, in social and political ways. In the edition published by the Rationalist Press Association in London in 1905, it had an introduction by Stanton Coit, in which he said that this was "the only organized religious movement which has come into existence and developed under the Darwinian method of viewing human events." At the same time, it had kept the emotional enthusiasm of German idealism.[22] This was another kind of creative evolution.

South Africa

When he arrived back in South Africa in December 1906, Gandhi had to face new disappointment and take up again a fight against the proposed law. For by the time their ship reached Capetown, on December 20, the excited self-congratulation of Mauritius had begun to fade. On December 6, the Transvaal and Orange River Colonies had been granted self-government, and it gradually became apparent that they felt free to make their own laws, in the assurance that the imperial government would not act against them. Thus British imperialism proved itself morally ineffective. It could not enforce its will upon the colonies, when the latter were set upon injustice.

On April 30, 1907, Gandhi wrote to *Indian Opinion* promising to lead active opposition to the Asiatic Registration Act. On May 7, that act got the Royal Assent, though Gandhi kept trying to persuade the colony not to enforce it. Thus on May 30 he wrote to the *Star*, appealing to the colonists to accept voluntary registration by Indians; and on July 14 he exhorted the Indians not to submit to compulsion. Such a registration, he told them, had never been imposed upon free men anywhere in the history of the world. He told the Indians that India's honor was in their keeping; an insult offered to a single innocent national insulted that nation as a whole, if accepted. His campaign was beginning.

On November 14, he appeared at Germiston in the trial of Ram Sundar Pundit, the captain of the antiregistration pickets there. The latter was sentenced to six months in jail and was made by Gandhi the first martyr and hero of the movement. A *hartal*, a sort of general strike, was observed by the Indians in the Transvaal in protest against the imprisonment, and Gandhi wrote an article in *Indian Opinion* in his praise, wrote letters for him, and went to see him in prison.

He reported, amongst other things, that Ram Sundar had much enjoyed the political poems written about satyagraha, especially those by Mr. Mehtab—who was none other than Sheikh Mehtab. In a jail interview, Ram Sundar said he had read all the jail-going poems. "I have been deeply moved by them, especially by the poems of Mr. Mehtab. When I come out, I hope to see a copy of these poems in the hands of every Indian in Germiston" (7:419). The reference may be to a book or pamphlet of poems that Mehtab brought out in 1905. Gandhi wrote a note to the editor of *Indian Opinion* on September 30 of that year, saying that the paper need not include any reference to it. (The note is too brief to support any speculation about its emotional significance.)

Perhaps, on the other hand, Ram Sundar was talking about the entries in a competition Gandhi organized in 1907 for the best poem in Gujarati on the subject of satyagraha. Although Mehtab did not win the prize, his poem was printed in *Indian Opinion,* and was introduced with a jocular comment on how it had insinuated itself into the editor's mind irresistibly.

The introductory comment suggested that the editor and the poet had talked about it together. We know that on January 2, the Camroodin company in Durban gave a dinner in Gandhi's honor; which it seems likely that Sheikh Mehtab attended, whether or not he was still living in the Camroodin house.

The poem cannot be made to yield us much knowledge about Mehtab. Both form and content were dictated by the terms of the competition; like all the other entries, it exhorted the readers to go to jail, and listed past and present Indian patriots (Tilak and Surendranath Banerji, amongst the contemporaries). But there seem to be more Muslim heroes mentioned than in the other poem (the winner of the prize) that we can compare it with. Mehtab used the pen name "Rasik," and there is some joking about his poetry being the crowing of a crow. (Mehtab was better known as a poet in Urdu—indeed is still remembered in Durban as a poet of moderate achievement.)

The reader may well be puzzled as to how to fit Ram Sundar's remarks together with the facts about Mehtab's poems as we know them. Perhaps it is most likely that the former had not really read the poems, but even that does not resolve all the inconsistencies.

To return to Ram Sundar's career, it turned out that he was, as Gandhi put it, "accustomed to license and bad habits," and fraudulent as a hero. He was not even a pundit, Gandhi says. (Immigration and the colonial life invited people to invent a past for themselves; one of the inspirations of Gandhi's stress on truth, was his resistance to this.) Though Ram Sundar knew some sanskrit verses by heart, he was, according to Gandhi, only an indentured laborer, who had deserted his indenture.

(In Sushila Nayar's biogaphical volume, *Satyagraha at Work,* the author gives a different account of Ram Sundar; saying that he was a genuine priest, who had studied at Benares, and had spent nine years in South Africa, and built a temple in Germiston. She does not allude to the discrepancy between her account and Gandhi's.)

The new movement needed moral heroes, all the more because Indians were not used to heroism, at least of the sort Gandhi wanted. He wanted the kind the British attributed to their own national traditions; steady, rational, public, communal heroism, breathing the self-respect of both the individual and the community, adorned with the precedents of Hampden, Pym, Latimer, and More.

Gandhi's disappointment was correspondingly bitter when Ram Sundar came out of jail in January and reneged. The government told him to get out of the colony in seven days, and he obediently left the Transvaal and the movement (instead of repeatedly breaking the law and returning to jail) thus answering to British expectations of Indians' instability of purpose. "Ram Sundar Pundit has deserted his temple, his congregation, and his brethren," said Gandhi in *Indian Opinion.* "Present struggle is purification. The dross is being separated from the gold, the chaff sifted from the wheat. . . . This struggle shows up all the flaws in the metal, to expose all the weak links in the chain . . . the result can only be a greater strengthening, a greater power of existence" (8:3).

He continued, "As far as the community is concerned, Ram Sundar is dead as from today. He lives to no purpose. He has poisoned himself by his own hand. . . . We should think of Ram Sundar as a demon, and guard ourself against being possessed by it."

Here we see again the hard side of Gandhi's idealism. Ram Sundar is publicly condemned as severely as Sheikh Mehtab was in private life. (Perhaps Gandhi linked them in his mind.) We must remember that in a sense Gandhi had to create by his voice alone a force of public opinion and a tradition. Many of his comrades did in fact soon cease their resistance or move away, after making bold declarations. Their political self-respect was unreliable. He had to generate a moral-social pressure that in other communities—he thought—sustained itself.

His imagery was often triumphal and military, like that of the Salvation Army. In the Transvaal, he said, the campaign had begun. Hitherto the two sides had only been storing up ammunition. Now the bugle sounded, calling Indians to wake up and mount a ceaseless vigil. This was a struggle that the gods themselves might well come down to watch. He spoke of it being between God and the Devil, between Rama and Ravana. He spoke often of lions: more than one article ended with: "Will the Indian lion wake up?"

But Gandhi also employed traditional religious imagery, which at first had most often a Christian flavor. Antiregistration placards said, "Loyalty to the King of Kings—Indians be free!" The crown of thorns was set in opposition to the crown of diamonds (South African mines had produced fine diamonds for the British crown jewels.) And on July 27, *Indian Opinion* said of the Indian resisters: "Gentle Jesus, the greatest passive resister the world has seen, is their pattern. What matters it to them if the rulers of the Transvaal reject their advances, if their overlord King Edward declares himself unable to protect them?"

This appealed to his Christian sympathizers, who were not insignificant as a presence on the scene. There was a committee of Europeans supporting the Indians, organized by William Hosken in 1908. Hosken was the manager of a gold mine, and had taken part in the Jameson Raid (which nearly provoked war between Boers and Rhodes' followers in Capetown). He was an imperialist but not a racist, and had supported the Baptists in the passive resistance in England. There were also several nonconformist ministers, like Doke, who supported Gandhi: Thomas Perry the Baptist, Charles Phillips the Congregationalist, John Howard the Wesleyan Methodist, N. Audley Ross, the Presbyterian (he too had praised the English Baptists.) Some well-known journalists also were highly sympathetic (as was the case in India later) notably Vere Stent, Albert Cartwright, and David Pollack.

By November 30, 1907, the last day when registration was possible, only eleven out of thirteen thousand Indians had registered themselves. On December 27, Gandhi was arrested, and the next day was tried and ordered to leave the Transvaal, but instead of leaving he addressed a mass meeting. (*He* was not going to run away.) Early in January, he reiterated the Indians' readiness to face imprisonment and deportation, and adopted the term *satyagraha* for what they were doing. On the tenth, he was sentenced to two months in jail.

Gandhi usually speaks of his times in jail in terms of pride, joy, and triumph, which suggest that his residence there was purely symbolic, and morally exalted—an experience very unlike the picture we get of prison in our own contemporary literature. But the reality was not so different; as we would expect from what van Onselen has told us about South African prisons. In Johannesburg, Gandhi was put into a cell with men who had committed crimes of violence and who degraded themselves and everyone around them, he says. He spent one night with black prisoners, in great misery and fear, he tells us; and a Chinese and a "Kaffir" played with each other's genitals. Both of them were in jail on charges of murder and larceny (9:148–49). They played with each other sexually, and at least one night Gandhi had to stay awake the whole night to protect himself from homosexual rape. It is hard to imagine anyone for whom such an experience would have been more upsetting.

In 1925 he spoke of the foul language and unnatural vice to be found in prisons. (It is not clear whether the institution he is writing about is in South Africa or India.) One warder was reputed to have killed another for the possession of one of the prisoners. Gandhi said he would not shock the reader with any details.

His dealings with the jail officials were less brutal but still grim and frustrating. From Volksrust he was sent to Pretoria, where he spent three hours polishing a varnished iron door (9:231). But he was able to do some reading. He carried his copy of *The Kingdom of God Is within You* to court. At the chief warder's request, he carried it in such a way as to conceal his handcuffs—a wonderful irony, as Gandhi said (9:240). And he learned by heart some exalted passages of Raychandbhai's verse, such as: "The sky rings with the name of the Invisible, I sit rapt in the temple, my heart filled with gladness."[23]

Private Life

But we must turn to Gandhi's family relations, to follow an important new thread in that tangle. In 1907 Gandhi's oldest son, Harilal, returned from India, bringing a wife with him. He had married the year before, without his father's consent, and indeed quite against his father's wishes. In South Africa he joined in Gandhi's political work, and went to jail more than once, but from this time on there was growing difficulty and strain between them.

In August 1908, Gandhi wrote proudly to *Indian Opinion* that "it was part of Harilal's education to go to gaol for the sake of the country." But this pride had much to do with Gandhi's conviction that modern education was "a thorough fraud," a conviction that Harilal did not—at least steadily—share. He was, Gandhi said, ambitious; as he himself had been, going to London.

Indeed, Gandhi's own evaluation of Western education fluctuated. Despite his disappointment in London in 1906, he began immediately to make arrangements for his nephew Chhaganlal to go to study there. Gandhi still thought, intermittently, that a training in England was of great value.

Then twenty, Harilal is described by Robert Payne as being tall, lean, and better-looking than the other Gandhi boys. (Gandhi described him in 1915 as "very handsome," not a word he often used.) He was proud of his hair, which he wore long, and parted in the middle. He was also serious, sympathetic to all suffering things, and personally engaging.

But though ambitious, it seems that Harilal also needed to be looked after and to be reassured. It seems appropriate that he should have fallen ill while he was in India, and should be nursed back to health by his host, and then should marry his nurse's daughter. He had little power of resistance to his father, in direct confrontation, but considerable power of resentment.

He was arrested four times in the satyagraha cause, as Gandhi boasted to Tolstoy; but in jail railed to his friend, Pragji Desai, saying that his father wanted him to be nothing but a pliant tool in his hands. He made himself the official defender of his mother's rights within the household, and plaintiff on her behalf.

In the autobiography Gandhi explains Harilal's rebelliousness by saying that his son had long been affected by Gandhi's own state of mind during his Sheikh Mehtab period—his period of "half-baked knowledge and indulgence." Harilal still (this was written in 1925) thinks those were Gandhi's best years. Gandhi says, "Why should he not think that at that time I trod the royal road followed by all the world and was, therefore, safe, whereas the changes effected later were signs of refined egotism and ignorance in me?" One might suggest also that the son was affected by his mother's state of mind as well as his father's—her bitter complaints against the father. She herself was to outlive her complaints but not he.

There developed thus something of an alliance between Harilal and his mother, against Gandhi and those they thought he favored, like his nephews, Maganlal and Chhaganlal—and Polak, whom Kasturba bitterly described as Gandhi's "first-born." Later his second and third sons, Manilal and Ramdas, said that their father had been hard on them, which in some sense of the word could hardly be contested; and that he treated them badly, which seems to mean that he did not give them special opportunities as his sons.

Gandhi was trying to turn his domestic ties into something like ideological links and to form a party out of his family; Maganlal and Chhaganlal were devoted disciples and workers for his causes, and were therefore closer to Gandhi than his sons. He was loosening family ties. In a letter to his cousins, who had reminded him to get his sons married, he said that that would only make them sensual, "and thus the tree of lust flourishes. I do not think this is religion, whatever others may say." As for property, the satyagrahis lived communally, at Phoenix and later at Tolstoy Farm, owning nothing individually. Gandhi was fond of individuals and places, and glad to be fond of them, but there were clear limits to his attachment. Eros was not his god.

Public Affairs and Ideas

While in jail, Gandhi managed to reread Tolstoy's *Kingdom* and began to translate another classic of the New Age—Ruskin's *Unto This Last*. Meanwhile, in London, his allies, like Sir William Wedderburn, Sir Mancherjee Bhownagree, and Mohammed Ali Jinnah, were busy on his behalf. Jinnah had been commissioned by the Anjuman Islam of Bombay to argue the case of the Transvaal Indians before the English people. And in November 1909 he, Gokhale, and others formed the Indian Committee in Bombay to collect funds to help those Indians deported from the Transvaal. Jinnah's career was to run curiously close and parallel to Gandhi's.

On January 28, 1908, a compromise letter was drawn up and signed by both Gandhi and Smuts, which exchanged a promise of repeal of the Registration Act for a promise of voluntary registration. On the thirtieth, Gandhi was taken out of jail and brought secretly to a confrontation and conference with Smuts in Pretoria. At the conference, Gandhi was immediately freed and addressed a midnight meeting of Indians a thousand strong. Next day all the satyagrahis were released from jail.

But there were soon disquieting rumors about what Smuts thought he had agreed to, as judged by his comments to his party. Moreover, Gandhi himself had involved the Indians' cause with subtleties. He had to explain to suspicious Pathans an apparent change of position, or at least of tactic. To register in obedience to the Black Act, he had insisted, would be a sin; but now he said that voluntarily to give their fingerprints would be the hallmark of a gentleman. They were not convinced.

In February 10, voluntary registration began, and Gandhi meant to be the first to offer his fingerprints, but on the way to give them he was struck down from behind with a cudgel by a Pathan, Mir Alam Khan, in the company of other Pathans. Mir Alam was, Gandhi tells us, fully six feet tall, and of powerful build. Gandhi fainted, with "He Ram" allegedly on his lips. Gandhi and his companions were kicked and beaten while they lay on the ground. Taken to Mr. Doke's house to recover, he asked that no vengeance should be taken against his assailant. Mr. Chamney, the registrar of Asiatics, came to the house eager to assure Gandhi of legal redress but Gandhi insisted instead that he be registered. (He also insisted on making himself a mud poultice, to the doctor's disgust.)

By February 29, 1908, 3,400 Indians had registered. On March 5, however, there was another attempt on Gandhi's life at a meeting in Durban (the lights were put out, and a Pathan carrying a big stick rushed the platform) and the next day, when he had a meeting with the community leaders of the Durban Pathans, they told him they believed he had betrayed them. The rumor was that he had taken fifteen thousand pounds to sell out.

This conflict followed sectarian lines to some degree. Gandhi tells us that all the letters blaming him for the compromise came from Muslims. Haji Ojer Ally ceased to trust him, as a Hindu, and many Muslims thought of wiring Jinnah to warn him against Gandhi—some Pathans did so. Some of them said: "Gandhi has totally ruined the Muslims and has been doing so for fifteen years" (8:99 and 100). There were many shifts in opinion, but from this point on Gandhi was frequently criticized by South African Muslims, especially the Natal merchants and the Pathans.

Polak wrote in 1909, "Perhaps Mr Gandhi's greatest regret during all the last three terrible years, is that so much of the communal energy has been used up in destructive criticism instead of in constructive social work, and he has only become reconciled to the situation by realizing that destructive criticism is essential to the communal progress and that the struggle itself has built up character as probably no deliberately undertaken constructive work could have done."[24]

The events surrounding registration followed an even more Kipling-like pattern than the Ram Sundar story did. As Kipling might have put it, the South African Pathans had been induced to put their faith in a babu, an educated, nonmartial, clever-talking Indian, who promised to lead them in a nonviolent revolution against the English masters. He turned out to be a man of many words, who did not keep his promises, and they were betrayed, so that they took their revenge with murderous violence and turned back to their firm but just English masters. (One such story is "The Head of the District.")

It was in terms of such legends that the English understood India, the empire in general, and their role as its rulers. Lord Milner actually referred to Gandhi as "some clever babu"; an Anglo-Indian term defined as having "a flavor of disparagement, as characterizing a superficially cultivated, but too often effeminate Bengali."[25] And many conflicts between Indians and English did fit those Kipling patterns, as this whole story would have done if Gandhi had run away or fallen silent. But on August 16, when he began a new phase of the campaign, Mir Alam and other Pathans admitted their error, burned their registration cards, and resolved to fight with him to the end. What we see here is Gandhi breaking the pattern of expectation in both English and Indian minds by the strength of his resolve and the clarity of his mind.

European Friendships

I said that Eros was not Gandhi's god, but perhaps one should say rather that he was a servant of Eros who struggled to be free. His letters to Kallenbach give us the most complete example we have of Gandhi's way of winning someone over; inducing them to work for a cause, while at the same time offering them a highly personal love. While reading these letters one has a glimpse of what he may have tried to say and write to Sheikh Mehtab.

Gandhi said that when C. F. Andrews asked if they could use each other's first names, he replied that that would be hard for him because he had always "kept a respectable distance from friends" (84:384). That exchange presumably took place in 1914. But the lack of first names between him and Kallenbach cannot be taken to signify lack of intimacy.

On June 21, 1909, he writes that he does not understand Kallenbach's extraordinary love for him. Their mutual attachment is proof of their having lived before in other bodies. (I think he means the feeling Westerners mean by saying two people are "meant for each other.") On August 30 the same year he writes, "You remind me of friendships of bygone years of which one reads in histories and novels. . . . But is that almost superhuman love to exhaust itself in delicate attentions to me and mine, or will it not compel you to the study you know you need so badly to complete?" (UC). This is a reference to Kallenbach's studies for a degree in architecture, begun in Germany in his youth, but still unfinished many years later.

On September 24, 1909, he tells Kallenbach that *his* photograph is the only one on the mantlepiece opposite Gandhi's bed in his London hotel room. His handkerchief also reminds him of Kallenbach, because it was part of their contract that Gandhi should use a new one every day. The pen he uses, "in each letter it traces makes me think of you." And so on. "If therefore I wanted to dismiss you from my thoughts, I could not do it. My nose is—well, it won't stop its action." All this shows "how completely you have taken possession of my body." He *is* Kallenbach. And the moral is, again, that Kallenbach should study; because "You cannot take no as an answer from yourself."

The issue of the handkerchief seems to show that Gandhi had—rather surprisingly—not acquired that item of Western politeness in London in 1888; or perhaps he had discarded it afterwards. But it is interesting to see Gandhi in the less-usual role of accepting discipline from others. In other letters, Kallenbach is allowed to have much to teach him about gardening, and about physical exercises and drill. Polak in their first years together taught Gandhi how to overcome annoying habits in public speaking: Gandhi used to hesitate, and draw in his breath sibilantly, seeking the word he wanted.[26] But it seems to have been clear that in both relationships Gandhi was the dominant one and the disciplinarian.

Gandhi and Kallenbach wrote to each other sometimes as "Upper House" and "Lower House," referring to the House of Lords and the House of Commons. While Polak and he wrote to each other as "Bhai" and "Chota Bhai," older and younger brother. In both cases, we note the superiority of Gandhi's role. But it was the playfulness of love that got expressed in those terms. "Dear Mr Kallenbach, The Upper House was delighted to receive a note from the Lower House, but the Upper House strongly resents and protests against the insult implied in the title used by the Lower House in addressing the Upper House. If the Lower House persists in such disrespectful and inappropriate language, all the liberty granted by the Constitution to the Lower House will be withdrawn, and the Lower House will be called upon to return to Phoenix" (UC). And in 1911, when Kallenbach went to Europe, and they drew up "Articles of Agreement" between them, embodying his promises to behave himself while away, the return he is promised is "more love and yet more love between the two houses—such love as, they hope, the world has not yet seen."

In all this Gandhi was clearly indulging the desire, (in both men) for what he elsewhere disapproved, as an "exclusive relationship." He wrote to Kallenbach, "I certainly did not like to part with you. But the parting was inevitable. Remember the meditation of the Yom Kippur, you must constantly check yourself" (UC). And again, later, "Nothing has pained me so much in leaving Johannesburg at the present juncture as your physical and mental condition. If I could have avoided going to Natal . . . ," he would have stayed, in order to nurse and encourage Kallenbach.

Kallenbach's profession, architecture, was one of Gandhi's lifelong interests, and one of the areas in which the Simple Life experimented; in simple structures, openness to sun and wind, economy of means, local materials, harmony with the landscape, and so on. Kallenbach had such ideas of his own, as we have seen. But his big commissions naturally were to design hotels, department stores, and so on, where those ideas could not be employed.

This kind of architecture and city planning was closely linked to the simple life, and to vegetarianism—the prospectus for Letchworth, the first Garden City, was printed in the *Vegetarian*. In 1909 Gandhi visited Whiteway, and also wrote to Kallenbach, "I should certainly like to push my nose into it [a plan Kallenbach was drawing up] and play the architect and give some of the newfangled notions I am bringing with me." In India, later, he was able to put his architectural ideas into practice at his ashrams.

Another side to Gandhi's emotional and relational life is shown in his letters to Millie Graham Polak. There was considerable debate or dialectic in this relationship, about the conflicting claims both of them made on Henry; Gandhi used to say that Henry had two wives. On November 14, 1909, Gandhi wrote from London to Millie—Henry being in India—saying that he and she differed and yet were the same, in that they both sought the truth. "You are my sister and brother, as well as Henry's wife." He wanted from her "a sister's full trust and confidence, not a daughter's obedience." He boasted that he had hastened their marriage (when Henry's father had wanted to delay it) and admitted that he was now keeping them apart, by sending Henry to India.

The next day Gandhi wrote to Henry, describing a scene at the home of the senior Polaks, where Millie had given a "harrowing account" of life at Phoenix to Henry's sisters, who were enthusiastic about going out to Africa, to become Gandhians. Millie admitted to not a single redeeming feature to the settlement, according to Gandhi, who reports her words in high good humor: filth, beetles everywhere, spiders, ants in the milk, bad water, no baths, people half-naked, snakes hanging from the trees, lift a plate and you find an insect under it. "It was a gloriously exaggerated description. I said not a word except that it was accurate." The effect was to turn Sallie Polak against the project, but not Maud, who remained enthusiastic about becoming Indianized.

Gandhi went on to worry about whether Maud's enthusiasm resulted from the glamour of his own personality: "If so, I should be shot on sight: as a power more for harm than good." In these years he began to refer to this glamour—which was evidently something established, in a sense taken for granted, and freely discussed in his circle. It was of course not something that had been attributed to him in earlier years.

The letter is full of gaiety and affection for Henry. A friend, praising Henry's work as editor of *Indian Opinion,* has called him a born journalist. "I have a better name for you," said Gandhi. "You are a born idealist." He was equally enthusiastic about Millie, calling her a wonder-worker in the way she looked after her two beautiful children.

In a letter to her of December 31 that year, he goes again into their differences, in the same style. It is evident that Millie has been complaining about the way he is affecting her married life. She is, he says, dearer to him than is his sister in India, whom he worships but from whom a gulf (of ideas) divides him. Nevertheless,

> Your brief letter haunts me. It fills me with sorrow and admiration for you. You have written it in grief, love, and resignation. . . . No, no, my dear Sister, you are not going to live away from Henry for ever. . . . No path can be considered right for him along which he cannot carry you. . . . You have cut a deep wound in my heart by telling me that your brief letter is to be the last for many months. . . . You have often given me the privilege of analysing you to yourself. . . . You have heroically sacrificed yourself on the altar of duty. But you have done so in bitterness not always free from resentment. . . . Will you not for my sake shake yourself free from the little

> morbidity of your nature? . . . Now do tell me what you would have me do? (UC)

He accorded Millie the status of a superior person—a strong nature, which he compared with his own. Sometimes he implies a closer resemblance between the two of them than there was between Gandhi and Henry. In a letter of April 24, 1910, he describes Henry as a tender flower, his spirits ruffled by the slightest breeze. "You and I divide him. . . . But alas! he can just now have neither you nor me. The publication and confiscation of the little book of mine [*Hind Swaraj*] have disconcerted him a bit." He wants Millie to apply to him, Gandhi, for money, and not to trouble Henry, who hates the subject.

This triangular relationship is a pattern we shall often see in Gandhi's life from this point on. He made alliance with the wife, daughter, or sister of his ally or rival, and sometimes (playfully) incited her to bring the man around to Gandhi's point of view. (He approached Henry's sisters in somewhat the same way.) Later we see this happening with Kamala Nehru, with Manibehn Patel, even with Mrs. Jinnah. In somewhat different form, we see it with Saraladevi Chaudhurani, the niece of Rabindranath Tagore. It was connected, in his mind, with his being as much woman as man. In 1939 he declared that in South Africa "I discovered that I was specially fitted to serve womankind" (70:313).

Henry Polak's sense of himself, as expressed in his letters, is not at all the tender flower (which is not to say that Gandhi was wrong). His tone is often tough and truculent. Thus on August 17, 1911, he begins a reply to "your astonishing and characteristic letter." "My Dear Bhai, You have a most delightful habit of directing at my devoted head bolts from the blue, and then imagining that things will proceed just as before." Gandhi is much too impulsive, and shows a subtle kind of selfishness and egotism. "Apparently you ask for martyrdom quite regardless of the fact that you may be conferring martyrdom upon others who are not so willing to receive it. . . . You must be either the prophet or the worker in everyday affairs" (UC).

The idea of "the prophet" was popular in sociology at that time (connected to the idea of "charisma") and it becomes clear that Polak has adapted these terms to deal with his sense of himself and his relations with Gandhi. Polak sees himself as a "worker"; one who fulfills various obligations to persons and causes. The prophet, on the other hand, throws off ordinary responsibilities, and the restraints of convention, creed, and nationality. The two functions cannot be combined successfully in one person. Polak clearly intended to remind Gandhi of obligations that, as a prophet, he forgot. On the other hand, the idea of his being a prophet was also deeply admiring. Moreover, it was congenial to Gandhi's own way of thinking, and so acceptable; just as Polak's fearless criticism of Gandhi must have been, since Gandhi asked for that so often.

Thus we find Polak writing later (in 1920), "I have been very painfully exercised indeed with regard to your various activities of late. Either I do not understand them or, if I do, I find it difficult to appreciate your point of view . . . you have a fatal gift of passing from subject to subject, losing yourself in each at a time, only to leave it unfinished and go on to the next" (UC). These were indeed very pertinent criticisms, as Gandhi admitted.

He and the Polaks lived together more than once, and they were very close allies. Millie says he had installed a Turkish cabinet bath, and a cold plunge and hip bath, in 1905, as the nucleus of a nature cure sanatorium. The failure of this sanatorium was a great disappointment to Gandhi. But he did, according to her, save Ba from pernicious anemia, considered to be a fatal disease.

They were a New Age family. The Polak children seem to have been named after New Age heroes: the older son was called Bernard and Graham (after Shaw and Wallas) as well as Waldo (from the Olive Schreiner novel); the younger was called Morris as well as Leon. It does not seem likely that this was exclusively Henry's influence.

Millie was a New Ager as a young woman, though she was not ready to sacrifice her marriage, and other interests, to the cause. (She was for instance interested in music, and we hear of her singing arias like the Jewel Song from *Faust* and "Il Bacio.") She was skeptical about Phoenix, and resentful of the rivalries and jealousies that surrounded Gandhi. But she too clearly felt for many years the glamour of Gandhi's personality, and of the adventure they were all engaged in. She took part, organizing meetings of Indian women, at critical moments. Her sisters came out to South Africa to stay with her, and Kallenbach is said to have wanted to marry one of them.

On occasion Gandhi apologized for overtaxing his friends. "That unfortunately is the price friends pay for close association with me," he wrote Kallenbach (UC). In 1913 he decided that the latter had been following Gandhi in his enthusiasms, and not acting out of his own convictions. "If you had an inner conviction, if your belief in the future life was unshakable, if you had become sick of the world unto death, . . . [Then he should boldly follow Gandhi.]" But as it was, Kallenbach *ought* not to think of living in Phoenix or India. Gandhi had been forcing his pace. Kallenbach should stick to his architectural practice and material advancement, while keeping up his interest in the simple life.

Gandhi tried to give him a different role in the movement. "Watch me just now, not with a friendly eye but with a highly critical and fault-finding eye" (UC). And again, "Please come and criticize . . . I know that in many things there is room for improvement. Only I cannot see it. I do need a friendly critic." This was perhaps a role that Polak could play better than Kallenbach, whose friendship was emotional, not to say sentimental.

Often Gandhi took a bracing tone to him: "You are in a self-scorching mood," he wrote on March 5. "Carried too far it makes one morbid. . . . If you have wasted forty two years then don't waste the forty third. . . . This heart-scorching is a species of subtle pride. At the bottom there is a desire to shine" (UC). The temptations of "subtle" pride were something they were all much aware of.

He often scolded Kallenbach for his affectional claims and resentments, in ways that are sometimes tender, sometimes not. Kallenbach has wrongly transferred all his affection to Gandhi: "And now you find your idol not satisfying you. This hurts you as if a dagger had gone through you. But why? Who am I? . . . Let the idol be broken. The residue will be a purer thing" (UC).

As for the severe tone: "Your letter of the 9th [1914] is petty, touchy, and spiteful. It has made me sad and shows that all your so-called reforms there are simply superficial. What you call a circular letter is no circular letter. It was addressed to you and Polak. [Kallenbach had apparently written, 'Please do not send me such circular letters henceforth.'] You are right, you are jealous, and wrongly so, of Miss Schlesin and Andrews." Because Miss Schlesin wrote the covering letter that accompanied Gandhi's, "it became an offense to you."

Soon after meeting Andrews, Gandhi wrote Kallenbach: "Mr. Andrews is a wonderful man, full of wonderful experiences" (UC). Soon he tried to reassure his older friend that he is still loved: "I sense your fear. The result has been and will be the opposite of that you have feared. All is gain for you and me." On February 27 he employs the rhetoric of love to soothe the other man. "Though I love and almost adore Andrews so, I would not change you for him. You still remain the dearest and the nearest to me and so far as my non-selfish nature is concerned I know that in my lonely journey through the world, you will be the last (if even that) to say goodbye to me" (UC). And again on April 17: "How curious! No matter how intimate I may be with Andrews or Gokhale, or anyone else, you will always be you to me. I have told you, *you* will have to desert me and not I you" (UC).

There were painful jealousies among these friends—one of the marks of the exclusive relationship—for instance between Polak and Kallenbach, each wanting to be closest to Gandhi. Kallenbach was the more effusive and personal in his devotion; Polak the more political and purposeful. (The two men look rather similar on photographs, partly because both wore pince-nez and both combed their hair back.) The problems inseparable from his "glamour" were to pursue Gandhi for the rest of his life. It was something not easily detached from his causes, for it was by means of his charm, partly, that Gandhi was able to extract so much work from other people.

In 1912 also Gandhi was jealously reproached by Kallenbach with being too much impressed by Gokhale, who toured South Africa that year. Gandhi replied, "Mr. Gokhale absorbed so much of my time because his possibilities are great and he has a very lofty character. . . . Naturally I want to see him as perfect a being as possible. He is my political teacher. For that reason also I would like to contemplate him in his perfection."

This attribution of perfection to another, however self-aware, is at odds with much in Gandhi's later character (though pious, he was in many ways dour and skeptical) but this is not the only case of it. It is implicit in his enthusiasm for Andrews (whom he repeatedly called a wonderful man) and explicit in a few sentences about Emily Hobhouse, the English idealist-reformer. "Miss Hobhouse has a divine face. I have never seen a diviner face. Gokhale by his features took me by storm. Miss Hobhouse has done likewise only more so. I felt like gazing at her in awe for hours." Gandhi liked to worship.

As for himself being worshipped, he certainly knew that was happening; he accepted it, and derived energy from it. After all, he *intended* to bring the light of heaven down to earth. But being treated as a Mahatma was painful to him as much as pleasant, and most of the time he tried to ignore it. Certainly most people in a situation anything like his give much more impression of eagerly sniffing up incense.

As Father Husband Brother

The stress that Gandhi's enterprises put on his family life can be glimpsed and guessed in a few external facts. On January 5, 1909, Harilal and others were remanded at Volksrust. On January 10 Kasturba, who had been seriously ill for three months, was operated on in Durban. Gandhi looked after her, but on January 16, he himself was arrested and deported; he returned immediately and was rearrested. On February 4, he brought Kasturba, still quite sick, to Phoenix. On the tenth, Harilal and others got sentences of from three to six months. When Gandhi himself was taken from jail to court in handcuffs as a witness on March 10, passive resisters congratulated Kasturba on his third imprisonment. The next day she sent a message to a meeting of Indian women in Johannesburg to say that had she wings she would fly to them.

The doctor insisted that she take beef tea, but Gandhi insisted on explaining to her what it was, and asking her to decide if she wanted to take it. (She did not.) He then had her carried—in a very enfeebled condition—to Phoenix, where he could look after her himself.

It is clear that family comfort and prosperity were sacrificed to the cause, and one is bound to suppose, furthermore, that the family members found themselves engaged in exciting acts, and using excited language, which they knew when they asked themselves all derived from Gandhi. (This criticism was brought up often: Kallenbach was said by skeptics to be Gandhi's puppet, and both he and Gandhi worried about whether he was.)

From jail, Gandhi wrote a letter to Manilal, on March 25, 1909, trying to put things right between them. "My dear son, Although I think you are well able to bear all the burden I have placed on your shoulders and that you are doing it quite cheerfully, I have often felt that you required greater personal guidance that I have been able to give you." But he does not really yield. "I know, too, that you have sometimes felt that your education was neglected. Now I have been reading a great deal in prison. I have been reading Emerson, Ruskin, and Mazzini. I have also been reading the Upanishads. All confirm that education does not mean a knowledge of letters—it means a knowledge of duty" (UC).

Though the letter was addressed to Manilal, he was asked to make copies for other people, and one can take it for granted that Harilal too was meant to read it. Manilal and Harilal seem to have been influenced by the Arya Samaj, which sent Bhai Parmanand as a missionary to South Africa in 1905, and in 1909 both him and Swami Shraddhanand. The former had taught at the society's Anglo-Vedic College. (Then a young man of twenty-seven, he was later to be sent as a political prisoner to the Andaman Islands because of his links to the revolutionary, Har Dayal.)

Gandhi was on his guard against the Arya Samaj. In *Indian Opinion,* he welcomed Professor Parmanand as a distinguished scholar, on July 21, 1905, but added: "I do not give my consent to the collecting of subscriptions for him." And he advises against giving the reception for him a religious, Hindu-revival aspect. "We are not yet ripe for missionary work. Indians in South Africa are not ready to receive any doctrines of reform" (5:20, 48). Parmanand, and the swami, reproached Gandhi with being insufficiently Hindu in his religion and his politics.

They were more ready to employ violence. While in London in 1909, he wrote commenting on the swami's speech about the assassination of Curzon-Wyllie, and on two of his letters, saying that he was grieved by all three. The swami's ideas about education would create a split between Hinduism and Islam, which would cause the death of Hinduism. But, he says, Hinduism will not perish, even at the hands of its priests. "I have respect for your knowledge; but I am pained at your behaviour." (9:377).

No full account of Harilal's dealings with that society has been compiled, but there are hints over the years that he often found in its Hinduist doctrines weapons with which to oppose his father. He wanted to go to study "in the Punjab" in 1911, and when he converted to Islam in the 1930s, it was the Arya Samaj that brought him back to Hinduism. It was a counterorganization to the Muslim missionary Hamadiya Islamia Society. Both originated in the Punjab. The Young Men's Hindu Association, too, was inspired by Arya Samaj ideas, and existed to retrieve lapsed Hindus.

In the letter already cited, Gandhi wrote about the wearing of the sacred thread, as the mark of the reborn upper-caste Hindu, which the Arya Samaj was trying to revive. "I respectfully disagree with the Swamiji in his propaganda. I think that the adoption of the sacred thread by those who have for years given it up is a mistake. As it is, we have too much of the false distinction between shudras and others." He went on to question the swami's interpretation of various prayers and upanishads.

He asked that the swami should leave behind some of his writings, if he left South Africa while Gandhi was in prison, or send some from India. But he went on to recommend Manilal to read the New Age writers, Emerson and Tolstoy.

Family relations did not break down completely. In 1911 Gandhi wrote to Harilal that he didn't like his views, but had no suspicions of his character, and therefore felt no anxieties about him. But in the spring of that year, Harilal left his home in anger, saying in a letter that he was breaking all his family ties. His letter, which followed the lines of one in a Gujarati novel—the letter-writer a man who ran away similarly—made his friends fear suicide, and they openly blamed and reproached Gandhi. Harilal had in fact taken refuge in the Portuguese colony in Delagoa Bay, where he took an assumed name, and planned to return to India. Kallenbach followed him, and persuaded him to come back. Even after long discussions with his father, he remained unreconciled, and went home alone to India, to begin a formal education again at the age of twenty-three.

By Gandhi's account, Harilal complained that his father had not admired his sons, or done anything especially for them, that he was hard-hearted, and had put them and their mother, not ahead of other people, but behind. No doubt all this was true. In 1914 Manilal also charged him with cruelty, though it is not clear what kind.

To some extent Harilal's resentment, and that of other family members, was aimed at Maganlal in particular. Gandhi sent the latter a bundle of Harilal's letters in 1911, saying: "If Harilal's or Manilal's or Ba's being unhappy with you, or their bitter words, make you think of leaving, you will be behaving as one separate from us and I shall find it difficult to do my duty to them and to you"; and "If you decide on leaving, Harilal's and Manilal's best interest cannot but suffer" (11:74 and 5). He explained that Harilal's anger was really directed at his father.

In his letters, Gandhi appears most often understanding and compassionate. He told Maganlal that the fault in the parting was not Harilal's but his own; Harilal was not to blame. He gave the latter some reasonable-sounding advice, and even warned him not to follow it simply because it came from his father. And to Harilal's wife, he wrote on February 18, 1912, "I can well understand your natural desire to be with Chi Harilal. I do not at all wish to come in your way in this. Live, both of you, as you wish and do what you like. I can have but one wish; that you should be happy and remain so" (11:237). He knew, he said, that Harilal would not do anything wrong.

However, like other people, Gandhi could and did sometimes write and reflect more nobly than he spontaneously acted. The quarrel with Kasturba described in the introduction was a good example of his severity; and so was his description of his feelings during the fast.

No doubt the stress and strain of fasting added to his misery at that moment. In those early fasts he lost his voice, and couldn't swallow or keep food down when he tried to eat again. Gradually he learned the art of fasting; he took water frequently, did muscle exercises in bed, and had two enemas a day administered to him.

His relations with his brothers were also difficult. Both had in effect severed relations with him. We do not know what passed between him and Karsandas, but Mohandas got bitter reproaches from Lakshmidas for having abandoned the family.

In a reply of April 20, 1907, Gandhi said that their outlooks differed widely. He too believed in the old traditions but not in age-old superstitions. Lakshmidas, he said, harbored hatred for his younger brother; this was because he was overcome by attachment (6:430). Gandhi now felt that his insurance policy in Ba's name (taken out because of his brother's bitter letters to him when he was in Bombay, fighting the plague) went against his conscience. Lakshmidas was apparently afraid that he would be burdened with looking after Ba and the boys if Gandhi died (6:432).

Mohandas agreed that his two brothers have a right to a share in his own earnings, but said he had already paid them nearly sixty thousand rupees, and they spent more than he on personal enjoyment. He has cleared all their debts, and they told him then that no more was needed. He answers some questions

Lakshmidas has put. Why did he go to England? To maintain the family's status—"to be well off and enjoy the good things of life." The risk was great, for all of them; they staked everything on his education. Because the relatives and family friends who promised to help did not do so, Lakshmidas had admittedly had to work hard. The disposition of some pieces of property mentioned by the latter Mohandas cannot now remember, "as father himself had started selling the property and we did the same after him." In any case, Lakshmidas has been extravagant, and squandered a lot of money on pomp and show, and in what Mohandas regards as "immoral ways." Above all, he himself is not the master of his earnings, because he had dedicated his all to the people. Thus he has not robbed his brother, or anybody else. No doubt Lakshmidas will be dissatisfied with these answers, but "I am quite helpless" (6:436).

Much later, Gandhi wrote to Srinivasi Shastri (in 1932) that his brother had banished him for fourteen years; this would be from the time of his 1901 visit to 1914. "Year after year he sent me curses by registered post" (51:102). Typically, the occasion of this remark was that Gandhi was asking Shastri for criticism as frank as Lakshmidas's. It is equally typical that he continued with a claim to have triumphed in that earlier quarrel: "I rejoiced in his curses. His curses were so many sparks of love—I won him. Six months before his death he saw that I was in the right."

On the other hand, Gandhi promised that he would look after his brothers' widows and dependents. (By the end of 1914, he had five such widows dependent on him.) Lakshmidas wrote shortly before his death, saying that his dearest wish was now to join Mohan in South Africa, and asking him to look after one of his sons. Both brothers died in this period; Karshandas on June 22, 1913, in Rajkot, and Lakshmidas on March 9, 1914, in Porbandar.

Followers

But if his relations with his immediate family were strained (though not unmixedly black) Gandhi found ardent disciples. We have mentioned Polak, Kallenbach, and other Europeans. There were also Indians; some of Dr. Mehta's family, and his own nephews, Chaganlal, Maganlal, and Jamnadas, the sons of his cousin Khushalal. And he formed a happy friendship with a man he surely felt to be close to him in sympathy, Joseph Doke, a Baptist minister.

Only eight years the elder, Doke was a man of delicate health and little schooling who had come to South Africa as long before as 1881; he had wanted to be a missionary in Africa, but was not thought strong enough. He had preached in New Zealand, where he had taken an interest in the Chinese immigrants, similar to the interest he now took in South Africa's Indians. One can see some similarities of temperament linking him and Gandhi; both had varied interests and talents, but subdued or sacrificed them all to moral enthusiasm.

They shared many of the same concerns. In 1911 Doke was reading books that interested Gandhi: Tolstoy, Maude's biography of Tolstoy, and Nordau's *Degeneration*. Doke's fiction expresses those interests. And he well understood and defined the dynamic of Gandhi's life. He wanted to call his biography

The Path Finder or *The Jungle-breaker.* In writing Doke's obituary, in *Indian Opinion,* August 23, 1913, Gandhi praised him warmly. Doke had no exclusive relationships (12:168); and his was not, Gandhi said, "a modernized or civilized Christianity. He practised the original" (12:176).

Earlier in his life Doke had the ordinary British prejudices. On a trip to India in 1885, he saw the subcontinent as: "Teeming in population, black with ignorance, horrible with idolatry, its beautiful marble palaces and inlaid tombs speaking of the high civilization of which we see only the ruins."[27] He contrasted the empty shell of the Jama Masjid in Delhi with the new Baptist college there, a hive of activity. Doke's, however, was a naive mind in the good sense also, and he learned from Gandhi, and others, how to expand his mental horizons.

Doke wrote two novels, in the same genre as Rider Haggard's romances, which show us certain ideas that were circulating amongst Gandhi's friends. The second, *The Queen of the Secret City,* was published posthumously, in 1916. The evil character is said to put Nietzsche's ideas into practice. Chapter 2 makes play with a lot of such ideas; for instance, that slavery is necessary to civilization. An anonymous postscript tells us that Doke had been studying Nietzsche, and was so impressed by the perniciousness of his teaching that he had written this book to show what the Will to Power means. The war that has broken out since Doke died shows how a nation can be debased by taking the Gospel of the Superman as its ideal.

Doke's death was followed within the year by the arrival in South Africa of C. F. Andrews, who in some sense took Doke's place in Gandhi's life. The two Englishmen were quick and clever, rather facile minds, and Andrews was another physically frail enthusiast; often said, later, when he grew haggard and bearded, to look like Christ. He was born in 1871 into a charismatic sect called the Catholic Apostolic Church, fundamentalist in its theology and led by people who spoke in tongues. Charlie went by means of scholarships to Cambridge and there formed a close friendship with a fellow undergraduate, Basil Westcott. Westcott's father, who became the bishop of Durham, and other members of the family, also became close friends with Andrews, who converted to the Church of England. It was due to them that he went out to India and fell in love with the subcontinent. He later called himself "twice-born"; the second time being in India.

There he came to sympathize with the nationalist cause, and formed a close discipular attachment to Rabindranath Tagore. At Gokhale's suggestion, he and a friend called Pearson went out to South Africa, to help Gandhi in the satyagraha struggle. Their Indian friends "lent them" to Gandhi. (This also was New Age politics.) When he was first presented to Gandhi, on January 1, 1914, Andrews bent down, in the Indian gesture of deference, and took the dust from Gandhi's feet. He had learned the gesture at Tagore's school in Shantiniketan. This offended Andrews's Anglican superiors, and indeed embarrassed Gandhi, who said, "Pray do not do that, it is a humiliation to me." But apparently Andrews persuaded Gandhi that he should accept such gestures if offered in India—another mark of the difference between the Indian and the South African milieux.

We now find ourselves, however, speaking of events that occurred in 1914, some years ahead of our chronological scheme.

Political Action

After the Smuts-Gandhi agreement of 1908, Gandhi advised his countrymen to register voluntarily. By May 9, 8,700 applications for registration had been received, and 6,000 accepted. Soon, however, Smuts made it clear that even Asiatics who had lived in South Africa before would have to register when they reentered, which was against the compromise agreement as Gandhi understood it. On May 16, Gandhi accused Smuts of foul play. But he himself was suspected of betraying his countrymen. The next day, Pathans assaulted the chairman of the British Indian Association. On May 26, that Association told the colonial secretary that they were withdrawing their voluntary registrations, and on May 30, Gandhi announced that satyagraha would begin again.

This campaign, he announced on July 2, would be on behalf of people not yet in South Africa—of the Indians who were prohibited from immigrating—and he suggested that everyone who had registered should ceremonially burn their certificates if the voluntary applications were not returned. One of the three prohibited categories was "educated Indians," and Smuts offered a compromise whereby the other two would be accepted only if Gandhi would agree to the exclusion of the educated. Gandhi of course refused, recognizing this as an attempt to exclude Indian culture and to admit Indians to South Africa only as laborers, as plantation fodder. So on July 16 hawking without licenses was begun. On July 27 Harilal Gandhi was arrested. And on August 16 and 23, the example of Thoreau being cited, 3,000 certificates were ceremonially burned.

James Hunt points out that the "educated Indian" issue was also a matter of legal symbolism.[28] The law was a powerful symbolic system to Gandhi, as well as an agency. He could not tolerate a legal barrier to the entry of educated Indians, even accepting the fact that the government would circumvent a liberal law and keep them out in some other fashion.

On January 16, 1909 Gandhi was arrested in Volksrust. Escorted to the Natal border, he immediately returned and was rearrested, and on the twentieth wrote to the press that the struggle had entered its third and final phase. On January 28, the Indian merchants of Johannesburg decided to operate without licenses and court arrest. Cachalia and Naidoo, and others, were sentenced to three months each on the thirtieth.

A British Indian Conciliation Committee, convened to petition Smuts, was formed by Haji Ojer Ally, George Godfrey, a Christian Indian, and Haji Habib, a Muslim born in Porbandar. They wanted to make a compromise with Smuts, and to send another deputation to London. Gandhi refused the first and did not see any point to the latter, but agreed to go. He sailed with only two demands, that Law 2 of the Transvaal should be abolished, and that six educated Indians should be allowed to enter every year.

1909–1914

In June of 1909, Gandhi left for London with Haji Habib, to represent the Indians to Whitehall. He wrote to Polak how reluctant he was to go; how little he now believed in talking to "the big men," and how much more effective were the satyagrahis who were in South African jails for their beliefs those who were practicing New Age politics. But his countrymen wanted him in London.

General Smuts and General Botha were already there, conferring with the ministers, dining at Buckingham Palace, making history. The British and the Boers had overcome the divisive memories of war, and the empire had acquired a great new dominion. The reality principle seemed to be on the side of the generals; Gandhi was going to have to appeal to a different principle.

Polak meanwhile sailed to Bombay, to appeal directly to the Indian people on their cousins' behalf, arriving there on July 21. His enthusiastic description of Gandhi's philosophy and personality fascinated some and disturbed more among the Indian leaders. Gandhi, who was sending detailed instructions to guide him through the maze of Indian politics, finally asked him not to write and talk so much about him, because of the reaction he might provoke (9:462). On October 6, he asked Polak instead to expound the idea that their real success in South Africa lay in the effort itself—"that we are giving ourselves the finest type of education, better than any university education. . . . We are presenting the Indian Motherland with a disciplined army of the future" (19:463). This was the idea for Polak to emphasize.

But, whether because of Polak's indiscretion or because of Gandhi's idealism, there was a reaction amongst Indian nationalists like the one Gandhi feared, and an invitation extended to him to be president of congress, in 1911, was withdrawn because of suspicions and resistance.

Johannesburg to London 1909

In the middle of his journey, just nine days before Gandhi landed in England, on July 10, Sir Curzon Wyllie, political ADC to the secretary of state for India, was shot by an Indian student associated with India House, at a reception held by the National Indian Association at the Imperial Institute in South Kensington. A Parsi doctor, Cowanji Lalkaka, who tried to help Wyllie, was also fatally wounded. The assassin, Madanlal Dhingra, was a disciple of V. R. Savarkar, who inspired the deed, and wrote the assassin's statement of purpose, including: "The only lesson required for India at present is to learn how to die, and the only way to teach it is by dying ourselves. Therefore I die, glorying in my martyrdom."[29]

Payne tells us that Savarkar had trained Dhingra for some months to commit an assassination. The young man had set out to shoot Lord Curzon on an earlier occasion, and on the morning of this, his successful attempt, Savarkar had given him a nickel-plated revolver, and told him not to return if he failed again.[30] Dhingra's prosecution was straightforward because a cook at India House turned King's evidence, but indeed there was no need for evidence, so far as Dhingra was concerned, with so many eyewitnesses. He was hung at Brixton prison on August 17. Savarkar, however, escaped, for the time being.

His connection was immediately suspected, but it could not be proven. He challenged suspicion; at a meeting of London Indians to make a statement deploring the assassination, he shouted his opposition. The *London Times* openly blamed the deed on the men of India House, who favored and committed political assassination. Krishnavarma was in France, so the editor being out of reach, the printer of the *Indian Sociologist* was condemned on the same day as Dhingra, and jailed for four months, because of the journal's declaration that patriotic homicide was no murder.

According to Manmathnath Gupta, Dhingra came of a rich family in the Punjab, and his loyalist father sent him to London to acquire English qualities. But he fell under Savarkar's influence, and had the latter's statement in his pocket when he fired. "I have conspired with none but with my duty. I believe that a nation held in bondage with the help of bayonets is in a state of perpetual war and since the guns are denied to me, I drew forth my pistol and attacked by surprise. Being a Hindu, I believe that an insult to my country is an insult to God. For the worship of my country is the worship of Shri Ram and the service of my country is the service of Shri Krishna." He offered his blood to the Mother, and prayed himself to return to the same Mother and to die again and again, until She was free. (Gupta, a secular revolutionary, adds, "I presume that this statement was prepared by Savarkar, who crammed as much Hinduism into it as possible."[31]

Gandhi declared that Dhingra was intoxicated, by a mad idea; he had been "egged on" to do it and his self-defense seemed to have been learned by rote. "Mr. Dhingra's defence is inadmissible. He has acted like a coward. He was egged on to do this act by ill-digested reading of worthless writings . . . , It is those who incited him to do this who deserve to be punished" (9:302). The reference was of course to Savarkar; who was in hiding, moving from one shabby lodging to another.[32] The whole story makes an instructive contrast to Gandhi's mode of political action.

He and Habib were to be in London eighteen weeks, much longer than his stay in 1906. They stayed at the Westminster Hotel, which was close to parliament, but older and cheaper than the Cecil: Gandhi paid three pounds, seventeen shillings, sixpence per week, instead of one pound, ten shillings per night. He saw much of Millie Polak and Henry's sisters. He and his friends ate lunches of fruit and nuts in his hotel room, spreading newspapers on the table in lieu of linen and cutlery, and ordering tea and toast from the waiter.

Parliament was in prolonged session, even though these were the summer months, because of difficulties in passing the Budget. The House of Lords refused to pass what the Commons proposed; because the former was a conservative body, while the latter felt it had a mandate for far-reaching Liberal reforms. Gandhi was shocked by reading of members sleeping on the benches when they were supposed to be taking important decisions. This crisis preoccupied the mind of the members of parliament, and made it harder for the deputation to get their attention.

The assassination, moreover, was a grave disadvantage to Gandhi's mission, because it seemed to justify all the distrust of and anxiety about the Indian nationalist movement, and put all the Liberals who sympathized with that movement into an awkward position. Gandhi could not but be tarred with the same brush. The printer who was sent to jail for printing *The Indian Sociologist,* Guy Aldred, was the man who had contracted to print Doke's biography.

(The latter had practically no sales, and Gandhi himself bought up most of the copies.)

Perhaps for these reasons, Gandhi's strategy this time was rather different than before. He secured the patronage of Lord Ampthill, a former viceroy, very conservative and imperialist in his politics, but devoted to India, and ready to work hard and honestly with Gandhi. He in turn secured the support of Lord Curzon, the greatest of the ex-viceroys. This was the most prestigious possible sponsorship for the deputation, but it left Gandhi unable to influence the action a lot of the time.

Because Lord Ampthill insisted on pursuing the method of individual diplomacy, and because of Lord Crewe's delays, there was little for the Indian deputation to do. At least between September 16 and November 3, according to Hunt, Gandhi was immobilized, as far as politics went.[33]

Lord Ampthill made pointed inquiries about Gandhi's contacts with the extremists, and Gandhi could honestly say that there were no such contacts in South Africa. Neither did he make any attempt to contact India House this time, but he told Lord Ampthill later that the extremists had sought him out (9:508). Surprisingly, however—despite his disapproval of the assassination, and despite Ampthill's attitude—Gandhi hosted a public dinner for Savarkar on October 24, the festival of Dussera; though he made the condition that there should be no political content to the speeches. The dinner was held at Nazimuddin's Indian restaurant. It was a sizable social occasion. About seventy attended, including a few Englishmen—one of them a Scotland yard detective. Bipin Chandra Pal and Virendranath Chatopadhyaya spoke, as well as Gandhi and Savarkar.

Gandhi spoke on the significance of Rama and Sita's long exile in the forest, and their ascetic self-preparation for a return to royal prosperity. Savarkar spoke about the demon Ravana, whom Rama had to slay, and Durga, the goddess of death and vengeance. The contrast between the speakers was thus a contrast between two female embodiments of virtue, Sita the gentle and Durga the fierce. (In 1927 Gandhi said that Savarkar and Krishnavarma had told him that the Gita and the *Ramayana* meant the opposite of what he thought [32:102].)

Savarkar fled to Paris in early 1910, because he was wanted by the police in connection with another assassination; this one in India and of A. M. T. Jackson, a district magistrate at Nasik, on December 29. The assassins had been arrested and letters from Savarkar found. He had sent a consignment of twenty Browning pistols to India, one of which had been used in the killing. He returned from Paris to London in March, however, and was arrested; and, despite several attempts to rescue him from Brixton jail, he was sent to India on July 1, 1910. He made a daring escape from the ship at Marseilles—wriggling naked through a porthole and dropping into the sea—but was recaptured as he ran along the quays. (Jayakar tells us that the porthole was twelve inches in radius, and he was thirty-six inches round the chest, so he must have scraped himself severely.) In India he was charged with conspiracy, along with some thirty others, and was sentenced to exile in the Andaman Islands. This was a different kind of courage and force than Gandhi could show, and the story thrilled many young Indians.

As was mentioned, Gandhi also had a brush with Swami Shraddhanand, partly a propos the swami's criticism of satyagraha (10:284). In his reply, Gandhi treated the swami as an enemy. He said the latter would ruin himself with his own hands, if people were patient. His ways and doings were crooked (10:355).

Thus Gandhi had contacts with Indian radicals and with English officials on this visit to London. But he also had more time to himself on this visit, and he used the opportunity to get in touch with the New Age. For instance, he paid a visit to Whiteway, the Tolstoy farm colony in the Cotswolds. This had been functioning for a decade, which was quite a long time for such an institution. The twelve colonists there, who had been members of the Croydon Brotherhood Church, took their big decision to move into the countryside in 1898. (That was just two years before the people of Monte Verita did, in Ascona, and twelve years before the setting up of the South African Farm.) Three of them officially bought the land, but they then burned the title deeds, so there should be no owning or owners. The twelve of them—some of whom were Quakers—lived communally and but also spontaneously. They shared even their clothes, and took no vows, made no promises or pledges even to each other. During their very first winter their money ran out, and they lived on potatoes and parsnips.

Though many left, many more came, with various intentions, and from various countries. Let us take as an example Francis Sedlak, the neo-Hegelian philosopher, born into a farming family in Moravia in 1873, whose life story reflects the New Age spirit in many ways. He ran away from home to join the French Foreign Legion. After a short time he deserted, was imprisoned, and returned home in time to be conscripted into the Austrian army; but soon preferred military jail to obeying military orders.

He studied anarchist doctrine in jail, and—as soon as he was free from the army—set out for England, where he had heard there was an anarchist colony in Newcastle. By the time he got there, the colony had been turned into a private enterprise; in which he took work; but soon set off for Russia, as fireman in a steamship, and had an interview with Tolstoy, who told him about the English colonies set up by Tolstoyans at Purleigh and Whiteway.

When Sedlak arrived at Purleigh (founded by Aylmer Maude) he discovered that it too had reverted to private property; but at Whiteway he finally found a welcome, and in fact stayed there till he died in 1935, living in a free union with Nellie Shaw, one of the original founders. He began as a Tolstoyan, but then was attracted to Theosophy, and finally turned to Hegel.

Like Gusto Graeser in Ascona, Sedlak was a figure of splendid manliness and perfect health—such are the terms in which the colonists described him. (It is notable that these living icons were most often male.) He went barefoot, dressed in white cotton pants and shirt, and wore his hair long. He was often asked to pose for a photograph by strangers, and compared with paintings of Christ's apostles, or Christ himself. The same thing happened to Graeser and other German New Agers. And Sedlak was a vegetarian and a nature curer. In a different way, Gandhi too had to embody his values; it is the fate of the New Ager.

There were then manifold likenesses between Whiteway and Ascona, and the two groups knew of each other. It is no exaggeration to say that they were both manifestations of the same idea. As for Gandhi's Farm, outside Johannesburg, that had an extra dimension of political action, since it sheltered the families of satyagrahis who were in jail. But the essential idea was the same.

London in 1909

Gandhi's London included the women suffragists. On July 29 the hunger strikers of the Women's Social and Political Union were presented to the public at a mass meeting in St. James's Hall, and Gandhi was in the audience. (The government had released them from jail, baffled by their tactics.) He wrote a long article about them for *Indian Opinion*. He met their leader Mrs. Pankhurst there, and Mrs. Pethick-Lawrence, who chaired the meeting. The latter was a Quaker, who had done settlement house work before she turned to the suffrage question. She remained in touch with Gandhi. But of all the feminists it was the deeply religious Charlotte Despard, who founded the Women's Freedom League, whom he most admired. The WFL avoided violence and property damage. Its members picketed parliament, in a campaign beginning on July 5, 1909, and by the end of September, they had celebrated their ten-thousandth hour of picketing.

On October 8, Gandhi spoke to the Union of Ethical Societies, on the subject of soul force. Bipin Chandra Pal attended, and in the question period said that soul force should be backed up by the physical kind. Gandhi replied that it would not then deserve the name of soul force. This conflict with other Indian spokesmen in London was developed further on October 24, at the Dussera dinner.

General Smuts had left London on August 29, to prepare for the celebrations of the new union, and of the coronation shortly to follow. He was confident that the Indians in the Transvaal were "sick to death" of the agitation. Back in South Africa he made the treatment of passive resisters harder, deported some to India, and imposed the law upon women and children as well as upon grown men.

Gandhi soon found that his official activity was as fruitless as he had predicted. The secretary of state for India, John Morley, told him that the imperial government could exercise little control over self-governing dominions; the tie between mother country and colonies was made of silk, and would snap if subjected to any tension.

Thus the treatment Gandhi got in London in 1909, and what he saw and read, drove him even further out of sympathy with modern ideology and brought him even closer to Tolstoy. When he reported the MPs falling asleep in parliament, he commented, "It does not seem likely that Western civilization will survive much longer" (9:354).

What he wrote in lighter vein betrayed the same exasperation. Writing about motoring to Kallenbach (who owned a car), he said, "If you saw the craze for it here [in London] and saw how poor people suffer from the infliction, I am sure your humanity would make you forswear motors for ever. They are an invention of the devil" (UC). Feeling forced by convention to wear boots instead of sandals, he grumbled that he had bought ill-health for twenty-two shillings, six pence when he could have bought health for eight shillings, sixpence. "But can a delegate walk about London in sandals?" (UC).

The city no longer exerted any charm over him. In an article for *Indian Opinion* in October, entitled, "This Crazy Civilization," he wrote, "London has gone mad over M. Bleriot [the pioneer aviator]. . . . We have trains running underground; there are telegraph wires already hanging over us; and outside, on the roads, there is the deafening noise of trains. If you now have planes flying in the air, take it that people will be done to death. Looking at this land, I at any rate have grown disillusioned with Western civilization. . . . It is beyond my understanding what good the discovery of the North Pole has done the world. . . . I for one regard all these things as symptoms of mental derangement" (9:401–2).

He had immediately met with his friend Florence Winterbottom, who gave him the letter to Ramsay MacDonald mentioned before. Gandhi later wrote that Winterbottom belonged to that class among the English who "seek out and befriend forlorn causes in the teeth of odium, ridicule, and opposition." We have called that class the members of the New Age. She was intensely English, he said, and yet international in her sympathies (33:20).

She took him to hear Stanton Coit speak on July 18, presumably at the West London Ethical Church. In the vestibule there he would have seen busts of Emerson and Josephine Butler (leader of the purity campaign); and Christ on the right, Buddha on the left, of the pulpit, supported by Socrates and Marcus Aurelius. The church was decorated mostly by Walter Crane, and was a temple of the New Age cult. (Coit and Gandhi had some ideas in common: around 1930, Coit passed from saying "God! Thou art Love," to "Love! Thou art God"; which will remind us of Gandhi's passage from "God is Truth" to "Truth is God."[34])

He and Maud Polak and Dr. Mehta went out on Sunday, August 29, to Whiteway. Gandhi enthusiastically described to Polak the place and the principal farmer, George Allen, a "magnificent specimen" though not a man of culture. There must have already been some contact between Whiteway and the Indians, for one of the South African students, Hoosen, the son of Dawd Mohammed, and a favorite of Gandhi's, educated partly at Phoenix, was staying at Whiteway, convalescing.

New Age ideas were in the London air. Gandhi read G. K. Chesterton's essay in the *Illustrated London News,* on September 18, advising young Indians to hold by their traditional culture rather than introducing the new ideas associated with Herbert Spencer. Gandhi was so delighted with this—which may have been provoked by the assassination, judging by its date—that he told *Indian Opinion* to print it. (Herbert Kitchin, the editor, thought Chesterton must be joking, and ended his column, "It is play—not serious thought.") Gandhi also liked a letter by Chesterton to the *Daily News* of October 22.

Chesterton preached a version of Ruskin's and Morris's enthusiasm for the culture of the Middle Ages.

Gandhi read Edward Carpenter's *Civilization: Its Cause and Cure,* which suggested that civilization might be a kind of disease that societies have to go through, and finally to escape from. Gandhi sent a long summary to Polak on September 8. He commented that Carpenter was afraid of his own logic, and where it would lead him. It was all a matter of theory in Carpenter, but for an Indian it was a matter of practical knowledge. India, in other words, was the homeland of the New Age. Gandhi was presumably also reading Geoffrey Blount's books, published by the Simple Life Press: *A New Crusade,* for instance, had been summarized in *Indian Opinion* in 1905, and was amongst the recommended reading listed at the end of *Hind Swaraj.*

Gandhi gave a speech at Hampstead which he reported to Polak on October 14, in which he put forward sixteen propositions. (Polak used these points in his book expounding Gandhi.) He began with Kipling's famous lines about the opposition of East and West. Gandhi said there was no such thing as Western or European civilization, but a modern civilization, which is purely material. Old-time Europeans were like Easterners. (He and General Smuts had agreed on that.) Modern medical science is a form of black magic. "I was entirely off the track when I considered that I should receive a medical training" (9:479). Railways and so on will have to go.

Before now, he said, Europeans had had much in common with Indians. Even now it is not the British people but modern civilization that rules India. East and West can meet if the latter throws modern civilization overboard, or if the former adopts it. But that second meeting would be in the Hall of Death, like the meeting to come between England and Germany. So the first, England's self-emancipation, is the thing to aim at. It is impertinence for the moderns to change the world by the means of speedy locomotion. India's salvation lies in unlearning what she has learned this last fifty years. These are the ideas of *Hind Swaraj,* in some ways more sharply expressed.[35]

The International Image of Gandhi

This was the time when New Agers—of various sorts—began to call the attention of the world at large to Gandhi. We have mentioned Doke's little book, and Polak's pamphlet, printed in India. While in London, Gandhi was also in touch with the Tolstoyan, Isabella Fyvie Mayo, in Aberdeen; she was writing three essays on Gandhi and his work which appeared in the *Open Road* in the spring of 1911. This monthly was a continuation of the *Crank,* which Arthur St. John edited. St. John was a Tolstoyan who had helped in the resettlement of the Dukhobors.

Mrs. Mayo got information from both Kallenbach and Gandhi for this project. Her first essay began by establishing Gandhi's relation to Tolstoy; and pointed out the further parallel that "intellectuals" could not recognize the true message of either, because they were dazzled by the literary work in Tolstoy's case, and the political work in Gandhi's.

She therefore avoided mentioning Gandhi's name, and India and Africa, in her first part. She quoted lavishly from *Hind Swaraj,* and ended by saying it had been governmentally proscribed, and asking: "In the name of wonder, what Government?" In part 2 she answered the question—the British government—and described his work. But she spent much of her space again quoting; and suggested that an Indian should challenge the government by reissuing *Hind Swaraj* with parallel passages from the New Testament.

In part 3 she summarized his life story, and quoted from a recent letter Gandhi had written: "In my opinion, those who work against Europeanizing India work for Humanity. In certain respects, living in a new country, I am in a better position to watch the baneful effects of the civilizing process on the natives of this continent."[36] She also quoted from Tolstoy's letter to him, and ended with a passage from the *Revelation:* "And the kings of the earth, and the great men, and the rich men, and the great captains . . . hid themselves in the dens and in the rocks of the mountains. And said . . . hide us . . . from the Wrath of the Lamb" (332).

Mrs. Mayo's was almost as sizable a portrait of Gandhi as Doke's, and contained much more of his doctrine—*Hind Swaraj* not having been written when Doke was at work on his book. Indeed, Doke was not as radical a New Ager as Mayo.

A little later, Gilbert Murray, the president of the Union of Ethical Societies, wrote an article about Gandhi's political activities, entitled "The Soul as It Is, and How to Deal with It."[37] This was read with enthusiasm by the Unitarian-Universalist minister John Haynes Holmes in New York, who thereafter made spreading the word about Gandhi his great cause in life.

In 1915 Romain Rolland, in Switzerland—in exile from France during the war because of his pacifism—read the Indian New Agers, Tagore and Coomaraswamy, on the subject of nonviolence and India's ancient culture. Devoting most of his time for some years thereafter to things Indian, Rolland wrote a short book about Gandhi in 1923. This brought the latter much wider fame, and several important disciples, like Madeleine Slade from England, and others from France and Germany, and even from India. (All these treatments of Gandhi assimilated him to Jesus Christ, in one way or another.)

Finally P. J. Mehta published *M. K. Gandhi and the South African Indian Problem* in Madras in 1912. He stresses Gandhi's "high moral character"—quoting the *Transvaal Leader*'s testimony, in a 1910 review of Doke.[38] This implied the bringing of domestic virtue to political practice; virtues like frugality, self-denial, gentleness. Mehta also declared that the basic principles of Indian civilization were self-sacrifice, self-control, and self-renunciation (50).

But from the point of view of the two men involved, this was above all the moment of conjunction for Gandhi and Tolstoy. In 1908, when Tolstoy reached eighty, he had received greetings from Gandhi among many other people, some more and some less eminent. That year, moreover, he got a letter about nonviolence from an Indian revolutionary called Taraknath Das, his reply to which turned out to be in effect addressed to Gandhi—his "Letter to a Hindu."

Its literal addressee was then living in Vancouver, Canada, and editing an insurrectionary magazine called *Free Hindustan,* which was very similar to

Krishnavarma's *Indian Sociologist.* It carried the same slogan: "Resistance to tyranny is obedience to God," and had on its cover quotations from Herbert Spencer. (Spencer was the very opposite of the New Age, for he defined civilization as ever-increasing complexity, and valued it therefor.)

Das had sent Tolstoy two copies of his magazine, and asked for an article, but at the same time had protested that nonviolence was self-defeating and undermined altruism as well as egotism. Tolstoy sat down to write a reply on June 7, the day he got Das's letter, but it took him 513 manuscript pages and six months before he completed it, having discarded twenty-eight tentative versions.

What Tolstoy said was that Hindus must resist England nonviolently, because to resist it violently would be to yield to the conquerors' ideology. (As Gandhi put it: Jesus refused to use soul force to turn stones into bread; but that is just what modern civilization does and what soul force refuses to do [10:246].)

Only by nonviolence could India retrieve an integrity it had already compromised, for the East India Company could never have enslaved two hundred million people if the latter had not accepted its values, its vision, its sense of the real. Only by practicing their own inherited nonviolence could Hindus defeat "the deeply immoral forms of social order in which the English and other pseudomoral Christian nations live today."[39]

Mankind must move to a new level of consciousness, and the law of love must rule instead of the law of violence. But this will happen only if men free themselves from belief in "all kinds of Ormuzds, Brahman, Sabaoth, and their incarnations as Krishnas and Christs, as well as from belief in science." Hindus must give us Hinduism, as they have known it. The old religions were no longer true. Like the "futile exercises of mind and memory called the sciences" (in which Tolstoy included law, history, anthropology) they obscure "the simple clear law of love, accessible to everybody and solving all problems and all perplexities" (96).

Gandhi read this letter-essay in 1909. He could not accept Tolstoy's brusque way with Indian religions, for his mind was highly sensitive to all affronts to cultural pride. There was a Voltairean and even a Nietzschean style to Tolstoy's performance in the world of ideas. Gandhi did not approve of using that style on any subject, but least of all on India and religion. But he was not a "church member" in any ordinary sense. And the main message of the "Letter to a Hindu" is almost exactly what Gandhi himself might have written, and on the subject dearest to his heart. Since he and his friends were already great admirers of Tolstoy, it must have been a powerful excitement for him to find himself thus corroborated. It is from the moment he read the letter that one can detect, as one would expect, a fairly constant scrutiny fixed by Gandhi on Tolstoy, even in the midst of other occupations.

On October 1 of that year, he wrote to Russia, asking Tolstoy to confirm that he had written the letter (which Gandhi had read reproduced in some unofficial form) asking if he could put it into print, and also asking if Tolstoy would give publicity to the nonviolent resistance to the state being mounted by the Indians in South Africa. Tolstoy replied immediately (he wrote on October 7) giving that confirmation and renouncing royalties. Gandhi made some unsuccessful attempts, with the help of Aylmer Maude, to get English newspapers, like the *Manchester Guardian,* to print it; but then resigned himself to distributing it as a separate pamphlet. With financial help from Dr. Mehta, he got twenty thousand copies printed. He wrote again to Tolstoy on October 11, giving some details of his work in South Africa, and in November sent Joseph Doke's biography of himself, which was just off the press.

From London to Johannesburg 1909

Gandhi sailed from London to Durban on *The Kildonan Castle,* and he translated "Letter to a Hindu" into Gujarati, and wrote a preface in which he said that its central principle was exactly his own. He gave it the title, "The Subjection of India—Its Cause and Cure," thus aligning it with Carpenter's book.[40]

The translation of Tolstoy and an essay of his own were written in tandem. Gandhi's own essay he entitled *Hind Swaraj,* meaning Indian home rule, with the further, punning, meaning of Indian self-control. (The same pun on self-government was made by American revolutionaries.) This is a discussion of the right kind, and the wrong kind, of home rule for India to work toward. In its appendix Gandhi listed as recommended reading six books by Tolstoy, two each by Ruskin and Thoreau, and one each by Socrates, Mazzini, R. C. Dutt, Henry Maine, and Edward Carpenter. (A good example of New Age reading.) The book is a Socratic dialogue between an Editor who represents Gandhi (the whole thing was written for the magazine he edited) and a Reader, whose opinions are those of the extremists—such as Savarkar or Krishnavarma—but whose submissive and respectful way of arguing is more that of his old friend, Dr. Mehta.

He wrote it in nine days, on 271 pages of the ship's notepaper. Introducing the argument, Gandhi said, "These views are mine, and yet not mine. They are mine because I hope to act according to them. They are almost a part of my being. But, yet, they are not mine, because I lay no claim to originality. They have been formed after reading several books" (10:8). He added that these views were also held by thousands of advanced Europeans (New Agers) and by millions of Indians (those untouched by "civilization"). They represented a return to ancient tradition.

The Reader says that young Indians are angry with their leaders and have turned away from congress, for instance, considering it an instrument of the perpetuation of British rule. The Editor defends congress, and even more the man associated with it, Gokhale. The Reader is perceptibly an adherent of Tilak, instead. But the Editor too is no constitutionalist. He says he finds parliaments and newspapers too merely expedient and insufficiently moral. He is disillusioned with modern civilization in general, and attacks law courts, medicine, hospitals, railways, and textile factories. The whole modern system is a poisonous Upas tree, its root immorality, its branches the parasitic professions (10:35). Lawyers have enslaved India to English law and English eloquence. Doctors induce us to sin, because they eliminate the naturally punitive consequences of self-indulgence. (Hunt points out that Gandhi's gives a more moral twist to arguments he takes over—from Carpenter on doctors, for instance, and from Sir Henry Maine on lawyers) (161).

Gandhi deplores the whole quality of modern life; people in modern civilization keep up their energy by using intoxicants and are unhappy when they are alone. The English at least have lost all interest in the God of Christianity, and worship money; and the Indians, in their turn, are losing faith in the religion that underlies all religions.

Indian civilization is better than the Western kinds, because it has lasted, while the Greeks and the Romans destroyed themselves. That is, village India lasted, largely unchanged by the cities, the palaces, the dynasties, the conquests, that rolled over it. The focus of Indian culture and even the tendency of Indian civilization is to elevate the moral being, because their forms are based on a belief in God, while modern civilization is essentially materialistic and appetitive. Our ancestors saw that the mind is a restless bird, and their social institutions caged it for its own good. (On other occasions, Gandhi calls the mind a drunken monkey.) But modern civilization is a mere congregation of chattering birds and monkeys since the need for limits has been forgotten. (This is one of the moments when Gandhi reminds us of Kipling, and his law of the jungle.)

However, the Indians' quarrel is not with the English, who are themselves suffering as a result of that civilization. He, the Editor, holds no more grudge against the king-emperor than against the Indian princes, and if the English could recapture their old nature they could be accommodated in India. They could even rule the country (through the Kshatriyas and the princes) if they would respect the culture.

The real evil is embedded deep in modern industry and the modern economy. "Machinery is the chief symbol of modern civilization; it represents a great sin . . . a snake-hole which may contain from one to a hundred snakes" (10:54). But those whom the Reader represents are eager to introduce it and all it involves into India. They think they are revolutionaries, but: "You want the Englishman's rule without the Englishman; the tiger's nature but not the tiger; you would make India English" (10:14).

Gandhi is perfectly aware that he is "going against history." But he repudiates history as a criterion of wisdom. "To believe that what has not occurred in history will not occur at all is to argue disbelief in the dignity of man" (10:40). Besides which, "history, as we know it, is a record of the wars of the world. . . . How kings played, how they became enemies of one another, how they murdered one another. . . . If this were all that had happened in the world, it would have ended long ago" (10:47). And by the same token, it is only in *their* history that organized violence is natural and inevitable. "Kings will always use their kingly weapons . . . [and] England is, I believe, easily influenced by the use of gunpowder. . . . But the fact is that India will not adopt arms, and it is well that it does not" (10:51, 42).

Political progress of the type that the modern system holds up to admiration—nation building—is a fraud. It does not build the kind of nations we want. Italy has won for itself the kind of freedom that suited Cavour and Garibaldi, but not the kind Mazzini dreamed of—"freedom for all the people of the land" (10:41). (Gandhi was himself a nation builder; it is as such that he is installed as the founder of modern India; but being a New Ager he wanted an ideal version of a nation.)

Violence cannot ever bring about true freedom. The Reader proposes to murder a few English by assassination and then raise an army to fight a war of liberation, admitting that perhaps a quarter of a million Indians might die in the course of it. The Editor, on the other hand, declares that India did not gain by, for instance, the murder of Curzon Wyllie. And of course he bases his feeling on something more profound than the calculus of profit. He quotes the Tulsidas line, "Pity is the root of religion, as egotism is the root of the body," and says that he believes this to be a scientific truth; and that that nation is great that rests its head upon death as upon a pillow. His politics, like his ethics, are based upon sacrifice.

Hind Swaraj, therefore, does not make sense of a modern politics kind, and Gokhale and Nehru and most of Gandhi's political allies in the years to come ignored it. (Those who saluted it have mostly been New Agers by temperament like John Middleton Murry.) In effect, Gandhi himself ignored it in most of his political activity. We can understand its relation to his public career only by remembering that ideological or vertical split in Gandhi, corresponding to the chronological or horizontal split in Tolstoy, which separated the man's religious self from his political self. The left hand wrote in a different script from the right hand. Gandhi was aiming toward religious results via political activities; but the passage from one to the other could not be smooth and continuous.

Hind Swaraj was published in *Indian Opinion* December 11 and 18, 1909, and issued in South Africa as a pamphlet in Gujarati in January 1910, but its distribution in India was proscribed by the government of Bombay (which ruled the Gujarati-speaking areas) on March 24. An English translation, with a foreword, was published by Gandhi's International Printing Press on March 30, and that was the version sent to Tolstoy. No Indian edition was published until 1919. Along with *Hind Swaraj, Sarvodaya* (Gandhi's Gujarati version of *Unto This Last),* and *The Story of a True Warrior* (his life of Socrates, also derived in fact from Tolstoy) were also prohibited by the Bombay government. And the magazine *Gujarat* had also been prosecuted for printing his translation of "Letter to a Hindu."

Gandhi sent Tolstoy a copy in April 1910. Having read *Hind Swaraj,* Tolstoy noted in his diary how close Gandhi's work was to his own, and how important, and on September 7 wrote to him at some length, saying: "The more I live—and especially now that I am approaching death— . . ." the more the eternal enmity between love and violence struck him as a fundamental truth.[41] This enmity was between more than feelings, being between two structures of ideas, and indeed of behavior. The whole of Christian civilization, so brilliant outwardly, had grown up on the self-evident and blatant misunderstanding that the two can be reconciled and combined—a self-contradiction sometimes conscious and cynical but mostly unconscious and sentimental. He could see that Gandhi, if no one else, had grasped the danger of that lie. Thus "Your work in the Transvaal . . . [is] . . . most fundamental and important . . . [and]

most weighty practical proof." This was Tolstoy's last long letter, and it is appropriate that it should have been addressed to Gandhi.

His only reservation was on the question of patriotism. Gandhi was alert to the dangers of Western-style nationalism, but he wanted Indians to go through a phase of patriotic virtue as a moral discipline, while Tolstoy was a fierce denouncer of all nationalism. He would have no truck with Gandhi's seventeenth-century British and eighteenth-century American heroes of national freedom. It is more than a mere coincidence that Aylmer Maude should have cited Pym and Hampden when he argued against Tolstoy that he failed to do justice to modern civilization. (He also cited Washington and Lincoln.) Pym and Hampden were WASP names representing a WASP complacency about WASP politics, which Tolstoy repudiated.

This led many of Tolstoy's disciples to dissent from him. For instance, Aylmer Maude said, in 1918, again arguing against Tolstoy: "I have tried to suggest reasons for believing that, however urgently the building may need repair, the foundations are as firm today as when they were first laid."[42] At just about the same time, Gandhi, however, came to agree with Tolstoy in finding those foundations shaky.

In November 1910 Tolstoy died, and on November 26 Gandhi wrote an obituary in *Indian Opinion,* saying: "He was for us more than one of the greatest men of his age. We have endeavoured, as far as possible, as far as we understood it, to follow his teaching" (10:369).

I have called this an opposite philosophy to Smuts's, but analytically it is identical; the two saw East and West as the crucial antagonists of world history, and they understood them in the same terms; they differed only in the value they assigned to those terms.

Emily Hobhouse recommended *Hind Swaraj* to Smuts in these words: "I like it *very much*—all about India and the harm English civilization is doing there. The book has already been prohibited in India (O foolish authorities! will you never learn wisdom?) but he means to devote his life to it in India, and I tell him he is undoubtedly qualifying for deportation from India. It is a book which you would have enjoyed at one period of your life."[43] The last sentence has the pathos of a New Ager's reproach to a former comrade.

Gandhi solicited opinions from all kinds of people, notably Gokhale and Wybergh, his Theosophical friend. No one liked *Hind Swaraj,* but Gandhi continued for the rest of his life to declare that it was the fullest statement of what he believed.

The Campaigns

Gandhi arrived home in Johannesburg eager to make changes in his life. He was heavily in debt, his faith in some of his British allies was shaken, and he wanted to give up the practice of the law.[44]

On June 1, 1910, the Union of South Africa was born; and on the same day Sorabji, one of the most persistent satyagrahis, was arrested for the seventh time. On June 30 another of them, Sammy Nagappen, was released from Johannesburg jail in a dying condition; he died on July 6, a martyr to the cause. It was also in June that Kallenbach gave his 1100-acre farm in Lawley for the accommodation of satyagrahi families; there were from sixteen to sixty people living there at a time.

Gandhi announced that Kallenbach was going to retire from the practice of architecture, and live in poverty; and in fact he taught carpentry, gardening, and sandal making on the farm. Polak returned from India on September 28, 1910.

Gandhi said that everyone should learn to weave (10:398). He was enthusiastic about traditional arts and crafts; and was reading Ananda Coomaraswamy, the scholar of Asian craft traditions (10:356). In 1911 he recommended *Gulliver's Travels* to Maganlal for its criticism of civilization (11:77). This was not the only time he recommended Swift, but at this point he was especially in sympathy with the scathing satirist. Maganlal should go on from Swift to Carpenter.

Intellectually and morally, Gandhi and Polak were flushed with aggressive zeal. Gandhi wrote to Polak in June or July of 1911 saying that the racist mayor of Durban was a cad and a disgrace to Judaism. On July 22 Polak wrote that he was going to make an enemy for life of Hollander [the mayor] by writing what he thinks of him, as one Jew to another. He also said that Gandhi had done him proud in an article in *Indian Opinion*.

On September 7 that year, however, Henry said that Millie was not looking forward to returning to South Africa, or to living at Phoenix, where she did not find the social intercourse she needed. It was hard for her to leave England. While he was there, we learn from a later letter, they had taken part together in a suffragist demonstration, where Mrs. Besant made a great speech. The Polaks had marched in the Indian section, and he had carried the elephant.

Descriptions of life on Tolstoy farm, in Gandhi's letters, are full of zest in the physical work—chopping and sawing wood, fetching water and doing laundry, rolling stones for the building's foundation. "I for one am a farmer and I wish you to become farmers," he wrote to Maganlal in August: "My way of life has completely changed here. The whole day is spent in digging the land and other manual labor instead of in writing and explaining things to people. I prefer this work and consider this alone to be my duty [presumably dharma in the original] . . . I regard the Kaffirs, with whom I constantly work these days, as superior to us. What they do in their ignorance we have to do knowingly. In outward appearance we should look just like the Kaffirs. . . . The body is like an ox or donkey and should therefore be made to carry a load" (10:308).

These are the Robinson Crusoe pleasures, here recaptured. "Having founded a sort of village we needed all manner of things large and small, from benches to boxes, and we made them all ourselves" (S:219–20). And as in Defoe's story, the reduction to material simplicity produced an exaltation of the spirit. This experience was profoundly important to Gandhi. "My faith and courage were at their highest in Tolstoy Farm. I have been praying to God to permit me to re-attain that height" (S:222). The difference is that in *Robinson Crusoe* the hero returns to England to enjoy the fruit of his labors—his exhilaration and exaltation of spirit reempower his love of his own civilization—whereas in Gandhi something like the reverse occurred.

Thoreau's self-simplification, reported in *Walden*, can also be compared with Crusoe's, but the South African Indians' setting makes Gandhi's story especially interesting, because it gives the ideas the three authors shared a large and political scope. The significance of Gandhi's pleasure is also increased by the decline of the same pleasures, or at least of the corresponding virtues, among the whites around him. (In 1908 Sir Percy Fitzpatrick of the Progressive Party of South Africa called upon the white man to "justify himself" by "out-working the native.") It was the brown-skinned Indian who began to practice those virtues that had been the pride and the moral prerogative of the whites.

In these years, as we have seen, Gandhi in some sense wanted to change his identity. In March 1914 he wrote Chhaganlal that the Gandhis had been a famous or notorious family: "that is, we are known to belong to a band of robbers." (Literally, of course, they were advisers to their princes.) If their elders had done some good to others, Gandhi said, it was incidental. Chhaganlal and Maganlal should cease to be Gandhis, and become farmers. Probably he was writing similar things to his brother Lakshmidas, and the other family members, for they quarreled bitterly with him by mail.

To Maganlal he wrote in 1911: "If we think of our own family . . . Please think of the hypocrisy, the corruption and the immorality of the members of our family who are occupying posts of executive officers" (10:373). And in the 1914 letter to Chhaganlal, "The life of service or political work which we have followed so far seems to me of the lowest order. . . . Without disparaging our elders. . . . At present, the family has fallen on evil days. Any member who failed to obtain a paid job would be on the streets. The highest our eyes can look up to is Narandas [the addressee's brother] slaving away in Bombay. Other members of the family just loiter about or, wallowing in the politics of [princely] states, manage to earn just enough for their food from day to day. All of them are busy multiplying, arranging marriages, etc." (12:381). They should become farmers or weavers.

In another sense the Indians became Europeans on Tolstoy Farm, only not ruling-class Europeans, but those outside or against empire. "We had all become laborers and therefore put on laborers' dress but in the European style, viz. workingmen's trousers and shirts, which were imitated from prisoners' uniforms" (S:224). Making their own wooden spoons there, like Crusoe himself, their own medicine, their own food, Gandhi and his friends were full of faith. "I had in those days as much faith in the nature cure of disease as I had in the innocence of children."

That faith was tested, and he reacted with a cruel severity, though the severity was indirect. Often he was himself the first victim, but not the only one. He beat his face when he found that Phoenix settlers had had spiced food brought in from Durban, and then lied to conceal the fact. At Tolstoy Farm he fasted on one occasion when there was sexual misconduct; but on another occasion he cut off the girls' hair, even though it was the boys who had taken the initiative.

January 8, 1913, he wrote to Kallenbach that the latter must not abandon the simple life. During this period of his life, Gandhi began to develop his ideas about diet and health more fully. He wrote a long series of articles for *Indian*

Opinion, later published as a book, on "General Knowledge about Health." He recommends vegetarianism, restraint of appetite, scrupulous cleanliness, nature cure with earth and water. Perhaps the most striking essay is the seventeenth, which appeared on March 10, 1913, and declared brahmacharya the most important of all the rules of health. Sexual activity fritters away our energies, our integrity, our health. "He who has conserved his generative fluid is known as *virayan,* a man of strength." (As his resort to Sanskrit words indicates, this was a traditional Hindu idea; but on the whole his philosophy of health was New Age.) We should, he suggests, store within our body the mysterious power which nature has bestowed upon us. Men and women are blinded by sexual passion; Gandhi himself on occasion had lost all sense under that influence. All the other passions derive from violations of chastity.

In saying this, Gandhi is tracing out, in another field, the consequences of his great principle of conservation, concentration, contraction, self-restraint, the opposite of the modern world's principle of expansion, exfoliation, self-multiplication.

Of course New Agers like Tolstoy have made the same criticism of modern civilization. "Our diet, our way of life, our talk, our sights which surround us, are all such as to excite our lust" (12:52). That quotation is from Gandhi, as is the next, but both could perfectly well be by Tolstoy. "People of the West have broken all bounds in this matter. They adopt various techniques so that they may have pleasure without being burdened with children" (12:48). Not that large families are what he recommends. In India, children have children, and the country is swarmed over with worthless creatures as with ants. The good is restraint, diminishment, singularity, sublimation.

His ideas about health were closely connected to Tolstoy Farm and his experiences there, and to Tolstoy's writings. On December 10, 1910, *Indian Opinion* included an extract from Tolstoy on Bondarev and the idea of bread labor. And Tolstoy's influence was strong in many matters. Gandhi sent Maganlal, as invaluable, Tolstoy's pamphlet, "The Relations between the Sexes," and wanted everyone at Phoenix to read Tolstoy. Even such surprising items as "Hadji Murat," a bloodthirsty adventure, are recommended in the book lists in *Indian Opinion.*

On July 15, 1911, he wrote, "A moment's thought ought to convince our friends that a nation cannot be built out of clerks or even merchants. 'Back to the land' is General Botha's advice even to the Europeans who, after all, do follow many useful occupations. ['Back to the land' was of course a New Age slogan.] The world lives on its farmers and those who are indispensible to farmers, e.g. carpenters. . . . We all live upon the great industry of the Natives and Indians engaged in useful occupations in this country. In this sense they are more civilized than any of us" (11:124).

As for aesthetic sensibility, Gandhi showed for the rest of his life an intense appreciation for "organic" phenomena, which we are surely justified in connecting with this experience. He wanted to come close to nature; we might remember that he had before this time himself delivered Kasturba of her fourth child. This is a stress of sensibility familiar enough among those who have read

D. H. Lawrence's or Tolstoy's novels, but not so common among those who, like Gandhi, read instead the *Ramayana* and the Bhavagad Gita. Here, for instance, is a passage from a letter about unpolished rice.

"I opened out one grain from the paddy and showed to those around the full unpolished grain. I had not seen it before. But in a heap of half-polished rice I saw a whole paddy grain. I immediately removed the husk with my fingernails. Out came the beautiful red grain from its husk" (60:86). It is a moment of birth he is evoking. As Madan C. Gandhi says, Gandhi found a dead polish in the smooth starchy texture of mill cloth. Homespun seemed to him soft, lovely, graceful, its coarseness the very weave of nature. And just so he loved the flour patterns on Indian doorsteps, and the light shed on banana-branch arches by earthen oil lamps.[45]

Politics

In 1911 the political situation grew calmer, and the Indians won some concessions. In January, India prohibited the export of indentured labor to Natal; in April, to all South Africa. The South African government presented a new Immigrants Restriction Bill, which the Indians protested against in March, and got amended. But in April, Gandhi agreed to suspend satyagraha, even without the amended bill being passed, in response to Smuts's desire for peace in South Africa during the coronation of George V, and in exchange for certain promises. Smuts promised that existing rights would be maintained, that former satyagrahis would be allowed to register, and that five or six educated Indians would be allowed to enter as settlers each year. A provisional settlement on these terms was agreed on in May.

In 1912 Gokhale visited Africa. As a member of the viceroy's council, he came with the power to negotiate with the authorities. In *Satyagraha in South Africa,* Gandhi writes: "I had been requesting Gokhale and other leaders to go to South Africa and to study the condition of the Indian settlers on the spot. But I doubted whether any of them would really come over" (S:237). It was important to Gandhi and his career, that it should be Gokhale who came; that the two should bind themselves to each other publicly in that way.

So Gokhale got permission from the secretary of state for India to make a six-week tour on his way back from England. As Gandhi says, "No Indian leader had been to South Africa before or for that matter to any other place outside India where Indians had emigrated." It was an imperial occasion; an occasion for the white colonists, too.

The Indians decorated the railway stations, and held public meetings in town halls. Gandhi's white friends were involved. Kallenbach designed the ornamental arch of welcome at Park Station in Johannesburg, and Gokhale stayed in Kallenbach's house, which was, Gandhi says, simple but full of art.

Gandhi deeply respected Gokhale, but there was some struggle of wills between the two men—Gandhi wishing Gokhale to make speeches in an Indian language, for instance. However, they resolved the conflict in laughter. There was a good deal of teasing competition, particularly about matters of health. Gokhale said, "You all seem to think that you have been born to suffer hardships and discomforts, and people like myself have been born to be pampered by you. You must suffer today the punishment. . . . I will not let you even touch me" (S:379).

Gokhale got from the government a promise that the three-pound tax would be removed, as would the racial bar from immigration; but Gandhi remained skeptical; and in fact that promise was not kept. Gandhi knew the men he had to deal with better than Gokhale, despite the other man's long political experience. Gokhale was of course the more moderate of the two, in temperament as well as policy. Romain Rolland decribed Gokhale as an Indian who hoped for a future like Canada or Australia for his country; whereas his rival Tilak hoped for a future like Japan. Gandhi wanted something different from both.

In April 1913 a new phase of the campaign began, and this time it involved women. It was provoked by the government's ruling that Indians must *prove* themselves legally married. This was again an issue of cultural honor, and Kasturba decided to join in the resistance activity herself. She was incensed by the thought that she and others like her were not wives in the eyes of the law, but concubines. Sonja Schlesin, as secretary of the Transvaal Indian Women's Association, announced that they would offer satyagraha. The police wanted no martyrs, and refused to arrest the first group of protesters, the Tolstoy Farm sisters, six of whom carried babies. But on September 16, Kasturba and fourteen others from Phoenix who had kept their expedition secret, and refused to give their names, were arrested, and she was given three months hard labor.

That was the day after satyagraha was revived. On October 2, Kallenbach and twelve more women "offered themselves." The event was widely reported; the Zoroastrian and Islamic Societies officially supported the Hindu movement. And although the Muslim political community, especially in Natal, was now resistant to and distrustful of Gandhi, one Muslim woman took the initiative and got herself arrested, in the same cause. She left Durban by train on October 8, seen off by a gathering of friends, who presented bouquets and refreshments. She was becoming a heroine of the movement. On the fourteenth, in Volksrust, she was sentenced to three months in jail with hard labor. This was Bai Fatima, the wife of Sheikh Mehtab.

Not much is known about Bai Fatima, or about Sheikh Mehtab's marriage. What is known derives from a biographical sketch inserted in the November 5, 1913, issue of *Indian Opinion,* as part of a process of drawing attention to her exploit. She had apparently attended classes in Arabic in the Grey Street Mosque Medressah (where Sheikh Mehtab taught) up to the age of ten. She did not learn Gujarati until after her marriage, and her father's name was Sherekhan. All this suggests an origin in the Punjab or further north. She is said to have read *Indian Opinion* faithfully, but she acted independently of both her husband and Gandhi in going to Volksrust, and there are some other indications of a bold and stubborn personality.

The October 15 issue of *Indian Opinion* included a public letter signed by her, and beginning "Dear Indian Brothers and Sisters"; but it is hard to know how much of this was really written by her. The letter gave three reasons for her going to jail: the government's discrediting of Indian marriages; its breaking its promise to Gokhale; and the need for Indians to defend their institutions. She said she was breaking the purdah she had so long observed, because of this crisis.

She took with her her mother, Hanifa Bai, and her seven-year-old son, and a man described variously as a servant and a friend of the family. (This grouping was against the strategy Gandhi had devised for this campaign, and suggests that she acted on her own initiative.) Sheikh Mehtab is not mentioned in the reports, except for the anecdote that his wife told him that since he was too poor to pay her railway fare to Volksrust, he should sell the jewels in her dowry. This anecdote was taken up and repeated by, for instance, Polak, in public remarks.

It appears that Bai Fatima refused to give her fingerprints, and there was some physical struggle between her and the police, which caused some indignation. The British Indian Association in Volksrust made an official protest. The little boy was not allowed to accompany her to jail, and was taken into the care of Mr. Badat, an Indian merchant in Volksrust, until he could be sent back to his father.

When she and her mother were released, from Pietermaritzburg jail, three months later, they were garlanded with flowers and given a triumphal reception in Durban, at Parsi Rustomji's house. A group came to Pietermaritzburg from Phoenix to welcome her, and all then entrained for Durban. There were receptions at stations on the way. At Malvern she was met by Parsi Rustomji, who brought flowers sent by the Zoroastrian Society; at Durban she was garlanded by Sonja Schlesin; at Rustomji's reception for her, Miss Molteno spoke; and so on.

Bai Fatima's action was not designed as a part of the campaign, but it was quite important in that she was a Muslim woman (the only one to take such an active step) and in that the Muslims of Durban had largely disassociated themselves from the satyagraha movement. It was calculated that only 3 percent of the people on the march were Muslims. Items about her appeared in *Indian Opinion* up to November 26, and then again in January.

The March

The first group of women, meanwhile, being left free, had returned to Natal and made their way to the Newcastle coal mines where they urged the miners to strike. The response was much greater and quicker than Gandhi had anticipated; he had in fact neither the money nor the workers to deal with the mass movement that was soon on his hands.

But on October 17 he himself went to Newcastle, and urged the indentured Indian workers there to strike until the three-pound tax was repealed. Seventy-eight did so, and four were arrested and given two weeks imprisonment; and as a result three thousand more decided to strike on October 20. These miners lived in houses owned by the mine company, and used its water and electricity. They were thus wholly dependent on their employers, so Gandhi decided that they could not stay at home to strike, but must "fare forth like pilgrims," selling what they could of their possessions, and abandoning the rest, bringing with them only blankets. On October 28, he led them on a march from Newcastle in Charlestown, the Natal border village, where two hundred arrived on the thirtieth.

On November 6, he led twenty-two hundred out of Charlestown and crossed the border to Volksrust. On November 11, Gandhi was sentenced to nine months imprisonment, to which another three were added. All the miners were sent back to their mines, now as state prisoners. All Indian labor in Durban struck, and the plantation labor, and there were mass meetings everywhere. Soon there were sixty thousand men on strike beside the satyagrahis in jail.

The men on the march were far from being satyagrahis themselves. In 1921 Gandhi said that he had had thieves and murderers as his associates in South Africa (20:62). And that there were Pathans on the march (20:465).

On December 11, the South African government appointed the Solomon Commission to investigate the situation, and on the eighteenth Gandhi and Kallenbach and Polak were released. He decided to boycott the commission. He did so against the advice of Gokhale, the viceroy, and Lord Ampthill, but he carried mass meetings of South African Indians with him. Meanwhile, the movement had more martyrs. An old man, Hurbath Singh, died in jail at the age of seventy; a girl, Valliamma, died of an illness contracted there at the age of seventeen, on February 22. Gandhi had already taken to wearing the costume of the indentured, out of mourning for previous martyrs to passive resistance, and he regularly reminded audiences of those who had given their lives for the cause.

Finally, in January 1914, a settlement was reached; the three-pound tax was abolished and monogamous Indian marriages were recognized as valid. Gandhi was free to return to India at last. He was by then a political and religious hero; at a farewell banquet in Johannesburg on July 14, a man presented Gandhi with his four sons, so that he should train them for national service.

Nevertheless, things were not so universally triumphant as they seemed, and Gandhi was bitterly criticized by some Natal Muslims (12:491). A meeting was held to object to Gandhi's settlement with Smuts; and there was considerable criticism and objection to his use of the money collected for the campaign. Mr. Ally criticized him. The newspaper report speaks of applause from "a section of the audience."

The Mehtabs

As a climax to this narrative of Gandhi's years in South Africa, let us remind ourselves of a shadowy presence at several of the ceremonies surrounding Gandhi's triumph and departure. At least at those in Natal, Sheikh Mehtab and Bai Fatima and their son were often amongst those surrounding him and amongst the few representing the still-faithful Muslims. Sheikh Mehtab and his pupils sang songs, composed by him for the occasion. For instance, for a reception for Andrews and Pearson, he had composed songs in both English and Hindustani. When the Transvaal women were released and welcomed home, on January 20, he sang a Hindustani song in their honor. At one of them, on July 15, he gave a speech in Gujarati, in Gandhi's honor. (He is not recorded to have performed at the reception for his wife.) Prabhudas Gandhi remembers seeing him often, after other Muslims had turned hostile, at Parsi Rustomji's house; where the satyagrahis and their sympathizers met. No doubt Mehtab and his family risked the displeasure of their Muslim patrons for their loyalty to Gandhi.

Since the Mehtabs do not appear again in the record of Gandhi's life, it will be well to sum up what little we know about the rest of their lives. In July 1915 we find Bai Fatima listed among the Durban donors to the Indian Women's Bazaar, along with Mrs. Polak, and her two sisters. She had no other children, though she adopted a young boy called Khan, and she herself died young, before her mother. There is no record of what her marriage was like, but the things we do know about Sheikh Mehtab suggest that he did not lead a domestic life. Of course, Indian men of his generation often did not mention their wives, however rich the marital relationship was, but he was known to the few people who still remember him in Durban as a peripatetic figure. He was well-known in the community; as a humorist, as a poet in Urdu, as a teacher (of music and of Gujarati, privately and at the Medressah) and as a deviser of *nataks,* a kind of musical theater with moral or patriotic themes. He too served the cause of Indian patriotism in his own way, though it was more aesthetic and desultory than Gandhi's.

His name recurs in the record of Gandhi's emotional life, as we shall see. When an unpleasant incident in the ashram in the 1930s reopened the wound of Sheikh Mehtab's long-past manipulation of his feelings, Gandhi's anger swelled out of all reason and control. On the other hand, when he wrote a comic poem for his grandson (apparently his only poem) he signed it Rasik, the Poet of Poets: that was the name Mehtab took for his comic poem about satyagraha.[46]

Pursuing Mehtab's ghost through the streets of the Indian quarter he inhabited, finding a building he slept in, and the grave where he lies, the theater where his nataks were put on, and the mosque he taught at, I found myself reminded of some aspects of Dublin at the same time, as Dublin is represented in Joyce's *Ulysses*—the world of Simon Dedalus, let us say. Reginald Reynolds says that the intellectuals of Delhi reminded him of those of Dublin, in their scathing and scatological wit, citing the phrase: "If he swallowed a nail it would come out a corkscrew."[47]

Obviously, this is a guess and not in any sense authoritative, but Mehtab may have become one of the convivial masculine presences of Durban, like those of Dublin, hearing and retailing gossip, reciting poems and songs, all bearing on the great national past and the deplorable colonial present; with a habit of laughter, a flavor of bitterness, and an encroaching shabbiness.

He did not, it seems, boast of his relationship with the Mahatma, or at least those who remember him did not make much of that association. According to Gandhi, Sheikh Mehtab "worshipped me from afar." This sounds like another of Gandhi's simplifications, judging by what we have seen of the other man's temperament. But we are in no position to be sure; and even if it could be called a falsification, it is almost certainly not inspired by complacent self-congratulation—that was not one of Gandhi's weaknesses. How then can we understand that phrase, and the last, posthumous phase of their relationship?

There had long been a struggle between the two of them over Gandhi's claim to be a moral hero and lawgiver, deserving deference from his old friend—his mischievous tormentor and quondam protector. Measured by almost any criterion, and whether or not one likes him, Gandhi had between 1893 and 1914 shown himself to be such a hero, and so had triumphed in that struggle—Bai Fatima's initiative alone would indicate that. If Mehtab had any share of that generosity of spirit that we seem to see in him, he probably did acknowledge that achievement. He acknowledged, we could say, the size of the djinn which had billowed out of the little bottle in Rajkot—timid little Mohan Gandhi—and with which he had been for thirty-five years unequally wrestling.

From South Africa to England 1914

Most of the inmates of Phoenix sailed from Durban to India, but Gandhi and Kasturba sailed from Capetown, on the *Kilfauns Castle,* and went to London first, because Gokhale was to be there, and Gandhi wanted to consult with him. Kallenbach accompanied Gandhi, planning to live with him in India. (His luggage, including books, went to India, and—he being interned in England during the war, and subsequently out of touch with Gandhi—were lost to him.) They debated the propriety of Kallenbach's possessing an expensive pair of binoculars; and Gandhi persuaded the latter to let him throw them into the sea.

When Gandhi left South Africa, he still believed in the British Empire, though tentatively. "Though Empires have gone and fallen, this Empire may perhaps be an exception . . . it is an Empire not founded on material but on spiritual foundations . . . the British constitution. Tear away those ideals and you tear away my loyalty to the British constitution; keep those ideals and I am ever a bondsman." And besides being an imperialist, he was, in a spiritual sense, a colonial—i.e., a life-experimenter.

On this voyage his mind must have turned toward India, and toward the new allies and/or rivals he would meet there, both constitutionalists and the revolutionaries. Most important to Gandhi were probably the latter. We have described those he met in London, led by Savarkar and Krishnavarma, and inspired by Tilak. However, the main center of Indian revolutionary thought, during Gandhi's time in South Africa, was Bengal. That province was not much of a presence in South Africa, or in London, and Gandhi had paid only brief visits to Calcutta, but once he arrived in India he would have to show off his paces there.

In Bengal both town and country were ruled by the *bhadralok,* a term that might roughly be translated as gentry, and there was a wide gap between them and the lower castes. They were landowners, but had a tradition of literary education and cultural responsibility. With the cultural revival called the Bengal Renaissance came a debate over how to develop that heritage: to blend into the modern world, or to revive the classical Brahminism of the past. The second was not as peaceful a choice as it sounded. It involved a cult of Shakta, the mother goddess of strength; in modern terms, violent revolution. Gandhi was going to have to find a way to redirect that energy in peaceful channels.

In 1906 a new Bengali weekly called *Yugantar* (The new age) had been founded, which was frequently prosecuted, and "breathed bombs in every line." It contained, for example, on May 20 that year, an article entitled "The Bengali's Bomb." *Yugantar* asked Bengalis to show themselves men in the way they died, if they could not do so in the way they lived. The journal was banned in 1907, but there were Yugantar groups, and related Anushilan (culture) groups. The Anushilan Samiti (the society for the promotion of culture) was founded in 1902, inspired by the ideas of Vivekananda, Sister Nivedita, and Bankim Chandra Chatterji. One of its supporters was Saraladevi Chaudhurani.

The main revolutionary textbook in Bengal was *Bartaman Rananiti* (The modern art of war) of 1907. It began with an article taken from *Yugantar,* in October 1906, saying that destruction was another form of creation. It described guerrilla violence as the natural way to cut out society's gangrene, and cited Japan's rise to power through war. It used the image of Time pointing to the power of the English rifle, and saying: "See, the warlike spirit is the artificer of the European palace; acquire the warlike spirit."

But the bhadralok's claim to patriotic idealism was not universally conceded. In 1900 the Muslims outnumbered the Hindus by 10 percent in Bengal as a whole, and were growing twice as fast, although they were predominantly poor peasants. The partition of the province that Viceroy Curzon decreed in 1905 was seen by the English, and by some of the Muslims, as an attempt to save the latter from dominance by the bhadralok. The latter, of course, claimed they were fighting for India's freedom, and their agitation progressed from peaceful protest to overt violence. Arabindo Ghose and his brother invoked the legends of Kali driving out the demons; and terrorist samitis were founded, to commit assassinations.

Arabindo, born in 1872, had a career in some ways parallel with Gandhi's, inasmuch as it was split between nationalist politics and religion, between Indian and Western culture. He and his older brother were sent to European schools in Darjeeling, and later in England. Arabindo passed the examinations for the Indian civil service, and returned to India in 1893. (This was a crucial year: it was when Annie Besant went to India, Vivekananda went to America, Gandhi went to South Africa, and Tilak organized the Ganapati Festivals.)

Arabindo went to teach in the princely state of Baroda, whose ruler promoted educational experiment. He lived as a brahmacharin, and sought spiritual inspiration, but studied political activism. He disagreed with the moderates' politics of petition. In 1902 he initiated his younger brother into revolutionary work, ceremonially putting a copy of the Gita and an unsheathed sword into his hands. Arabindo himself practiced marksmanship, something Gandhi was never to do.

The agitation against the partition of Bengal succeeded, in that the two parts were reunited in 1912, when the English moved their capital to Delhi. But the movement had not been entirely triumphant for the bhadralok, because it had revealed their unpopularity with other groups, notably the poor and the Muslims. Rabindranath retreated to literature, Bipin Chandra Pal to England, and Arabindo Ghose to religion.

During his jail sentence in 1908 the last-named underwent a change of heart, and came to believe in purely spiritual energy. When he was freed, he left British India for Pondicherry, one of the tiny remnants of French territory in India, and set up an ashram there. He practiced a quietistic meditation, combined with a philosophy that can remind one of Teilhard de Chardin. Some followers of Gandhi passed from his ashram to Arabindo's, and vice versa.

The Bengal agitation was something for Gandhi to measure himself against and to learn from, when he began his own agitation in India a decade later. In many ways he followed its example; for instance in dramatizing the issue of foreign imports, which he and the Bengalis fought with the cry of "Swadeshi," homemade. He tried hard to make an alliance with the current leaders of Bengal, and to some extent succeeded with C. R. Das. He found in Saraladevi Chaudhurani a woman who was identifying herself with the forces of Shakta. But in the long run his movement was to be non-Bengali; despite being a rejuvenation and extension of the Bengali initiative.

However, the forces of world history were, as Gandhi sailed toward Southampton, preparing an event that was to make these choices in India temporarily unimportant. The assassination of the Grand Duke Ferdinand at Sarajevo brought Austria to declare war on Serbia; Germany joined Austria; Russia joined Serbia; France joined Russia; Germany attacked France, going through Belgium. And as Gandhi's ship arrived in England, on August 4, 1914, World War I, known as the Great War, engulfed the British Empire also. This meant, to name only the personal consequences impinging on Gandhi, that Gokhale could not be in London, that Kallenbach could not go to India, and that Gandhi had to decide what attitude a nonviolent man should take up toward this major explosion of violence.

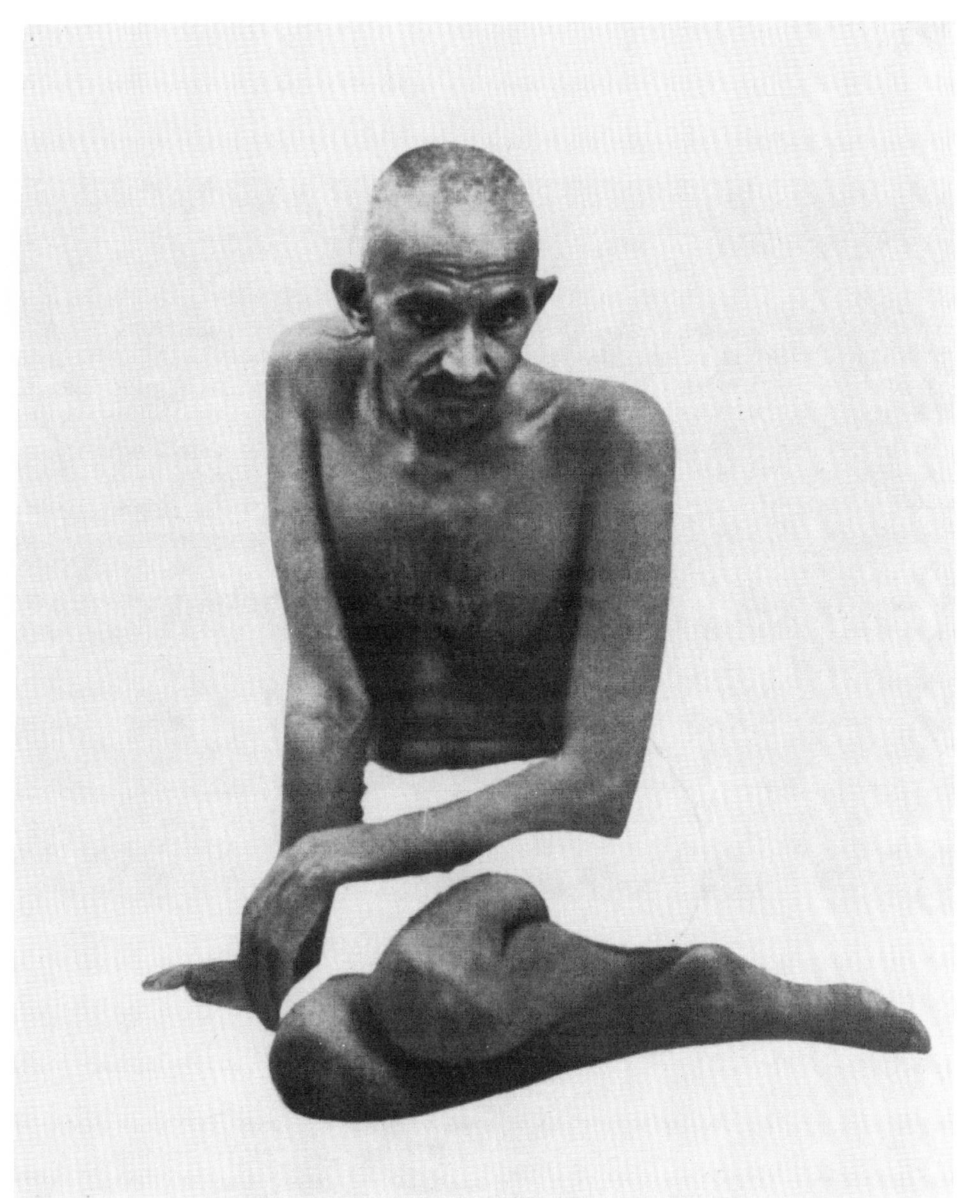

1. Gandhi.

2. The student Gandhi with English vegetarians.

3. Gandhi's great teacher, Tolstoy.

4. Gandhi in Johannesburg in 1906.

5. Gandhi and Sonja Schlesia, and other office workers.

6. Saraladevi Chaudhurani, an important woman friend.

7. Saraladevi Chaudhurani graduating from college.

8. Gandhi in London in 1931.

SIX

VIOLENCE AND NONVIOLENCE

Now, when the story of Gandhi's life is half told, is a good time to step out of the narrative stream, in order to examine in more depth some of the major ideas that are a key to its meaning. One of those is Gandhi's philosophy of nonviolence; another is his declaration of anger: "I shook with rage." That is a deliberate manifestation of violence. Despite appearances, the two are rooted in each other, as Gandhi himself perceived.

A boy-and-man's experience of impotence, such as we have traced in Gandhi's early years (impotence in matters of force) can lead to quite different reactions: to the renewed pursuit of force by indirect and "cultural" means—in his case, political leadership; or to its renunciation, and the assertion of the superior values of peace and gentleness. This gentleness asked to be called feminine, as the force asked to be called masculine. We find both in Gandhi. The personality he presents was built up by these, and by other, various and strenuous, kinds of psychic "work," done in reaction to that early experience.

The second idea is perhaps the more obvious. Gandhi is justly famous as a man of peace. His satyagraha was the greatest application of the principle of peace on a political level that the world has ever seen, and as a private person Gandhi was the embodiment of gentleness for many who knew him. And this was not composed of acts of virtue, achievements of willpower, it was continuous and rooted in his character.

The Rajkumari Amrit Kaur said, "We found in him not only a 'Bapu'—a wise father, but what is far more precious, a mother."[1] Erikson says that in nursing his father, Gandhi's love of nursing displaced the Oedipal wish to rival him.[2] That displacement could be discerned in his relation to the British Empire, and his supplying an ambulance corps to the British army in time of war was like his nursing his father.

Gandhi gathered round him, to work for his various causes, primarily mild and gentle, even timid, people. Krishnadas, his principal secretary for a few months in 1921, records Gandhi's saying about the noncooperation campaign, "It is time people realized that only mild and gentle people should enlist themselves on our side in the battle."[3] When he planned a Bardoli campaign, he said he chose that place rather than Ahmedabad because of its meekness—Ahmedabad and Bombay were too wealthy for his purposes, and wealth meant pride (22:396).

Krishnadas himself was of that mild and gentle type. He was a highly valued aide to Gandhi, editor of one of the Gandhi newspapers for a time, but he presents himself as full of shyness, and alarms, always hanging back and needing to be pushed forward, even to do acts of service to Gandhi. He doubted his own worthiness; he longed to wash Gandhi's clothes; he wrote poetic prose about nature. Physically and socially feeble, he was prone to headaches and alarms, and frightened by crowds and violence.

Krishnadas was not of course a political leader, but we find a similar psychological type in Rajendra Prasad, Gandhi's chief lieutenant in Bihar, and later president of free India. Prasad tells us in his autobiography how he could never swim or climb trees, and had nothing of the adventurer in him. "I am by nature shy and bashful" (A:83). He was a great winner of school-prizes and treasurer of testimonials by his teachers and superiors. His book about Gandhi is entitled *At the Feet of Mahatma Gandhi.* (Bombay: Asia Publishing House, 1961) where he described Gandhi as being like the river Ganges (Mother Ganga) in all her aspects.

A vegetarian, and a khadi-and cow-enthusiast, Prasad never smoked tobacco or drank alcohol—the familiar drugs of fire. Even Patel, a political ally, found Prasad too mild. He was a temperamental opposite to Nehru: their supporters constituted two mutually opposed parties. Prasad's biographer says Nehru's temperament was poetic, "and his imagination wove dreams, governed by his egotism, wherein he sees himself as the centre of things, and people created for him to fulfil his dreams."[4] Prasad, on the other hand, was the reverse of an enthusiast or a self-dramatizer; being in his moments of strength all cool mild reason.

There were also people of very different psychological types who worked closely with Gandhi: Vallabbhai Patel, Chakravarti Rajagopalachari, and so on. Of course, whatever their individual temperaments, the terms on which they cooperated with Gandhi were always nonviolent. However, he continued to have to deal with the violence in them and in himself—he needed to overcome both the fear and the anger left in his own psyche by his early experience. And he also had to deal with violence in others, often more literal or habitual than his own.

There was something almost magical about the mature Gandhi, in his power of winning over people of a great variety of kinds, getting work from them, establishing moral authority over them. But of course this power was not really magical, not completely automatic or unfailing. There were always men like Jinnah and Ambedkar, who hated him mercilessly; and there were neutral-seeming circumstances in which he was impotent. The sessions of the Round

Table Conference in London form one example. On some political committees—to take another instance, the Viceroy's Subjects Committee in 1918—he had nothing to say, and counted for little.[5] And there is a story of how, going to see the viceroy at Viceregal Lodge, he was asked to wait in an office where the aides-de-camp sat and talked, and how ill at ease he showed himself in that company. With such men he had nothing to say.

In Krishnadas and Rajendra Prasad we see the type to which Gandhi himself primarily belonged, and which held a certain psychological hegemony over the satyagraha movement. He was more various than the others at that type, as well as more forceful, but at the root of his temperament was still the experience of knowing himself feeble. He always acknowledged that experience. And with that went fear, humiliation, resentment, and anger—as well as the commitment to peace and goodness.

The Pursuit of Force

On the other hand, Gandhi did pursue, and achieve, a specifically masculine forcefulness. For instance, when he used the phrase "I shook with rage" to describe his reaction to legislation against Indians, he did not write that phrase apologetically; he was claiming to be a man and a leader. And he was so understood. People as tough-minded as Vallabhbhai Patel acknowledged his claim, and obeyed him scrupulously, sometimes blindly. Patel himself said so, about himself; and Prasad said, about the great industrialist G. D. Birla, that Gandhi "made use of many" like Birla, and the latter "obeyed him like a soldier."[6] Birla himself, in the introduction to his memoir, says, "A saint is not very difficult for the world to produce, and political leaders are put forth in plenty, but real men are not to be found in abundance on this earth. Gandhiji was a man among men—a rare specimen not produced by the world even once in a century" (xvi).

In politics, as in other matters, manliness meant force, and force meant, on occasion, rage. After the Russia-Japan War Gandhi wrote "The people of the East will never, never again submit to insult from the insolent whites" (8:324). The man of peace did not write such things with any sense of being inconsistent, apparently. On occasion, moreover, he explicitly refuted the charge of moral inconsistency—which was often put forward, by Indians as much as by Englishmen. For instance, the Servants of India Society criticized his enrolling the forces of hatred and violence under the banner of love in 1921 (19:362). And Saraladevi Chaudhurani made the same accusation, in private letters, at that time.

Gandhi replied that he did not create political hatred, but did use its energy. In 1920, he used the phrase "disciplined expression" often: saying that it had become the fashion to ascribe hatred to noncooperators, but: "I make bold to say that the only way to remove hatred is to give it disciplined expression" (19:80). He claimed that by conserving his anger he turned it into energy. This formula applies convincingly to some instances of his behavior, but not to all. His political language was often highly emotional, and bound to arouse anger in others, rather than to discipline it. It was often ambivalent. During the same campaign, when Gandhi advised students *not* to leave their government schools for his own *vidyapiths,* his argument was that, however discontented, they should stay in the official schools *unless they had a choking sensation when they approached the building* (19:110). Clearly, this was a test of the students' sincerity that set a high value on fierceness of feeling.

Throughout his life, therefore, but perhaps especially in the noncooperation campaign of 1920–22, Gandhi employed a rhetoric of rage. He spoke in terms of death (settling problems of conscience his followers brought up with the recommendation to die rather than yield) and blood (the swarajists would have to wade in blood before they succeeded) and destruction (of the British Empire) and fire (literal bonfires of foreign cloth, and metaphorical flames engulfing the imperial institutions) and so on. Many of his friends, as well as his opponents, were made nervous, some were horrified, by this destructiveness. After riots in Bombay he fasted and suspended action; and in 1922 after Chauri Chaura, Gandhi halted his whole movement, at enormous political cost. He acknowledged "Himalayan blunders." But his later speeches and writings were, from time to time, charged with the same emotions.

When challenged about the emotion inspiring many of his followers, during that campaign, he even admitted that their nonviolent noncooperation was based on malice and hatred, but claimed that in effect he could disinfect those emotions for them; because "a noble action, whether done with love or hatred, cannot but yield fruit" (19:136).

"Shook with rage" is of course a phrase out of a well-worn rhetoric, and perhaps the reader does not take it very seriously. But it recurs, and is echoed in other phrases; and in Gandhi's case one is unwise ever to discount his rhetoric as simply or conventionally exaggerated. We should at least begin with the literal image of that frail body shaking, and the urge to destroy overcoming that iron self-control.

Whether we deplore that image or welcome it, our response will be shaped partly by its discordance with the better known image of Gandhi the sad sufferer, the man of prayer, the cadaverous faster—or the playful grandfather surrounded by smiling disciples and children—in either case, the saint of nonviolence. How can the two go together? When a prince of peace displays himself shaking with rage, is it not ugly, and a proof of hypocrisy? That was certainly what his opponent Ambedkar said. "If a man with God's name on his tongue and a sword under his armpit deserves to be called a Mahatma, then Gandhi was one."[7] He often called Gandhi a humbug, and compared him with Uriah Heep.

However, a little acquaintance with Gandhi's writings will show us a third profile between the martyr and the militant, which is more central to his behavior than they, from the point of view of political dealings. This Gandhi was a tough-minded realist, who both thought and acted in terms of strength. He made things happen—made others do things they could not or would not otherwise do. Gokhale said Gandhi made ordinary men into the stuff of heroes. This was true enough. But Gandhi's own bleaker, grimmer language is more to the point here. He often said that a satyagrahi had to be *hard*—as well as strong. As early as 1909 he wrote thus to Kallenbach about the *weakness* of his codelegate to London, Haji Habib: "Smuts can feel it and so can Lord Crewe. What wonder then if both of them be in no hurry to end the struggle!" (UC). Gandhi himself was strong.

Habib had wanted to accept what the British offered, while Gandhi had refused. He said he would say no even if the whole Indian community asked him to say yes. However, it is better, he concluded, that Habib should be in London, under Gandhi's eye, than elsewhere, making mischief. This is a toughness of tone Gandhi quite frequently employed (UC).

Men of traditional religion, like Raychandbhai and Ramana Maharishi (a Hindu saint contemporary with Gandhi) felt that he was imperiling his soul by occupying himself so much with worldly matters. And on the other side, English officials were sometimes shocked to hear him talk coolly of the numbers of deaths to be expected if—in some particular instance—a city riot or a communal war broke out. They accused him of hypocrisy. But leaders of men have to think of such numbers. The Englishmen were shocked at such language because they didn't believe such a naive, New Age man could be a political leader. They thought that was *their* language.

In their dealings with Gandhi, the English, and Ambedkar too, were probably influenced by one of the cliché images of Anglo-Indian fiction—the fakir or mullah who established a leadership by preaching religion, but who was secretly preparing an armed uprising against the British raj. This figure is to be found in stories by Kipling and Flora Annie Steel and Sara Jeannette Duncan and Edmund Candler and Maud Diver. In fact, many elements of Gandhi's personality fit in with that image—may even have been shaped by it. As we have seen before, the Indians and the Anglo-Indians were both very alert to promptings in the air—the same promptings, often.

Even more strikingly, Gandhi often exhorted Indians to be proud and strong and even fierce—to leave behind passivity and to act on their resentments—to enter into struggle and become lions. We shall see that after the Jallianwalla Bagh riot and massacre in Amritsar in 1919, he declared the humiliating punishments imposed by the British (Indian men were forced to crawl in the dust along a lane where an Englishwoman had been assaulted) to be worse than the deaths inflicted. Honor and manhood were the issues for him, not peace and justice.

For him, politics came to life when a point of honor was at stake. He was not much interested in the extension of the democratic franchise, or only as a symbol, not in its employment. He didn't expect or want the Natal Indians to use their votes in 1894—merely to hold on to them. In those ways he was more like Kipling or Nietzsche than like a political idealist of the modern democratic kind. There was something archaic and legendary about his politics. We have noted already that his ideal India was a Rajput state; and that he thought a benevolent autocrat the best kind of authority. He liked to personalize issues, by summing up all of India in his own person, and all of—for instance—the South African whites in General Smuts, or all of the Muslims in Jinnah, and he would then deal "chivalrously" with the opponent. He was ready to call off the Indians' campaign in 1913, in order not to embarrass the government when it was dealing with striking railwaymen; and to delay action at the time of the coronation of George V, to allow Smuts to celebrate the event with imperial dignity.

Moreover, though we have no reason to doubt his love of peace, we must be struck by his respect (so rare among pacifists) for the military virtues—both individual heroism and group discipline. He wanted his satyagrahis to be soldiers. And in a speech in Calcutta in 1902, Gandhi said, "As a Hindu, I do not believe in war, but if anything can even partially reconcile me to it, it was the rich experience we gained at the front. It was certainly not the thirst for blood that took thousands of men to the battlefield. If I may use a most holy name without doing any violence to our feelings, like Arjun they went to the battlefield, because it was their duty. And how many proud, rude, savage spirits has it not broken into gentle creatures of God?" (3:223).

Also in an article for the *Times of India,* on June 16, 1900: "It was wonderful to see how with clockwork regularity, over fifteen thousand men with heavy artillery and transports broke camp and marched off, leaving behind nothing but empty tins and broken cases" (3:138). He had a Kipling-like sensibility (see the scene of the regiment breaking camp in *Kim*) to the efficient movement of masses of men and material.

It is not surprising that some Indian liberals deplored Gandhi's stress on "physical" courage, as something that separated him from them. They felt that they were just as devoted as he to nonviolence, but in a more refined way. Thus his friend, Srinivasa Sastri, wrote in a letter in November 1932, that Gandhi often seemed to "de-throne nonviolence from its place of honour, and crown the pinch-beck god of physical courage instead."[8]

He aroused the South African Indians by talking of adventure—taking his examples more often from English history than from Indian. He printed poems about adventurers from Columbus to Napoleon, in *Indian Opinion*. Adventure was the consecrated imagery of imperialism, but Gandhi was ready to adapt it to anti-imperialist purposes.

We have seen his readiness to recruit an ambulance corps to support the British army in South Africa; and we shall see him recruiting Indians to fight in the 1914–18 war in Europe. He was always ready to imagine scenes of bloody slaughter as occasions of courage and virtue. He accepted in advance the likelihood that Hindus and Muslims would fight each other when the English withdrew from India. He described to the members of the Sabarmati Ashram a day he foresaw when they might be mowed down by British bullets, and the pride and joy with which he would sacrifice them.

So far this discussion has focused on political behavior, but Gandhi was a sincere politician, in the sense that there was no disjunction between his politics and his temperament, at least as he understood the latter. Moreover, he thought in terms of cultural psychology, understanding for instance "the Muslim" simultaneously as an individual psychology and as a political group. We have seen this idea, which included also aptitudes for violence, in his relations with Sheikh Mehtab.

His friend was able to deal in violence much more easily than Mohan himself was, and he directed—most often in playful form—some of that violence at Mohan. An important strain in the latter's early experience was fear; the more generalized and persistent result of that fear was humiliation; and the reaction against that humiliation took the form of anger. We saw that sequence in some of the events of 1893; the conflict with the British agent in Porbandar, the anger and humiliation, and the protest against the colonists in Durban.

The anger manifested itself more openly and proudly in politics than in private life, or even than in nonpolitical aspects of public life. His politics were masculinist, his other activities were—in one sense—feminist, or androgynous, as has been pointed out. However, even in domestic matters, Gandhi wrote to Chhaganlal Joshi in September 1915, "I myself am fighting with the demon of Anger these days. The moment anyone in our circle makes a mistake, this adversary Anger rides on my back" (41:412). And in 1934 to Premabehn Kantak, "None of you know the [strength of] anger in me. I alone can know it. I wouldn't describe as anger what Lilamati or Gangaben have observed in me. I suppress most of the anger which I feel. Gangaben and others could have seen only what remained of it. . . . Because I don't think it necessary to be careful with people who are intimate with me, they occasionally get a glimpse of the anger in me, but, being kind to me, they forget it" (59:419).

It is also significant that Gandhi liked to associate with men of violence—as well as with men of strength and courage. One example is Chhotelal Jain, a former terrorist, indicted in the Delhi Conspiracy of 1915, who was converted to nonviolence by reading Gandhi, and came to live at the ashram, working at all sorts of humble employments: kitchen-work, spinning, Gandhi's correspondence.

When Chhotelal died, Gandhi accused *himself* of violence toward him. "I could not tolerate any imperfection in him and so he had often to bear the brunt of my impatience, as, perhaps, only one or two besides him have born . . . I had hoped one day to discharge my debt towards him by offering him as a sacrifice at the altar of Hindu-Muslim unity, untouchability, or cow protection. . . . Chhotelal was in the front rank of the few who, to my knowledge, had the strength and capacity to claim this privilege."[9] Here we see how the nonviolent man, operating in the world of life-and-death, absorbed the force and the violence of men by nature very unlike himself, making himself harder than they.

Another similar Ashramite was Balwantsimha, who heard of Gandhi in 1919 while serving in the Indian army in Aden. After hearing the news of the Jallianwalla massacre: "We, therefore, discussed amongst ourselves the possibility of our returning to India by land, after massacring our few British officers." In 1921 he began to read Gandhi. When a police inspector pounced on Balwantsimha like a wildcat, seizing his throat and sitting on his chest, the other laughed, repeating Gandhi's name in his mind.[10]

But in his dealing with Gandhi all this violence was reversed. "My relations with Bapu were like those of a child with his mother" (40). Balwantsimha looked after the cows at the ashram. When he wrote to Gandhi protesting—in the name of the cow—some interference with his work, Gandhi replied, "I have heard the roaring of the lion as well as the mooing of the cow"—a reference to the *simha* of Balwantsimha, which means lion. (Gandhi was often compared with other men in terms of a pair of animals, the other man being the lion—for instance, Tagore was seen as a lion and Gandhi as a mouse.)

If we conclude, then, that Gandhi had some elements of violence in him, or encouraged some kinds of violent thoughts in himself, while others he drove away, the question becomes, which kinds were which?

Let us look first at his recorded behavior. We can say immediately that he never fired a gun, slashed with a sword, or even punched. (Nehru, on the other hand, did use a *lathi* against rioters, on occasion.) He did not inflict physical violence upon others on the battlefield, or in his daily life. If we think of the violent scenes in which we see Gandhi involved, he is most often the victim: when he was pulled off the coach on the way to Pretoria, when he was assaulted by Mir Alam, when he was assassinated; or in much smaller incidents, as when Sheikh Mehtab grabbed him, in the Beach Villa house. Or else he is deliberately passive, as in his work as schoolteacher at Phoenix or Tolstoy Farm, where he struck himself instead of the boy who annoyed him, and on another occasion had Polak beat a troublesome pupil on his behalf.

The exceptions to this general description are scenes with women; as when he half-put Kasturba out of the house in Durban, or when—according to Sonja Schlesin—he slapped her face, because she—as a young girl—smoked in his presence. When Gandhi discussed the sort of "violence" a woman might legitimately employ to defend herself, he explicitly accepted such slaps or scratches as innocent. They were not what was meant by violence. His own physical acts were of that innocent kind.

Describing the stagecoach scene, he said, "When I held on to that bar, I was mentally prepared for death. I could not have inflicted any serious injury on my assailant. If, however, I had lost hold of the bar, I would have slapped or bitten. That would not be violence" (51:24).

He did not impose systematic pain even upon himself, as some religious penitents do—he did not wear a hair shirt, for instance. There was pain associated with his fasting, of course, but it was incidental. Nor did he cherish or appropriate the violence others did to him. Imaginatively, after all, a person can be deeply involved with, can in a sense appropriate, the violence that someone else inflicts upon him/her. Gandhi was on guard against that. This showed itself in his disapproval of the English women suffragists. We can take an example from one of the movement's leaders, Sylvia Pankhurst, who wrote to her mother from Holloway jail, "I am fighting, fighting, fighting. I have four, five, six wardresses every day as well as the two doctors. I am fed twice a day. They prise open my mouth with a steel gag, pressing it in where there is a gap in my teeth. I resist all the time. My gums are always bleeding. My shoulders are bruised with struggling, while they hold the tube into my throat." Gandhi printed this in *Indian Opinion* for July 5, 1913. It is significantly different from his accounts of his own prison life, and different precisely in the quantity of violence it asserts and shares, with which it infects the reader—which is one reason why he disapproved, while admiring, the Pankhurst branch of the suffrage movement.

He prepared himself for death daily. Krishnadas reports an occasion during the riots in Bombay when the people in the ashram heard a noisy bunch of Parsis approaching along the road, and Gandhi thought they were coming to kill him, and was glad that the long-promised sacrifice was finally to be demanded of him.

In the 1930s he wrote about another martyr: "My ahimsa will also be perfect if I can die similarly peacefully with axe blows on my head. I have always been dreaming of such a death. . . . How noble that death will be—a dagger attack on me from one side, an ax blow from another," etc.[11] It is clear from his language that he was preparing himself for the event, imaginatively. He was anxious about that test, and in some sense eager to have it over with. The day before his death he told his companions that they would know he had been a true Mahatma only afterwards; if he died by a bullet and with the name of Rama on his lips.

Many of Gandhi's readers, especially Westerners, see something morbid in such declarations, but he himself saw the readiness for death as a necessary part of courage.

The Masks of Terror

Perhaps an unconventional definition of, or way of imagining, courage is a useful key to understanding Gandhi's complex attitude to violence. If we speak of courage simply as the opposite of cowardice (as Gandhi himself spoke most often) we find ourselves thinking in terms of the virtues, and then "moral" courage or cowardice eclipses the "physical" kinds—the primary, premoral experience of violence—so completely that the latter loses all interest. But that primary experience was of great interest and importance to Gandhi. Speaking of these matters in *Satyagraha in South Africa,* he wrote, "Knowledge which stops at the head and does not penetrate to the heart is of but little use in these critical times of living experience" (S:171). In the ordinary sense of heart, Gandhi's indifference to death was surely heartfelt; but in the critical moments of action—the lived experience—even that was of little use. It could not abolish fear.

So let us speak rather in Nietzschean fashion about a premoral domain of violence; and about a kind of behavior, of the emotions as well as of the body, in which the ultimate polar realities are the terrifying and the terrified. We might think of these states of being as like giant masks, or the grotesque incantations and dances of the Japanese theater; assumed to impress the opponent, known or unknown, and intended to infect him or her with panic.

The Japanese film *Rashomon* first gave many Westerners some sensory images of that, and they are useful in constructing a psychology of violence. Of course our actual experience of terror is various and amorphous. It is not always a face-to-face matter; often two groups are involved, or one person and a group, or some persons and an unknown thing. The degree of terror varies with the kind and with the individual. Gandhi, for instance, seems to have been naturally brave about, perhaps exhilarated by, being at sea, even when the ship was in a storm; there is no record that he was afraid on the battlefield. However, he was afraid of many things; and all his experiences of terror, various as they were, can be seen as occurring between two persons or groups.

When two such individuals come into conflict in the domain of violence, and accept the rules of that domain, each has the aim of putting on the terrifying mask, and forcing his opponent to be terrified; the latter is then encumbered with the shattered remnants of his own violence. To use the terms of modern thrillers, A takes away B's gun, and threatens B with his own gun. But such conflicts do not necessarily involve guns, and when they do, they are not necessarily about shooting. They are about the imbalance of power between two people—about terror.

The man or woman of courage is one who can enter into the domain of violence and stay steady; uninvaded by the flood of its feelings—panic, collapse, disruption—not forced into the posture of the terrified. But most people acquire that courage by becoming familiar with that domain, those feelings, wrestling the terrifying mask from the opponent, and being able on occasion to assume it. That is why people learn to box and wrestle, to fence and shoot. Gandhi however would not, indeed could not, do those things, "I cannot pull the trigger against my worst enemy" (23:30); and he could not make up his mind whether to recommend them.

At the end of 1926 he gave a speech when he opened a gymnasium, and said that only a man capable of violence could be capable of nonviolence; and that physical training was one way to acquire the capacity for violence (32:443–44). But though they had swords and daggers in the ashram, and though they were persecuted by a community of thieves nearby, Gandhi's advice was that the inmates should not practice their use—only lathis (49:259–60).

The ashram, he said, should defend itself. But Gandhi himself would not take up arms for that purpose. He had "deliberately renounced the path of living by killing others." So for him, and a few others, there was a different path—dying to live (23:468). His dharma is not to resist others' violence. But since he has never successfully communicated this idea to others, he has given up trying (26:508).

As we have seen, Gandhi was one of those who—up to at least eighteen—found himself often terrified. Sheikh Mehtab was just one of those who wore a dominating mask, but he came close to Gandhi for a long time; and though the two boy/men were other things to each other, their relations included that conflict over force. (Gandhi says that Mehtab often threatened him.) It became Gandhi's need to escape the feelings of terror, but by a nonviolent discipline, not by assuming the mask of terror. (I spoke before of two forms of action, the more masculine one of traditional politics and the more androgynous one of satyagraha: only the second, the more radical, could prevail against terror.)

Both aspects of terror were known even to this devotee of peace, as he admitted when he accused himself of anger in the family. And this was true of political situations, too. When Gandhi saw Untouchables trembling with fear in his presence, because he was a caste Indian, he was deeply upset. In Orissa in December 1927, he wrote how, "the bitter cup of sorrow and humiliation was filled." A man threw himself flat on the ground in front of Gandhi, would not look up, and thrust straw into his mouth, in token of self-abasement (35:407). He was terrified to be in Gandhi's presence, and the latter "writhed in agony." He knew that he was wearing, despite himself, the mask of terror.

This was just as much what he hated as the opposite: when the Pathan warriors or the British officials put on the mask of terror to subjugate *him*. When Gandhi describes the Jallianwalla Bagh massacre, we see both the masks of terror, and the hope of abolishing them. "We played into General Dyer's hands because we acted as he had expected. He wanted us to run away from his fire, he wanted us to crawl on our bellies and to draw lines with our noses. That was a part of the game of 'frightfulness.' When we face it with eyes front, it vanishes like an apparition."[12]

Gandhi wanted his followers to walk into the no-man's-land of violence and put back its magic—make it vanish like an apparition—transform its emotional economy into something different. This is what he did in his great political campaigns.

He often succeeded, and therefore became a Mahatma of peace. But he also failed; sometimes his followers became terrifying; and sometimes they became terrified. He also failed more intimately when he saw within himself an irreconcilable conflict, an impossibility. This happened to him in the course of his recruiting campaign in 1918, as we shall see. Then he saw the disabling truth that most people see most of the time, that the domain of violence is not an illusion, an apparition, but an ever-imminent reality. Nor is it a field of action for the civic virtues; but a different psychological terrain, which is ruled by those who are violent or who can be violent on occasion—those who can wear the mask of terror.

That is only common sense. When Gandhi proposes to erect a statue to the Christian soldier, General Gordon, who will be represented not carrying a sword or even a cane, but folding his arms and offering himself to his opponents; or when he describes any great soldier, possessing the warrior virtues, as one who is ready to die for his beliefs; we know that he is falsifying things (28:21). He is describing not warriors but martyrs. On the other hand, we cannot take this to be just Gandhi's individual aberration. The great religions, including Christianity, enshrine the faith that we should never be violent. That is not common sense, but it is just as vital a part of our culture.

A terrorist cultural psychology (terrorist in the sense that it involves wearing the masks of terror) had long been a part of imperialist ideology in India. In the eighteenth century (1780) the Englishman Robert Orme saw the Indian as "the most enervated inhabitant of the globe. He shudders at the sight of blood, and is of a pusillanimity only to be excused and accounted for by the great delicacy of his configuration. This is so slight as to give him no chance of opposing with success the onset of an inhabitant of more northern regions." This is the mask of the terrified.

In the nineteenth century, Macaulay wrote that: "The physical organization of the Bengalee is feeble even to effeminacy. He lives in a constant vapor bath. His pursuits are sedentary, his limbs delicate, his movements languid . . . he would see his country overrun, his house laid in ashes, his children murdered or dishonoured, without having the spirit to strike one blow." And James Mill in his *History of India* I, p. 480, makes the same analysis of Hindus as a whole. "Few pains, to the Hindu, are equal to that of bodily exertion; the pleasure must be intense which he prefers to that of its total cessation." Even the official 1858 report on India said the Hindu character was feeble, slow, and irresolute, and an Englishman did three times the work of an Indian.[13]

Gandhi was thus answering to a national and historical need in India, as well as to his personal and psychological need. He was inventing courage. Naturally, other Indian nationalists, as well as Gandhi, tried to reverse the psychology of terror. On the other hand, his self-declared model, Gokhale, and the other moderates, were much less likely to attempt that than his enemies, like Tilak. The politics of the former was less aggressive and masculinist. Gandhi was unlike both of the other two, going further than either.

The artists and political leaders of India (such as Bankim Chandra Chatterji and M. N. Roy) had tried to produce images of aggressive Indians. In the preceding generation, Bankim Chandra Chatterji (1838–94) wrote novels about the conflicts of the Moguls and Pathans, using astrological symbolism and heavy with a sense of fate. The most famous of these was *Anandamath* (1880), which contained the song that became the national anthem, "Bande Mataram." The novel is about a band of sanyasis rebelling against the English in 1772–74. They are dedicated to the service of Durga (the goddess Bankim identifies with their mother country) employing all means, including violence, in that service. This novel became a bible for secret societies, and its hero, Satyananda, became their model.

The Bengali revolutionaries took sanyasi names for themselves out of that novel, and sang the anthem, part of which Arabindo translated thus:

> Terrible is the clamorous shout of seventy million throats,
> And the sharpness of swords raised in twice seventy million hands
> Who sayeth to thee, Mother, that thou art weak?
> For thou art Durga holding her ten weapons of war.

Another book much read by the revolutionaries was Arabindo's *Bhabhani Mandir,* published anonymously in 1905. Bhabhani was another manifestation of Durga, and the tutelary goddess of Shivaji, who named his sword after her. The book proposes that a temple be erected to Bhabhani. She is the Infinite Energy that sets the Wheel of the Eternal to work; she differs in form in each age, appearing sometimes as Renunciation, sometimes as Piety, but sometimes as Durga. In our age she has been Lakshmi (Wealth).

"Wherever we turn our gaze, huge masses of strength rise before our vision, tremendous, swift, and inexorable forces, gigantic figures of energy, terrible sweeping columns of force. All is growing large and strong. The Shakta of war, the Shakta of wealth, the Shakta of science. . . . Everywhere the Mother is at work. . . . We have seen the slow but mighty rise of the empires of the West, we have seen the swift, irresistible and impetuous bounding into life of Japan."

Some Shaktis are white and pure, others are black; and in 1905, Arabindo said, India was weighted down with the inertia and impotence of the latter. "Rushing and billowing streams of energy must be poured into her [India], her soul must become, as it was in the old times, like the surges, vast, puissant, calm and turbulent at will, an ocean of action and of force."

The early career of M. N. Roy, the Bengali who became the leader of the Indian Communist Party, answered to the stories and ideas of Arabindo and Bankim. In 1906, before he became a communist, he went to Hardwar to become a sanyasin. He swore loyalty to Jatin Mukherji, who called himself the commander in chief of revolutionary forces in India. Then Roy engaged in acts of sabotage; derailing a governor's train in 1907, and bombing a mayor's house in 1908. The life of revolution involved a great deal of secrecy and disguise and sacrifice. When Roy committed crimes, other men confessed to them, and took the punishment for them. The same was true, we have seen, of V. R. Savarkar, the Maharashtran. There were many such at that time.

Gandhi's movement was strikingly different, being so devoted to nonviolence, and yet it was equally an attempt to meet violence in others and to master it in himself.

Saraladevi Chaudhurani

One of the most striking cases of a Gandhi-like concern with both violence and nonviolence is to be found in the woman with whom he came to have his most important love relationship. Saraladevi Chaudhurani grew up in the heart of the Bengali intellectual aristocracy, and was familiar with the ideas of Bankim and Arabindo before Gandhi was.

In her autobiography, she wrote about her Tagore siblings and cousins,

> As children, we used to sing Rabimama's [her uncle Rabindranath Tagore's] songs exhorting us to wipe off the records of Bengal's shame. As an adult, I realized that the biggest cause of shame was our reputation for cowardice. That is what had to be erased. Holding a weapon in your hand does not necessarily drive out cowardice. But training in arms would at least give you the knowledge of how to hit the attacker without actually killing him. . . . It is this confidence that enables the trained person to employ arms in self-defence. When attacked, a dog will bare his teeth, a cat her claws; even the insects will bite. Why should Bengalis keep quiet under infinite aggression? Why should they be so lacking in humanity, in self-respect?

All this is clearly in line with Gandhi's thinking about courage.

She continued:

> I also realized one other thing. The hand and the mind must work in unison. Even in the old days, when the Bengali was an adept at using *lathis,* his mental muscles had not been exercised for generations. If he

> could not overcome that lethargy and train his mind to welcome action, and get into the habit of taking action, the hand that held the *lathi* would not rise instinctively in times of need. The heroes of ancient times used to say that the best power is physical power. Along with that, the sages used to say, power comes from the energy of Brahman. What this meant was that the mind and the body work on each other.[14]

We are familiar with this conviction, and also its ambiguity, or even paradox, in Gandhi.

Saraladevi (also known as Sarla) was a writer as well as a musician. "My pen reverberated with the power of Shiva's trumpet and invited Bengalis to 'cultivate death.' The first piece I wrote after coming back [from a few months in South India] was the first note sounded on that *rudraveena*. [We might translate this as "war-trumpet," although the *veena* is a string instrument.] To Bengalis, who were primarily concerned with their personal safety, the instrument brought a new message—don't become the passive victims of death, court it." For Saraladevi, the concept of death should not lead to grief, much less despair. It was closely associated with that of adventure and courage and a kind of playfulness. What she went on to say sounds quite like the British adventure writers.

> Defy death and confront it in play, pleasure, hunting, consciously and unconsciously, in tending the victims of plague, of fire, of drowning, in saving the lives of others. Learn your geography by travelling around the world, not by walking your finger across the map. Sail the high seas, go to the Sahara desert, climb Mount Everest. And your main resource will be [that of the ancient sadhus] a strong and healthy body. This is the greatest treasure man can have. And to have it, Bengalis must start a sustained regimen of physical culture, like the other races in India. (125)

Her concern for the strength of Bengalis was very like Gandhi's concern for that of Gujaratis. Saraladevi gives very few dates in her book but it seems that at this point she is referring to the time of her meeting with Gandhi, in 1901. They were close in their general position even then.

> I invited the readers of *Bharati* [the Tagore journal that she edited] to send me descriptions of incidents where a Bengali man, angered by insults offered either to himself or to his wife and family [by the British] had taken the law into his own hands and sought physical compensation for that insult, instead of being overcome by his feelings or taking recourse to the courts. . . . Suddenly, before anyone understood what was happening, a literary forum which had been reserved for the soft footsteps of the goddess Saraswati, was transformed into the dance arena of the terrible lord Shiva, and everyone was forced, voluntarily or involuntarily, to dance to that rhythm.

Saraladevi became known for her militancy; she was hailed by the title of Bengal's Joan of Arc. Young men gathered round her. "I selected some of these visitors and formed a special group. I would place a map of India in front of them and make them take an oath—that they would serve this country with body, spirit and wealth. And then I would tie a red *rakhi* (wrist band) around their wrists as a badge, or emblem of their offering of themselves. . . . Not that this group was any kind of secret society. But since an undisclosed resolve has greater power, I encouraged the members to keep all this to themselves" (126).

Later on, Saraladevi decided to institute a Bengal festival of courage, and found that the second day of the traditional Durga Puja had formerly been assigned to listening to tales of heroism and bravery. She revived that custom.

> Bengali mothers would once again have to be inspired to instill courage into their children. These timid mothers would have to be transformed, so that they instructed their sons in physical culture, games and being active. How could our country have reached the present state of decrepit ignominy, when at one time it was a part of our religious observance for mother and son to unite to promote the glory of the native land? My heart wept for us. By now many boys called me "Mother." And in the past, unknowingly, I had bound the red band of courage on their wrists. Now that I realized that I had only done the duty of a mother, I decided I would continue the practice as extensively as possible. This was the command of the motherland. (140)

She was a mother of power, a Durga.

When she met Gandhi, in 1901, she tells us, she saw him only as a possible South African contributor to her journal. It was nearly twenty years before she began to focus her powers of enthusiasm on him. And presumably he was not then reading much, if anything, of what she wrote. But they were aware of each other. Polak, we know, stayed with Saraladevi in Lahore, on one of his trips to India; and he seems to have reported Gandhi's achievements in glowing terms, privately as well as publicly, to everyone he met.

"The 'worship of the brave' continued in Bengal. I started bringing out booklets under the serial title of 'Heroes of Bengal.' Then I organized a festival in honour of Pratapaditya's son Udayaditya. [These two men were feudal lords in Bengal, who led armed resistance to the Muslim conquerors.] In those days the paper *Bengalee,* edited by Suren Banerjee, was the most important English paper brought out by a Bengali. All the details concerning my festival were reported with enthusiasm in this paper. 'Saraladevi is springing one new surprise after another on the country.'" *Bangabasi* asked, "Has the goddess Durga come down to earth herself? A daughter has awoken in a Brahmin home, the glory of Bengal has returned." The idea of shakti, the female power, being embodied in Durga and other goddesses, and—in the first decade of the twentieth century—being associated with national revolution, invited women of imagination to act out that role, in one way or another.

In what has been quoted, the writer was of course describing these events long after they occurred (probably forty years after) and was moreover excited with her own achievements. But we have testimony in Gandhi's letters to her and about her between 1920 and 1922 that she was for him too an embodied idea, a radiant personality—a shakti.

The Bengali revolutionaries passed among themselves *Chandi,* a book about Durga (also called Kali and Shakti) who destroyed the demon Chanda. The myth was that when the gods were driven from their kingdom by the demons, they created Durga to defend them. Thus they combined the idea of revolution with the image of shakti. Saraladevi herself told Gandhi that her husband called her the greatest shakti in India, and her writings show that she herself thought along those lines. She seems to have been the best known of all the women who attempted to embody that image in Bengal.

The Doubt about Nonviolence

Predictably, both of these militant friends came to feel dissatisfaction and doubt about nonviolence; and of the two, Gandhi is the one we must devote most time to. The experience of the war had come close to Gandhi, in England and then in India. He volunteered to serve in an ambulance unit both in France and in Mesopotamia, and then he volunteered to recruit other Indians to fight as soldiers. Thinking about such matters was bound to be painful to a man of nonviolence.

On August 3, 1917, he wrote to his Danish friend, Esther Faering, that only a few individuals could achieve innocence, and no nation could. Nations will always fight. "A nation to be in the right can only fight with soul-force. Such a nation has still to be born. I had hoped that India was that nation. I fear I was wrong." For himself, he would always let himself die rather than kill; that was *his* fate; but as for advising another: "Where I know there is want of will altogether [a paralysis] I would advise him to exert his will and fight. There is no love where there is no will" (13:485). The word *will* here has a ring of manly pride that might make one think of Lawrence or Hemingway.

Thus in the rational part of his mind Gandhi gave room to the idea of violence as an acceptable means to a political end (not for him, but for others) in that period of his life. That was above all in 1918, when he recruited for the British army. The whole episode must be given careful study, but let me quote in advance from a remarkable letter he wrote to C. F. Andrews on July 6, 1918. The latter has just before tried to reassure Gandhi about Indian nonviolence, but Gandhi cannot accept the reassurance.

> I must attempt in this letter to reduce my own [difficulties] to writing. They just now possess me to the exclusion of everything else. All the other things I seem to be doing purely mechanically. This hard thinking has told upon my physical system. I hardly want to talk to anyone. I do not want even to write anything, not even these thoughts of mine. I am therefore falling back upon dictation to see whether I can clearly express them. I have not yet reached the bottom of my difficulties, much less have I solved them. The solution is not likely to affect my immediate work. But of the failure I can now say nothing. If my life is spared I must reach the secret somehow.

As we shall see later, he never did reach that secret. But in this letter he goes on to challenge Andrews's declarations that, first, Indians repudiated "bloodlust" in times gone by. "Is this historically true?" Gandhi asks—though historicism was an unusual intellectual tactic for him to employ.

> I see no sign of it in the *Mahabharata* or the *Ramayana,* not even in my favourite Tulsidas. . . . I am not now thinking of these works in their spiritual meanings. The incarnations [figures like Krishna] are described as certainly bloodthirsty, revengeful and merciless to the enemy (14:474). . . . The battles are described with no less zest than now, and the warriors are equipped with weapons of destruction [as powerful] as could be possibly conceived by the human imagination (475). Even among the Jains the doctrine has signally failed. They have a superstitious horror of blood(shed), but they have as little regard for the life of the enemy as an European.

Andrews had also said that nonviolence had become an unconscious instinct with the Indians, which needed only to be awakened, as Gandhi had shown. The latter replied,

> I wish it were true. But I see that I have shown nothing of the kind. When friends told me here that passive resistance was taken up by the people as a weapon of the weak, I laughed at the libel, as I called it then. But they were right and I was wrong. . . . And I contend that they will not regain the fearless spirit until they have received the training to defend themselves. *Ahimsa* was preached to man when he was in full vigour of life and able to look his adversaries straight in the face. It seems to me that full development of body-force is a *sine qua non* of full appreciation and assimilation of *ahimsa.*

He was writing this shortly before he got to know the woman who was following the same train of thought.

We should not overlook the application of these remarks to the person to whom the letter was addressed, and to the writer too. There was no "full development of body-force" in Andrews. He, and Joseph Doke, were like Gandhi, frail men, incapable of violence, certainly men of great moral courage, but excitable and ineffective in certain ways—easily despised by men of force; in direct confrontation "light on their feet." (The current association of that phrase with gay men could be misleading, but I find the implication of a nonviolent and nonforceful manhood helpful, and worth the risk of misunderstanding.) These were men of the same temperament as Gandhi himself—suffering saviors. He far surpassed them, of course, but he grew from a similar root. He became a man of power, in some measure because he asked himself these questions and acted on the answers.

As we shall see, Gandhi soon broke off this sequence of thought and in a sense turned his back on the problem. He returned to making propaganda both for nationalism and for nonviolence. But in a deeper sense the thought of their mutual contradiction never left him, and indeed had been there before.

The Complex Encounter

Violence had always been important to Gandhi as part of his imaginative diet, because of his early experience of fear and humiliation. We have looked at his dealings with Sheikh Mehtab, his determination to understand and appropriate his manliness. That was mostly playful, but later Gandhi had to imagine death and killing, in order to be ready for it, whenever it came. He of course expected his own assassination, more or less always. Moreover, he had incited others to expect death, and to run the risk of it.

But—and this may be even more disconcerting—he also had to accept violence in order to be able to deal with men of violence; amongst whom were to be named some of the nationalist leaders and revolutionaries. His dealings with Sheikh Mehtab were to be repeated in his dealings with, for instance, the Muslim brothers, Mahomed and Shaukat Ali. They embodied the Muslim fierceness on the public and political stage, and as long as they acknowledged Gandhi as their leader he possessed their strength.

The same pattern is visible in his relationship with Abdul Ghaffar Khan and his brother, the Pathan leaders, as far as Gandhi's side of that relationship goes. Saying "I shook with rage" he entered the world of men. Condemning Ram Sundar, for instance, he claimed to embody himself the criterion of manliness. It has been pointed out how often Gandhi used the language of virility and emasculation in political matters. This was a deep part of his psychological being from as far back as we can trace, and remained there till the end.

Our nonviolence should be the nonviolence of the Pathans, he wrote in 1938. "A Pathan boy is fearless . . . [He finds pleasure in fighting.] . . . I have seen one standing unmoved in the midst of blood gushing from many wounds. . . . I myself have not yet reached this stage. There is a lot of cowardice in me. I talk of satyagraha, no doubt. But in the face of killing I cannot have the fearlessness of the Pathans" (66:436). And later, "I am afraid of every little thing" (66:449).

With representatives of the other martial races (Gandhi names the Sikhs, the Gurkhas, the Rajputs) he had less-dramatic personal relationships, but he did appeal to them, in their character as martial, and appealed to their example in his dealings with people of his own type, like the Parsis and the Jains and the Kathiawari banias. It was one of the most constant of his themes, that his bania followers must learn to become Kshatriyas. He himself had become a Kshatriya. (He played with all the caste identities, it is true, but this shift from the bania to the Kshatriya carried the most serious weight.)

Among his own closest followers, Vallabhbhai Patel was a Patidar, as we have seen; a Gujarat caste that one might suggest carried something of the suggestions of "yeoman" in English history; or—more fanciful but more specifically similar—the heroes of the Icelandic sagas. Patel was generally considered a hard and fierce man, the disciplinarian of the swaraj movement, and sometimes compared with Bismarck.

It must be largely a coincidence that Patel was so closely bonded to his brother Vithalbhai, while the Ali Brothers and the Khan Brothers were generally known by that title, "Brothers"; but it is not perhaps entirely coincidence. Gandhi appreciated the masculine character brought out by close fraternal relations—as well as the sisterly and androgynous relations mentioned before. In any case, Gandhi established over Patel and the Khan Brothers the sort of ascendancy that he only attempted with Sheikh Mehtab and the Ali Brothers. In this way his life was a triumph. He came to dominate the dominating.

The Triumph over Fear

The theme of violence is not, of course, the only one in Gandhi's psychology. But it is possible to see many of the other themes as deriving from it—because of massive psychic work done in response to the early experience of fear, humiliation, and anger. It is one particular kind of such work that we see as most striking in Gandhi, one particular source of power he tapped. He *reversed* his feelings. One can learn from the experience of one emotion, however unwelcome, the shape of its polar opposite—and so learn where to find that and how to install it. All that one needs is the (enormous) will to do so. Gandhi was in this sense a self-made man, to an unusual degree—he was a voluntarist, as J. P. Narayan said.

For instance, his profound love of peace is clearly a contradiction of his tendency to anger; his preoccupation with lavatories and night soil contradicts his fastidiousness; the strenuous asceticism of the fasts and the vows is a contradiction of his early greed; his pride in being Indian is a contradiction of the humiliation to which he was subjected by the British; the extraordinary moral and physical courage he developed contradicts his fearfulness; and so on.

We have noted his enthusiasm for vows, which offended so many of his closest friends, for instance Sonja Schlesin and Henry Polak, and Charlie Andrews. Such vows are a way of mobilizing the psychological and moral force necessary to the reversal of the congenital or ordinary. Gandhi said that life without vows is "insipid"—overrelaxed, flabby. Vows are a more self-conscious equivalent of those involuntary "decisions" that Gandhi reported. They seem to be a kind of moral muscle.

Gandhi remarked that his friend Andrews, on the other hand, held himself free to do the will of God as that revealed itself to him from moment to moment. "This attitude has answered his purpose. I should be undone" (33:127). This is interesting because the two men were similar in many ways, but different in this matter. Andrews was in many ways feckless. He spent or more often gave away whatever money he had, and turned to his friends for more. Andrews, Gandhi said, had a trusting nature; Gandhi himself had not (32:481). Gandhi kept very careful accounts, and in fact did not give money away. He controlled all the circumstances of his life, including the psychological ones. Gandhi would have been undone without vows because the knots that held him together would have been loosed.

He uses the same image in this passage of 1929. "The world would go to pieces if there was not this element of stability or finality in agreements arrived at. . . . India would perish if the firmness of the Himalayas gave way. . . . A person unbound by vows can never be absolutely relied upon. . . . To shirk taking of vows betrays indecision and want of resolution."[15]

On the other hand, according to a letter written to Mira Behn in 1927, about the prayer meetings at the ashram, prayer was not a large feature of Gandhi's devotional life early on. "The value of prayer dawned upon me very late in life, and as I have fair capacity for imposing discipline upon myself, I have by patient and painful striving been able now for some years to conform to the outward form. But do I conform to the spirit? My answer is: No." The proof of that he offers is that when he prays, his mind wanders; and that is what goes wrong at Ashram Prayer Meetings (34:205). We can surely see prayer here as an opening up of oneself, a yielding to something outside and beyond—thus having a different psychological character from vow taking—less voluntarist. Andrews was a man of prayer.

Judith Brown, in *Gandhi, Prisoner of Hope,* also sees anger at the root of his psychology, though she looks at it from a different angle. She suggests that both his ceaseless activity and his troughs of depression were repercussions away from an unacceptable and inexpressible anger, which was directed "at his own physique and personality, at the stubbornness and cruelties of his compatriots, at the untrustworthiness of his closest"; an anger directed at himself and others.[16] He found that one of the benefits of his periods of silence was that they "ate up" his anger.

He was thus keenly aware of his anger; of which his wife and sons, but also friends like Gokhale, reminded him. Sometimes he praised it, as an source of energy, like sex. "I have learned by bitter experience, through a period of close upon thirty years, the one supreme lesson, namely, to conserve my anger, to control it, and just as heat conserved is transmuted into energy, so also our anger, conserved and controlled, can result in a power that becomes irresistible throughout the world."[17] Sometimes, however, he called this a harshness in him, destructive to others and to himself.

He described how he lost his temper when people disturbed him at night on a train, in order to take darshan of him. "I beat my forehead, but that had no effect. I did that again." Gradually he recovered his peace, and this was the fourth time in his life that he had employed that tactic successfully. It is of course better not to feel anger, but "When, however, a person simply cannot control his anger, the best way to work it off is to strike oneself" (19:373–75).

He accepted the prospect of violence in the struggle he was leading. "We will probably have to go through a sea of blood before we are through" (19:161). But, what does it matter? If the British leave, and the Pathans and the Gurkhas attack India from the north, what does it matter? The Rajput, the Sikh, and the Muslim warriors will combine to defend us. Moreover, he said, violence is morally necessary. Death will be more manly than submission (19:172). "I do really believe that anarchy will be preferable to continuance of the orderly humiliation and emasculation of a whole nation" (19:213).

He wanted to cultivate the virtues that grow alongside violence, and he sometimes thought they could not be acquired without engaging in the latter.

Sometimes he thought they could be. Naturally he preferred somewhat ambivalent formulas. Nonviolent noncooperation does not mean cowardice, he said: it means the spirit of manliness in its perfection (19:12).

Voluntarist Psychology

There are of course several ways to analyze or describe Gandhi's psychology. Erikson sees the ultimate key in Gandhi's rebellion against his father, and all fathers; and his determination to rise above them morally. And this was linked to an unconscious aggression against his sons. Gandhi wanted to be a son above all sons, and a father to no son—that is one of Erikson's formulas.[18]

On the whole it seems best simply to alert the reader to this other approach, so different from my own; but I will make one comment. Erikson says this quasi-Oedipal theme is played out at critical times in the lives of all great innovators; but despite this apparent generosity—linking Gandhi's behavior to historical greatness—it seems impossible to follow Erikson's account of his subject without condemning Gandhi. Erikson's psychology is implicitly so much on the side of domestic happiness, or of the younger person, that he does not even read the relationships between Gandhi and his sons as reciprocal; he sees them as Gandhi dealing with Another. Gandhi's treatment of his sons was certainly often—though by no means always—very hard; but I do not want to enter into the argument of how much we must reproach him. My approach allows me to avoid passing judgment on that matter, I hope.

I have mentioned the paradox of voluntarism within Gandhi's advocacy of nonviolence. We could follow that clue further. He told the students at Hindu Benares University in 1916 to terrorize themselves; to turn the cannon of aggression around, to fire the other way. He reversed the natural direction of his and his followers' emotions. "Passive resistance must revive. . . . We must learn the lesson again of finding pleasure in pain."[19] In all these cases he turned feelings back upon themselves. He cites a hymn with the lines, "It is by my fetters that I can fly / It is by my sorrows that I can soar" (8:146).

In his angry letter about Kasturba, quoted in the introduction, Gandhi proceeded directly from his anger at her behavior to his delight in all he has learned from her, and his need to deepen and strengthen the power of love in him. We have seen that also in his congratulating others on their wounds, their imprisonments, the sufferings of their relatives. Grief turns into joy, pain into pleasure, defeat into triumph—because he wills them so to do. This is clearly an ascetic and voluntarist psychology, quite unlike the erotic psychologies that have been more popular in the West in this century.

For instance, we find a criticism of voluntarist psychology in chapter 12 of D. H. Lawrence's *Women in Love*. The character Hermione describes how a great doctor cured her of various neuroses by having her deliberately perform the obsessive act (biting her nails, for instance) when she had no desire to do so—against her wish. The triumph of will over wish would not only break those habits, but energize her whole psyche. The character who represents the author, Birkin, retorts angrily that it is fatal to use the will like that—it is an obscenity.[20] He believes implicitly in the opposite strategy, in directing the will away from the psyche, leaving the latter free from compulsion. Gandhi's psychology is more like the doctor's.

In 1939 he wrote, from Rajkot, where he was leading an unhappy and unsuccessful satyagraha protest, "I am making a ceaseless, strenuous effort not to be irritated. My heart is overflowing with good-will, even for Virawala [his opponent there]" (69:31). Clearly the second sentence is what he wanted to feel—and so did feel when he exerted his will. The space between the two sentences was not—from his point of view—hypocrisy or self-deception, but simply the move from what he felt despite himself to what he felt by desire. But such a move is just what psychotherapies of the Lawrentian kind forbid.

At times, therefore, we today are likely to accuse him of mistaking intended feelings for real ones. But Gandhi was quite alert to himself, and surprisingly sophisticated in some of his formulations. He was well aware that, as he put it, there were two sides to his nature, the severe and the loving. The former, he said, had estranged many—including his wife, his son, and his brother. Somewhat more surprising is what came next in his argument. Students of psychology, he said, declare that both these phases of the mind arise out of the same cause. He went on to use this proposition to justify the apparent inconsistency of his policies.

He said this apropos of his angry-and-loving feelings about England, and of his parallel ambivalence about his political rivals in the Swarajist party (led by Motilal Nehru), with whom he was then at odds. He had to assume a fierce attitude in order to awaken England, but later he would be her friend. His quarrel with Motilal was in the later phase; he now laid down his arms and surrendered. "I shall be humble and hope to unite all through my humility" (25:62).

In another place he used the Jekyll-and-Hyde image about his own psychology. He says he does not read articles praising or dispraising him: "Praise I do not need, as I am sufficiently proud of myself without outside help. Condemnation I refrain from reading, lest the Hyde in me get the better of the Jekyll and do violence to my nonviolence" (24:6). Here we are struck most by a play of fancy and wit, which is certainly as typical of Gandhi as his harsher language. Just a few days after writing that passage he complains humorously that he is being blamed for someone else's misdeeds. "I being the meek cow, all ticks come and settle on me" (24:73). He often called himself a crank, or a madman. "I am certainly mad in the sense that every honest man should be" (26:331). This is sometimes no more than a grace of manner; at other times, it signals the profound paradox of his nature.

Perhaps the side of Gandhi's personality most remote from the theme of violence was his humor. He was humorous in a very ordinary and rational way. For all his psychological extremism, it comes as no surprise, and as no paradox, to see him remonstrating with a too-scrupulous follower, "But there is such a thing as common sense in the world," he writes in *Young India* in 1929 (41:155).

Extraordinary as his actions could be, he kept in touch with the ordinary.

After what he described as an "outpouring of my soul," he continued, "I alone have to be carried away in [this] current. Others have not to. If, on seeing the current that is carrying me, a similar current begins to flow in them, they may let themselves be carried away by it" (22:85). He was a very reasonable idealist. "I do not mind having to find out that nonviolence is an impracticable dream. . . . For me . . . I would love to contemplate the dreamland of nonviolence in preference to the practicable reality of violence. I have burned my boats, but that has nothing to do with any of my co-workers" (23:4).

In a comparable way, his discourse always avoided the shocking. Printing someone's letter about the horrors of jail in his newspaper, he said, "I have removed some of the descriptive passages from the letter" (22:126).

His was in many ways a commonsense persona, and he addressed a commonsense audience—a normal audience. We see this in the dry way he used the term *lunatic*. He often said the ashram was a kind of hospital. "In jest I have called it a 'Home for Invalids.' I am physically and even mentally an invalid and I have collected about myself a crowd of invalids. I have even likened it to a lunatic asylum—by no means an inappropriate comparison. . . . But luckily lunatics are unaware of their lunacy. And so I regard myself as sane."[21] This one might call a philistine point of view; sane and insane are very simple opposites.

Even in this matter, however, we note the challenge and teasing of his wit: the roots of which Erikson found in the boy Mohan's twisting of dogs' ears. He addressed an Ashramite as "Dear Mother Superior, I have to address you like this, you are so solemn. I must laugh or I shall burst."[22] There is often a flavor of such teasing in his jokes. Thus he accused a Congress man of wearing mill cloth to spite him. "Surely not to spite you, Mahatmaji?" No, but why grudge me the bliss of imagining that."[23] And about the people who want to take darshan of him: "Are they observing my asinine properties?"[24]

On the Salt March, pointing out that the British might remove the salt from their announced destination, so that the satyagrahis must think of alternatives in advance, he said, "Let it not be said that within the mighty British Empire there is no salt to be picked up. That would be to the discredit of the Empire."[25] And part of the joke was a previous reference to the disguised CID men in his audience.

At a railway station, a journalist asked him, "Will Congress accept office?" "Why, do you want to be a minister? . . . [And then] Please let me use your hat as a begging bowl." Then the first person he presented the hat to was the owner. He even asked doctors for a fee before he would let them examine him.[26]

He was essentially ironical and self-ironical. When he helped Sushila Nayar learn English, one of the first sentences he had her memorize was, "Cranks, faddists, and madmen often find their way to the Ashram." He added, "And I am the maddest of them all."

There is not therefore much in what is written here that would surprise Gandhi, however little he might like its tendency. These aspects of his own psychology are all ones he pondered. *Courage,* for instance, was one of the words most often on his lips, and he was clear that Ba, for instance, was in some ways braver than he.

He was very psychologically aware of other people. He for instance worked on other leaders very personally. When Tilak died, and when C. R. Das died, Gandhi professed himself lost, which at first seems exaggerated, since neither of them were close allies of his. But it will seem a natural word when we realize that he had been focusing on that particular individual, and had to start almost from scratch with his heirs. "His [Das's] consent was as a good as a draft in my hand which I could cash" (27:305).

He was in many ways a realist. He did not recommend simply the moral essence of manliness. He wanted his followers to impose and obey a military discipline, and he sounds like Kipling as he describes it. A soldier may disobey his officer only at peril of his life. "He may not come to you afterwards to lodge a complaint." He has made his choice, and military duty requires implicit obedience (19:187).

On the other hand, there is never any question of Gandhi himself taking up a weapon, or himself breathing in the atmosphere of violence. For good or for ill, "This hand will never fire a rifle." He speaks on political topics as if he were a man who dealt in violence, but he is not such a man. A man who deals in violence, he says, will have tiger skins, deer horns, swords, and guns on his walls. He has seen this at Viceregal Lodge in Simla, and in Mussolini's house in Rome. "The sword in Mussolini's hall seemed to say 'Touch me and I will kill you' . . . I was given a salute with arms, a symbol of violence." The charkha, on the other hand, in the ashram hut, symbolized nonviolence (78:76). It is implicit that Gandhi himself could never live with tiger skins and guns.

The Persistence of Fear

Gandhi's concern with these issues—at the existential level too—continued all through his life, in a variety of forms. He did not leave them behind when he left Rajkot. In *Satyagraha in South Africa,* and other places, he laid a stress on Kallenbach's size and strength that was prompted by his sense of his own smallness and weakness, and was echoed in many other such alliances. He talked often in 1920–21 about his physical weakness. His four sons, for instance, are all strong enough to destroy him, as far as bodily strength is concerned (19:160). A fifteen-year-old boy can knock him down (22:293).

That aspect of Kallenbach was an echo of Sheikh Mehtab, and Shaukat Ali was to be another ally he referred to always in terms of size—and of contrast with himself. In 1925, despairing over the Hindu-Muslim hostility, he declared that if the two sides decided they could achieve no unity without bloodshed, that he would challenge Shaukat Ali to a duel. "I know that he can twist me around his thick fingers and dash me to pieces. That day Hinduism will be free." We must not, he said, let the *goondas* (ruffians) do the fighting for us (25:168). We must do it ourselves. That grotesque fantasy of a duel between the violent and the nonviolent is surely very suggestive.

In *Satyagraha in South Africa* he describes how, when his life was threatened by Pathans, a self-appointed bodyguard, including a trained boxer, for a time accompanied him everywhere and insisted on sleeping next to him. It was Gandhi's principle to entrust his safety to God, and his habit to sleep outdoors, so he continued to do so, and these men therefore had to do the same.

In this passage he did not talk about his own timidity, or not in any confessional terms. (*Satyagraha in South Africa* was a discourse in which Gandhi was presenting to the Indian reader heroes to emulate, including himself.) He simply added: "I must confess that I was weak enough to feel safer for their presence. I wonder if I could have slept with the same ease if the guard had not been there. I suppose I should have been startled by some noise or other" (S:171). He goes on to admit that there had been other times when he felt afraid, despite his acceptance of death; because—to use my more dramatic language—terror is a domain of its own.

But he himself could use dramatic language on occasion. Looking back on this question of courage, in 1938, he talked quite frankly, beginning as so often with praise of the courage of the Pathans. "I myself have not yet reached this stage. There is a lot of cowardice in me. I talk of satyagraha, no doubt. But in the face of killing I cannot have the fearlessness of the Pathans. If I have to go and face such a situation, my heart's one wish would be to escape alive. If perforce I do go, my heartbeats would quicken." He gave the example of the Bombay riots of 1921, when he had to put himself at risk. "I wanted to save myself but what could I do? I was the leader. How could I protect Anasuyabehn? I saw mounted police advancing towards us. . . . My heart trembled. . . . As soon as they arrived the people ran helter skelter" (66:436). There is an account by a British officer (not necessarily to be believed) of Gandhi "skipping out of the way" of the police on that occasion.

He remained conscious to the end of the problem of timidity for the nonviolent, for instance for many in the ashram. "In Gujarat and Kathiawar children turn pale at the very mention of the Pathan. [Our ashram girls] try to make a show of bravery. But it is only a make believe. During a communal disturbance they dare not stir out of their homes if there is a report of even a casual Pathan being about." They tell Gandhi that they know he is right about the need to conquer fear, but they also know that when the time comes they won't be able to do so (68:41).

And anger as much as fear remained a problem. In November 1946 he wrote, "I am not able to say today that nothing irritates me or has irritated me." He confesses the fury he felt at the extravagance of a flag-raising ceremony at which nuts and raisins were distributed. "I flared up madly. I lost my balance. You may use any adverb or adjective you may like to describe it. It was then I discovered my failure. This loss of self-control has cost some years of my life" (86:11).

In 1947 he was still talking of his timidity, "the vague fear which is so unbecoming in a man. . . . To sleep alone in a room was an act of bravery for me. I hope I have lost that cowardliness. Yet I do not know what would be my state" in a forest at night. Certainly, he said, in him fear was harder to control than sexual excitement (88:101).

Thus the problem of fear was not anything that Gandhi could overcome and put behind him, once and for all. If one thinks of courage as a virtue, and fear as a moral failing, he made himself into a very brave man. But if one thinks of them as psychological traits, he remained timid and fearful. He had not gone through the ordeals of young manhood, and so he did not have manly courage.

The Wages of Fear and Shame

In consequence, Gandhi remained for some people a little man, psychologically as well as physically, all his life. He was so seen by many of the governors and viceroys, even the "religious" Lord Irwin, who always referred to him as little. And one does indeed see him, in some photographs, sitting as primly wrapped up in his shawl as if he expected it to be snatched from him. Ranjee Shahani describes a hypothetical Indian politician's first sight of Gandhi, saying to himself, "I can knock him down with one blow. He is as humble as any peasant in the countryside. I'm sure he would stand in the gutter if I asked him to."[27] Needless to say, any such politician found that there were formidable powers in Gandhi; but that does not mean that that judgment was entirely mistaken.

This contrast between Gandhi's meekness and his forcefulness was misread by many of his enemies and counterplayers, as mean-spiritedness or hypocrisy. Dr. Ambedkar, for instance, attacked Gandhi on many grounds: "Treachery and deceit are the weapons of the weak, and Gandhi always used those weapons."[28] And he called him "the most dishonest politician in the history of India." Such remarks are useful to remind us of the resistant element in Gandhi's environment, but useless as a way for us to understand Gandhi or our feelings about him. However, Ambedkar also called Gandhi "elvish," meaning not full-size, not human, or least not normal, lacking something; and that does afford us some insight. The same feeling, after all, gives its flavor to Sarojini Naidu's affectionate term, "Mickey Mouse" (and "Tweedledum and Tweedledee," applied to him and Kasturba). Perhaps it is there again in the image of Ariel, which both General Smuts and Llewelyn Powys associated with Gandhi.[29] In all these cases there is some reference to his physique, but more to his psychology.

Ambedkar's remark is the most useful, because it declines to yield to the playful and comical charms of Gandhi's looks and manner. It continues to resent Gandhi's "less than full-size" character. It reminds us of the way he failed to meet the demands of manliness.

Arthur Koestler says that Gandhi seduced many young women into chastity, and the phrase is something more than a witty paradox. (Koestler discusses the topic in *The Lotos and the Robot*.[30]) We have seen already something of his extraordinary power of charm, and his boldness in pursuing those he saw were attracted to him. There were in fact cases, as we shall see, in which he was in competition with another man for the favor of a young woman—and sometimes he was the victor, in getting her to share his bed. She chose chastity and devotion over marital love. In at least one case, she was already married to the other man.

The resentment that arouses is reflected indirectly in the reactions of, for instance, the viceroys and governors to him. Like Ambedkar, they saw him as an elvish energumen. Lord Milner in South Africa called him "some clever babu"; Lord Wavell, "a malevolent old politician"; Lord Willingdon, "the most Macchiavellian bargaining little political humbug." And the archetypal Churchill phrasing, "a half-naked fakir, of a type well known in the East." They all express a psychological distaste, which is part of a caste hostility. These men had all acquired their manhood by going through adolescent contests in masculine forcefulness; they resented those who entered the world of power without having gone through that, or bearing its imprint. This was true of a lot of men in the military and civil services.

We see something related in the contempt such men avowed for proto-Gandhi figures like Andrews. G. D. Birla, in a letter of 1934, wrote, "I had a long talk yesterday at my house lasting for about two and a half hours. Mr. Muggeridge, the new man, came with him. . . . Somehow or other, I find that these men do not take to Andrews and such with great kindness. They have no opinion of his intelligence and unfortunately have a sort of prejudice which I had not discovered until now."[31] Gandhi was aware of this, without sharing it. No doubt some felt that about Doke, and—especially in Gandhi's early years—about Gandhi himself.

Other official observers expressed puzzlement, rather than hostility, but it seems to derive from the same perception. We are told that Smuts in 1914 took a sympathetic interest in Gandhi as an unusual type of humanity, whose peculiarities were "not devoid of attraction" for the student. "The workings of his conscience are inscrutable to the Occidental mind . . . a curious compound of mysticism and astuteness." The same year Lord Crewe called him a "hopeless and impracticable person for any kind of deal, but with a sort of ardent, though restrained honesty." While, again in 1914, Sir Benjamin Robertson called him "very subtle-minded and always ready to change his ground at a moment's notice. . . . He has a terrible amount of conscience and is very hard to manage."[32]

No one is likely to align him- or herself with Lord Crewe or Sir Benjamin Robertson against Gandhi. But it is helpful to see him through their eyes—and not through the misty halo of the Mahatma—if only because that perception is linked to his own early self-perception. We have a lot to learn from seeing him clearly; for this is what we should have seen ourselves, and should see if such a man came again. When a phenomenon even of his size appears amongst us, it still looks to many of us absurd or distasteful.

He of course set out to be a Mahatma, although he made jokes about the enterprise, and no doubt was sincerely embarrassed by it. "It is easy enough to be a Mahatma. If one makes a fuss of eating and drinking and wears a langoti, one can easily acquire the title of Mahatma in this country" (43:330). As a title he preferred, he said in 1930, "salt-thief."

Gandhi and Women

Gandhi's identification of himself with women was obviously one of his ways to escape contamination with violence, but it was more than that. For instance, it related to spinning: five times as many women as men supported the khadi movement in 1930, by his count (43:189). And he more than once declared that progress in civilization consisted in introducing into it more womanliness, more of the love and self-sacrifice of woman, the mother of man.

Nirmal Kumar Bose said that by becoming a woman Gandhi tried to circumvent his sexuality, and he compared him with Ramakrishna, who pursued womanhood so intensely that he allegedly menstruated.[33] But Gandhi's womanliness was not of that quasi-physiological nature; it had more to do with socially constructed gender than with sex. It had to do with meekness, self-sacrifice, and compassion.

He often talked like a contemporary feminist. In 1926, dealing with a range of topics, including diet fanaticism, he added: "Why is there all this morbid anxiety about female purity? Have women any say in the matter of male purity? We hear nothing of women's anxiety about men's chastity. Why should men arrogate to themselves the right to regulate female purity?" (32:89–90). And a little later, "The ancient laws were made by men. The women's experience, therefore, is not represented in them. . . . Only women can raise women" (32:488). At the end of 1929, he spoke of the subjection of women, and said the root of the evil lay in man's greed for power. "Man has always desired power. Ownership of property gives this power" (42:5).

He expressed the same ideas in relation to people in his circle. When Jeki, Dr. Mehta's daughter, reluctantly went to Aden to join her husband, Manilal Doctor, Gandhi said, "I cannot bear to see the miserable condition of women. I would, if I could, save every woman from the burden which her husband in his sensuality puts upon her" (36:70). When his grand-niece, Manu, whipped off her sandal, when a man made a nuisance of himself in a public place, and either threw it at him or struck him with it, Gandhi was pleased (84:295).

In other ways, however, and notably in the scandal of his physical contacts with women, he was and is disapproved by most feminists. At the end of his life, when the scandal broke in 1947, Gandhi more than once said that the ideas he was putting into practice were not new to him. He had believed in making physical contact with women for fifty years (or, in one place, forty-five years). That puts the beginning at around 1900. That was when his last son was born, and when he began to want to end his sexual relations with Kasturba.

On another occasion (1929) when reproached for his freedoms, he said he began to put his hands on others' shoulders in 1891, when he returned from England, and used to take the children of the extended family out for walks. It is probably significant that recreational walking, and cross-gender contact, were especially common in New Age circles in the West. But clearly this was different from his later behavior, since these were children and relatives.

After realizing in 1900 that he wanted to renounce sex, he found the task beyond his strength until, in 1906, he took the vow of brahmacharya. However, what everyone gathered from his description of this was that it was straightforward renunciation, while—as we have seen—it in fact covered an arc from renunciation to something ardently positive. Feeling himself absolved from the ordinary restrictions upon contact with women, as long as he felt no sexual desire, he could develop new powers of love.

There is no record of his behavior in South Africa crossing the strictest lines of propriety. Nor did he develop a "spiritual marriage" with a woman such as he attempted later in India. The only woman with whom he exchanged letters like those with Saraladevi was Millie Polak. Probably the fact that she was English would have prevented anything more developing in that case; and there is every sign that she was dedicated to building a close and loving marriage for herself. Indeed, Gandhi often said that in South Africa he felt that he had conquered the sexual problem.

In the first few years back in India, he found that he had not: especially in his relationship with Saraladevi in 1919 and 1920. That may have been prepared for by his relations with her friend, Anasuyabehn; with whom he was friendly from the time of his settling near Ahmedabad in 1915. In the mill strike of 1917 she was of immense use to him, and he to her. There is no reason to suppose that their relations were erotic, but it is worth noting that he issued a bulletin about the strike every day, over her signature. The identity of mind that implies is bound to be something very deeply felt. When he announced the fast that formed a part of that strike, she immediately did the same. The experience of profound sympathy and admiration, from a woman who had had the best of both India's and England's education, must have been exciting to Gandhi, and immediately thereafter he met another such who had much less of the restraint and reserve one seems to see in Anasuyabehn. Saraladevi had dreams of being the greatest shakti in India; also we have Gandhi's word for it that he was deeply attracted to her.

When that relationship was broken off, Gandhi had a series of close encounters with Mira Behn, Nilla Cram Cook, the Rajkumari Amrit Kaur, and others. The freedoms he allowed himself included his hand on a woman's shoulder, or his arm along her shoulders, while walking. (On occasion it might be a man, but far more often a woman.) The touching hand was Gandhi's, except in the case of massage, which he received from a woman, from Mira Behn and from a niece of Kallenbach, who passed on the technique to Sushila Nayar. (Forms of massage were practiced in India, but it seems to have been men who gave it to men, and vice versa.) Then at night he slept next to women. And finally came the taking of a woman into his bed, when they were both naked.

There are records of complaints on July 29, 1929 (UC) and in 1935 J. P. Narayan complained about Gandhi's influence on his wife, Prabhavati (who was one of those who slept with Gandhi). Before that, Gandhi had told J. P. that Prabhavati had chosen the life of a virgin. Indeed, the ashram was, amongst other things, a society for the promotion of virginity.

At the same time, Gandhi continued to be severe against "freedoms" taken by others. In 1933 for instance, he said that passion is like a snake in one's bed (54:160). There should be no privacy and no exclusive relationships in the ashram (ibid 200) and boys should not even be friends with girls (54:211). We shall see some unpleasant examples of his severity and suspiciousness in his dealings with Pyarelal and Sushila Nayar in the next chapters.

It is also important to note that three or four times he examined his conduct, avowed that he had been wrong (*arrogant* and *vain* are words he uses) to allow himself freedoms he denied to others, and renounced them. But he returned to them. This return can be seen as a renewal of faith in his brahmacharya; but perhaps it can also be seen as a yielding to temptation.

But if he was trying to do something beyond his strength, he did not wholly fail. At the end of his life, he was strongly tempted to feel that he had failed: in politics, with India partitioned and engulfed in something like civil war; and amongst his friends, who were appalled by or disapproving of his experiments in brahmacharya. But he held on to his course, despite both kinds of failure, and continued to believe that the two were connected. He was overheard to say, "If I can do this [his brahmacharya] I can still beat Jinnah."

And in a sense he demonstrably succeeded. The last photographs of the old man walking with his disciples or approaching a prayer meeting—approaching his assassination—his hands on the shoulders of his white-khadi clad attendants, are profoundly moving. What we see is the saint with attendant virgins, an image that recalls great religious images of the past, not by artificial or superficial imitation, but by profound coincidence.

The saint, the martyr, and the virgin, together bringing peace—these were not just visual images; in Calcutta in 1947, a city on the brink of terrible mutual slaughter, it was processions of young women and girls, of both communities, who walked across the city to Gandhi's lodging and brought peace. There has surely been no greater realization of no greater hope in all history.

SEVEN

SABARMATI AND INSURGENCE

· 1914–1921 ·

In this seven-year period, Gandhi became the leader of the nationalist movement in India; and he did so as Mahatma Gandhi. He surpassed rivals who were better established and more in tune with the times, and mobilized the country via its traditional culture. He also went through two very upsetting experiences: doubting the truth of his message of ahimsa, nonviolence, and feeling an erotic attraction that endangered his vow of brahmacharya; for a Mahatma, experiences more disorienting than we can easily measure. One sign of this was that no one wanted him to talk about either experience.

Gandhi left South Africa a famous man, on whom many eyes were focused in expectation. But by the time his ship reached London he had become obscure; because the Great War had broken out, and all eyes in England, and elsewhere, were turned to the battlefields of Europe. Beside obscurity, moreover, this event brought him a grave problem. How was the exponent of nonviolence to behave in a situation of violence? He was not one to take the easy option, and turn his back on the fighting self-righteously, as if he had nothing to do with it. In England, as in South Africa, he knew he was accepting the protection of the empire, and so, as he saw things, owed its armies his support.

Gandhi's ship arrived in London on August 4, 1914, the day England joined France and Russia in making war against Germany and Austro-Hungary. He left on December 18, having made an unsatisfactory attempt to lead a volunteer Indian ambulance corps in support of the British army, and having been sick much of that time. Since his health and his power to cure disease were so important to him, the second also was a major defeat.

Gandhi took part in the corps drills, and walked two miles to reach the place where they were held, in damp weather, and so caught a pleurisy from which he could not get better. He was keeping to a diet, he tells us, largely of ground nuts, ripe and unripe bananas, olive oil, tomatoes and grapes. He refused milk, cereals, pulses. His first doctor, Jivraj Mehta, said he must take milk, but Gandhi had taken a vow against that. He asked the advice instead of the vegetarian doctor Allinson, whom he had known in 1890. Allinson advised him to live on brown bread, raw vegetables grated fine, and raw fruits; he also advised keeping all the windows of his room open twenty-four hours a day. Gandhi did all this—getting the fanlight broken to let air in—but he did not fully recover, and had to spend most of his time in bed. It began to seem that he would never regain his health as long as he stayed in England. He wrote to Maganlal, "To me this country seems like poison" (12:533).

This time he hated living in London, because of the climate of opinion as well as the literal climate. It is worth noting, however, that he had told Joseph Doke that London was of all places where he would choose to live, after India: and presumably he said that as late as 1908, since it appears in the biography Doke wrote; perhaps it was the experience of 1909 that changed his mind.

Certainly when he was there in 1914 he found he hated the speed, the noise, the size, the ugliness, the artificiality, the nationalist and military excitement, all of which in their ugliest forms animated England—and the other European countries—in the days of war.

He had come to London on his way home because Gokhale was to be there, but the latter was delayed in France, and they did not actually meet until September 18. On August 8, however, a reception was given for Gandhi at the Hotel Cecil, and amongst those present were several new acquaintances with whom he was to have significant relations: Lala Lajpat Rai, Mohammed Ali Jinnah, Sarojini Naidu, and Ananda Coomaraswamy.

Of these four the last is especially interesting to us because his link to Gandhi has received so little attention in earlier Gandhi biographies, and because that link leads us directly to the spinning wheel, the most important symbol in the whole armory of Gandhism.

One of the puzzles of Gandhi's development is to know how and why, when and where, he began to develop his faith in spinning. It was not something he had always known, practically, or even conceptually. In 1915 he had never seen a spinning wheel, he said; "never" apparently including his years as a child. There were of course no wheels in South Africa; and when he got to India in 1915 he went about Gujarat quite blindly *looking* for a wheel—and had the greatest difficulty in finding one.

The idea came to him, he says, in London, in 1909; and it was then so much a mere idea or word to him, and an *English* word, that he confused it with the weaving loom. "I did not know the difference between a loom and a spinning wheel in 1908 though I had written about the latter in *Hind Swaraj* then" (26:458). (He meant 1909; he habitually made the mistake of dating his book a year early.) In England, the home of the textile factory, Gandhi found the wheel that that factory had abolished.

Who then, in the circles Gandhi moved in, suggested to him the importance of spinning? The answer must surely be the New Age followers of Ruskin and Morris. Homespun cloth was then—is now—one of the symbols of that intellectual world; it has remained familiar to English readers in a hundred satires on New Age phoniness, for instance, novels by Evelyn Waugh and Kingsley Amis. "Homespun" and "Folk-dancing" have long been reliable triggers for laughter in England, except of course among New Agers themselves.

In India, later, Gandhi kept receiving from English friends, to quote in *Young India*, passages in praise of spinning taken from Ruskin (Gandhi quoted from *Sesame and Lilies* in 1926) and from George Macdonald, the Scots author. And Polak sent him a Welsh spinning wheel—Wales and Scotland, and Ireland, the peripheral parts of Great Britain, were especially associated with spinning and weaving. Leading propagandists for those crafts were Mr. and Mrs. Godfrey Blount.

Gandhi recommended Mr. Blount's *A New Crusade* (1903) at the end of *Hind Swaraj*, and Mrs. Blount published *The Story of a Homespun Web: A Simple Guide to Spinning and Weaving*, in 1913. The first, which had been summarized in *Indian Opinion*, described a typical New Age organization, the Fellowship of the New Crusade, which claimed Ruskin as its master, and quoted from three books: Ruskin's *Queen of the Air*, and Tolstoy's *Slavery*, and Blake's *Jerusalem*. Its message can be given in a single passage. "Machinery has been the Devil's instrument to seduce us from the paths of Peace. It is going to lead us into war . . . [because of] the deadly perfection of what the machine does."[1]

Blount also put out *The Gospel of Simplicity, a Plea for Country Life and Handicrafts*, in 1906. This said that our enemy is the modern disease of apathy. We have lost "faith" (7). And we would do better to be underfed and overworked agricultural laborers than to cramp our lives with these shackles of gold (8). In England, unfortunately, it was probably too late to restore the people to the land (11). *Our* revolution would have to proceed along individual lines. (It is easy to see how well this would fit with Gandhi's sense that the New Age's main destiny lay in India, not in England.) The author was designer to the Peasant Arts Society, and to the Haslemere Handweaving and Peasant Tapestry Industry. Dr. Mehta tells us that he once visited the Haslemere handloom factory, which he found in such thriving condition that it could not produce enough cloth to fill all the orders.[2]

Mrs. Blount's also is a book redolent of the English New Age and the naive mind; quoting Ruskin, and promising easy and immediate salvation—in ten years England could be renewed, if women began to spin again.[3] It plays on the vocational origins of the words *spinster* and *wife* (spinning and weaving) as Gandhi also did. At the end, the author urges her readers to get in touch with her, which is another of the marks of a New Age book.

Mrs. Blount wants to see spinning revived not as a commercial activity but as a home industry; it is to add a joy to labor, and to help make life sacramental

(2). We are disinherited of tradition, she says, in a significant phrase; materialism has stolen our joys and privileges. In the Middle Ages a woman was identified with her spindle, as a man was with his spear (7). But women have given up their birthright of lovely labor.

These are the ideas Gandhi prepared to put into practice in India. In fact the connection between spinning and Indian nationalism had already been established—in England. One of the best known of Morris's lieutenants in the crafts movement was C. R. Ashbee, who ran a guild and school of handicrafts in the little village of Chipping Campden; an art community in which also lived A. K. Coomaraswamy and his wife, Ethel Partridge, who practiced embroidery and dyeing and weaving, and her brother, who was a silversmith. Ashbee was the high priest of arts and crafts in England.

Coomaraswamy had bought the printing press that Morris had used for the Kelmscott Chaucer, and used it to publish pamphlets demanding swaraj for India. He was a friend of A. R. Orage and A. J. Penty and the other *New Age* magazine writers. He was also a friend of Tagore and of the Irishwoman, Margaret Noble, Vivekananda's disciple,who had taken the Hindu name, Sister Nivedita. These people constituted the world of Indian cultural nationalists in England, in the decade 1900–1910.

Coomaraswamy was born into a New Age, mixed-race family. He was the only son of a Sinhalese father (the first Hindu called to the bar in England, and the first Asian given a knighthood) and an English mother. The two became acquainted in the New Age congregation of Moncure Conway at the South Place Chapel. The father was knighted in 1874, and died soon after. Brought up in England, by his mother and other female relatives, the son went to Ceylon as a young man, and became interested in its arts and crafts. He married Ethel Partridge there in 1902. He also became interested in anti-imperialist politics. In 1908 he attended a meeting at Caxton Hall to protest Gandhi's imprisonment; and in 1914 he spoke at the Hotel Cecil reception for him.

In *The Arts and Crafts of India and Ceylon* (a New Age title in itself) published in 1913, Coomaraswamy quotes Ruskin and praises traditional societies. He says that in feudal and theocratic cultures ploughmen speak as well as courtiers; while in progressive democracies, the workers are disinherited of their culture, and the different social classes have no bonds to tie them to each other. The criteria of culture, according to Coomaraswamy, are aesthetic: so the absence of beauty from art, or of happiness from life, condemns a civilization. But beauty and happiness cannot be sought as such. They are received as a reward when tradition is preserved.[4]

Coomaraswamy was traveling in India for most of 1909 and 1910, and so missed Gandhi's visit to England. He stayed with Tagore in Calcutta; a closely kindred spirit. The pair of them should perhaps be called aesthetic rather than cultural nationalists; their position was certainly not the same as Gandhi's; but it was a New Age position, all the same. At that time, indeed, Tagore's cultural politics was closer to Gandhi's than it came to be later. He had published *Swadeshi Swaraj* in 1905, which prescribed a quite Ruskinian program of activities, including road building, education, arbitration, and the maintenance of community water supplies.

Clearly, some nonaesthetic values are recommended there. And at the beginning of the Bengal Partition agitation Tagore led public processions in the name of quite political demands. But political conflict was not a field in which he was at ease. He withdrew from the agitation when the violence began, and his values reconfigured. He continued to set a high value on village life and village culture; but he and Coomaraswamy cared most about art, and hoped aesthetic values would gradually take the place of political ones.

Gandhi too, of course, wanted "mere politics" to yield to other values. Thus the scorn Coomaraswamy expressed for politics and economics in *Art and Swadeshi* sounds quite like Gandhi's in *Hind Swaraj*. "It is the weakness of our national movement," said Coomaraswamy, "that we do not love India; we love suburban England, we love the comfortable bourgeois prosperity that is to be some day established when we have learned enough science and forgotten enough art to successfully compete with Europe in a commercial war."[5] But there is a more narrowly aesthetic sound to his essay on Tagore's poetry—included in the same volume—which said that "nations are destroyed or flourish in proportion as their art flourishes."[6]

Coomaraswamy and Gandhi knew of each other's ideas. We find frequent traces of Coomaraswamy's ideas or those of his circle in *Indian Opinion;* which cites enthusiasts for Indian art like E. B. Havell, of the Calcutta School of Art, who became a friend of Coomaraswamy. When Sir George Birdwood declared that there were no *fine* arts in India, only folk arts (in a speech to the Royal Society of Arts in 1910) Havell, Coomaraswamy, Walter Crane, and William Rothenstein protested. They and Roger Fry founded the India Society.

Henry Polak told Raja Singam, the author of a book about Coomaraswamy, that it was Gandhi who first talked to him about the latter, and he did so in South Africa. Gandhi recommended Coomaraswamy's *Essays in National Idealism* to Maganlal in 1910; and P. J. Mehta mentioned the same volume in his 1912 biography of Gandhi.[7] In India Gandhi discussed with Kalelkar Coomaraswamy's *Domestic Handicrafts and Culture,* and wished the author would devote all his energy to implementing those ideas. Most important, in 1914, Gandhi sent word to Ethel Partridge Coomaraswamy that he wished to see her, and she went to London and explained to him the crafts of which was a master. She had learned weaving after separating from Coomaraswamy. This is the testimony of Philip Mairet—an editor of the *New English Weekly,* the successor to the *New Age*—whom she married in 1913.[8] (The Mairets moved from Chipping Campden to Ditchling, another arts-and-crafts center, associated with Eric Gill and Bernard Leach the potter.)

Coomaraswamy was a New Ager of the erotic wing. He read Blake, Whitman, and Nietzsche, extolled aristocracy and genius, and preferred intuition over intellect. In *The Dance of Shiva* (a series of essays published in the *Athenaeum* in 1915) he said, "The heart and essence of the Indian experience is to be found in a constant intuition of the unity of all life, and the instinctive and ineradicable conviction that the recognition of this unity is the highest good and the uttermost freedom" (4). This, he said, was the universal gospel of Jesus, Blake, Rumi (the Muslim poet), and Lao Tze. But only in India had this gospel been made the basis of education and of sociology (in the caste system). Europe too needed to find and install its true aristocracy.

Coomaraswamy describes some of Shiva's dances as symbols of Hindu culture. In the night of Brahma, nature lies inert and impotent until Shiva dances in pulsing waves. The destroyer Shiva (like Nietzsche's Dionysus) destroys the fetters that bind the soul—the ego, with its illusions and its deeds. All this is intuited in some European thought—he cites Nietzsche; and in some European music—for instance, Scriabin's *Poem of Ecstasy.*

The book is an important contribution to the post-Nietzschean thought of the times, and stands comparison with the culture-criticism of both D. H. Lawrence and W. B. Yeats. It includes a chapter on the status of women in India, and Coomaraswamy credits women with preserving the cultural heritage that men endanger. This all belongs to the New Age movement, but of the anti-ascetic and therefore un-Gandhian kind. Ironically, as we have seen, it was from Coomaraswamy's circle that Gandhi seems to have received crucial ascetic ideas, like spinning.

It was also from Coomaraswamy that Romain Rolland took his calling to interpret India to the West, a vocation that in the 1920s became very effective in spreading the image of Gandhi throughout the world. (Gandhi spoke of the Frenchman constituting himself his chief advertising agent.) Rolland kept a journal from 1915 to 1943 of his thoughts on things to do with India, published under the title *Inde* in Paris in 1960. It begins with notes on an article by Coomaraswamy in the *New Age*. This article dealt with the issues of militarism and capitalism, about which Rolland too was then troubled, and it said that India could play an important part in the world's greatest Kulturkampf, which was the war between East and West. Rolland went on to read Coomaraswamy's two volumes on the arts and crafts of India and Ceylon, and grew excited. He saw that this idea of the East was big enough for him to devote the rest of his life to it: "My chest is bursting. . . . If I am granted ten or twenty more years of life, I would wish to lead the mind of my race on to the high places of the world."[9]

Coomaraswamy led Rolland, predictably, to Tagore. In 1916 Rolland read reports of Tagore's speeches in Japan, which warned that country against "developing" by following the model of Europe. Letters passed between Rolland and Tagore, who arrived in Switzerland on a visit in 1921.

Rolland was very active in spreading his friends' ideas. He wrote a preface to a French edition of *The Dance of Shiva* in 1922; and 1923 was the year of Hermann Hesse's *Siddhartha,* about the Buddha, the first part of which was dedicated to Rolland. (Rolland and Hesse were wartime allies in pacifism, and in Orientalism, and powerful influences in the fragmentary New Age of the 1920s and 1930s.) The book on Gandhi came out just a year later.

It was above all Gandhi who embodied the East in the way Rolland wanted to imagine it, and the encounter between the two was to do honor to both. A pacifist and a former disciple of Tolstoy, Rolland was intellectually the most distinguished New Ager in Europe. Tagore and Coomaraswamy he could understand easily enough as variants on himself: Gandhi was fundamentally different.

Paradoxically enough, what Gandhi found in England was a vision of India as much as an argument. The vision we find in the Orientalists, English as well as Indian, inspired his politics. Take for instance this passage by Sir George Birdwood.

> Outside the entrance of the simple village street, on an exposed rise of ground, the hereditary potter sits by his wheel, moulding the swift-revolving clay by the natural curves of his hands. At the back of the houses, which form the low, irregular street, there are two or three looms at work in blue, and scarlet, and gold, the frames hanging between the acacia trees, the yellow flowers of which drop fast on the webs that are being woven. In the street, the brass and copper-smiths are hammering away at their pots and pans, and further down, in the verandah of the rich man's house, is the jeweller working rupees and gold mohars into fair jewellery, gold and silver earrings . . . taking his designs from the fruit and flowers around him, or from the paintings and carvings of the great temple, which rises over the groves of mangoes and palms at the end of the street above the lotus-covered village tank."[10]

This evokes in landscape form all that Gandhi wanted to preserve—to defend against the invasion of European, factory-made substitutes.

1914

To return to London in wartime: Gandhi quickly raised his ambulance corps amongst the Indians in England. As before, he had offered his volunteers for any kind of military duty, but the authorities preferred medical workers. He had decided in South Africa that one should not support a war even by nursing, but once in London at war he realized that he was implicitly accepting the protection of the armed forces, since he did not retreat to the mountains, renouncing the advantages of civilization. "I do not yet possess the spiritual strength necessary for this."

His project did not run as smoothly as its South African predecessors. Colonel Richard J. Baker, who was the director of the Field Ambulance Training Corps, was not willing to allow the Indian group any autonomy within the military structure. Gandhi threatened satyagraha when Baker appointed NCOs without consulting him, but—partly because he was sick—he was not able to conduct an effective campaign.

Many of his friends of course did not approve the project. Olive Schreiner, who was in London, wrote him that she was struck to the heart with sorrow to hear that he had offered to serve the English government in this evil war—this wicked cause. She had hoped to meet him and Kasturba, but now refused to attend one of his meetings. The break between them was not final, however, and Kallenbach remained friends with both. He helped Schreiner to get the foods she needed for her diet, and ran errands for her.[11] And she did attend the farewell reception given Gandhi in December at the Westminster Palace.

Gandhi tells us that he was often visited on his sickbed by Charles Roberts, the under secretary for India, and his wife, Lady Cecilia Roberts. They found him milk-substitutes, and recommended doctors, but nothing cured him. Finally the Robertses persuaded Gandhi that he was never going to recover in England, and that he could not serve his countrymen there; and he allowed them to find him a quick passage home. He admitted, "I feel that I hopelessly mismanaged my constitution in the past."[12]

Kallenbach was not allowed to accompany him and Kasturba to India, where he hoped to settle, because he was still a German national. They hoped he would soon get permission to follow them, but in fact he was to spend most of the war years in internment in England. He and Gandhi parted in sorrow at the station for Tilbury in December, 1914, as Kallenbach recalled later.

From England to India

Gandhi and Kasturba took with them what was left of the dried fruit they had brought from South Africa. (They could not rely on a ship's supplying them with vegetarian food.) He was still sick, and was supposed to wear a Mede's Plaster round his ribs till he got to the Red Sea, but took it off quite soon. He found that he did indeed feel much better when he got to the different climate of the Suez Canal. He had discussions with an English feminist aboard the ship, and wrote letters to Kallenbach in London and Maganlal in Shantiniketan.

In his letters to Kallenbach he said that London had made him sick, and warned Kallenbach against its influence.

> I notice that I have lost much in London in mental equilibrium. My mind wavers and longs for things which I had thought it had laid aside. How we are deceived! We fancy that we have got rid of particular desires but suddenly we discover that they were only asleep in us and not dead. No, London has done me no good. Instead of returning to India a man full of health and hope, I am returning a broken man, not knowing what he is to do or be in India. . . . So beware of London, a City of Darkness. Let the Inner Light shine upon you. . . . I am free of the place and yet it haunts me" (UC).

He sent Kallenbach: "a personal touch before I reach India. . . . I have been harsh to you, apparently cruel even, rude too as you thought. But the words came out of the purest love. If I did wrong it was not because I loved you less but because I loved you too well. I became impatient to see you do what I thought was the right thing. Pardon me then if I hurt you as I know I did. You made no secret of it. I did not heed it. I hope I did right in not heeding it."

That relationship, and the whole South African adventure, was now behind Gandhi. He was on his way to a land where the scope of his action was to be immensely expanded. His scene was now transferred from South Africa, only one of the components of the British Empire, to India, a subcontinent of three hundred millions, and itself an empire or series of empires.

India was the kingpin of the whole British imperial structure, without which the rest of it would collapse; and it was the greatest trophy of the royal hunt of white empire across the world. And on this new scene Gandhi was to lead, not a minority that was almost a bystander in the conflict between black and white, but the majority group, the Hindus; and was to lead them in outright defiance of the whole modern world.

He would need, of course, to find or make for himself a position of leadership. In general, two great projects were on his mind, the abolishing of untouchability, and the forging of Hindu-Muslim unity. These had been minor problems in South Africa, but would be major in India. Gandhi thought a lot about caste in these months, and especially about the position of Untouchables in Hindu culture, with its quasi-religious sanctions. On May 1, 1915, he said he was beginning to study his religion, and if he found untouchability to be an inseparable component of Hinduism, he would renounce it. But as for the caste system in the sense of the four *varnas,* that he endorsed. (It was very like the system of the four estates in Christendom—knight, priest, peasant, merchant—which Ruskin appealed to, and which could be used to criticise modern society radically as much as conservatively.)

Gandhi decided that the discipline of *varna* had on the whole benefited India—by introducing a series of negatives and separations into the culture. "Our society was organized according to *varnavyavastha* [division by vocation] for the purpose of self-control, that is for self-denial. It is a vain effort to replace this structure by a single community" (13:301). The last phrase meant that he thought the mobility and indiscriminate mutual competitiveness of Western society made it self-destructive.

As for Hindu-Muslim relations, Gandhi had already, in South Africa, had bitter experience of how much mutual suspicion lay beneath the surface, and undermined attempts at united action. He wanted to build an Indian nation, united in a struggle for national liberation. But he had to face the Muslim dissent formulated in intellectual terms by Sir Syed Ahmed Khan, the founder of Alighar College. Sir Syed declared that India had never been and could never be a nation, that democratic institutions presupposed a social homogeneity not to be found in India, that the interest of Hindus clashed with those of Muslims, and that Muslims should align themselves with the raj.

Syed Ahmed Khan had dissuaded Muslims from joining in congress activities. In 1883 he declared, "I object to every congress—in any shape or form whatever—which regards India as one nation."[13] He was the leading Islamic "liberal" of his time; liberalism meaning in the 1870s the attempt to reconcile Islam to Christianity and Western civilization. His college was designed to bring European science and literature to Muslims, and to make them good citizens of the empire.

This meant it was not exclusivist; and in 1882 it had 57 Hindu pupils out of 259. Syed Ahmed Khan's successors there were, however, more orthodox, more "Islamic," than he. Around 1900 there had been a shift in the balance of Muslim thought, giving an advantage to orthodox revivalism, like the shift there had been in Hindu thought twenty years before. This made national union more difficult.

The Muslim revival was led by the Wahabis, heirs to the eighteenth-century reformer, Shah Wali-ullah of Delhi. They stressed the value of pure Islamism, and so prepared the way for communal political conflict. Some were militant, and had set up a state in the Northwest Frontier Province, which lasted from 1830 to 1870, and where some rebels joined them when the mutiny was put down. They kept alive the dream of an Afghan or Pathan invasion of India, which alarmed many Hindus, and made them feel the need for British protection. Gandhi protested against that fear, but shared the image of the Pathan.

An idea of Pan-Islamism, moreover, which tended to override national loyalties, came to the fore at the end of the nineteenth century. The idea was to mobilize the international community of Muslims, to resist the cultural imperialism of Christendom; a resistance that could make trouble for England in India. After 1880 the sultan of Turkey, who was also the caliph of Islam, made Pan-Islamic propaganda of this kind, and so did some Indian reformers whose work influenced Iqbal, the future prophet of Pakistan, an all-Muslim state in the subcontinent. As put into political practice by Iqbal and Jinnah, Pan-Islamism was to become a major problem for Gandhi at the end of his life.

Jinnah's future organization, the Muslim League, was founded in 1906, after a deputation to Simla had solicited British approval. In its beginning, the British fostered the league, as they had congress. But according to A. C. Niemeijer, in *The Khilafat Movement in India* (Hague: Mouton, 1972) around 1910 some of the Muslim middle class grew more dissident, feeling that England was hostile to them. This was true of the political journalists, the Ali Brothers and Maulana Azad, and Dr. Ansari. Gandhi was to look for a chance to ally such Muslims with the Hindus against the British, instead of with the British against the Hindus.

But these projects were far from being realistic plans, and the man who sailed toward India in early January 1915, though he was a famous name in congress circles, was, in many practical ways, nobody in the world of Indian politics. He had no important constituency and only one powerful alliance (with Gokhale), in which he was the minor partner, and his style was unimpressive if measured against that of most political leaders. Neither in position, personality, nor oratory was he comparable with Tilak, Annie Besant, or Pherozeshah Mehta, and if he was comparable in personality with Gokhale, he was the latter's *chela,* and less impressive intellectually. Indeed, a dozen lesser figures stood between him and that highest level of national leadership; figures like Lala Lajpat Rai, Bipin Chandra Pal, C. R. Das, and in somewhat separate fields, Pandit Malaviya, the spokesman for Hindu orthodoxy, and Rabindranath Tagore, the Nobel prize-poet and international celebrity. Because of his ignorance of the scene, Gandhi had promised Gokhale to make no public pronouncements for the first twelve months after his return. And Gokhale died soon after Gandhi's return, before he could do anything for him.

And yet, despite all these disadvantages, by the end of 1921, after a year of nationalist nonviolent noncooperation, it was to be clear that none of these other figures could defeat Gandhi in the competition for the leadership.

India

There were receptions in Gandhi's honor in Bombay when he arrived, but the demonstrations of respect were not of a fervent enthusiasm. His views seemed revivalist and backward-looking. The secret abstracts of the Bombay police described his speeches as colorless, and the reminiscences of those who were there confirm that impression.[14] He grimly deplored the silver caskets and so on presented to him: somewhat unsuitable, he said, for someone with neither a roof over his head nor locks on his doors (13:3). He wrote to Kallenbach that he was perfectly sick of the addresses presented to him.

What he said on these occasions was not so striking as what he sounded like and what he looked like. He and his family wore Kathiawari village costume, and spoke in Gujarati, distancing themselves from British models, and he asked the other speakers to do likewise.

One of those other speakers was the Anglicized Mohammed Ali Jinnah, whose English was perfect, but who could only flounder in Gujarati. Twenty-seven years later, Gandhi said, "Jinnah has hated me ever since I made him speak Gujarati."[15] In another typical maneuver, Gandhi enlisted Mrs. Jinnah in the same cause; he suggested that she should coax her husband into learning Gujarati or Hindustani; she should begin herself speaking to him in those languages.[16] It seems likely that Jinnah resented that too. He was never a willing recruit to Gandhi's teasing games.

Gandhi wrote to Maganlal—who was still in Shantiniketan with the Phoenix settlers—that he had shed tears of joy to see India, but had found that Bombay was "the scum of London" (13:4). (This was perhaps a version of his better-known remark that Indian cities were the blotting-paper impress of English ones.) He was looking for a place to settle, and was choosing between Rajkot, Porbandar, and Shantiniketan. None of the big cities attracted him. The contrasts of wealth and poverty, and the vulgar and ugly uses of wealth, alike appalled him. In June he felt like crying out for help; Kasturba was sick again, and the filthy roads and closets in Bombay disgusted him. "If I had to live in Bombay for a year I would die" (UC).

Hallam Tennyson, a follower of Vinoba, has described Bombay as being the very opposite of Gandhi's India: every inch carved with gargoyles, gods, lotuses, garishly painted, its jute and sugar millionaires eating off gold plate. He said they worshipped the Golden Calf and not the Golden Mean.[17]

On another occasion, however, Gandhi wrote Kallenbach that though India's cities were plague-spots, India was still a place of spirituality. This was in May 1915; he said that on the surface he saw nothing but hypocrisy, humbug, and degradation, but underneath was a divinity he missed elsewhere (UC). Clearly, he wanted to believe that it was a place in which New Age values could be made to prevail.

In these years he went through much bewilderment and depression, waiting for some line of action to become clear and attractive to him. Much of actual

Indian politics was repugnant to him, and he was more dependent on intuition or inspiration than he had been before. In South Africa, at least to begin with, he had followed well marked-out and plausible patterns of activity. Only in 1913, with his army of pilgrims, and with sixty thousand men on strike, had he begun to take enormous risks, and needed to derive enormous sanctions from within himself. From now on, that would habitually be the case, and it put a great strain on him. No one else understood politics the way that he did, so though he asked for people's advice he must often go against it.

Circumstances in his immediate family were no better. On April 22, 1916, he wrote Kallenbach, "If you were here, you would go out into the jungle and like Job give way to crying bitterly. Such is the misery we are passing through just now" (UC). Being with his family (probably his extended family) Gandhi said he had felt like a stranger, in the midst of many who thought they knew him. Maganlal was the only one who stayed loyal.

On July 26, 1915, Gandhi had written that they had a handloom in the ashram. He had also taken in an Untouchable, and Kasturba was angry, and she and others might leave the community. A little later Gandhi reported that Maganlal's wife and children had also left, and Maganlal himself was in such torment that he was absentminded and hopeless. Gradually the crisis was overcome, and the ashram reconstituted itself, but it was not easy.

In 1917 Gandhi heard that Kallenbach was out of England, in Switzerland: and invited him to visit India when the war was over. But the peace that came in 1918 seemed to him only the prelude to bloodier strife. (He felt the same at the end of World War II; the peace arrangements of nations organized to make war upon each other rarely seem substantial to a mind like Gandhi's.)

Henry Polak wrote, on one occasion sending his regards to Saraladevi Chaudhurani. (He had met her before, and must surely have known about Gandhi's relationship with her, but we don't know what he thought.) Polak had arrived in India in 1916, and Millie wrote how pleased he must have been to have Gandhi to himself when he arrived; as often, her letter sounds a little jealous. She and the children followed him. Gandhi hoped that Henry would make a career for himself in India, but in fact his future lay in London, where he represented Indian clients before the privy council (the highest court of appeal in the empire) and was a lobbyist for India with the government, in all sorts of matters.

For the first twelve months at home, Gandhi traveled and observed and reflected. The India he chose particularly to explore lay midway between British or princely power and the revolutionaries. He sought out those who were reconstructing Indian culture. Soon after landing, he went to see Gokhale's Servants of India Society in Pune; and to Tagore's school at Shantiniketan in Bengal, founded in 1901, where about twenty children from the Phoenix settlement were staying; and then to the Arya Samaj school in Hardwar. All three were educational and reformist rather than political.

Cultural Style

Gandhi's politics were always educational and cultural, and if they now seem strikingly traditional, they were then also Westernizing and modernizing. He introduced Western styles of action and Western traits of character into Indian politics. He was not the only or the first Indian politician to do that—one could point both to the parliamentarians like Pal, and to the revolutionaries like the Indian Communists. But the New Age traits Gandhi embodied were peculiarly proper to—if also opposed to—modern ideology. Erikson says that traditional Indian life moves toward fusion—a tendency that may derive, he says, from the cult of the mother goddess: Gandhi, he says, tried to create bulwarks within that flow—bulwarks like punctuality, accuracy, factuality, responsibility.

The diary, for instance, was something Gandhi valued, as a way to know oneself, and to concentrate one's mind and will. He asked members of the ashram to keep a diary, kept one himself, and required it of people who were to join in satyagraha during World War II.

Cleanliness, above all public and communal hygiene, was another modern value as important to Gandhi as to Westerners, and with the same moral resonance, as we have already seen in his South African years. In India he associated the need to cleanse particularly with temples, and their combination of gold (and jewels) with filth (and blood). He hated the confusion of the spiritual with the animal, the sacred with the sacrilegious—everything Tantric. His cleanliness symbolized a zeal to keep those things separate, to exalt the one and repress the other. Most modern enthusiasts for the East serve exactly the opposite zeal.

The most obvious symbolism of cleanliness has to do with sexual purity or asceticism, of course. We have seen that the first half of Gandhi's adult life coincided with a Purity Campaign in England, and in the second half he tried to make his *swaraj* movement another such campaign, in India. In 1926 he printed a series of articles under the heading of "Towards Moral Bankruptcy." They were translated from a French book, *L'Indiscipline des Moeurs,* by Paul Bureau. He spoke of the role of chastity in the West, where it was a small but inexhaustible reservoir of purity and strength (31:260). When he read the Indian erotic-religious poem, *Gitagovinda,* the same year, Gandhi found the experience a torture (31:158).

When he settled in Ahmedabad, he planned to work upon his municipality like the great city leaders of the West—say Joseph Chamberlain in Birmingham. He meant to extend the city by opening new suburbs, and to build parks and to organize supplies of pure milk. He had had, he said in 1924, a dream of an ideal city; but the Rowlatt Acts agitation blew away those schemes (25:40–41). Such schemes represented one of those paths he did not find the time to follow.

Gandhi was then modern in morality and politics, but that modernism was combined with a traditionalism in dress, food, language, body-style—and in the tradition of religious asceticism. He taught his followers to be ready for self-sacrifice and to drive toward *moksha*. His political leadership was also religious, as he said. As he rose up toward eminence and leadership, he sank down toward simplicity and poverty.

Thus as far as eating was concerned, he took a vow in April 1915 to limit to five the number of foodstuffs he would consume in any one day, and to eat nothing after sundown. In 1921, he began to observe total silence on the Monday of every week, sitting at his wheel or his prayers, working alone or replying with notes to those who came to see him, enclosed within a transparent shell of isolation. And as far as clothes went, by the end of 1921 he had reduced himself to a loincloth and a shawl. He had shaved off his moustache and refused to replace the teeth he had lost. He had discarded the apparatus and prostheses of modern civilization and was an Indian villager. He was also, by the same token, man naked, unadorned, and unprotected. He was a living manifesto against Western, and indeed any other, high civilization.

By the same token, many other political nationalists resented him. We have seen how Jinnah resented being forced to speak Gujarati. About Subhas Chandra Bose, Gandhi told friends they must accept that Bose would always be an enemy, because he could never pardon Gandhi's wearing of the loincloth (41:379). For some people, political or not, Gandhi's naïve style was irresistible; for many others it was intolerable; and—to return to the three kinds of educational politics listed before—Gokhale's Servants of India inclined to the latter.

In 1915 Gokhale tried to persuade his servants to elect Gandhi a member, ultimately to become his own successor as first member. He himself promised financial support for Gandhi's projects. But the servants were nervous of Gandhi's radicalism. They were more cautious and reformist by temperament, religiously agnostic, and discreet in their interventions.

The Tagores

Of the three educational options, it was the middle one, Shantiniketan, Gandhi was most often to visit; and with its resident genius, Rabindranath Tagore, he was to conduct the most interesting and fruitful debates, on and off during the years to come. Perhaps this was because Tagore, like Gandhi, did not so much expound a system as sum up a number of ideas in his own person. Or perhaps it was because they both belonged to branches of the New Age, and so had something in common. In any case, their debate itself was often a phenomenon of the New Age in India.

They were courteous, but not without severe mutual criticisms. Tagore saw in Gandhi "a fierce joy of annihilation."[18] The bonfires of foreign cloth, for instance, seemed to Tagore to express a symbolic desire to destroy much that was beautiful. While Gandhi told Mahadev Desai—more privately—that Tagore's greatest fault was that he lacked fearlessness (353). In this context of political or cultural action Gandhi himself can of course be called unequivocally fearless. And we know that courage was always a major criterion for him.

In cultural terms, Gandhi probably felt that the Brahmo Samaj too lacked courage. Rabindranath Tagore's father and grandfather had been leaders of the Brahmo Samaj, and he returned to it after his political activities in the middle of the first decade of the twentieth century. He became editor of its journal in 1911, and began to recommend its teachings as a (gentle and indirect) cure for Bengal's problems. The history of the Tagore family was much entwined with the history of the sect. Devendranath Tagore had joined the Samaj in 1842, and accepted Keshub Chandra Sen as coleader in 1862. In Rabindranath's time—so many members of the family being artists—the Tagores turned the sect toward aesthetic values.

In terms of religion the sect was more congenial to Gandhi than was the Arya Samaj. But in terms of cultural politics, the Brahmos were too emotionally refined and intellectually elite. Emotional refinement Gandhi could take for granted in himself, and it was not valuable to his cultural politics. It was the cultural "virility" of the Aryas that he needed to harness to his purposes, and the Brahmos were too refined for most nationalists. Tilak had refused to consider Brahmo Samajists Hindus at all, and Bankim had declared against them, "God is not only love incarnate, He is also infinite Power."[19]

Tagore is an important person for us to understand, being clearly opposed to or unlike Gandhi in most ways. He was a man of extraordinary personal beauty, as well as talent, and his life had been lived almost exclusively in the world of art. In his 1912 "Reminiscences" he said how he had hated school and discipline. He felt he owed everything to vision and nothing to knowledge.[20] He began to publish poetry when twelve, and to act on the stage when sixteen. In "What Is Art?" of 1916–17 he speaks on the side of art for art's sake, and against the puritanism that questions enjoyment (227). Art is exuberance, opposed to thrift and purpose; and individuality, as opposed to science and generality. Personality and an exalted hedonism are the great values.

In *Gitanjali* he says, "I have tasted of the hidden honey of this lotus that expands on the ocean of light, and thus was I blessed—let this be my parting word.

"In this playhouse of infinite forms I have had my play and here have I caught sight of him that is formless" (307).

Under Rabindranath's direction, Shantiniketan became a treasury of Indian folk and fine art. Traditions like arati (torches circling the faces of those to be honored) and baitalik (singers going round the ashram by moonlight) were observed there in their most exquisite forms. Visitors were greeted with banners, arches, processions of singers and dancers. There grew to be a large collection of pieces of rare Indian art (five thousand pieces in 1945), and thousands of Chinese texts, and objets trouvés. One of Rabindranath's brothers led the renaissance in Indian painting—which Rabindranath himself later joined in.

The institutional center was a high school and a university, devoted above all to art; there were about 125 students there in 1915. But the institutions were secondary to the personality and the artwork of Tagore and one or two friends. So Pyarelal says in his "Shantiniketan Pilgrimage" in *Harijan* 1945. It was a paradise of art, a private kingdom. G. Ramachandran spoke of Tagore looking like an emperor as he advanced down one of the Shantiniketan avenues.[21]

During his first stay at Shantiniketan, in 1915, Gandhi persuaded the pupils at the school to take over the scavenging of the place and the preparing and serving of their own food. Implicitly he was criticizing the lax and self-indulgent character of the place—which reflected that of its founder. (There were also traces of caste prejudice in the arrangements there.)

Tagore raised no objection, though he doubted (rightly) whether the pupils' enthusiasm would last. In fact it did not long survive Gandhi's departure. But both he and Gandhi dissolved the harsher feelings about each other (much better than Mrs. Besant did in her comparable relations with Gandhi). There were many occasions for such bitter feelings. For instance, Charlie Andrews was devoted to both masters, and divided between them. On the whole he gave his primary loyalty to Tagore—possibly because Tagore needed him more, probably because he found the poet's mind-set more congenial.

And there was also a genuine conflict of ideas. As early as 1893 one can find an anti-ascetic poem by Tagore, "On the Doctrine of Maya," attacking that doctrine, which could have been written with Gandhism in mind.

> Joyless country, in tattered decrepitude dressed,
> Burdened by your own sagacity, . . .
> Birds and beasts, creatures of many species,
>   bereft of fear, have breathed here for ages.
> To them, this created world is a mother's lap,
>   but you, old dotard, have faith in nothing![22]

Many of Andrews's reproaches to Gandhi, about the burning of foreign cloth, and more generally about his ascetic celebration of poverty, can be taken to come from Tagore to some degree, and Gandhi was aware of that. For instance, when Gandhi founded his ashram at Kochrab soon after his visit to Shantiniketan, Andrews wrote warning him against moral tyranny, and emasculation of his followers through the celibacy vow.

Gandhi understood the situation. In a letter to Andrews in September 1921, he wrote about reports he heard of dissension in Shantiniketan. "You yourself are torn by internal conflict," he says. "I know that you will find your peace. Whether I lose you in the struggle or keep you, you will remain the same to me even as Polak is. [Polak had separated himself from Gandhi, disapproving of the nonviolent noncooperation campaign.] I know too that you will do as the spirit leads you. I want you not to be sad on my account" (21:98).

Returning to Calcutta in 1921, after a trip to Europe, Rabindranath gave lectures against Gandhi's boycott of schools, saying that India needed Western science, and that Gandhi's movement rejected reason itself. Tagore was no longer a radical New Ager. On February 1, 1922, he wrote an open letter warning his countrymen against violence; because too much was at stake. This was published two days before the bloodshed at Chauri Chaura, an event that reinforced its teaching.

Gandhi replied, "My experience has proved to my satisfaction that literary training by itself adds not an inch to one's moral height and that character-building is independent of literary training. [And Tagore's] . . . whole soul seems to rebel against the negative commandments of religion. . . . In my humble opinion, rejection is as much an ideal as the acceptance of a thing."[23]

Tagore's attitude is summed up in a frequently quoted couplet,

Deliverance is not for me in renunciation,
I feel the embrace of freedom in a thousand bonds of delight.

It is useful to see the antithesis between those lines and one of Gandhi's favorite passages in *Song Celestial* (Arnold's translation of the Gita):

If one
Ponders on objects of the sense, there springs
Attraction; from attraction grows desire,
Desire flames to fierce passion, passion breeds
Recklessness.

At this time, Tagore's accent in his poems and plays "was increasingly on the dynamic aspects of reality—on life's élan and ever-changing forms, its movement and fluidity, its inexhaustible youth and energy, its urge for freedom and adventure."[24] These are the signs of the Nietzschean-aesthetic version of the New Age.

When Gandhi began the burning of foreign cloth, as part of his noncooperation campaign, Tagore disapproved. He wrote Andrews (in public letters published in the *Modern Review*) "I refuse to waste my manhood in lighting fires of anger and spreading it from house to house . . . it would be an insult to humanity if I use the sacred energy of my moral indignation for the purpose of spreading a blind passion all over my country. It would be like using the fire from the altar of sacrifice for the purpose of incendiarism" (115). This one might call a Brahmo position.

The differences between Gandhi and Tagore were therefore great. If Gandhi was a prophet, Tagore spoke as a poet, claiming all sorts of exemptions from ordinary duty. Gandhi told Tagore that Shantiniketan lacked discipline. The other man laughed and said he was a poet, and Shantiniketan was for his amusement. He could only sing, and make others sing (22:366). In a piece dated March 5, 1921, (he had been in Europe, collecting funds for Shantiniketan) Tagore described hearing a voice tell him: "Your place is on the 'seashore of worlds,' with children; there is your peace, and I am with you there.'. . . But while I play, the whole creation is amused, for are not flowers and leaves never-ending experiments in metre? Is not my God an eternal waster of time?"

To some extent the debate was conducted in terms of color. Tagore and Andrews spoke of cherishing the bright reds and blues, and even the tinsels, of art, while Gandhi wanted pure white khadi, which we might associate with dharma. Andrews wrote at the end of 1924 about the art renaissance in Bengal, saying Indians should enjoy the glorious primary colors again, scarlet, gold, and blue, not just the white of khadi. Gandhi replied that Indians would not lose their color sense; they might and should lose their tawdriness (25:424–25).

Rabindranath spoke in the name of art and play, and Gandhi accepted that, while giving such terms moral and political meaning. Apropos of the arrest of Lala Lajpat Rai he wrote:

> Once when I was talking with the Poet about the Jallianwala Bagh Memorial and trying to persuade him to interest himself in it, he replied, 'What poetry is there in it to attract me? Only what is poetic can have interest for me, a poet. In Jallianwala Bagh, unsuspecting men who had been trapped were shot down. Such an incident cannot inspire new life in people. It merely illustrates their utter helplessness. Does it deserve a memorial?' There was deep meaning in this criticism. . . . I said that, if the public forgot Jallianwala, it would be incapable of creating poetry. . . . But now the Poet has got a poetic subject. A lion like Lalaji [Lala Lajpat Rai] will not be helplessly led into jail. (22:204)

Thus Gandhi translated aestheticism into the current event of Rai's protest and jailing.

In 1925, Gandhi came to Tagore to ask him to endorse the charkha, the supreme emblem of *his* New Age. Congress had just adopted it. But he did not get what he wanted. Tagore wrote an essay called, "The Cult of the Charkha," saying that in India life was leveled down into death and the charkha would level it even more, until people turned against life itself. India needed to rediscover man's wealth of diversity.

Their disagreements were thus highly public, but they remained polite, and their goodwill sincere. Tagore remained an ally and admirer. When he attacked nonviolent noncooperation, Gandhi wrote that those attacks were "written in anger and ignorance," but he bore no grudge. Later, in 1934, after Tagore had attacked him again, Gandhi wrote that he had "made amends." Tagore always, Gandhi said, got excited, wrote something angry, and then corrected himself (57:155). Gandhi controlled himself better.

Rabindranath's arguments with Gandhi must be read as just one, though the most famous, of the voices in the Tagore camp. Not that the others all agreed with him. Rabindranath's older brother, Dwijendranath, known as Borodada, was Gandhi's enthusiastic adherent, and was usually on his side against Rabindranath. In 1925 he attended a discussion between Gandhi and his brother at Shantiniketan, and told the former, "I am speaking all this in the exuberance of joy. I have seen with my own eyes things I dreamt of but never expected to see. *You* are making me speak so. You have taken away my gloom and I hope that the memory of these days may pull me through the dreary journey that may still be before me."[25] On the other hand, Rabindranath's nephew, Soumyendranath, published a communist book in France in 1935, attacking Gandhi as a traitor to the people and a servant to capitalists.[26]

And then there was another participant, silent in public—Saraladevi Chaudhurani. She seems at first to have found in Gandhi a welcome ally in her long quarrel with her uncle. We have seen that she had inclined in an Arya Samaj direction, against Rabindranath. After Gandhi took the national lead with the satyagraha movement, she became his principal lieutenant in the matter of the charkha and khadi.

But she shifted position more than once. She too was distressed by the violence of Gandhi's noncooperation campaign, and quarreled with him over it:

and was ready at other times to accuse Gandhi of having forgotten the martial traditions of Hinduism and being under the sentimental influence of Christianity and Buddhism.

On the whole, Gandhi found in the Tagores a keen-witted appreciation, but a sharp self-differentiation. They were occasional allies but not close comrades. But in Rabindranath he found another exponent of New Age cultural philosophy, worthy of being matched against him.

Annie Besant

Gandhi's relations with Mrs. Besant, perhaps because she was a rival political leader, were more difficult than those with Rabindranath. They showed how far she had come from her New Age beginnings toward a more ordinary idea of politics. With her there was no debate worthy of the name. In 1918 she said, "Gandhi believes in suffering, and he is not happy if he achieves his object through normal evolutionary methods. He wants to build character through suffering. That is not my way. He is the martyr type and believes more in suffering than in achievement."[27] She had renounced naïveté for expertise. She did not want him for president of congress: she told Rajendra Prasad that "he's very good for other kinds of work, but he's not a politician."

She had made accommodations to the Indian status quo. In 1915, Gandhi paid a visit to her establishment at Adyar, near Madras, but when he found that the school for Untouchables there was only a shed, he refused to stay the night.[28] That was one of several points of disagreement over moral principle.

Mrs. Besant was still a major figure in nationalist politics. In 1917, then sixty-nine, she was interned, briefly, by the government. She had begun to publish *New India* in 1914, and was the high priestess of a home rule movement, which she started in 1916. (Tilak's parallel organization was five months older.) She wanted hers to be like Redmond's Irish Home Rule League.

There were several elements of rivalry between her and Gandhi, and she opposed him over noncooperation, as "the representative of dark forces."[29] She thought passive resistance would lead to violence. In 1919 Gandhi was offered the leadership of the Home Rule League built by her and Jinnah; but he said "There cannot be two swords in one scabbard,"[30] and proposed changing the name to Swarajya Sabha. She and Jinnah never forgave him for dividing and thus destroying it.

Gandhi's Choices

While Gandhi was at Shantiniketan, Gokhale died, on February 20, 1915, and it soon became apparent that the other members of the Servants of India Society would not choose Gandhi to be his successor. In fact Srinivasa Shastri, a classic liberal, took Gokhale's place; he and Gandhi maintained an affectionate mutual opposition to the end of their lives; unlike Jinnah and Besant, Shastri *was* able to respond to Gandhi's teasing challenges.

Gandhi had to start on his own, and in May he founded an ashram at Kochrab; using a bungalow owned by a barrister friend. This was not far outside Ahmedabad, and supported financially by local merchants. The most prominent figure amongst those merchants was Ambalal Sarabhai (Erikson suggests that the latter supported Gandhi because he recognized in him a kindred spirit—a kindred combination of the manly voluntarist with the maternally concerned person.)[31]

The ashram at Kochrab had about twenty people in it, many of them originally from Phoenix, Tamils, and Telugus by birth. Newcomers took nine vows, including fearlessness, the love of swadeshi, and resistance to untouchability, as well as more traditionally moral ones. It was a New Age ashram, but a specifically Indian one. As we know, Gandhi soon took into the ashram a family of Untouchables, a move that outraged Kasturba and many of his supporters. He almost had to close the ashram down.

He soon moved it to Sabarmati, because of an outbreak of plague in Kochrab. The landscape of the ashram at Sabarmati was described by Verrier Elwin thus:

> On the further bank I could see in panorama many of the forces against which Gandhi was in revolt. There were the tall chimneys of the factories which were helping to destroy the hand-spinning industry. There was the palace of the Collector, symbol of a foreign domination which had done so much to ruin the quiet peasant life of the villages. Opposite were the low roofs of the simple dwellings of the ashram. The forces of the world and the forces of the spirit were here in vivid symbol arrayed, against one another—machine-force against soul-force, force of arms against love-force.[32]

Gandhi's love-force was however complex in character. He wanted to arouse the Indians to pride and to independence; though at the same time he often warned students against terrorist methods. He advised them to terrorize themselves instead. Thus there was an ambivalence to the message that young people and others took from him. His rhetorical ornament, as was mentioned before, was full of fire and blood, while most often his explicit message was "spin and pray." A striking case of this was his speech at the opening of the Benares Hindu University, which he gave on February 6, 1916.

This university was Mrs. Besant's creation (she was handing over what had been her Central Hindu College to Pandit Malivya) and she presided over a platform crowded with princes and rajahs who glittered with jewels and satins. The university was to revive and reincarnate the glorious heritage of Indian high culture, reuniting princes and poets. This was not a New Age idea of India, nor were elaborate ceremonies of any kind to Gandhi's taste. He was a private man, and also irritable and impatient; it is notable how often, at the innumerable events held to honor him, he began by scolding his hosts or his audience.

This time, when he got up to speak at the opening ceremony, there had already been two days of speeches, and he was, under the surface, exasperated. So were many of the audience, because, in the interests of security, many students who might have caused trouble had been detained. Their friends were eager listeners to Gandhi.

He had been complaining for some time of the excess of feasting and speechifying at Indian events, and of their too elaborate politeness, which suited a different idea of culture—a nonnaive mentality. (At a ceremony in South Africa, making a similar complaint, he had explained that he was a Tolstoyan, and consequently out of place at such events.) In this speech he complained of the speakers' use of English, of the dirt around the famous temples of Benares, of the vulgar luxury of the rajahs in their satin pajamas, and of the detectives guarding the viceroy. The speech of course included praise of the new university and a warning against terrorism, but what came across also was the undercurrent of anger.

He was giving "disciplined expression" to that anger. His exasperation came across inspiringly to some of the students in the audience—one of whom was Vinoba Bhave, who there began to follow Gandhi—but ungraciously to the people of the platform. Mrs. Besant interrupted him, and prompted the princes to walk out.

In that incident we see in epitome Gandhi's complex personality and challenge to his rivals and followers. He called for Hindu tradition—but not the rajahs' tradition; for humility—but equally for pride. To those who had ears to hear, like Vinoba, it was all consistent in its complexity. But to the princes, and Mrs. Besant (no longer a New Ager) and the terrorists, and the communalists, it was a bewildering mishmash, intellectually confused and morally distasteful because of its religiosity.

Another major cause was swadeshi, a slogan that for most Indians meant the use of Indian cloth instead of foreign, but which Gandhi defined much more broadly. On February 14, 1916, he described it as self-restriction to the use and service of one's immediate heritage; one's indigenous political institutions, one's ancestral religion, and all the goods produced in one's own country and region. Indeed swadeshi also implied the propagation of Hindi as a national language that all Indians should learn. Gandhi devoted a lot of time to this last cause in this period. In January 1917, he drew up his prospectus for a National Gujarat School, in which no English would be taught for the first three years. He thought that the learning of English as a national language not only wasted six years of the student's life, but left him nervous, insecure, afraid of examinations, afraid to make a mistake, an imitator.

The Campaigns

At the beginning of 1917 Gandhi was approached at the congress session by a man he did not know called Rajkumar Shukla, who told him of the plight of the indigo workers around Patna. The indigo industry had been injured by the development of synthetic dyes in Germany, and the planters were passing on their losses to the growers, and treating them as serfs. Gandhi went to Bihar, and recruited some Indian lawyers in the region to take down the depositions of twenty-five thousand workers. (Some of these lawyers became his ardent followers for the rest of their lives, like Rajendra Prasad and his brother.) He was ordered to leave the district but refused and was arrested. He drew up a report that the lieutenant governor treated courteously, and the latter's commission refunded 25 percent of what had been exacted by the planters.

As usual, Gandhi was concerned with more than the immediate objective. In 1925 he looked back to this Champaran campaign, and said that for four months seventeen lakhs of people hovered round him, doing nothing. "They were satisfied to draw a little warmth from one whom they considered to be their true servant, but they would not work" (27:33).

In February to March 1918 he was involved in a strike by cotton-mill workers in Ahmedabad. This posed Gandhi a difficult problem because the leader of the mill-owners was Ambalal Sarabhai, who supported Gandhi's ashram financially; but an attractive one, because the owner's sister, Anasuyabehn Sarabhai, was advising and encouraging the workers. (She was a close ally of Gandhi's; she had studied in England, and knew the settlement houses in London.) Gandhi fasted to make the strikers hold by the terms that they had begun with, and a settlement was reached. He was therefore again successful, but he felt uneasy because his fast had had some character of moral blackmail against the owners. (According to his idea, one should fast only against one's friends.)

This is a good example, as Erikson has pointed out, of Gandhi's way of personalizing political conflicts, and making them part of a family plot. Thus he wrote Ambalal on December 21, 1917, "I think you should satisfy the weavers for the sake of Shrimati Anasuyabehn at any rate. . . . There is only one royal road to remove their discontent: entering their lives and binding them with the silken thread of love. . . . How could a brother be the cause of suffering to a sister?—and that, too, a sister like Anasuyaben. I have found that she has a soul which is absolutely pure."[33]

In the course of this campaign, Gandhi engaged in the first of his seventeen fasts unto death, in which he allowed no one else to join. He also wrote daily leaflets under the name of Anasuyabehn. He had to do everything, because no one else understood the full scope of his tactics and strategies.

There was also a campaign in Kheda, another part of Gujarat, organizing the peasants to unite in a refusal to pay excessive government taxes on their crops. There had been a bad monsoon in 1917, damaging the crops, and there was a provision that whenever crops were injured by 25 percent the tax rates should be renegotiated. Vallabhbhai Patel helped organize that campaign. We see how quickly Gandhi was acquiring followers and lieutenants.

In Bengal, he got to know C. R. Das, another powerful political personality. Gandhi says he approached the meeting with suspicion and awe. Das was famous for his stormy speeches and hot temper and extravagance, and Gandhi had heard of Das's roaring practice and still more roaring eloquence (27:268). Das was said to have spent fifty thousand rupees on his trip to the Punjab after the Amritsar Massacre. Gandhi referred to him as the polished Pandit with the terrible jaws, making him sound like Motilal Nehru (27:270). But according to Gandhi Das became really spiritual at the end of his life; he had a guru to consult and wanted to retire from the world. He used naive language to Gandhi, "If we are good, we can make the British good" (27:299).

Gandhi was quickly becoming a legendary character. When he traveled by train, third class, there were anecdotal scenes—he was the humblest person in the compartment, standing when others sat. Then when someone found out that his name was Mohandas Gandhi, everyone stood up in his honor. He was known to be watched by the police and CID men in disguise, and his fellow travelers tried to defend him against them. These are scenes like those in *Kim,* but now they featured a New Age Indian hero.

Private Life

Gandhi's immediate family was split up in this period. After a brief reunion in early 1915, Harilal again parted from his father in anger. His wife died in 1918, and his children were put partly under Gandhi's care, partly under that of Harilal's wife's sisters. Ba stayed with her husband, sometimes accompanying him on tours, for instance in Champaran, but the old jealousies persisted. Gandhi asked her to be a mother to Maganlal, now the manager of the ashram, who had parted from his parents and made Gandhi's work his own: who had so trained himself that he could carry it on after him. But she still resented the usurpers who had displaced her sons.

Gandhi had hoped his widowed sister, Raliatbehn, would join him at the ashram and become a mother to the many children there. That would be true *vaishnavadharma*—not the conventional pieties she practiced—he told her reproachfully; and seeing her he would have some reminders of their mother constantly about him. But in her eyes Gandhi was still an outcaste because of his trip to England. The world did not regard him as "defiled," but she did.

There was also a quarrel between Gandhi and his second son, Manilal. The latter gave Harilal money that had been entrusted to him, and so Gandhi banished him from the ashram for a time. He went to Madras and took lessons in weaving. Later he went back to South Africa, to be in charge of Phoenix, and to edit *Indian Opinion* there.

Ramdas suffered from ill health, and found it difficult to decide on a career, or to persevere with one, once it was chosen. Devdas was the one who maintained most independence of his father. Indeed, he figures in the record more often as reproving and disapproving the latter. According to Shahani, Devdas said, late in life, that he had revered his father but could not love him; that everyone around Gandhi had to pretend to be good; and like Jesus he wanted everyone to sacrifice themselves. Devdas grew tired of being a figure in a stained glass window.

But the great tragedy of Gandhi's family relations continued to be those with Harilal, who was from several points of view degenerating. In 1918 he wrote to tell his father that he had been accused of losing (embezzling) thirty thousand rupees of his Madras employer's money. On May 1, Gandhi wrote back, "I got your letter in Delhi. What shall I write to you? Everyone acts according to his nature" (14:385). Gandhi did not cut off relations, for in November he wrote about a task of translating something into Gujarati that Harilal had undertaken.

Public Activities

It was also at this point that spinning became more than a word to Gandhi; indeed it became of prime importance in his program. A widow called Gangabehn Mazmudar had taken up, at his instance, the search for spinners in Gujarat, and finally found some Muslim women who remembered the skill, and agreed to spin if she would promise to buy what they produced. She also found an old wheel in a lumber-room in Baroda, which carpenters could copy.

In an interview in *Hindu* he said, "I want every man, woman, and child to learn hand-spinning and weaving. . . . Even a few decades back, every village had its handlooms and the people were wearing only clothes woven therefrom." He developed a whole culture of ideas associated with these activities. On October 5, 1919, his paper, *Navajivan,* announced a five-thousand-rupee prize for a portable wheel, made of indigenous components, which could take on ten spindles simultaneously. He wanted every home to have its own wheel, as it had its own oven.

He was never himself a good spinner—nor indeed very deft with his hands at anything. "I am a lame duck in so far as spinning is concerned. I love it, I work hard, and pay great attention to it but the speed simply does not come" (44:68). Sometimes he blamed his failure on his passion for doing two things at once. He read at meals, dictated while spinning, read in the toilet (54:452).

On April 11, 1918 Patrick Geddes wrote to him approving the idea of unifying Hindi and Urdu, and suggesting festivals to encourage Indian folk songs and folk literature; he offered Wales with its Eistedfodd as a model, also Ireland and Provence. (Geddes was a British New Age architect and town-planner Gandhi was in touch with.) Geddes was closer to Tagore than to Gandhi in his ideas, but they were all comrades in the New Age cause.

As far as Hindu-Muslim tensions went, Gandhi thought he had found in the Khilafat project something to unite all Indians, and in the Ali Brothers the Muslim comrades he needed. He summoned his readers on October 27, 1920, to help the Muslims. "An avalanche has descended upon the seven crores of Muslim brothers. A ferocious Empire is out to make mincemeat of their religion. . . . Islam is eclipsed, like the moon, possessed by a demon called the British Empire, and you must free it."[34]

The Ali brothers, who belonged to a family of landowners in the state of Rampur, were to be important to Gandhi for some years. Shaukat Ali was born in 1872 and went to work in the Opium Department in the state of Baroda in 1896; in 1911 and 1912 he was secretary to the Aga Khan. He turned to religion earlier than his brother Mohammed, founding the Servants of the Kaaba Society in Lucknow in 1913. Shaukat was known as the Big Brother, because of his physical size, which was matched by an aggressive and suspicious temperament. He was suspicious of many Hindus, for instance, Motilal Nehru, but for a long time he trusted Gandhi.

Mohammed Ali was six years younger; he went to Oxford to study for the Indian civil service, but did not pass the examination. Like Shaukat, he lived extravagantly, spending six hundred pounds a year in England, at that time a very large sum. Later Gandhi called Mohammed the most improvident and unmethodical of all public workers (30:273).

The brothers were then unlike Gandhi in temperament, and in ideology also. They had studied at Aligarh, where an idea of Islamic exclusivism was stressed. Following Sir Syed's line, Mohammed Ali wrote to Gokhale in 1908 that the

Muslims were a nation without a country, and could not join the Hindus in congress.

In the two brothers, but especially in Shaukat, Gandhi found a political ally who answered to the same idea of the Muslim as Sheikh Mehtab. Gandhi does not draw that connection in so many words, but we, reading him describe them, cannot but be struck by the recurrence of the same ideas. Shaukat Ali was boisterous, exuberant, untrustworthy, physically aggressive—the temperamental opposite of Gandhi. He was no spinner. But this time Gandhi began the relationship as an adult, and with some advantages over his counterplayer from the point of view of political strength. In the long run he was to be disappointed again; and in a parallel way, granted the distance separating the political from the domestic.

Recommending to his readers the Ali Brothers' conversion to spinning, Gandhi said that they had lived in luxury and were in love with silk and muslin. (Here we see a likeness to Kallenbach.) He used to boast that when he and the Ali Brothers addressed meetings of Muslim women, the latter had to be blindfolded, but he was allowed to use his eyes. They were not androgynous brahmacharis (86:98). He persuaded them to spin, but there was always a paradox and comedy about their performance. Reporting the spinning statistics in *Young India,* Gandhi said that the Big Brother had made a mighty effort but could only send one *tola* of indifferently spun yarn (25:15).

Mohammed Ali had failed to become a teacher at Alighar, and he went back to Rampur and then to the state of Baroda. He founded the newspaper, the *Comrade,* in Calcutta in 1910, which aimed to inculcate territorial patriotism in Indian Muslims without sacrificing their Pan-Islamic sympathies. This became an important publication with the outbreak of the Balkan Wars in 1911, taking Turkey's side. The circulation rose to 8500, and he also began an Urdu daily in 1913.

At this point Mohammed Ali was familiar with the European countries' Press, rather with that of Islamic countries like Egypt, Turkey, and Morocco.[35] He had written for the *Times of India* and was a favorite with Anglo-Indian readers, and hoped for a job with the governor of Bombay. He also edited a paper in Urdu.

Shaukat Ali took his political cues from his younger brother. Big Brother was an incarnation of the principle of genial violence, in the way that Sheikh Mehtab had been. He had occasional fits of rage when he beat people up, and more often indulged in buffoonery and horseplay. He had to be restrained from attacking Jinnah on one occasion, and Ambalal Sarabhai on another. He took up Pan-Islamism; and founded the society to organize trips to Mecca, which at first talked of buying destroyers and airplanes to protect the holy places. In the decade before the war, he took to wearing Muslim dress and beard, calling it a protest against Europe and Christendom.[36]

Gandhi made overtures toward the Ali Brothers as soon as he returned to India. In April 1915 he addressed the Muslims of Delhi in the presence of Mohammed Ali, who thanked him afterwards. Later in 1915 Shaukat Ali and his brother were interned for 4½ years for Pan-Islamic propaganda that was implicitly anti-British. During that time, he became religious, and read the Qur'an through. Gandhi did not see them throughout that period, but he appealed to the government on their behalf, and wrote to them in internment, forging an alliance for the future.

Violence and Nonviolence

On March 30, 1918, Gandhi gave a talk on Indian civilization at Indore, which expressed an idea that preoccupied him at this time; of the unique character of India's vocation. "India alone is the land of karma, the rest is the land of bhoga [enjoyment]. I feel that India's mission is different from that of other countries. India is fitted for the religious supremacy of the world. . . . India can conquer all by soul-force" (14:53). Similar ideas were held about Zion's vocation, by some Jews.

Later in that year, however, he came to doubt that. He wrote to Andrews on July 6, full of perplexity, saying that the ancient Indians did *not* repudiate war (this is the letter quoted in the last chapter). Hindus were as eager to fight as Muslims—simply less able to do so. Such thoughts were connected to his recruiting campaign. This was the worst failure of all his campaigns, but at the same time strangely impressive.

Gandhi asked the government to make him its chief recruiting officer on April 30, 1918. He hoped to get twenty men from each of the six hundred villages of Kheda. This was work that most nationalist leaders did not touch and for which there was no constituency in Gujarat. There were eight hundred thousand Indians serving in the British forces, but they came from areas and groups that had few dealings with congress.

Gandhi wrote to other national leaders, asking them to take up the same work, but without success. Tilak did agree to recruit five thousand in Maharashtra, if Gandhi would guarantee a certain proportion of commissions—which he would not. One striking exception to the general rule was Saraladevi Chaudhurani, who had been given an official commendation by the authorities in Lahore for having done such work. She felt, as much as Gandhi did, and quite independently, the importance of military training, as a means of restoring Indian courage.

Such recruitment was work usually done by British agents, and among the martial races. Its discourse was quite different from that of nationalism. Gandhi found himself saying to his audience many of the things Sir Michael O'Dwyer said in the Punjab; complaining, for instance, that although four hundred thousand men from that province joined the army during the war, only seventy of them came from among the university students (of whom there were ten thousand). He had to praise martial loyalty and valor, and to deplore the educated middle class that refused to defend its country or to respect those who did. And the work involved him in endless debates over how he could reconcile this work with his opposition to violence. No wonder he wrote to his old friend, Dr. Mehta, on July 2, "You must be watching my work of recruitment. Of all my activities, I regard this as the most difficult and the most important. If I succeed in it, genuine *swaraj* is assured" (14:468).

One of the arguments he advanced for Indians enlisting was political partnership. If Indians wanted to have the benefits of being treated as equals in the empire, they must take a part in its defense comparable with the part the British took. Gandhi himself had twice volunteered for service in this war, in France and in Mesopotamia, because he had convinced himself that he owed the empire that sacrifice in return for accepting its military protection. He would also say, as he did in Nadiad on June 17, that swaraj without military power would be useless, and joining the army was the way to acquire military power.

Another way in which Gandhi defended his position was by saying that he recommended military training only to those who did not believe in satyagraha. Nonviolence was the higher calling, but: "That the whole of India will ever accept satyagraha is beyond my imagination." Thus he had one message for one part of his audience, another for another. This was philosophically realistic, but morally confusing, for it left his listeners free to assign themselves to an identity, or to invent a new one.

It is one of Gandhi's most striking characteristics that, while identifying himself as a man of a special type, an ascetic and savior, he also addressed the whole range of human types and invoked the criteria of cultural normality, of reason and tradition and culture. He spoke to those unlike himself, and of all of them, he was most importantly concerned about men of violence, and their place in society, and their virtues.

He described himself and his type from the outsiders' point of view. "There can be no partnership between the cat and the mouse, between the ant and the elephant." He cheerfully implied, or declared, that he himself, and the groups he belonged to, *were* mice and ants; which meant they must become something better.

"Any stout fellow can successfully intimidate us. If a Pathan were to come here and start hitting out with the lathi, we would all run away. An overbearing Kabuli, entering a compartment already crowded, will get the people to vacate the seats . . . and occupy the room for four" (14:437). He often said in this period that he was training to cease to be a bania and to become a Kshatriya. "*Satyagraha* is a soldierly instinct, and Banias are largely associated with money-making rather than with fighting for a cause. Hence, I have the fewest co-workers from among fellow-Banias" (16:78). His movement's prime aim is purification, or the revival of the Kshatriya spirit. And perhaps his most epigrammatic formulation of the idea comes in a letter to Andrews. "You cannot teach *ahimsa* to a man who cannot kill" (14:444).

He was very unsuccessful in this campaign. He got very few volunteers, and very hostile audiences. The Kheda peasants refused to supply him even with food and transport. In early July he said he had won no recruits; by the end of the month, a hundred.[37]

This idea involved him in debate and doubt of himself, much more than did his ideas of sex, for on this issue he was strongly drawn in two opposite directions. In *Young India* on October 20, 1921, we find him saying: "The sooner we are left free to fight, the better for our manhood, our respective religions, and our country. It will not be a new phenomenon if we fought ourselves into sanity. The English carried on internecine warfare for twenty-one years before they settled down to peaceful work. The French fought among themselves with a savage ferocity hardly excelled during modern times. The Americans did nothing better before they evolved their commonwealth. Let us not hug our unmanliness for fear of fighting among ourselves" (21:319). This is an example of Gandhi citing the lessons of history, which he usually repudiated. It is also an example of why he had finally to repudiate them. The lessons of history, as it has usually been written, are not in accord with the gospel of a New Age.

He had a sufficiently clear and convincing formula, that a man must be capable of violent resistance before he was capable of nonviolence. But that principle involved him in many difficult questions of application, which tormented him especially in the summer of 1918. "It is clear that, before I can give a child an idea of *moksha,* I must let it grow into full manhood. I must allow it to a certain extent to be even attached to the body. . . . What is the meaning of having a vigorous body? How far should India have to go in for a training in arms-bearing?" (14:476).

He fell ill on the very day he wrote one of these letters of self-scrutiny.[38] Erikson draws our attention to the importance of this breakdown, but explains it as deriving from Gandhi's concern with the role of father and son: Gandhi wrote a letter to the viceroy in which, Erikson says, he implicitly offered to become the latter's nurse-son; and the next day wrote to Harilal one of those letters in which—as Erikson thinks—he so often repudiated his own sons.

Gandhi wrote to his son Ramdas, July 28, 1918, that if the latter were with him, Gandhi would have sent him into the army; Ramdas was at that time in South Africa, with Manilal. "I have come to realize that this is our paramount duty. A young man must learn self-defence. I have not forgotten the insults inflicted upon you by that Pathan. I have defended you but that gave me no satisfaction. . . . Ahimsa is the extreme limit of human strength" (UC). He had given the same advice to Harilal, to join the army, he said. He did not, however, tell Devdas, who was available, to enlist. He justified this difference on the grounds that Devdas was doing too important work. One may doubt if he would have actually sent Ramdas, had he been there—but Gandhi did many things one would have doubted.

On July 17 he wrote to Hanumantrao at the ashram:

> I do believe that we shall have to teach our children the art of self-defence. I see more and more clearly that we shall be unfit for *swaraj* for generations to come if we do not regain the power of self-defence. This means for me a rearrangement of so many ideas about self-development and India's development. (14:485)

Twelve days later he wrote to Mashruwala:

> In what manner should the children learn to use their strength? It is a difficult thing to teach them to defend themselves and yet not be overbearing. Till now, we used to teach them not to fight back if anyone beat them.

> Can we go on doing so now? What will be the effect of such teaching on a child? Will he, in his youth, be a forgiving or a timid man? My powers of thinking fail me. Use yours. (14:515–16)

On the same day he wrote to Andrews.

> I must indulge myself again. I begin to perceive a deep meaning behind the Japanese reluctance to listen to the message of a Prophet from a defeated nation. [Tagore had gone to Japan, preaching pacifism, and had been coolly received.] War will always be with us. There seems to be no possibility of the whole human nature becoming transformed. Moksha and ahimsa are for individuals to attain. Full practice of ahimsa is inconsistent with possession of wealth, land, or rearing of children. (14:509)

As a last example of his power of imaginative projection at this time, we might take a letter of July 28 to Maganlal: "I have come to see, what I did not so clearly see before, that there is nonviolence in violence. This is the big change which has come about. Brahmacharya consists in refraining from sexual indulgence, but we do not bring up our children to be impotent" (14:505). As we have seen, Gandhi more than other men knew what it was like to feel impotent. He had sought potency—and especially in political matters or by political means—ever since his youth.

Gandhi found this recruiting work exhausting. His fatigue was caused by the physical strain of the speeches, and the disappointing results (some days he walked twenty miles, and found no one who listened to him at the end of them), but perhaps even more because of the moral perplexities just mentioned, which it evoked in him.

Tagore told Romain Rolland in 1926 that Gandhi had been in a state of collapse ever since the recruiting campaign—nearly ten years before. This was not true in any simple sense, but there are reasons to believe that the crisis left a severe mark on Gandhi. For instance, Rolland wrote him disagreeing with his rationale in that matter on March 7, 1928; and Gandhi immediately thereafter became eager to come to Europe to meet Rolland.[39]

Erikson tells us that whatever the physical nature of Gandhi's original illness, he was suffering from a nervous breakdown in the last months of 1918.[40] His intimate friend, Rajendra Prasad, tells us in his autobiography that Gandhi was full of indecision and self-doubt after the recruiting campaign; a very rare condition for him. He often wept and said, "I do not know what God's will is."[41] It does not seem, indeed, that Gandhi ever resolved the problem. His activity, from then on, had a shifting foundation; but of course his was a dialectical mind, and he was used to shiftings.

Indeed in many ways this internal debate shows us Gandhi at his most impressive. It shows his imaginative flexibility and willingness to imagine points of view and modes of being quite unlike his own. As he took over the leadership of the nationalist movement, he was drawn both to nonviolent values and to others that express the whole range of human strength, including the soldier's kind. He came down on the side of the first, but he seems to have ended the debate, and escaped—from the tangle of feelings to which there was no solution—by virtue of a dangerous illness.

In his extreme distress of mind, he fell sick of dysentery, and again could not cure himself by his own nature-cure methods. (Perhaps because there was some connection between the distress and the sickness.) He was taken into Ambalal Sarabhai's house, for better nursing, but this in some ways increased his distress. He complained that "the luxurious living in that palatial house had started corroding my mind." The doctors told him he would not recover unless he drank milk. He had taken a vow against doing so, but Ba persuaded him that he had been thinking only of cows' milk when he took the vow, and that goat's milk was another matter. Gandhi was quite clear that he was in some sense cheating, but he accepted the cheat, drank the milk, and recovered.

He wrote to his sons, when he thought he would not survive, on October 2 (his birthday). To Harilal he said he was leaving them an inheritance of character, not money: to Devdas, that he must show the strength of a Kshatriya, and keep his father alive in his actions.

He was seriously ill for several months, throughout the rest of 1918 and the beginning of 1919. On October 1 he was at death's door, and in January had to submit to an operation, and then to the ultimate humiliation, the breaking of his vow. He knew goat's milk was a compromise, and felt that he had "lost lustre." But he wanted to live, and to work, as he admitted.

Public Crisis

And suddenly a national cause arose, and his response to it made him the nation's leader. It was provoked by the Rowlatt Bills, which the government introduced to give itself emergency powers to deal with insurrection, conspiracy, and revolution, including powers to investigate revolutionary movements. The Rowlatt Commission was appointed on December 17, 1917, and reported in April the next year. The bills legitimized preventive detention, with no right of appeal. Indignation against them was rife in India, and a general need was felt to give that indignation expression.

On February 9, 1919, Gandhi wrote: "The Rowlatt Bills have agitated me very much. It seems I shall have to fight the greatest battle of my life" (15:88). And soon he was writing letters to the press, explaining satyagraha and distinguishing it from comparable tactics like boycott. He began touring again, though he could not stand to speak, and Mahadev Desai often had to read out his speeches for him.

There was nationwide agitation from March 1 to April 18, 1919. There was a day of prayer and humiliation, and an appeal to the viceroy, and a hartal on April 6. At the last, proscribed books by Gandhi, including *Hind Swaraj* and his translations of *Unto This Last* and *The Death of Socrates*, were sold.

Naturally there was opposition to Gandhi's initiative. The liberals objected to direct action against the acts, and G. S. Khaparde, Tilak's henchman, poured scorn on Gandhi's philosophy, and on the Satyagraha pledge. "One touch of a whip," said Khaparde, "would deter the Gujaratis from their determination."[42] Gandhi demanded complete obedience, if he was to direct a noncooperation movement. Jinnah objected to that. The Muslims as a whole were divided over the movement; but some joined in; and what they did, Judith Brown says, gave noncooperation bite and power, but was always near to violence.[43] Gandhi strove, and with considerable success, to link swaraj to the Khilafat movement.

In May of the same year Gandhi took control of two weeklies, *Young India* and its Gujarati equivalent, *Navajivan,* which had a circulation of forty thousand. He launched a noncooperation campaign; for instance returning his South African medals to the viceroy, as some others did also. In his letter to the viceroy, after Amritsar, Gandhi called O'Dwyer totally unfit to be lieutenant governor of the Punjab, and the viceroy's treatment of the crime lighthearted. In Europe the condoning of such a crime would have resulted in bloody revolution by the people. "They would have resisted at all cost the national emasculation such as the said wrongs imply"[44] (53).

The Rowlatt Bills, aimed at suppressing protest, provoked much more, in large groups and small, and those responsible for maintaining order grew very uneasy, especially in the Punjab. Thus in Amritsar, the holy city of the Sikhs, on April 13, 1919, thousands of people gathered in the Jallianwala Bagh, and the British general Dyer, having given an order to disperse, opened fire upon them. His troops were Gurkhas and Baluchis, martial races, like the Pathans, often employed by the British against other Indians.

There were about 6,000 people in an area the size of Trafalgar Square, and 1,650 rounds were fired (the aim shifting to where the crowd was thickest); 1,516 casualties resulted, 379 were killed, and more than 1,000 injured. Severe repression followed; three days before, an English schoolmistress had been assaulted, and Indians were now forced to crawl along the lane where that happened. And news of the shooting was kept secret for a long time.

The news was suppressed for a while, but when it was known, this event, known as the Amritsar Massacre, of course caused an immense shock of indignation throughout India, and indeed the outside world. The nationalist leaders had to take some action that would seem equal to the occasion, and it was Gandhi who seized the opportunity. In the second half of 1919 he was primarily concerned with the tragedy and its aftermath.

Gandhi headed the Congress Commission on the Punjab Disorders and drafted the congress report—the Indian answer to the government report. He then launched a noncooperation campaign. He asked Indians to return all honors, titles, and medals they had received from the British government. He asked plaintiffs and lawyers to boycott the British courts, and officials to refuse to discharge their offices. And finally, soldiers should lay down their arms, and citizens should stop paying taxes. Naturally, there was a wide variation in the degree to which people followed these guidelines, but for a brief time the city of Bombay had in effect two systems of authority, the government-instituted, and the Gandhi-instituted.

When he went to the Punjab to investigate, he stayed at the house of Pandit Rambhuj Datta Chaudhuri, a Lahore lawyer and editor of a nationalist journal. The pandit was in jail for earlier political activities, but his wife, Saraladevi Chaudhurani, had invited Gandhi to stay with her. As we know, Saraladevi was in her own right an important figure in the nationalist movement, both in Bengal, where she was born, and, after her marriage in 1910, in Lahore. But before we examine Gandhi in the close-up of an intimate relationship, let us fill in the background of public events.

Public Affairs

We have seen that Gandhi was in Amritsar at the beginning of 1920. He appealed for donations to a Jallianwala Bagh Memorial Fund, and wrote the congress report on the massacre. There were riots in Bombay in 1921, because the Hindus and Muslims were boycotting the Prince of Wales, while other groups, like the Parsis, were not, and so different groups of Indians came into conflict with each other. Beyond these matters, he was concerned with two larger causes, Khilafat and noncooperation.

The Khilafat movement, already mentioned, was a protest against the Allied Powers' disposal of the sacred places of Islam. Medina and Mecca had been part of the Turkish Empire, and so under the rule of the caliph. With the defeat of Turkey in the War of 1914–18, that empire collapsed. The Khilafat movement was an attempt to get them returned to Islamic custody. Gandhi supported this, and even hoped at one point to be sent to London to speak for India's Muslims. (This would have been like Polak being sent to India to speak for the South African Indians.) In the event, it was Mohammed Ali who went.

This was a New Age cause, dear to Gandhi's heart because it was a matter of religion, and one in which the Hindus might—partly by force of numbers—help their Muslim brothers. But neither the Western powers, nor most of the Indian Muslims, could take such a religious idea as serious politics. And the movement died when Turkey came under the rule of the secular leader, Kemal Ataturk.

In 1920, however, England and her allies were moving toward the Treaty of Sèvres, intending to confiscate Turkey's European territories, and to put the Near Eastern ones under British mandate. This was what the Pan-Islamic movement had feared, and congress adopted the issue of Khilafat, largely at Gandhi's urging. Participation in some Khilafat activities was made conditional on belonging to congress.

Gandhi inaugurated the noncooperation campaign on August 1, 1920, the third Khilafat Day. The aim was to induce the nation to boycott the institutions of British rule—the army, the law courts, the schools, the universities, the administration—to give up any career in such institutions, and to set up their own institutions to replace them. Thus on November 15, in Ahmedabad, he became chancellor of the Gujarat Vidyapith, the Indian "university" set up in his own province. On September 8, both the congress and the All India Khilafat Committee had passed his resolutions on noncooperation.

Of course spinning and khadi were associated causes. So was the return by Indians of British medals and titles—on August 1, 1920, Gandhi returned the medals he won in South Africa, and Tagore refused to employ his title. Noncooperation also meant the boycott of the Prince of Wales on his visit to India.

Nationalist propaganda became more aggressive. On April 13, 1921, Gandhi recommended the adoption of a national flag, "to live and die for"; and in a speech at Ahmedabad declared, "We want a swaraj which should be Ramrajya"—that is, he wanted the Western idea of nationalism combined with the Hindu legend of peace and justice.

On July 31, he began his campaign for swadeshi, to bring economic and therefore cultural independence, by setting alight a bonfire of foreign cloth in Bombay. He had appealed to merchants to stop the import of cloth and to keep the price of Indian cloth down. (In October he began to spin for half an hour every day before his second meal.) In December Harilal was arrested for his part in a Gandhian demonstration. There were riots in Bombay; so serious that Gandhi fasted because the people had dishonored the "check" he had presented: he said he had to draw upon God for further credit. Fasting was the naive man's style of keeping control over the movement; it was equally Eastern and Western, but few of his friends approved it.

He needed someone with a double cultural education, someone with strong sympathies with both nonviolence and violence, and preferably someone who knew the best of Bengal, to complement his own Gujarati heritage. He found all these things conjoined, in a woman, the niece of Rabindranath Tagore.

Saraladevi Chaudhurani

Saraladevi's father, Janakinath Ghosal, was an important figure in the early years of congress; he had been a close associate of Allan Octavian Hume in setting the institution up; and was one of its two secretaries during the 1901 meeting that Gandhi attended. But Ghosal was in England during much of Saraladevi's childhood, and in several ways her heritage via her mother was more important. Her mother, Swarnakumari, herself active in literature and the nationalist movement, was the sister of Rabindranath Tagore, and took part in public life.

Ten women (from Bombay and Calcutta) attended the congress of 1889. One of these was Swarnakumari Devi. She was also interested in Theosophy, and worked for swadeshi. The Tagore women had much easier access to public life than most women, but the gender split worked against them too. For instance, the Tagore men, including Rabindranath, disposed of their daughters and sisters in marriage in a way quite at odds with their professions of liberality. And in literary matters there seems to have been a similar inequity. Saraladevi therefore inherited from her mother a certain conflict with Rabindranath. Swarnakumari was five years older than her famous brother, and wrote early in literary forms that he took up later, and for which he became famous—for instance, opera, and a kind of long philosophical poem. She was already writing, when, at thirteen, she was married to Ghosal, then a deputy magistrate. She wrote novels, plays, songs, poetry, which were widely read in her day. *Kahini* (1898), a novel of love-relationships, set in contemporary Bengal, was published in England, and had a second printing. But she was known everywhere as Rabindranath's sister, and resented that.[45]

Saraladevi, born on September 9, 1872, grew up in the Tagore house in Jorosanko, in Calcutta, and followed the poet, to some degree collaborated with him, in various artistic enterprises, above all in music. The large family, living together in a large mansion, were nearly all involved in the arts, some being executants—singers, actors, painters—others being also composers and writers. However, the Tagores who published had another audience, much broader than the family and their immediate social circle. In some cases that audience was international; especially of course Rabindranath, who as noted won the Nobel Prize for Literature (in 1913), the first time it was given to an Asian.

Swarnakumari, busy with writing and reading, did not take part with the other women in the daily cooking and vegetable-chopping sessions. Nor did she give her child much affection, according to the latter's autobiography. Saraladevi complains of being handed over to a stern nanny and a stern tutor. Her famous uncle also often appears in that story being furious at something Saraladevi did—though it is also clear that he was extremely important to her. Perhaps because both these relationships were difficult, we seem to see in Saraladevi a reaction against Brahmo Samaj ideas—a preference for Arya Samaj ideas—and also a general emotional insecurity, perhaps instability. Though enthusiastic by temperament, she was full of grievances, with a sense of being unappreciated; and indecisive—in that, for instance, she allowed herself to be disposed of by her family at crucial moments.

Though close to her uncle in the talents and interests they shared, she and he were not mutually supportive. His favorite was another niece, Indiradevi Chaudhurani. There was something of a court around Rabindranath, and Saraladevi found herself in the position of competing for his favor; and, because she felt herself to be really more rival than courtier, she was a less-comfortable companion for him than her competitors.

A Tagore scholar says, of his relations with another woman writer, "Not that Tagore himself had ever sought a peer figure in a woman. Like most male heterosexual artists even up to this day, he needed women more as sources of inspiration . . . than as friends on equal terms."[46] Even later in life, after Saraladevi's widowing and her return to Calcutta, their relations were strained. She was again editing *Bharati,* and reproached him with preferring to publish elsewhere.

Saraladevi was animated and emotional, and prone to reversals of feeling. Thus it may not be insignificant that she speaks of her propensity to laugh "at the slightest possible excuse." Gandhi said, "Your laughter is a national asset. Laugh away!"[47] But we know of her deep melancholy and dissatisfaction, and so her laughter was also, one might guess, the mark of an unstable temperament. (It is worth noting that in this anecdote Gandhi makes her a national figure; and that her husband said she was the greatest shakti in India; her size and scope were obviously larger than average. And she herself is the source of both anecdotes.)

Saraladevi's attention was drawn to politics early; she remembered the Ilbert Act agitation, and the black badges her schoolmates wore when the nationalist Surendranath Bannerji was arrested. She had an admirable schooling; the Brahmo Samajists being in favor of women's education. By her own account,

Vivekananda told Sister Nivedita that Saraladevi had had the perfect education. She attended the Bethune School, where she met many women who were to become prominent. In order to study physics she went in the evenings to the Science Academy, with male relatives standing on either side of her. After getting her degree in English, she went on to study French, Persian, and Sanskrit. She sang "Bande Mataram" on the congress platform. She composed patriotic songs, and issued a collection of them, *Satagan*. She knew Calcutta celebrities like Bankim Chatterji and Vidyasagar socially.

In 1895 she went to teach at the Maharani's Girls School in Mysore, and did so in a conscious bid for independence, but returned home after a year or so, having fallen sick. She edited *Bharati* for some years after her return, advocating Hindu-Muslim unity, amongst other things. She published pieces by Gandhi and others. In 1902 she started social service and physical culture clubs in Calcutta, and opened Lakshmi Bhandar shop to sell homespun on Cornwallis Street in 1903. In 1904 she won a gold medal for exhibiting improved textures in swadeshi cloth. (She thus knew about spinning and weaving long before Gandhi did.) In 1905 she gave new life to the Sahid Samiti, which trained its members in political meetings and boxing and wrestling. She addressed meetings of all-male societies, for instance, a martial arts gymnasium, an *akhara*. Sumit Sarkar, in *The Swadeshi Movement in Bengal* (1973) says she was the only woman leader in the movement.

When she went to live in Lahore, she worked for women's education in the villages round the city. She took over the editing of *Hindustan* when her husband was jailed, and brought out an English language edition that was praised by Ramsay MacDonald. In 1910 she founded the Bharat Stri Mahamandal, which spread education for women, and worked against purdah and child-marriage. This organization eventually had branches all over the country. She also made a cause out of persuading Bengali young men to join the army. In 1917 she joined Margaret Cousins in her Votes for Women organization.

She entered into a significant discipleship to Vivekananda, before the comparable one to Gandhi. (She had published Sister Nivedita, and written about Vivekananda in *Bharati*.) Vivekananda wanted her to accompany him on tours abroad, representing Indian womanhood, but her family did not approve of the scheme. She attended his ashram at Mayavati in the Himalayas, heard lectures on the Upanishads, and planned a journey to Tibet; but in 1905 was summoned back to Calcutta by her family to marry Pandit Chaudhuri, whom she saw only the day before the wedding. He was already twice a widower, an Arya Samaj activist, and editor of *Hindustan*.

This was the time of the agitation in Bengal, and it is possible that the Tagores wanted to find Saraladevi a protected position, where she would not be so involved. She was suspected of complicity in smuggling arms; and was warned by C. R. Das not to go out alone after dark, because the police were planning to have her assaulted, and to blame her young men for it. She also reports consulting Atul Prasad Sen in Lucknow on her journey home to get married, who said there was nothing wrong with Pandit Chaudhuri, but he feared the national movement was going to be weakened by her withdrawal from it.

Saraladevi is described in the Indian *Dictionary of National Biography* as an eminent feminist after the Victorian pattern—"ardent, passionate, headstrong"—and a typical member of the Tagore family. B. R. Nanda, in *Gandhi: Pan-Islamism, Imperialism, and Nationalism,* says that Saraladevi typified the new genre of young Bengalis, "pulsating with patriotic fervor." She was consequently dissatisfied with Brahmo Samaj gentleness. Rabindranath had returned to those ideas after his flirtation with political activism, but Saraladevi wanted something more.

Her autobiography is evasive in certain matters, both of fact and of feeling. For instance, she gives no hint of her relationship with Gandhi. And she generally does not make clear whether she is formulating her idea as it seemed to her then, or as it seems at the time of writing. But she seems to have aspired to the position of Durga, or Shakti (or Bhabani, or Bangabhoomi, local versions of the female deity). There was a lot of mythical speculation in Bengal then about the power of the goddess, and it was to be expected that a woman with Saraladevi's remarkable gifts and excitable temperament should play that part. There was, however, a strain of timidity and uncertainty in her that pulled her back from decisive self-commitment.

When she met Gandhi she was about thirty, three years younger than he. She revived national festivals, staged patriotic plays, helped run a girls' school, organized clubs, and was at the heart of the nationalist movement. Just a year after her first meeting with Gandhi, she wrote his friend Gokhale, on March 31, 1902, about his beautiful speech on the budget in the Imperial Council—to which the viceroy's reply had been merely frivolous, she said. She had been thinking about Gokhale's resolution to devoted himself solely to politics. "It is this habit of sacrifice which we want cultivating in Bengal."[48] That speech raised Gokhale's stock high with many people.

But art was as much Saraladevi's concern as politics. She speaks of a ritual of mutual enrichment between her self and the god of music who inhabited the depths of her heart. Despite the tensions between her and her uncle Rabindranath, she says that Rabimama (her uncle) was the priest of that ritual; which gives him a very special position in her inner life. She had an absolute passion for music, and in that house it was he who knew best what she was doing.[49] She brought him folk songs, and he adapted them.

Both of them faced the dilemmas of translation and transposition, and the double audience, Indian and English. It is worth noting that some of Saraladevi's early work for her uncle was transposing some of his songs into Western musical terms. Later on, of course, she and many others believed in conserving the indigenous culture, and there was criticism of Rabindranath for translating his own poetry into English. It seems likely that the personal conflict was involved in the cultural one.

Saraladevi's mother became very interested in theosophy for a time, and founded the Ladies' Theosophical Society of Calcutta. Madame Blavatsky was a frequent visitor to the Tagore house, and Saraladevi herself was cured of neck pains by the mesmeric powers of the Theosophist Colonel Olcott. And after the interest in theosophy waned, Saraladevi's mother and friends worked for the poor, in ways like those of the women's settlement houses in the West.

She describes going as a child to a debate between Rabindranath and the famous Bengali novelist, Bankim, on the question of how truth should be respected. Her uncle spoke for truth as an absolute value and duty, the novelist spoke for certain reservations or adaptations in, for instance, political situations. She was on her uncle's side at the time but later she decided that she had not done Bankim justice. It is for *children* that truth is an unqualified value; adults have to discriminate. This represents a recoil from the pure idealism of the Brahmos toward political activism. Gandhi of course asserted the duty of perfect truth, and clashed with Tilak on that and other moral issues. (Tilak said the Indian languages had no word for *conscience,* and so he rejected it.) (37:267). These are parallel conflicts, Gandhi vs. Tilak and Rabindranath vs. Bankim: Saraladevi was drawn in both directions but came down on the side of the second.

The Brahmos did not worship idols, and Saraladevi never saw such rituals of worship in her home. She was intensely moved when she was taken to watch the "arati" ritual at the Bishweshwar temple in Benares; but Rabindranath was furious when he heard of her response, she says. He was opposed to the cult of Kali, and to the terrorist politics associated with that cult. More generally, he believed that the divine powers were transcendent and invisible, and though it was appropriate to flesh them out in song and legend, one must always remember that these were metaphors. (His writing recalls the Symbolism and Expressionism fashionable in the West at that time, his poetic rhetoric being studded with capitalized abstractions.)

Saraladevi's cultural loyalties were quite different. When she married, her in-laws were very impressed that she joined in their traditional ceremonies, despite her Western education; she even defended polygamy for men whose wives were infertile. She became a model for the woman's movement in Lahore. Rabindranath had retired from the activist politics he had endorsed, but Saraladevi continued them.

In 1904, when war broke out between Russia and Japan, she (like Gandhi in South Africa) tried to raise an ambulance corps to serve beside the Japanese troops. Her social work took the turn of encouraging patriotic action and martial arts. She persuaded a group of boys to devote their annual meeting to a display of wrestling, fencing, boxing, and to call it Pratapaditya Festival, after a Bengali hero of Hindu resistance to Muslims. The newspapers reported the occasion. *Bangabasi* commented, "What a wonderful sight! No speeches, no table-thumping—only the evocation of the memory of a Bengali hero, a display of arms by Bengali youths, and the distribution of prizes by their leader, a Bengali woman." This festival, and the other celebrating Pratapaditya's son, at which a sword was displayed on the stage and flowers were offered to it, were comparable with Sheikh Mehtab's work in Durban. She used the same word for that kind of patiotic theater, *natak*. Thus Gandhi's friendship with Sheikh Mehtab may have prepared him to appreciate Saraladevi when he met her.

However, Rabindranath was disapproving about the festival, because he thought Pratapaditya did not deserve hero worship; he himself in one of his plays had portrayed Pratapaditya unfavorably. Saraladevi protested that Pratapaditya was a political, not a moral hero, and that he was Bengal's equivalent for Tilak's hero, Shivaji. (On the other hand, when she was told some young radicals were using violence to raise money, with Tilak's approval, she made a journey to Pune, to protest.) The debate over these issues, a debate between two kinds of idealism, prepared Saraladevi to appreciate Gandhi's nonviolent politics.

"Around this time"—Saraladevi gives few dates—she read a story by Kipling about the Northwest Frontier Province, and the contempt in which the Pathans hold a Bengali civil service officer put in charge of them (It must be the story alluded to before, "The Head of the District.") Saraladevi was so angry that she wrote a letter to Kipling, "For the indignity you have heaped on my race, I summon you to come forward—come and fight a duel with any of my Bengali brothers. I give you five years to prepare. Train yourself to use any weapon of your choice, guns, swords, whatever." (Thinking of the person Kipling, as distinct from the author, there is a grotesque comedy to this idea, comparable to Gandhi's idea of himself dueling with Shaukat Ali.)

Having written this letter, she had to discover Kipling's address before she could mail it. While she was trying to do so, someone advised her to wait and give herself five years to train Bengali boys in martial arts, in order to be ready for the Englishman. She searched around in Calcutta until she found a Muslim instructor called Professor Murtaza, and set up the club at her family home, buying swords, shields, knives, lathis, and so on. She took the roll call, and presided over the whole enterprise.

Some people began to refer to her as "Debi Chaudhurani." This is the name of the heroine of a novel by Bankim. She was a village girl abandoned by her husband, but trained by a famous dacoit in Sanskrit, the Scriptures, and physical fitness. She then led his gang in robbing the rich to pay the poor. (It was a coincidence that Saraladevi was to acquire that name, by marriage, some time later.)

The Chaudhuri couple lived in Lahore in 1919, and they now became Gandhians, sending their son to be educated at his ashram. They invited Gandhi to Lahore, though the Pandit was in jail by the time Gandhi could get there, on October 17, 1919. Gandhi and his entourage stayed with Saraladevi, and she traveled with them. She took up the cause of swadeshi (which she and Rabindranath had propagated in the 1905 agitation in Bengal). She gave song recitals, made speeches, and opened a shop for khadi.

This was the woman Gandhi met in 1919; someone ideologically though not socially similar to himself. They were both concerned to renew India's culture by renewing its virility, as manifested in acts of physical courage and aggression. For various reasons, however, they were not themselves going to take up arms; they spoke *for* virility, and not as virile. By a curious coincidence, their position was like that of their enemy's major spokesman, Kipling. Speaking for Anglo-India, though himself no warrior, Kipling wrote stories and poems that made heroes out of soldiers and rulers, and asked England to identify itself with the latter, and not with the merchants who had first gone to India—in the nineteenth century dismissed as "box-wallahs." In Hindu terms (which fit the case exactly) he spoke for the Kshatriya and against the bania.

So did Gandhi. The latter had read a lot of Kipling, but there seems no evidence that the writer influenced him, except as one particular vocalizing of the Anglo-Indian mood. But that mood certainly did affect the nationalism of Gandhi and others. The English in India were assuming on imperial posture, and altering their sense of their identity, becoming aristo-military, and rejoicing in those powers. The Indians had to find their own version of them.

Socially, Saraladevi was very unlike Gandhi. When he wrote about her, after 1919, he always drew attention to her Tagore connection, and sometimes said she was of "the Indian nobility." He particularly reported the connections between her and Rabindranath—saying, for instance, that the latter approved her khadi sari.

Her song, "I Bow to India" is known everywhere, he says, and her gift for music exceeds even that for poetry; she had prepared her husband's song for performance by boys and girls at the 1919 congress. Since it could almost serve as a satyagrahis' anthem, Gandhi had it printed on the front page of *Young India,* on February 29, 1920.

On the same day, Gandhi's other weekly *Navajivan* published her essay-poem entitled "Bandhu" (Brother) which Gandhi described as a perfect poem. On March 30 he offered to interpret it to those readers of *Young India* who had been puzzled. (It was written in the somewhat enigmatic style of Rabindranath.) Time can be either a brother to us or an enemy—it is the latter when we are plunged over our heads in pleasures or in grief. The first part describes how much at peace she felt in Bolpur (the Tagore estate where Rabindranath set up Shantiniketan). Part 2 is about the opposite feelings that came from living in the city, in a house full of furniture, and with only a glimpse of the sky, framed in a window.

In *Young India* for March 24, 1920, Gandhi reports a speech Saraladevi made in Hindi at the ashram, on the banks of the river Sabarmati, on February 27, entitled "The Message of the Punjab." She described the Punjab as the holiest place in India; proud of the glory of the past that lies buried in the inexhaustible ruins of the Vedas. But now degenerate Punjabis value physical power over moral force. (She cited Herbert Spencer and his idea of Infinite and Eternal Energy, obviously a Western parallel to shakti.) The Punjabis are degenerate when they refuse to sign Gandhi's satyagraha pledge, and accept British violence without retaliation. At the end of her talk, just after sunset on the banks of the river, she sang her husband's song, "Never Lose heart."[50] Singing, composing, exhorting, against a background of the river and the sunset, Saraladevi cut a very different figure from Kasturba, and we should not underestimate the attraction of her gifts. Next to her, Kasturba was dull. On February 1, 1945, Gandhi wrote to Munnalal Shah, "Perhaps you do not know how many of my plans came to nothing because of Ba's limitations" (79:84).

Under Gandhi's inspiration, Sarla again took up spinning, and *Young India* often reported her activities. In May 1920 she and a Muslim woman were declared the heroines of the Khaddar movement, which was linked to the Khilafat movement. Gandhi quoted her letters often in *Young India;* describing how she had decided to wear khadi to the Khilafat Conference; and to wrap up her bedding inside a holdall, in the Indian style, when she traveled, instead of using a European trunk: "Whether to be smart and fashionable as of old, or to be simple and common only. I have at last chosen to be the latter. But it is taking time and trouble to assimilate the new method" (17:428). She says she has been getting women to take the vow of swadeshi.

On July 7, 1920, the joint secretaries of the Punjab branch of the Bharat Stri Mahamandal report in *Young India* on three meetings of women (one meeting attracted more than a thousand) all deeply interested in the way Saraladevi traced the causes of India's deep poverty. She herself wrote that the women were more impressed by her coarse but beautiful khadi sari than by her speech. She has been charged by them to open a shop where they could buy the like.

In 1921 she published a pamphlet, "At the Point of the Spindle." "I heard Mahatma Gandhi's call to the students of the Gujarat National College to give up their scholastic studies for a year and to take to spinning six hours a day, and I have read his appeal to Young Bengal. I wish to convey to you their full import as it has dawned on the heart of at least one of you—a child of Bengal. . . . It was on ashes of the spinning wheel that the foundation of the British Raj was laid" (3) The battery of the spinning wheel alone can bring about a bloodless moral revolution that will withstand England's doubly destructive—in both physical and moral ways—machine power (15).

She was a friend of Anasuyabehn Sarabhai, and Gandhi wrote to the latter on October 27, 1919: "Sarla's company is very endearing. She looks after me very well." And after his own break from her, he inquires from the Sarabhais about her health.

On February 9, 1920, to Narahari D. Parikh, talking about Dipak attending the ashram, Gandhi wrote that this was the third time she had sent her son away from her (he would be about thirteen). Her old mother was not pleased; nor the pandit, but he did not stand in her way. She wanted Dipak to become a scholar and a man of character. The ashram must arrange for him to learn Sanskrit and Bengali.

Saraladevi traveled together with Gandhi, both giving talks on swadeshi and swaraj and Khilafat. Sometimes Shaukat Ali accompanied them. There was some consciousness, on their part and their audience's, that their union was unusually or unconventionally close—she was in some sense his wife. A Bombay Secret Abstract of July 25, reports a speech by Gandhi in which he said that he took Saraladevi, rather than his literal wife, all over India, because she understood the principles of swadeshi better.

It seems clear that—whether consciously or not—Gandhi was tempted to take over, or marry to his own purposes, the dynamism of pre-1910 Bengal. He had done so in the matter of swadeshi, and he was tempted to do so in the matter of Saraladevi, the embodied Durga. He thought of Bengal as violent: "The atmosphere in Bengal has always been surcharged with violence which is the reason for the lesser dissemination of my ideas there" (64:346). Perhaps he felt he could conquer that violence, as embodied in a woman. He and she together would certainly have made an extraordinary political phenomenon. But their personal relationship was unstable.

On August 23, 1920 Mahadev Desai entered in his diary that seven or eight letters were received from Saraladevi during the Madras tour. "They indicate her suspicion about [name erased] her charge that Bapu was dazzled by him, and her complaint that Bapu's letters betray 'mental exhaustion.' She says that for Bapu's sake she had made an inordinate sacrifice. She put in one pan all the joys of life and pleasures of the world, and in the other, 'Bapu and his laws,' and committed the folly of choosing the latter." After this, Gandhi took to signing his letters to her the Law Giver, or L.G.[51]

Her relationship with Gandhi is worth studying because it was personal to a more striking degree than his other relationships. It was erotic, in the sense that word carries when applied to novels. The letters beween them that survive do not express the alliance of comrades—though that must have been a large part of what passed between them—but a love relationship.

It is surely no coincidence that both of them should have been devoted to the powers of war—often related to the powers of ardent love. Their ideas must have reinforced their mutual attraction. We are bound to wonder what might have happened between them if they had met before, instead of after, the torment of Gandhi's recruiting campaign, his illness, and his capitulation to the doctors. He had allowed himself to take milk only in order to work for India; and he had come up against his limitations as never before. He must have been more on guard than ever against temptation, including the lures of Eros. Without that recent warning, might he have embarked on the adventure of a relationship with a political heroine like Saraladevi? There are signs that he might.

Writing to her in spring, 1920, he more than once says he has dreamed of her, calls her the greatest shakti in India, says, had she been there, she would have dragged him from his bed to watch the sunrise, and so on. He dreams of her leaving her husband, and coming to him. (This leaving does not seem to mean breaking off their marriage, but merely taking a journey.) And whether or not sexual pleasure was consciously in question (later he said it was, for him) the relationship was erotic because she invited him to explore her personality.

On August 23, 1920, he wrote: "Your letters have your usual self. Some of them decidedly despondent and skeptical and suspicious" (18:191). She has complained about his companions (Narahari Parikh and Maganlal are mentioned) because they criticized Gandhi's intimacy with her. (Others who were disturbed were Mathuradas Trikumji, Devadas Gandhi, Mahadev Desai.) He replied that they were his superiors, because they were so jealous of his character, which was their ideal. They want to run no risks and they are right. "I would surrender all the world to deserve a love so pure and unselfish."

Turning to her, he wrote: "You should be proud of their jealousy and watchfulness. . . . You asked for a reward of your great surrender. Well, it is its own reward. With deep love, Your L. G." (18:193). In an earlier letter, he had said that she must enslave India by becoming India's slave in thought, word, and deed: she must get rid of her inertia and give her music to the nation.

He was obviously proud of this relationship, for a time. On August 10 he wrote to his old friend Kallenbach: "I have come in closest touch with a lady who often travels with me. Our relationship is indefinable. I call her my spiritual wife. . . . It was under her roof that I passed several months at Lahore in the Punjab" (18:130). But he was also troubled. To her, on August 24, he wrote: "Your letters have caused me distress. You do not like my sermons. And yet so long as you remain a schoolgirl, what should I do except give you sermons? . . . What is the reward of your having given years to acquiring perfection in piano playing? You give all for the cause you represent because you cannot do otherwise" (18:193). He asked her to do household work in her home—to become a complete woman.

After that there is a gap in the letters we have from him until December, when he wrote, on the eleventh, "I have certainly not betrayed any annoyance over your complex nature, but I have remarked on it. . . . I refuse to call an indefinable complexity a piece of art. All art yields to patient analysis and shows a unity of design behind the diversity on the canvas. You are hugging your defects even when they are pointed out by a friend in a friendly manner. I do not feel vexed but it makes my task of helping difficult. What art can there be in moods, in fits and starts?" (19:80). Simple natures are called so only because they are understandable and yield to treatment. And again, more yieldingly, and with a kind of metaphysical wit: "I love you more for loving me less for any hate you may see in me" (19:137).

What he refers to is the hatred that was expressed in his noncooperation campaign—the hatred of "I shook with rage"—which she had written to deplore. But what concerns both her and him more is her demand for reassurance as to her place with him, and the mysteries of her temperament.

Her stress on her own complexity reminds us of her Tagore heritage, and of contemporary developments in art. The mystery of art was not something Gandhi was sympathetic to—precisely because it was often, as in her case, an alternative to purposeful action.

Answering her reproaches, on December 14, 1920, he wrote, "My love for you is not a task. It is one of the keenest pleasures of my life" (19:107). But finally, on December 17 he wrote again in his new voice but bidding her farewell. He did not want to develop that new voice; he was closing the door that had opened before him.

> I have been analysing my love for you. I have reached a definition of spiritual wife. It is a partnership between two persons of the opposite sex where the physical is wholly absent. It is therefore possible between brother and sister, father and daughter. It is possible only between two brahmacharis in thought, word and deed. . . . For this special partnership to subsist, there must be complete coincidence, not from faith, but from knowledge. It is a meeting between two kindred spirits. (19:138)

Such people can never be physically wedded.

> Are you spiritual wife to me of that description? Have we that exquisite purity, that perfect coincidence, that perfect merging, that identity of ideals, the self-forgetfulness, that fixity of purpose, that trustfulness? For me I can answer plainly that it is only an aspiration. I am unworthy to have that companionship with you. I require in me an infinitely higher purity than I possess in thought. I am too physically attached to you to be worthy of enjoying that sacred association with you. By physical attachment, I here mean I am too much affected by your weaknesses (ibid).

But despite this last phrase, Gandhi said later that the physical attachment meant also sexual attraction.

They have sharp differences, and must accept something more like a brother-sister relationship. "This is the big letter I promised. With dearest love I still subscribe myself, Your L. G." (ibid).

She had had criticisms to make of him. As we saw, in 1920 she wrote to Gandhi that noncooperation was based on hatred, and that she felt less love for Gandhi, for the hatred he directed against others. Such a movement, she said, might be taken up by lesser men than he.

Later, after the break between them, she wrote about his description of a Rajput gathering, the Rajput Parishad of Vartej, where he had remarked that the volunteers carried swords, and the air was full of military swagger. The swords were not, she pointed out, the signs of violence but the mark of the Rajputs' dharma. Gandhi was imposing his dharma on theirs, critically (24:400). Here, and in another letter, she accused him of a Christo-Buddhist, as opposed to a Hindu, frame of mind. Hers was an Arya Samaj criticism, and by that time she and he were at odds. Gandhi published her letter, as from "a fair friend," in *Young India*.

He commented in his reply that she, and other highly educated people, were hostile to the charkha (24:401). She asked him to publish the whole of her letter (24:470). He wrote to Rajaji on August 24, 1924, that the fair friend was Saraladevi. "She wants to bombard me with more stuff, but I have refused to give further accommodation." The period of intimacy was over.

We have few photographs of Saraladevi—they make her appear a handsome and impressive woman—and (in English) few descriptions. In one of the latter, an American, Gertrude Emerson, described in some articles she wrote for *Asia* in 1922 meeting her at Shantiniketan, and taking a railway journey with her. Emerson says that the most prominent women to identify themselves with Gandhi were then Saraladevi, Sarojini Naidu, Anasuyabehn, and Basanti Devi, the wife of C. R. Das.[52]

On the journey, Saraladevi wore coarse black khadi and a scarf over her iron gray hair, and no rings or bangles, but the soles of her feet were hennaed in the traditional manner. She was spinning, and tried to persuade some Muslim women who got into their railway compartment to take up swadeshi. When they said a khadi sari must be hot and uncomfortable, she told them, "This is not the time to think of comfort."

Sharing her lunch, she told Gertrude Emerson of how she had broken caste tradition by combing the hair of her washerwoman's three children. She had to overcome feelings of pollution as she did so; and washed her hands afterwards like Lady Macbeth. When her Brahmin friends suspected what she had done, she had to confess, and noticed that they avoided taking food from her hands thereafter.

Emerson asked Sarojini Naidu whether there would be violence if Gandhi were jailed. When Naidu said yes, Emerson said that was not what Gandhi wanted, but Naidu replied: "Mahatma Gandhi is a great man, too great to understand the frailty of ordinary human nature. Mahatma Gandhi does not know what violence really means" (202). This was typical of the way Gandhi's political allies handled his "greatness," but Saraladevi came closer to him than they.

Gandhi often referred back to this relationship in a veiled way. In 1932 Mathuradas Trikumji wrote a play about divorce, taking up—we gather from Gandhi's letters—a liberal attitude toward that institution. Gandhi was not pleased, and asked his friend to imagine what would have happened if Gandhi had divorced Kasturba: with whom would he have then rushed into marriage? Gandhi does not say when such a remarriage was a possibility, but the only plausible time is in 1920, and the woman is Saraladevi. Gandhi's question would have extra point since Mathuradas was one of those who warned Gandhi against his feelings for Saraladevi at that time.

In 1936, when discussing birth control and marital experiment with Margaret Sanger, Gandhi brought up the long tradition of polygamy in India, which made it more vulnerable than the West to the new freedoms, which had proven dangerous enough there:

> Now I don't ask this question to put you in a corner. This is the argument I have with a woman with whom I almost fell. [Saraladevi approved of polygamy under certain circumstances.] It is so personal I did not put it into my autobiography. We had considered if there can be this spiritual companionship. . . . I came in contact with an illiterate woman. [That is, he married Kasturba.] Then I meet a woman with a broad, cultural education. Could we not develop a close contact, I said to myself? This was a plausible argument, and I nearly slipped. But I was saved, I awoke from my trance, I don't know how. For a time it seemed I had lost my anchor. I was saved by youngsters who warned me. I saw that if I was doomed, they also were doomed.

In other places he makes it clear that the "youngsters" included his son, Devdas, and his secretary, Mahadev Desai.

Before that, in the early 1920s, he wrote that he was once nearly lost "through placing too much confidence in my own self." On another occasion he was saved by an adulterous friend: the second was of course the time in England; the first must be his relation with Saraladevi. He said he had to be on guard against moha, always (23:430).

In 1933 he reflected that he had all but fallen a few years before, but had been saved by the thought of Kasturba, and that of Devdas, Mahadev, Mathuradas, and others, who leaned on him. "Their love chained [me] so tightly and strongly that I could not burst through the bond although the flesh was pulling hard enough to tear the chains to bits and rush into hell-fire" (53:229).

Finally, in 1947 he wrote in his diary of never having sought the company of a woman "with a view to satisfying my passions" with one exception (87:99). The singleness of the exception (since his encounters with prostitutes were always grouped together, and anyway he never went to them of his own accord) surely points to Saraladevi. And he spoke of his seeming triumph over sexual temptation in South Africa, saying that, by contrast, in the early days back in India he had had to battle fairly hard. That cannot be anyone but Saraladevi (88:101).

Gandhi cut himself off from his friend, but not completely. He wrote a note of introduction to a new journal, *Bharati,* which she proposed to edit from Lahore in March 1924. She had turned her attention back to spiritual matters, leaving her husband to study in the Himalayas. After Pandit Rambhuj died in 1923, Saraladevi took her son back to Calcutta.

Dipak remained in touch with Gandhi. In March 1926, Gandhi wrote to him, "If you are keen on military training, how can I stop you? Do as your mother says. My opinion in this regard differs from hers. I therefore do not want to confuse your mind." (We see there that Gandhi then took the nonviolent position, against even military training, and Saraladevi had again taken up that cause. They kept shifting. Neither is to be identified with one of these positions. Both are to be identified with the concern about those issues.)

She wrote to Gandhi occasionally, and obviously studied his activities. When he announced a fast in 1924, she wrote to him appealing to him not to, and talking sadly of his vicarious suffering and the Christian influence upon him (25:203, 209). In 1930 she founded a girls' school in Calcutta, Bharat Stri Shiksha Sadan. In 1935 she turned away from education as a major cause, toward spirituality, finding guidance in a guru called Bijoy Krishna Dev Sharma.

EIGHT

IN AND OUT OF JAIL

· 1921–1931 ·

In this decade, Gandhi was sent to jail for a sentence of six years, of which he served two, and then for another; and voluntarily withdrew from political life for more than one period. Yet he remained the leader of India and its figurehead, both within India, and in the outside world. His circle was enlarged by the addition of several Westerners, most notably Madeline Slade, who took the Indian name, Mira Behn. He wrote his two full-length books, the autobiography and *Satyagraha in South Africa.* And in 1930 he won international acclaim for leading the Salt March.

At the beginning of the decade, the wave of noncooperation that Gandhi directed was cresting throughout India. The British government's position was almost untenable; some of its leaders afterwards admitted that they had felt themselves within a hairbreadth of defeat, and some historians have agreed with them. They think that if Gandhi had persisted, the moderate nationalists in India would have allied themselves with the extremists under his leadership.

But Gandhi's feelings about what was happening were never as simply exultant as those of other nationalist leaders, because for him the nonviolent character of civil disobedience was always of first importance, and he did not feel secure about that. He would have succeeded only by allying himself to the violent. Afterwards he said he had been praying for defeat because of what he felt in the air. There had been so much violence that "I was actually and literally praying for defeat."[1]

His friends, like Rabindranath Tagore and Saraladevi Chaudhurani, had warned him about the hatred that was inspiring his followers in their action, and, as we know, he had acknowledged the truth of that. He had answered their warning with the declaration that he could disinfect that emotional violence; and continued his own "disciplined expression" of political hatred. But of course he was not blithely indifferent to that danger.

However, there was more to the nationalist movement than civil disobedience, and 1921 was the annus mirabilis of the spread of spinning and khadi, and of the theory of nonviolence. Lala Lajpat Rai and C. R. Das, and Motilal Nehru and Abul Kalam Azad, became converts to these doctrines—or at least these practices—at that time. (There was always a difference between those who believed in the philosophy of satyagraha, for whom its laws were absolute, and those who employed its techniques as long as they were successful.)

Though Gandhi wrote consistently in warning against anarchy and destructiveness, it is easy to detect a note of New Age exhilaration in his comments on the dynamism and the sheer mass of the movement, like this of December 1921: "Freedom is to be wooed only inside prison walls and sometimes on the gallows, never in the council chambers, courts, or the schoolroom . . . she builds her temples in jails or on inaccessible heights." He says he would have loved to see Motilal and Jawarhalal Nehru handcuffed together and made to walk to prison (22:10). His "loved to" expresses not malicious glee but idealistic enthusiasm; the conflict between Gandhi's usage and ours is typical of many other differences.

The congress marquee that year was made of khadi and decorated by artists from Shantiniketan; another sign of the New Age character of this nationalism. On January 26, 1922, Gandhi wrote: "India is slowly getting to be a holy land, aye, a purified country" (22:271). And in later years, for instance, early 1927, he looked back to 1921 as a period of enthusiasm when everyone was eager for sacrifice and miracles were happening—"the heroic days when people were excited about khadi."

He planned a satyagraha campaign in Bardoli. But on February 4, 1922, only a few days before that campaign was to begin, a procession of civil resisters at Chauri Chaura (in Gorakhpur, in the United Provinces, eight hundred miles from Bardoli) after coming into conflict with the authorities, surrounded a police station, killed twenty-one policemen, and set fire to their bodies. They had been chanting Gandhi's name as a slogan, considering themselves part of his movement, and he felt responsible for what they did. His teaching had aroused the people, excited them to public emotion, incited them to public action, and so he was responsible for what they did, even when that went against his explicit instructions.

On February 8, he wrote that, for the third time, he had received a shock on the very eve of mass civil disobedience, and so had canceled the campaign, to the dismay of his allies and followers. They said that this retreat would disgrace India before the world (22:377). But Gandhi wrote to Nehru on February 19: "I assure you that if the thing had not been suspended, we would have been leading not a nonviolent struggle, but essentially a violent struggle. It is undoubtedly true that nonviolence is spreading like the scent of the otto of roses throughout the length and breadth of the land, but the foetid smell of violence is still powerful, and it would be unwise to ignore or underrate it. The cause will prosper by the retreat."[2]

Gandhi obviously wanted to escape from the position that made him responsible for the killing of others, in the future as well as the past, and he needed to find a median between that desire for innocence and his contrary vocation and ambition, to be politically effective. On March 2, he declared that he hated his command of a huge majority (which was what brought him his responsibility). He would feel safer, morally, without it. "I have always been in a minority . . . [But] I have begun to wonder if I am not unconsciously allowing myself to be 'exploited.' I confess that I have a dread of it as I never had before. My only safety lies in my shamelessness. I have warned my friends of the commitee [the All-India Congress Committee] that I am incorrigible. I shall continue to confess blunders each time that the people commit them" (22:501).

The feeling in the country was of course very bitter, amongst Anglo-Indians as well as nationalists. When the government prosecuted those held responsible for the killings at Chauri Chaura, 172 were condemned to death—though finally only 19 suffered that penalty.

Two of the people Gandhi most needed to explain himself to were the Nehru father and son. To Jawarharlal he wrote: "I see that all of you are terribly cut up over the resolution of the Working Committee [to cancel the campaign]. I sympathize with you, and my heart goes out to Father" (22:435). As usual, Gandhi treated his own decisions, and even his emotions, as irrevocable facts, and looked sympathetically on the problems they created for others—whose decisions and emotions were *not* given facts, but struggling, fluctuating, tendencies.

"Above all, whatever you do, don't be disgusted with the spinning wheel," he continued to Nehru. "You and I have reason to get disgusted with ourselves for having done many things and having believed many things, but we shall never have the slightest cause for regret that we have pinned our faith to the spinning wheel or that we have spun so much good yarn per day in the name of the motherland" (22:437).

It was a general habit with Nehru's friends to address him as a man only reluctantly, or only half, a politician. When they said "you and I" most of them allied themselves with him as men of sensibility, of soul, of poetry. Gandhi named him a spinner, a New Ager, and it seems likely that the spinning wheel was—in those early years—the key to, the sign of, the hope for, a Gandhian Nehru. Not many politicians did like to spin—certainly not Motilal Nehru—and that decidedly feminine aptitude in Jawaharlal was the key to Gandhi's influence over him and ultimately to Gandhi's nomination of him as his heir. (In fact, of course, Jawaharlal became his father's heir after all, but that was not predetermined in 1922.)

In a letter from Gandhi to Dr. Ansari, August 1927, he talks about Motilal in the context of persuading Ansari to accept the presidency of congress. (The letter is a masterpiece of persuasive prose.) When congress comes to power, he says, "The law, diplomacy, military and the rest, we shall leave to Motilalji and company; and if Panditji thinks that Shaukat Ali would be good company, he may throw at him the military departments" (34:304–5). Gandhi speaks in terms of "you and I," who are not interested in power, as those others are. This does not make insincere Gandhi's professions of esteem and friendship for Motilal, but it reveals the distance and difference ever-present between them. He once referred to Motilal as being as much at home in the intricate paths of diplomacy as Gandhi was with the charkha (38:107).

With the end of civil disobedience, the immediate danger to the government was over, and it was free to act. On March 10, 1922, Gandhi was arrested, and was charged the next day with writing three inflammatory and disaffected articles that appeared in *Young India*. A week later he was tried in Ahmedabad, and, though treated very courteously by the judge, committed to six years in jail. The indictment was headed, "Imperator v. Mr. M. K. Gandhi." Judge Broomfield bowed to the prisoner before him, as to his moral superior; he said Gandhi's was a saintly life; but the law was no respecter of saints. A judge had to administer a system, although his sympathies might be naive. Broomfield had worked in India since 1905, and liked Indians, but he was part of the administrative system.

Gandhi's speech in his own behalf remarkably combined—along the same lines as earlier writings—his two main statements about his political leadership. He acknowledged more than legal guilt: "Thinking over these [*sic*] deeply and sleeping over them night after night, it is impossible to dissociate myself from the diabolical crimes of Chauri Chaura, or the mad outrages in Bombay and Madras. . . . I knew that I was playing with fire" (23:114, 115).

But on the other hand:

> I would still do the same. . . . I had either to submit to a system which I considered had done irreparable harm to my country, or incur the risk of the mad fury of my people bursting forth when they understood the truth from my lips. . . . I am, therefore, here to submit not to a light penalty but to the highest penalty. I do not ask for mercy. . . . To preach disaffection towards the existing system of Government has become almost a passion with me. . . . By the time I have finished my statement, you will, perhaps, have a glimpse of what is raging within my breast to run this maddest of risk a sane man can run. (23:114–15)

What is raging within his breast is what shook him with rage before.

The Revolutionary

And besides the British government, there were Indian revolutionaries he had to explain himself to. Gandhi was opposed by a group of "working-class militants" in public debate, from 1921 on, according to Manmathnath Gupta. The latter's friend, Sachindranath Sanyal, who had been released in 1918 after confinement for taking part in a Bengal conspiracy, wrote to Gandhi, and Gandhi published the letter (signed "Revolutionary") and his reply in *Young India* on February 12, 1925.

Sanyal had described Gandhi's idea as "an imperfect mixture of Tolstoyism and Buddhism and not a chemical mixture of East and West. You adopted the Western method of Congress and Conferences and tried to persuade the whole nation to accept the spirit of ahimsa, irrespective of *desh, dal,* and *patra* like Tolstoy, but which was a matter of individual *sadhana* [method] with Indians" (26:137).

Desh, dal, and *patra* mean place, time, and person. Thus what the revolutionary points to as Western and Tolstoyan in Gandhi's doctrine is its universal applicability, its overriding of the Hindu patterns of thought, which allot a different dharma to each social group. The same point was to be made about the Tolstoy-Gandhi doctrine of bread-labor, later. This Western universalism can be seen, from a Hindu point of view, as a kind of potential radicalism. (Of course it becomes truly radical only when it is taken seriously by an activist like Gandhi or Tolstoy.)

It is an insistence on the "one thing needful," which overrides, for instance, the *varnashrama* doctrine that at different stages of a man's life different duties impinge on him. From a Western point of view, of course, this moral radicalism is merely natural. It belongs to conservatives as much as to radicals, and the difference between them lies all in the way they apply it. But using a world-historical perspective, we can see that the Western view is typical of the modern world, which is characterized, comparatively speaking, by a sort of existentialism—the assertion of self-determination, or self-creation—the assertion therefore of permanent change, the constant social evolution that alone makes possible self-determination.

But some young men, Sanyal's letter continues, dare to go against Gandhi's wishes: "These are the Indian revolutionaries. They have now decided to remain silent no more and therefore they request you to retire from the political field or else to direct the political movement in a way so that it may be a help and not a hindrance to the revolutionary movement" (26:138). Sanyal claimed that the revolutionaries had saved Indians from their fear of death.

Gandhi replied that if he were convinced that India wanted a bloody revolution he would indeed retire, for he would have no part of that (26:140). Later he said that the revolutionaries' sacrifice, nobility and love, though genuine, were not only a waste of effort, but "do and have done more harm to the country than any other activity" (26:486). They were ruining India's tradition. For though India had had armies and warfare, militarism was never the normal course of Indian life. "The masses, unlike those of Europe, were untouched by the warlike spirits" (26:488).

In another letter, the revolutionary [Gupta] denied this, saying that his comrades "are entering villages, and have been successful everywhere. Can you not believe that they, the sons of Shivaji, Pratap, and Ranjit [past leaders of revolt] can appreciate our sentiments with more readiness and depth than anything else? Don't you think that armed and conspired resistance against something satanic and ignoble is infinitely more befitting [Indians]?" (26:490).

In reply, Gandhi relied in effect on the doctrine of castes again: "Are we all descendants of these heroes [Shivaji, Pratap, Ranjit] in the sense in which the writer intends it? We are their countrymen, but their descendants are the military classes." The three men named were heroes of Maharashtra, Rajasthan, and the Punjab respectively.

It is clear that Gandhi was uneasy in this area of dispute. For how, if India was divided in this way, could he the nonviolent bania speak for the military classes? He was not a revolutionary in the sense they were, since he was a New Ager. He was—as usual—soon frank about his difficulty. Sanyal asked what Gandhi thought about Washington, Garibaldi, Lenin, Kemal Pasha, and de Valera, the heroes of nationalist revolution. "This is a hard or rather awkward question. . . . It is highly likely that, had I lived as their contemporary and in the respective countries, I would have called every one of them a misguided patriot" (26:491). He took refuge, as Tolstoy did, in a denial of historicism. Even if Indians had always had been warlike, that was no reason why they should go on being so. "I positively refuse to judge men from the scanty material furnished to us by history." More fully, he said: "As it is, I must not judge them [the heroes of violent revolution]. I disbelieve history so far as details of acts of heroes are concerned. I accept broad facts of history and draw my own lessons for my conduct. I do not want to repeat it insofar as the broad facts contradict the highest laws of life."[3] Those highest laws are the ones recognized by the New Age.

In response to the question. "Will your *swarajya* government keep armies?" he replied, "Alas, in my swaraj of today there is room for soldiers. . . . I have not the capacity for preaching universal nonviolence to the country. I preach therefore nonviolence restricted strictly to the purpose of winning our freedom" (114). He suffers this incapacity because: "I have yet anger within me, I have yet the *divait bhava* [duality] in me."

It is also worth noting that on March l, 1927, Gandhi went to call on another revolutionary, V. R. Savarkar, the Hindu-nationalist, who was then living in exile in Ratnagiri. (He had been released from his jail in the Andaman Islands.) Savarkar represented another kind of revolution, in some sense right wing or communalist. Gandhi said his visit expressed his regard for Savarkar, as a man who loved the truth and would lay down his life for it; and praised him for having seen before Gandhi did the need for Indians to resist the British Empire. He offered to find two or three days to come again, so that they two could discuss national issues together, but the other man declined, saying that they could correspond instead.

There was no public controversy between these two in the 1920s; their debate had taken place in London in 1906. But Savarkar attacked Gandhi severely in print (in the newspaper *Shraddhanand*) from the Hindu nationalist point of view, and it was to be revolutionaries of his group who would finally kill Gandhi. This meeting occurred just about halfway between their first meeting in London, and Gandhi's assassination in 1948.

The Ashram

Gandhi was released after serving only two years of his six-year sentence because he fell sick with appendicitis. He was operated on by a British prison doctor, Colonel Maddock, and as usual developed a personal friendship with him and with the doctor's wife. He was not, however, happy about having the operation. He described his disease as being the result of infirmity of thought and mind; but so was the cure. "If I was absolutely free of egotism, I would have resigned myself to the inevitable; but I wanted to live in the present body."[4]

It was also a failure that he could not cure himself by nature cure. He acknowledged the value of Western diagnoses, but sought to avoid the surgery or drug-therapy associated with them (23:372). He wrote to a fellow enthusiast at the ashram, "This breakdown in the application of Nature-cure is a tragedy of my life. Not that I have lost faith in it, but I have lost confidence in myself" (23:262).

He did a lot of reading in jail, and some thinking about literature and art, still along the lines of Tolstoy. One of the few books of literary criticism we know that Gandhi read—and the only one he refers to with enthusiasm—was Upton Sinclair's *Mammonart* of 1924. This is an echo of Tolstoy's *What Is Art?*, though it also recalls such New Age writers as Shaw and Wells. They are all enemies of "Art for art's sake."

Religious writers, Gandhi said, had the greatest hold on mankind. "They have made a greater impression on me," than men of letters like Mark Twain or Emerson. On November 13, 1924, he wrote, "Jesus was to my mind a supreme artist, because he saw and expressed Truth. . . . True art takes note not merely of form but also of what lies beyond. . . . True art must be the evidence of the happiness, contentment and purity of its authors."[5]

He copied out some of Gretchen's lines from a translation of Goethe's *Faust*:

> My poor sick brain is crazed with pain
> And my poor sick heart is torn in twain. (25:77)

He evidently found that those lines expressed feelings of his own, which reminds us of the contrast between his dry humor and his deeper feelings.

He also read Sir John Woodroffe's books on Tantric Hinduism, including *Shakti and Shakta*. It is likely that Gandhi's interest in that subject was awakened by his relations with Saraladevi Chaudhurani, and it is typical that he should study that aspect of Indian culture as it was presented in an English book. Woodroffe was a judge in Bengal, where the *shastras* communities were to be found. He took the pen name of Arthur Avalon, which was practically an announcement of occult sympathies, and so an act of New Age allegiance. Woodroffe compared the shastas with the Dionysian mysteries.

Tantra, as Woodroffe expounds it, is linked to magic, and to goddess worship; but also to worship by means of meat, wine, and sex—the opposite of the ascetic traditions. At the same time it is linked to Aryan racism, and carries the usual fear of decadence. Woman is deified and adored as is *parashakti*. Thus tantrism is all about power, bodily, spiritual, and sexual. Woodroffe's works were published by the Theosophical Press at Adyar.

Gandhi does not tell us that he was convinced by Woodroffe, much less that he himself ever practiced a kind of Tantrism, but nevertheless his late practices were a kind of sexual experiment (judged by the standards of Hindu asceticism) in the search for power.

After his time in jail and his convalescence, Gandhi retreated to the ashram. As Judith Brown says in *Gandhi and Civil Disobedience*, in the 1920s Gandhi seemed a spent force politically, and he seemed to turn inward, referring increasingly often to his "inner voice," and fasting more often. This was not true of 1929–31, when he resumed national leadership, but the decade began with the dramatic reversal after Chauri Chaura, when Gandhi canceled the civil disobedience movement, and continued with the handing over of congress to his Swarajist opponents. He called on his followers to accept political impotence, to devote themselves to spinning and other "constructive work," and he himself retired to the ashram.

He repeatedly named the latter as his "best work." He said it was his best and only creation, and the world would judge him by it. He called it his creation or his body. It was, in all its imperfections, the material manifestation of his spirit, and by it he was to be judged. His speeches and even his ideas showed what he claimed to be; the ashram showed what he was.

He also said that the ashram atmosphere was not favorable for philosophical studies, but it was for manual work. We recognize his familiar distrust of the intellect: "I am convinced that we have had an overdose of philosophical and political studies" (23:307).

The permanent core of the ashram were people who had lived with Gandhi in South Africa, and had come back to India with him. Many of them were there as members of family groups, bringing up children, getting them married, and so on. (People who newly joined the ashram, on the other hand, were asked to take a vow of celibacy, though this was not enforced in any uniform way.)

The members of this core were not intellectuals, nor politically active, nor spiritual seekers of a very developed kind—though there were such people there too. The ashram was not a monastery. Newcomers often remarked on how undisciplined the community was; because it was made up of such disparate types, and because Gandhi's attention was so often distracted from it. When Vinoba Bhave began his ashram at Wardha, it was much more monastic.

As noted, Gandhi was sometimes a severe disciplinarian, both with individuals, and in his public pronouncements. But his remarks of that kind should be read in the context of ashram life. Partly just because of his restless curiosity and vitality, and partly because of his warmth of personality and charm, the severity was less oppressive in the long run—though no less wounding at the moment—than it reads. There was a lot of interplay between him and individual members, some of whom felt free to challenge him. Others, of course, revered him breathlessly.

Narayan Desai, the son of Mahadev Desai, has described the ashram as it was when he was a child there, in his *Blessed Was It to Be Young—with Gandhi*, (Bombay: Bharatiya Vidya Bhavan, 1967, 1988). His father, Gandhi's secretary, will be described more at length in the next section. Though so young, Narayan was well placed to register the force of the leader's personality. The little boy called Gandhi Bapu, Father, and his literal father Kaka, or uncle; he says that the former was strong like the sun, the latter mild like the moon. (53)

Narayan Desai tells us of striking figures at the ashram, like Premabehn Kantak, who acted as teacher to the children, and tried to impose a rather severe discipline on them. (Gandhi told her, "You are by nature harsh, curt, reserved" [47:33].) There was also the hanger on, Ismailbhai, a CID spy, who bribed the children with sweets to tell him what the adults said to each other.[6] There was Bhansali, a former professor of French, who took a vow of twelve years' silence, though Gandhi made him speak God's name. Bhansali is supposed to have sewn up his lips in penance for having cried out when someone trod on him as he slept. He performed great feats of asceticism, of the kind attributed to sages in the epics. He rolled on cactuses till he was covered with thorns, and fasted for sixty-three days in protest against an act of rape (for the first fifteen of those days he kept walking).

Premabehn deserves our attention because she described and analyzed her relationship with Gandhi. She came from a middle-class family in a small town in Maharashtra, the only daughter, with four brothers, and emotionally close to her father, Sudhir Kakar tells us. She heard Gandhi speak at her college in Poona; and went to touch his feet, or his knee, since his feet were folded beneath him. He started and returned her greeting. "If he but knew that by touching him my heart had blossomed forth with incomparable pride! With that pure touch an electric current ran through my body and I walked home lost in a world of bliss."[7]

As she grew older she quarreled with her father, and found herself repelled by the idea of marriage. She wanted an extraordinary life. At the age of twenty-three she went to Gandhi, and told him she wanted to work with him and do something tremendous. As he usually did, he discouraged such ambition, but gently enough to encourage her also. Kakar tells us she dreamed that she was a girl in Gandhi's lap—sweet milk flowed from his breast, she was soaked in it, and woke in alarm. Premabehn half-managed the ashram, in her rather severe style, during his absence, and wrote Gandhi long letters when he was in jail. In 1939 she set up an ashram of her own in Maharashtra. After Gandhi's death she drifted back to the tutelage of yogis and mystics—rather like Saraladevi.

Some of the seekers after spiritual revelation came and went between Gandhi and more traditional saints and sages and experimentalists in a different style, like Arabindo. (For a time, Harilal was an Arabindo-chela.) These included trusted familiars who worked at Gandhi's practical enterprises. For instance, Kaka Kalelkar, the schoolteacher, and Jamnalal Bajaj, the businessman, were both interested in meeting holy men; and Gandhi did not forbid it. Jamnalal had spent some time with Ramana Maharishi; and Gandhi recommended that Kalelkar do the same, but he decided, "One master is enough for me."[8]

As for himself, Gandhi said later that friends had recommended to him taking Ramana Maharishi, Arabindo, or Sahabji Maharaj of Agra, as his guru. It does not seem that he ever seriously entertained the idea of joining any one of them as their chela (88:70).

Bajaj came of a wealthy and pious Marwari family. He had fallen under Gandhi's spell by the end of 1915, and asked Gandhi to adopt him in 1920. He represented one type of those who were attracted to the Mahatma, and required fostering from him.

There were of course non-Indians in the ashram, who stayed for varying lengths of time, and their accounts of the ashram are especially illuminating. Reginald Reynolds, who went out to India in 1929 to "make amends for all the degradation that Indians had suffered from the British," nevertheless found "some rather bogus people" in the ashram. As the word *bogus* suggests, Reynolds brought the sensibility of 1920s England to his experience. When the Ashramites asked him which civilization he preferred, he answered, "Western, decidedly," and noted that they looked quite hurt.[9]

Gandhi himself Reynolds first found to look very old, but otherwise ordinary. "I saw him at first as a kindly, practical, sensible, unemotional person of devastating sincerity; but I knew there must be more than that about him and hoped that time would disclose the rest" (15). Later he wrote in his journal that Gandhi seemed to him as remote as a great Catholic saint, because with his views on "sex and other sociological questions, I personally cannot agree." (48) Reynolds was most concerned with the ecological side of Gandhi's work.

The Calling of Disciples

The most significant group among Gandhi's contemporaries to emerge during this period were his close disciples. The calling of followers was a large part of his work, especially in his first few years in India, and their relations with him, their typology, and the other callings they followed *as* his disciples, together constitute an interpretive context for him in our minds. Though he had had both friends and followers in South Africa, Gandhi's first six years in India included a rather different calling of other, distinctly younger men, to help him in his work. The friends of earlier days had been mostly Englishmen or Europeans, and so were somewhat independent, while the Indian followers of those years seem to have been comparatively submissive or inarticulate.

The calling of Prasad and Patel has already been mentioned. In Gandhi's dealings with such men, moreover, and with Nehru and Rajaji, there was an element of alliance. Gandhi told Mahadev Desai that when Patel came the two of them would discuss a fast he was proposing to start "politically." He explained that this was because, "My relations with Vallabhbhai are not on a religious basis, as they are with you."[10] Men like Patel were figures of independent political power, leaders themselves. Their relation with Gandhi was not an alliance of equals, and they were in important ways his followers too. But the phenomenon of "calling" is best studied in other types.

First come those who were so close to him to him as to be like his arms or legs. Mahadev Desai was of an artistic-poetic type, physically delicate and charming, sympathetic and responsive, and always in danger of being seduced by new ideas or personalities. (Erikson goes into more detail on the matter of seduction in the literal sense.[11]) He was a naive mind, more completely naive than Gandhi himself—though certainly not in the depreciatory sense simple-minded. He became Gandhi's secretary, and wanted to become his Boswell, having strong feelings for literature. We find Gandhi reproving this ambition in 1921: "If extensive notes on Johnson's talks were taken, they have conferred on the world no incomparable benefit that I know of. We do not at all look at this matter merely from the point of view of literature" (20:501). Desai became Gandhi's favorite son, replacing Harilal.

He was chosen by Gandhi in 1917 in Ahmedabad, where he had been a lawyer and inspector of coöperatives. Not being very successful at the law, he had taken to collecting folk songs and examples of the dialect of the peasants of his district. Gandhi wrote to him: "I have found in you the young man I have been searching for these two years. I have spoken like this to only three people before—to Mr Polak, Miss Schlesin and Shri Maganlal. Leave everything else and come to me. But go to Hyderabad and enjoy yourself for a year, and the moment you feel you are losing yourself, come and join me."[12] This is Desai's account of the letter, given to his friend Parikh, who wrote a biography after Desai's death. Desai added that he had felt tired of life, but now (a day or two after hearing from Gandhi) everything seemed worthwhile. Desai's wife, on the other hand, sometimes felt herself deserted; and Gandhi was often hard on Mahadev himself. But it seems clear that on the whole the latter was reassured by the discipline and never deeply doubted that he had found his vocation.

Mahadev wrote in Gandhi's style, and could tell people what Gandhi would say in reply to no matter what question. (On the other hand, Erikson complains that Mahadev falsified Gandhi's language, subduing its variety and subtlety.)[13] Taking notes, he could run ahead and complete a sentence before Gandhi himself could. He made sense out of Gandhi's spoken remarks, when they rambled or took shortcuts. People said, "We will know what he said when we get Mahadev's notes."[14]

Gandhi scolded Desai for being so easily seduced (in the metaphorical sense). "You are extremely pliant, and this I point out not as a merit in you, but as a defect. You succumb completely to the atmosphere around you. You do not display the mettle to resist and rise above a debasing environment. . . . You are like a painter who cannot help depicting obscenity in his portrait, if he chanced to see an indecent scene."[15]

Pyarelal, who joined Gandhi as another secretary, tells us that it was as a high-school boy that he first heard of Gandhi, in a speech Gokhale made in Bradlaugh Hall in Lahore, after his return from South Africa. He says he was more struck by the factual news, that Gandhi's wife and sons were going to jail for their beliefs, than he was by the impassioned eloquence of Lajpat Rai, who spoke at the same meeting. Six years later, when Pyarelal was a student at Government College, came the news of the Amritsar Massacre, and he heard Gandhi and two other nationalist leaders speak, and again found the former quieter but more effective. "I had found my Master. Thereafter I was his man."[16] As such phrasing suggests, Pyarelal saw Gandhi as a Kipling hero—with certain radical changes. *Man* and the attributes formed from it, *master* and *soldier* and *epic,* were key terms for him.

In other words, Pyarelal affected a tougher and heartier tone than Mahadev; but Romain Rolland recorded a conversation with him, during Gandhi's visit to Villeneuve, which makes it appear that Pyarelal felt himself to be quite the reverse of tough and hearty. He spent a lot of time sunk in his own unhappiness, convinced of his own unattractiveness and ineffectiveness. Gandhi remarked that Pyarelal had an "inferiority complex," in a letter of October 26, 1940; he thought that other people despised him (UC). Pyarelal needed a lot of attention from friends to keep him on an even psychic keel.[17] Later we shall see how much effort this demanded from Gandhi.

In December 1930 Gandhi wrote Narandas Gandhi that when he and Pyarelal were together in jail, it was like tethering a goat near to a wolf. "A goat tied in front of a wolf will grow thinner every day even if you feed it on the finest grass. . . . I blame myself a good deal for what used to be" (44:371). Presumably he means that Pyarelal had been worked beyond his capacity.

Pyarelal has described how Gandhi trained him in matters of physical and intellectual service. Gandhi warned his secretaries against overstatement by having them read critically Milton's exaggerated praise of freedom in *Areopagitica*. (Gandhi used to deplore the idea of studying freedom in English books, instead of practicing it in Indian reality.) He and his fellow secretaries also learned practical skills, like how to fetch and carry food and drink, and how to find out addresses from Bradshaw and the *Posts and Telegraphs Guide*. They had to do these things in no slapdash way, but with as much efficiency as they would if they were serving British officers or officials.

Above all, there was always, with Gandhi, a great deal of humor and charm in the interplay of personalities, along with the seriousness and severity. Gandhi disapproved of "the tea habit," but would on occasion fetch a tray from a station cafe to the train for his secretaries while they slept.[18]

Amongst the politicians, pride of place may be given to Jawaharlal Nehru, on the grounds of his subsequent eminence, though not on the grounds of any greater affinity with or understanding of the Mahatma. In 1919, as Gandhi rose to national fame, Nehru was thirty years old, the youngest of the four who were to be considered Gandhi's principal lieutenants and possible political heirs: the other three being Rajendra Prasad, Vallabhbhai Patel, and Chakravarty Rajagopalachari (usually called Rajaji). Nehru was also at that time the only one of the four with no satyagraha experience. Prasad had been thirty three years old as a satyagrahi in Champaran, Patel was forty-three as organizer of the Kheda campaign, and Rajaji was forty during the Rowlatt satyagraha. Although we may say that none of the four was fully in accord with their leader, it was surely Nehru who was furthest from him, intellectually as well as temperamentally.

The Nehrus

Jawaharlal was the son of one of India's most brilliant lawyers, a self-made man and brash exponent of English life-styles, who designed his promising son's education in order to make him a national leader. Motilal Nehru drove to the law courts with liveried servants behind a fine pair of horses, and lived in a house equipped with modern English comforts, including wine and cigars.

He was a kingly man, with a fierce temper and a hearty laugh. Jawaharlal seems to have loved his father fairly steadily, but he felt the pressure of a powerful will upon him. "I admired Father tremendously. He seemed to me the embodiment of strength and courage."[19] But he also feared him.

B. R. Nanda described the schoolboy Motilal thus. "Athletic, fond of outdoor sports, particularly wrestling, brimming over with an insatiable curiosity and zest for life . . . his quick wits and high spirits landed him in many an escapade, from which he was extricated by Principal Harrison and his British colleagues, who conceived a strong liking for the intelligent, lively, and restless Kashmiri youth."[20] This is the type of Sheikh Mehtab, in more richly endowed form—so Gandhi found himself facing a familiar antagonist in his struggle to attach Jawaharlal to himself. (When the latter showed Gandhi a photograph of Motilal without a moustache, so that the hard lines of the mouth were visible, Gandhi said, "Now I see what I have to fight.")

Motilal attended a meeting of congress in 1888, and was a delegate in 1889. In 1896 he became an advocate in the Allahabad Court, and in 1909 won the right to plead before the privy council, the highest court in the empire. In his early forties (i.e., before Gandhi's return to India) his income, which derived mostly from property cases, was counted in five figures of rupees. He lived in the Civil Lines, with the English and the Eurasians. In 1900 he moved to another house, called Anand Bhavan, which became famous for its luxury. There his life was thoroughly anglicized, or westernized. In 1904 he imported a motor car, and bought himself a Lancia in Italy in 1909. But the family life retained some traditional aspects. In Anand Bhavan the women were deeply religious, Nanda says, though the men were lightheartedly agnostic.

The life there blended the patriarchal with the modern. When too old for the sport himself Motilal set his servants to wrestling, and shouted to encourage them (11). Jawaharlal found his father generous, his mother gentle; he admits that he himself played his father's role toward his mother. He was the prince and heir apparent of the palace. He was, like a literal prince, weighed on his birthdays, and his weight in grain given to the poor. He had of course every advantage, educationally. He had a Theosophist tutor between 1902 and 1904. (Motilal was initiated into the society by Madame Blavatsky, his son by Mrs. Besant.) Then in 1905 Jawaharlal was entered at Harrow in 1905, and from there went to Cambridge.

Jawaharlal was the instrument of his father's will, though at the same time his own willpower was cultivated. According to his biographer, the male heir of a Hindu family is often "a little idol adored by grandparents, uncles, aunts, and sisters; his wayward will is a law unto itself."[21] Except of course when it crossed the will of such a father as Motilal.

We are bound to guess that the young man's attraction to Gandhi was in part a rebellion against his father. In 1919 Jawaharlal had joined Gandhi's Satyagraha Sabha; on July 5, 1920, Motilal wrote him, "So far as your following the request of Gandhiji is concerned, there is nothing to be said. That is more or less a matter of sentiment of a kind which does not enter into my composition."[22] Motilal's tone was stiff, but he soon came to see the need to be flexible, if he was not to lose his son.

For Jawaharlal to choose Gandhi was to refuse his patrimony of luxury and worldliness. This became true in a literal sense. When Motilal followed his son into Gandhi's camp, everything in the Anand Bhavan life-style had to change—cars, clothes, food and drink, from Englishness to Indianness, from modernity to tradition, from splendor to simplicity. Swadeshi was more of a revolution for them than for anyone, and their bonfire of foreign cloth must have been one of the biggest. Gandhi remarked afterwards that their change did not last long.

Even Motilal's legal practice had to go. According to his daughter, Krishna Nehru Hutheesing, he said to Gandhi: "You have taken my son; let me keep my practice." But Gandhi replied, "No. I want you and every member of your family."[23] And Motilal was, like his son, able to appreciate that answer, that sense of style. (Jawaharlal spoke of Gandhi on one occasion being in his "best dictatorial vein. He was humble but also clear-cut and hard as a diamond."[24]) There can be no doubt, however, that there was at first a struggle between father and son. Going to Calcutta by train, Motilal had been used to take a whole first-class compartment to himself; when one day he saw his son traveling third class on the same train, he said to Rajendra Prasad, with tears standing in his eyes, "Look at this boy. . . . This is a time when he should be enjoying himself but he has given up everything and has become a sadhu."[25]

The son was rebelling against his father ideologically or religiously. Motilal is supposed to have said to Gandhi, "I don't believe in your spirituality, and am not going to believe in God, at least in this life."[26] Jawaharlal was not a "man of religion," to use his own terms, but he was an idealist, and found ordinary politics and legal practice sordid, so he turned to Gandhi in relief.

He said, "I was simply bowled over by Gandhi, straight off. . . . [He] was like a powerful current of fresh air."[27] He wrote to his father from jail in 1922 that he shuddered to think what he had been becoming before the Noncooperation campaign: the uninspiring conversation of the Bar Library, the sordid side of human nature. "We remain in the ruts and the valleys, incapable almost of looking up towards the mountain tops" (90).

In the long run, however, Jawaharlal was to follow his father in such matters, though not without some continuing loyalty to Gandhi. In a letter to the latter in 1933, about Gandhi's crusade for the Harijans, he begins, "Not being a man of religion, my interest is largely confined to the social aspect and to the wider issues involved" (53:505). And when India won her freedom, Nehru guided it in directions quite opposite to Gandhi's; a personal and political development that had tragic significance, for Indians and others who ponder this story.

I hope my readers will not find it frivolous of me to ask them to think for a moment of the end of Kipling's *Kim*, when the gifted and charming hero and his Holy One come to the parting of their ways. The novelist has made us believe in a strong personal affection between the two, and also in a true reverence on Kim's side. We believe this enough for the fictional image to stand for, or stand with, historical examples of such deep reverence—even Nehru's for his Mahatma. But in the final analysis, for all his wisdom, the Lama is a Dostoyevskian idiot, in his ignorance of the world; and Kim is called to deal with worldly realities. For Nehru, Gandhi's political and cultural philosophy was equally foolish. The younger man's protracted and recurrent farewell to his mentor—starting with the radio eulogy after the assassination—deserves to be bracketed with the last pages of *Kim* permanently, so that the two may amplify each other.

In the letter last quoted, Nehru continues that his jail solitude and the sight of the Himalayas from jail have driven him in upon himself, "and I have grown a little contemplative, in defiance of heredity and family tradition and personal habit! But that is a thin veneer which I am afraid will rub off at a little provocation. How can the Ethiopian change his skin?" (53:505). He thinks of Buddha's grief about Brahma's indifference to the world he has created.

✓That last reflection is typical of what "religion" meant to Nehru, and it was quite different from what it meant to Gandhi. But Gandhi was able to respond to many of Nehru's sides, and his reply to this letter catches something of Nehru's own tone. "I have dashed to pieces all Vallabhbhai's hope of becoming a good Sanskrit scholar. He can't concentrate on his studies in the midst of the excitement of Harijan work and the daily dish of spiced criticism which he enjoys like the Bengal footballers their game" (53:310). The gay and gallant tone they shared was modern-British, and in Nehru it went along with comparable qualities of character, which Gandhi much appreciated. His romance with Nehru was one of the signs of how much he *was* in tune with the modern world.

Motilal Nehru rose to the challenge. He formed a genuine alliance with Gandhi, and engaged in poverty and simplicity as if they were great adventures and the newest and most elite forms of privilege. He wrote a letter to Gandhi in 1921, comparing the trip he was then taking to Mussoori with his old hunting trips, on which he had taken English food, etc. "The *Shikar* [hunt] had given place to long walks and the rifles and guns to books, magazines and newspapers (the favorite book being Edwin Arnold's *Song Celestial* which is now undergoing a third reading). . . . 'What a fall, my countrymen!' But really, I have never enjoyed life better."[28] The Nehrus were a princely family, and the son remained a Nehru. He came round from his initial rebellion, no doubt because of his father's tactful response, and his own tone of voice about Gandhi came to resemble Motilal's.

Handsome, intelligent, brave, sensitive—Nehru had to worry mostly about having too many advantages. He was always praised in extravagant terms, by Tagore, by Naidu, and even by Gandhi. He had moreover a kind of princely carelessness, which echoes even in his writings. He writes letters to his daughter to pass the time in jail, and other people insist that they be published. He entitles one book *A Bunch of Old Letters*. He was full of the spirit of adventure, much cultivated in England then. He talks of the "exciting adventure of Man" and asks Indira to imagine the Aryans. "Can you not see them trekking down the mountain passes into the unknown land below? Brave and full of the spirit of adventure, they dared to go ahead without fear of the consequences. If death came, they did not mind, they met it laughing. But they loved life and knew that the only way to enjoy life was to be fearless."[29] And he makes a confident claim on happiness, for himself and for his daughter. "This letter has become much too dismal for a New Year's Day letter. That is highly unbecoming. Indeed, I am not dismal, and why should we be dismal? . . . And you, my darling one, on the threshold of life, must have no dealings with the dismal and the dreary" (477).

Nehru wrote to Gandhi on July 28, 1930, "For myself I delight in warfare. It makes me feel that I am alive. Events of the last four months in India have gladdened my heart and have made me prouder of Indian men, women and even children than I had ever been, but I realize most people are not warlike and like peace and so I try hard to suppress myself and take a peaceful view." He was announcing his conversion to nonviolence while in jail, and it seems implicit that he felt his love of "warfare" introduced no impediment between him and Gandhi (44:468).

There were periods of Jawaharlal's life, moreover, especially periods in prison when he was young, when he was quite Gandhian, when perhaps he seriously doubted his career and his calling. One outward sign of that is that he became an expert spinner. On September 1, 1922, he was sending home ten thousand yards of finespun yarn; he was not interested in any but finespun, he tells us. (Vinoba, so much closer to Gandhi in vocation, in 1932 suggested that Gandhians should spin only coarse yarn.)

The woman Nehru married was in some ways more intimate with Gandhi than with the other Nehrus. The marriage was not an entirely happy union, and Kamala Nehru presumably sought counsel from the Mahatma. But Gandhi was always discreet about that triangular relationship, between himself, Nehru, and Kamala. She was often sick, and as usual Gandhi was eager to help find a cure. In 1929 we find him urging the merits of Kuhne's baths and sunbathing (38:360).

The Patels

Patel, who was fourteen years older than Nehru, was jealous of the latter's relations with Gandhi, and offended by the freedom of his behavior with their joint leader.[30] Nehru would sit in a place next to Gandhi, even when elders were present, and would joke and read aloud items in the newspapers. This went against Patel's more traditional and severe sense of decorum.

Vallabhbhai Patel has already been described. He came to know Gandhi in Ahmedabad, first seeing other men at his club become enthusiastic adherents, and then hearing Gandhi himself, and being impressed by the plainness of his speech. He reminded people of Tilak, seeming arrogant and standoffish, but he subordinated himself to Gandhi much more than Nehru did (130). He accepted all Gandhi's initiatives and decisions.

His brother Vithalbhai, on the other hand, opposed spinning, and supported—like Motilal Nehru—the nationalist party's entering the councils in the 1920s. Gandhi once called him a sort of successor to Pherozeshah Mehta. The Patels' fraternal interrelationship exemplified traditional hierarchy, as was said before. They had agreed that Vithalbhai should go into politics, while Vallabhbhai made the money, and their transactions were quaintly hierarchical in style. (When the former came to the house, the latter undid his laces and took off his shoes, in token of service, and silently filled his pockets with money.)

This agreement was not so extraordinary as it may seem. Gandhi tells us that he and his friend Dr. Mehta had an agreement for a time that the latter would set up a bank in Gujarat on which Gandhi could draw freely. Mehta was to make money to his heart's content, and Gandhi was to spend it on national work to his heart's content (40:133).

Patel was most often silent in Gandhi's presence; and spoke of himself as his soldier, obeying orders. "When it comes to obeying an order, there is no soldier like me" (69). He and Rajaji were the only two who did not question Gandhi's decision after Chauri Chaura. At the All India Congress Committee meeting in 1924, returning to a session after an absence, Patel would say, without finding out what had been said, "I support Gandhi." He was known as a blind follower. He renounced his law practice in 1919 (as part of noncooperation) and took to khadi wholeheartedly (90). Kheda saw Gandhi as a saint, Patel as a hero (a son of his native soil) though the two cooperated closely (69). He was very much of his province and position in society. He never tried, or claimed, to speak for the Muslims. He was a Hindu politician.

When he spent time with Gandhi in jail, he showed a different side, by entertaining Gandhi with his sardonic jokes, and insisting on preparing his dates and tomatoes for him to eat. They came closer than ever before. But later it seems that they reverted to being allies rather than friends.

Pyarelal says that Patel surrendered his judgment and will to Gandhi, and Gandhi himself said: "When I am there, the Sardar's thinking is paralyzed."[31] With everyone, his style was stern and inexpressive: Patel himself said, "Other people can find relief in tears. I cannot weep but it reduces my brain to pulp."

His daughter, Manibehn, devoted herself to her father, but found more parental tenderness in Gandhi and Kasturba. His biographer speaks of Patel's "imprisoned tenderness."[32] Vallabhbhai himself explained his silence thus: "It's a trait in the family. Until I was thirty I didn't utter a word if elders were around. . . . Older ones scarcely spoke with youngsters" (127). From 1927 on Manibehn communicated with her father via Gandhi. In letters, it seems, Patel could use quite a sentimental rhetoric, but not in speaking to her. As for his wife, who died young, the biographer could find out nothing about her, from either relatives or friends of the family. Politics took up Patel's emotional as well as his intellectual life.

In 1929 Gandhi backed Nehru to be congress president. He thought that Nehru would rally the young behind the party, and that the responsibility would sober him (181). Patel followed him as president. In all this we see Gandhi's power. Vallabhbhai's brother Vitalbhai had wanted the post, and was very disappointed that—not having allied himself to Gandhi—he was denied it. He went abroad, in part to have some surgery, and died there.

Vallabhbhai Patel was fund-raiser, candidate chooser, and later supervisor of provincial ministries, as well as busy in Gujarat politics. As a personality, he was compared with Bismarck. He himself said, "If I had not met Bapu, I might have ended up like Virawala" (a corrupt minister in Rajkot against whom Gandhi led a satyagraha in 1939).

Two More Disciples

A somewhat different type from both Nehru and Patel, less romantic than the former, more cynical than the latter, was Rajaji, the Brahmin leader of Madras. Gandhi, he said, saved him from having to choose between either terrorism or cynicism. Born in 1878, he was an intellectual and a wit, but also a prohibitionist and khadi man, being morally and religiously conservative. He never left India, or, one might say, the nineteenth century. But his familiarity with traditional English literature, and what one might call his temperamental Englishness in intellectual matters, were complete.

Pyarelal has a good essay on Rajaji in *In Gandhiji's Mirror*. He says that Rajaji "attained his greatest height in the year following his discovery of Gandhiji and Gandhiji's discovery of him, during the [early] phase of satyagraha and noncooperation."[33] He and Gandhi got on well; they had a similar playfulness of mind, and fastidiousness.

At that time, Pyarelal says: "The scepticism and doubts that later assailed [Rajaji's] spirit had not yet made their appearance" (184). As to those latter, Pyarelal speaks of Rajaji's "unbounded faith in the sovereignty of reason" (185). That seems to mean his lack of faith in other things; and translates also into his "limitless faith in the weapon of diplomacy" (186). Such a temperament might be thought to be irreconcilable with the naive mind of the Mahatma, but in fact Rajaji remained devoted to Gandhi.

Finally, the closest of Gandhi's disciples in many ways was Vinoba Bhave, who carried on the work in the 1950s and 1960s, concentrating on land reform. He took a vow of celibacy at twelve. Socially a timid and silent person, he is supposed never to have looked people in the eye while Gandhi was alive. He was more of an intellectual than Gandhi was, being both a mathematician and knowing fifteen languages. He was also more of an ascetic, living almost exclusively on curds for most of his life.

Vinoba heard Gandhi's speech at Benares Hindu University in 1916. He had just left home, at the age of twenty-one, to make his way either to Bengal (and revolution) or the Himalayas (and mystical retreat). He had the same sense of options as Kalelkar. He found in Gandhi, he says, "not only the peace of the Himalayas but also the burning fervor of revolution typical of Bengal. I said to myself that both of my desires had been fulfilled."[34] After questioning Gandhi about his speech by letter, Vinoba appeared at the ashram on June 7, 1916, and from that time devoted himself to Gandhi—though most often he kept himself at a certain distance, as Gandhi always wanted.

"It was indeed God's boundless grace that brought me to Gandhiji, impelled me to sit at his feet. . . . My heart and life are firmly established at Gandhiji's feet.[35]. . . I kept testing him, whether or not he tested me. . . . I met Bapu and at once fell in love with him. That was because of the unity of his inner and outer state. Then again, it was Bapu who initiated me into the philosophy of karma-yoga (3). . . . He talked as a mother, responded as a mother, and people unhesitatingly ran to him" (8).

Vinoba was a Chitpavan Brahmin, like Savarkar and the assassins, and felt a comparable call to a patriotic destiny. As a child he used to read Tilak's magazine aloud to his mother. "Only I can know what I have found in the ashram. It was an early ambition of mine to distinguish myself by a violent deed in the service of the country. But Bapu cured me of that ambition. It is he who extinguished the volcano of anger and other passions in me." He was relieved to find in Gandhi someone who outreached and encompassed him. "Deprived of your blessings I find the world a howling desolation. Pray commend me to God so that he may make me a worthy offering for the great Sacrificial Fire you have lighted."[36]

On the other hand, Gandhi never considered himself Vinoba's guru, in the full sense, nor did Vinoba consider himself a disciple. But he found in Gandhi "the man of steadfast mind" described in the Gita; and Gandhi called him the son who outdoes the father. He wrote to Vinoba in 1918: "I do not know in what terms to praise you. . . . I accept your own estimate and assume the position of a father to you. You seem almost to have met a long-felt wish of mine. In my view, a father is, in fact, a father only when he has a son who surpasses him in virtue" (14:188). He told Desai that Vinoba was a great man, a phrase he applied to no one else.

Gandhi found all of these variously gifted men, called them to him, and involved them in his movement.

Westerners

Besides the Western admirers at a distance, like Rolland and Geddes, there were, first and last, quite a number of women disciples of Gandhi who were drawn to him both personally and to work for his causes; nearly all of whom came to live in India with him.

The first, and in some ways the most spectacular case was that of Madeline Slade. Her father, Sir Edmund Slade, had been commander in chief of the East Indies Fleet of the Royal Navy, and, after his retirement from that position, chairman of the board of governors of Anglo-Iranian Oil. He was therefore an important figure in the complex of British power and profit in the East, and his daughter's defection was a dramatic gesture of repentance by (in the name of) British culture as a whole.

She was quite conscious of that symbolism. She chose Gandhi to be her real father; she addressed him and referred to him as "Bapu," and when they first met, on November 7, 1925, she kneeled at his feet, and he raised her, saying, "You shall be my daughter." Even more dramatically than C. F. Andrews, Madeline Slade chose to be Indian rather than English; she took the name Mirabai or Mirabehn, after the famous mystical poet, wore the sari, shaved her head, took a vow of celibacy, and so on. (Between 1927 and 1930, incidentally, Andrews was out of India, traveling or in Woodbrook. He wrote frequently, urging Gandhi to come to terms with the viceroy.)

Mirabai was one of the poets Gandhi most often quoted, and she is said to have been close in her religious feeling to the Vaishnavites of Gujarat. But she was by birth a Rajput princess, the only daughter of Ratna Sing, and grew up in Merta, a Rajput fortress city, in the first half of the sixteenth century. Her grandfather had captured Merta from the Muslims, and populated it with Hindus. Her family had a tradition of devotion to Krishna.

In 1516 Rana Sanga, the king of Mewar and leader of all the Rajputs, married her to his heir, Bhoja Raj. But Rana Sanga himself married a woman whose son became king of Mewar and persecuted Mirabai from 1531 on. There were attempts to poison her. Her marriage was childless and she called herself a virgin in her poems. Her husband is supposed to have persecuted her, too. She mingled with the wandering sadhus who visited the town, and probably became another such ascetic. Her poems were about her love of her Lord, using the language of sexual and romantic love.

Some of the most important women in Gandhi's life bore some resemblance to Mirabai. The Rajkumari Amrit Kaur, for instance, was a literal princess, who came to serve Gandhi. Saraladevi Chaudhurani was a child of the Tagore "royal family." Madeline Slade was the daughter of an Admiral and the Chairman of Anglo-Persian Oil. And Nilla Cram Cook was something of a wandering poet. Saraladevi and Mirabehn had beautiful voices and sang to him. They were all imposing personalities, physically and psychologically.

Born in 1892, Madeline Slade had always been a misfit in her family and class—though she clung to her mother—and developed immoderate enthusiasms for trees and animals and everything that represented a world opposite to the social one she was born into. As she grew older, it was the masters of art she adored—notably Beethoven, to whom she awoke at fifteen, and one particular executant of Beethoven's music, Charles Lamond; she arranged a public concert for him in 1912; and then Romain Rolland, the French intellectual and novelist who had written about Beethoven.

In 1924 she read Rolland's book about Gandhi, and immediately wrote to the latter; and booked her passage to India before getting a reply. She had spent the years 1909 to 1911 in India, when her father commanded the Eastern Fleet, and it was by no means rare for Anglo-Indians, especially the women, to feel a romantic devotion to that country. She soon realized that she was being too precipitate, so deferred her passage for a year, during which time she prepared herself for life in India, learning to spin, to speak Urdu, to sleep on the floor, and so on.

Once at the Ashram, Mira made herself very useful to Gandhi, in many aspects of his work and correspondence, notably in the organization of khadi work, and later in setting up model dairies and centers of village regeneration. Gandhi sent her on many missions through the country by herself, partly because she was too dependent on him, in terms of emotional attachment. He devoted considerable effort to freeing her from that dependence. Thus he wrote on March 22, 1927: "I want you to be a perfect woman. I want you to shed all angularities . . . do throw off the nervousness. You must not cling to me as in this body."[37] She gave him his massage.

She seems to have had hysterical fits at the thought of his fasting, and at having to leave him, even temporarily. She was denied access to him once when he was ill because her emotionality made her dangerous to a patient with high blood pressure. Even telling of this being turned away, afterwards, her language indicates how violent her emotion was, at being excluded. "The words hit me like a thunderbolt" (197–98).

She became for Gandhi the prize and the problem that Chertkov was for Tolstoy; because of her anxious possessiveness and her instinct for conflict, as well as because of her executive ability and authoritative training. Gandhi too was drawn into the emotional vortex of their troubled relationship. He sent her away, and then wrote: "Now that you are away from me, my grief over having grieved you is greater. No tyrant has yet lived, who has not paid for the suffering he has caused. No lover has ever given pain without being more pained." It is no accident that his language should recall that of one of his letters to Saraladevi, and the two women had similar strengths and weaknesses. "Such is my state. What I have done was inevitable. Only I wish I did not lose temper. But such is my brutality towards those I love most" (61). Thus he offered her tenderness as well, and did after all allow her a special relationship. But he told her, for instance, in 1931: "I was on a bed of hot ashes all the while I was accepting your service" (88). She was often difficult for the others to deal with, both because of her need to be first with and closest to Gandhi, and because of her imperious temperament. Even more than Gandhi himself, Madeline Slade was a New Age figure, in her Orientalism, her devotion to other species, and her temperament of enthusiasm. The novelists who wrote satires on the New Age (Waugh, Orwell, Sayers) could have used her as a model for one of their characters.

Between her and Gandhi it was, finally, a love relationship. On September 23, 1932, during his fast, he wrote to her: "The thought of you corrodes me. I wish you could be at peace. Do write daily and wire tomorrow your condition" (51:131). And later: "The seven years [of their relationship] seem like a dream. As I remember the terrible scoldings I tremble. . . . As I look back upon the past I realize that my love was impatient" (51:98). And she wrote him, when he was about to begin a fast, in 1933: "God gave me light to recognize His messenger . . . in you. He will therefore give me strength to go through everything and anything for the fulfilment of His word through you. . . . My love would be a poor thing, if it failed at this supreme moment and gave way to misery and desperation. And that is my cry, borne on the wings of a love which knows no bounds."[38]

This rather fulsome rhetoric was the mark of the older disciples, the men like Andrews as well as the women like Mira. The generation that came of age after the World War I had a different intellectual temperament, marked by a dandy sense of humor. Reginald Reynolds and Verrier Elwin, though in practice New Agers, had an astringent and satirical wit that made them sound quite different.

There were other women, the patterns of whose relations with Gandhi were less stormy. Among the early names we may mention Esther Faering, a Dane, Helene Haussding, a German, Antoinette Mirbel, a Frenchwoman, and a little later Nilla Cram Cook, an American, and Mary Barr, an Englishwoman.

Of these the first, quite unlike Madeline Slade, deserves some attention here.

Esther Faering came to India in 1916 to teach in a Danish missionary school. She and Anne Marie Petersen were sent out to visit experimental schools, including that at Sabarmati, in 1917. Because of the political situation, she and her friend were forbidden to return there or to correspond with Gandhi. They resigned and went to Sabarmati, but Esther fell sick.

She was a frail and sensitive person, physically and psychologically. She married an Indian doctor called Menon, and then moved to England and spent eight years at the Woodbrooke Quaker Settlement in Birmingham. She received many letters of spiritual direction from Gandhi, and no stormy relations developed between them. These cases, as we glimpse them from time to time, will illustrate both the effort and the skill this disciple relationship drew out of Gandhi, and the variety of response he elicited from those who followed him.

Via Madeline Slade important messages passed between Gandhi and Romain Rolland. On March 31, 1928, the latter wrote her that he was a pacifist, but "I am not dedicated to the cause of peace alone, or of social action. I am, on one side a religious nature, in my way, which is free. I am on the other side a European intellectual, an artist, whose principal effort is directed towards the living understanding of all human souls. I consider that my principal role is to understand and to declare, to be a sort of arch which unites the spirits of men and women, of people and races."[39]

Later he asked her to tell Gandhi that for them both the new enemy was the octopus of finance; the international conspiracy of financiers and industrialists, which had been working in secrecy the last twenty or thirty years, with governments and the press their tools (306). The workers were the only force left to resist them. "We" must defend Russia against the other countries. Soviet justice was hard but impersonal: Lenin had no personal hatreds (314).

This was what Gandhi was to hear from Nehru. It was the prime example of systematic thinking about politics in those decades. Gandhi never entirely accepted it, and remained more open to the representatives of capitalism than his Socialist friends approved. Rolland was upset that Gandhi didn't mind being misreported, or being watched by the police—by Gandhi's implicit faith that he could defeat these systematic forces by his naive force of goodwill (608).

The triangular relationship of Gandhi, Mira, and Rolland led to some interesting formulations, on Rolland's part, of the different kinds of spirituality involved in art and religion, in India and Europe. He called Beethoven "Our European Mahatma, our strongest mediator between the life of the senses and the eternal life . . . his music is for us the highest form of prayer."[40]

Perhaps the most striking service Rolland did for students of Gandhi and Tagore was to show how much the first could be measured by the same intellectual-aesthetic criteria as the second. He criticized Tagore's constant traveling and hypersensitiveness, and registered very exactly Tagore's egotism. While he wrote Gandhi the same year, "All egotism dies in your presence, because you give the example. And he who writes, like me, bows before him who acts, like you."[41]

Muslim Allies

To pick up the thread of the Khilafat cause, we must return to the spring of 1919, the year when Italy, Greece, and France attacked Turkey. The Muslim

League in India was angry, and in February 1920 there was a Khilafat Conference. Those who took part in the movement were supposed to participate in the noncooperation campaign also. The Khilafat Deputation, including Mohammed Ali, sailed from Bombay to London that month, and in the summer there was a *hijrat* (religious emigration) to the North West Province and Afghanistan. There were 750 *mujahadin* in Peshawar early that year; 18,000 by August, and 30,000 by September.

In May 1920 the terms of a proposed peace treaty with Turkey were published, which gave the sultan Constantinople. The Ali Brothers were somewhat appeased by this provision, but still protested publicly. This Treaty, which was signed at Sevres in mid-1920, removed European territories from Turkish rule, and placed Arab territories under Allied mandate. Gandhi tried to keep the issue alive. On March 23, 1921, he wrote in *Young India* that every Muslim must try to maintain Turkey's temporal power. But it was hard to keep up Indian enthusiasm, and Gandhi's Western friends were shocked by his support for Turkey, especially because of the scandal of the Armenian massacres.[42]

In August 1921 also came the rising of the Moplahs in the south of India. These belonged to a poor Muslim community, on the Malabar coast, stirred up by Khilafat propaganda. A Khilafat king proclaimed himself, and the Moplahs attacked the Hindus. (Mrs. Besant held Gandhi responsible for this outbreak of violence.) There were 2300 casualties, 40,000 arrests.

Khilafatists and their volunteer corps were the most turbulent element in the noncooperation movement, when the Prince of Wales came to India in 1921. The extremists among them wanted a refusal to pay taxes to be part of the campaign. Gandhi demurred, and his withdrawal after Chauri Chaura was taken to be a betrayal. (The sequence of events, and the division of sympathies, remind us of the registration campaign in South Africa.)

In 1925 Gandhi announced that he and the Ali Brothers no longer agreed about everything. They no longer appeared together on speaking engagements. They differed over the Kohat riots. He admitted failure in his attempts to overcome the Hindu-Muslim split. The best he could offer was: "If we propose to break one another's heads, let us do so in a manly way" (May 1, 1926). And into the space left by Gandhi's defeat stepped Mohammed Ali Jinnah.

Mohammed Ali Jinnah

Jinnah's career ran curiously parallel to Gandhi's. He was born in 1876, only seven years the younger. His parents too were Kathiawaris, who moved to Karachi only when he was born. His father was a merchant, who traded in hides and gum arabic. He belonged to the Khoja Muslims (converts who retained their Hindu caste and family classifications) and Jinnah is a Hindu name. Indeed, like Gandhi he spoke Gujarati as a child in his father's house. Like Gandhi again, Jinnah went to London to study law; but he was only sixteen when he arrived there, being a more precocious mind and personality.

Like Gandhi, he was married before he went to England (in the year Gandhi left); and like Gandhi he lost his mother (but Jinnah lost his wife also) before he returned. During his three year stay, he listened to parliamentary debates often, and admired the oratory. He also toured in a theatrical company, and played Romeo. He was a handsome man—a striking presence—and an effective speaker; his theatrical and rhetorical personality was the very opposite of Gandhi's. During those years he was taken up by Dadabhai Naoroji, the veteran Indian nationalist, who recognized his potential. Jinnah helped Naoroji fight parliamentary campaigns. Gandhi revered Naoroji, and corresponded with him later, but did not establish a personal friendship.

Back in Bombay, from 1897 to 1900, Jinnah had to start from scratch, as Gandhi had tried to do from 1891 to 1893. But Jinnah succeeded; he faced penury at first, but soon he was earning more than any other lawyer in the city. He was elegantly English in his clothes, wearing a monocle on a gray silk cord, a buttonhole and a stiff collar, and also in his manners; for he addressed people as "my dear boy," and carried a long ivory cigarette holder. He had something of a mania for cleanliness, avoiding the touch of others, and washing his hands every hour—so it was said. The opposite of swadeshi in his ideas and personality, he never mastered even Urdu, and was—by most accounts—almost openly uninterested in Islam as a religion. But he was passionately interested in national politics when they were played according to parliamentary rules; in fact, politics seems to have been his hobby, as well as his profession. He was taken up by Gokhale, and Pherozeshah Mehta. He at this time aspired to be the Muslim Gokhale.

Sarojini Naidu's early book about him was entitled *Mohammed Jinnah: Ambassador of Unity*, and the unity in question was that between the Hindus and the Muslims of India; which was then his and her cause. Those who were intensely concerned with Hindu-Muslim unity attached themselves to Gokhale, rather than to Tilak.

Though the Muslim League was founded in 1906, Jinnah stayed aloof until 1913. Three years later the league and the congress concluded the Lucknow Pact, in which the latter yielded in principle to the demand for separate electorates for Muslims. All these concerns and relationships, together with Jinnah's work for the Transvaal Indians, suggest how very close his work was to Gandhi's in those years. There were even sympathies of temperament, suggested by both men's extreme fastidiousness—neither was in any sense hearty; psychologically as well as physically, both had a certain fragility. But while Gandhi sought authenticity by rooting himself in the depths of the human condition, Jinnah defiantly identified himself with the superficies—with current styles of elite dress, behavior, and action. Jinnah's way of solving the Hindu-Muslim problem would be for the duly constituted leaders of each community to consort with each other ceremonially, and to deplore the violence committed at a lower level—which would continue, but within bounds.

At the Nagpur Congress in December 1920, Jinnah told an Indian journalist: "Well, young man, I will have nothing to do with this pseudoreligious approach to politics. I part company with the Congress and Gandhi. I do not believe in working up mob hysteria. Politics is a gentleman's game."[43] This journalist describes Jinnah's skill as a debater: his sense of his opponent's weaknesses; his simple language and dramatic gestures—for instance, he stabbed the air with a forefinger and consulted his notes with his monocle.

He denied, then, the ultimate meanings that Gandhi dealt in; and curiously enough "No," and the other modes of negation seemed to dominate his rhetoric. Nehru, who had a similar elegance though a broader and richer nature, described him as an incarnation of negativism. Agnes Smedley, who knew him in Berlin in the 1920s, described him as "cold, sleek, cruel-faced."[44]

Jinnah's mind was by and large inaccessible to Gandhi; he was an example of the systematic mind in politics—his interests being exclusively political. *System* in this sense does not mean philosophical rigor; it means the reduction of the individual's possibilities and the concentration on a limited range of interests and emotions.

Other Indian Counterplayers

Another curious link betwen Jinnah and Gandhi was Sarojini Naidu herself, for after 1914 she devoted herself to Gandhi's cause, becoming one of the most colorful figures in his entourage; she became attached to him rather than to Jinnah. She, Jinnah, and Gokhale (the last was for her, too, *the* master of the older generation) were all in London in April and May of 1914, and it seems likely that it was then she accepted the hopelessness of a personal attachment to Jinnah, confiding in and consulting with Gokhale about the matter.

Naidu was born in 1879, ten years after Gandhi, into a Brahmin family of artists and intellectuals. She composed poetry very early, in a Pre-Raphaelite ornate style, and she was cursed with that Swinburnian fluency against which modern taste has reacted. She may have turned away from poetry and toward politics for that reason. But in politics, too, she seems always to have embodied effusive speech in others' eyes.

Involved in politics, then, she first took up women's causes. She became a notable orator, but Gokhale once told her: "You are typically Hindu in spirit. You begin with a ripple and end in eternity."[45] And after a speech in 1925, when everyone was applauding, Motilal Nehru asked, "But what did she *say*?" (338) This did not mean that she was solemn or sentimental in ordinary conversation—on the contrary, she was comical, sensible, and witty. She was above all a colorful presence, dramatic in gesture, impulsive in speech, and dressed in vivid saris, gold bangles, chains and brooches, and twin tiger-claw clasps. Her address to congress in 1925 gives us a taste of her style: "I, who have rocked the cradle . . . I, who have sung soft lullabies . . . I, the emblem of Mother India, am now to kindle the flame of liberty."[46]

It is therefore interesting that Naidu should have devoted much of her later life to Gandhi (traveling with him, nursing him through the Untouchability fast, going to jail with him in 1942) while his career gradually came to a head-on collision with Jinnah's.

She was, at least superficially, irreverent about Gandhi; calling him Mickey Mouse, and refusing to follow his example as far as austerities went. She laid easy claim to a broader wisdom than he—telling Gertrude Emerson that he had no idea what violence would be like. But one must suppose that at heart, and in silence, she took him more seriously than she took other people. When he began to fast in the fall of 1932, he wrote her a possibly farewell letter, saying, "If I die I shall die in the faith that comrades like you, with whom God has blessed me, will continue the work of the country. . . . I think that I understood you when I first saw you and heard you at the Criterion in 1914" (51:71). That last sentence sounds like a claim to know the serious person beneath her personality.

Of course her relation with Gandhi was nothing like that she had with Jinnah; it was not in the least erotic in any ordinary sense—perhaps it was most like the teasing comradeship and enjoyment of oppositeness he had with Sonja Schlesin; nor is there any reason to suppose that she chose the one man to spite the other. If there was any connection in her mind in 1914 between the new loyalty and the old, most likely it was that she chose someone as unlike Jinnah as possible, as an escape from the griefs that relationship brought her. But for Jinnah there was almost certainly—over time—a large emotional significance to her choices. He was to undergo a series of losses, of fields of action open to him (congress and the Home Rule League) or of people devoted to him, like Naidu, who turned to Gandhi instead. That experience I think one must connect to the resentful assertiveness and negativism that shows itself in his dealings with Gandhi and the Gandhian cause. In 1942 he told Louis Fischer that both Gandhi and Nehru had begun their careers by working *under him* in the Home Rule League.

Naidu was another of that group of Indian Orientalizers, of whom the most famous was Rabindranath Tagore. Gandhi differed from the Orientalizers by engaging in politics, and within politics, by engaging in noncooperation. But he also differed from another group of significant contemporaries by refusing to engage in revolution or terrorism. Amongst these the most important in his story was Vir Savarkar; but we should mention Virendranath Chattopadhyaya.

The latter was a brother of Sarojini Naidu, lived in Krishnavarma's house in London and met Gandhi there, in 1909, attending the Savarkar dinner. Chattopadhyaya left England for Germany in 1910, and spent nearly all his adult life in exile in Berlin. Nehru was influenced by Virendranath in the 1920s, and felt obliged to explain to him his drift away from socialist toward nationalist politics. In 1929 Virendranath warned him that he was being trapped by the cunning "Mahatmaji," and that he must split congress, in order to destroy "a patched-up unity and clear the way for a solid anti-imperialist movement." Gandhi stood on the other side of Nehru, and exerted the stronger pull. He was in a better position to aid Jawaharlal's career.

Educated Men

Gandhi spoke of "educated men" as being resistant to his leadership, as we know. One of the most interesting testimonies to consult when considering that idea is K. M. Munshi's, eminently an educated man himself, and frankly resistant, but yet responsive. Luckily he wrote a partial autobiography, published in 1940: *I Follow the Mahatma*. Munshi was an advocate at the High Court of Bombay, home minister in that city under the British, and a writer of plays and novels.

Munshi's interest in politics began in 1903 at the congress meeting at Ahmedabad, when he was in his first year of college at Baroda. He was in many ways a typical patriotic radical. Arabindo was his teacher, and "I was one of the ardent band of 'revolutionaries' who talked of Garibaldi and the

French Revolution, and hoped to win India's freedom by a few hundred drachms of picric acid."[47] He also followed the congress extremists when they split from the moderates in 1907, believing in swadeshi, boycott, karmayoga—the cult of violence and the worship of the motherland.

Under Mrs. Besant's influence, he and some friends began a *Young India* journal, which later became Gandhi's. They also decided to bring Gandhi in as President of the All-India Home Rule League. Munshi says: "I was one of the last to yield on the point; [because] I then considered Gandhiji's ways uncertain, arbitrary, and unpractical" (3). As we saw in the introduction, Munshi accepted Gandhi's way of explaining this resistance by saying that he and his friends were "educated men."

When Gandhi did join their league, they found that they had to follow his ideas. He disapproved of a boycott, for instance, as full of hatred, and said he would resign if they insisted on it. "We were aghast; our sense of democracy was shocked. What was the use of a committee, we argued, if every member threatened to resign, if outvoted."

Munshi felt also humiliated by the mildness of Gandhi's language, in defining their demands, and so in 1920 he left the Home Rule League. He could not believe in Gandhi's peaceful illegalism. Munshi devoted himself to his legal work and to literature, in which field he preached Art for Art's Sake. In May of 1928, however, he was agitated by news of the Pathan soldiers being used by the government against the peasants of Bardoli; in June he was even more agitated by Gandhi's success. "I hated myself for these conflicting emotions, threw mere prudence to the winds, and resigned" (34).

When Gandhi launched the Dandi march, Munshi at first hung back, but became very uneasy: "Genghiz Khan and Napoleon enforced conscription at the point of the dagger and the bayonet. But this man's method of conscription was worse; it tortured not the body but the soul. Every day of his march brought me tense excitement and insufferable agony. I felt like a thrice-cursed slave tied to a millstone of luxurious living, destined to grind and to grind forever. . . . When Gujarat was rising like one man, why was I, who always talked of its greatness, staying away from the fight? . . . I could not resist this any longer, and surrendered" (81). He resigned from the council, rejoined congress, made salt, and got arrested.

Munshi's written story thus ends with the triumph of Gandhi, but in fact his political life continued to present him with more dilemmas and resistances to Gandhi. "Educated men" never found it easy to be Gandhians.

Public Events

On January 3, 1926, Gandhi announced that he was retiring from public life for a year, to concentrate upon the ashram. He suffered a breakdown from strain that March, and in the second half of the year wrote: "I still have enough strength to be left alone to think and do my work, but the ability to talk to a group, to guide and to explain things to a succession of people coming to me, to humour them, to get angry and get work out of them, has all but left me" (34:285). In 1927 he suffered from two mild strokes.

But in the second half of 1928, Gandhi gradually emerged from his political retirement. He had watched with skepticism the efforts of various nationalist leaders to unite in their response to the government's Statutory Commission, but he himself participated—from the ashram—in the Bardoli satyagraha, which was directed by Patel. This ended successfully in August, and Gandhi said the success had been made possible by the ashram's training of the participants. "The way to constitutional *swaraj* may lie through Lucknow [where the other leaders met]. The way to organic swaraj, which is synonymous with Ramarajya [Rama's rule—the golden age] lies through Bardoli (37:212). And he wrote to Andrews: "Bardoli victory . . . has almost restored the shattered faith in non-violence on the political field" (37:200). That restoration may have happened to his own faith as much as other people's, for his Salt March was a kind of extension of the Bardoli satyagraha, covering the same territory, and relying similarly on Patel's organization and the ashram members.

In 1928 a congress commission headed by Motilal Nehru submitted a report demanding home rule. This "Nehru Report" seemed to some Muslims too Hinduist in its thrust, and was the occasion for Jinnah to leave congress and to ally himself to the Ali Brothers, who were demanding separate electorates for their religion. Shaukat Ali was very suspicious of Motilal, and Hindu-Muslim relations were bad. At the end of November 1928 Gandhi wrote the former reproachfully for his speech at the Cawnpore Congress, which included "terrible threats and exaggerations," declaring for instance that all Hindus were slaves. Shaukat even said that Gandhi had used Khilafat funds for his private travel (38:129).

At the Lahore Congress at the end of 1928, Gandhi resumed national leadership, identifying himself with radical ideas and sponsoring the resolution demanding complete independence. This was, he said, a matter of honor: "Organizations like men . . . must have a sense of honor and fulfil their promises" (42:424–25). And this sense of honor was also a sense of power. "The nation wants to feel its power even more than to have independence. Possession of such power is independence" (42:426). In such apostrophes of honor and power, Gandhi was of course far removed from his first master, Tolstoy, who had recoiled from patriotic politics and its chivalric language. In this matter Gandhi was scarcely a New Ager at all, but a romantic patriot. Gandhi's praise of Nehru was in fact literally chivalric, for he called him a "knight sans peur et sans reproche," one pure as a crystal, the jewel of India, truthful beyond suspicion, and so on (41:499).

Gandhi continued, however, his diet experiments. On June 5, 1929, he announced that he had given up milk again. "Praise be to mother almond, I may perhaps start saying the same about linseed oil. Please do not make light of these experiments of mine. They are as dear to me as the struggle for swaraj" (UC). Gandhi saw the two as connected, though for most people, of course, they were widely separate.

In 1929 the viceroy, Lord Irwin, announced that a Round Table Conference would be held in London to discuss India's future. Gandhi cautiously welcomed the announcement (to Nehru's displeasure) but saw Irwin on December 23 to ask for some guarantees that such a conference would accept as a starting point the idea of Dominion Status. The viceroy could give no such assurance, and so, at the congress meeting soon after, total independence was made India's goal, and the Round Table was boycotted.

Congress's immediate demands were a ban on the liquor trade, and a revaluation of the rupee; the halving of the land revenue, arms expenditure, and officials' pay; a protective tariff on foreign cloth; a release of political prisoners; the disbandment of the CID; and the right to carry firearms.

Gandhi, moreover, was charged with devising some form of civil disobedience, and he came up with the refusal to buy salt, because of the tax imposed on it by the government. He would lead members of the ashram to the seacoast, where salt could be (illegally) picked up free. This led to the great Salt March that aroused all India, and for which Gandhi was again imprisoned. Gandhi wrote a letter to the viceroy, Lord Irwin, which Reginald Reynolds took to Delhi. Irwin had been an early advocate of home rule for Ireland, and was a devout High Anglican. Gandhi however described the reply as stony. "On bended knees I asked for bread and I have received stone instead." Seventy-nine satyagrahis left the ashram, including one Christian and two Muslims. The oldest was Gandhi, who was then sixty-one.

A bullock cart was put at Gandhi's disposal, but he walked all the way. On the march, Gandhi often said that he would not return to the ashram if he was unsuccessful. Rather than that, "my dead body will float in the ocean." Afterwards, since the government abstained from arresting him, he announced his intention to stage a raid on the government salt works at Dharasana, and this drove the British to imprison him.

Mira Behn described his arrest, quoting the Gospel account of the scene in the Garden of Gethsemane. "At the dead of night, like thieves they came to steal him away. For when they sought to lay hands on him, they feared the multitudes, because they took him for a prophet."[48] The attack on the Salt Works also attracted worldwide attention. His place there was taken by Sarojini Naidu, and 2500 congressmen were involved, facing four hundred police.

His sons played a part. Pyarelal describes how he and Manilal Gandhi grew weary of the delays and half-measures that prevailed in the satyagrahi camp while deciding how to move upon Dharasana. He presents himself and his friend in the light of adventure heroes. Devdas, meanwhile, Gandhi sent to the Northwest Frontier. He wanted others to go there, too, because of the rising of the Khudai Khitmagars, so exciting a development in satyagraha.

Altogether sixty thousand people followed Gandhi into jail, and in several Indian cities life was brought to a standstill. In the Northwest Frontier Province, in April 1930, Abdul Ghaffar Khan, the man they called the Frontier Gandhi, was arrested. There were riots in Peshawar, and the army's armored cars were attacked. The troops retreated, and Abdul Ghaffar Khan was released. The Khudai Khitmagar ran the city, from April 25 to May 4. Here Gandhi for the first time saw, or heard of, numbers of Pathans calling themselves his followers, and satyagraha in the hands of a martial race.

Released so that he could negotiate with the viceroy, Gandhi agreed, though with misgivings, to attend the second session of the Round Table Conference in London. There was a Gandhi-Irwin Pact, which the Liberals, M. R. Jayakar and Srinivasa Shastri, helped to create. They acted as intermediaries between the government and the radicals, and were intermediary in several senses. Shastri apparently told Irwin that Gandhi's leading characteristic was an unconscious vanity. That may be true, in the sense that Gandhi felt himself to be a man of destiny, as a man like Shastri could not. But the remark needs to be understood also as showing how the naive and the systematic minds conflict.

Autobiographical Writing

Gandhi was of course a voluminous writer, and left behind him about ten million words, which means he wrote an average of five hundred words a day for fifty years. In this ten-year period that he spent largely in retirement, he produced his two major books, the *Autobiography* and the *Satyagraha in South Africa*. The autobiography appeared in *Navajivan* from November 29, 1925, until February 3, 1929, and, translated, in *Young India* in the corresponding issues, a week later. It was begun in 1921, and resumed while Gandhi was in Yeravda Jail.

"Autobiography" is a somewhat misleading title, and was foisted upon the book by publishers who did not understand the New Age. The title he gave his story, *My Experiments with Truth*, is a New Age slogan—not in the sense that other New Agers often used that phrase, but in the sense that it promises any instructed reader New Age themes and sympathies.

As for the other book, it is eminently educative and "relevant" writing, in the line of nationalist historiography. He began writing it on the same day as he began reading Motley's *Rise of the Dutch Republic* (22:186). He had also read the quite similar J. R. Green's *History of the English People*, which he referred to as giving us history without kings.

In the introduction, Gandhi says: "But our present fight is epic in character. . . . The reader will note South African parallels for all our present experiences in the present struggle to date. . . . I have neither the time nor the inclination to write a regular detailed history. My only object in writing this book is that it may be helpful in our present struggle." In this book, and outside as well, he quite regularly compared events, persons, friendships, from his South African years with their equivalents in India.

Obviously Gandhi's two books are not to be considered literary achievements of the same order as, for instance, *War and Peace* and *Anna Karenina*. His writing is nevertheless remarkable from a literary point of view, because of the range of tone, of humor, reasonableness, solemnity, and tenderness that he can coax out of his limited instrument, but also because of the purity of effect that is given by that very limitation. That purity was the charm of the folk tale for Tolstoy, and the aesthetic reason why he took up that form and left the novel.

At the beginning of the autobiography, Gandhi says that a friend had protested to him that that literary form was peculiar to the West, and had never been written in the East except by those under the Western influence. Gandhi's reply was that his was not a real autobiography, and that the experiments he describes were in the the spiritual field. In effect, he is saying that it is about a soul, not a self. (The same could be said about premodern autobiographies in the West, such as St. Teresa of Avila's.)

One sign of that is how rarely Gandhi evokes the feel of his day-to-day living, of the empirical flow of his experience; his closest approach to doing that is his narrative of his first few days in South Africa, when crucial events followed so fast upon each other that the reader has that sense of complete knowledge.

In this period he also did a lot of writing besides his two main narratives. He wrote quite a long series of essays that could be put together as a book (indeed Rajaji did just that) on his "Jail Experiences." These represented an extension of his readers' consciousness, in a simple, nontranscendent sense, for Gandhi wanted to familiarize them with life in jail as part of training their imaginations for political action and cultural regeneration. He wanted them to be ready for hardships, for social ignominy, ready to identify themselves with "the insulted and injured." But if one compares his essays with Dostoyevsky's *House of the Dead*, one sees how little Gandhi gives us of the rawer facts and rawer feelings of the experience. When, for instance, he lets the reader know that incidents of homosexual rape occurred where he was imprisoned, the fact is signaled (not described) by the phrase "unnatural vice." Gandhi treated literature as one of the habits of polite culture, which should represent only a polite selection from the range of experience. Modernism, from Dostoyevsky on, has included more and more impolite material, extending its harmonic range by including the shrieks and groans of the reader's (and the writer's) consciousness and sense of taste as they struggle against so much that challenges and offends.

Perhaps the most striking aspect of Gandhi's literary work is something that can be conjoined directly with Tolstoy's popular writing. His letters and newspaper articles contain many narratives and anecdotes, direct addresses, and expositions of an idea that can together suggest a whole "literature for the people." The forms are short and simple, the style is clear and unpretentious, the range of effect is from a modest gay inventiveness to a severity of logic and a mood of memento mori. It is a religio-pastoral literature, reminiscent of that of the Christian Middle Ages.

One example is Gandhi's letter to the ashram children, written from Yeravda Jail, soon after his arrest in 1930.

> Little Birds, Ordinary birds cannot fly without wings. With wings, of course, all can fly. But if you, without wings, will learn how to fly, then all your troubles will be at an end. And I will teach you.
>
> See, I have no wings, yet I come flying to you every day in thought. Look, here is little Vimala, here Hari, and here Dharmakumar. And you also can come flying to me in thought.
>
> There is no need for a teacher for those who know how to think. The teacher may guide us, but he cannot give us the power of thinking. That is latent in us. Those who are wise get wise thoughts.

Tell me who, amongst you, are not praying properly in Prabhubhai's evening prayer.

Send me a letter signed by all, and those who do not know how to sign may make a cross.

Bapu's Blessing. (63:406)

This is the side of Gandhi that can aptly be compared with St. Francis of Assisi, the side most often turned toward the general public by his Christian admirers after Doke: when there came a shift of taste towards a medieval and "Catholic" sensibility. Notable names in England were Laurence Housman, Verrier Elwin, and Reginald Reynolds.

One of the signs of this was the "ecological" stress on other species, which we find in Gandhi himself. He told Kasturba to recite the *Ramanama*, the names of Rama, which are "familiar to the very animals and birds, the very trees and stones of Hindustan through many thousand years. . . . You must learn to repeat the name of Rama with such sweetness and such devotion that the birds will pause in their singing to listen to you—the very trees will bend their leaves towards you, stirrred by the divine melody of that name" (57:446).

Another example, slightly more complex, is a joint effort by him and Mira Behn, published in *Young India* for December 5, 1929, called "Our Brethren the Trees." Mira Behn tells of asking a volunteer to pick some babul leaves for her, and how he brought her a great bundle. She went to Gandhi to show him how the leaves were all "asleep" (tightly folded) because it was dark. Gandhi was indignant; leaves were living creatures, not to be torn off at night, and why so many? She should know "how deeply it pains me that people pluck those masses of delicate blossoms to fling in my face and hang around my neck. . . . Yes, Bapu, I know—I understand, said I, hanging my head in shame. . . . Often have I put my arms around the trunk of an old mighty tree and listened to his hushed words of wisdom and peace. . . . How could I have been so heartless?" (42:238). (When Gandhi's disciples wrote about their dealings with him, they usually presented themselves as children standing before an adult, being scolded or being consoled.)

Then Gandhi's brisker and drier commentary begins. "Let not the reader call this sentimental twaddle. . . . India had cultivated no small respect for trees and other sentient beings." He goes on to cite figures of legend, like Damayanti and Shakuntala.

This literature was spread by other Gandhians, for instance in their narratives of the Gandhi campaigns. Mirabehn made the story of his midnight arrests (in 1930 and 1932) sound like the Gospel story of Jesus' arrest before the Crucifixion. Rajendra Prasad wrote about Champaran, Mahadev Desai about Bardoli, in *The Story of Bardoli*; about which Rabindranath Tagore said that it had the spirit of the Epic Age in its narrative of the triumph of moral right over arbitrary power. In fact, of course, such writing is epic only by a paradoxical transvaluation of the term; it is epic transformed into pastoral, external battle translated into internal psychological terms. That is clear in Pyarelal's title for his pamphlet about the fast of 1932, "The Epic Fast." The story of a fast can only paradoxically be compared with, say, *The Iliad.* The real significance of such terms is to testify to our sense that time has been turned back, and that we are escaping from the sordid empiricism and complexity of the modern into an earlier, naiver, nobler age—a New Age.

Gandhi usually presents his allies and himself as "in love with" each other, able to deny each other nothing, making each other the gift of a favorite disciple. They plead with each other, they yield, tears of joy spring to their eyes, and so on. It all rings very oddly in the modern ear, Indian as well as Western. Nehru wrote to Dr. Ansari on October 10, 1931, about the negotiations at the Round Table in London: "There seems to me too much sugariness in its procedings, at least so far as our side is concerned. That of course is Gandhiji's way, and we must not complain. But a little pepper would add to the taste."[49]

As usual, one can find an answer to this complaint in another place in Gandhi. In 1925 a correspondent protested against Gandhi's editing of his letter (in publishing it) and said he himself always followed W. L. Garrison's motto; "I will be as harsh as truth, and as uncompromising as justice." Gandhi replied, "I do not mind harsh truth, but I do object to spiced truth. Spicy language is as foreign to truth as hot chilies to a healthy stomach . . . truth suffers when it is harshly put" (27:183).

Gandhi did not use such terms as *pastoral, epic,* or *idyll,* but he did use the Indian terms for *qualities*—terms that can be applied to anything from food through art to temperaments—*tamas* (dark, gloomy, inert, or chaotic), *rajas* (fiery, passionate, energetic, or enthusiastic), and *sattva* (marked by peace and reason, and what I have called pastoral). Touring in the United Provinces in 1924, Gandhi found a sheet of paper thrown into his car by a peasant, which he found to be covered with verses by Tulsidas. Gandhi talked about this incident at some length, for he found it significant and moving. "Historians have testified that nowhere in the world are the peasants as civilized as in India. This sheet of paper is proof of it. . . . I firmly believe that in our country it is not *tamas* which rules supreme but *sattva* . . . people who have such ideas [as that peasant] have a *sattvik* civilization" (41:356–57).

Aesthetics

We can guess some of Gandhi's ideas about art from Upton Sinclair's *Mammonart,* which he admired. He wrote Sinclair, asking for more of his books. This was one of a series Sinclair published himself, each of which asked a question like "Who Owns Journalism?," "Who Owns Education?," and in this case "Who Owns Art?"

"From the dawn of human history," Sinclair wrote, "the path to honor and success in the arts has been through the service and glorification of the ruling classes; entertaining them, making them pleasant to themselves, and teaching their subjects and slaves to stand in awe of them." But this is of course concealed from both the writer and the reader (Sinclair was most concerned with literature among the arts). He discussed six "art-lies," which mystified art. The first and prototype of the six was "Art for Art's Sake," the aesthete slogan—

which Gandhi used in just the same way. Like Gandhi, Sinclair accepted the label Puritan for himself in art-matters. And both believe that art should belong to the people, not to the ruling classes.

In denial of "Art for Art's Sake," Sinclair asserted that all art is propaganda, but sometimes consciously so, sometimes unconsciously.[50] Literary critics, Sinclair said, set Jesus and Tolstoy, the conscious propagandists, in opposition to Shakespeare and Goethe, the would-be pure artists. Then they acclaim the "realist" art of the latter as superior to the "idealist" art of the former. But what about the writers of the Gospels? Sinclair asked. Set Jesus against Shakespeare, and Buddha against Goethe, and leave it to common sense to decide. This argument was attractive to Gandhi, who referred to Jesus as a supreme artist.

The other field of aesthetics in which Gandhi was active was that of architecture and furnishing. "If you gave me a contract for furnishing all the rich palaces, I should give you the same thing for one-tenth of the money, and give you more comfort and fresh air, and secure a certificate from the best artists in India that I had furnished your houses in the most artistic manner possible."[51]

Gandhi had a stronger and more confident sense of aesthetic values in architecture and decor than in literary matters. But he once called out to his secretary, Krishnadas: "Krishna, see what a beautiful article I have written! It is indeed a piece of beauty; see how I have described the condition of present-day India." It was a piece entitled "Death Dance"; which includes the passage.

> The Councillors want their fares and extras, the ministers their salaries, the lawyers their fees, the suitors their decrees, the parents such education for their boys as would give them status in the present life, the millionaires want facilities for multiplying their millions, and the rest their unmanly peace. The whole revolves beautifully around the central corporation. It is a giddy dance from which no-one cares to free himself, and which, as the speed increases, the exhilaration is the greater. But it is a death dance, and the exhilaration is induced by the heartbeat of a patient who is about to expire. [52]

The article itself, and Gandhi's comment on it, show us a literary artist.

Private Life

Gandhi's relations with his sons continued to be difficult, especially in matters to do with marriage. When Manilal thought of marrying in the early 1920s, Gandhi wrote that it was up to him, but "As long as you do not think of marriage, you stand absolved from your past sins. This atonement of yours keeps you pure. . . . Take it from me that there is no happiness in marriage. . . . I cannot imagine a thing as ugly as the intercourse of men and women." All our physical enjoyments are unclean (23:101–2).

In 1927 he wrote that Devdas's state was pitiable. He wanted to marry Rajaji's daughter, but Rajaji did not approve, rightly in Gandhi's opinion. The daughter, Lakshmi, was happy as she was, but Devdas had "gone mad after her and is pining. He wishes to obey me, but his soul rebels against him." He is angry, thinking that Gandhi stands in his way. Devdas has used the term *pleasure-loving* about himself, but *pleasure-loving* is rather a mild word (35:339). "I see clearly that his impure desires are the cause of his many diseases." Devdas's thoughts run after sex-pleasure, and since he cannot see this clearly, it consumes him secretly.

Gandhi himself was not without similar problems. Only a few pages after this entry in the *Collected Works*, we find him reporting about himself that in the last two weeks he has twice had involuntary discharges in his sleep. He is unhappy about this, but not seriously afraid. He remembers the long struggle it was for him to come to see Kasturba as a mother (35:379).

He wrote to Louis Ritch that "Harilal has practically forsaken me. He drinks, eats and makes himself merry. But he is a brave boy in one sense that he makes no secret of his vice and his rebellion is an open rebellion. If he had not done his creditors down, I would not have minded his other lapses" (36:61).

Gandhi wrote to his grandson, Kantilal (Harilal's son) in June 1927, that he regarded Harilal as suffering from a kind of disease. Harilal was now telling people that Gandhi had forsaken his dharma as a Hindu and was propagating Buddhism. He wrote in letters to the press that he wanted to get his sons away from Gandhi's bad influence. Kantilal wrote for permission to go to see his father. Gandhi wrote that he should go only if he could "reform" Harilal, and that was a task Kantilal was not yet ready for—but he should make up his own mind (34:18–19).

In his political but also affectional life, Gandhi seemed to be coming to a parting of the ways with Nehru, who had apparently, Gandhi said, been suppressing his protests for years (35:470). The differences between them "appear to me to be so vast and radical that there seems to be no meeting ground between us." Gandhi was grieved to lose such a comrade (January 17, 1928). Nehru had written on the eleventh that he could not understand how "a national organization can have as its ideal and goal dominion status. The very idea upsets and strangles me" (35:543). "Above everything I admire action and daring and courage," and that was what he had found in Gandhi. It was not his ideas he liked. He thought Gandhi misjudged the West; and he disliked the "Moral Bankruptcy" series of articles Gandhi had run in *Young India*, and later as a series of pamphlets—a purity campaign. Nehru was not a New Ager in his intellect.

From Bombay to London

Gandhi sailed to London on the *Rajputana*, and his physical presence was captured on film when Egyptian journalists and cameramen came aboard the ship at Port Said. His thoughts about the Round Table Conference were highly skeptical, but he seems to have approached his meeting with Romain Rolland with intense if imprecise expectations. He had for some years thought of making a trip to Europe, and had explained his readiness to go by his eagerness to meet "the wisest man in Europe."

Rolland and he were, however, very different types, who met on only one, though a profound, plane of being. For instance, though Rolland was above all a writer, Gandhi had read nothing he wrote, not even the book about himself. He wrote to Rolland that he felt he knew him via the friends they had in common—above all, Mira Behn.

Once before when Gandhi was wondering whether to make the trip, he left it to Rolland to decide if he should, and Rolland said no. We know from the latter's journal that he was very aware of the chance of mutual disillusionment, just because of their high expectations. Because they were both men of goodwill, and because of the high plane on which they did know each other (at least, Rolland knew Gandhi) they were not to be disillusioned. But neither was it to be a great occasion of mutual enlightenment.

At the conference, Gandhi's misgivings were justified, and the nationalists were outmaneuvered, though Gandhi himself had a personal success with the English press. There were twenty-three representatives from the princely states, and sixty-four from British India. Gandhi as usual claimed to represent all India.

He stayed with Muriel Lester at Kingsley Hall settlement house in Bow, in the East End of the city, among the soap factories and warehouses. Both Polak and Sarojini Naidu were annoyed about that, because they had found for him much more elegant quarters. He was accompanied by Devdas, Pyarelal, Mira Behn. He wore his shawl and sandals, and went for long walks in the early morning, just as at home. He saw old acquaintances like Ramsay MacDonald the prime minister (MacDonald had manifold connections with the Indians) and Harry Snell, the under secretary for India. Both of them had been members of the Ethical Culture Society.

Winston Churchill refused to see Gandhi. On February 23, 1931, he had made a famous attack on him, in a speech to the West Essex Unionist Association. Churchill described the nauseating and humiliating spectacle of seeing this former Middle Temple lawyer, now a fakir of a type well-known in the East, striking half-naked up the steps of the viceroy's palace to confer with the representative of the king emperor. In Churchill's anger as well as in Rolland's regret, in the authoritarian as well as the systematic mind, we can see a hardening of the line against Gandhi's naïveté since 1920. The 1930s were not going to be a good decade for Gandhism.

Congress had sent no delegates to the first session of the conference, and at the 1931 meeting Gandhi said the other delegates were nominated by the government, not representatives of the people. The Untouchables' leader, Ambedkar, said Gandhi insulted the noncongress delegates: the princes, the Untouchables, the Muslims. The most important of the nine committees, according to Ambedkar, was the one on the Minorities, of which MacDonald was chairman. There was sharp conflict and bitter resentment between Gandhi and Ambedkar.

In London Gandhi met various celebrities, like Charlie Chaplin and G. B. Shaw. The latter said, "You and I belong to a very small community on earth"; he meant the New Age. Shaw also told reporters, "He is Mahatma major, I am Mahatma minor."[53] What they might have discussed, but presumably did not, was Shaw's *Saint Joan*, a play about a New Age hero on trial, written in the year following Gandhi's great trial of 1922. This above all was the work that wins Shaw the title of laureate of the New Age. There seems no reason to suggest that Shaw was thinking of Gandhi as he wrote that play, but he is writing about the central themes of Gandhi's politics and spirituality, in the form of a life story also significantly like his own.

Andrews arranged for him to visit Manchester, the capital city of the English cotton industry, which was suffering from both the depression and the swadeshi boycott in India. He made much more effect on such visits and in interviews with the press than in the Round Table meetings. He made jokes about his dhoti—Englishmen wore plus fours, he wore minus fours, when he went to Buckingham Palace, the king was wearing enough for both of them. The king was not well disposed to Gandhi, and admonished him not to speak against England's soldiers in India.

Gandhi also met old friends, like Henry Salt and the Polaks, and Mr. Charles, the maître d'hôtel at the Dorchester Hotel, who claimed old acquaintance with Gandhi, having taken dancing lessons together with Gandhi in 1888. Gandhi remembered him as "Charlie."[54] He saw a lot of the Quakers, who were prominent in all committees to do with India. Gandhi went, for instance, to Woodbrook in Birmingham, a Quaker center, where Andrews stayed. He met there Horace Alexander and Jack Hoyland, friends of Andrews and Reynolds. Esther Faering also lived there, with her Indian husband. Lord Sankey said that Gandhi had surrounded himself with churchmen, cranks, and faddists, on his visit to England.

France and Italy

When the conference ended, Gandhi visited France, Switzerland, and Italy, whence he sailed for India. He went to France on his way to Switzerland, to spend five days with Rolland. The Frenchmen who might have welcomed Gandhi, however, were preoccupied with the waning power of the League of Nations, and the waxing power of Fascism. Their imaginations were captured by Russian communism. This generalization included Rolland, who spoke almost immediately to Gandhi about Lenin.

Rolland played his guests some Beethoven, which made a sacramental moment for him and Mira. Beethoven was the European Mahatma, as Rolland said more than once—the equivalent, for a secularized and aestheticized society, of religious spirituality. It must also have been a great moment for Gandhi's secretaries. Mahadev Desai was extremely responsive to European art, and had read much of Rolland. Gandhi had more than once reproved Mahadev for losing himself in that pursuit. Rolland tells us that Pyarelal was especially penetrated by the cult of Beethoven.[55] As for Gandhi himself, he said, at the end of the recital, "Il doit être beau, puisque vous me le dites." (Presumably he actually said, "It must be beautiful, since you say so," but we have only Rolland's words.)

It is an interesting coincidence, and somewhat more than accidental, that one of the few pieces of fiction by Tolstoy that Gandhi knew was "The Kreuzer

Sonata." In this story, Tolstoy wove together the themes of Beethoven, and the cult of music, and eroticism, and hysteria, and put his readers on their guard against aestheticism. Few readers in the West have been able to follow Tolstoy's feelings about this, but Gandhi of course did. When he and Rolland spoke of art, it became apparent that the latter thought of it in Sturm und Drang terms, in which the work of art was born in the suffering of the artist. Gandhi associated it rather with truth and joy.

Judging by later remarks of hers, Mira/Madeline found the social occasion of her two masters' meeting difficult; in Switzerland and in Rolland's presence, she seems to have felt herself—with her sari and shaven head—to be playing a part.[56] In 1934, when she saw Rolland again, she had the same feeling. Rolland remarked in his journal that she was a violent nature, and not at all an intellectual.[57]

As for the two principals, what passed between them was mostly a matter of Rolland educating Gandhi in the current state of world politics, notably the crisis in capitalism and the rise of Fascism. For despite his acute appreciation of Gandhi, Rolland was turning toward systematic thought. He wrote as early as 1923: "le monde n'a recu de plus cruelles deceptions que des grands 'liberaux' bourgeois: Gladstone, Wilson, etc" (58). "The world has received no greater disappointments than from the great liberal bourgeois: Gladstone, Wilson, etc." That implied clearly the triumph in Rolland's mind of Marxist socialism, at least at the level of ideology. The Frenchman had a pessimistic vision of great conflicts to come between East and West (85).

Although Gandhi was of the two the man of action, and the world-historical figure, he was of course a naive mind, in more than one sense, when compared with Rolland. Though the latter was unusually capable of appreciating the great naifs, like Tolstoy and Gandhi, he was himself a man of knowledge—what the Hindus call a *jnana yogi*. Some Swiss friends of his, Edmond and Yvonne Privat, came to meet Gandhi, and they accompanied him back to India, to live in the ashram. But Rolland himself met Gandhi only during the days at Villeneuve.

He particularly warned Gandhi against allowing himself to be exploited by Mussolini when he got to Italy. Gandhi naturally formed his own judgments. Though he was indeed cautious—he refused to get out of the train in Rome until the right people to greet him arrived—he was of course used to dealing with such problems. (At the practical level, he was much more used to them than Rolland.) He did not join in the standard left-wing condemnation of Fascist Italy, but he was under no illusion about Mussolini, as a personality or as a national leader.

Gandhi went to Mussolini's office in the Palazzo Venezia, where the anteroom walls were hung with weapons and armor. He recognized their symbolic meaning, and found more of what he wanted in two other encounters, which had an opposite symbolism. He met and talked with Tolstoy's oldest daughter, Tania. And during a visit to the Vatican, he was profoundly moved by a crucifix on the high altar of the Sistine Chapel: "It was not without a wrench that I could tear myself away from that scene of living tragedy. I saw there at once that nations like individuals could only be made through the agony of the Cross and in no other way" (48:434). This we may see as implying a theory of nationalism opposite in emotional character to the exhilarated rhetoric about Nehru as a knight of chivalry, a jewel of India, a hero of youth, and so on. In this affirmation that the Cross is at the heart of all life, including politics, he rejoined Tolstoy.

He boarded the *Pilsna* for Bombay at Brindisi on December 14, 1931.

NINE

POLITICS AND CULTURE

· 1931–1941 ·

In this decade, the development of both Fascism and Communism in the West made things difficult for Gandhi, because those ideologies seemed authoritative to young Indian politicians, like Subhas Chandra Bose and Jawarlalal Nehru, and because a naive mind like his found it hard to use the language of either system. His following abroad also became attenuated, for the same reason. But he managed to maintain his position of power. At the same time, he felt himself drawn to act more boldly upon his faith in a brahmacharya that included (for him) physical contact with women. This contact too involved him in difficulties, because of the chastity expected of a Mahatma by others, but also because of his distrust of ordinary sexual excitement, in himself and in other people.

From Brindisi to Bombay

Gandhi sailed together with Rolland's Swiss friends, the Privats. Aboard the ship was also a young English missionary, Mary Barr, who got to know Gandhi, and became one of his followers. She had attended Kingsmead School as a student, like Reginald Reynolds and Jack Hoyland and Horace Alexander, and then taught ten years in a mission school in Hyderabad.

She remained in touch with Gandhi in India, and avoided the emotional excitement and mutual jealousy that entangled so many other women disciples. Her testimony is sensible, and it is the sensible sides of Gandhi it refers to: she recognized promptness and thrift as two of Gandhi's "specialties," and mentioned also his attentiveness to others' needs and plans. Her friend Mary Chesley, a Canadian Quaker, and *her* friend, Mary Ingham, all came under Gandhi's influence. Mary Chesley left him all her money when she died.

On this voyage, Gandhi must have been thinking a good deal about the situation awaiting him in India, and about the one behind him in Europe. But above all, he must have been thinking about the British government's impending action on behalf of the Untouchables. He knew that he had a determined enemy in Dr. Ambedkar, but even more that he had a monstrous social problem to solve. Most Indian politicians were deeply aware of the shame that the Untouchable problem brought India in world opinion, but were unwilling/unable to do anything about it. They saw it as a legacy of the past, which was melting away, or would melt away (at some unspecifiable rate of slowness) as India modernized itself, politically and otherwise. Gandhi, on the other hand, was a karma yogi, and had to act.

Public Events in India

He arrived back in Bombay on December 28, 1931, to find his followers Nehru and Abdul Ghaffar Khan already in jail, and the viceroy unwilling to negotiate with Gandhi himself. On New Year's Eve, then, on his advice, congress resumed civil disobedience. On January 4, Gandhi himself and Vallabhbhai Patel were arrested. Congress committees were declared unlawful, as were national schools, *kisan sabhas* (peasant societies) and other Gandhian institutions. Thousands of congress workers were interned or detained, and there were no-tax campaigns in Gujarat, Karnatak, and Bengal.

Besides the sharply focused campaigns, like the one in Rajkot in 1939, and the individual satyagraha of 1941, in this decade we can see Gandhi leading two long-term and manifold projects: this fight against untouchability, launched in 1932; and his revival of village culture via village industries, launched two years later.

Gandhi showed himself deeply concerned about the problem of untouchability—the imposing of a cruel inferiority on millions, on quasi-religious grounds—all through his years in India, from 1915 on. And at the Round Table Conference it became clear that the need for action was a pressing one, when the British, with the support of many Indians, proposed to give minorities separate electorates, to save them from being overborne in elections by the Hindu majority. Gandhi saw this—partly because of the religious piety natural to him—as a "vivisection" of his culture. He was willing to have seats in legislatures reserved for Muslims and Sikhs, but not for Untouchables, who were, he insisted, Hindus.

As soon as he returned to India, and before the Communal Award was announced, he wrote a series of directions for "Temple Entry Satyagraha," in which he defined the problem as essentially religious. First of all, in time and in importance, Untouchables must be welcomed in Hindu places of worship. Belief in temples and temple worship were necessary preconditions for satyagrahis engaging in such campaigns, although their belief must of course be enlightened. Satyagrahis were not to force actual barricades, when they were erected in front of temples, and formal legislation was, as usual, to follow, not precede, the conversion of public opinion. Thus the changes were to be a religious reform, coming from inside Hinduism; caste-privileged reformers should lead such satyagraha. This would be followed by other, nonreligious, changes.

On August 17, 1932, Ramsay MacDonald, the prime minister, announced the British government's Communal Awards, which gave the electoral districts to the Scheduled Classes (the official name for the Untouchables). Gandhi said this would divide India up and set some Hindus against others; and that he would fast to death if it were enforced. He acknowledged the mistreatment of Untouchables by the caste Hindus, but insisted that this was a sin that they must expiate; if they did not, Hinduism, and India, would die.

In September Gandhi began his fast in protest, and first Dr. Ambedkar and then the British government yielded. Then, having defeated the government's scheme for helping the Untouchables, he was left with the responsibility of serving them in his own way.

Gandhi tried to remove the religious endorsement that propped up the practice of Untouchability. He engaged in dialogue with the leaders of orthodoxy about the fundamental teachings of Hinduism, and the status and meaning of the *shastras* (the holy law books). He got support from Dr. Bhagwan Das and from Acharya A. B. Dhruva for his contention that the shastras did not enjoin untouchability. But he did not proceed on the whole by scholarly argument about the holy texts, which he always admitted he knew less well than many others. (The Arya Samaj joined with orthodox Hindus in reproaching Gandhi with his ignorance.)

His argument was that truly *sanatana* (orthodox) Hinduism could change in this matter because it had always been changing. It had been a dynamic faith, growing to meet new social conditions; a lived faith that was at root a lived morality. When Hinduism became rigid and rule-defined and book-derived, it lost its natural health. (This was Tolstoy's theory of religion: one might call it a New Age theory of religion.) Gandhi turned away from party politics toward this cultural work, and so gave a new turn to the national movement that led ultimately to the suspension of civil disobedience.

On February 11, 1933, he began to publish a weekly called *Harijan*. He introduced that term, meaning Child of God, to replace the humiliating "Untouchable." Ten thousand copies per issue were printed. And the usual Gandhian disciplines were enforced. On April 29 a new fast was announced, to war against "impurity" among the Harijan workers.

On January 15, 1934, a severe earthquake occurred in Bihar, causing a lot of distress. On January 24, Gandhi declared that he saw it as a divine chastisement, imposed on India for the sin of untouchability. Tagore protested that that was an unscientific view, which promoted the superstitiousness that hampered Indian civilization. Gandhi said he had a right to make such connections for himself, though he did not declare them as facts that other people had to acknowledge as such.

Village Culture

Not long after launching the Harijan campaign, he began his second great effort, on behalf of village industries. In the last quarter of 1934 he retired from congress and set up the A.I.V.I.A., the All-India Village Industries Association; for the "economic, moral, and hygienic uplift of the rural population."

J. C. Kumarappa—a Christian Indian, professionally trained in the West—was its secretary. Soon it was serving 5,300 villages and supporting, amongst others, 200,000 spinners. Gandhi said that India's villages had become untouchable and invisible to the cities, so that just by fixing city Indians' gaze upon the villages the campaign would achieve a great deal. *Nai Talim*, Gandhi's basic education, which excluded the teaching of English (and so could offer matriculation in seven instead of eleven years) and included manual work along with academic studies, became an integral part of the village program.

This was an obviously New Age form of resistance to technocracy and industrialization, which Gandhi, like Tolstoy, thought always exploitative. "They say that the control over these hidden forces of nature enables every American to have thirty three slaves. Repeat the process in India and every Indian will be thirty three times a slave"[1] Of a congress meeting he said, "We sit here under electric lights, at the expense of the poor." In the first months of the war he said (as Godfrey Blount had said before the First World War) that Europe's cities, monster factories, and huge armaments were so intimately related one could not exist without the other. The erstwhile village republics of India were the nearest approach to a civilization based on nonviolence.

Besides spinning and weaving, tanning, oil pressing, soap making, beekeeping, hand husking of rice and hand grinding of wheat, the making of paper and of *gur* (like molasses) were recommended. Gandhi, as always, went into great detail, both technological and economic. He did not expect townsmen to buy these things, but the other villagers, who amounted, after all, to 90 percent of the country's population. Local industries, supplying local markets, were what he wanted. "Large-scale, centralized industries in India . . . must mean starvation of millions" (90:104). He had scientific tests performed to prove that rice when polished lost vitamin B along with its pericarp, that cow's milk was more nutritious than buffalo's milk, and that gur was 33⅓ percent more nutritious than sugar. He recommended adding raw green leaves to the villager's diet, and said that everyone must become a scavenger, offering detailed prescriptions for digging lavatory trenches, six inches wide by one foot deep. Because of the habit of public defecation, he and his disciples cleaned up the streets of the village of Sindi, near Wardha.

The AIVIA, he said, could become a living link between the intelligentsia and the illiterate masses. It could turn city dwellers into real helpers and servants of the villagers. If it was the students he thought should work with Harijans, it was the middle class he invited to carry the message of the wheel to the villages—because it was they who had bartered away the economic independence of India for a mess of pottage. He himself now wrote with a reed pen and swadeshi ink on swadeshi paper.

Ashram Life

During Gandhi's journey to Europe, and the prison sentences both before and after that, he kept in touch with the ashram people by means of correspondence, especially via Narandas Gandhi (brother to Maganlal) and Premabehn Kantak, who together managed the community. These letters reveal mostly (though not exclusively) the gentler side of Gandhi. As playfully as he wrote to the children, he wrote to his friends about the cats in the jail. The mother cat had a fancy for vegetarian dishes. When in pain, about to give birth, she would caress the prisoners, and insist on being caressed by them (51:57). Gandhi devoted considerable time to observing the cats.

When he set off on the Salt March, he said he would not return to the Sabarmati Ashram until he was successful. He seems to have wanted to give it up, as a sacrifice. And he set about doing so as soon as he got out of jail. First, however, he planned a new march, by thirty-three comrades from the ashram, to go from village to village, staying one day and one night in each, and to last until all of the comrades had been arrested. In fact the party was arrested before the march could begin.

Since he spoke of the ashram as his body, his self, we are bound to ask if this wish to renounce it was a form of suicide. The ashram had not been a conspicuously successful enterprise. There were often problems with animals (troops of monkeys and dogs who made life difficult, especially for believers in nonviolence) with thieves from outside, and with squabbles and scandals within. But perhaps Gandhi would have replied that for him to separate himself from this body of his was more like a fast than a death. He kept in touch with the people there, from a distance.

Gandhi also said he was leaving, after eighteen years of ashram life, because its constructive activities would be endangered by association with his campaigns. Clearly these explanations overlap each other. Perhaps we should also remember Gandhi's constitutional restlessness and desire to begin again.

The ashram was a sizable institution; there were then 107 inmates (forty-two men) excluding those in jail. The fixed property was worth 350,000 rupees, the movable 300,000 rupees. He offered it to the government, who did not want it, and it continued as before, though Gandhi did not live there. He himself finally moved to Wardha, in Central India, as we shall hear.

One of the troubles of the ashram had long been a neighboring community called the Chharas, who were habitual thieves (52:117). Gandhi had written to the collector, asking if it were a good policy to settle such a community near the ashram. He acknowledged that the ashramites were afraid of the Chharas (52:195). He wrote to Mary Barr about the stealing: our neighbors steal by day and night, without compunction, he said: we work among them, hoping they will leave the ashram alone, but they don't. This was another defeat for soul-force.

Nilla Cram Cook

A woman disciple who stayed in the ashram during the early 1930s was the American Nilla Cram Cook, who had engaged in Untouchables work, and was a fellow New Ager. Though in most ways unlike Madeline Slade, she too had psychological problems relating to her father, and found in Gandhi, at least temporarily, a solution to those problems. She was, however, a less-dignified figure, by ordinary moral standards. She carried with her an aura of scandal, of sexual and other kinds. In her autobiography, *The Spirit's Pilgrimage*, Madeline Slade wrote about Nilla thus: "Nilla was a sprite, dancing and singing her way through life like a bird. Earnest she was too, but it was an earnestness of exaltation, and one fine morning we found that she had flown from the nest." She was found far away, dancing by herself, "all alone in the woods of Lord Krishna."[2]

In other words, she had suffered a mental disturbance, and with it, much more quickly and theatrically than Madeline Slade, a relapse to the way of life she had followed before meeting Gandhi. It was decided to send her home to America. "Bapu was pained," said Slade. "It was clear to me that, in spite of the extraordinary escapades, he had seen much more in that passing spirit than the rest of the world at that time" (180).

✓ It is not possible to say how important the relationship with this woman was to Gandhi. Obviously, it was much briefer than many others, and tangential to the line of his practical activity. On the other hand, she represented to him an erotic-aesthetic version of the New Age more vivid than it seems likely he saw in anyone else. In any case, for those who want to see Gandhi in relation to our own life-options, what passed between them must be of great interest.

For Nilla Cram Cook, dance, and eroticism, were essential parts of the New Age philosophy. She had read Coomaraswamy's *Dance of Shiva* with enthusiasm, and she knew other such books by comparable writers. Like Coomaraswamy, she believed in Shiva Nataraja as the Lord of Dancers or Actors—the cosmos his theater, himself his own audience. Originally this was no doubt, Coomaraswamy says, an intoxicated dance in honor of a pre-Aryan hill god. Later it became a ceremony to honor dance as divine. In the chapter "Sahaja," Coomaraswamy discussed the sexual mysticism of the Tantric Buddhists of Bengal—taken up in the fourteenth century by the Brahmin priest Chandidas, who was excommunicated for falling in love with a low-caste washerwoman. Chandidas claimed to have transcended desire for her. "To attain salvation through the love of women, make your body like a dry stick." This was a sexual love without passion and without children; a love incompatible with marriage; a Tantric form of love.[3]

Though Coomaraswamy does not discuss this explicitly, he had worked quite closely with Sir John Woodroffe, whose main interest was Tantrism, in the Indian Society of Oriental Art, in 1910 and later. For instance, Coomaraswamy gave a lecture on art in Woodroffe's house in Calcutta in 1910. A Coomaraswamy scholar has remarked on their sharing of ideas.[4] *The Dance of Shiva* (1915) bears the marks of that cooperation, and Nilla Cram Cook was already prepared to respond to Tantric ideas.

To understand this woman, it is well to begin with her father, for in many ways her relationship to India and to other things was a continuation and fulfillment of his. George Cram Cook, famous in theater history as a founder of the Provincetown Players, and an early producer of Eugene O'Neill, followed a course of intellectual self-emancipation familiar in the 1890s, discarding an early transcendentalism for an erotic philosophy of life.

This was a New Age eroticism, which did not present itself as the enemy, rather as the ally, of spiritual values like anarchism and pacifism. Teaching at

Stanford, Cook read Tolstoy and Kropotkin, and left teaching for farming. He also read Arnold's *Light of Asia*. Next followed his pioneering work with the Provincetown Players and, after World War I, his move to Greece, where he hoped to revive and adapt the ancient Greek theater. He married Susan Glaspell, the feminist, and began to make a cult of India, as a culture even older than Greece.

When he died, he left an essay entitled "Write a Dance," imagining a theater in which the great creation myths could be staged; a building of many domes, a theater of light and dance. Nilla took up the project, declaring that Buddha, Christ, and Allah were all names for Dionysus.[5]

Cook died in Greece in 1922, but his daughter soon made her way from there to India, in a gesture of repentance like, but also unlike, Madeline Slade's: a repentance by the West of its cultural imperialism. She had grown up in Provincetown and California. Her mother, who had been a Dalcroze dancer, worked at Prince Hopkins' school, Boyland, in Santa Barbara, California. Hopkins was a pacifist, and so suspect during the war. Upton Sinclair also was a friend of her mother's.

Nilla traveled between her divorced parents' homes—she said she had crossed the continent ten times before she was twelve—imbibing the spirit of Greenwich Village, espousing the dance and eroticism, and compared by her peers with Isadora Duncan. She saw the *Light of Asia* danced on the Los Angeles hills (a performance put on by the Theosophical Society) when she was five or six. It was a dance before Buddha, using fire and incense and a lotos throne. Seeing similar things in the sunset, Nilla danced them by herself on the Pacific seashore.

In the summers she went to a Camp Fire Girls Camp on Thunder Mountain, near South Haven, Michigan, which had an American Indian ritual, where all religions were given the same dignity. She loved the camp but got expelled, for preaching against Jehovah.

Her life was lived on the edge of sordid scandal, sexual, financial, psychological. Edmund Wilson knew her in the 1920s in the world of the Provincetown Players. In his memoir, *The Twenties*, he describes meeting her at a party in 1926, where she behaved with exhibitionist craziness. At the same time, she was a scholar. She talked of Homer and Plato, and claimed to know how ancient Greek had been pronounced. She had had three years of Sanskrit.

Nilla declared that the Kamasutra should be taught in schools, instead of "these books by women doctors," and embarrassed everyone at the party by shouting "I am free-ee-ee" at the top of her voice.[6] Wilson thought that many of her poses were probably suggested by her idea of Millay. Malcolm Cowley knew Nilla then and, in a letter to the author, gives a similar account of her.

In Greece she had helped revive ancient arts, woven her own cloth, married a poet called Nikos Proestopoulos at seventeen, and borne him a child at nineteen (by her own account). The Proestopoulos family was related to the Sikelianoses, one of who was married to Eva Palmer of New York, who revived the Delphic Festival. Another of the Sikelianoses was married to Raymond Duncan, whose son Menalkas was a friend of Nilla. There was therefore a tangle of such Greek-American families, all to some degree interested in reviving Greek art; a New Age settlement. Whitman was an important influence on many of them.

But Nilla soon left her husband, and traveled further east with her baby, arriving in India. In Kashmir she persuaded some brahmin priests to accept her as a Hindu. Moving south, in Bangalore she produced a performance of Nataraja dances, in the spirit of her father's work in Greece, but then involved herself in the picketing of temples, in protest against their exclusion of Untouchables. She herself had been denied entry. She joined forces with the Harijan enthusiasts and joined in the street cleaning. When her activity of this kind was reported in the press, she came to Gandhi's attention, and he wrote asking her to come to see him in Yeravda Jail in 1932.

Ramakrishna of the Deena Seva Sangh in Mysore had advised her to write to Gandhi. She had put on a play at the university, and gave a lecture to the Untouchables' League in Bangalore, where she met young men like him and Rudramini, an Untouchable student in training to be a priest, and Ramaswami. One at least of these young men was in love with her, and they shared erotic dreams.

The first letter preserved from Gandhi to her is dated January 18, 1933, and begins: "My Dear N., I have your two interesting and instructive letters. It is very great work you are doing." (This work was temple picketing and street cleaning, in which she was helped by a group of young Gandhian volunteers; they were taking on themselves the dharma of the outcastes.) Gandhi said he wanted to meet her, whenever it was convenient.

But on February 12 he wrote to say that he had heard an attack upon her character; that the friend she had sent to see him—one of her young men—seemed unbalanced; and that her own letter smelled of the hysteric. He then wrote asking about her to various people whose names she had given him. She went to see him, and in March he wrote to Ramachandra, saying: "She has led for years an utterly immoral and extravagant life and has been an utter stranger to truth" (54:7). Moreover, "some of the young men at least who have surrounded her do not seem to have behaved well." Now she had promised to make a public confession, and to lead a beggar's life in Harijan quarters, abstaining from all public activity.

Nilla was her father's pupil in the philosophy of New Age eroticism. She saw herself as a reincarnation of Mary Magdalene, as Anna Kingsford had.[7] She was also interested in the Indian ideas of Shakti (230). By her own account, she had written Gandhi that her life had been a moral hell from his point of view, since he disapproved of "the sensual world," while she adored it (307).

"I did not relish these reminders of Protestant puritanism," she wrote in *My Road to India*. However, she did go to Yeravda, where she found Gandhi so ugly that she nearly ran away; instead, however, she listened to what he had to say, and when charged, confessed everything to him, and accepted his recommendation that she should embrace poverty.

She argued with Gandhi boldly, telling him she did not believe in jail for civil resisters, who should be out in the world, working. She wrote an article for *Harijan*, saying the latter should refuse to take professional training, to become doctors and lawyers. (This would be a convincing position from a New Age point of view; it was after all close to Gandhi's own.)

Gandhi was as shocked by her financial as by her sexual sins. He told a friend: "She was open to the advances of practically every person, and she was no better after her acceptance of Hindu religion. She has debts amounting to nearly 10,000 rupees spread over Europe and India. She has traveled under a false name" (54:27). Her public confession, which was addressed to "Dear Mahatmaji," and written for him, laid the stress on her unpaid debts.

She wrote: "And I want the general public to know that as an aspirant to social service I have been a great hypocrite."[8] But from a New Age point of view, the erotic dimension of her style is far from merely sinful. She called herself a mother to the young men she worked with, *and* to Gandhi. He replied disapprovingly: "I did not like the subscription to your note. 'Your son' looks unnatural and theatrical. . . . You ought to shed all hysteria and unnaturalness" (54:26). Her motherhood was that of Magna Mater, the great female deity whose lovers are her children. Gandhi wrote reproachfully to Rudramuni, who was a Harijan priest, "N. tells me that you are talking about spiritual marriages or spiritual friendships bordering on marital relations. This is nothing but playing with fire and an echo of very subtle sensuality" (54:121). Knowing what we do of his relations with Saraladevi, we can understand what emotions the idea of a "spiritual marriage" aroused in him.

Later he wrote to the same man, "You were all working together, the central attraction being N. Devi, at that time not a fountain of purity. You cannot divest yourself of all responsibility for all that happened during that period" (54:230). And in April, to another of the young men who claimed to have been unmoved by any sexual passion while passing the night with Nilla, Gandhi said flatly that that was impossible for "any person who is not utterly impotent or who is not a god. . . . You were no baby, nor was N. playing the part of mother when she forgot herself and the limitations of sex which God has imposed on us human beings" (54:124).

This was a rejection of all the moral claims of Tantric Hinduism. In the last years of his life, however, we shall find that Gandhi took a different attitude, and practiced something comparable with what he here condemns in them. By exceeding those "limitations of sex," he then sought to increase his spiritual power. Indeed, he then allowed himself freedoms in touching women that upset and scandalized some of his followers.

Gandhi was so concerned about the Nilla scandal partly because the Untouchable work was part of his campaign, and was done in his name. It was a situation like Chauri Chaura ten years before; other people's faults were injuring his cause; only this time the scandal was sexual. Moreover, he felt, as he said, like a father toward these young men, whom he must have met when he was in Bangalore. But he was also impressed by Nilla, saying that she had great capacity for sacrifice and service, and that she had great ability and wide knowledge.

He was impressed by her knowledge of the *Mahabharata,* and her potential as a teacher, for instance. He was also moved by the moral mess she had gotten into. In a statement in *Harijan,* following on her confession, he said her life had been one of lewdness, untruth, and extravagance, because she was brought up in a bohemian family, where the very name Jesus was taboo. "One word to the young men who fell under N.'s spell . . . ," he wrote in a public letter. "It shows the need for the young to maintain brahmacharya up to the age of twenty five" (55:8–9). Here brahmacharya obviously means just chastity.

Nilla went back from Yeravda to Bangalore, now seeing herself as a great sinner, and gave away her saris and jewels, shaved her head, wore a monk's robe, and wrote Gandhi a letter every day. Going further to extremes (against his advice) she went to live in an Untouchable temple in a poor village of Mysore, where, by her own account, she ceased to menstruate, so completely had she renounced her former Aphroditean self. When her health began to break down, Gandhi ordered her by wire to return to Yeravda, and sent her from there to the ashram. Like Madeline Slade, she was devoted to Gandhi personally and exclusively, rather than in the rest of the community there, and was upset by the scavenging imposed on her. She speaks of the "terrible consciousness of human physiology" this forced upon her.

Of course her earlier philosophy had focused upon human physiology, but under the aspect of Eros, of beauty and pleasure. Now she had to see death and corruption—she had to see all the things she had avoided seeing before. She refused to look after herself, and no one could do anything with her.

When Nilla ceased to menstruate, she thought it was because she had transcended the sexual condition, but Gandhi thought she was simply pregnant, and he was glad of it. He said an illegitimate child would be a test for her and for the ashram. But he had no doubt that she could in time become entirely spiritual. "You have in you the making of such a woman" (55:190). (At this point in her development, we might compare Nilla with Natasha Rostov, Tolstoy's character in *War and Peace*; after Prince Andrei's death, she felt called to a spiritual destiny, though the novelist calls her back to a different destiny of marriage and motherhood. Gandhi encouraged Nilla to follow the first.)

He could not, however, give her the time and devotion that would have been needed to confirm her in her new vocation. Quite apart from her psychological and moral instability, her mind and imagination were harnessed to other life-choices. Soon he was writing to her: "I wish you will forget Pythagoras, Bacchus, and the *Mahabharata.* Why should you brood over the past when you have to re-enact the *Mahabharata* at the Ashram?" (54:167). He wanted her to move forward, morally, but her imagination needed huge spaces of freedom. Her letter of May 13 was "too imaginative and poetic for me. You have plenty of poetry in you. Your imagination knows no bounds. I want you to transmute these into an inexhaustible power for real service. We have all to aspire after being childlike" (55:209). But she relapsed psychologically, fell ill, and eventually ran away from the ashram.

His encounter with Nilla inspired him—half consciously—to undertake a fast of purification in 1933. "I can see that she has had a large share in persuading me to undertake this fast. I did not know this. If there is anything which can give her strength, it will be this fast, and, if I have made any mistake in sending her there [to the ashram], the fast is the only thing which can undo it" (54:153). He wrote to her with some of the emotion he showed to Mira. At first: "My spirit hovers about you as a mother's about her lost child. I would love to own you as a child, but I have not got that faith in you yet. It may be no fault of yours, but there it is" (54:102). But soon: "I can't put you out of my mind" (55:164).

On October 9, 1933, after prayers, Nilla disappeared. Gandhi made a public statement about her on the seventeenth. He asked people not to give her money, or to be tempted by her. She had honestly tried to restrain her passions; and if she is still alive, he will not give up hope for her (56:102, 106).

Nilla took her place in the sequence of remarkable women who came close to Gandhi: Saraladevi, Mirabehn, and later Amrit Kaur. Nilla was different because hers was a brief episode, because she did less for him, and because of the more obvious instability that always threatened her; but she belongs in the sequence because of her gifts and the impression of moral and intellectual size she gives. These women were all queens or princesses. Amrit Kaur was a literal princess, and the others deserve the title if it is used freely.

When Gandhi was released from jail, he ordered Nilla to eat and wash and sleep on a bed. He nursed her himself, as he nursed Madeline Slade when she suffered from typhoid in 1936. He taught Nilla, she says, "to be a girl again," and told her she must dance again. One more reliably recognizes his voice in his remark: "Nilla has lost the tenant in her upper storey. But let's hope we will be able to rent it out again soon."[9] In many ways, he played father to her, as he had to Madeline Slade, and Nilla acknowledges this. "In the role of Bapu's daughter I straightened out an uncompleted relation to Kyrios Kook" (411). This is how she refers in her book to her father, for it was the name the Greek peasants had given him. Finally, she and her little boy were sent home to the care of relatives in America. Her story of that part of her life, *My Road to India*, ends with the quotation from Tagore of the lines about freedom lying in the thousand bonds of delight.

Her idea world had always more in common with Tagore than with Gandhi. Her subsequent career is something we cannot follow here, but it was a remarkable one. In New York she put on a dance performance, "The Song of Daphnis," with music by Nicholas Roubanis. In Persia she founded a national ballet company. She was also involved in Middle East politics in Jerusalem.

Another of Gandhi's Western women disciples, Margarete Spiegel, a German Jewish schoolmistress, who had lost her job in Berlin because of her race, arrived at the ashram at exactly the same time as Nilla. She had been drawn to pacifism during the Great War, and Tagore had been a favorite author for her. Then she read Rolland's book on Gandhi, and went to India for two months in 1932.

She was enthusiastic about all things Indian, including Hinduism, but Gandhi told her to stay loyal to Judaism. She returned to Germany; whence she sent Gandhi a copy of *Parsifal*, which he liked. Fired from her job on April 1, 1933, because of her race, she came to India to settle. Emotional in some simpler sense than applies to Nilla, Margarete fasted against Gandhi's fasting, to his annoyance. She was much less gifted than Nilla—or so at least Gandhi judged—but she stayed in India, and for a long time corresponded with Gandhi. She reappeared in his life-story later.

Sexual Scandal

In the autumn of 1935 (September 21) Gandhi wrote an article in *Harijan* in response to scandalized rumors about his habit of putting his hands on the shoulders of ashram girls and women. He titled the article "Renunciation," because he was giving the practice up (61:436–37). As noted, he first began that habit in 1891 when he returned from England. In those days it was the children of the family he touched that way when they walked together. Later be began to lean on the shoulders of women (much more rarely on men) and to accept massage at their hands, and to sleep next to them.

A few years before 1935, he had been told that such things offended the accepted notions of decency. After discussion with those involved and with others, he had disregarded this; but recently coworkers at Wardha had again said the habit set a bad example. More discussion followed, and a case of a young man of the ashram who was taking liberties with one of the girls surfaced at the same time. Gandhi therefore decided to renounce the freedom he had allowed himself, though he did not really believe in a brahmacharya that required a wall of protection by forbidding any contact. This is one of the first public signs of the scandal to come.

In 1936 he underwent a lot of mental turmoil about these issues. On December 3 and 4 of 1935, Margaret Sanger had her interviews with Gandhi, as part of her world propaganda tour for birth control. (She went on to meet Tagore, who greeted her much more acquiescently.) Gandhi talked frankly with Sanger and gave her "an intimate glimpse of his private life," according to Mahadev Desai. He told her, for instance, that on one occasion he had been tempted to leave his wife, because of his attraction to a woman "of broad cultural education"—that is, Saraladevi Chaudhurani.

The Rajkumari Amrit Kaur remembered long after how Gandhi's talks with Sanger grew tense and strangely exciting, as if long-buried trains of thought were emerging. They left Gandhi exhausted. He was taken to a hospital in Bombay and only three days later he suffered a breakdown in his health that lasted two months, and was very painful to him because it involved an episode of involuntary sexual excitement. He attributed the latter to the rest from work and pampering with food that doctors had imposed on him because of his exhaustion. He was disturbed and disgusted because he had thought that he had, to use his own phrase, "become a eunuch for this work."

However, the question of affectionate physical contact with women was, as we have seen, a widely ramified and long-lasting preoccupation and problem; not simply a part of his attraction to Saraladevi. Gandhi resolved more than once to give up these practices—which, as he acknowledged, he disapproved in others—but he did not in fact do so.

On May 21, 1936, Gandhi wrote to Premabehn Kantak that in South Africa he had involuntary discharges at intervals of several years, but in India the intervals were of several months. He put his self-betrayals down to his indulgence in sex between the ages of fifteen and thirty.

In the late 1930s Edward Thompson reported that the rumor was circulating in England that Gandhi had ceased to be a saint—was sleeping with women. Gandhi was able to refute those charges, quite convincingly; but what was really in question, for those who knew him, was not covert sexual pleasure, but a claim to have transcended ordinary limits. The rules of Indian celibate asceticism felt to Gandhi—in relation to himself—negative and destructive. They had only prudential value, and he could not make up his mind to obey them.

In counterpoint with these sexual anxieties came other problems caused him by his secretary, Pyarelal. In these transactions, we see Gandhi's parental concern for Pyarelal and his sister Sushila in various combinations; that concern was combined with romantic feelings on their part for people of their own age; with sexual feelings on their part, conscious or not, suspected by Gandhi; and with Gandhi's own sexual feelings. In this relationship, at least, the Nayar siblings, though variously gifted, show themselves emotionally unbalanced, and Gandhi too is unstable from time to time.

The evidence for all this lies in several dozen notes that passed from Gandhi to the other two, which made reference also to their notes to him, and other relationships. (These are to be published in the supplementary volumes of the *Collected Works*.) Since the story has never been told, we have not much context in which to interpret these epistles—many of which are naturally so fragmentary as to be cryptic, because they were messages passed between people who had been and were living in close contact with each other. Moreover, we have only Gandhi's side of the correspondence to read.

The story begins with Gandhi addressing Pyarelal in love, and the first picture we get is of the latter as a romantic, despairing, self-dramatizing lover. The object of his unreciprocated passion was Yoga, the niece of Narayan Moreshwar Khave (UC). Gandhi was not sympathetic to romantic love, and in March 1935 noted drily that his secretary expected a vision of God while blinded with lust. He wrote to Mathuradas Trikumji about him, saying that no one but God could save Pyarelal from the situation he was in. His good must lie in finding peace in his work in a village.

Later he wrote to Pyarelal comfortingly: he may rejoin Gandhi (who was presumably at Segaon) unless he would not then remain cheerful (UC). On December 1, Gandhi told Pyarelal that his duty was simply to get well. On February 17, 1936, he reported that Yoga wanted to marry a Maharashtra Brahmin: Pyarelal should therefore forget her and henceforth love the Yoga of his imagination.

On February 28, 1936 (after the interview with Margaret Sanger and its consequences) Gandhi struck a more bracing note, and declared himself pained by Pyarelal's behavior; the latter must wake up, and dedicate himself to work (UC). On March 17, "I do not understand your behavior. I am extremely pained. . . . What are you doing, with whom, and for what purpose?. . . You have brought shame to the training I gave you."

Later, Gandhi received a letter from Pyarelal, which announced itself "a final farewell," but Gandhi has refused to accept it as such (UC). Pyarelal seems also to have doubted the sincerity of Gandhi's interest in his problems. "Your saying that I heard you out the last time out of kindness is the limit of unbelief. . . . I listened to your tale about your uncle with such interest that even today I can repeat it almost in your very words." From this point, however, Gandhi began to quail under the other man's emotional desperateness.

On May 18, he wrote that he found Pyarelal's case amazing. Pyarelal's love apparently did not need any response; a perfect love was born in an imperfect man. Pyarelal seems to have proposed going to work among the lepers, and as a fakir (UC). Gandhi replied, "I consider the service of the lepers, etc., the greatest thing only if you can stick to it. I did believe that Yoga would not have approved of your becoming a fakir. Those days are gone. Faith is the only thing left for the present age. For that, I would regard renunciation the best thing. . . . You still do not have mental poise. You are not at peace." Therefore Pyarelal's place was with Gandhi.

On June 29 Gandhi turned his attention to Pyarelal's sister, who had come to spend time at the ashram. He promised the brother he would try to win Sushila's heart. Gandhi had not realized that she needed a father. Like so many others, Sushila quickly became devoted to Gandhi, and from this point on, we see Gandhi himself as much entangled with the brother and sister and as much the victim of that tangle, as they themselves were. Sumitra Gandhi once told Ved Mehta that the ashram was like *Peyton Place*, and these letters give some support to that comparison.[10]

On January 23, 1937, Gandhi wrote very emotionally to Pyarelal, who had evidently threatened suicide, apropos of Yoga's engaging to marry another: "My fear of you does not allow me to do anything. But lest I should repent later I am overcoming my fear of writing to you. Why am I afraid? Is it because you have always been scared of me? But you had no reason to do so, while I have every reason to fear you. Must you still torment me? Have some pity on me. . . . Why should you fight against God? Suicide is an affront to God." Dispel my fear, Gandhi begs; "let me sit in peace." He persuades Pyarelal that the latter has no need to strain himself to satisfy Gandhi: "I would be satisfied even if you only make rotlis [bread] for me. I would be satisfied even if you just remained before my eyes. . . . I am always praying to God that he may grant you good sense and I may not lose you" (UC).

We gather that Pyarelal threatened to do himself various kinds of harm (UC). Thus on September 4, Gandhi asked: Is Pyarelal fasting because of Yoga's getting engaged to marry someone else? If so, this is not right. Three days later he says that everyone, at the ashram and in the family, is scared of Pyarelal—his mother, his brother, his sister, Mahadev. Kasturba can hardly bring herself to speak to him, and Gandhi too has become upset. "Your silence, your appearance and then your mutterings. Every fibre of my being became filled with tension." On November 22: Gandhi is sick, Sushila in tears; Pyarelal has shouted everyone down, and left the ashram, announcing some terrible step. "Will you not wait till I recover or die?" Gandhi asked.

After that comes a break in the notes preserved, but other strands of sexual anxiety remained tense. At the beginning of April 1938 Gandhi acknowledged having had another erotic dream. By April 30 he was despondent, having lost the self-confidence he had even one month earlier. He confided a good deal in Mira Behn at this point; telling her that his two great experiments, in brahmacharya and in ahimsa, lived and died together (this was no figure of speech, in Gandhi's view) and that he much needed support—a rare acknowledgment of weakness (67:76). He told her he would change his ways in the matter of touching (67:79). He acknowledged that he should not have had one law for himself and one for others; that was vanity and jealousy (67:104). After his vow not to touch women in 1935, he had reverted to his old ways at Segaon, as regards Ba and Sushila; partly because they were so upset when he stopped touching them. On September 17, 1938, he gave up even that freedom (67:362). Meanwhile, the complicated tensions between him and Pyarelal and Sushila resumed.

On April 16, 1938, Gandhi wrote to Sushila. "Lately you have been figuring in my dreams. Shall I call it attachment or love? Be that as it may, you have become a big question for me" (UC). But he is writing because their mother says he is taking away both of her children: Sushila should go back to her mother. "At least today your place is not with me. . . . If Pyarelal finds his moorings it will be well." On the same day, Gandhi wrote Pyarelal: "You have become part of me. If I cannot help you, I am worthless." We also learn that Sushila is fasting for Pyarelal's sake, because he is fasting.

On April 18, Gandhi wrote that he had accused Sushila of some kind of sexual feeling for or contact with Mahadev. She has been weeping; Gandhi is now weeping. He has had a reversal of feeling, and withdraws the suggestion. "A wicked person sees everyone as wicked. Do I also belong to that same category? How very perverted I must be to imagine even for a moment perversity in a pure hearted girl like you." She should go and stay with her mother. "It is too true that I have ruined the life of a saintly man like Pyarelal. Is that not enough?" (UC).

In May of this year (1938) there was a great deal of tension between the three. In letter of May 10, Gandhi again seems to feel sure there was something between Sushila and Mahadev, even if unconscious. Stupid Sushila (*stupid* was an affectionate term he applied to her) did not want Mahadev to read her letter. But: "I will not let you remain stupid for ever. You are not a goddess, nor is Mahadev a god. The future is bright if this illusion has been dispelled. I consider both of you simple-hearted. The only difference is that you have not experienced lust. Mahadev has done so in full measure. He is a married man after all. But the god of love is subtle. You were both unaware of his attack" (UC).

On the same day: "There is a churning going on in my heart. . . . I bathe alone." (Before, Gandhi had taken his baths in Sushila's presence.) Here we see how the emotional relations of the three were mixed up with Gandhi's other problems. On May 11, the following day, he wrote to Pyarelal: Sushila is causing Gandhi worry—she may break down. "Your profound love can save her. Her bitter experiences here will be like medicine to her." Gandhi wrote on his way to the Northwest Province.

On May 14: "A great burden will be off my mind if she [Sushila] returns to her original self." Pyarelal is with Sushila in Delhi. She is unnecessarily angry with herself. Her brother should console her. "I see myself distressed and senile." Gandhi says he is learning to give more weight to others' opinions than to his own (UC).

On May 15: Gandhi wrote Pyarelal about an angry letter that the latter had sent to Mahadev. "Mahadev has been terribly hurt by your letter. He has been crying. . . . However, it is just as well that you have expressed through this letter whatever was weighing on your mind." Mahadev had written a letter full of anguish, but Gandhi did not let it go. They should all write to him, and not to each other (UC). Gandhi has committed a grave sin: he has seen wrong where none was, and then insisted that they see it.

May 16 he wrote to Sushila. "Stupid daughter Sushila. . . . Forget your own unhappiness and share mine." He presumably meant "enter into my feelings of being guilty" (UC). The same day, writing to Pyarelal, he said he had had a letter from Mirabehn about his touching women. Perhaps he is thrusting his own faults on Sushila and Mahadev. "If you [Pyarelal] remain composed I may regain my self-confidence."

On May 18, writing to Pyarelal, he reverted to the previous topic, taking responsibility for what happened. "Your letter to Mahadev is shocking. It would seem [Pyarelal seems to think that] of all the people you are the most distressed." Gandhi thought it should be *he* who felt worst. Mahadev's great sorrow was that he had lost his place with Pyarelal. And the same day Gandhi wrote to Sushila, "Oh the things that sexual impulse makes us do!" He accepted her version of "the night of the 9th" (UC).

To Pyarelal, who had given a scientific analysis of Gandhi that the latter agrees with, Gandhi wrote that he wanted to discuss with him something sexual, which presumably had to do with his [Gandhi's] contact with women. "I submitted to Mahadev, Rajaji, etc., because I am a little scared of them myself. We shall see about it when I have acquired confidence in myself." That note of regained confidence is very typical; presumably Gandhi now felt that he had yielded to those named against his better judgment, and was ready to resume his old practices (UC).

In a later letter, however, he reverted to feeling that in all these incidents he had played the part of Satan. But at least he then looked on the crisis as being over. However, two letters later, he wrote in distress to Pyarelal (on May 27): he had gathered from Ba that Pyarelal plans to run away. "If you want to throw pepper into a raw wound you will do that too."

On June 1 (still in 1938) he wrote to Sushila that he had made a terrible mistake, thinking that he, and he alone, might touch women. This was a terrible arrogance. "My whole life has been shaped in the belief that there is nothing wrong about innocent physical touch of women." Gandhi seems to be repudiating that belief, once and for all, but the reader of this correspondence will have his doubts. On June 2, he wrote a note for all the ashramites, saying that on April 7 he had had a dirty dream.

On July 11 he wrote to Pyarelal: both brother and sister were fasting, and Gandhi could not bear to look Sushila in the face. (The question of whether she has ever known sexual desire seems to be reopened.) Soon thereafter he told Pyarelal he could not reason with him; if he [Gandhi] tries to talk, he will burst into loud wailing.

Notes of this kind continued through the end of 1940, and we have of course only the ones that have been preserved. (Toward the end of 1938 Gandhi proposed a different woman for Pyarelal to marry, but we don't know how the latter responded.) In *Harijan* on November 4, 1939, Gandhi defended publicly his habit of taking a bath with Sushila in the room, and her massaging him. However, at the beginning of the following year, Gandhi tries to separate himself from Sushila. On February 14, 1940, he does not want her to regard herself as functioning exclusively as his physician. She has said she will leave him for good if she is not allowed to be that. He replies that she is therefore not to come on the tour with him. It was not, however, easy to dissolve those bonds. In a letter to Pyarelal, July 18, 1940, Gandhi says that Sushila is more absorbed in him than Pyarelal is. "Hence I would even make her sleep by my side without fear." Also in this letter comes a significant sentence, with which we can close this episode. Gandhi says he has always, from childhood, taken greater liberties with women than with men.

Family Life

Margarete Spiegel reappeared in Gandhi's life-story, making an offer to marry Harilal, in the spring of 1935. It was in 1934 that Harilal returned to the family and promised to turn over a new leaf. In September and October of that year we find Gandhi writing to Harilal, welcoming him back. He had been out of his father's sight for a long time, but not out of mind, inasmuch as so much of Harilal's behavior (drunkenness, embezzlement, debauchery) was reported in the newspapers, and a good deal of that behavior was directed against Gandhi or other members of the family. Harilal had quarreled with his brothers, calling them charlatans for emulating their father. He wrote long letters of denunciation to Gandhi (as Gandhi's brother had) and threatened to send copies to the press; he did send copies to Gandhi's friends.

On the other hand, Harilal wrote in 1933, when his father's intention again to fast was announced, begging his father not to do so, and saying he would do anything he was told, and what was his dharma? No one knew how seriously to take such appeals (55:128).

There had been a conflict between father and son over the custody of the latter's daughter, Manu. (This Manu Gandhi was not the young woman who figured in the Noakhali scandal in 1947.) Harilal had demanded that she be taken from the aunt Bali with whom she lived, and given to him. Gandhi advised Manu to harden her heart against her father in 1932.

Gandhi said Harilal had written a letter to his father with a trembling hand, no syntax, and words, even his signature, left incomplete (49:498). He thought the people of the ashram should not let Harilal stay with them. He always stayed a few days, spent the time in his habitual pleasures, and then sought shelter elsewhere, using the ashram's address to seem respectable. He got worse, rather than better, when he stayed there (49:316).

Gandhi wrote to Devdas, "Harilal's glass is always red. He goes about drunk and begs from people. He holds out threats to Bali and Manu. Even in this, his motive is to force Bali to give him money" (50:92). He is now threatening to sue Bali. All this, Gandhi concludes, is his own fault, since Harilal was born in his period of self-indulgence. As a young man, Gandhi had craved inwardly for pleasures of the senses, and that is why Harilal is the way he is (55:239).

Harilal's face was by the 1930s blotched, ravaged, and sinister, according to Robert Payne. His hair was long and unkempt, his body undernourished. Narayan Desai reports seeing Harilal grey, thin, dressed in rags and lacking teeth.[11] He was notorious, because of his father; the gutter press wrote often about him, and company promoters used his name. He carried a copy of the Gita, and Tilak's commentary, everywhere with him.[12] These texts were signs of his allegiance to the Arya Samaj or to Savarkar's Hindu Mahasabha.

Gandhi had toughened his mind, or at least his tone of reference, against the distress his son caused him. Reporting on his family to a friend, he said: "Harilal remains drowned in casks of liquor, or say rather that his belly is always full of them. Thanks to their weight, how can he shoulder any other burden?" (55:241). To Manilal, he wrote that Harilal spent whole days immersed in a tub of liquor (61:353) and that he was sanctifying his anatomy in the holy Ganges of liquor (61:465).

On July 23, 1934, Gandhi wrote that Harilal used to be brave, but that his false friends had deprived him of his capacity for self-reliance. Now he wanted to engage in a business in patent medicines, and alleged that "all of you" (family members) have approved it (58:233). On September 19, the same year, Gandhi agreed cautiously that Harilal could marry some suitable widow (59:27). Gandhi was of course wary of recommending such an ineligible bridegroom, especially since a recommendation from the Mahatma would carry so much weight. He asked Narandas if Harilal could be given some work in khadi or with Harijans.

Harilal had written from Porbandar, where he was again studying the Gita (59:78). He should begin work in khadi by hawking, Gandhi said, before he opened a shop. Gandhi asked if Harilal was still drinking, and cautiously began to pay his expenses. In October, evidently beginning to hope, he said he got letters from Harilal regularly, and was keeping them (59:155). Gandhi told his son to keep a diary, and Manu was teaching her father to spin. In February 1935, the father invited his son to come and stay at the ashram, and he did so (60:226, 245). He took Balvantsimha's room: Gandhi asked the latter to move out, telling him that Rama had come to dwell in Harilal's heart (60:383). A little later, Gandhi wrote to Harilal that he quite understood his desire for sexual satisfaction, but he could not arrange a marriage for him, as Harilal would surely understand (60:410–11). Was he going to be able to give up smoking? (The tone of all these letters is gentle.)

Amala (Margarete Spiegel) wrote in that spring of 1935, proposing to marry Harilal. Presumably she knew of his wish to find a wife, but it seems clear that Gandhi was surprised, and had not prompted the proposal. He told Harilal that he would have to tell Amala how simply their children would have to be brought up, in Wardha. He was doubtful about the proposal—this was a side of Amala he had not known, he said.

The scheme fell through, and Harilal returned to Rajkot, still wanting a suitable wife. Gandhi would help him in only a limited way. "I may accept his marriage but I can't welcome or like it. Still, I do wish that his marriage should be a happy one." He would like it if Harilal worked with them, but he could not recommend him. "I liked his staying here. He did whatever work he could and was friendly with everybody." Harilal said he had no longer any passion for drink or sex, though he still smoked three cigarettes a day (61:37). The next day Gandhi wrote to Harilal's sister-in-law about Manu getting married, and about Harilal's interest in arranging that. He would have no objection if Bali and Harilal together arranged it. Later, Harilal has the idea of making a living by selling watches, an idea Gandhi disapproves, but without anger (61:90).

Soon, however, he wrote to Manu that he had sent both her letters on to Harilal. "This chapter is becoming more and more painful" (61:139). Harilal had been writing frightful things to his father. As for Manu, Gandhi is willing to arrange her marriage, but it will be out of caste. If she agrees to that, does she want to come to live with him till it is arranged? Soon he writes that Harilal is off the rails again and has left his job. Narandas has promised him some work in the school in Rajkot. Gandhi sends Narandas copies of all his letters to Harilal; he should beware (61:199).

When, soon thereafter, Harilal disappeared again, Gandhi said to Narandas Gandhi: "Leave him to his fate." But by one of those curious coincidences of public with private life, in October 1935 Gandhi's other enemy, Dr. Ambedkar, declared that Untouchables should abandon Hinduism and convert to some other religion. As soon as he had "thrown his bombshell," as Gandhi said, Christian missionaries, Muslims, and Sikhs, all came forward to compete for the new recruits.

Conversion was in the air. And soon Gandhi heard that Harilal had gotten a job with the municipality at Nagpur, by means of threatening to convert to Islam unless they gave him one. P. M. Naidu got him the job; the news was given by Gandhi in a letter of March 3. (Let us note that these events came after the Sanger interview, and contemporaneously with the hectic exchanges between Gandhi and Pyarelal and Sushila.)

Then Harilal *did* convert; on May 29, 1936, at a great mosque in Bombay, the Jamma Masjid, he was received as a Muslim and took a new name, Abdullah, in front of a large congregation, to whom he made a wildly applauded speech. He was besieged by admirers, vying to shake his hand, and so on (63:5).

(A Muslim Brotherhood wired Gandhi, affecting to expect his own conversion to follow.)

Gandhi gave the news to his readers in *Young India*, adding the background of Harilal's addiction to drink and "houses of ill fame," and his living on charity, and borrowing from Pathans at a heavy rate of interest. Till recently, Gandhi said, Harilal had gone in fear of his life from Pathan creditors in Bombay. He had told his parents in April how amused he was by the efforts of various missionaries to convert him.

Gandhi thought he saw the hidden hands of some "responsible Muslims in society" behind all this (63:23). The scandal over Harilal and his conversion was certainly part of Hindu-Muslim squabbling. We might note that Gandhi's early Muslim allies were by this time growing old and dying (Dr. Ansari, the Imam, Abbas Tyabji, the Ali Brothers). They were not replaced by others we could count as equivalent, except in the case of the Khan Brothers.

Harilal's was not a sincere conversion. He had apparently told his father only three weeks before that he would do anything to make some money. November 10 he announced publicly that he was thinking of reconverting (64:23). And during the winter of 1936 he did in fact revert to Hinduism. His son, Kantilal, went to see him, but found him such a distressing spectacle that he wept and left.

There was some attempt to keep these things from Gandhi, but he wrote to Kantilal that he must not be protected from them. "I must learn to endure unhappiness and get used to it." This was, he said again, his punishment for his share in Harilal's sins. Kasturba's loyalties seem to have been undivided. She wrote Harilal a letter (that is, she dictated one for Devdas to write) which was wholly on Gandhi's side, saying quite unequivocally that the father's heart was full of love for the son, despite the latter's behavior.

The Arya Samaj continued to play a part in Harilal's life. Some of its members helped reconvert Harilal to Hinduism, but could not save him from alcoholism. He stayed with a swami after his reconversion, and Gandhi corresponded with a member of the samaj (perhaps the same swami) about his son for a time (64:97). Reports came to Gandhi that Harilal was seen in many parts of India, traveling by train from one big city to another, his hair long enough to brush his shoulders, his face gaunt and toothless, ravaged by drink and tuberculosis.

His mother and father one day at a railway station heard the familiar cries of "Mahatma Gandhi ki-jai!" interrupted by "Mata Kasturba ki-jai," and there was Harilal, dressed in rags and carrying an orange (begged from a passerby) that he presented to his mother, ignoring his father. He insisted that she should eat his orange, not he. When the latter spoke to him, Harilal replied, "I have only one thing to say to you—if you are so great, you owe it all to Ba."[13] And when his mother wrote to him reproachfully, he said, "Someone else wrote it, and she signed her name."[14] He wrote a thirty-two-page open letter/pamphlet, addressed to Gandhi. And yet his brother Devdas says that, though self-willed and obstinate, people could not help loving Harilal.[15]

Devdas's own relations to his father were at least on the surface serene and affectionate, although his life-style was far from Gandhian. He became editor of the *Hindustan Times* (owned by his father's friend, G. D. Birla) and lived like other well-to-do journalists. The other two brothers were unstable, in mood and occupation. Manilal lived at Phoenix and edited *Indian Opinion*, but was always uncertain if he should not be in India; Ramdas changed jobs every few months. In both cases the wife was the stronger character, and in some ways closer to Gandhi. But their relations with their father were not bitter.

Manilal, according to Pyarelal, did not like the looseness of discipline in the ashrams in India, compared with what he had been put through in South Africa. Ramdas made a similar complaint, but declared that the brothers' education had done them no harm.[16] He is described by Sushila Nayar, who remembers him in 1928, as being then a very good-looking and gentle young man. He joined Manilal at Phoenix briefly, but left because he could not accept all the disciplines imposed there. He took a number of six-month jobs, for instance, in tailoring. Gandhi had hoped he would find a career in nursing, but he needed to be looked after himself.

Harilal's son, Kantilal, began to correspond with Gandhi in this period, about his father and about his own desire to attend medical college. Gandhi persuaded Devdas and Manilal to support their nephew there. But Kantilal seems to have had (understandably) complex and stormy feelings about his grandfather. Gandhi wrote him a very emotional letter on September 7, 1936, saying, "You made me cry so much," and accusing him of cruelty to someone else in the Gandhi circle. At other times, Gandhi says he was deeply hurt, and "I am very much afraid of you. You are so touchy" (64:335).

We do not have Kantilal's letters, but it does not seem, from Gandhi's, that the grandson accused him of mistreating Harilal; but he did demand, quite roughly, to be independent. What is surprising is Gandhi's language of fear and weeping. This is not a language he used before, even within the family, but, as we have seen, in these years he uses that language also with Pyarelal and Sushila. It is perhaps a reminder of the emotional frailty of the boy we saw in Rajkot and London, so easily frightened and plunged into grief. That early self, with its strains of what we might call emotionalism, had been disciplined severely, and subdued to purposeful courage and calm and humor, but now it surfaced again.

Gandhi began to feel old and acknowledge a loss of self-control. In a speech on March 25, 1938, sitting next to his old friend, Kishorelal, he said: "I have become old, I lose my temper, I am not prepared to listen to anything; should he [Kishorelal] then forsake me?" (66:418). And again, "I am afraid of every little thing" (66:449).

Old Age

These crises in his emotional life coincided chronologically with Gandhi's sense of being outmoded by modern ideas: the new systems of thought we associate with Marx and Freud, with socialism and Fascism. These things made him feel old.

Gandhi began referring to himself as an old man in 1921, when he was only fifty-two years old. Some other people, notably government Englishmen, tended to see Gandhi as feeble and sickly and old beyond his years. But Gandhians and American journalists saw him as the reverse. Viceroy Irwin described Gandhi to the king thus: "Small, wizened, rather emaciated, no front teeth," and so on. Louis Fischer, on the other hand, says that his body did not give the impression of age; his skin was soft and smooth with a healthy glow, and his beautiful hands (big and expressive, with well-formed fingers) did not shake like an old man's.[17] Ved Mehta quotes Woodrow Wyatt as saying that Gandhi looked like a polished nut, all bright and shiny, with no spare flesh. "He gleamed, you know. His chocolate-colored skin was smooth, healthy, and young-looking, and shone all over."[18]

This gleam (no doubt owing something to his oil massage) was a literal-minded version of the luster of the brahmacharya of which Gandhi spoke. Francis Watson gives us a similar description of Gandhi in 1939: "shining with that look of coppery well-being . . . the bat-like ears, the flitting smile, the coiled energy in the angular body, the snowy scrap of clothing."[19] But the well-being was not complacent or complaisant. Watson asked him how Europe's rush toward Armageddon could be stopped: "With a smile as wan as the solution he answered: 'Give up your ill-gotten gains'" (33).

The objective facts about his looks are clear enough. He was only five feet five inches tall; in these years the veins in his temples protruded, his fat nose pointed downwards, and his lower lip pushed up to meet it. And the semiobjective fact is that he—like Tolstoy—was ugly. This is not to say that it was unpleasant to look at them. In fact, the late images of both are most often impressive and moving. But they were never beautiful young men, and their later selves show that.

That marks them off from men like Edward Carpenter, Francis Sedlak, Havelock Ellis, and Walt Whitman, also heroes of the New Life, whose complacently cultivated old-manly beauty goes with a certain complacency and limitedness in their thinking. Tolstoy's form, and Gandhi's form, was never beautiful like theirs; our men's circumscriptive line never completed itself. They never fully realized a natural self, at least in youth, and that was both cause and consequence of the way they reached out unrestingly to the reality beyond.

In late descriptions there is often a stress on Gandhi's youthfulness and gaiety, his jokes and his laughter. There is certainly some truth to this, but it was a secondary or paradoxical truth, and what was primary was almost the opposite. Nehru said Gandhi's eyes were often full of laughter "and yet were deep pools of sadness"; and Hanse Mehta said "There must have been something terribly pathetic about him, for I always felt deeply moved in his presence."[20]

But a certain kind of gaiety he did have. Nehru said Gandhi radiated lightheartedness. "There is something childlike about him, which is full of charm. When he enters a room he brings a breath of fresh air with him which lightens the atmosphere."[21] What kind of lightheartedness this was is perhaps best explained by Vinoba in *The Third Power*, when he says: "I laugh a good deal nowadays, partly because although there is plenty to weep about nothing is gained by weeping. I laugh also because I have discovered a way to make all India happy, if only people will accept it, and I think of the happy future. And I laugh also because this world does not appear to me to have much reality."[22] But of course both Vinoba and Gandhi had to deal with "this world."

Public Events

To return to his public life, in October 1934, Gandhi decided to leave congress because he was "obstructing its growth." He believed that his leaving it would "rid it of hypocrisy." Congressmen apparently felt they had to pretend to Gandhian attitudes and motives that they did not feel. He felt sure that in their minds progress toward independence was all-important, at the cost of even the spinning wheel, which was to him the "emblem of human dignity and equality" as well as "the nation's second lung." Congressmen still objected to his raising the issue of untouchability, and did not share his concern about the means by which their aims were achieved. So he "chose the path of surrender," as he had before in 1925.

A government of India Act was passed in July 1935 that set up dyarchy (the sharing of power) in the center, and in the provinces legislatures with—apparently—more independence than before. Both congress and the Muslim League at first decided to reject this scheme, but controversy developed, and Gandhi was called in as an advisor by Nehru and other congress leaders.

During his fast in 1934, Gandhi read G. D. H. Cole's *What Marx Really Meant*, and made his comments. Nehru complained that he used the word *socialism* quite against the way everyone else did. Gandhi replied that he had looked it up in the dictionary (58:315). This could be described as a conflict of understanding between an ethical or New Age socialist and a scientific or Marxist socialist. Later—in September 1935—we hear that Gandhi is reading a book on Lenin (61:461).

Gandhi had noted that Nehru was unhappy with him. In September 1934 Gandhi wrote: "I seem to be going in a direction just opposite of what many of the most intelligent Congressmen would gladly and enthusiastically take, if they were not hampered by their unexampled loyalty to me" (59:4). This must surely refer to Nehru, as well as others.

So Gandhi was going to force a break by proposing amendments that include a stress on nonviolence, more spinning, shrinking the membership of congress from six to one thousand, and so on (59:9). For himself, Gandhi wanted to turn his back on congress politics, and bury himself in a Northwest Frontier village—the Khans' village of Utmanzai. He was going there, among other reasons, in order to challenge the Indian fear of the Pathans—of the "Afghan menace . . . which we dread so much."

Gandhi also spoke of absorbing himself in Indian village work, to the exclusion of politics and everything else. On August 26, 1935, he wrote: "This village work is so taxing and baffling that if I could help it I would stop all writing and simply busy myself in a village and there work away for all I am worth, and that I should love to do [in] perfect silence" (61:369). It was no doubt the silence that attracted him as well as the work.

In this period Gandhi also mooted the idea of a chain of fasts unto death—an amplification of his own fasting. Those involved would of course be carefully chosen, and only when the first one died would the second one take his place. This idea kept recurring over a long period, but was never put into effect.

This was the religious side to Gandhi. His style in writing to Nehru was different. He used a quite sprightly or British tone with him: Rajaji has just *dropped in;* Ansari has *packed* Devdas *off* to Simla; he himself has Mira *on his hands* with bad fever (61:406). On inspection day in jail, Patel never has any requests, but with Gandhi never a day passes but, "I have some request to make. But I do not know which is the happier. Why may not I be as happy as he, if I can take my defeats without pulling a long face?" (53:309–10).

Patel displayed motherly qualities otherwise unknown, in jail. Gandhi and Patel had apparently come closer to each other there, "like husband and wife." In Kaira they worked together for months but Patel only came to see Gandhi on business. In jail they drew their cots side by side and talked of the joys and sorrows of life (like Kallenbach and Gandhi).[23]

Long sentences were imposed on nationalist leaders in this period. Patel was kept in Yeravda Jail for thirty months, starting in 1932, and nearly three years in the keep at Ahmednagar. There were twelve nationalist leaders there, including also Nehru, Azad, Ali, Kripalani, and Pattabhi. These experiences brought them together, but the twelve just mentioned differed too much to use the opportunity to discuss issues or to prepare for power.

Gandhi sent Mahadev to the Northwest Frontier in 1938, and he himself paid a brief visit to Peshawar in May; and again in the following October. He saw the Khudai Khitmagars, who were volunteers for social and economic reforms, in some sense Gandhians—and who were therefore persecuted by some other Pathans (68:1). Gandhi addressed himself directly to that persecution and to Hindu-Muslim mistrust. People believed he had come to Peshawar, he said, to sap the Pathans' strength. The Frontier Province is the bastion of Islam in India, and the Pathans are the masters of the sword and the rifle, and "mine is an attempt to emasculate them." He had eloquent replies to such charges.

Friends and Enemies

The relations between Gandhi and Nehru were complex. In some ways Nehru was full of youthful confidence in the international left wing to which he belonged, and felt condescending at best to Gandhi. But in the early 1930s Nehru's letters strike a plaintive note. In May 1934, hearing that Gandhi was fasting again, Nehru said, "Religion is not familiar ground to me, and as I have grown older I have definitely drifted away from it" (65:438). Above all, Gandhi's fasting was something he could not like. "It is hard to be so far from you, and yet it would be harder to be near you. This crowded world is a very lonely place, and you want to make it still lonelier. Life and death matter little, or should matter little. . . . I have loved life—the mountains and the sea, the sun and rain and storm and snow, and animals, and books and art, and even human beings—and life has been good to me" (65:439). We cannot but think again of Kim and his Holy One.

In August 1934, Nehru wrote of the shock he had received when he heard of the reasons Gandhi advanced for withdrawing from civil disobedience: "I had a sudden and intense feeling, that something broke inside me, a bond that I had valued very greatly had snapped. I felt terribly lonely in this wide world. I have always felt a little lonely even from childhood up. But a few bonds strengthened me, a few strong supports held me up. That loneliness never went, but it was lessened. But now I feel absolutely alone, left high and dry on a desert island." He felt that reactionaries dominated congress and that, "Inside or outside the legislature I function as a revolutionary" (58:460–61).

Gandhi was not plaintive toward Nehru—that was a crucial difference between them—but he did use a considerable variety of tones with him, all with the general intention of warmth and gaiety. Without falsifying himself, Gandhi found a dozen ways to charm and attach Nehru. In September 1933, for instance, when the Hutheesing family made an offer for Nehru's sister, Gandhi acted as marriage broker.

In the same year, moreover, Gandhi wrote to Nehru that he had heard from Saraladevi, who was proposing her son Dipak to be Indira Nehru's husband. Gandhi had replied that Indira would choose for herself. But he added to Nehru that he thought Dipak would be a good match (56:79).

Kamala Nehru died abroad in the February of 1936. Gandhi saw her in Bombay before she sailed. After her death he said she had had more peace of mind than ever before. "Her mental disturbance had vanished" (62:17). He claimed to have known her intimately for years (62:209).

This period of conflict and cooperation with Nehru seems to have introduced a yet warmer phase in their feelings for each other. Nehru, Gandhi explained to others, "mistrusts the human race a little . . . he therefore places his faith in the class struggle" (65:119). One hears the echo of Gandhi's curious tenderness for Nehru, answering perhaps the latter's plaintiveness. One might both object that Gandhi mistrusted the human race much more than a little, and ask on what grounds he should feel himself to be so much more serene than Nehru. (We have seen how stormy his relations were with intimates like Pyarelal.)

The explanation seems to lie in that paradoxical lightness of heart, that "faith" we have before remarked in Gandhi (and Tolstoy). They did not "place their faith in the class struggle" because they refused to take seriously half the "facts" of life, remaining convinced that half of the latter were temporary and mistaken, that the only substance to past, present, and future is the will of God. To them, people like Nehru and Harilal and Sonia Tolstoy seem pathetically self-oppressed.

At this time Nehru's autobiography was published. Gandhi read it and claimed to be closer to him in feelings than ever before, although further away from him in opinions. He told Nehru that it was a brilliant literary production, but he was too hard on the liberals, like Shastri (62:172). Nehru was of course by then a leader in the international left wing.

Among Gandhi's new disciples prominent in this period, perhaps the most striking figure was Abdul Ghaffar Khan, "the Frontier Gandhi." Born into a wealthy Pathan family in 1890, he attended a mission school and was inspired by its teacher, the Reverend Wigram, to dedicate his life to serving his people.

His older brother had gone to London to study medicine, returning home in 1920; and Abdul would have liked to study engineering in the West, but his mother objected. He turned his attention to politics, became a leader in the Khilafat movement, founding Gandhian national schools, and was jailed more than once in 1919.

Noncooperation swept over the province at that time. In 1921, having been given another (three-year) jail sentence, Abdul Ghaffar Khan began teaching religion in jail. There was trouble in the province in 1924 and 1927 and again in 1930. The Khan brothers launched the red-shirted Khudai Khitmagar movement in 1929–30. In 1931 they met Gandhi at the congress meeting. In 1934 they were banished from their home province and went to Wardha, and the younger brother gave his daughter to Mira Behn to educate. They were resentenced to three years more banishment that December, but in 1937 the doctor Khan Sahib became prime minister of the province.

From the political scientists' point of view, the Khudai Khitmagar was a tenant-artisan movement, popular among the lesser Khans.[29] In the middle of 1930, they nonviolently occupied Peshawar, and achieved the disarmament of some of the elite forces of the Indian army.

Politically, they were the rival and alternative to the Muslim League, which was to triumph historically in the province. In that area the league was then only the party of urban lawyers and non-Pathans, though later, when the threat of Hindu rule became more pressing, it won over the big khans, and came to power by the time of India's partition.

In 1938, as we know, Gandhi twice toured the Northwest Frontier Province with his new friend. It was only thirty-eight thousand square miles, which included settled districts, a tribal belt, and an independent territory. It had been the preserve of military and political officers, and was quite remote from the rest of India. Gandhi would have liked to test the efficacy of satyagraha by settling in that province, if the viceroy had let him.

Gandhi was of course profoundly excited by this attempt to evolve nonviolence in a martial race. It was the answer to his life quest, in a sense. The Pathans, as we know, had great personal significance for him. The brothers' movement brought to political life all the themes of his psychology—fear and violence getting transformed into love and peace. The Khan Brothers promised Gandhi the kind of politics he wanted.

When Gandhi toured the province, there were one hundred thousand Khudai Khitmagars, faithful to their Badshah (King)—Abdul Ghaffar Khan. Pyarelal says, "Never shall I forget the ecstatic exultation of the soul which filled him [Gandhi] throughout that memorable tour."[25] But he remained cautious, intellectually; unsure of how deep the Pathans' nonviolence went, and unsure of what he and Abdul Ghaffar Khan could do for each other.

As exotic a figure as the Khan in another way was the Sikh princess, the Rajkumari Amrit Kaur, born 1889, who entered Gandhi's ashram in 1936.

(She had been following his ideas since 1915.) Her family was one of those partly assimilated by the British. Her father was a Punjab maharaja who could not hold the throne because he was a Christian, and her uncles held high positions in the government. She was sent to Sherborne School in England for her education, and became a tennis star. This time the third figure in the triangle involving Gandhi and a gifted woman was her brother, a retired surgeon, who had been the important man in her life. The Rajkumari was a feminist, and became minister of health in the free India.

A very affectionate relationship developed between her and Gandhi, though not without its storms. She wept when he scolded her, and he reproved her tears as a sign of pride. We see again the pattern of the princesses with whom he dealt: Saraladevi, Mira, and Amrit Kaur; who addressed him as Law Giver, Bapu, and Tyrant.

In 1935 Tyrant wrote the Rajkumari many letters that have been preserved, making many references and sending many messages to her surgeon brother "Shummy." As usual, Gandhi tried to negotiate between the disciple and the other man. Shummy complained at the end of 1935 that Gandhi was coming between him and his sister (62:270). Later, in 1936, Shummy wrote that Amrit had returned to him from Gandhi a sick woman, and he was very disappointed all round. Gandhi wrote her that she must win Shummy back (63:242, 251). If Shummy wanted her to eat meat, she should do so.

Before the Rajkumari joined the ashram, she did a number of things on the edge of public life, like running a khadi store, and putting on a production of the Sanskrit classic *Shakuntala*. But nothing less than personal service of Gandhi would satisfy her, for personal as well as public reasons. He resisted her impulse to spoil him with gifts. For instance, in early 1936 Gandhi wrote to her that she could send him apples only when she got them free. "I know there [is] little logic about it. But it is some restraint on my greed and if you like yours also—mine to take and yours to give. We won't quarrel about which is worse. It would be well for us both to give it [up] simultaneously and thus avoid at least one cause of war between us" (62:15).

When he enjoys a relationship he writes this witty and playful prose. He described his room to her, with different people in each corner. Houselessness is one of the marks of the bhakti, and he is "playing all sorts of pranks, trying to play the bhakti." In a postscript he says this is silly stuff, but a way for him to relax (63:218).

Other of the later disciples can be aligned with Abdul Ghaffar Khan, like Prithvi Singh and Balvantsimha, inasmuch as they were all three by birth and temperament men of violence, who submitted themselves to Gandhi. The first and the third have already been described.

Prithvi Singh was a Sikh who developed revolutionary ideas in Canada before World War I, and in 1914 led a band of revolutionaries back to India. He received a life sentence for his part in the Lahore Conspiracy case in 1915, and began to serve the sentence in the Andamans; but escaped in 1922. For the next fifteen years he lived in hiding. A powerfully built man, he taught gymnastics and trained young revolutionaries.

Converted to nonviolence, he came to Gandhi on April 18, 1938, entrusting him with his fate. Gandhi wrote to the district magistrate responsible, offering Prithvi Singh back to justice, but also accepting responsibility for him if he were set free. The Sikh had in fact to go to jail again for a year, where he occupied himself at the spinning wheel, and thereafter played a prominent part in the Gandhian entourage; though Gandhi later came to distrust him.

For instance, Prithvi established a physical training camp at Ghoga, fifteen miles from Bhavnagar, with 340 boys and sixty girls. On August 9, 1940, Gandhi wrote that Mira Behn was looking upon Prithvi as a husband for herself. The similarity to Amala's interest in Harilal will of course strike the reader; the woman disciple, devoted to her master, who wants to marry someone close to him. There was a circuit of desire linking Gandhi's intimates, which had sexual as well as other meanings, and Gandhi himself was clearly part of it.

"She believes that her love for him is the result of her previous life. Prithvi Singh regards her as a sister. [Gandhi had told him he must see all the women of the ashram as such.] Mira Behn is pining for him here. . . . It is a question of life and death for Mira Behn. [She] is worthy in every way. . . . Mira Behn does want a child and that too by Prithvi Singh." So it is, Gandhi says, Prithvi's duty to agree (72:371–72). However, it does not seem that he *did* agree, and soon we hear that Prithvi wants to leave the ashram, because of disagreements with other inmates.

Prithvi had written out, years before, a *Scheme of Physical Training*. Gandhi said he liked it and hoped that experts in the field would study it (73:235). His lieutenant, Acharya Kriplani, officially opened Prithvi's gymnasium, giving it Gandhian sponsorship. Gandhi was again trying to find a nonviolent form of force. On March 8, 1941, Mira Behn was still harping on marriage.

To turn from friends to enemies, in 1935 Jinnah returned to India from England, to reorganize the Muslim League for the new elections to provincial legislatures. But in those elections the congress triumphed and the league got only one out of the 86 Muslim seats in the Punjab, and none in Sind and the Northwest Frontier. It did well only in Bengal. Subsequently the league took up the idea of Pakistan: and in 1944 it got 75 seats in the Punjab, 115 in Bengal, 30 in Sind, and 75 percent of the total of Muslim votes (as opposed to 4.4 percent in 1937). The way opened for Jinnah to put a stop to Gandhi's plans, and congress's, for a united free India.

As Ved Mehta says: "Gandhi had had many previous adversaries in his life, but none of them had ever aroused his passion or made him despair as Jinnah did."[26] And despite the latter's august impersonality, when he speaks to or about Gandhi, the note of malevolence makes itself heard. Gandhi appealed to him in February 1938 not to make civil war between the league and the congress, reminding him of the nationalist hopes that had inspired both men in 1915, and asking him why he had changed.

Jinnah replied: "Evidently, you are not acquainted with what is going on in the Congress press—the amount of vilification, misrepresentation, and falsehood that is daily spread about me—otherwise, I am sure, you would not blame me. . . . I would not like to say what people spoke of you in 1915 and think of you today. . . . I think you might have spared your appeal and need not have preached to me on your bended knees to be what you had thought I was" (66:182). We are reminded of what Nehru said of Jinnah: "With all his strength and tenacity, he is a strangely negative person, whose appropriate symbol might well be a 'no.'"[27]

Gandhi too said that Jinnah's heart was full of a canker of suspicion, but: "When I am gone, he will realize and admit that I had no design on the Muslims and that I had never betrayed their interests."[28] This trope, "when I am gone," was of course what Gandhi also said about Nehru's resistance to his New Age ideas. It expresses Gandhi's half-guilty sense that they found his personality an obstacle, an oppression. (He had, after all, chosen to be unlike other men.)

Not far second to Jinnah in hostility to Gandhi was Dr. Ambedkar, whose career, like Jinnah's, was frustrated by Gandhi time and again. In the 1937 elections, out of 151 seats reserved for the Scheduled Castes (the Untouchables) 139 went to congress, and only 12 to Ambedkar's Independent Labor Party. By an analysis of the statistics, however, Ambedkar offered to show that by itself the congress won only 73, and without Untouchable votes would have had only 38. The first count he called a wicked lie by congress and Gandhi, claiming to represent the Untouchables. He said bitterly that Gandhi delighted in his reputation as savior of the Untouchables even more than in that of champion of swaraj or protagonist of ahimsa.

In a chapter entitled "What Is Gandhism?" Ambedkar says that Gandhi's economic ideas were a familiar brew that came out of Rousseau, Ruskin, and Tolstoy—"there is always some simpleton to preach them."[29] The word *simpleton* is of course the hostile synonym for naive. Ambedkar was a good example of the systematic mind, a lawyer and socialist, trained at the London School of Economics. Life is animal, he declares, and the only thing that divides the brute from man is culture. A democracy cannot accept such ideas as Gandhi's. "The genius of Mr. Gandhi is elvish, always and throughout. He has all the precocity of an elf with no little of its outward guise. Like an elf he can never grow up" (284).

Ambedkar developed this argument into a book, entitled *What Congress and Gandhi Have Done to the Untouchables* (Bombay, 1947). In it he claimed that Gandhi was full of caste feeling; and attacked also Mrs. Besant ("she felt great antipathy towards the Untouchables") and Tilak ("one of those social Tories and political radicals with which India abounds") (3, 13).

When Ambedkar heard of Gandhi's assassination in 1948, he was at first silent, and then said, "My real enemy has gone; thank goodness the eclipse is over now."[30] And in the BBC program *Talking of Gandhiji* (ed. F. Watson and M. Brown, London: BBC, 1957) Ambedkar spoke of Gandhi opening his real fangs only to him. This is the tone and the image (the wolf in sheep's clothing) that one guesses to lie behind the discretion of Savarkar and Jinnah and others.[31]

Ambedkar wanted to modernize India, and in the process to destroy Hinduism. He often quoted Harold Laski, and was in sympathy with Laski's London School of Economics socialism. As part of his opposition to Hinduism, Ambedkar supported the splitting off of Pakistan, and ordered his followers to convert to Buddhism. Temperamentally he admired, and aspired himself to be, the bold and manly and realistic leader. "Napoleon always charged from the front," he often said. Treachery and deceit were the weapons of the weak, and he ascribed that politics to Gandhi—"the most dishonest politician in Indian history," with his "pernicious saintly idiosyncrasies. . . . If a man with God's name on his tongue and a sword under his armpit deserved to be called a Mahatma, then Gandhi was one." He often called Gandhi a humbug, and compared him with Uriah Heep. At best he compared his attitude to the Untouchables with Lincoln's attitude to the Negroes; citing Lincoln's remark that it was the Union he really cared about, not the slaves. By inference, it was the glorification of Hindu India that Gandhi really cared about, and his love for the Untouchables and the rest of his protestations were propaganda. (This—translated into Muslim terms—was of course what Jinnah also said.)

But, finally, what strikes one most in Ambedkar's testimony is the intensity of hatred he directed at the other man, which helps us to understand the situation in which Gandhi lived and died—the bubble of adoration and service, transparent and lit up to attract everyone's attention, while outside it the storms of jealousy and hatred lashed toward him. Ambedkar wrote: "Is Gandhi a Mahatma? I am sick of this question. . . . I hate all the Mahatmas, and firmly believe that they should be done away with . . . because they try to perpetuate blind faith in place of intelligence and reason."[32]

Among Gandhi's congress rivals, the most striking late figure was Subhas Chandra Bose (1897–1945). Bose was born into the Kayastha caste in Bengal—the caste that managed the city of Calcutta and had grown rich on British trade. His father was a well-to-do lawyer and a social reformer, his mother a "Hindu wife and mother"; in other words, he had the same sort of family background as Nehru. He grew up an introverted rebel against his family's Edwardian and seigneurial style; he decided to become a sanyasi statesman, and cut everything else out of his life.

He went to Cambridge in 1918, to prepare himself for the Indian civil service examinations, and became very English in style. In 1921 he began to write to C. R. Das, offering to devote himself to the nationalist cause in Bengal, and recommending the congress keep a research staff. He met Gandhi at this time, but did not like what he saw, although he always acknowledged Gandhi's power to arouse the masses.

In 1928 he became president of the All-India Trade Union Congress, and at the congress meeting in Calcutta led a procession accompanying President Motilal Nehru in a triumphal chariot, Bose wearing the semimilitary uniform of his Youth Movement, the members of which demonstrated with black flags against Gandhi. By 1930 he was mayor of Calcutta. He cited the model of the nineteenth-century Italian independence movement, but employed the semimilitarist style also of contemporary Fascism in Italy and Germany.

The issues between him and Gandhi always included the legitimacy of violence, and generally speaking all political realism or unscrupulousness. Bose believed in realpolitik. In April 1939 Gandhi wrote him: "I wholly dissent from your view that the country has never been so non-violent as now. I smell violence in the air I breathe. . . . We seem to differ as to the amount of corruption in Congress. My impression is that it is on the increase. I have been pleading in the past many months for a thorough scrutiny."[33]

Arrested in July 1940, Bose was released in November when he threatened to go on hunger strike. In January 1941 he disappeared and made his way to Afghanistan and—with an Italian passport—through Russia to Germany, where he gave broadcasts over Radio Berlin in April 1942. He then left Europe by German submarine, and made his way to Japanese-held Singapore. There he formed the Indian National Army (the INA) from units of Indians who had surrendered with the rest of the British army in Southeast Asia. The INA fought in Burma, and was intended to lead an invasion of India itself, but the defeat of the Axis powers frustrated that scheme. Bose himself died with his hopes, in 1945.

What he stood for may be summed up as efficiency, in the party and the state. He was not a great orator, but a good organizer and disciplinarian, just as in the world of mind he was efficient. He admired the German army, and liked to see men, in or out of uniform, looking spruce and well turned-out. He clearly had some of the potential to become a dictator like his contemporaries in Europe, and in his conflict with Gandhi, we see how the latter might have met the challenge of, say, an Indian Mussolini.

Gandhi was enmeshed in a network of hostilities that were getting sharper. He now had many bitter enemies, both personal and ideological. Bose was declared ineligible for congress office for three years, because he had infringed congress discipline. Jinnah said that Hindu-Muslim unity was foundering on the rock of congress Fascism—meaning Gandhism—and Savarkar said, "Henceforth our politics will be Hindu politics," and exhorted Hindus to repudiate congress leadership and reclaim their power. Gandhi sensed the anger in the air. "Each is arming for the fight with the other. The violence that we had harboured in our hearts during the non-cooperation days is now recoiling upon ourselves" (67:132).

Sevagram Ashram

Meanwhile Gandhi's second ashram had come into existence, unintentionally. He wanted to live alone and to avoid the ashram life, including the feverish intimacy with the Nayyar siblings. But there had also long been disappointment at the highest levels of the All India Village Industries Association, about the village work done by Gandhian volunteers; the villagers were sometimes hostile, and complained that the worker lived off them and was a threat to their meager resources. So in 1936 Gandhi decided himself to experiment in their work.[34]

In 1934 Jamnalal Bajaj had recommended Wardha, at the geographical center of India, to be the headquarters of AIVIA. Vinoba Bhave established an ashram there. When he left Sabarmati, Gandhi tried living in the village of Sindi, near Wardha, but it was not sufficiently isolated to suit his purposes.

In the summer of 1936, Gandhi settled in the smaller village of Segaon, where Bajaj owned 75 percent of the land. This was a very poor community of 639 people, mostly Untouchables, with no post office, no medical care, no food supplies beyond the most primitive, and difficult to reach in rainy weather. Gandhi tried to improve their lives—with no great success—by methods that we can recognize as very modern though also Gandhian. Of the four hundred adults, he said: "They could put 100,000 rupees into their pockets if only they would work as I ask them. But they won't. They lack cooperation; they do not know the art of intelligent labor. They refuse to learn anything new." One hears there the voice of the modernizing Gandhi.[35]

Despite Gandhi's intention, little by little another circle established itself around him, as it had done before. (He was at all times under pressure to allow first this and then that friend to live with him.) With the ashram situation, the nervous agitation also returned. In June 1940 there was a crisis over a torn letter and a missing pen, which upset Gandhi out of all proportion to its triviality. Gandhi fell into a fever of suspicion, demanding that the person responsible confess.

Mahadev Desai argued against Gandhi's fury, seemingly in vain, in person and by letter. As was increasingly the case, Gandhi was not to be reasoned with, and announced he would go on a fast. But this time, without warning, he called it off, after receiving Mahadev's last letter. (We see Gandhi taking as well as giving in these last years.) What is of most interest in this incident is that Gandhi traced his storm of the nerves and emotions to the way the incident had evoked in him traumatic memories of Sheikh Mehtab: he had thought someone was making him suspect someone else, just as Mehtab had so successfully done, in Rajkot, and in Durban.

Mira found Segaon for Gandhi, and almost everyone except her disapproved the scheme of his settling there. It was very inconvenient, as a center for a national movement; until 1940 visitors had to walk the distance from Wardha. There were many snakes, including the highly poisonous kraits; and malaria, dysentery, typhoid, and enteric fever were endemic. Gandhi himself soon fell sick and was sent away, and when he returned he found a loosely organized ashram gradually developing.

In terms of its interaction with the surrounding population, the Segaon cottages were like a settlement house, a rural Hull House, experimenting in how to make a decent life out of the raw materials available to the villagers. Gandhi devoted, for instance, a lot of time to medicine there. There was a regimen of enemas, sponge baths, steam inhalations, mud packs, and wet sheets. He taught Harijans to follow these methods, and used only iodine, quinine, castor oil, and sodium bicarbonate, doing it all himself, till Sushila arrived.

The population was mostly Harijans of four subcastes. They were all denied access to temples, barber, tailor, water-carrier, schools, roads, wells. When Gandhi first arrived, the Headman said he could not drink from the Harijan well, but gradually yielded and even ate Harijan-prepared food at the ashram.

The villagers refused to cooperate in the sanitation Gandhi introduced. Seventy villagers promised to help in road making, but only fifteen or twenty did, till he reproached them. Khadi was only a partial success; but by 1946 20 percent wore it. Gandhi started tanning classes, which included showing them how to make use of the meat and bones with which they were paid for their work on the hides. Gandhi invented a quilt made of newspapers and cotton waste and old saris.

We have a description of Gandhi's cottage there written by Nandalal Bose, the Shantiniketan artist. The wall and floors were plastered with cow dung. There was a net in one corner, with sheets and pillow for sitting and resting. A few packing cases contained letters and files. Another case covered with khaddar served as a writing desk, with a bottle of water, a bamboo basket, and a Gujarat lota [container] of bell metal covered with an iron-sheet pipal leaf. "Is it not beautiful?" Gandhi asked. "It bears the impress of Nature; moreover, a blacksmith of this very village has made it and given it to me as a token of his love. It is very precious to me." Bose says Gandhi, in his loincloth, looked like a sword of fine temper, kept unsheathed.[36]

Gandhi insisted on the exhibition of Indian art, of the many kinds that Bose knew, at congress meetings. At the Gauhati Congress they used, "Assam bamboo, Assam mud, Assam khadi and Assam labor were responsible for the very simple but artistic huts created on the Brahmaputra bank." Then came the session at Faizpur, using Bose's decor—a truly village congress. The *Times of India* said, "Everything is crude in the extreme . . . . A bamboo city." The following year Haripura, where Bose's exhibits demonstrated the evolution of art (51). Gandhi spoke of the art and beauty in the spotlessly white khaddar and its soft unevenness. "After all, all true art can be expressed not through inanimate power-driven machinery, but only through the delicate living touch of the hands of men and women."

In this setting, Mira Behn came into her own. She had always had a passion for country life. In April 1935 Gandhi wrote that she was absorbed in garden work all day. She was the "whole-hogger" amongst them (61:1). But even Bhansali, whose religion was contemplative, was gradually persuaded to take on some work—to spin yarn that could be made into a dhoti for Gandhi (61:5–7).

Kallenbach and Palestine

Despite being buried in this little village, Gandhi was still the focus of national and indeed international attention. In 1936 Moshe Shertok, or Sharett, the head of the Political Department of the Jewish Agency, sent Immanuel Olsvanger, a scholar who knew Sanskrit, to India. The agency wanted to elicit from Gandhi some statement of sympathy with the Zionists; It was generally known that the Muslims in particular, and Indians in general, sympathized with the Arabs, and regarded Zionism as another form of Western aggression. To have Gandhi dissent from that opinion could be useful to Zionists in a number of ways.

Olsvanger had lived in South Africa, in the 1920s, and knew Kallenbach. He suggested that the latter should accompany him to India. Kallenbach said, "None of us should refuse the call for service, when it arises. I am coming."[37] However, Olsvanger got there first. He arrived in Bombay on August 12, 1936, and was well received by Sarojini Naidu, who took him to see Nehru. Polak was in India then, and was ready to help (though no Zionist). Nehru, however, said the Arabs were the nationalist party in the situation, and Zionism was a movement of Jewish high finance.

Olsvanger saw Gandhi at Wardha, but conceived no respect for him. He regarded Gandhi as a sham saint; in his diary referring to him as *das Laemmel*, which implies a naive simpleton (the latter was Ambedkar's term). He thought both Nehru and the Aga Khan more impressive.

In March 1937, Olsvanger and Shertok met Kallenbach in London. The latter went on from there to Palestine and visited the kibbutzim. He reached Gandhi on May 20, and stayed with him till in July. They were again as deeply delighted with each other as before. Kallenbach wrote Shertok, "A father and brethren could not bestow more love and kindness on me. . . . It is a different world to the West, with which our people and we, I feel sorry to say, have assimilated ourselves so fully. This is no doubt one of the reasons why we have not been able so far to overcome our difficulties in Palestine, with its Eastern habits and culture."(32)

Gandhi was proud of his old friend and told others that Kallenbach's firm had four branches, and he employed thirty-five architects. He told a Captain Strunk, a German officer then visiting the Ashram, that Kallenbach had been a hot pro-German during the war. He approved Kallenbach's plan to settle in Palestine, and the idea of Zion as a goal, but not the Zionists' proposed means, of getting the British to protect them. Kallenbach asked the Jewish Agency to send Gandhi material on Zion. Via Gandhi, Andrews became interested. He was deeply impressed by Ahad Ha-am and Dr. Magnes. He wanted to go to Palestine, to write a new Life of Jesus, and Kallenbach was ready to put money at his disposal, could the scheme have been put into practice (Andrews died in 1940.) Kallenbach rejoined Gandhi in early 1939, and urged him to speak out on Palestine and on the Nazis. Gandhi was reluctant but did so in *Harijan* on November 26, 1938, criticizing the Jews' call for a National Home. He said Palestine belonged to the Arabs. This provoked the well-known letters of protest by Martin Buber and Judah Magnes in February 1939. Gandhi probably never saw those letters (47).

National Politics

At the end of 1936 and beginning of 1937, nationalist politics again began to intrude upon Gandhi's attention. Though congress had decided to work against the new constitution England offered (it was only divided about whether to do so from inside or outside the legislatures) the party had campaigned hard in the general elections, and as we know had won majorities in six out of eleven provinces. Nehru was still against congressmen taking office, but Gandhi supported Rajagopalachari and Patel and Prasad, who were for it.

Gandhi acted as mediator between the two parties—and between congress and the government—and so he returned, in mid-1937, to a position of political leadership, and in a context of suddenly increased political power. Many workers in the Gandhi Seva Sangh were bewildered by this turn back to politics, and by the recommendation of entry into the councils, which he had so opposed in the past.

In February 1938, congress met at Haripura, under Subhas Chandra Bose, who was reelected for the Tripuri session in 1939. Gandhi (suspicious of Bose) said he should choose a new working committee, the old one being Gandhian and therefore anti-Bosian in its view, and that if the All-India Congress Committee did not approve that new group, Bose should resign. This is what happened on April 29, 1939, and on May 3, Bose founded a new political party called the Forward Bloc.

It was typical of Bose's methods that he had founded centers for spreading information about India in the great cities of Europe. Gandhi disapproved; he seems to have suspected the European countries, and to have been suspicious even of America. For Gandhi, England was the only antagonist he knew.

Of course the work begun earlier continued, and of course Gandhi continued to invent new strategies and respond to new situations. But the outbreak of war brought the prophet of nonviolence a number of problems other politicians did not have to face, and to know that he could not carry most of his followers with him in the strategy he would have preferred had a semiparalyzing effect upon Gandhi, however much he might protest that he spoke and acted for himself alone.

There was trouble in Rajkot, and Ba (a daughter of Rajkot) went there first to help in the popular resistance to the Thakkore, and his advisor, Virawala. Gandhi joined her because of the threat of hooliganism, which would provoke violence in the authorities, as it had in Travancore and other places (69:7). He said that there was a growing conviction that the princes were beyond reform, but he disapproved. He hoped to win over Virawala as he had won over Smuts. But the effort was exhausting and the result dissatisfying. "Rajkot seems to have robbed me of my youth. I never knew that I was old." Now his hope "seems to have been cremated" in Rajkot (69:168–69).

On July 3, 1939, Rajaji and Patel led the Congress Working Committee to make the offer to England to fight alongside her in exchange for independence. (Like Gandhi, Abdul Ghaffar Khan disagreed and so resigned.) On September 15 congress returned to Gandhi, since the British had not responded to the offer. However, on December 23, 1941, he resigned, because the congressmen were not really nonviolent.

Gandhi wrote letters to Hitler in July 1939 and December 1941.[38] Such letters, and his articles on the plight of the Czechs and the Jews under Germany, were obviously naive in the pejorative sense—though also in better senses. Amrit Kaur and many congressmen wanted to see Germany defeat England. Gandhi wanted to give England unconditional moral support (he did not want to see the Allies defeated) but the Congress Working Committee preferred to dissociate themselves from the Allies and to demand a declaration of the empire's war aims, and their application to India. The congress ministries resigned; which gave a large opportunity for the Muslims to replace them.

His campaign of individual satyagraha in 1941 was striking in its style. The AICC asked Gandhi to lead individual civil disobedience and in September he gave the word; one leader at a time was to be arrested; the only issue raised was to be freedom of speech—freedom to speak against the British war effort.

On October 1, 1941, Vinoba Bhave made the first such demonstration and was arrested. Nehru, who was to have been the second, was arrested before he could speak. By May 1942 fourteen thousand were in jail. The restriction of the issues to free speech, and the small scale and dignity of the proceedings, made it less spectacular than other campaigns. Gandhi disciplined the movement severely; he refused to let Bose's Forward Bloc participate in the action because they were not nonviolent, and he expected prospective satyagrahis to keep a logbook of the constructive work they were doing.

One after another, congress leaders "offered satyagraha" individually, having given the authorities full notice in advance. Gandhi himself did not provoke arrest, and maintained friendly relations with other viceroys so as not to embarrass the British government in its hour of crisis. This could be called "classical" satyagraha, marked as it was by restraint, decorum, and gravity. It was an epitome of much that had been done elsewhere, but this time in a purer style and better taste. "This is to be an example of unadulterated non-violence," Gandhi said. But it was also less powerful as a political spectacle than, say, the Salt March.

In the summer of 1940—the summer of Germany's conquest of Northwest Europe—there were strikes and demonstrations in Indian cities, marches and train stoppings in the countryside. The league claimed to have organized ten thousand meetings of Muslims on April 19 alone, and in the Punjab armed bands of Sikh Khaksars, who hid out in mosques, roamed the countryside threatening Hindus. The latter demanded some effective defense. On June 29 congress finally said it could not agree 100 percent with Gandhi about nonviolent resistance. Even Rajagopalachari, perhaps his closest supporter in such matters, declared for armed resistance and brought Patel over to his views. But Gandhi persuaded the All India Congress Committee to declare its faith in the principle of nonviolence as a method for India after independence.

There followed the 1942 Quit India campaign, whose weaknesses were opposite in character. This was a mass movement, it was not under Gandhi's control, and it soon ceased to be peaceful. Gandhi was arrested as soon as he had launched it, on August 8, and was thrust into seclusion, and away from the other leaders. He felt more effectively isolated there than he had in other imprisonments.

TEN

TRIUMPH AND RUIN

· 1941–1948 ·

In this last decade of his life, Gandhi spent a long period in jail. He lost some of his most intimate companions to death; notably his wife and Mahadev, who was like a son to him. He also lost the battle with Jinnah, and had to accept the partition of India, and the setting up of an independent Muslim state. Furthermore, he was involved in a sexual scandal that alienated followers and admirers who had been loyal to him for forty years, and that undermined his position as Mahatma, even among his closest friends. But his work in bringing peace to Calcutta and to Noakhali was as remarkable as anything he ever accomplished.

Japan's attack on Pearl Harbor, bringing both that country and America into the war in December 1941, put India into much more immediate military jeopardy. Singapore fell to the Japanese in February 1942, and there was soon fighting in Burma, close to the Indian border. Gandhi also regretted America's entry into the war. He wished she had instead remained arbitrator and mediator between the warring nations. As for American aid, even if it undermined British power in the subcontinent, Gandhi knew that such aid carried with it American influence, which would bring India into the modern world, and prevent her from ever becoming a New Age country.

Moreover World War II, like World War I, brought with it many problems for the preacher of nonviolence: not only how could the nonviolent resist the armed forces, of an invader or of the British, but also, how could they cooperate with armed forces, of either kind? How could they take any effective action?

Even close friends came to doubt the great principle. Gandhi wrote to Agatha Harrison that she had hinted—and Polak had said—that Gandhi's nonviolence would not have stood the strain of being in wartime England, and seeing German bombs drop near him. He said only that perhaps that was true, and he did shed a silent tear, reading of damage done to the Houses of Parliament, St. Paul's, and Westminster Abbey. He had a strong sentimental feeling for England.

Gandhi wanted India to offer only passive resistance to invaders, and Mira Behn went to visit the areas that would be first affected by a Japanese invasion, to make plans for such defense. But Nehru then persuaded Gandhi to agree both to accept defense by the British army, and even to support the latter (the Indians acting as voluntary allies) in return for England joining the antifascist alliance with Russia and China. However, Gandhi's leadership was not very effective. The civil disobedience campaign of individual satyagraha he had inaugurated was suspended after a year, and the Working Committee accepted Gandhi's resignation from its leadership (which carried the responsibility to devise forms of civil disobedience) because he and they were at odds.

However, in 1942 he sent Mira Behn to the committee, then in session at Allahabad, to present the text of a demand that the British "Quit India" immediately. This was adopted as congress policy, and Gandhi led India into action again; saying, "this unnatural prostration of a great nation" must cease if the victory of the Allies is to be ensured. In parenthesis after "great nation" he added—defying Jinnah and Ambedkar—that India was just that, and not a complex of many nations. He promised that India would cooperate with Great Britain if it were free. He still opposed the policy put forward by Nehru and Rajaji, of armed resistance to the Japanese.

This last would have meant military cooperation, which Gandhi resisted. However, he foresaw unwillingly but unflinchingly that a free India would be militarist itself. "I expect that with the existence of so many martial races in a free India, national policy will incline towards a militarism of a modified character."[1] In any case, such cooperation was not to be. The British were not about to quit India, and there was talk of a scorched earth policy, like that employed in Russia, to frustrate the Nazi invasion. But Gandhi also disapproved that, which was being praised as heroic by the Allies. He did not want to see anything similar in India.

Jail Reflections

As soon as the "Quit India" campaign was announced, in August 1942, Gandhi was arrested and confined in a palace belonging to the Aga Khan, together with Kasturba, Mira Behn, Sarojini Naidu, Mahadev Desai, and others. Six days later Desai died; and in 1944 Kasturba died: from this point on Gandhi began to lose close followers to death by natural causes. While in jail, he was allowed no access to the press, and was in general sequestered much more completely than he had been in his other imprisonments. The authorities were less amenable than they had been. Churchill was prime minister of England, and he had always been more hostile than others to Gandhi.

Gandhi's health, physical and also psychological, suffered more this time than in other imprisonments. After his release in 1944, he was found to be suffering from malaria, amoebic dysentery, and acute anemia. And while in jail he wrote letters expostulating with both Viceroy Linlithgow and his successor, Viceroy Wavell, in which Gandhi sounds more plaintive and self-pitying than we expect him to be.

Part of the nationalist movement, including some of his close followers, engaged in violent resistance to the war effort, including industrial and communications sabotage, profiting by Gandhi's absence to follow their own desires. Things were done against his wish without the deed being acknowledged. It is often supposed, for instance, that Patel secretly approved of the sabotage. Some of those "underground" were more violent than others: there was a split between the forces led by Sucheta Kripalani and those led by Aruna Asaf Ali; the latter party being more violent.

In jail, meanwhile, Gandhi read Marx's *Capital*, and admired the author's erudition, but thought he made things more complicated than they need be. Gandhi spoke as a naive mind, judging an elaborate system of thought: "I think I could have written it better, assuming of course I had the leisure for the study he has put in."[2]

He knew how many of the most gifted young Indians found in Marxism something more congenial than they found in Gandhism, and he tried to combat its attraction. In 1940 he wrote, "The socialistic conception of the West was born in an environment reeking with violence. I hold that the coming to power of the proletariat through violence is bound to fail in the end. What is gained by violence is bound to lose before superior violence."[3] And again, "Insofar as Bolshevism is based on violence and denial of God, it repels me."[4] In June 1947 he quoted a passage from his morning prayers, and added: "What can Lenin add to this? Why are we so much infatuated with him?" (88:132).

Similarly, when Richard Gregg offered him a Freudian-psychological explanation for India's violence in November 1947, Gandhi found that the explanation mystified rather than clarified the problem (90:2). Freud was as repugnant as Lenin to him. The answer to the question Gandhi raised was surely that Lenin (and Freud) was an example of the systematic mind; the prayer, and Gandhi himself, were naive; and that young activists preferred the former.

In August 1942, Gandhi told Pyarelal that Marx, "has the knack of making even simple things appear difficult." When the secretary said that Marxists were like Gandhians in putting a high value on manual work, Gandhi disagreed, saying that Marx wanted to replace the hand with the machine, and—even more important—Marx approved of violence. "The difference between violence and nonviolence is fundamental. It cuts at the very root of the Marxist theory. If you alter the foundation the whole superstructure will have to be changed" (76:468).

On the other edge of the political spectrum was the legend of Subhas Chandra Bose, who with the help of the Japanese raised an Indian National Army among the Indian prisoners of war. This had fought in Burma against the British and was intended to head an invasion of India. In broadcast appeals he made to India, Bose associated himself with Gandhi; he said the struggle inside India was Gandhi's conception, and Bose's followers should obey him, while the struggle outside India was Bose's. In response, Gandhi was discreet. He talked of Bose's life being full of perilous adventure and romance, and perhaps thought of Savarkar's early exploits (89:104). He certainly, more privately, said that he didn't want to build up the Bose legend.

But the immediate problem was the demand of the Muslim League, under the leadership of Jinnah, for a separate Islamic nation, according to the theory of Pakistan developed by the poet Iqbal. The word was derived from the name of various provinces populated by Muslims in the north of the subcontinent: Punjab, Afghani, Kashmir, and so on, which meant the defeat of the united India cause for which Gandhi had worked for forty years. Indeed, Jinnah dreamed of a Muslim Empire that would include Russian Turkestan and four western provinces of China, as well as Pakistan and its immediate neighbors.

With so much going against him, we can guess that Gandhi felt one of his recurrent recoils away from orthodox politics—the field dominated by Jinnah on the Muslim side, and Savarkar on the Hindu, not to mention Ambedkar and the British. And there were moments, increasingly frequent ones, when all his enemies joined forces. In October 1939, Savarkar and Ambedkar and some liberals had jointly protested that congress could not speak for all Hindus, while Jinnah had long advanced the same protest on behalf of Indian Muslims. Soon after, a correspondent said Gandhi should make Jinnah negotiate directly with Savarkar and the Mahasabha, since these were the ultimate opponents; and Gandhi admitted the logic of that proposal. Indeed, he encouraged his opponents to make alliance. He congratulated Jinnah on giving his opposition to congress a national character (making it an opposition in the parliamentary sense); by joining forces with Ambedkar and by going to see Savarkar. (Jinnah replied by repeating that there could be no national opposition in India because it was not a nation, but a continent containing many nations.)

Gandhi acknowledged that Jinnah was winning the political battle—in the short run—against all odds. "Mr. Jinnah is doing something very big. Nobody had ever dreamed that in this day and age Pakistan would become a possibility. . . . Today my tongue, my words, have lost their power. But he still has that power" (88:134). What Gandhi had been able to do in the 1920s, Jinnah could do in the 1940s.

Gandhi remained of course a great public institution and a valuable congress property. But just for that reason, many people criticized his staying at Birla House when he went to Delhi, and the building of statues in his name (78:26). A preacher of poverty and simplicity who traveled in a chauffeur-driven car could easily seem hypocritical. And in practical politics, he had less power than ever before.

As freedom approached, his ex-lieutenants became busy with national and international politics. Gandhi tried to take consolation from Nehru's emotional dependence on his being in Delhi. Nehru had in the past argued with Gandhi and "made me feel confused over so many issues." But now he would be heartbroken if Gandhi hesitated to attend AICC meetings. However, Gandhi saw for himself that he was little use there. He wrote to Nehru. "Would I be of much use in Delhi as an adviser or consultant? I fancy I am not built that way. My advice has value only when I am actually working at a particular thing. I can only disturb when I give academic advice" (89:117). India was however able to provide him with many particular things to work at.

What Jinnah had to say about Gandhi in public we know, and what he and Savarkar said in private we can guess. From Ambedkar we have only a few phrases, but those are startling in their venom. "I've a feeling I know him better than most other people, because he had opened his fangs to me, you see, and I could see the inside of the man."[5]

To what extent these men's political actions may be linked to their personal hatred of Gandhi is not easy to say, but some connection there was. Of necessity, they did hate Gandhi's populism, pacifism, internationalism, and antipoliticism, and the result of their behavior was to disable those policies and finally to eliminate Gandhi. They hated peace worse than their opponents in war.

Gandhi seems to have worked more with women in this last period, just one example of how the New Age elements in his complex were becoming more prominent. In 1944 he spoke to a group of women, saying, "I have repeated times without number that nonviolence is the inherent quality of women. For ages men have had training in violence. In order to become nonviolent they have to cultivate the qualities of women. Ever since I have taken to nonviolence, I have become more and more of a woman."[6] In the photographs of the last campaigns and fasts, Gandhi is surrounded by women, especially young ones.

Release

Another major sign of his turn away from politics toward New Age concerns was that around this time he wrote a letter to Nehru reaffirming his *Hind Swaraj* ideas. He also renewed his interest in nature cure, into which he poured a great deal of his energy for two years after his release from jail. In 1945 he spent nine months in a nature-cure establishment in Poona, and when he gave up that work in March 1946, it was to become a village doctor in Uruli Kanchan, on the outskirts of the city.

He spent some of the time in the clinic supervising Patel's treatment. It seems, however, that the two men were out of sympathy; perhaps because of the power politics in which Patel was involved. On October 21 Gandhi said that he and the Sardar did not talk to each other; it was only the nature cure that held them together (81:460).

Saraladevi Chaudhurani and Kallenbach both died in 1945. The latter left some of his fortune to South African Indians, most to Zionist enterprises in Palestine. His five thousand books went to Hebrew University. His remains were buried in Kibbutz Dagania Cemetery, near those of Aaron David Gordon, the Tolstoyan theorist of self-labor.

As for the former, Gandhi had sometimes, in his political distress, evoked her memory, singing in her melodious voice, the lines from her husband's poem, "Never admit defeat even if you should lose your life" (88:145). He also thought of Mira's beautiful singing. The voices of women, uplifted in song, could console him for the misdeeds of men.

At the end of the 1930s Saraladevi had visited the ashram. She was sick, and Gandhi consulted Dr. Dinshaw of the Pune nature-cure clinic about her case. We gather that her spleen was swollen. Gandhi thought she should put herself under Dinshaw's care. If, on the other hand, she followed the orthodox medical route, she must begin to take quinine. He wrote this to Amrit Kaur and asked her to read it to Saraladevi; his tone friendly, but busy. She should not worry about the bill, if she goes to Dinshaw. Otherwise she must go to the Civic Hospital, and no false modesty should deter her.

Judging by these few brief letters of his, Saraladevi seems to have turned back to consult Gandhi as a guru, at the end. Thus on June 2, 1944, he wrote her that he could not guide her from his sickbed: she must do as much service as came her way; he asked after Dipak (77:298). In early November he wrote to her to come to the ashram whenever she wanted—she had fallen sick when he expected her, so she should come when she recovers. On August 19, 1945, he wrote her again that Dipak had given him a sorrowful account of her health; and soon thereafter she must have died.

After her death, Dipak immediately married Chhaganlal's daughter, Radha, one of the families most closely connected to Gandhi, and the Mahatma was asked to solemnize the wedding. It is said that Dipak's mother had, somehow, prevented the marriage as long as she was alive.

Mira Behn and Prithvi Singh were also involved in emotional conflicts with Gandhi, who had written to Prithvi in May 1941, seeming to withdraw his support from the gymnasium scheme. "I shall not be able to guide you much, because in a gymnasium you have to teach the use of weapons for self-defence and the defence of others. So act according to your own lights. . . . It is to be seen how far you can take up responsibility for training in violence" (74:43). We cannot teach the use of the sword, Gandhi said; though to snatch it from the murderer would be nonviolent defense. But in such circumstances one must above all be ready to die.

Acharya Kripalani had officially opened the gymnasium in Bombay, with forty-two students, on October 26, 1941. But Gandhi seems to have been more excited by a scheme of Abdul Ghaffar Khan in the following month. This was a big nonviolent defense camp organized by the khan in the Northwest Province, with workers from the Punjab, Kashmir, and Baluchistan. Five hundred people attended, as well as guests. They lived in tents, and the whole cost only 1,500 rupees. There were prayers and village cleaning, and three hundred spinning wheels, plied daily.

By 1942 Gandhi was saying that Prithvi had lost faith in Gandhi, and their friendly relations were over. On May 23, he said that Prithvi Singh must announce this publicly. Kedarnath and Kishorelal Mashruwala were severing connections with him (76:141). But this was not the last of the dealings between Gandhi and Prithvi Singh.

In 1944 Gandhi wrote to Mira Behn both about Prithvi, and about money she had deposited with the ashram and now wanted. Prithvi had been found out extorting money, and making indecent advances to girls (UC). Gandhi had been becoming suspicious for some time. Prithvi had not been sincere about nonviolence, Gandhi said. He had set out to deceive Gandhi; and it was now generally believed that he, and via him the Communist party of India, was exploiting Mira.

Mira Behn gives no account of all this in her books. She apparently did not accept Gandhi's view of Prithvi, and there was bad feeling between Gandhi and her. At least, he decided he must return to her the money that she had deposited with the ashram. Gandhis letter of June 12 addressed her as Dear Miss Slade. By July 18 he had returned to calling her Mira, but in the last few months of his life they were distant from each other, both literally and emotionally.

Other things did not change. Agatha Harrison asked if he would not ask people to grow flowers as well as vegetables, since color and beauty were necessary to the soul. Gandhi replied, "No. Why can't you see the colour of beauty in vegetables? And then there is beauty in the speckless sky. But no, you want the colours of the rainbow, which is an optical illusion. We have been taught to believe that what is beautiful need not be useful" (76:265). This was a replay of the reproaches of Tagore and Andrews, twenty years before. (At the same time, in 1942, Gandhi asked Horace Alexander to play the part Andrews had played in the past—and Polak before him—of pitiless cross-examiner of Gandhi.)

Sexual Scandal

It was surely another, indirect sign of Gandhi's turn toward New Age hopes, that he followed a new quest for new powers of brahmacharya, and so there was also a recurrence of the sexual scandal. On March 7, 1945, he wrote to Gosibehn Captain that Khurshedbehn (they were both Naoroji's granddaughters) was with him, and was disgusted about his contacts with women. He asked if his addressee was similarly disgusted (UC). He continued with apparent calmness that there was quite a storm brewing, and he contemplated making a statement. Munnalal Shah at the ashram, for one, had asked Gandhi about what was happening, and Gandhi had answered with full details of names and places.

He did not say much in that reply about his intentions or rationale, but we can supply that information from other sources. Gandhi was intensifying the powers of brahmacharya in himself, but also in the young women around him, by the physical intimacy that he sometimes calls maternal. We have already seen the circuit of desire that included Gandhi and Mira Behn and Amala, and the men they wanted to marry; what we now see is a similar circuit, but with younger women, who have never known sexual desire. He wanted to make their virginity into a positive force. With them he hoped to build a power of caritas that could make itself felt even on the plane of actual politics.

He wrote to Munnalal Shah briskly, "Why need you feel embarrassed? This problem cannot be solved in that way. Ask me any question without the slightest hesitation." He had named four women as having shared his bed. But he expects they will tell Gandhi, "'We were not objects of your experiment; we slept with you as with a mother'" (79:212). Those involved were the Rajkumari, and Prabhavati (married to J.P. Narayan) and Lilavati and Amtussalaam (two long-term inmates of the ashram). Another three, Abha, Kanchan, and Vina, do not count as parts of the experiment, since they slept with him so rarely. Of those three, he said, Kanchan seems to have taken no interest in brahmacharya, and so slept with him reluctantly—though he did not know that at the time. (Kanchan seems to be the woman of that name married to Munnalal.) Gandhi then stopped the experiment, realizing that Kanu (Abha's husband) and Munnalal were upset. He also advised the women to tell the two husbands and Bhansali.

The remark about Kanchan implies that the others *did* take an interest in brahmacharya, and were partners with Gandhi in the experiment; which was a matter of proud faith. In another letter on the same day, Gandhi added, "If I completely give up sleeping together, my brahmacharya will be put to shame. . . . It is true that people may indulge in licentiousness by imitating me. Who can stop it?" The implication here is that since whatever he does may lead others astray, he cannot allow that to inhibit him. "I claim that whatever I have done I have done in the name of God. I go to bed reciting His name. I have got up with His name on my lips. So it is in my dreams, whether alone or with some woman. What God will make me do in days to come He alone knows" (79:216). Kishorelal seems to have been the leader of the critical party.

Gandhi also wrote to Pyarelal about his relations with Gandhi's grandniece, Manu, who had spent a lot of time with Gandhi and Kasturba, for instance during the years in the Aga Khan's bungalow, and was in 1947 to be the main participant in the experiment that cause such scandal. Pyarelal now was in love with Manu, and had been writing to her. Manu, like Yoga, seems not to have returned Pyarelal's feelings, and Gandhi from this time on kept Pyarelal at a distance, physically. Manu and Gandhi had long been very intimate.

In early 1945 Gandhi wrote to his cousin, Jaisukhlal, Manu's father, in Porbandar, that he had had Manu sleep with him three nights, hoping to correct her sleeping posture (79:45). On February 5 he wrote to her that he worried about her: she was restless and always crying. She was keeping something from him. She apparently thought it was out of hostility that Sushila told her not to come to class—really it was because she had been sick with a cold (79:96).

Gandhi was thus developing his brahmacharya, but he took a quite different attitude to other people's sexual lives. Some he urged to avoid all contact with the opposite sex; others he urged to marry. For instance, at this time he got many requests for advice from Munnalal Shah, who had made a brahmachari marriage, but who found that his wife was not satisfied with it (81:141). To him Gandhi gave the commonsense advice that he should give Kanchan sexual satisfaction.

Gandhi was a New Age teacher even in matters of sex, remarkably bold and explicit and experimental. He is best compared with the psychotherapists of the New Age. But his own experiments in brahmacharya must not be confused with what he taught others.

Family Life

In 1941 Harilal went to stay with Ba in Delhi for a few days, but then disappeared without explanation in May. In 1942 he fractured his hand, and Gandhi was the one who sent him to the hospital. His recurrent professions of repentance were not to be trusted, Gandhi judged; he was drunk much of the time, and had lost all sense of truth (76:10). On April 11, Gandhi asked Devdas to tell Harilal that he would help him get admitted to some jail or asylum temporarily, while he recovered self-control. He wrote to Harilal that he would be delighted if the latter had turned over a new leaf. "Mine is an arduous pilgrimage. I invite you to join it if you can" (86:376).

At the time of Kasturba's last sickness, she and Gandhi were in prison. The sons assembled in nearby Pune. On January 26, 1944, Harilal asked to see her but was refused permission because he was drunk. On February 17 he *was* admitted and was given permission to come again, but he failed to turn up. On February 21, he reappeared and saw her, but was drunk again. Kasturba beat her brow in anguish to see him, and the following day she died.

Later Harilal went to Mysore, where his son Kantilal lived, by then a doctor and married. There he seemed to become amenable to social discipline, for a time. April 19, 1945, Gandhi wrote to Kantilal's wife, Saraswati, "The victory over Harilal, which was denied me, has come to you two." They were right, he said: if Harilal could get rid of two vices, he could be the best of all brothers. Gandhi declared himself very happy with the change. On May 3, he wrote to the same person, apparently agreeing with her, "I would consider it a great triumph if you can win over Harilal. Do not leave him and do not bring him this side. He is so stubborn by nature that he relapses into his old ways again and again" (80:61). And "If you two can reform Harilal, I shall feel that you have accomplished a great thing" (80:216).

There was a struggle between the Gandhi family (especially the Mahatma) and Harilal's disreputable friends, each side trying to free him from the opposite influence. In February 1947, Gandhi wrote that "Harilal knows that when he has shed his evil habits he will be welcome in Sevagram." But those who nursed his evil habits were his enemies (87:2).

Partition

The Labor government had come to power in London in 1945, and despite Churchill's wholehearted opposition, set about freeing India. After the failure of the Cripps Mission, Lord Louis Mountbatten was sent out to be the last viceroy, to oversee the transfer of power. He was so popular that he stayed on as the first governor-general of the free India. Mountbatten was over six feet tall, a military hero and fond of wearing a uniform; fond of the limelight, color, parades, games, gadgets. He and his wife were brilliant and popular figures, socially not unlike Nehru, and belonging to the post-Victorian generation in England.

Churchill made many speeches like that of September 28, 1947, where he said: "The fearful massacres which are occurring in India are no surprise to me. We are, of course, only at the beginning of those horrors and butcheries, perpetrated upon one another with the ferocity of cannibals by races gifted with the capacities for the highest culture and who had for generations lived side by side in general peace under the broad, tolerant and impartial rule of the British Crown and Parliament."[7] Morally speaking, Gandhi probably felt that Churchill—like his other enemies—had triumphed. They had shown that India was incapable of governing itself as a whole, and even of keeping the peace locally. On the occasion of his seventy-eighth birthday on October 2, 1947, Gandhi said, "Where do congratulations come in? It will be more appropriate to say condolences. There is nothing but anguish in my heart."[8] He said that Patel, amongst others, found that nonviolence did not serve his purposes once he acquired power; and that he himself realized that theirs had not been true nonviolence.

At the end of July 1946 the Muslim League withdrew from the Cabinet Mission's national negotiations, begun by the British, and launched Direct Action. Gandhi told Louis Fischer that Jinnah was an evil genius, not just a lawyer (85:514). He looked upon himself as the savior of Islam. Fischer protested, "But Jinnah is cold. He is a thin man. He pleads a case, he does not present a cause." Gandhi replied. "I agree he is a thin man. But I don't consider him a fraud. . . . I learned that he was a maniac." We know that Gandhi had formed this opinion in 1944: he had come to see Jinnah as a religious fanatic.

Once India was divided, the communal hatreds became uncontrollable. Forty-five million Muslims were left living in Hindu India. Altogether twelve million people migrated from there to Pakistan or vice versa. Ultimately there were seven million homeless in India, one million of whom were in Delhi, doubling the city's size. It was one of the great migrations of history; one column was eight hundred thousand strong. But the worst of it was that these migrations all provoked more manifestations of purely destructive violence. There were columns of women, five hundred at a time, who had been stripped naked; there were hundreds of thousands of mutilated and murdered bodies.

In 1947 the Muslims were only 25 percent of the population of India, but in the Northeast and the Northwest they were in the majority. The population of Bengal and the Punjab was 60 percent Muslim, but the league was not powerful there. It was strong in the United Provinces, where Hindus were in the majority, and where in 1916 the Young Muslims and the ulema had broken free from the landowners' control.

Partition left many ends loose, especially in the princely states, which had to choose either Delhi or Karachi to be their rulers. India made a military invasion of Kashmir, where the Maharaja was Hindu, although the majority of the population was Muslim. Gandhi did not protest, though he certainly grieved over the imperialism of Indian policy. He realized he had labored under an illusion—that Indians were nonviolent. But he believed that but for that illusion India might not have developed to the point she had.

A Free India

By mid-1947 it was accepted that partition was inevitable, and all Gandhi's causes seemed forgotten: brahmacharya, swadeshi, spinning, nonviolence. If he were prime minister, he declared, "I would stop all machine-driven flour mills, and restrict the number of oil-pressing factories but install the indigenous mills all over the country. . . . I would close all the cinemas and theatres" (88:17). This declaration was a defiance of all that his lieutenants were doing.

Nehru was his dear friend but he was going to betray Gandhi's fondest hopes for India. Gandhi wrote Jawaharlal that the hope of peace and justice rested on the organization of India as a society of villages as he had declared in *Hind Swaraj* nearly forty years before. Nehru replied: "I do not understand why a village should necessarily embody truth and nonviolence. A village, normally speaking, is backward intellectually and culturally, and no progress can be made from a backward environment. Narrow-minded people are much more likely to be untruthful and violent."[9]

Pandey says that during Gandhi's tours, from October 1946 to March 1947: "He was not missed in Delhi, where Nehru and Patel had taken upon themselves the sole responsibility for making policy decision and planning strategy." They were deeply committed to purposes that conflicted with his, and that seemed to make nonsense of past enthusiasms. Nehru had called khadi the livery of freedom. Gandhi now observed, "not if it is the consolation of cranks and paupers only" (86:21).

Nehru and Patel and Ambedkar cooperated in setting up the new state. (Gandhi insisted that Ambedkar be given a place in the cabinet.) When the constitution was drafted, Ambedkar said, "The love of the intellectual Indian for the village community is of course infinite if not pathetic. . . . I hold that these village republics have been the ruination of India. . . . What is the village but a sink of localism, a den of ignorance, narrow-mindedness, and communalism? I am glad the draft Constitution has discarded the village and adopted the individual as its unit."[10] Nehru was therefore more in sympathy with Ambedkar than with Gandhi.

Gandhi told Jehangir Patel that partition was the work of four men, Nehru and Patel, Jinnah and Mountbatten, who did not consult him. "I was tempted to feel that my whole life's work had been destroyed."[11] What was lost was not only national independence, but ahimsa—and the penalty was not only the divided political structures, but the appalling bloodshed and the national shame. Gandhi feared, for a time, that the Allied powers would intervene to reimpose order.

Noakhali

In Lahore, in the Punjab, Hindus and Sikhs were isolated in the Old City, and water supplies were cut off; women and children coming out with pails to fill were butchered; geysers of sparks arose from blazes in six places. And in Amritsar, nearby, the Number 10 Down Express came in on Independence Day with no one aboard but murdered bodies, and the sign "This is our Independence gift to Nehru and Patel." Nehru threatened an aerial bombardment of Bihar in early November, as the only way to stop the fighting.

Gandhi decided to go to Noakhali, in Bengal, where the Muslim majority of the population had taken up arms against their Hindu neighbors. Noakhali was a jigsaw of islands in the water-logged delta of the Ganges and the Brahmaputra, forty miles square, and inhabited by 2.5 million people, 80 percent of whom were Muslim. Gandhi mentioned it as a promising center of khadi, because of the 55,000 weavers there, in 1925. The Muslims had rioted against their Hindu neighbors, burning, raping, pillaging, murdering.

The villages were separated by canals and streams, which were crossed by hand-polled ferries or by rope and bamboo bridges. Single-file paths, often jagged with pebbles and roots, led through mango orchards and palm groves, by scum-slicked ponds with geese and ducks, and through jungle to the next village.

Of all Gandhi's campaigns, this last one, which began on January 1, 1947, may be both the most beautiful and the most troubling to his admirers. It was the most compassionate, inasmuch as it was directed against the violence the Hindu villagers there had suffered, and the threat of more such; but it was also the one with a hidden underside of sexual scandal.

Asked about his plans, Gandhi said, "I don't know what I shall be able to do there. All I know is that I won't be at peace with myself unless I go there" (86:52). Later he said it was the cry of outraged womanhood that had peremptorily called him to Noakhali (86:65). He went there with a small group of companions, including Nirmal Kumar Bose, a teacher of anthropology at the university of Calcutta, who had compiled anthologies of some of Gandhi's writings. He was to serve as secretary and translator, but also to teach Gandhi Bengali. He was at the same time making Gandhi a collection of all Jinnah's speeches, in chronological order.

Bose had met Gandhi at the end of 1945, and offered to serve him, but only in some intellectual capacity. He refused to go to Sevagram to scavenge. Payne says Bose was fascinated by the movements of Gandhi's mind and his defiance of logic. But it is clear that he was as caught up in a personal dialectic as most of Gandhi's companions.[12] He seems always to have been raising objections, and withdrawing from Gandhi. He got on badly with Sushila Nayar, in whom he sensed possessiveness and secrecy and hysteria. (She was also engaged in a long-drawn quarrel with Munnalal Shah.) Bose had, of course, an academic training, and a systematic mind, but he came to Gandhi after reading Tolstoy and Kropotkin.

As for Gandhi, he personalized the politics of Noakhali, even more than usual. He wrote in his diary, "I can see there is some grave defect in me somewhere which is the source of all this" (86:302). Brahmacharya was to be the remedy for that defect.

Gandhi first assigned one of his companions each to a village; though he took Bose and Parasuram (a stenographer) with him. He had been staying in Shrirampur, but on January 1, announced that for the next seven weeks he would walk barefoot from village to village, living on charity, with four companions. This would be his "last and greatest experiment," to "re-kindle the lamp of neighborliness." He would visit forty-seven villages, and cover 116 miles.

As they set out each day, his little group, going single file, sang Tagore's song,

"If they answer not your call, walk alone, walk alone." In each village he begged for food and shelter, preferably from a Muslim, and went from door to door till he found it. He persuaded two village leaders, one Hindu, one Muslim, to live together and each to vow to fast to death if the other condoned communal violence. He inspected latrines and wells, and suggested improvements: "The lessons which I propose to give you during my tour are how you can keep the village water and yourselves clear," he would tell the villagers. "What use you can make of the earth, of which your bodies are made; how you can reinforce your vital energy from the air which surrounds you, how you can make proper use of sunlight."[13] It was the doctrine of the Simple Life, as he had heard it in London sixty years before.

He expected the Muslim League to send him volunteers, but they did not come. At first he was met with courtesy and indeed reverence, by Muslims as well as Hindus. But there were propagandists for rival ideologies in Noakhali, and later Muslim children were driven indoors away from Gandhi, a Muslim spat in his face, the bridges he was to cross were sabotaged, the trees carried slogans, "Go home for your own good," and some had glass shards and human turds placed on them for his bare feet. Whole villages had been burned down, women raped, many forcibly converted or forcibly fed beef. There was bitter hatred, legends of vendettas and communal violence. In many places all he could do was listen to the tales of horror, see the ruined buildings and lives, and then, rather than console, exhort them to courage and forgiveness. "I have come to Bengal not to give consolation but to bring courage."[14] But he did console, by the closeness of his attention and the gentleness of his presence. One feels the difference between him and Nehru when the latter writes him: "In quality or lack of it there is little to choose, to my mind . . . [between Hindu and Muslim rioters]. They all represent utter degradation and depravity."[15] These things drove Nehru to anger (and of course to horror); one hears of him seizing a lathi and attacking Hindu rioters in Delhi.

Gandhi had some ineffective police protection but he eluded it. Manu and Abha massaged Gandhi's feet with a stone, prepared his food, looked after his clothes, and so on. And other people often came to see him, including journalists and photographers. There are many pictures of the white-clad party going in single file along narrow village paths, and in yet another village looking at ruined houses and mutilated corpses.

He quarreled with Sushila, when she insisted that he take his familiar companions with him, including herself. He shouted at her, and then slapped himself (86:238–39). Parasuram left him, disapproving of something, presumably related to the scandal (86:246). Gandhi wrote in his diary, "Does India have the ahimsa of the weak, and not of the strong?" (86:335). Could he find a new source of strength? He complained that he couldn't find the truth, in an atmosphere of exaggeration and falsity. His oldest friendships had snapped. "Truth and ahimsa fail to show the attributes I have ascribed to them" (86:138).

Perhaps because it was so immediately picturesque and unequivocally spiritual (lacking the aggressive political element of the Dandi March) the feeling of the Noakhali Pilgrimage is closer to sentimental piety than some of the other campaigns. But the sexual scandal attached to it has done more than anything else to make Gandhi seem a whited sepulcher. The scandal was publicly suppressed even then, but a circle of people in the Gandhian movement knew about it at the time, and that circle spread out rapidly.

Sexual Scandal

The core of the scandal, as we know, was that Gandhi asked the young girls of the ashram, which in Noakhali meant Manu, to share his bed. He suffered from shivering fits at night, and he wanted them to warm him. (Erikson points out that this is the first time in Gandhi's life in which he admitted to a need that someone else could satisfy; and that here for once he was daughter as well as mother.[16]) But it was also a test, or better a development, of his and their purity and love.

The rumors of scandal soon followed Gandhi to Noakhali. At the end of 1946 he wrote to Manu's father, who had expressed alarm about an atmosphere of impurity there, reassuring him about Pyarelal (86:221). On January 6, 1947, he wrote to Pyarelal that he had a letter from Nirmal Kumar Bose for him and his sister to read. (He'd also had a long talk with Devdas, evidently about related matters.) Manu, he said, had developed a terrible dislike for things, and if Pyarelal comes, it would be aggravated. "I came to know about it from Nirmal Babu's letter afterwards" (UC). She has lost her equanimity, and Kishorelal's letter, presumably also about the scandal, played a part in her upset. As for Pyarelal, "If instead of worshipping her, you worship God—if it is possible for you to do that—then everything will become easy" (UC).

Gandhi's old friends did not even profess to understand what he was doing, at the time or after Gandhi's death. To Kripalani he wrote that his sleeping with Manu had lost him the support of Patel, Kishorelal, Devdas, and probably Rajaji. He said he had lost caste with them. Professor Swaminathan, the editor of Gandhi's *Collected Works*, described Gandhi's sex experiments as a desperate, anguished striving to find a way to discover his identity (86:ix). And Vinoba, as close to him intellectually as anyone ever came, was equally baffled. "I must confess, the last chapter of his life . . . remains a mystery to me" (86:x).

Yet it is not so difficult to align what Gandhi was doing with Tantric or indeed with Christian practices, amongst Roman Catholics especially. (Gandhi used to point out to Andrews in the 1920s and before, that Protestants were eccentric in their distrust of chastity.) Francis Watson described Manu as being as sweetly immaculate as Saint Rose of Lima, and that idea is what shines out of the later group photographs.[17] It was there in earlier photographs, too, for instance those of the noncooperation campaign, but not so decidedly. In the Salt March, for instance, only men were allowed to take part. The shift to women, or rather to maidens, as the leading figures, is a mark of the late period.

Mira Behn said that in her dreams Bapu was often mixed up with her mother. We have heard of something comparable in Premabehn's dreams. And Gandhi himself "was" a woman, as we know; indeed Manu's book about him was entitled *Gandhi: My Mother*. Such women as Mira and Premabehn—commanding and capable of severity—continued to play a large part in the movement. It was the men who, comparatively speaking, removed to a different platform: Nehru and Patel and the other political figures. But amongst the women, it is the maidens who most strike the eye and the imagination.

The matter came to a head because the young secretary, Bose, protested to Gandhi against what he was doing. Bose had found (not that they were hiding, but he was apparently unprepared for what he saw) Gandhi and Manu in bed together on December 12. But it is important to realize that his objection was not that Gandhi was indulging his sexual appetites. No one suggested that in print, and I would guess that no one who knew and understood Gandhi even thought it. What Bose objected to was the strain imposed upon the girls by so complete a flouting of ordinary propriety, plus—a related matter—the emotional hysteria of mutual jealousy, competitiveness, and possessiveness that surrounded Gandhi.

It is, I think, possible that Bose himself was speaking out of his own involvement in that group hysteria. Between him and Sushila Nayyar, who had herself on occasion slept with Gandhi, there developed a sharp irritation that might be called jealousy; she certainly accused him of "a dirty mind."[18] On the other hand, common sense would certainly endorse his judgment. Any hesitation to agree must base itself upon the feeling that this was not a commonsense matter; that these young women, not to mention Gandhi himself, were most uncommon creatures in their mutual relations. They were engaging in a spiritual experiment. That they were unable to explain this afterwards is not so surprising; a certain simplicity of the mind was part of the experiment.

Erikson reports Bose overhearing Gandhi say to himself, "If I can master this, I can still beat Jinnah."[19] He believed, as we know, that ahimsa and brahmacharya went together. Strength in the latter form would bring strength in the former.

At the beginning of 1947, Gandhi described his behavior with Manu to S. C. Mukherji and asked his opinion (86:414). He said that Kishorelal, Patel, Devdas, Swami Anand, and Narahari disapproved, while Vinoba passed no judgment. He talked about the matter in an interview, saying this was part of his *yajna* (or penance) (86:420). He declared that had done the same things in thought for fifty years (86:466).

In February 1947 he had a discussion with A. V. Thakkar, and told him too that this was not an experiment, but a part of his yajna. (He realized what disapproval the word *experiment* opened him up to, though he still used *research,* sometimes.) If he were to give the yajna up, "to please Mrs. Grundy," he would be sacrificing brahmacharya. He told Thakkar he had asked himself in Noakhali, "Why does the spell not work? May it not be because I have temporized in the matter of brahmacharya?" Temporizing means that he had not lived up to his faith. Thakkar accepted what Gandhi said, but suggested giving up the practice for the time being. Manu also suggested that they should. In the course of this discussion Gandhi declared that the prospect of being debunked as a mahatma greatly pleased him; but of course he, like them, had a great deal invested in his being a mahatma (77:14–16).

On March 15 and 16, he had more discussions, with two longtime coworkers, Swami Anand and Kedar Nath. This time he admitted that he should have asked for the previous consent of other people, before beginning his experiment, and that that was a serious flaw. They said that he was weakening the moral order of society, and what was he gaining? He declared that he was still recommending the old ideas of prudence in sexual matters to other people; but he thought the ninefold wall Hindus had built around brahmacharya was not good, and he had never believed in it. As we know, in South Africa he had read writers like Havelock Ellis and Bertrand Russell, who believed in a purity independent of usages. "My research runs somewhat in that direction" (87:90).

His friends said that in the past he had always put before the public opposite, and more familiar, moral ideas. He counterattacked by reproaching them with caring more about a fancied breach in brahmacharya than about anything else, and protested (a rare note of self-pity) that he was "not so lost as you seem to think." They concluded: "We cannot say we have been convinced. We feel unhappy."

He and Nirmal Kumar Bose exchanged letters on the same topic. On March 17 Gandhi said again he had held the same views for forty-five years. Bose said he had joined Gandhi in Noakhali because Gandhi was trying a new experiment in nonviolence of the brave (87:270). That phrasing is ambiguous, but "experiment" seems to hint that he knew some part of what was happening; for what was new in Noakhali was this interpretation of brahmacharya. In any case, Bose made sensible criticisms—and Gandhi made sensible enough replies. He protested against Bose's argument that he was demeaning women: Ba had been his inferior when she was the instrument of his lust, he said, not when she lay beside him like a sister (87:104). And "What is brahmacharya? It is the way of life which leads us to the Brahman" (88:58).

On March 18 Gandhi reported the interview with Thakkar and Kedar Nath to others; and said that only in one case in his life had his touching of women ever had anything lustful about it. This seems to refer to Saraladevi, since a few days before he mentioned in his diary the one time he had sought the company of a woman for sensual reasons. Now he says of that occasion, "I was carried away in spite of myself and but for God's intervention I might have become a wreck" (87:108). This is the language he used to refer to the Saraladevi relationship when he talked to Margaret Sanger.

On March 1 Kripalani wrote to say that he had the fullest faith in Gandhi, but his letter made it clear that he was also full of doubt. Sometimes he had thought that Gandhi was employing people as means, not ends; sometimes that he was not conserving the social good. But he felt sure that could not be true (87:533).

Not everyone knew everything (it is not clear how much Nehru, for instance, was kept informed) but those who did were of course exchanging letters and meeting, in distress and perplexity. On March 16 Bose wrote to the others that he had always thought that morally Gandhi "represented a hard, puritanic form of self-discipline, something which we usually associate with medieval Christian ascetics or Jain recluses." When Bose found out in what the experiment consisted, he saw in it the reason for his companions' jealousy and emotional imbalance. But he would still stand by Gandhi if the other parties were willing and if the public was told (87:535).

Bose did in fact return to Gandhi; he was with him in Calcutta later; and he and the others managed to prevent news of the scandal from reaching national or international papers. But there was great tension within the movement. Gandhi's friends at the Navajivan press, and the Gandhi newpapers, were noncooperating with him, as he said.

Gandhi left Noakhali in disgrace; the fact that that disgrace was private rather than public may have made it even sorer. But in Calcutta he was restored to power and was able to exert a force for peace as never before. Grace followed upon disgrace.

Calcutta

From Noakhali, Gandhi went on to Bihar briefly, and then to Calcutta. He had intended to be back in Noakhali for August 15, 1947, Independence Day, but the city authorities were very nervous about what would happen in Calcutta, the greatest trouble spot in India for communal rioting, after the Punjab. First Mountbatten and then Shaheed Suhrawardy, the Muslim mayor of the city, asked him to be there to help prevent riots. Gandhi at first agreed to be there for two extra days on his way to Noakhali, at the prompting of Mohammad Usman, a former mayor. But then Suhrawardy flew in from Karachi and begged him to stay longer.

Suhrawardy had worked with Gandhi in Bengal in the days of noncooperation, and had been one of his spinners. Patel and Sykes say that Suhrawardy had more recently referred to Gandhi as "that old fraud," and Gandhi had been warned not to trust him.[20] But Gandhi remembered him as a young man who said he felt like a son to Gandhi (90:260). Amongst Muslim politicians, Suhrawardy was not one of those closely allied to Jinnah. But he was in 1947 a prime example of the communal politician; forty-seven years old and a pillar of the Muslim League, he had a reputation as a gourmand and womanizer who had made a fortune selling on the black market grain intended for the starving. He was said to have a private army of goondas, and to have licensed the riots of Direct Action Day by telling his followers that the police would not interfere.

Gandhi was asked to stay in Calcutta on August 10, and agreed to, on two conditions: that the Muslims of Noakhali pledge safety to the Hindus there, and that Suhrawardy come to live with him, night and day, unprotected, in a Calcutta slum. At one point Gandhi suggested that he should become Suhrawardy's secretary, and make sure that the Hindus listened to him (87:453). For his part, the old Suhrawardy would have to die, and the new one wear the garb of a mendicant. Gandhi told Suhrawardy to go and consult with his daughter.

Gandhi arrived on August 13 at 151 Beliaghata Road (according to the authors of *Freedom at Midnight* a decayed mansion, looking like a Tennessee Williams stage set). It stood in a Hindu district, but on the border of a Muslim slum, Miabagan, which had recently been the scene of raids and a massacre. People were awaiting Gandhi there with cries of traitor and a shower of bottles and stones, as he stepped out of the car. The Hindus accused him of being interested only in the Muslims. "You wish to do me ill and so I am coming to you," he said. And when Suhrawardy joined him there, a barrage of rocks was discharged against the house.

A miracle happened almost immediately, recalling the early Khilafat days. A band of girls, both Muslim and Hindu, had walked through the city at night to come to Gandhi in the morning (another example of the power of the maiden idea) and that afternoon thirty thousand people attended his prayer meeting. When Suhrawardy admitted to an angry crowd his responsibility for the Muslim Direct Action, their mood reversed itself, and they cheered him. He and Gandhi toured the city by car, and there were cries of "Gandhiji, you have saved us." Later there were crowds of up to a million attending his prayer meetings. Gandhi wrote to Mira Behn that it was too sudden to be true, and was anyway not his work (89:58). He was proven right.

Bose's notes on those events shows us how Gandhi was involved in interplay with those around him. When he told Bose (who acted as his translator) to tell a bereaved mother that the Lord giveth and the Lord taketh away, Bose refused. And when some young men ready for violence asked for Gandhi's blessing, he gave it to them (because he had nothing better to offer). Bose could not deliver that message, and asked for an explanation.[21]

On August 31, Hindus brought him a bandaged man whom they claimed had been attacked by Muslims, and demanded from Gandhi the lives of all the Muslims in the house. Gandhi tried to throw himself among them in order to be killed. On September 1, there were more riots. Hindus led by RSS men (of the Rashtra Swayamsevak Sangh) attacked the Muslim slums, and there was a murder with grenades on Beliaghata Road, which Gandhi went to inspect minutes after it occurred. That night he decided to fast to death unless the communal leaders swore to prevent any more violence. His fast was designed to act not upon the goondas but upon those behind them (542).

Gandhi lived on water and bicarbonate of soda. The next morning he was already missing one heartbeat in four, and his voice was a whisper. Almost immediately there was an effect. A band of twenty-seven goondas came to beg his forgiveness; then those responsible for the grenade murder brought him their weapons and asked for punishment—he had sent them to a Muslim quarter, to take its defense.

The leaders worked out a joint declaration and on September 4 he broke his fast. (The same day Delhi went up in flames.) Suhrawardy knelt at his feet weeping, to offer him the first drink of lemon juice. (This reduction of adults to children, which disturbs many of us as an attack on our reason, is an essential party of Gandhi's political therapy.) And in fact there was no more major violence in Calcutta.

Rajagopalachari said: "Gandhi has achieved many things, but there has been nothing, not even independence, which is so truly wonderful as his victory over evil in Calcutta."[22] And Mountbatten had written Gandhi, before that, "In the Punjab we have 55,000 soldiers and large-scale rioting on our hands. In Bengal, our force consists of one man and there is not rioting. . . . [I] pay tribute to my One Man Boundary Force" (302). Mountbatten's letter was premature; it was written on August 26, and on the thirty-first the trouble began again, when

Surawardy had left, thinking the trouble was over. But, as we have seen, the forces of peace finally triumphed. This was an example of history making a pun with the idea of force.

Gandhi set off by train to the Punjab, but when he got as far as Delhi, found it to be in such a dangerous situation that he could not leave it. He found the Muslim population in terror of their lives, and taking refuge in the courtyard of the Jamma Masjid, and in the ground of Humayun's Tomb. At the Purana Qila Fort, seventy-five thousand people awaited evacuation, but had hidden stores of arms and ammunition. A curfew was in operation, and was lifted for only a few hours each day. Jinnah and Liaquat Ali Khan had no control over the situation, from Karachi, and Nehru and Patel in Delhi very little. Patel had decided he had to treat all Muslims as potential traitors to the new state of India.

Gandhi went to the Fort with three of his young women, and though he was greeted with cries of "Death to Gandhi" *(Gandhi Mordabad),* he was able to abate the fever somewhat. But on October 2 he said to Patel: "What sin have I committed that He should have kept me alive to be witness of these horrors?"[23] And the question could not seem entirely rhetorical, for there were many who felt that Gandhi, as the leader of national liberation, was indeed responsible.

He must have felt something like that himself. He had passed Independence Day in Calcutta, and was asleep at the midnight at which India became a free nation. He refused to celebrate the event. He told the students who came to him for a message for the occasion: "This is a sorry affair." He arrived in Delhi only three days after Nehru and Patel had in effect handed power back to Mountbatten, in an appeal for his help. Communal violence seemed inevitable, and with a million refugees in the city, seemed also limitless.

Gandhi said the refugees must learn to adapt, as the English, driven out of Johannesburg into Natal during the Anglo-Boer War, had adapted to new conditions—for instance, taking up new trades and professions. One who had been an engineer worked with Gandhi as a carpenter. But the Indians had not learned this virtue, the experimenter observed (90:351).

His prayer meetings were repeatedly interrupted by young Hindus who objected to his reading of verses from the Qur'an, and he also got abusive mail. But he abounded in plans. He wanted to send the refugees back to their native villages and to get the Muslim houses of Delhi, taken over by Hindus, vacated; so that their owners could return. He also wanted India to send to Pakistan forty-million dollars of the Reserve Bank's holdings; this had been agreed to be Pakistan's share of British India's capital, but Nehru and Patel had decided they could not hand over such a sum, to be used against themselves. On January 28, 1948, Gandhi saw Mountbatten, then governor general, to announce his intention to fast until Nehru and Patel changed their minds. This fast was to be a fatal step in the march of events toward his assassination.

Thoughts of Death

Gandhi returned to thoughts of the attempted assassination in South Africa—he expected another such attempt—and the role of Pathans in his life. Mir Alam had been even taller than Badshah Khan, he said.

Gandhi, like Tolstoy, began early in life to speak about his death; and from the birth of satyagraha on, it became a constant reference. In his last years he (again like Tolstoy) often wanted to die. "I am a spent bullet," Gandhi said; "I may last a year or two more"; as Tolstoy said, "I have a criminal desire for death." They had long before then begun to practice death in their living. It was the energy with which they dived down toward self-extinction, pressing into imaginative depths of dissolution most men never enter, that lifted them up again over other people's stature.

They practiced the death of the ego in their physical asceticism and in a dozen disciplines of mind and imagination. They died daily and eagerly; it was in consequence that they lived another kind of resurrected life. This both soothed and irritated other people in alternating and escalating waves of impulse. One sees that clearly in the group reactions to Gandhi's fasts. In Calcutta in 1947 he was pelted with stones when he arrived, with rose petals a few days later; in Delhi groups publicly chanted "Let Gandhi die," and then knelt at his bier sobbing and groaning.

The Assassins in Pune

It is not surprising that, throughout his life, those who were in conflict with Gandhi tried to turn their own weapons against him—they too spoke of dying and killing themselves. When Gandhi fasted, his opponents often fasted against him; when he campaigned against untouchability, some Brahmins lay down in front of his car, halting his self-sacrifice with their own. Indeed Godse, Gandhi's main assassin, had been a great admirer of his work and his principles. Godse too had worked for the reform of caste and the elimination of untouchability. "My respect for the Mahatma was deep and deathless," he said in the dock. He had gone to jail with other Gandhians, before he met Savarkar; and he claimed to have studied the former as much as the latter.

Nathuram Godse was thirty-eight, and his main coconspirator, Narayan Apte, was thirty-four, in 1948. Both were Chitpavan Brahmins (as was Savarkar himself) and members of the Hindu Rashtra Dal, founded by Savarkar in 1942, as a secret society at the heart of the Rashtra Swayamsevak Sangh, which was the paramilitary arm of the Hindu Mahasabha. All the members of the Hindu Rashtra Dal had to be Chitpavan Brahmins and took an oath of loyalty to Savarkar as dictator.

The two men were quite different superficially. Apte dressed in smart British clothes, drank whisky, ate luxuriously, and was a womanizer. While Godse was puritanical, hypersensitive, afraid of women. (According to *Freedom at Midnight* he fled a hospital at the sight of a nurse, and left home to avoid his sisters-in-law.) He was, according to Manohar Malgonkar, brought up as a girl, to ward off evil fate, because his older brothers had all died. "Born in a devotional Brahmin family," he said in the dock, "I instinctively came to revere Hindu religion, Hindu history, and Hindu culture."[24] He was the theoretician among the conspirators, the intellectual. He was taught tailoring by American missionaries, but long found no practical career for himself.

In 1929, however, his family moved to Ratnagiri, which was Savarkar's place of exile within India, once he returned from the Andaman Islands. In 1929 the latter was forty-six, and, according to Malgonkar, "a soft, pale man, with the face of a family priest."[25] Collins and LaPierre speak of his drawn and sunken cheeks, and cruel and sensual lips. Godse made acquaintance with Savarkar, and soon became his secretary. In 1937 the new Bombay government of congressmen (installed by Gandhi, in effect) released Savarkar from his sentence, and he returned to Pune, with Godse in attendance.

Pune, 120 miles from Bombay, was the ancestral city of the Chitpavan Brahmins, the city of Tilak and his tradition of Maharashtrian nationalism. Pune was where a bomb had been thrown at Gandhi in 1934. Savarkar was twice elected president of the Hindu Mahasabha, membership one million, whose doctrine was explicit Hindu imperialism. He taught that all save Hindus should leave India, or accept secondary status; that Gandhi had usurped Tilak's position, and perverted his mission; that nonviolence was a coward's philosophy.

In 1944 a new newspaper, *Agrani* (The forerunner), appeared in Pune. Its first issue contained a portrait of Savarkar, with Godse as editor and Apte as manager. In 1946, when communal hatred became widespread and respectable, this paper began to prosper. In 1947, celebrating the acquisition of a new press, Godse called for Gandhi's death. Suppressed in 1947, for calling for a Black Day of protest, it reopened under a different title immediately. (The Black Day was one of Savarkar's Hindu-nationalist demonstrations against the partition of India, against Muslims and their friends—a Hindu equivalent for Jinnah's Day of Direct Action.) The paper's last issue would carry the news of the assassination perpetrated by Godse.

Why did Godse kill Gandhi? In the name of "sound nation building." He decided that it had been a dangerous error, "to imagine that the bulk of mankind is, or can become, capable of scrupulous adherence to these lofty principles," of Gandhism. He saw that Gandhi had "developed a subjective mentality," and showed "childish insanities and obstinacies," and so his existence "should be brought to an end immediately."[26] Putting it another way, he said that Gandhism meant Muslim rule over all India.

Apte had had plans to blow up Jinnah and his asembly in Delhi, to blow up a Pakistan ammunition train, and to lead a commando raid into Hyderabad. His violence was more multidirectional. In 1946 he already knew one of the other conspirators-to-be, Vishnu Karkare, an illiterate but politically minded Brahmin, who ran a boardinghouse in Ahmednagar. Karkare and six other Hindu Mahasabha workers had gone to Noakhali at the same time as Gandhi did. They too were rallying the Hindus there, with their own message of militant Hinduism, opening Vir Savarkar relief centers, and wearing chain mail under their shirts for protection. Karkare had returned humiliated by the failure of their efforts, which were counteracted by Gandhi's, and talking of revenge.

He went to see Godse and Apte, who already also knew Digambar Badge, who was to become the state's witness in the trial after taking part in the conspiracy. Badge ran a storehouse of weapons (he sold chain mail and tiger claws as well as pistols and knives) and supplied the conspirators with the means of assassination. He and his servant, Shankar Kistayya, had little of the political idealism of Godse and Apte. Shankar, who was supposed in an early plan actually to shoot Gandhi, never knew who Gandhi was.

The last of the conspirators who needs to be named was Madanlal Pahwa, whose home was in territory taken over by Muslims and whose father had been the victim of violence. He had made money and amassed money in Ahmednaggar and organized a gang in a Bombay refugee camp, blackmailing store owners. In Pune in January, he and Karkare agreed with the plan to assassinate Gandhi.

The leaders of the group were clearly Godse and Apte. But it was in Savarkar that the idea of Hindu nationalism had been embodied and became infectious. He had fought Gandhism for forty years. The conspirators themselves were in one sense or another his agents; perhaps carrying out his orders or advice, probably carrying his blessing, certainly inspired by the hatred he had generated. That hatred was a vortex swirling around Gandhi, and sustained by cross currents from Jinnah and Ambedkar and many other sources. For instance, Godse and Apte sought arms and got advice from Dada Maharaj, the head of an affluent Vaishnava sect in Bombay, the Pushtimarg Vaishnavites. But above all they visited Savarkar in his Bombay home, Savarkar Sadan (guarded by armed men day and night) immediately before the assassination.

The Victim in Delhi

Gandhi's death bears a certain resemblance to Tolstoy's, although the latter's was of course a death by natural causes in the literal sense. But Tolstoy was driven to run away from home by the extreme unhappiness of his family situation, to which his wife and other members of the family contributed. It was then a domestic tragedy, while Gandhi's was a political tragedy. In both cases, those most immediately involved were almost irrelevant. I have argued the case for seeing the two in parallel, in *Tolstoy and Gandhi*.

As for Gandhi, himself like Tolstoy subjected to such pressures of hatred, he reacted with a similar mixture of exhaustion and activity, death wish and hopeful enterprise. Brokenhearted by the first actions of the new India, and the slaughterhouse slop already staining his new creation, Gandhi spoke often of dying. On the day before the assassination, he told Manu that only if he died from a bullet and with "He Ram" on his lips, would he have been a true mahatma. But at the same time he had planned another major campaign—a pilgrimage to Pakistan—and was on the last day of his life drawing up a new constitution for congress.

He met constant reproach and accusation from young men, like Bose in Noakhali, and J. P. Narayan in political matters. Above all, Gandhi was like Tolstoy in that both managed to absent themselves from the scenes of their ostensible triumphs, in politics and literature respectively. Gandhi absented himself from the Independence Day celebrations, Tolstoy canceled the plans for a literary celebration of his eightieth birthday, and finally, of course, absented himself from Yasnaya Polyana itself.

Gandhi's slogan of nation building had announced a cult of political militancy, and he had grave problems to do with power. It was not so much (as far as we know) that he doubted his own use of it, as that he aroused his followers' appetite for it. So much of his early effort had been directed at winning self-respect for them and teaching them to win it; teaching them to demand freedom, to defy oppression, to follow a steady resolve through years of disappointment, to fight—even in the simple sense of learning to shoot a gun, wield a bayonet, and maneuver as a military unit. (One of the demands he made in 1930 for his countrymen was the right to bear arms.) Indians had to cease to be a depoliticized and demilitarized race incapable of self-government; they must become a free nation like the English. Indeed, they must be freer, acting spontaneously against constituted authority.

And at the end of his life Gandhi found that his teaching was realized in the form of communal riots, the Indian National Army, the military branch of the Hindu Mahasabha, and the military academies of Nehru and Patel. If Tolstoy had Midas's touch, making his stories valuable properties that his heirs fought over, Gandhi had Mars's touch, Shiva's, which turned everyone military.

Before going to Calcutta, in August, Gandhi's home in Delhi had been the Valmiki Temple in Reading Road, a sweeper's colony. On the open space there, where Gandhi held his prayer meetings, the military branch of the Hindu Mahasabha also held its drills and parades, at which its men saluted the flag of Mother India the Terrible, Kali. And the man of the hour, as far as the newspapers went, was Lord Mountbatten, the last viceroy, a modernized Kipling hero who always appeared in uniform and loved to wear his medals. Nehru and he became great friends. Gandhi had created a state, a great country, and its greatness consisted in military power, which Mountbatten symbolized better than he.

Nehru was turning away from Gandhi personally, and there were hundreds of signs in state policy and practice of the same tendency politically. Gandhi was distressed at the prompt establishment of military academies in India. He was distressed at the invasion of Kashmir, a classic result of the power conflict between Jinnah and Nehru. Kashmir was a territory of eighty-four thousand square miles, with a population of 4½ million, of whom 77 percent were Muslim; but the Maharajah was Hindu. Nehru wanted the ruler to bring his state over to India, while of course Pakistan had a (better) claim to any state so predominantly Muslim. The Maharajah himself wanted to keep his independence from both, but when Jinnah sent armed Pathan raiders across the border (ostensibly nothing to do with Pakistan) the maharaja appealed to India for help, and Nehru flew in an army that annexed the territory to India.

In 1947 the leaders of India rejected the flag with the spinning wheel design that had been congress's emblem. Gandhi's charkha was replaced with the *Dharma Charkha* of the ancient King Asoka. It was the sign carried by Asoka's conquering soldiers, signifying his law, and was flanked by two lions signifying force and courage. Gandhi observed that the new leaders were saying that Swaraj did not belong to old women but to warriors; he also observed that the new flag was not made of khadi cloth, but of a beautiful new material made from glass. Nehru assured him that it was the same flag, only modified by "the exigencies of art." Gandhi had of course thought a good deal about those exigencies. "However artistic the design may be," he said, "I shall refuse to salute a flag which carries such a message" (89:10).

Pyarelal says that in December 1947, Gandhi was "the saddest man one could picture." "If India has no further use for nonviolence," he said, "can she have any for me?" He said Nehru and Patel were "hypnotized by the glamor of the scientific process and expanding economies of the West" (89:369). He kept letting them know of incidents of corruption and extravagance in the new state. He distrusted the elite who were going to rule India and proposed that they should be sent "with their town-bred bodies" to live in a village, to drink from the pool where the villagers bathe and water their cattle, and to "bend their backs under the hot sun as they do." He abhorred Westernization as much as ever.

He was as grieved at India's industrialization as at her militarization and bureaucratization. "God forbid that India should ever take to industrialization after the manner of the West. The economic impact of one single tiny island kingdom is today keeping the world in chains. If an entire nation of three hundred million took to similar economic exploitation, it would strip the world bare like locusts."[27] As we know, he wrote to Nehru that the hope of peace and justice rested on the organization of India as a society of villages as he had declared in *Hind Swaraj* nearly forty years before.

And yet beneath the enthusiasm of the new leaders lay something close to despair. In the very letter in which Nehru rejected Gandhi's call for simplification, and declared his own faith in the modern world, if it would but follow the dictates of common sense and common decency, he ended, "but the world seems bent on committing suicide" (546). This was of course Gandhi's starting point, but Nehru could reach it only as an ending, a giving up. This was Gandhi's bitterest disappointment.

One of his last letters was to Mira Behn, and was written on January 16, 1948, sadly weary and disappointed. "I see that you are destined for serving the cow and nothing else. But I seem to see a vital defect in you. You are unable to cling to anything finally. You are a gipsy, never happy unless you are wandering. You will not become an expert in anything and your mother [the cow] is also likely to perish in your lap" (90:431). Similar reproaches had of course long been made to Gandhi himself; by Polak, for instance.

The Final Scene

To put the assassination in sharpest focus, we must concentrate on the events that followed from the beginning of Gandhi's fast, on January 13, 1948. There were journalists and photographers outside Birla House, where he spent his last days, though none was there to record the actual assassination. When he began his final fast, the first day cost him 2 pounds of his weight, reducing him to 109 pounds. His kidneys were also failing to eliminate the water he drank.

These last fasts were especially dramatic—biological melodramas—because of the daily bulletins full of numbers. At the end, the hero rose from his deathbed, renewed in his strength, and had carried the people with him through the fiery gates.[28] Sushila sang "When I survey the wondrous Cross" at the end of the last one.

On that first day Patel yielded over the money, but Gandhi demanded an agreement between all the community leaders in Delhi (similar to the one he had got in Calcutta) promising that they would cooperate to prevent the outbreak of any more violence. In Pakistan people began to be anxious for Gandhi's life. But in Delhi itself the public response was sluggish and resentful. In the bazaars people said, "When will that old man stop bothering us?" The communal leaders' signatures were finally secured on the morning of the eighteenth, and he took his first sip of orange juice.

From the point of view of rival politicians, this was, like the others, a performance. And from the point of view of a people whose blood lust had been aroused by Black Days and Direct Action Days, and the riots and killings they produced, it was an inhibition. Gandhi and his peacemaking were both resented. As he lay on his cot on the first day of his fast, he could hear hostile slogans chanted: "We want blood for blood," and "If he wants to die, let him die." When Nehru heard the last, he stopped his car and jumped out to tell the chanters (West Punjab Sikhs) that they would have to kill *him* before they said that again in his presence. His indignation and horror were no doubt sincere, but every politician must have felt, about one or another of Gandhi's fasts, "If he wants to die, let him die." Some sense of unwelcome complicity with the demonstrators may have fueled Nehru's anger. Jinnah sent a wire urging him to live and work.

In Bombay on the fifteenth, having seen Savarkar, the conspirators examined the weapons Badge had brought them, and found that the pistols were unreliable, homemade weapons. On the nineteenth, in Delhi, they attempted some target practice, and found that one would not fire at all and the other would not aim. Godse and Apte then made another trip, went to Gwalior, and got a decent pistol from the leader of the RSSS. And on the twentieth they made their first attempt to kill Gandhi, which failed because various small things went wrong, and Badge lost his nerve and failed to fire. Madanlal Pahwa was arrested for setting the time bomb that was to have been the others' signal. The details are sad and ludicrous.

Recovering from his fast, Gandhi planned a pilgrimage on foot to Pakistan, for which he had received Jinnah's permission. He dispatched Sushila Nayyar there, to make detailed plans. His idea was to lead as many Hindu refugees in India as he could back to the homes they had been driven from in Pakistan, to guarantee their safety with his life, and then perhaps to lead back Muslim refugees to India. (In Lahore, he had said he would spend the rest of his life in Pakistan, and perhaps in the Northwest Frontier Province [89:10].) Jinnah had agreed to the scheme, though insisting that Gandhi must have a military guard while there.

Suhrawardy had gone to Karachi on September 18, trying to reconcile the two countries. He had a jocular meeting with Gandhi when he returned. Jinnah had told Suhrawardy that he had let Gandhi take him in (89:307).

Gandhi had fixed February 13 as the date of his departure, from Wardha.

Meanwhile of course he was busy with other things, like the constitution for congress, designed to redirect its activity to village work again; and on the afternoon of January 30 he was arguing with Patel to withdraw the resignation from the cabinet that he had just offered because of a quarrel with Nehru.

Because of this argument, Gandhi was—most unusually—a few minutes late for his prayer meeting. As he approached the dais, along a corridor through the crowd, Godse stepped forward to meet him, saying, "Namaste, Mahatma." Then he pushed Manu aside with his left hand and fired point-blank three times. It was 5:07 P.M. Gandhi sank to the ground with "He Ram" on his lips, according to Gurbadu Singh, a Gandhian businessman who was there. Karkare said it was just the guttural rasp, "Aagh!"

CONCLUSION: THE GREAT ABSENCE

When one retells a story like Gandhi's, one realizes what intentions have shaped earlier tellings. It becomes obvious, in this case, that, while Gandhi was alive, and for the forty-odd years since his death, his friends and disciples suppressed the evidence of one side of his life; notably the scandal that in muffled form exploded in Noakhali. They suppressed it in part against his wish, though we should not blame them exclusively. There is not necessarily anything sinister about intentions like theirs. A great man like Gandhi is a source of power to his party and nation; and it is a loss when his greatness is besmirched.

Indeed, they quite sincerely felt that he was a source of power to mankind as a whole. Gandhi was a savior, one of that small number whose legend is preserved from century to century; like the Buddha and Jesus Christ. But this time the savior was our contemporary, and the religious dimension was embedded in everyday life.

Of course, such a figure is always vulnerable to malicious gossip, which seeks to bring the extraordinary down to the size of ordinariness. It was therefore the work of those who recognized that religious dimension to foster it and protect him—if necessary, against himself.

Gandhi remarked as early as 1925 that "those who keep guard over me are trying to make a perfect man out of me" (28:74). He did not mean that they were altering the facts, but by 1947 their project did involve concealing them. Earlier, in his correspondence with Saraladevi, when he was preparing to break off his relations with her, he had spoken of their love for him—his guardians'—as something that he would do anything to deserve. He wanted to be a perfect man (were he to read this, he might say, "Don't you? Why not?") and to be known as such was a natural consequence.

His friends were making him a heroic myth, writing about his fasts as epic stories, and so on. Gandhi was often uneasy with that process; referring to it under the name of "being a Mahatma." When the trouble came to the surface in Noakhali, he said the prospect of being debunked as a mahatma greatly pleased him (87:15). But of course he had joined in—indeed, initiated—the enterprise.

Naturally, anyone investigating Gandhi in India still runs up against resistance from the vested interests linked to the word *mahatma*. Erik Erikson says he found the true Gandhians the least helpful to him in his research.[1] He divides those close to Gandhi into two groups, the true Gandhians, and those who escaped the full ashram experience, and were ready to admit to some ambivalence about it. People in his position, including me, are bound to have some animus against the first.

Erikson described all India as being in a permanent state of mild mourning for Gandhi. I had few contacts among Gandhians, and saw what I would rather call a state of discreet sullenness. When Indians heard I was writing about Gandhi, they dropped the subject of my research completely. My landlords, whom I saw every day, never referred back to it in all the months I lived under their roof, when it would have been—so far as I can see—the easiest possible topic for small talk. They took cover, it seemed to me, against the likelihood of embarrassment or boredom.

I explained this to myself by means of an analogy with literature. During my leisure hours in Delhi I reread Dickens, including *Great Expectations*, and I found that the twentieth-century history of India reminded me of that novel; not for the plot or characters but for the authorial presence. Dickens's Pip longs to be a gentleman and—as soon as he gets the chance—abandons his true friends, Joe and Biddy, for London and Estella; he knows his guilt, and Dickens repeatedly points it out to the readers. But they—knowing that they would have done just the same as Pip themselves—resent that imputation of guilt; resent the novelist's manipulation of their feelings.

That is what Indians feel today. India's great expectations were of becoming an independent state, breaking away from the British Empire, becoming the largest democracy in the world, and so on. The liberation of August 1947 was like Mr. Jaggers's annunciation to Pip of the fortune he had inherited. The subsequent disillusionment in both cases I pass over. What is poignantly interesting is—in the Indian half of our equation—the reproach incarnate in the figure of Gandhi, and spelled out by Gandhians—those who chose to stay simple and naive, the equivalents of Joe and Biddy. As we read the novel, we accuse the writer of bad faith in his condemnation of Pip. We say, "Pip *could* not make that choice, *nobody* could, *you* couldn't." (Heaven knows Dickens was full of great expectations, if anybody ever was. He did not want to be simple or naive.) In the case of Indians, there is no one for them to address their protests to but Gandhi. They are not living under the spell of a great novelist, but another kind of spell, another great imagination; and they are enmeshed in a various yet single discourse (the modern world) that makes Gandhism an inescapable false pathos, always reproachful.

As far as I myself am concerned, my feelings for Gandhi are not diminished by knowing all I now know about him. They are of course changed. He is in some ways (not all) reduced in scale; and that is a loss. But it is not so much a loss of Gandhi to my gallery of legendary heroes as a loss of the legendary dimension itself. I think that loss is balanced by a gain, but even if it isn't, there is nothing I can do about it. Situated as I am in the geography of culture, being what I called a professional writer and reader, I have to see him in these terms. And I have to see the Gandhians' story of his life as the creation of a heroic myth.

To say so much and no more is to imply that the truth is unheroic. But I think the idea of heroic myths may lead us in a more interesting direction, if we distinguish between different kinds thereof. At first glance the mythology Gandhi engaged with seems as Hindu as possible. The motifs of costume (sandals and loincloth) and activity (spinning and praying) and ideology (brahmacharya and ramrajya) are all archaically oriental. But on reflection we can see something British beneath those trappings—and not just another case of the New Age connection. This kind of heroism comes to us from the authoritarian mind of the British Establishment.

Joseph Campbell, in his *The Hero with a Thousand Faces*, has made a well-known analysis of all the heroic myths of the world, breaking their heroes' lives down into three phases, of departure, of initiation, and of return. The hero departs from home and family and way of life—loses him/herself; in a strange land is challenged severely and, triumphing over those challenges, is initiated into new truths; and returns to his/her people with the liberating gifts won abroad.

These are very large loose categories, which include so much that they tell us very little. But recently there has been an adaptation of Campbell's categories to a particular historical situation that makes them more useful, and also brings them close to Gandhi. In "Heroic Myths of Empire," John M. MacKenzie discusses the second half of the nineteenth century in England, and analyzes four heroes' lives as myths: David Livingstone, the African missionary; Henry Havelock, the Indian army man who died in the mutiny; Charles Gordon, the imperial soldier who fought in China and the Sudan.[2] (The fourth hero, T. E. Lawrence, is less well suited to my purposes—and indeed to MacKenzie's.)

These three Victorian Englishmen went out into lands far from home, profoundly separated themselves, suffered, and died. Indeed, Gordon and Havelock were killed there by enemy soldiers. But they sent home to their countrymen, in the form of the legend of their lives and deaths, religious and political truths that reanimated their culture. In Livingstone's case, there was no literal martyrdom, but there was Stanley's famous quest for him, which all the world read about with bated breath as it was reported.

The religion, of an Evangelical Protestant kind, was very important in all three cases; all three men were themselves pious and were treated as saints. And Havelock's soldiers, like Cromwell's, were so referred to. In the second half of the nineteenth century in Great Britain, there was both a cult of military heroism and an assimilation of the army in battle to the moral struggles of Christianity, especially battles fought by the army in the empire.

Like Gandhi's, these men's diaries, journals, letters, were preserved (much published and republished) but also edited, to make heroic and patriotic myths. There was a plethora of biographies, and plays or entertainments written about them; and widely reproduced paintings and sculptures. Anecdotes, like that of the woman at Lucknow who put her ear to the ground and heard the approach of Havelock's Scots pipers coming to rescue the garrison, were taken up in song and story and music-hall sketches. Institutions like the Gordon Clubs, to inspire working-class youths, were set up in their names, and many other institutions, like the Church Army and the Boy Scouts, carried their message and legend. So did the great body of late nineteenth-century boys' literature, by G. A. Henty and the writers for the *Boys' Own Paper*, for instance.

We remember little of this mythifying, because, even in its own day, it was opposed by literature and the intellect, in well-known meanings of those terms. Heroic myths usually are. We remember them best in the form of ancient jokes—men like these heroes were the strong and silent men of the stiff upper lip, and the earnest men of *The Importance of Being Earnest.* (It is appropriate that Oscar Wilde should both be the source of several of those sardonic phrases, and should have represented decadence to Gandhi.)

These men became heroic myths by virtue of a cultural process specific to one place and time in British history—and indeed to one part of British culture. Gandhi became a comparable though greater myth in Indian history. He could not be part of exactly the same process as them: because he was an Indian; because he came too late; and because his New Age was set in a different part of British culture. Nevertheless he and some of his admirers were deeply influenced by that cultural process, as I have pointed out along the way of his life story—such as the moments when Gandhi reminds us, in one way or another, of a story by Kipling. Gandhi was certainly an earnest man and a hero, in that Victorian sense. That fact won him many of his admirers, and perhaps more of his detractors, English as well as Indian.

In Gandhi's heroic myth there was a double exile, a double departure and return: the first, his time in London as a student, 1888–91; and the second, his time in South Africa, 1893–1914. I would suggest that we can consider the two one, and the place of sojourn England, most importantly New Age England. I think it a pardonable exaggeration to say that Gandhi was never in the Africa of the Africans. He lived in the English cities of Durban and Johannesburg, and the wasteland of Phoenix and Tolstoy Farm—places consecrated to New Age experiment. From that distant land he returned to India in 1914 with his gifts, of the spinning wheel, nature cure, swadeshi, and above all satyagraha. Those were, as I have argued, New Age gifts to a rather striking degree. (Gandhi drew on Indian sources also—the two are not mutually exclusive; the New Age covered both, with its Orientalism.)

If we see his life in these terms, we shall be struck by the likeness-in-difference between his heroic myth and the three MacKenzie discusses. Gandhi's life was a heroic myth, by dint of both his efforts, and those of his disciples. But certain features of Gandhi's myth were different from the Englishmen's, because he was an Indian. He went *from* the exotic and peripheral land *to* the homeland;

that was where he met his challenges and whence he brought back his secret truths. To call England the homeland implies seeing both countries from the English point of view, but there is evidence that Gandhi—and other Indians—did see both England and India that way. India was the supreme New Age legend. That was another of the messages of Orientalism, that India was the great alternative to the West and its great corrective.

What difference did it make, that the direction of Gandhi's journey was in reverse, in the terms of cultural geography? I think it made for some confusion of feeling, some oversimplification of thought, to see India as the world-historical alternative. But it also made for a gaiety, impudence, and sparkle to his career that was missing from theirs. He was stealing his opponents' moral secrets, English as well as Indian, he was on both sides of all the splits. There was, as Ambedkar said, something elvish about Gandhi—earnest but elvish, "always and throughout."

Of course he was serious—he was, precisely, "more earnest than anybody else." Quite seriously he presented himself as a regenerative myth; just as he—and other Indians—had seen Victorian English heroes as regenerative myths. In *Indian Opinion* he often offered his readers the example of Nelson and Cromwell and Hampden, in just the same terms as English moral teachers did—especially the Evangelical and Nonconformist churchmen. Livingstone, Gordon, and Havelock were roughly the same kind of figures as those other three.

But there remains of course an element of antithesis or paradox in assimilating him to the heroes of empire: Gandhi was the great denier of empire, and he was famously nonviolent. What had he to do with Havelock, or with the heroic myths that propped up the British Empire? But that is the source of the gaiety and sparkle I spoke of. New Agers often *are* paradoxical; they are elvish. They reject the rules of the game, the lessons of history, the nature of man. If we follow them, they liberate us—and enchain us with more lasting shackles.

Not that the influence of the imperialists on those they ruled was felt only by Gandhi. The Indian nationalist movement had been studying the heroes of the West since long before Gandhi came on the scene. The Indian patriots admired English heroes, but also French, Italian, Irish ones. Gokhale and Tilak imitated the Jesuits. For a variety of reasons, it was more tactful to focus on Mazzini or Garibaldi or the Irish revolutionaries than on Gordon or Havelock, but many of the same morals could be drawn from all those stories.

The Victorian heroes were debunked after 1918, throughout the West. The most famous title in the literature of debunking was Lytton Strachey's *Eminent Victorians*, which was published that year, and took up where Wilde left off in making fun of earnestness. Being an anti-imperialist, Gandhi should have become a hero of the twenties' intelligentsia. That he did not, that—among Indians—Nehru instead did, needs surely to be explained by Gandhi's naive and earnest style (Nehru was not earnest in that sense) and by his nonsystematic mind.

The only first-class literary mind that was in tune with Gandhi's was George

Bernard Shaw, who stayed loyal to the New Age. It must seem a paradox to praise Shaw for loyalty, when in his plays he so often betrayed what he believed in for laughs. (As he said, he preached what Henry Salt practiced, and "passed his time" writing plays on those texts.) But if we look at the topics he took up, we must surely be struck by his writing *Saint Joan* in the year after Gandhi was put on trial in Ahmedabad—the trial in which he triumphed morally over his prosecutors.

There is no reason to suggest that Shaw was thinking of Gandhi as he wrote the trial scene in that play. But he was certainly celebrating a New Age hero: a woman, a naif, a leader of nationalism, and a saint, confronting representatives of the authoritative and the systematic minds (the Inquisitor, the Bishop, and the Earl of Warwick) on trial for her life.

The similarity between those men set in authority and the people Gandhi confronted, time after time between 1906 and 1948, will perhaps become most evident if we think of his Indian rivals as well as the Englishmen—Jinnah, Ambedkar, Savarkar. They were his Bishop and his Inquisitor. And the reverent but tough-minded tone that Shaw took toward Joan in his preface was—one might suggest—the tone in which biographers of Gandhi should address him.

Once given that clue, we should be struck by a number of resemblances between Gandhi's life and Shaw's plays. There is, for instance, a constant reference in the plays' prefaces to New Age people and things familiar to Gandhi. The New Age world we need now laboriously to reconstruct around Gandhi, is all there in Shaw's prefaces. In the plays, that historical specificity is lost; they seem, at first sight, to move away from the prefaces in the opposite direction: toward abstract patterns of farce and paradox. But at a second reading that is not entirely true. It seems that the New Age mentality envisaged humankind in terms of a typology, a grouping of types, which we find both in Gandhi's sense of self and choice of friends, and in Shaw's gallery of characters.

Let us take *Androcles and the Lion*, the play on the theme of ahimsa, written just before World War I. (It belongs as a document with *Hind Swaraj* and "The Moral Equivalent of War.") The central character, Androcles, a timid tailor, is contrasted with Ferrovius, a name chosen to remind us of *ferocious,* and which will remind *us* of Gandhi's early mentor and oppressor, Sir Ferocious Mehta. In Shaw's play, these two are both early Christian martyrs, rebels against authority, thrown to the lions to make a Roman holiday. But they are very different. Androcles is a natural Christian, a satyagrahi who enacts his religion because he cannot help doing so—who does not preach it. Ferrovius is a natural gladiator, who loves the idea of meekness, but finds it easier to kill his enemies.

The stage directions tell us that Androcles is "a small, thin, ridiculous little man, who might be any age from thirty to fifty-five. He has sandy hair, watery compassionate blue eyes, sensitive nostrils, and a very presentable forehead . . . his arms and legs and back, though wiry of their kind, look shrivelled and starved."[3] Change the colors to suit a Hindu, and it would be hard to find a better description of Gandhi. As for Ferrovius, the would-be Christian, he is an armorer "of dangerous character and great personal strength," and "a powerful choleric man in the prime of life" (942, 946). It is a central paradox of the play that these two opposite types should be found side by side engaged in ideological conflict with authority. In Gandhi's life we think of his conjunction with Shaukat Ali; but we also think of Sheikh Mehtab and Kallenbach and all those Pathans. Gandhi constantly aligned himself with Ferroviuses. Do we deduce from this that Shaw knew Gandhi? Surely we deduce rather that—being New Agers—they employed a similar typology. (We find no such types in D. H. Lawrence's novels, or Virginia Woolf's, or T. S. Eliot's plays, or Noel Coward's.)

For a last example let us take *Major Barbara*, the play about the Salvation Army and the armaments industry, written in 1905. We can pass over the facts that the armaments king is said to derive from Gandhi's patron, A. F. Hills, and that the professor of Greek is avowedly modeled on Gilbert Murray (who was one of the earliest propagandists for Gandhi in England). What is most to the point is the characterization of Barbara, the woman unable to rest in the social or political privileges she was born into, and energetically impelled to change the world by her own strength. She is the play's comic heroine. She is a type Shaw admires, and yet plays his wit upon, self-defensively.

It is the type of Madeline Slade, Mira Behn, and indeed of several of the women with whom Gandhi had his most significant relationships. I have described them as imperious "princesses," and pointed out the rather disconcerting jocularity with which Gandhi challenges them, calling himself their Tyrant, their Bapu, their Lawgiver. That is the key in which the exchanges between Barbara and her father (and other men) are played.

We should surely see an important truth to Shaw's remarks to Gandhi in 1931. He said, you will remember, that the two of them belonged together in a very small group, and that he, Shaw, was mahatma minor to Gandhi's mahatma major.

Of all the many writers about Gandhi in India, the most satisfactory is the very Shavian T. K. Mahadevan. His essays of 1950–72, titled *Gandhi My Refrain* (Bombay: Popular Prakashan 1973), are Shavian, both in the clarity and speed of the writing (and the excessive epigrammaticism) and in the loyalty to Gandhi's extremism. This is expressed in a comic style, but it is as genuine a loyalty as Shaw's was.

Mahadevan recommends unilateral disarmament, for instance, and insists on the simple but appalling dangers of war. But he emphasizes the transpolitical character of Gandhism. We must celebrate Gandhi as a man of ideas, not as a man of historical achievement. *Jnana* or understanding always precedes *bhakta* or devotion. Even in the world of ideas, moreover, Gandhians must accept the position of minority, whose task is always a corrective one.

Mahadevan's jnana-Gandhi (which can remind us of Rajaji's adaptation of Gandhi) is only one aspect of the man, but it is surely a major one. Mahadevan responds energetically to all Gandhi's ideas, and translates them into language in some ways sharper. He says that people (including those who call themselves Gandhians) think that violence and nonviolence are incompatible, seeing the world in black and white: but life is in fact a web in which each interpenetrates the other. Gandhi bracketed nonviolence with truth, but cared more for the latter. Gandhians, Mahadevan says, have done the opposite (93).

Mahadevan has applied Gandhi's teaching to contemporary problems. "At bottom, the human crisis is a crisis of excess. Pollution, population, and all the rest of it are just symptoms. . . . And the only way out of the excess—simplistic as it may sound—is to abstain, abjure, abnegate, give up" (219). This is pure and perfect Gandhism.

Unfortunately—for cogent reasons—Mahadevan's name is anathema in Gandhian circles today. In the preface to *Gandhi My Refrain*, he wrote: "In the pursuit of ideas I am as fickle as a harlot. I go to bed with one idea and wake up with another!" He recurred to Gandhi only as a refrain. Mahadevan's dazzling self-display—so far from earnestness—must always have made the Gandhians uneasy, and in the years since that book was published, he has intensified his ambivalence about his teacher, and reached—and passed—the point of direct attack.

In his foreword to a book by Manmathnath Gupta, Mahadevan kicks the mahatma around the intellectual arena like a football. He cannot find anyone who used the first-person singular with such unabashed abandon as Gandhi, who was so full of himself: "Such cocksureness in an ill-stocked mind, wearing blinkers to boot, is fraught with great danger: the nation was reduced to a sacrificial lamb to sate the megalomania of a doctinaire. . . . This in brief is the quintessence of modern India's continuing tragedy: was our 'freedom' worth the very high price we paid for it?"[4]

In the previous year, Mahadevan tells us, a private member of parliament introduced a bill to make any tarnishing of Gandhi's image a cognizable offense. Mahadevan had thereupon written a letter to a national daily, saying that Gandhi was the greatest disaster to have overtaken modern India. Nonviolence was political and moral nonsense. He traced "the process of India's enfeeblement [which] began long ago. First the tirthankara Mahavira, then Gotama the Buddha. Then came a mythical moksha, and then nonviolence—'and all was lost'" (v/vi).

The book to which Mahadevan wrote this preface is called *Gandhi and His Times* (New Delhi, 1982). The author, Manmathnath Gupta, had had a long career as a revolutionary nationalist, beginning a series of jail sentences in 1921 while still a boy. He argued with Gandhi (as "Revolutionary") in the pages of *Young India,* it may be remembered. Though by no means so brilliant a writer as Mahadevan, his attack on Gandhi is interesting, and in some ways undeniable.

Gupta admits the importance of *Hind Swaraj* (which is even now a cause of intellectual scandal to many Indian Gandhians). But it is important to him because it openly attacks the heroes of the Indian revolution—for instance, Gandhi uses the British word *anarchists* for them. Chapter 4 is called "Tilting Indian Culture in Favor of Nonviolence," and Gupta objects (surely with justification) to Gandhi's attempt to make Indian culture out to be essentially or ancestrally nonviolent. He quotes the many scholars who have described the ancient Aryans as essentially warriors. Indeed, "Hindu culture unfortunately needed violence, as much as it needed nonviolence" (54). Gupta also says with justification that Gandhi *knew* that the Gita did not teach nonviolence. As we have seen, Gandhi would on occasion acknowledge that. One sees why most often he would deny it, but Gupta is more in the right.

These direct attacks on Gandhi are intellectually exhilarating, in the Indian atmosphere, whether you describe that as mild mourning or as sullen silence. But they remain a mere starting point, which has yet to be developed. Mahadevan's later writings—those that have come to my notice—founder in an excess of malice and mere fireworks. It is the indirect attacks on Gandhi that are blunting his thrust more effectively, even when they are written by sincerely devoted Gandhians.

In the last twenty-five years the largest part of the work done on Gandhi has tried to assimilate his ideas and practices to contemporary social science. *Gandhi and Social Sciences* (Delhi: n.p., 1970) prints essays from one of the seminars held to celebrate the centenary of his birth. "This book is a pioneering attempt at establishing Gandhiji's approach to the study of Social Sciences." The introduction contrasts Gandhi with Marx and Lenin, who are more congenial to social science.

One of the leaders in this initiative was J. P. Narayan, the greatest Gandhian politician of the period after 1960, and the one who came round to Gandhi after his death. The Gandhian Institute of Studies at Varanasi, intended to promote Gandhism by the same method, was founded by J. P. Narayan and Sugata Dasgupta. J. P.'s essay in the first general report says that one reason Gandhi has come to seem irrelevant in India is people's failure to interpret him in modern terms—i.e., social-science terms.

This was also, as we have seen, an attempt to defend Gandhi from attacks from the left. Nirmal Kumar Bose, in his introduction to *Gandhi in Indian Politics* (Bombay, 1967, xi), quotes A. B. Shah, saying: "The broad features of a theory of man and society that is generally acceptable to scholars in this area have been fairly clear for many years now. Judged from its standpoint, Gandhi's world-view appears incredibly naive." But a defense like Bose's or Narayan's will not serve Gandhi, because he was not a systematic but a naive mind, with all the implications that this book has tried to point out.

Another way in which Gandhi has been taken care of is by putting him into the aesthetic heavens, alone or in conjunction with Tagore, as a portentous constellation. Sucheta Kripalani said, "Gandhi was the form and Tagore was the content, Tagore was the imagination and Gandhi was its concrete expression." The two worshipped at the same shrine of Truth, but at different corners.[5] Nehru, who exalted Tagore over Gandhi after their deaths, says the same sort of thing: "Even in his [Gandhi's] death there was a magnificence and complete artistry. It was from every point of view a fitting climax to the man and the life he had lived."[6] Ashis Nandy does something similar in his essay on the assassination. The police as well as the assassins collaborated with Gandhi, Nandy says (70).

This we might call the Shakespeareanizing of Gandhi—others abide our question, thou art free. "Effortlessly transcending the dichotomy of orthodoxy and iconoclasm. . . ." This is a good example of the systematizing character of even the aesthetic mind.

It is, however, too easy to laugh at these efforts to assimilate Gandhi, and such laughter will probably be punished by fate. The best anyone can do is to swallow Gandhi whole. The powers of digestion of the systematic mind are enormous, but he is too tough for them. *Of course* he does not fit into Indian intelligence now, just as he did not fit into Indian politics then. Of course India fails to meet his challenge. But the same would have been true of every other country he might have been born into.

Thus Gandhi remains a puzzle—one I have tried to explain by distinguishing the naive mind from the other kinds, and the New Age from other phases of history. But he was other things also. Not meant for a hero by either nature or culture, he made himself both a towering horizon figure, and a subjectivity so rich in intricate meanings that he deepens our sense of the human.

NOTES

A lot of Gandhi's correspondence, and of letters written to him, has been collected in archives in India without yet being printed in his *Collected Works,* or indeed in any other form. I refer to those letters, but, because there is no guarantee of when they will be published, or whether the printed versions will follow the archives' cataloging, I have alluded to that material simply as "unpublished correspondence," with two exceptions. There are two large collections of letters, one between him and Henry Polak, and the other between him and Hermann Kallenbach, both housed at the Indian National Archives, which I allude to as the "Polak Papers" and the "Kallenbach Papers."

Introduction: The New Age Scene and Scenario

1. Charles Chatfield, *The Americanization of Gandhi* (New York: Garland, 1974), 284.
2. Parenthetical citations in the text such as "(19:289)" refer to Mahatma Gandhi's own writings. (See bibliography under GANDHI.) The "19" refers to the volume number in the *Collected Works of Mahatma Gandhi,* 90 vols. (Ahmedabad: Navajivan, vol. 1, 1958). The "289" refers to the page number. (A:24) refers to *An Autobiography,* page 24. (M) refers to *My Dear Child.* (H) refers to *The Healthy Guide.* (S) refers to *Satyagraha in South Africa.* (UC) refers to Gandhi's unpublished correspondence.
3. D. G. Tendulkar, *The Mahatma,* 8 vols. (Delhi: Ministry of Information, 1951, 1954), 2:134.
4. Kallenbach papers.
5. Polak papers.
6. S. Radhakrishnan, ed., *Mahatma Gandhi* (London: Allen and Unwin, 1939, 1949), 191.
7. K. Mashruwala, *Gandhi and Marx* (Ahmedabad: Navajivan, 1951), 21.
8. N. K. Bose, *Lectures on Gandhism* (Ahmedabad: Navajivan, 1971), 112.
9. Pyarelal, *Mahatma Gandhi, Part 2: The Last Phase* (Ahmedabad: Navajivan, 2 vols., 1956, 1958), 1:7.

10. Ananda K. Coomaraswamy, *Selected Works* (Princeton, New Jersey: Princeton University Press, 1977), 2:325.
11. *Gandhi Marg,* 14:5.
12. K. M. Munshi, *I Follow the Mahatma* (Bombay: Allied Publishers, 1940), 3.
13. M. R. Jayakar, *The Story of My Life,* vol. 1 (Bombay: Asia Publishing, 1958).
14. Jayakar, 355.
15. See Bernard Porter, *Critics of Empire* (New York: St. Martins Press, 1968).
16. George Santayana, "The Poetry of Christian Dogma," in *Interpretations of Poetry and Religion* (New York: Scribners, 1900), 76–117, 86.
17. Pyarelal, *Mahatma Gandhi, Part 1: The Early Phase* (Ahmedabad: Navajivan, 1965), 10.
18. W. Wellock, *Off the Beaten Track* (Varanasi: Sarvodaya Press, 1963, 209–10.
19. Jawaharlal N. Nehru, *A Bunch of Old Letters* (New York: Asta Publishing, 1960), 234.
20. Millie Polak, *Mahatma Gandhi* (Madres: Natesan, 1931).

Chapter 1: Porbandar and the Past: 1869–1876

1. C. D. S. Devanesen, *The Making of the Mahatma* (Madras: Orient Longmans, 1969), 143.
2. Fatima Meer, *Apprenticeship of a Mahatma* (Durban: Premier Press, 1970), 143.
3. Ranjit Shahani, *Mr. Gandhi* (New York: Macmillan, 1961), 3.
4. Quoted by Robert Payne, *The Life and Death of Mahatma Gandhi* (New York: Dutton, 1969), 24.
5. Erik Erikson, *Gandhi's Truth* (New York: Norton, 1969), 108.
6. Chandrashankar Shukla, *Reminiscences of Gandhiji* (Bombay: Vora, 1951), 110.
7. Erikson, 109.
8. Joseph Doke, *M. K. Gandhi: An Indian Patriot in South Africa* (London: Indian Chronicle Press, 1909), 19.
9. Jawaharlal Nehru, *The Discovery of India* (New York: John Day, 1960), 335.
10. Prabhudas Gandhi, *My Childhood with Gandhiji* (Ahmedabad: Navajivan, 1957), 81.
11. Shahani, 30.
12. Devanesen, 7, 27.
13. Agehananda Bharati, *Asians in East Africa* (Chicago: University Press, 1972), 305.
14. Quoted in R. A. Huttenback, *Racism and Empire* (Ithaca: Cornell University Press, 1976), 14–15.
15. Quoted in James Hunt, *Gandhi in London* (New Delhi: Promilla, 1978), 49.
16. Hugh Tinker, *A New System of Slavery* (New York: O.U.P., 1974), xiv.
17. Tulsidas, *The Holy Lake of the Acts of Rama,* tr. by W. Douglas Hill (Cambridge: University Press, 1952).
18. See Edward C. Dimock et al, eds., *The Literatures of India* (Chicago: University Press, 1974).
19. Tulsidas, xxxvii.
20. Wendy Doniger O'Flaherty, *Hindu Myths* (London: Penguin, 1975), 36.
21. Romain Rolland, *Prophets of the New India* (New York: A. and C. Boni, 1930), 371.
22. H. Spodek, "On the Origins of Gandhi's Political Methodology: The Heritage of Kathiawad and Gujarat," *Journal of Asian Studies* 30, February 1971, 371–72.

Chapter 2: Rajkot and the Present: 1876–1888

1. Prabhudas Gandhi, *My Childhood with Gandhiji* (Ahmedabad: Navajivan, 1957), 17.

2. J. M. Uphadhyaya, *Gandhi's Early Contemporaries and Companions* (Ahmedabad: Navajivan, n.d.), 9.
3. [illegible] K. Bose, ed., *Selections from Gandhi* (Ahmedabad: Navajivan, 1947), 176.
4. Fatima Meer, *Apprenticeship of a Mahatma* (Durban: Premier Press, 1970), 11.
5. Elinor Morton, *The Women in Gandhi's Life* (New York: Dodd Mead, 1953), 20.
6. "Gandhi and Mrs. Sanger," *Asia*, November 1936, 700.
7. D. Kalelkar, *Stray Glimpses of Bapu* (Ahmedabad: Navajivan, 1950), 115.
8. Fatima Meer, *Portrait of South African Indians* (Durban: Premier Press, 1969), 115.
9. J. M. Uphadhyaya, *Mahatma Gandhi—A Teacher's Discovery* (Ahmedabad: Navajivan, 1969), 18.
10. Erik Erikson, *Gandhi's Truth* (New York: Norton, 1969), 135.
11. Sudhir Kakar, *Intimate Relationships* (Delhi: Viking, 1989), 88.
12. Robert Payne, *The Life and Death of Mahatma Gandhi* (New York: Dutton, 1969), 39.
13. Uphadhyaya, *Early Contemporaries*, 67.
14. P. Gandhi, 122.
15. Stanley Wolpert, *Tilak and Gokhale* (Berkeley: University of California Press, 1962), 45.
16. P. Gandhi, 25.
17. Uphadhyaya, *Early Contemporaries*, 7.
18. Joseph Doke, *M. K. Gandhi: An Indian Patriot in South Africa* (London: Indian Chronicle Presses, 1909), 33.

Chapter 3: Metropolis: 1888–1893

1. Stephen Hay, "The Making of a Late Victorian Hindu," *Victorian Studies*, Autumn 1989, 79.
2. See, for instance, James N. Farquhar, *Modern Religious Movements in India* (New York: Macmillan, 1915).
3. Annie Besant, *Jainism* (Adyar: Theosophical Publishers, 1949), 13.
4. Digish Mehta, *Shrimad Rajachandran* (Ahmedabad, n.p.: n.d.), 4.
5. Robert Payne, *The Life and Death of Mahatma Gandhi* (New York: Dutton, 1969), 79.
6. D. Mehta, 29.
7. Rajmohan Gandhi, *Patel* (Ahmedabad: Navajivan, 1990), 4, 5.
8. R. Gandhi, 4; quoted from David Hardiman, *Peasant Nationalists of Gujarat* (Delhi: O.U.P., 1981), 43.
9. R. Gandhi, 170.
10. D. Mehta, 9.
11. Mahadev Desai, *Day to Day with Gandhi* (Ahmedabad: Navajivan, 1968), 137.
12. Mary Barr, *Bapu* (Bombay: Book House, 1949), 4.
13. Payne, 63.
14. Hay, 78.
15. David Bebbington, *The Nonconformist Conscience* (London: Allen and Unwin, 1982), 11.
16. Bhikhu Parekh, *Colonialism, Tradition, and Reform* (New York: Sage, 1989), 204.
17. Hay, 79.
18. Susan Budd, *Varieties of Unbelief* (London: Heinemann, 1977), 43.
19. Hay, 84.
20. A. F. Hills, "Prospectus" of *The Vegetarian*, first issue.
21. P. J. Mehta, *M. K. Gandhi and the South African Indian Problem* (Madras: Ganesan, 1912), 47.
22. Hay, 96.

23. *Lucifer,* November 1987, 173.
24. Quoted in Raghavan Iyer, *The Moral and Political Thought of Mahatma Gandhi* (Delhi: Oxford University Press, 1973), 28.
25. Leo Tolstoy, *The Kingdom of God Is within You* (Lincoln, Nebraska: University of Nebraska Press, 1974), 9.
26. Edward Carpenter, *The Art of Creation* (New York: Macmillan, 1904), vii.
27. Harold Monro, *Collected Poems,* intro. F. S. Flint (London: Cobden-Sanderson, 1933).

Chapter 4: Durban and Politics: 1893–1902

1. H. Rider Haggard, *King Solomon's Mines* (New York: Dell, 1961), 30.
2. Maureen Swan, *Gandhi: The South African Experience* (Johanessburg: Ravan Press, 1985).
3. Quoted by Ved Mehta, *Mahatma Gandhi and His Apostles* (London: Penguin, 1977), 102.
4. R. A. Huttenback, *Gandhi in South Africa* (Ithaca: Cornell University Press, 1971), 133.
5. G. H. Calpin, *A. E. Kajee* (Durban: Iqbal Study Group, n.d.).
6. Vishnu Padayachee and Robert Morrell, "Indian Merchants and Dukawallahs in the Natal Economy c. 1875–1914," *Journal of South African Studies,* 17:1, March 1981.
7. Robert Payne, *The Life and Death of Mahatma Gandhi* (New York: Dutton, 1969), 106.
8. Digish Mehta, *Shrimad Ramachandra* (Ahmedabad, n.d.), n.p.
9. Pyarelal, *Mahatma Gandhi: The Discovery of Satyagraha—On the Threshold* (Bombay: Seva Prakashan, 1980), 398.
10. Pyarelal, 6.
11. Erik Erikson, *Gandhi's Truth* (New York: Norton, 1969), 179.
12. James Hunt, *Gandhi in London* (New Delhi: Promilla, 1978), 43.
13. Cited in *Gandhi Marg,* 1957, 199.
14. Judith M. Brown, *Gandhi: Prisoner of Hope* (New Haven: Yale University Press, 1989), 155.
15. Pyarelal, *Mahatma Gandhi, Part 1: The Early Phase* (Ahmedabad: Navajivan, 1965), 2:383–84.

Chapter 5: Johannesburg and Satyagraha: 1902–1914

1. Ranji S. Nowbath, "Smuts and Gandhi," in the 100th anniversary issue of *The Leader,* South Africa.
2. Bernard Porter, *Critics of Empire,* (New York: St. Martins, 1968), 88.
3. Pyarelal, *Mahatma Gandhi, Part 1: The Early Phase* (Ahmedabad: Navajivan, 1965), 353.
4. Joseph Doke, *M. K. Gandhi: An Indian Patriot in South Africa* (London: Indian Chronicle Press, 1909), 6.
5. C. K. De Kiewiet, *A History of South Africa* (New York: O.U.P., 1940), 154–55.
6. Charles van Onselen, *Studies in the Social and Economic History of the Witwatersrand* (London: Longmans, 1982), 1:103.
7. P. J. Mehta, *M. K. Gandhi and the South African Indian Problem* (Madras: Ganesan, 1912), 38.
8. Prabhudas Gandhi, *My Childhood with Gandhiji* (Ahmedabad: Navajivan, 1957), 156.
9. Ruth First and Ann Scott, *Olive Schreiner* (New York: Schocken, 1980), 234.

10. Phyllis Lean, *Fifty Years of Theosophy* (South Africa: n.p., 1949), n.p.
11. Quoted from the *Jewish Chronicle,* 1913, cited in Gideon Shimoni, *Gandhi, Satyagraha and the Jews* (Jerusalem: Jerusalem Papers on Peace Problems, 1977), 13.
12. Robert Payne, *The Life and Death of Mahatma Gandhi* (New York: Dutton, 1969), 145.
13. "Israel Zangwill," *Encyclopaedia Judaica,* 932.
14. Polak's biographical sketch of Gandhi of 1909, quoted in James Hunt, *Gandhi in London* (Delhi: Promilla, 1978), 48.
15. Erik Erikson, *Gandhi's Truth* (New York: Norton, 1969), 194.
16. Mehta, 31.
17. Hunt, 103.
18. David Bebbington, *The Nonconformist Conscience* (London: Allen and Unwin, 1982), 144.
19. Hunt, 91.
20. P. Gandhi, 94.
21. Hunt, 148.
22. W. M. Salter, *Ethical Religion* (London: Rationalist Press Association, 1905), 7.
23. Payne, 194.
24. Quoted in Hunt, 108.
25. R. A. Huttenback, *Gandhi in South Africa* (Ithaca: Cornell University, 1971), 132.
26. Chandrashankar Shukla, *Incidents of Gandhiji's Life* (Bombay: Vora, 1949), 232.
27. W. E. Cursons, *Joseph Doke: The Missionary-Hearted* (Johannesburg: Christian Literature Depot, 1929), 33.
28. Hunt, 111.
29. Hunt, 134.
30. Payne, 204.
31. Manmathnath Gupta, *Gandhi and His Times* (Delhi: Prakashan, 1982), 14.
32. Payne, 204–5
33. Hunt, 121.
34. Gustave Spiller, *The Ethical Movement in Great Britain* (London: n.p., 1934), 91.
35. D. G. Tendulkar, *The Mahatma* (New Delhi: Government Press, 1951), 1:107.
36. Isabella Fyvie Mayo, "Another Wise Man from—the East," *The Open Road,* May 1911, 331.
37. See the *Hibbert Journal,* 16:2, January 1918, 191–205.
38. P. J. Mehta, 2, 3.
39. Kalidas Nag, *Tolstoy and Gandhi* (Patna: Pustak Bhandar, 1950), 82.
40. Hunt, 155.
41. Nag, 71.
42. Henry Gifford, *Leo Tolstoy: Critical Heritage* (London: Penguin, 1972), 167.
43. William Hancock and Jean van der Poel, *The Smuts Papers* (Cambridge: University Press, 1966), 3:173–74.
44. Payne, 229.
45. Madan C. Gandhi, *Gandhian Aesthetics* (New Delhi, n.p., 1969), 61.
46. Payne, 329.
47. R. Reynolds, *A Quest for Gandhi* (New York: Doubleday, 1952), 184.

Chapter 6: Violence and Nonviolence

1. S. Radhakrishnan, ed., *Mahatma Gandhi A Hundred Years* (New Delhi: n.p., 1969), 216.
2. Erik Erikson, *Gandhi's Truth* (New York: Norton, 1969), 129.
3. Krishnadas, *Seven Months with Mahatma Gandhi* (Ahmedabad: Navajivan, 1959), 216.

4. K. L. Panjabi, *Rajendra Prasad* (New York: St. Martins, 1960), 204.
5. G. A. Natesan tells of his silence there, in D. G. Tendulkar, *Gandhiji: His Life and Work* (Bombay: Karnatak, 1949), 214.
6. Foreword to G. D. Birla, *In the Shadow of the Mahatma* (Calcutta: Orient Longmans, 1953).
7. B. R. Ambedkar, *Gandhi and Gandhism* (n.p.: n.d.), 9.
8. V. S. Srinivasa Sastri, *Letters of V. S. Srinivasa Sastri,* ed. T. N. Jagadisan (Madras: Rochouse and Sons, n.d.), 90.
9. D. G. Tendulkar, *The Mahatma* (New Delhi: Government Press, 1951), 4:167.
10. Balwantsimha, *Under the Shelter of Bapu* (Ahmedabad: Navajivan, 1962), 11.
11. R. K. Prabhu, *This Was Bapu* (Ahmedabad: Navajivan, 1954), 3.
12. Bharatan Kumarappa, ed., *Non-Violent Resistance* (New York: Schocken, 1961), taken from *Young India,* 2-20-1921.
13. Francis Hutchins, *The Illusion of Permanence* (Princeton, New Jersey: Princeton University Press, 1967).
14. Saraladevi Chaudhurani, *Jhibaner Jhava Pata* (Life's fallen leaves) (published only in Bengali, translated into English by Chitrita Banerji), 135.
15. *Young India,* August 1929.
16. Judith J. Brown, *Gandhi: Prisoner of Hope* (New Haven: Yale University Press, 1989), 194–95.
17. Mahadev Desai, *Day to Day with Gandhi* (Ahmedabad: Navajivan, 1968), 3:223.
18. Erikson, 320.
19. Tendulkar, *The Mahatma,* 1:139.
20. D. H. Lawrence, *Women in Love* (New York: Random House, 1922), 157–58.
21. Tendulkar, *Gandhiji,* 198.
22. Chandrashankar Shukla, *Incidents of Gandhiji's Life* (Bombay: Vora, 1949), 205.
23. Dilip Kumar Roy, *Among the Great* (Bombay: Jaico, 1950).
24. N. K. Bose, *My Days with Gandhi* (Calcutta: Nishana, 1953), 89.
25. Shukla, 215.
26. Tendulkar, *Gandhiji,* 225.
27. R. Shahani, *Mr. Gandhi* (New York: Macmillan, 1961), 88.
28. B. R. Ambedkar, *Gandhi and Gandhism* (Jullundur: n.p., 1970), 121.
29. S. Radhakrishnan, ed., *Mahatma Gandhi* (London: Allen and Unwin, 1939, 1949), 238.
30. Arthur Koestler, *The Lotos and the Robot* (New York: Harpers, 1966), 149.
31. Birla, 142–43.
32. R. A. Huttenback, *Gandhi in South Africa* (Ithaca: Cornell University, 1971), 325–26.
33. Bose, 1.

Chapter 7: Sabarmati and Insurgence: 1914–1921

1. Geoffrey Blount, *A New Crusade* (London: Simple Life Press, 1903), viii.
2. P. J. Mehta, *M. K. Gandhi and the South African Indian Problem* (Madras: Ganesan, 1912), 47.
3. Mrs. Geoffrey Blount, *The Story of a Homespun Web* (London: Vineyard Press, 1913), 29.
4. Ananda K. Coomaraswamy, *The Arts and Crafts of India and Ceylon* (London: T. N. Fouldnis, 1913, 1963), xi.
5. Ananda K. Coomaraswamy, *Art and Swadeshi* (Madras: Ganesh, 1912), 88.
6. Roger Lipsey, *Coomaraswamy: His Life and Work* (Princeton, New Jersey: Princeton University Press, 1977), 84.
7. Mehta, 69.

8. S. Durai Raja Singam, *Ananda Coomaraswamy: Remembering and Remembering Again and Again* (n.p.: Petading Jaya, 1974).
9. Romain Rolland, *Inde: Journal 1915–43* (Paris: Vineta, 1951), 11.
10. S. P. Sitaramayya, *Gandhi and Gandhism* (Allahabad: Kitabistan, 1942), 517, appendix 2.
11. Ruth First and Ann Scott, *Olive Schreiner* (New York: Schocken, 1980), 34–35.
12. R. Payne, *The Life and Death of Mahatma Gandhi* (New York: Dutton, 1969), 281.
13. B. N. Pandey, *The Indian Nationalist Movement 1885–1947* (New York: Macmillan, 1979), 15.
14. B. R. Nanda, *Gandhi, Pan-Islamism, Imperialism, and Nationalism* (Delhi: O.U.P., 1989), 172.
15. Rajmohan Gandhi, *Patel* (Ahmedabad: Navajivan, 1990), 41.
16. Mahadev Desai, *Day to Day with Gandhi* (Ahmedabad: Navajivan, 1968), 2:141.
17. Hallam Tennyson, *India's Walking Saint* (London: Gollancz, 1955), 29.
18. Payne, 350.
19. Howard Spodek, "On the Origins of Gandhi's Political Methodology: The Heritage of Kathiawad and Gujarat," *Journal of Asian Studies* 30:5, February 1971, 361–73.
20. Amiya Chakravarty, *A Tagore Reader* (Boston: Beacon, 1966), 85.
21. G. Ramachandran, *Gandhigram Thoughts and Talks* ed. K. C. R. Raja, (n.p.: Gandhigram, 1964).
22. Rabindranath Tagore, *I Won't Let You Go,* tr. Ketaki Kushari Dyson (London: Bloodaxe, 1991), 94.
23. Bharatan Kumarappa, ed., *Nonviolent Resistance* (New York: Schocken, 1961).
24. Sibnarayan Ray, "Tagore-Gandhi Controversy," in Sibnarayan Ray, ed., *Gandi, India, and the World* (Bombay: Indian Committee for Intellectual Freedom, 1970), 112.
25. Mahadev Desai, *Gandhiji in Indian Villages* (Madras: Ganesan, 1927), 105.
26. Jawaharlal Nehru, *A Bunch of Old Letters* (Bombay: Asia Publishing, 1960), 164.
27. Kanji Dwarkadas, *Gandhiji through My Diary Leaves* (Bombay: n.p., 1950), 19.
28. G. A. Natesan, in D. G. Tendulkar, *Gandhiji: His Life and Work* (Bombay: Karnatak, 1944), 214.
29. Rajendra Prasad, *At the Feet of Mahatma Gandhi* (New York: Asia Publishing, 1961), 78–79.
30. Francis Watson, *The Trial of Mr. Gandhi* (London: Macmillan, 1969), 123.
31. Erik Erikson, *Gandhi's Truth* (New York: Norton, 1969), 299.
32. Verrier Elwin, *The Tribal World of Verrier Elwin* (Bombay: O.U.P., 1964), 52.
33. Pandey, 50.
34. Desai, vol. 3.
35. A. C. Niemeijer, *The Khilafat Movement in India 1918–1924* (Hague: Mouton, 1972), 57.
36. B. R. Nanda, *Gandhi: Pan-Islamism, Imperialism, and Nationalism* (Delhi: O.U.P., 1989), 134.
37. Payne, 328.
38. Erikson, 371.
39. Romain Rolland, *Rolland-Gandhi Correspondence* (New Delhi: Ministry of Information, 1976), March 7, 1928.
40. Erikson, 372.
41. Rajendra Prasad, *Autobiography* (Bombay: Asia Publishing, 1957), 104.
42. Nanda, *Gandhi: Pan-Islamism, Imperialism, and Nationalism*, 182.
43. Judith M. Brown, *Gandhi's Rise to Power* (Cambridge: University Press, 1972).
44. Pandey, 53.

45. Susie Tharu and K. Lalita, *Women Writing in India* (New York: Feminist Press, 1991).
46. Ketaki Kushari Dyson, *In Your Blossoming Flower Garden* (Delhi: Sahitya Akademi, 1988), 5.
47. Saraladevi Chaudhurani, *Jhibaner Jhava Pata,* 107.
48. Cited from Gokhale Papers by B. R. Nanda, *Gandhi and the Nehrus* (London: n.p., 1974).
49. Chaudhurani, 31.
50. *Young India,* March 26, 1920, 70–75.
51. Desai, 2:217.
52. Charles Chatfield, *The Americanization of Gandhi* (New York: Garland, 1976), 189.

Chapter 8: In and Out of Jail: 1921–1931

1. D. G. Tendulkar, *The Mahatma* (New Delhi: Government Press, 1951), 2:91.
2. Jawharlal Nehru, *A Bunch of Old Letters* (New York: Asta, 1960), 24.
3. M. B. Rao and S. G. Sardasi, *The Mahatma* (Bombay: People's Publishing House, 1969), 109.
4. Tendulkar, 2:120.
5. Louis Fischer, *Life of Mahatma Gandhi* (New York: Harper, 1950, 296.
6. Narayan Desai, *Bliss Was It to Be Young—with Gandhi* (Bombay: Bharatiya Vidya Bhavan, 1988), 9.
7. Sudhir Kakar, *Intimate Relationships* (Delhi: Viking, 1989), 110.
8. Desai, 67.
9. R. Reynolds, *A Quest for Gandhi* (New York: Doubleday, 1952), 9.
10. Mahadev Desai, *The Diary of Mahadev Desai,* vol. 1 (Ahmedabad: Navajivan, 1953), 4.
11. Erik Erikson, *Gandhi's Truth* (New York: Norton, 1969), 310.
12. N. D. Parikh, *Mahadev Desai's Early Life* (Ahmedabad: Navajivan, 1953).
13. Erikson, 60.
14. N. Desai, 54.
15. Mahadev Desai, *Day to Day with Gandhi,* vol. 1 (Ahmedabad: Navajivan, 1968), 100.
16. Pyarelal and Sushila Nayar, *In Gandhiji's Mirror* (Delhi: O.U.P., 1991), 8.
17. Romain Rolland, *Inde: Journal 1915–43* (Paris: Vineta, 1951), 352.
18. N. Desai, 14.
19. Jawaharlal Nehru, *Towards Freedom* (New York: John Day, 1958), 21.
20. B. R. Nanda, *Motilal Nehru* (Delhi: Ministry of Information, 1964), 3.
21. B. R. Nanda, *The Nehrus* (London: Allen and Unwin, 1963), 62.
22. Nehru, *A Bunch of Old Letters,* 17.
23. Krishna Nehru Hutheesing, *We Nehrus* (New York: Holt Rinehart, 1967), 34.
24. Nehru, *Freedom,* 53.
25. M. Saksena, *Motilal Nehru* (Delhi, n.p., n.d.), 7.
26. Louis Fischer, *Gandhi: His Life and Message for the World* (New York: Signet, 1954), 92.
27. Dorothy Norman, *Nehru: The First Sixty Years* (London: Bodley Head, 1965), 42.
28. Saksena, 103.
29. Jawaharlal Nehru, *Glimpses of World History* (New York: n.p., 1962), 13.
30. Rajmohan Gandhi, *Patel* (Ahmedabad: Navajivan, 1990), 98.
31. Pyarelal and Nayar, 183.
32. R. Gandhi, 46.
33. Pyarelal and Nayar, 183.

34. S. Radhakrishnan, *Vinoba and His Mission* (Wardha: n.p., 1948).
35. Kantilal Shah, *Vinoba on Gandhi* (n.p.: n.p., 1973), ix.
36. *Gandhi Marg,* 2:64.
37. Madeline Slade, *The Spirit's Pilgrimage* (New York: Coward McCann, 1978), 93.
38. Elinor Morton, *The Women in Gandhi's Life* (New York: Dodd Mead, 1953), 200.
39. Rolland, 237.
40. Romain Rolland, *Rolland-Gandhi Correspondence* (New Delhi: Ministry of Information, 1976), entry for April 25, 1928.
41. Rolland, *Inde,* 180.
42. Gideon Shimoni, *Gandhi, Satyagraha, and the Jews* (Jerusalem: Papers on Peace Problems, 1977), 23.
43. Durga Das, *India from Curzon to Nehru and After* (London: Collins, 1969), 76.
44. Agnes Smedley, *Battle Hymn of China* (New York: Da Capo, 1943, 1975), 14.
45. Padmini Sengupta, *Sarojini Naidu* (London: Asia Publishing, 1966), 79.
46. Morton, 159.
47. K. M. Munshi, *I Follow the Mahatma* (Bombay: Allied Publishers, 1940), 2.
48. Tendulkar 3:38.
49. Judith M. Brown, *Gandhi and Civil Disobedience* (Cambridge: University Press, 1977), 246.
50. Upton Sinclair, *Mammonart* (n.p.: n.p., 1924), 9.
51. *Young India,* October 6, 1927.
52. Krishnadas, *Seven Months with Mahatma Gandhi* (Ahmedabad: Navajivan, 1952, 1959), 256.
53. Tendulkar, 3:126.
54. Sir T. B. Sapru told this story to Pyarelal; see *In Gandhi's Mirror* (239).
55. Rolland, *Inde,* 385.
56. Slade, 147.
57. Rolland, *Inde,* 385.

Chapter 9: Politics and Culture: 1931–1941

1. D. G. Tendulkar, *The Mahatma* (New Delhi: Government Press, 1951), 4:3.
2. Madeline Slade, *The Spirit's Pilgrimage* (New York: Coward McCann, 1978), 179–80.
3. Ananda K. Coomaraswamy, *The Dance of Shiva* (New York: Sunwise Turn, 1924), 132.
4. Roger Lipsey, *Coomaraswamy: His Life and Work* (Princeton, New Jersey: Princeton University Press, 1977), 87.
5. Nilla Cram Cook, *My Road to India* (New York: n.p., 1939), 45.
6. Edmund Wilson, *The Twenties* (New York: Farrar, Straus, Giroux, 1975), 277.
7. Cook, 381.
8. *Harijan,* May 6, 1933.
9. Cook, 399.
10. Ved Mehta, *Mahatma Gandhi and His Apostles* (New York: Penguin, 1976), 54.
11. Narayan Desai, *Bliss Was It to Be Young—with Gandhi* (Bombay: Bharatiya Vidya Bhevan, 1988), 73.
12. R. Payne, *The Life and Death of Mahatma Gandhi* (New York: Dutton, 1969), 470.
13. Payne, 475.
14. Desai, 73.
15. Payne, 469.
16. Pyarelal and Sushila Nayar, *In Gandhiji's Mirror* (Delhi: O.U.P., 1991), 101.
17. Louis Fischer, *Gandhi: His Life and Message to the World,* (New York: Signet, 1954), 141.

18. Mehta, 3.
19. F. Watson, *The Trial of Mr. Gandhi* (London: Macmillan, 1969), 13.
20. Jawaharlal Nehru, foreword to Tendulkar, *The Mahatma,* 1.
21. Penderel Moon, *Gandhi and Modern India* (New York: Norton, 1969), 12.
22. Vinoba Bhave, *The Third Power* (n.p.: n.p., 1972), 103.
23. Rajmohan Gandhi, *Patel* (Ahmedabad: Navajivan, 1990), 221.
24. Ian Talbot, *Provincial Politics and the Pakistan Movement* (Karachi: O.U.P., 1988).
25. Pyarelal, *A Pilgrimage for Peace* (Ahmedabad: Navajivan, 1950), v.
26. Mehta, 168.
27. Dorothy Norman, *Nehru: The First Sixty Years* (London: Bodley Head, 1965), 548.
28. M. Chalapati Ram, *Gandhi and Nehru* (Bombay: Allied, 1967), 26.
29. B. R. Ambedkar, *Gandhi and Gandhism* (Jullundur: n.p., 1970), 283.
30. Bhagvan Das, introduction to B. R. Ambedkar, *Gandhi and Gandhism.*
31. F. Watson and M. Brown, *Talking of Gandhiji* (London: Longmans Green, 1957), 10.
32. Ambedkar, 119.
33. B. N. Pandey, *The Indian Nationalist Movement 1885–1947* (New York: Macmillan, 1979), 131.
34. V. T. Patil, ed., *Studies on Gandhi* (Delhi: Sterling, 1983), 126.
35. B. R. Nanda, in *Gandhi Marg,* January 1980, 621.
36. See "The True Artist" in D. G. Tendulkar, ed., *Gandhiji: His Life and Work* (Bombay: Karnatak, 1944).
37. Gideon Shimoni, *Gandhi, Satyagraha, and the Jews* (Jerusalem: Papers on Peace Problems, 1977), 29.
38. Payne, 486.

Chapter 10: Triumph and Ruin: 1941–1948

1. *Harijan,* June 17, 1942.
2. Louis Fischer, *Life of Mahatma Gandhi* (New York: Harper, 1950), 331.
3. D. G. Tendulkar, *The Mahatma* (New Delhi: Government Press, 1951), 5:225.
4. Fischer, 331.
5. F. Watson and M. Brown, *Talking of Gandhiji* (London: Longmans Green, 1957), 10.
6. Quoted in Pyarelal, *Mahatma Gandhi, Part 2: The Last Phase* (Ahmedabad: Navajivan, 1956), 1:45.
7. Tendulkar, 8:138.
8. S. Radhakrishnan, *Mahatma Gandhi A Hundred Years* (New Delhi: n.p., 1968), 10.
9. B. N. Pandey, *Nehru* (New York: Macmillan, 1976), 252.
10. Quoted by Mark Thompson in V. T. Patil, *Studies on Gandhi* (Delhi: Sterling, 1983), 145.
11. Jehangir Patel and Marjorie Sykes, *Gandhi: The Gift of the Fight* (Rasulia: Friends Rural Centre, 1987), 158.
12. R. Payne, *The Life and Death of Mahatma Gandhi* (New York: Dutton, 1969), 521.
13. Larry Collins and Dominique LaPierre, *Freedom at Midnight* (New York: Avon, 1975), 38.
14. Watson and Brown, 103.
15. Pyarelal, 2:15.
16. Erik Erikson, *Gandhi's Truth* (New York: Norton, 1969), 110.
17. F. Watson, *The Trial of Mr. Gandhi* (London: Macmillan, 1969), 264.
18. Ved Mehta, *Mahatma Gandhi and His Apostles* (New York: Penguin, 1977), 203.
19. Erikson, 404.

20. Patel and Sykes, 162.
21. Payne, 540–41.
22. Collins and LaPierre, 310.
23. Payne, 552.
24. Payne, 637.
25. Manohar Malgonkar, *The Men Who Killed Gandhi* (Delhi: Macmillan, 1978), 29.
26. Payne, 638.
27. Pyarelal, 2:589.
28. Payne, 554.

Conclusion: The Great Absence

1. Erik Erikson, *Gandhi's Truth* (New York: Norton, 1969), 64.
2. John M. MacKenzie, *Popular Imperialism and the Military* (Manchester: University Press, 1992), 109–38.
3. Bernard Shaw, *Nine Plays* (New York: Dodd Mead, 1937), 933.
4. T. K. Mahadevan, foreword to Manmathnath Gupta, *Gandhi and His Times* (Delhi: Prakashan, 1982), v.
5. K. N. Vaswani, ed., *Sucheta: An Unfinished Autobiography* (Ahmedabad: Navajivan, 1978), 73.
6. Quoted as epigraph to Ashis Nandy's essay, "Final Encounter: The Politics of the Assassination of Gandhi," in Ashis Nandy, *At the Edge of Psychology* (Delhi: O.U.P., 1980).

GLOSSARY

ahimsa: harming no one and nothing
anjuman: association
aparigraha: owning nothing
ashram: site of religious community
asteya: not stealing
atman: breath, spirit, soul
bajra: a kind of vegetable
bania: of the commercial caste
bhadralok: the gentry in Bengal
bhajan: hymn
bhakta: religious devotion
brahmacharya: renunciation of sexual activity
brahmin: of the priestly caste
charkha: spinning wheel
chela: disciple
dacoit: robbers or thugs
dharma: duty or obligation
dhoti: cloth tied round the waist
diwan: chief administrator
duragraha: mute reproach
goonda: rowdy or thug
harijan: child of God, Gandhi's word for Untouchable
hartal: general strike
ishvar: supreme being
juwar roti: maize bread
kanthi: necklace of tulsi beads
khadi: homespun cloth
khutput: intrigue
ki-jai: hail to
kisan: peasant
kshatriya: of the warrior caste
lathi: stick
maya: what seems real but is not
moha: enthusiasm
moksha: freedom, found in the vision of God
nai talim: Gandhi's theory of education
natak: nationalist theater
neem: tree with edible but bitter leaves
paharaj: shirt
pandal: marquee
puggree: turban
rana: prince
rotla: Indian bread
sabha: association
sadhana: method
sanyasi: religious wanderer
satyagraha: nonviolent activism
shastra: holy book
shakti: female power
shudra: of the agricultural caste
smitri: a treatise
swadeshi: locally made
swaraj: home rule or self rule
tampura: recitation of poetry
tola: a measure of weight
tulsi: plant with religious associations
upashraya: monastery
vaishnavadharma: the dharma of those who worship Vishnu
vakil: attorney
vanaprastha: giving up domestic life
varna: caste
varnashrama: division of life into stages of development
vidyapith: Indian-style university

BIBLIOGRAPHY

Ambedkar, B. R. *Gandhi and Gandhism.* Introduction by Bhagwan Das. Jullundur: Beem Patrika, 1970.

———. *What Congress and Gandhi have done to the Untouchables,* Bombay: Thacker, 1945.

Ashe, Geoffrey. *Gandhi.* New York: Stein and Day, 1968.

Baig, Tara Ali. *Sarojini Naidu.* New Delhi: n.p., 1974.

Balwantsimha. *Under the Shelter of Bapu.* Ahmedabad: Navajivan, 1962.

Barr, Mary. *Bapu.* Bombay: Book House, 1949.

Bebbington, David. *The Nonconformist Conscience.* London: Allen and Unwin, 1982.

Besant, Annie. *Jainism.* Adyar: Theosophical Publishers, 1949.

Bharati, Agehananda. *Asians in East Africa.* Chicago: University Press, 1972.

Bhave, Vinoba. *The Steadfast Wisdom.* N.p.: n.p., 1966.

———. *Talks on the Gita.* N.p.: n.p., 1970.

———. *The Third Power.* N.p.: n.p., 1972.

Birla, G. D. *In the Shadow of the Mahatma.* Bombay: Orient Longmans, 1953.

Blount, Geoffrey. *The Gospel of Simplicity.* London: Simple Life Press, 1906.

———. *A New Crusade.* London: Simple Life Press, 1903.

Blount, Mrs. Geoffrey. *Story of a Homespun Web.* London: Vineyard Press, 1913.

Bolitho, Hector. *Jinnah.* London: John Murray, 1954.

Bose, N. K. *Lectures on Gandhism.* Ahmedabad: Navajivan, 1971.

———. *My Days with Gandhi.* Calcutta, Nishana, 1953.

Bose, N.K., ed. *Selections from Gandhi.* Ahmedabad: Navajivan, 1947.

Bristow, E. J. *Vice and Vigilance.* New York: Macmillan, 1977.

Brown, Judith M. *Gandhi and Civil Disobedience.* Cambridge: University Press, 1977.

———. *Gandhi: Prisoner of Hope.* New Haven: Yale University Press, 1989.

———. *Gandhi's Rise to Power.* Cambridge: University Press, 1972.

Budd, Susan. *Varieties of Unbelief.* London: Heinemann, 1977.

Carpenter, Edward. *The Age of Creation.* New York: Macmillan, 1904.

Chakravarty, Amiya. *The Tagore Reader.* Boston: Beacon, 1966.

Chalapati Ram, M. *Gandhi and Nehru.* Bombay: Allied, 1967.

Chatfield, Charles. *The Americanization of Gandhi.* New York: Garland, 1976.

Chaudhurani, Saraladevi. *Jhibaner Jhava Pata* (Life's fallen leaves), published only in Bengali.

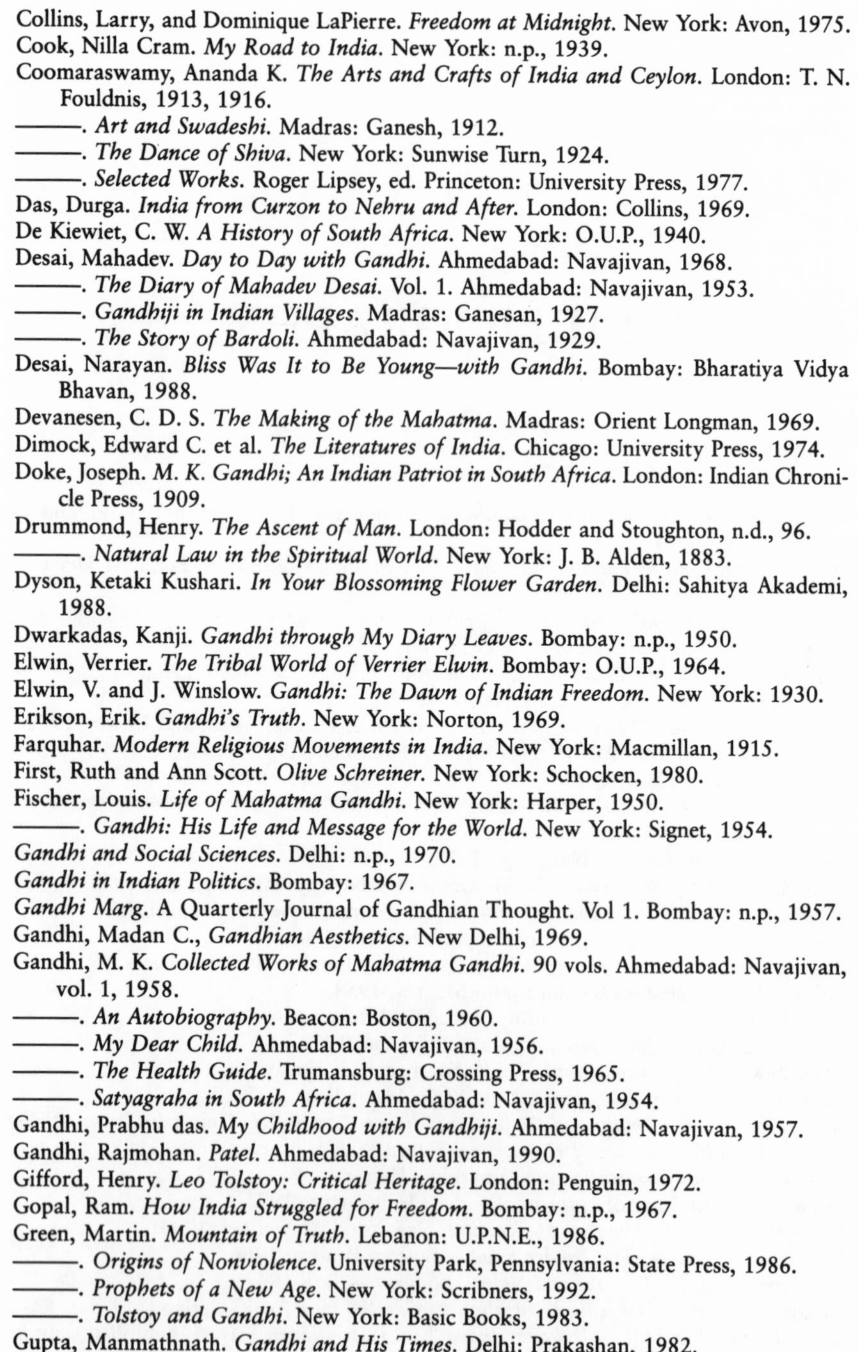

Collins, Larry, and Dominique LaPierre. *Freedom at Midnight.* New York: Avon, 1975.

Cook, Nilla Cram. *My Road to India.* New York: n.p., 1939.

Coomaraswamy, Ananda K. *The Arts and Crafts of India and Ceylon.* London: T. N. Fouldnis, 1913, 1916.

———. *Art and Swadeshi.* Madras: Ganesh, 1912.

———. *The Dance of Shiva.* New York: Sunwise Turn, 1924.

———. *Selected Works.* Roger Lipsey, ed. Princeton: University Press, 1977.

Das, Durga. *India from Curzon to Nehru and After.* London: Collins, 1969.

De Kiewiet, C. W. *A History of South Africa.* New York: O.U.P., 1940.

Desai, Mahadev. *Day to Day with Gandhi.* Ahmedabad: Navajivan, 1968.

———. *The Diary of Mahadev Desai.* Vol. 1. Ahmedabad: Navajivan, 1953.

———. *Gandhiji in Indian Villages.* Madras: Ganesan, 1927.

———. *The Story of Bardoli.* Ahmedabad: Navajivan, 1929.

Desai, Narayan. *Bliss Was It to Be Young—with Gandhi.* Bombay: Bharatiya Vidya Bhavan, 1988.

Devanesen, C. D. S. *The Making of the Mahatma.* Madras: Orient Longman, 1969.

Dimock, Edward C. et al. *The Literatures of India.* Chicago: University Press, 1974.

Doke, Joseph. *M. K. Gandhi; An Indian Patriot in South Africa.* London: Indian Chronicle Press, 1909.

Drummond, Henry. *The Ascent of Man.* London: Hodder and Stoughton, n.d., 96.

———. *Natural Law in the Spiritual World.* New York: J. B. Alden, 1883.

Dyson, Ketaki Kushari. *In Your Blossoming Flower Garden.* Delhi: Sahitya Akademi, 1988.

Dwarkadas, Kanji. *Gandhi through My Diary Leaves.* Bombay: n.p., 1950.

Elwin, Verrier. *The Tribal World of Verrier Elwin.* Bombay: O.U.P., 1964.

Elwin, V. and J. Winslow. *Gandhi: The Dawn of Indian Freedom.* New York: 1930.

Erikson, Erik. *Gandhi's Truth.* New York: Norton, 1969.

Farquhar. *Modern Religious Movements in India.* New York: Macmillan, 1915.

First, Ruth and Ann Scott. *Olive Schreiner.* New York: Schocken, 1980.

Fischer, Louis. *Life of Mahatma Gandhi.* New York: Harper, 1950.

———. *Gandhi: His Life and Message for the World.* New York: Signet, 1954.

Gandhi and Social Sciences. Delhi: n.p., 1970.

Gandhi in Indian Politics. Bombay: 1967.

Gandhi Marg. A Quarterly Journal of Gandhian Thought. Vol 1. Bombay: n.p., 1957.

Gandhi, Madan C., *Gandhian Aesthetics.* New Delhi, 1969.

Gandhi, M. K. *Collected Works of Mahatma Gandhi.* 90 vols. Ahmedabad: Navajivan, vol. 1, 1958.

———. *An Autobiography.* Beacon: Boston, 1960.

———. *My Dear Child.* Ahmedabad: Navajivan, 1956.

———. *The Health Guide.* Trumansburg: Crossing Press, 1965.

———. *Satyagraha in South Africa.* Ahmedabad: Navajivan, 1954.

Gandhi, Prabhu das. *My Childhood with Gandhiji.* Ahmedabad: Navajivan, 1957.

Gandhi, Rajmohan. *Patel.* Ahmedabad: Navajivan, 1990.

Gifford, Henry. *Leo Tolstoy: Critical Heritage.* London: Penguin, 1972.

Gopal, Ram. *How India Struggled for Freedom.* Bombay: n.p., 1967.

Green, Martin. *Mountain of Truth.* Lebanon: U.P.N.E., 1986.

———. *Origins of Nonviolence.* University Park, Pennsylvania: State Press, 1986.

———. *Prophets of a New Age.* New York: Scribners, 1992.

———. *Tolstoy and Gandhi.* New York: Basic Books, 1983.

Gupta, Manmathnath. *Gandhi and His Times.* Delhi: Prakashan, 1982.

Haggard, H. Rider. *King Solomon's Mines.* London: n.p., 1886, and New York: Dell, 1961.

Hancock, William and Jean van der Poel. *The Smuts Papers*. Cambridge: University Press, 1966.
Hardiman, David. *Peasant Nationalists of Gujarat*. Delhi: O.U.P., 1981.
Hay, S. N. "Gandhi's First Five Years." In D. Capps, et al., eds. *Encounter with Erikson*. Missoula: Montana University, 1977.
Hunt, James. *Gandhi in London*. Delhi: Promilla, 1978.
Hobson, J. A. *Imperialism*. London: J. Nisbet, 1902.
———. *The Psychology of Jingoism*. London: Grant Richards, 1901.
Hunt, J. D. *Gandhi in London*. New Delhi: Promilla, 1978.
Hutchins, Francis. *The Illusion of Permanence*. Princeton: University Press, 1967.
Hutheesing, K. N. *We Nehrus*. New York: Holt Rinehart, 1967.
Huttenback, R. A. *Gandhi in South Africa*. Ithaca: Cornell University Press, 1971.
———. *Racism and Empire*. Ithaca, Cornell University Press, 1976.
Iyer, Raghavan. *The Moral and Political Thought of Mahatma Gandhi*. Delhi: O.U.P., 1973.
Jayakar, M. R. *The Story of My Life*. Bombay: Asia Publishing, 1958.
Kakar, Sudhir. *Intimate Relationships*. Delhi: Viking, 1989.
Kalelkar, D. *Stray Glimpses of Bapu*. Ahmedabad: Navajivan, 1950.
Koestler, Arthur. *The Lotos and the Robot*. New York: Harpers, 1966.
Krishnadas. *Seven Months with Mahatma Gandhi*. Ahmedabad: Navajivan, 1959.
Kumarappa, Bharatan. *Nonviolent Resistance*. New York: Schocken, 1961.
Lawrence, D. H. *Women in Love*. New York: Random House, 1922.
Lean, Phyllis. *Fifty Years of Theosophy*. South Africa: n.p., 1949.
Lipsey, Roger. *Coomaraswamy: His Life and Work*. Princeton: University Press, 1977.
MacKenzie, John M. *Popular Imperialism and the Military*. Manchester: University Press, 1992.
Rajagopalachari, C., trans. to *The Mahabharata*. 18th edition. Bombay: n.p., 1976.
Mahadevan, T. K. *Gandhi My Refrain*. Bombay: Popular Prakashan, 1973.
Maitland, Edward. *Life of Anna Kingsford*. London: Field and Tuer, 1895.
Maitland, Edward, with Anna Kingsford. *The Perfect Way*. London: Field and Tuer, 1890.
Malgonkar, Manohar. *The Men Who Killed Gandhi*. Delhi: Macmillan, 1978.
Mashruwala, K. *Gandhi and Marx*. Ahmedabad: Navajivan, 1951.
Meer, Fatima. *Apprenticeship of a Mahatma*. Durban: Premier Press, 1970.
———. *Portrait of South African Indians*. Durban: Premier Press, 1969.
Mehta, Digish. *Shrimad Rajachandran*. Ahmedabad: n.p., n.d.
Mehta, P. J. *M. K. Gandhi and the South African Indian Problem*. Madras: Ganesan, 1912.
Mehta, Ved. *Mahatma Gandhi and His Apostles*. New York: Penguin, 1977.
Monro, Harold. *Collected Poems*. London: Cobden-Sanderson, 1933.
Moon, Penderel. *Gandhi and Modern India*. New York: Norton, 1969.
Morton, Elinor. *The Women in Gandhi's Life*. New York: Dodd Mead, 1953.
Munshi, K. M. *I Follow the Mahatma*. Bombay: Allied Publishers, 1940.
Nag, Kalidas. *Tolstoy and Gandhi*. Patna: Pustak Bhandar, 1950.
Nanda, B. R. *Gandhi and the Nehrus*. London: n.p., 1974.
———. *Gandhi: Pan-Islamism, Imperialism, and Nationalism*. Delhi: O.U.P., 1989.
———. *Motilal Nehru*. Delhi: Ministry of Information, 1964.
———. *The Nehrus*. London: Allen and Unwin, 1963.
Nandy, Ashis. *At the Edge of Psychology*. Delhi: O.U.P., 1980.
Nayar, Sushila. *Satyagraha at Work*. Ahamedabad: Navajivan, 1989.
Nehru, Jawaharlal. *A Bunch of Old Letters*. New York: Asta, 1960.
———. *The Discovery of India*. New York: John Day, 1960.

———. *Glimpses of World History*. New York: n.p., 1962.
———. *Towards Freedom*. New York: John Day, 1958.
Niemeijer, A. C.. *Khilafat Movement in India*. Hague: Mouton, 1972.
Norman, Dorothy. *Nehru: The First Sixty Years*. London: Bodley Head, 1965.
O'Flaherty, W. D. *Hindu Myths*. London: n.p., 1975.
Pandey, B. N. *The Indian Nationalist Movement 1885–1947*. New York: Macmillan, 1979.
———. *Nehru*. New York: Macmillan, 1976.
Parekh, Bhikhu. *Colonialism, Tradition, and Reform*. New York: Sage, 1989.
Parikh, N. D. *Mahadev Desai's Early Life*. Ahmedabad: Navajivan, 1953.
Patel, Jehangir, and Marjorie Sykes. *Gandhi: The Gift of the Fight*. Rasulia: Friends Rural Centre, 1987.
Patil, V. T. *Studies on Gandhi*. Delhi: Sterling, 1983.
Payne, R. *The Life and Death of Mahatma Gandhi*. New York: Dutton, 1969.
Porter, Bernard. *Critics of Empire*. New York: St. Martins, 1968.
Prabhu, R. K. *This Was Bapu*. Ahmedabad: Navajivan, 1954.
Prasad, Rajendra. *At the Feet of Mahatma Gandhi*. New York: Asia Publishing, 1961.
———. *Autobiography*. Bombay: Asia Publishing, 1957.
Pyarelal. *Mahatma Gandhi, Part I: The Early Phase,* Ahmedabad: Navajivan, 1965.
———. *Mahatma Gandhi, Part 2: The Last Phase*. (2 vols.) Ahmedabad: Navajivan, 1956, 1958.
———. *A Pilgrimage for Peace*. Ahmedabad: Navajivan, 1950.
Pyarelal and Sushila Nayar. *In Gandhiji's Mirror*. Delhi: O.U.P., 1991.
Radhakrishnan, S., ed. *Mahatma Gandhi*. London: Allen and Unwin, 1939, 1949.
———. *R. S. Vinoba and his Mission*. Wentha, 1948.
———. *Mahatma Gandhi A Hundred Years*. New Delhi: 1969.
Ramachandran, G. *Gandhigram Thoughts and Talks*. N.p.: Gandhigram, 1964.
Ramachandran, G., with T. K. Mahadevan. *Gandhi: His Relevance for Our Times*. New Delhi: n.p., 1967.
Rajagopalachari, C., tr. and ed. *The Ramayana*. Bombay: n.p., 1975.
Rao, M. B., and S. G. Sardasi. *The Mahatma*. Bombay: People's Publishing House, 1969.
Ray, Sibnarayan. *Gandhi, India, and the World*. Bombay: Indian Committee for Intellectual Freedom, 1970.
Reynolds, R. *A Quest for Gandhi*. New York: Doubleday, 1952.
Rolland, Romain. *Mahatma Gandhi*. Paris: Delamain and Boutelleau, 1924.
———. *Prophets of the New India*. New York: A. and C. Boni, 1930.
———. *Inde: Journal 1915–43*. Paris: Vineta, 1951.
———. *Rolland-Gandhi Correspondence*. New Delhi: Ministry of Information, 1976.
Roy, Dilip Kumar. *Among the Great*. Bombay: Jaico, 1950.
Rudolph, L. and S. Rudolph. *The Modernity of Tradition*. Chicago: University Press, 1967.
Saksena, M. *Motilal Nehru*. Delhi, n.p., 1961.
Salter, William. *Ethical Religion*. London: Rationalist Press, 1905.
Santayana, George. *Interpretations of Poetry and Religion*. New York: Scribners, 1900.
Sastri, V. S. Srinivasa, ed. T. N. Jagadisan, *Letters of V. S. Sastri*. Madras: Rochouse and Sow, n.d.
Sengupta, Padmini. *Sarojini Naidu*. London: Asia Publishing, 1966.
Shah, Kantilal. *Vinoba on Gandhi*. N.p.: n.p., 1973.
Shahani, R. *Mr. Gandhi*. New York: Macmillan, 1961.
Shaw, Nellie. *A Czech Philosopher on the Cotswolds*. London: Daniel, 1940.
———. *Whiteway: A Colony on the Cotswolds*. London: Daniel, 1935.

Shimoni, Gideon. *Gandhi, Satyagraha, and the Jews*. Jerusalem: Papers on Peace Problems, 1977.

———. *Jews and Zionism*. Capetown: O.U.P., 1980.

Shukla, Chandrashankar. *Incidents of Gandhiji's Life*. Bombay: Vora, 1949.

———. *Reminiscences of Gandhiji*. Bombay: Vora, 1951.

Sinclair, Upton. *Mammonart*. N.p.: n.p., 1924.

Singam, S. D. R. *Ananda Coomaraswamy: Remembering and Remembering Again and Again*. N.p.: Petading Jaya, 1974.

Sinha, M. P. *The Contemporary Relevance of Gandhi*. Bombay: n.p., 1970.

Sitaramayya, S. P. *Gandhi and Gandhism*. Allahabad: Kitabistan, 1942.

Slade, Madeline. *Gandhi's Letters to a Disciple*. London: Gollancz, 1951.

———. *The Spirit's Pilgrimage*. New York: Coward McCann, 1978.

Smedley, Agnes. *Battle Hymn of China*. New York: Da Capo, 1975.

Spiller, Gustave. *The Ethical Movement in Great Britain*. London: n.p., 1934.

Swan, Maureen. *Gandhi and the South African Experience*. Johannesburg: Ravan, 1985.

Swinson, Arthur. *Six Minutes to Sunset*. London: Peter Davies, 1964.

Tagore, Rabindranath. *Creative Unity*. Calcutta: n.p., 1971.

———. *I Won't Let You Go*. K. K. Dyson, tr. London: Bloodaxe, 1991.

Talbot, Ian. *Provincial Politics and the Pakistan Movement*. Karachi: O.U.P., 1988.

Tendulkar, D. G. *Gandhiji: His Life and Work*. Bombay: Karnatak, 1944.

———. *The Mahatma*. 8 vols. New Delhi: Government Press, vol. 1., 1951.

Tennyson, Hallam. *India's Walking Saint*. London: Gollancz, 1955.

Tharu, Susie and K. Lalita. *Women Writing in India*. New York: Feminist Press, 1991.

Tinker, Hugh. *A New System of Slavery*. New York: O.U.P., 1974.

Tolstoy, Leo. *The Kingdom of God Is within You*. Lincoln, Nebraska: University Press, 1974.

Tulsidas. *The Holy Lake of the Acts of Rama*. W. Douglas Hill, tr. Cambridge: University Press, 1952.

Uphadhyaya, J. M. *Mahatma Gandhi—a Teacher's Discovery*. Ahmedabad: Navajivan, 1969.

———. *Gandhi's Early Contemporaries and Companions*. Ahmedabad: Navajivan, n.d.

Van Onselen, Charles. *Studies in the Social and Economic History of the Witwatersrand*. London: Longmans, 1982.

Vaswani, K. N. *Sucheta: An Unfinished Autobiography*. Ahmedabad: Navajivan, 1978.

Watson, F. *The Trial of Mr Gandhi*. London: Macmillan, 1969.

Watson, F. and M. Brown. *Talking of Gandhiji*. London: Longmans Green, 1957.

Wellock, W. *Off the Beaten Track*. Varanasi: Sarvodaya, 1963.

Wilson, Edmund. *The Twenties*. New York: Farrar, Straus, Giroux, 1975.

Winsten, Stephen. *Salt and His Circle*. London: Hutchinson, 1951.

Wiser, W. W., and C. V. Wiser. *Behind Mud Walls*. Los Angeles: University of California Press, 1963.

Wolpert, S. A. *Tilak and Gokhale*. Berkeley: University of California Press, 1962.

INDEX